Changing Industrial Relations in Europe

Changing Industrial Relations in Europe

SECOND EDITION

Edited by

ANTHONY FERNER AND
RICHARD HYMAN

Copyright © Blackwell Publishers Ltd, 1998

First published as *Industrial Relations in the New Europe* 1992
Reprinted 1993, 1995
Second edition published 1998

2 4 6 8 10 9 7 5 3 1

Blackwell Publishers Ltd
108 Cowley Road
Oxford OX4 1JF
UK

Blackwell Publishers Inc.
350 Main Street
Malden, Massachusetts 02148
USA

All rights reserved. Except for the quotation of short passages for the purposes of criticism and review, no part of this publication may be reproduced, stored in a retrieval system, or transmitted, in any form or by any means, electronic, mechanical, photocopying, recording or otherwise, without the prior permission of the publisher.

Except in the United States of America, this book is sold subject to the condition that it shall not, by way of trade or otherwise, be lent, resold, hired out, or otherwise circulated without the publisher's prior consent in any form of binding or cover other than that in which it is published and without a similar condition including this condition being imposed on the subsequent purchaser.

British Library Cataloguing in Publication Data

A CIP catalogue record for this book is available from the British Library.

Library of Congress Cataloging-in-Publication Data

Changing industrial relations in Europe / edited by Anthony Ferner and
   Richard Hyman. — 2nd ed.
        p.   cm.
   Previous edition published under the title: Industrial relations
in the new Europe
   Includes bibliographical references and index.
   ISBN 0–631–20550–0. — ISBN 0–631–20551–9
   1. Industrial relations — European Economic Community countries.
   2. Industrial relations — Europe.   I. Ferner, Anthony.   II. Hyman,
Richard.   III. Industrial relations in the new Europe.
HD8380.5.C48   1998
331'.094 — dc21   97–24520
                                                                          CIP

ISBN 0–631–20550–0
ISBN 0–631–20551–9 (pb)

Typeset in 10 on 12pt Sabon
by SetSystem Ltd, Saffron Walden, Essex
Printed and bound in Great Britain by MPG Books Ltd, Bodmin, Cornwall

This book is printed on acid-free paper.

Contents

List of Contributors

José Barreto, Research Fellow, Instituto de Ciências Sociais, University of Lisbon

Jon Erik Dølvik, Researcher, FAFO (Institute for Applied Social Science), Oslo

Paul Edwards, Deputy Director, Industrial Relations Research Unit, University of Warwick

Anthony Ferner, Principal Research Fellow, ESRC Centre for International Employment Relations, Industrial Relations Research Unit, University of Warwick

Robert Fluder, Fellow at the Institute for Sociology, University of Zürich

Janine Goetschy, Chargée de Recherche, CNRS (Centre National de la Recherche Scientifique), Université de Paris-Nanterre

Mark Hall, Senior Lecturer in Industrial Relations and Senior Research Fellow, Industrial Relations Research Unit, University of Warwick

Beat Hotz-Hart, Professor of Economics, University of Zürich, Vice-Director of the Swiss Federal Office for Economic Policy

Richard Hyman, Professor of Industrial Relations, University of Warwick

Otto Jacobi, Laboratorium Europa – Independent research centre for industrial relations in Europe, and German member of TRANSFER, quarterly journal of the ETUC

Berndt Keller, Professor of Labour and Social Policy, University of Konstanz

Anders Kjellberg, Associate Professor, Department of Sociology, University of Lund

Nicos D. Kritsantonis, Personnel Director of a Greek company

Kari Lilja, Professor in Organization and Management, Helsinki School of Economics and Business Administration

Paul Marginson, Professor of Industrial Relations, School of Business and Economic Studies, University of Leeds

Miguel Martínez Lucio, Lecturer in Industrial and Labour Studies, University of Leeds

Walther Müller-Jentsch, Professor of Codetermination and Organization, Ruhr University of Bochum

Reinhard Naumann, freelance researcher at the CIES/ISCTE (Centro de Investigação e Estudos de Sociologia), Lisbon

Ida Regalia, Associate Professor, Department of Social Sciences, University of Turin

Marino Regini, Professor of Industrial Relations, Institute of Labour Studies, University of Milan

Steen Scheuer, Lecturer, Institute of Organization and Industrial Sociology, Copenhagen Business School

Keith Sisson, Director, Industrial Relations Research Unit, University of Warwick

Torgeir Aarvaag Stokke, Researcher, Fafo (Institute for Applied Social Science), Oslo

Franz Traxler, Professor of Industrial Sociology, Centre of Business Administration, University of Vienna

Gary Tunsch, Inspector at the Ministry of Labour and Secretary of the National Conciliation Office, Luxembourg

Jim Van Leemput, member of the Study Group in Technological, Economic and Social Change and Labour Market Research (TESA) and acting Secretary of the Board of Administration of the Vrije Universiteit Brussel

Jacques Vilrokx, Professor of Industrial Relations and Labour Economics, and Director of the Study Group in Technological, Economic and Social Change and Labour Market Research (TESA), Vrije Universiteit Brussel

Jelle Visser, Department of Sociology, University of Amsterdam and Max Planck Institute for the Study of Societies, Cologne

Ferdinand von Prondzynski, Professor of Law and Dean of the Faculty of Social Sciences, University of Hull

Jeremy Waddington, Senior Lecturer in Industrial Relations and Senior Research Fellow, Industrial Relations Research Unit, University of Warwick

David Winchester, Senior Lecturer in Industrial Relations, University of Warwick

Preface to the Second Edition

The first edition of this book was published at a time of great transformation in Europe with the dramatic collapse of the regimes of the 'Iron Curtain', a term which itself now seems quaintly historical. The past five years have seen less radical, but nonetheless fundamental, change in Europe, with the deepening of economic and monetary integration in the European Union – including the incorporation of three more member states, the increasing impact on national economies of the forces of internationalization, and the continuing transformation of the structure of production in most countries.

Change has prompted a wide range of industrial relations responses, some of which would not have been expected from the vantage point of the early 1990s. In editing this new edition, we have naturally been anxious to preserve something of the depth of historical context that was a feature of the first edition, but we decided that the focus of contributions should shift more towards understanding and explaining recent developments. Some of the historical description has therefore been pared away; readers who require more detail will still be able to refer to the relevant chapters of the first edition, which stands as a 'volume of record', or to the ample bibliographies of the individual country contributions.

We also decided as editors (and in this our concerns coincided with those of our publisher) to reduce the length of the volume. In designing the first edition we felt that existing multi-country texts were superficial in their brevity, and we aimed for comprehensiveness. This time we have urged our contributors to concentrate on the key issues of analysis and explanation, on telling the main 'story', if necessary at the expense of often transient institutional detail. We hope that the book will benefit from greater clarity and focus, and as a result appeal to a wider audience, including both interested non-experts and students at undergraduate and postgraduate level.

We were inevitably faced with the question of whether to include in this second edition chapters on the countries of eastern Europe (we included three overview chapters in the companion collection, *New Frontiers in European Industrial Relations*). We eventually decided that an 'opening to the east' was impracticable because it would have added excessively to the length, and hence the cost, of the volume. In addition, well-anchored analysis of developments in these countries is still difficult. Perhaps in another 5 years the systems will have bedded down and a more secure tradition of analysis will have emerged. At that point, some fascinating comparisons will become possible – between, for example, the nature of the democratic transition in the industrial relations systems of eastern Europe and in countries such as Greece, Portugal and Spain.

The work of revision has represented more than a desultory updating of statistics. All the chapters have been 'streamlined' and several have been completely rewritten as well as thoroughly revised and updated. In some cases, events in the intervening 5 years have called for significant changes in the analysis and conclusions. Some – the Norwegian and Dutch contributions, for example – have relatively optimistic stories to tell; others, notably the Germans, are markedly more pessimistic than 5 years ago. One chapter – Italy – has been written from scratch. In the first edition, we wrote it ourselves as last minute 'stand-ins'. Despite the favourable reception our chapter received, this time we felt that it should be written by Italian experts. We were able to bring in two highly respected Italian authors, who have produced a particularly subtle and sophisticated analysis.

The title of the first edition, *Industrial Relations in the New Europe*, was intended to signify the context of great transformations taking place at the beginning of the decade. The new Europe is no longer so new, though it is still undergoing dynamic change. A change in title was therefore called for. We toyed with the idea of *Industrial Relations in Western Europe*, but felt that this was both too prosaic and slightly antiquated in tone. Eventually, to convey the idea of events moving on, we decided upon *Changing Industrial Relations in Europe*. We accept, however, that the volume is not as comprehensive as such a title might imply, in that it excludes the former eastern bloc countries – for the reasons we have explained.

As in the first edition, we have not tried to impose a rigid structure on authors. Within a framework of shared themes and issues, we have given them relatively free rein to highlight the elements that they see as crucial for the understanding of their own country. As before, our primary editorial job has been to ensure that the chapters attain a common high standard of readability, clarity and consistency of argument.

We would like to acknowledge the institutional support of the Industrial Relations Research Unit (IRRU), whose Centre for International Employment Relations Research is funded by the UK Economic and Social Research Council. Finally, we would like to thank our colleagues in IRRU, and our contributors from sixteen other countries around Europe, for their commitment to the project which has enabled us to complete it on schedule.

Introduction: Towards European Industrial Relations?

ANTHONY FERNER • RICHARD HYMAN

The first edition of this volume appeared in 1992, on the eve of the completion of the Single European Market. Since then we have seen the enlargement of what was then the European Community and is today the European Union (now encompassing all but two of the countries which we cover). We are also digesting the key consequences of the agreement reached at Maastricht: first, the new impetus to social regulation at EU level; second, the adoption of a firm timetable and criteria for Economic and Monetary Union, scheduled to commence soon after this new text appears.

In our original introduction we addressed the familiar question: is convergence or continuing differentiation the key characteristic of industrial relations in the countries of western Europe? We sketched the complex interactions between cross-national forces commonly regarded as the impetus towards convergence, and the persistence of nationally specific institutions, patterns of historical experience, and strategic choices. In our view, developments in our seventeen countries in the intervening 5 years justify the cautious assessment which we then proposed. Rather than rehearse the same general arguments here, in this new introduction we focus on four specific themes, all relevant to the underlying question: are the pressures towards convergence becoming stronger, so that the outlines of a common European industrial relations system can be discerned (or, more pessimistically, is there a common erosion of the distinctive national regulatory processes which constitute industrial relations)?

First, we examine the question of 'internationalization'. Cross-national economic integration has been increasingly identified as the key challenge to the viability of 'strong' national regulatory regimes; but the meaning (and indeed the existence) of 'internationalization' have been hotly debated. At least some of the issues involved have been significantly clarified by recent developments, both in the real world and in academic debate. Second, we revisit some of the key themes of industrial relations analysis at the beginning of the 1990s, when many writers discerned an irresistible trend towards decentralization and flexibility. It seems obvious that such arguments were exaggerated; in many countries the regulatory capacity of the higher-level 'social partners' has survived, and they have often been active participants in the innovative developments of the 1990s, which have redirected or even in some cases reversed the trends visible at the beginning of the decade. We suggest tentative explanations for the emerging patterns. Third, we confront the question: how far has 'internationalization' eroded the regulatory capacity of the national state? In some respects, neo-liberal biases in state policies have been reinforced by the monetarist criteria of EMU entry. Yet paradoxically the 1990s have seen, in some countries, the revival of the 'neo-corporatism' which a few years ago was almost universally regarded as defunct. We consider some of the reasons, and also discuss the regulatory competence of the supranational 'Euro-state'. Finally we return to one of the core themes of our original introduction: the capacity of national institutions to respond to transnational pressures. Five years ago, we suggested that the very different patterns at national level could be understood as reflections of the contrasting strength and adaptability of institutional systems; we now consider how far our analysis stands up, particularly in the light of the critical German experience.

Internationalization: a Complex (and Contested) Dynamic

'Internationalization' has become one of the central concepts of the decade. Often used loosely, it generally refers to a number of interlinked dimensions. First, international markets have expanded through the removal of trade barriers – manifested in the GATT agreement of 1994, the growth of regional trade blocs, and the incorporation of former communist countries into the world economic system. Despite the liberalization of world trade, the evidence suggests a process of 'triadization' rather than 'globalization', in that interactions are much more intense within the three main trading blocs – Europe, North America, the Asian-Pacific – than between them (e.g. Hirst and Thompson 1996; Ruigrok and van Tulder 1995). Second, sectors of economic activity – notably business services – previously conducted within national economies have been opened up to international competition. Within Europe, a major impetus has been provided by the liberalization of sectors such as telecommunications and electricity supply, in the context of European integration. This has often been accompanied by the privatization of monopoly state utilities. Even central government services have been subject to 'marketization', through contracting out often to large multinational service providers. Third, the liberalization of financial markets has gone hand-in-hand with advances in microelectronics and telecommunications to permit non-stop trading in shares, securities and currencies. The 'short-termism' seen by many as a cause of Britain's economic ills – whereby managerial decisions on production and investment are dominated by preoccupations with immediate financial results – may thus infect corporate behaviour (and government priorities) cross-nationally. The EMU project is in one respect a response to these developments, aiming to remove the scope for speculative pressures on individual currencies; but the convergence criteria with their emphasis on financial rectitude reinforce the risk that the 'real economy' will be subordinated to purely monetary considerations. Fourth, the organization of production has become increasingly internationalized through the activities of multinational corporations (MNCs) which integrate their productive activities across national borders. MNCs are the dominant actors in the internationalization process: UN estimates suggest that they own around one third of the world's private productive assets (UNCTAD 1994). A high and rising proportion of stocks and flows, both of inward and outward foreign direct investment, is concentrated in Europe (Ruigrok and Van Tulder 1995; Jones 1996).

There has been considerable debate in recent years about the impact of 'internationalization', and in particular of the activities of MNCs, on national industrial relations systems. For some (e.g. Reich 1991), MNCs are forces for international homogenization. They act as 'transmission belts', bringing the practices of country-of-origin business systems into host countries, and undermining nationally specific regulatory regimes. A number of key mechanisms have been identified. The first is a form of 'social dumping'. Streeck (1992), among others, has argued that capital mobility allows MNCs to engage in 'regime shopping', moving (or achieving their objectives by threats to do so) to countries where the industrial relations regulatory regime is least onerous; this is bound to exert a downward pressure on employment standards as MNCs play one country off against another. As Erickson and Kuruvilla (1995) demonstrate, the higher productivity of the economically more advanced countries within Europe is not nearly enough to compensate for the gap in wage rates between high and low wage countries; as a result, MNCs have great and increasing economic incentives for relocating production. Second, and relatedly, the international integration of corporate operations, organizational structures and management systems allows companies to make effective 'coercive comparisons' (e.g. Mueller 1996). In effect, they can scan their international operations to identify 'best practice' (best, that is, for corporate returns; for example, in the use of flexible work organization) and then, if necessary, use the implicit or explicit threat of disinvestment to impose common standards across plants in different countries. Third, the growing integration of international operations and markets has led MNCs to develop common approaches to managing 'human resources', through the dissemination of international policies on training, management development, performance management, participation and involvement, and so on.

In the traditional phase of 'polycentric' international operations, MNCs generally gave their subsidiaries considerable autonomy to respond to national markets. Subsidiaries therefore tended to adapt to national industrial relations regimes. Now, MNCs are more likely to impose common patterns of employment relations across their operations internationally. The outcome of such forces is the emergence of company-based employment systems (Marginson and Sisson 1994). Pressures exist for the big multinational players to converge, as the history of lean production has shown. But considerable differences in corporate strategies are still likely, as MacDuffie (1995) has argued in the case of the car industry. One implication is that patterns of industrial relations *within* countries, even within the same sector, are likely to become more heterogeneous: rather than the British or Swedish model, one would be forced to talk of the GM or Ford model, or the

Toyota or Peugeot pattern. *Cross-nationally*, there would be increasing 'corporate isomorphism' (Ferner 1997). The employment practices of Ford in Germany, Spain or Britain would increasingly resemble each other. Traditionally, one of the stumbling blocks to the convergence thesis has been the existence of strong national regulatory institutions that have imposed country-specific practices on even the most internationally integrated of enterprises. An interesting thread of research in recent years has examined the robustness in practice of such institutional constraints, notably in Germany, the paradigm of the highly regulated industrial relations system. There is some evidence to suggest that foreign multinationals in Germany have a significant margin of manoeuvre even with respect to such fundamental aspects of the German system as workforce representation through works councils, and industry bargaining (e.g. Mueller 1997).

Locke (1995), too, points to increasing intra-national diversity, arguing that new practices in work organization, for example, are more likely to be adopted in greenfield sites, in the context of major technological innovation, in sectors where international competition is strongest – e.g. cars, steel, electronics – and where the social partners are able to forge constructive partnerships at corporate level. These widening variations suggest that patterns of employment relations respond to many factors other than the national institutional environment. At the same time, differences between national institutions in Europe are being squeezed from above, by the increasingly solid supra-national framework provided by EU regulation in the social area. In short, the (somewhat paradoxical) picture that emerges is one of increasing diversity within national systems but of increasing convergence between them.

Equally, however, other areas of research have provided strong grounds for believing that national systems can and do resist the homogenizing tendencies of 'internationalization'. First, to focus on company-based employment systems is to miss the point that MNCs are not 'stateless' players transcending nationality – as in Reich's vision (1991) – but are themselves normally embedded within a country-of-origin business system that strongly influences their behaviour (Ruigrok and Tulder 1995). Second, recent research has considerably deepened our understanding of the complex historical and institutional bases of nationally specific industrial relations systems. Crouch (1993), for example, has insisted on the continuing legacy of such elements of pre-capitalist social organization as the guild structure. Work on 'national business systems' has shown that participation in the international economy is compatible with a great variety of ways of organizing, controlling and financing productive activity, managing markets, educating and training the labour force, and so on (Whitley 1992; Whitley and Kristensen 1995). Moreover, many of these aspects remain unaffected by the incursions of multinational corporations. Thus, according to Köhler and Woodard (1997), despite intense pressures to homogenization in the international machine tool industry, important national differences in the organization of work – for example, in the degree of task differentiation – remain. These are related to different national traditions in the organization of skills and the division of labour.

Third, despite some high profile cases such as the transfer by Hoover of production facilities from France to Scotland in 1993, social dumping may not be as prevalent as has been feared. One reason is that national states are not totally defenceless against some manifestations of social dumping, for example the use by employers of cheap labour from other EU countries: as our contributors report in this volume, legislation was passed in Norway in 1992 to reduce social dumping by making it possible for collective bargaining parties to extend the terms of an agreement to all employees in the activity concerned; on similar grounds, the rarely used provisions of German labour law for extending the terms of collective agreements were invoked in the construction industry in 1996. A second reason is that the image of footloose MNCs responding rapidly and frequently to differences in unit labour costs and in standards of employee protection is an exaggerated one. It is clear that MNCs are motivated by a variety of factors other than wage costs, notably by industrial peace, the skills of the labour force, the provision of infrastructure, government investment incentives, the need to be in national markets, and so on.

We may thus conclude that the pressures of 'internationalization' are real and substantial, but neither unilinear nor overwhelming in their industrial relations consequences. We share in part the position of Hirst and Thompson (1996), that the idea of 'globalization' can be both a rhetorical device and a self-fulfilling prophecy in its logic of fatalism; yet we would differ from their tendency to dismiss the seriousness and novelty of many of the recent developments in the international economy. The processes which the term identifies do have significant disruptive potential, not least in industrial relations. What is also clear is that some types of institution – and national system – are more vulnerable than others. It is such differences which we address in the remainder of this introduction.

Collective Regulation: 'Social Partnership' Under Strain?

When we were preparing the first edition, the notion of 'social partnership' had an alien ring to the English speaker; and where our authors had written 'social partners' we substituted 'employers and trade unions'. Here, certainly, there has been a sea-change in our own country, and in this respect at least we have now used a lighter editorial touch. Yet is continental 'social partnership' itself under threat?

First, the concept itself requires clarification. It is, first of all, not universal in continental Europe but common where there is a significant catholic tradition; in the Nordic countries, by contrast, the phrase 'labour market parties' is more usual. 'Social partnership' cannot be taken as a synonym for industrial peace and harmony: paradoxically, the term is often most familiar in countries with the strongest traditions of militancy and class conflict. What the idea of 'social partners' implies however (and here the Nordic concept is virtually identical) is, first a societal recognition of the different interests of workers and employers; second, an acceptance – indeed encouragement – of the collective representation of these interests; and third, an aspiration that their organized accommodation may provide an effective basis for the regulation of work and the labour market. Implicit also is the notion that encompassing organizations (Olson 1982) and centralized regulation are the optimal features of an industrial relations system. Is such a conception now obsolete?

| The Ambiguities of Decentralization

In our first edition we stressed the onward march of decentralization, driven by companies' pursuit of flexibility in order to respond to fast-changing markets. But we also suggested that there was great variation between countries in the extent, the pace and indeed the meaning of decentralization. Events of the past few years have clarified the picture somewhat. There has been a notable growth in the importance of the company level. The tendencies to 'micro-corporatism' in countries such as Italy have been confirmed, and are reported also in countries such as Finland, as larger companies attempt to respond to mounting international competition (and to the internationalization of their own operations). It now appears, however, that what we called 'centrally co-ordinated decentralization' (Ferner and Hyman 1992: xxxvi) has been the major tendency. Decentralization has largely taken the form of a controlled and co-ordinated devolution of functions from higher to lower levels of the system; this has strong parallels – possibly not altogether accidental – with the widespread pattern of co-ordinated devolution of managerial responsibilities that has taken place within large corporations in recent years. This picture is confirmed by the research of Traxler (1995). Using a similar categorization, of 'organized' as opposed to 'disorganized' decentralization, he finds that most European countries that have decentralized industrial relations (and a number have not) have done so in a co-ordinated fashion. Thus, in Germany or the Netherlands, as our contributors explain, opening clauses in industry agreements have become increasingly important, allowing greater flexibility of practices (notably over working time) at company level, but the principle of industry bargaining has not – so far – been seriously challenged. The disorganized decentralization of industrial relations is marked only in the anomalous case of Britain, a pattern it shares with the USA.

In general, firms have exerted little pressure for radical decentralization: in case after case our contributors report that while employers are anxious to see greater flexibility at corporate level, they wish also to preserve the framework of labour peace provided by a structure of higher-level agreements. One might hypothesize too, that employers are also keen to 'take flexibility out of competition': in small and medium companies, and in countries, regions or industries where the appropriate human resource management skills are scarce and training systems underdeveloped, the potential for employers to develop innovative new employment relations policy in respect of work organization, employee involvement or performance management is likely to be limited. The suggestion of a straight-forward logic of decentralization (Katz 1993) underestimates the ambiguities and contradictions of the process: the costs as well as the benefits (for employers) of company-specific regimes. For managers themselves, a 'free' labour market is commonly perceived as a mixed blessing.

In some respects, the degree of higher-level co-ordination has increased in the 1990s. This appears to be true in Spain, France, the Netherlands and most strikingly in Italy. In all these countries, recent central confederal agreements have (in some instances for the first time) formalized the respective competences of different levels of bargaining. In Italy, major reform laws 'negotiated' with the social partners have been passed. Such agreements, while maintaining the integration of the system, have also tended to devolve greater autonomy to lower levels, for example through powers to rescind or undercut the terms of higher-level agreements. Overall though, the representative status of the central actors on the employers' side – hence their position as 'social partners' – has often been buttressed rather than further weakened.

The Adaptability of Trade Union Movements

Can the same be said of trade unions? Here, certainly, the issues are more problematic. The literature of the past decade (Crouch 1992; Golden and Pontusson 1992; Leisink et al. 1995; Visser 1994 and 1995) has overwhelmingly identified unions as the major victims of internationalization and of the dissolution of 'articulated' industrial relations systems. While cohesive, solidaristic union movements may have proved better placed to withstand the challenges, these characteristics themselves are seen as undermined by hostile circumstances. Among the features commonly emphasized are the decline of the manual working class, and particularly of those sectors in which 'mass' trade unionism had its strongholds; the differentiation of interests between 'winners' and 'losers' in economic restructuring; the perceived common interest between management and workforce at establishment level in securing competitiveness in a harsher product market environment with the consequent pressures to 'company egoism' and 'wildcat co-operation'; the contradictory interests of tax-payers and public employees (often of course the same persons) generating new and divisive conflicts.

Again, the evidence of our national chapters is that this is not the whole story, and that there are very different national stories to be told. The 'decline of the national trade union' (Locke 1995) is not universal; or to make the point differently, in trade unions as among employers we can identify *both* a trend to devolution and differentiation *and*, in many countries, new strategies and structures for articulation between levels and accommodation between interests.

Here, a key point to emphasize is the danger of a narrow 'collective bargaining' focus on trade union dynamics. The devolution of bargaining certainly implies parallel pressures within unions and union movements. However, unions are not only – even in the 'Anglo-Saxon' industrial relations systems – collective bargainers pure and simple. National unions are bearers of collective traditions which can provide legitimacy and vocabularies of motive to representatives at lower levels – as Hege and Dufour (1995) have emphasized in their study which demonstrates surprising affinities between workplace activists in France and Germany. They are also custodians of employee interests beyond the individual workplace. That distinctive 'European' notion, the 'social wage', is a neat example of the intersection of different agendas of representation: unions (and their members and broader constituencies) are concerned not only with the nominal wage or salary but also with the size of tax and other deductions, and with the social benefits and entitlements which their contributions provide. In many countries, the institutionalized role of the unions in the administration of the social welfare system contributes to membership stability (as in Belgium and most Nordic countries) or at least assigns them a 'public status'. More generally, one of the typical connotations of 'social partnership' is precisely that unions have a legitimate role in representing employee interests over all these agendas. This legitimacy has indeed been increasingly questioned in several countries, as our contributors show; but such challenges have, in most cases, had limited impact. Our Dutch chapter provides a cogent analysis of one case where the ability to share in the brokering of trade-offs between these different interest agendas has sustained the institutional robustness of trade unionism despite severe membership decline. This connects closely to our following theme.

The Role of the State: Changing Capacities and Strategies

The corollary of the 'internationalization' thesis, as has already been seen, is the erosion of the regulatory capacity of national states, the victims of 'regime shopping' by MNCs and of the stern criteria of fiscal rectitude within financial markets.

Many of the developments of the 1990s can be read in this light. In retrospect, what may be identified as one of the decisive episodes of the decade is the *Standort* debate in Germany: the argument that the strongest economy in Europe was being undermined by high wages, excessively restrictive labour market regulation and expensive social benefits, so that investment was inhibited and disinvestment encouraged. Whether or not the analysis was correct (our own authors discover little supportive evidence) is almost beside the point: its assumptions have driven public policy discussion and thus are 'real in their consequences'. The *Bundesbank* has continued to use its deflationary capacities to discipline wage bargainers, which is nothing new; what *is* a significant change from the 1980s is a more systematic government commitment to deregulation and the first serious efforts to rein in the welfare state. Whether all this amounts to the removal of the 'social' from the 'social market economy' is a moot point. Certainly the Kohl government is a belated participant in the state-sponsored pursuit of 'flexibility' and market liberalization, which in many other European countries was already far advanced by the end of the 1980s. Indeed the *Standort* controversy might be viewed as a direct response to the initiatives of Germany's competitors; but if so, it has given another powerful twist to the downward spiral of deregulation.

The Maastricht convergence criteria have reinforced these tendencies. Most governments have indeed faced powerful endogenous pressures to reduce the public debt, and thus to contain the expanding costs of public welfare; but the desire to join the fast track to the single currency has given such concerns new urgency. Countries which have committed themselves to first-wave EMU entry have ruled out the use of currency devaluation as a means of maintaining international competitiveness. The governments of France, Germany and Italy – to identify only the larger EU countries – have all cited EMU as the rationale for major inroads into public expenditure, provoking in the process new levels of social and industrial conflict. The Maastricht rules imply a competitive deflationary bias which individual governments will find it very difficult to withstand. The pessimistic conclusion is that European governments are perforce taking an active role in the unravelling of national post-war settlements.

Yet other readings are possible. The central argument of Hirst and Thompson (1996) is that 'globalization' is a myth and that the impotence of national governments is largely self-imposed through political choice. The title of a recent symposium, *States Against Markets: the Limits of Globalization* (Boyer and Drache 1996) implies a similar message – though the specific analyses and arguments of its contributors convey a more sombre account. The underlying thesis could be summarized as follows: the capacity for an autarchic economic (and hence industrial relations) regime is increasingly constrained by cross-national economic integration; but precisely because the integration which bears most heavily on European states is *internal* to Europe itself, the social regulation of market forces can in principle be reconstructed at EU level. This is not the place to revisit the issue of the nature and limits of the European 'social dimension': its achievements may be deemed pathetic in comparison with the pace of economic (de)regulation at European level, but are not to be dismissed out of hand. The meaning of the 'social dimension', like that of 'Europe' itself, is a terrain of struggle rather than a predetermined outcome. Streeck has written (1996: 313) that 'the European nation-state appears obsolete and alive at the same time: obsolete as the wielder of effective sovereignty over "its" economy, and powerfully alive as the most effective opponent of the recreation of internal sovereignty at the international level'. In their insistence on 'subsidiarity', most European governments ally with both national and multinational capital in blocking a possible transnational route to the socialization of the market. But this is political choice rather than economic necessity, strategy more than structure.

Meanwhile it is important to add that 'economic imperatives' may be contradictory in their implications, and are likely to be mediated – or indeed obstructed – by political contingencies at national level. 'Internationalization' notwithstanding, it is surely also noteworthy how far distinctive national 'state traditions' in industrial relations have persisted – or even been (re)invented. In the early 1990s, it was normally taken as self-evident that tripartite or bipartite concertation – or 'neo-corporatism' – was dead and buried. It had been useful to governments (and employers) as a vehicle of wage restraint in an era when trade unions possessed significant labour market strength, but was superfluous when unemployment exerted its own disciplines on bargainers and when employers were preoccupied with the pursuit of company-level flexibility. Deconcertation has certainly been a feature of some countries: as in Sweden, where SAF decided in 1990 to withdraw from tripartite labour market agencies, giving the Bildt government the green light to remove the unions also. The return to office of the Social Democrats has brought no significant moves towards the restoration of the former 'Swedish model' (nor, one might add, is a Blair government likely to reverse the demolition of tripartite institutions in Britain during the 1980s). But on the other hand, in countries like Austria corporatism has never gone away. In Spain, central agreements have reappeared in recent years after a period of quiescence, while the tripartite Economic and Social Council was at long last established in 1992; in Portugal institutionalized tripartism has been attempted over the past decade, with variable success. In Ireland, the succession of central agreements has continued with Partnership 2000, which strengthens the component of general political exchange by tying centralized wage co-ordination to a policy agenda for tackling problems of social exclusion. In the Netherlands, the tendencies, set in train by the 1982 Wassenaar accord, to long-term co-ordinated wage restraint appear to have been consolidated in recent years following the 'New Course' of 1993.

How is one to explain the persistence and indeed the revival of central co-ordination and concertation in Europe in the 1990s? In some cases this may be the product of the special 'geosocial' conditions of many of the 'peripheral' countries of western Europe. 'Distances in the Netherlands are small,' writes Visser in explaining that country's corporatist tradition; and the same could be said of Austria, Finland, Ireland, Norway and Portugal: restricted physical distance (at least between the main populated areas) facilitates centralized networks of key actors in close interaction. But it is clear that the phenomenon is far more widespread than this. Despite recent strains, conservative governments in both France (up to 1997) and Germany have still displayed a preference for pursuing change through agreement with the 'social partners'. The most dramatic case is however Italy, where a succession of governments in the 1990s have brokered bipartite and tripartite deals and have thus engineered the formal reconstruction of corporatist concertation.

A first element of explanation is provided by Regalia and Regini in this volume. They ascribe resurgent concertation to the imperatives of the latest phase of international competition, which has made the state arena a key factor in national competitiveness (Regini 1997). While flexibility at the micro-level in response to dynamic markets was important in the 1980s and remains so, it is also imperative to keep costs down within the economy as a whole as international competition intensifies: hence the abolition of the Italian *scala mobile* wage indexation system in the 1990s. Moreover, some of the key components of indirect labour costs – notably state and employer contributions to retirement pensions and other social benefits – come within the sphere of state action. One element in the economic context is undoubtedly the impact of the Maastricht convergence criteria; economy-wide control of costs assumes added urgency.

Second, the persistence of long-term, structural mass unemployment, with the associated dangers – increasingly manifest – of social breakdown, exclusion and right-wing extremism has prompted national responses: most notably in France, where the 1993 five-year employment law spawned a series of central agreements.

In France and elsewhere, state action to reduce employers' contributions has been an important part of the trade-offs to tackle unemployment. In Spain, too, the unemployment problem has been a major factor in central employer–union relations in the 1990s, while a major tripartite pact on employment was signed in Italy in 1996. Britain, long in the thrall of the political conviction that the market would resolve the problem without the need for state (let alone concerted social-partner) intervention, remains an isolated exception to such general trends.

Third, reform of welfare and social security systems has come to the top of the political agenda as governments battle to meet the criteria for economic and monetary union in a context of rising demands on the system caused by wide-scale unemployment, an ageing workforce, and so on. In many countries, the 'social partners' have a central role in the management of welfare systems through tripartite institutions, or through powers in effect delegated to them by the state. There has been at least an initial presumption, therefore, that the reform of welfare and social security will involve unions and employers' organizations. Efforts by governments to exclude the social partners – in particular the unions – from their reform plans have tended to be unsuccessful: witness the failure of Berlusconi's initiatives in Italy, or the outbreak of mass protest in France in December 1995.

Observers have pointed to major differences between the emerging 1990s corporatism and the classic 1970s variant. Traxler (1995 and in this volume), for example, speaks of a move from 'demand-side' to 'supply-side' corporatism. A similar notion underlies Regini's (1997) analysis. He argues that current concerta-tion tendencies are less inherently unstable than were corporatist experiences in the 1970s. Rather than a set of exchanges of benefits as before, which could often not be delivered, current concertation tends to be structured round the devolution of competences for policy-making to organized interests. In other words, it is *regulative*, rather than *redistributive*. This very quality may prevent a rift appearing between central players and their rank and file – an inherent problem of 1970s corporatism – since articulation between different levels in the system is one of the prime subjects of concertation.

All this is to indicate that states possess a key role in the reconfiguration of the relationship between social regulation and markets (including labour markets). To speak of deregulation, as Standing (1997) insists, is a misnomer: markets are one particular medium for *regulating* social relations; and to alter an established pattern of interdependence between market regulation and other regulatory processes can require forceful and disruptive intervention. At the same time as governments pursue at least potentially unpopular initiatives, their own legitimacy is often fragile: self-evidently in Italy, with the discrediting and disintegration of the former 'political class' in the 1990s, but also apparent in most other European countries with declining electoral allegiance to centre parties and increasing support for those on each extreme (often united in their opposition to the main drift of European integration). Concertation with the 'social partners' is in such circumstances a means of borrowing legitimacy or, to put it differently, of sharing the blame. On this reading, we can anticipate a continued revival of neo-corporatism – albeit with very distinctive national colorations – for the foreseeable future: only so long as the 'social partners' themselves are willing to play their part. For the unions in particular this involves very sensitive strategic choices, and typically reflects less a hope for gain (as in the 1960s and 1970s) than a fear of even greater loss.

Institutional Transformation or Institutional Rigidity: Ambiguous Still?

In the first edition we argued that the 'stickiness' of institutions, especially when enshrined in law, raises the question of how national industrial relations models respond to change. We suggested that institutions mediated common external forces in a variety of ways and with greater or lesser degrees of success. The key dimensions of the strength and the degree of rigidity of institutions helped explain the different trajectories of national industrial relations systems in the 1980s. For example, strong and inflexible institutions could not accommodate changes in markets and employment through evolutionary adaptation, leading to institutional crisis; the British and Swedish cases are examples of 'forced transformation' of institutions. By contrast, where institutions were weak and 'raw' power relations relatively untrammelled, transformations in economic structure created little pressure for institutional change, and the actors – particularly employers – could exert a good deal of strategic choice. Finally, where regulatory institutions were strong but flexible – notably, the German dual system of sectoral bargaining and workplace representation – economic change could be accommodated and its challenges successfully met. We argued that the nature of change in such systems depended on the sources of strength and flexibility: arrangements able to respond to the 'productivistic' agenda of employers at the company level were more likely to do well.

Five years on, these perceptions have been subjected to some important real-world testing, enabling us to refine the notion of institutional strength and flexibility. The key case is in many ways that of Germany. The optimism of our German authors in 1992 has given way to a more sombre evaluation. In particular, the incorporation of the east has been a more complex and less tractable process than foreseen. Despite the formal adoption of the west German institutions of industrial relations, there are indications that these are not functioning with the same efficacy as in the west. East German actors have not been socialized into the patterns of behaviour and attitudes that are the invisible prerequisite for the operation of the dual system. There appears, moreover, to be a danger of the 'contamination' spreading westwards as employers make coercive comparisons across Germany, undermining the system from within.

These problems suggest a first critical, if obvious, observation about the roots of institutional efficacy: that the strength of institutions does not only derive from strong formal arrangements, but from an 'invisible' web of actors' perceptions and strategies, and of 'tacit skills' and experience in operating the arrangements. This institutional 'culture' is what breathes life into potentially strong institutions. Where, as in Germany, there is a sudden, traumatic disruption of the invisible web of understandings, previously strong institutions may be endangered even without changes in their formal character. In other countries, such as Spain, France or Portugal, strong statutory regulation has not equated to institutional strength since it has been unmatched by a developed culture of institutional 'operation'. A rather similar point is implicit in the analysis of works councils in France and Germany by Hege and Dufour (1995). They show that actors need to adopt the appropriate strategies and interrelationships if statutory institutional provisions of worker representation are to operate effectively: in particular, councils are likely to be ineffective where they do not establish strong links with external unions.

Second, the German case also suggests that the challenges of economic transformation require different kinds of institutional responsiveness at different times. In the 1980s, the key requirement was for 'productivity coalitions' to allow flexibility in working practices at the level of the company in order to meet international competition, adopt new technology, respond to fast-changing markets, and so on. The German model gained its 'flexible strength' from its consistent ability to restructure the organization of work within its institutional constraints. Britain, by contrast, was forced into a traumatic transformation of workplace relations because strong (informal) institutions of job control did not permit smooth adaptation.

The systemic requirement of workplace flexibility is still important throughout Europe. But as we suggested above, there are additional pressures: the incorporation of new regions into the world economy, the rise of new international competitors, and in particular the sudden opening up of a large pool of relatively skilled, very cheap labour on the eastern borders of the European Union, have changed the terms of the debate (e.g. Deutschmann 1994). Perhaps the crucial change in the 1990s is that 'quality' and 'cost' competitiveness are no longer alternatives: success depends increasingly on the ability to combine high quality and reliability with competitive costs. Hence there are now much greater pressures for the control of labour costs, even in economies that have previously competed on the basis of flexible 'quality production'. While workplace flexibility posed only limited problems for the German system, labour cost pressures are much more threatening to the premises of the high-skill, high-wage German model, and to the aspirations and expectations of German employees. The challenge of meeting low-wage competition is likely, therefore, to be what Locke and Thelen (1995) call an 'institutional sticking point': by this they mean that a crucial issue thrown up by economic transformation threatens the accommodations and interests that lie at the heart of the national model.

As Locke and Thelen stress, comparative institutional analysis needs to take into account the fact that institutional sticking points are likely to be different from country to country. They argue, for example, that in Sweden, employers' demands threatened the viability of the traditional model because they called into question the solidaristic approach to wages that was vital to the self-identity of the Swedish labour movement. On the other hand, a challenge to central solidaristic wage determination is unlikely to be a crunch issue in different national systems. For example, the author of our chapter on Austria stresses that the strong, formalized institutions of Austrian corporatism are not dependent on low wage differentials, and have not been threatened by a widening of differentials in recent years. Norway provides an interesting and somewhat puzzling case. Like Sweden, its solidaristic pay ethos is a core element of the model. Unlike Sweden, however, it has come through the 1990s with solidarism relatively unscathed. The solution seems to lie in the very different form of engagement of the two countries with the international economy: Sweden's is based on a strong manufacturing export sector dominated by major multinationals, while Norway's rests predominantly on natural resources – particularly oil – still largely under state control.

Third, developments in several countries in the last few years suggest that institutional robustness and successful adaptation rely on a peculiar combination of flexibility and rigidity. The 'flexible rigidity' of the German system traditionally rested on the combination of the rigid statutory definition of the dual system, together with great flexibility of outcomes in the area of work organization. One reason the German system has run into difficulties – as with the significant problems experienced in implementing flexible working-time arrangements – may be that economic transformation has thrown it up against areas like working time where there has been considerable *substantive* regulation by law and generous social benefits which are highly symbolic outcomes of trade union struggles in previous decades.

Elsewhere, a trend towards a strengthening of *procedural* formalization has gone hand-in-hand with *substantive* flexibility. One aspect of this is the way in which in Spain, Italy and elsewhere, central agreements have drawn up new, more explicit procedural rules governing bargaining relationships at different levels, while at the same time, leaving more autonomy for each level to decide the substantive content of agreement. As the Italian contributors argue in this volume, this proceduralization has been driven by the need to enhance the stability and predictability of the system. In general, as mentioned earlier, therefore, more of the detail of industrial relations practice is being filled in at lower levels of the system, with opt-out and opening clauses, with the spread of minimum pay rather than 'normal' pay systems as in Denmark, and so on. In short, what in the 1980s was regarded as 'wildcat co-operation' at company level is becoming increasingly legitimized and institutionalized.

One question for the future is whether such institutional tweaking to allow increasing substantive flexibility will pose long-term threats to the robustness of institutions. The widening space for strategic choice, particularly by employers, at company level may come to exert cumulative pressure for change on institutional arrangements. As Locke (1995) argues, recent years have witnessed the uneasy coexistence – often with the same companies, and sometimes even at the same time – of strategies of quality production and low-cost competition. While substantive flexibility may be the order of the day, the increasing resort by employers to low-cost options is likely to stick in the institutional craw in countries like Germany. Will adaptation then take place through negotiated adjustments, or through the weakening or collapse of hitherto robust institutions (cf. Locke 1995: 25)?

▌ References

Boyer, R. and Drache, D. (eds) 1996: *States Against Markets: the Limits of Globalization*, London: Routledge.

Crouch, C. 1992: The fate of articulated industrial relations systems, in M. Regini (ed.) *The Future of Labour Movements*, London: Sage, 169–87.

Crouch, C. 1993: *Industrial Relations and European State Traditions*. Oxford: Clarendon Press.

Deutschmann, C. 1994: Present restructuration policies of multinational companies in Germany and their impact on industrial relations and human resources. Paper presented to European Commission Human Capital & Mobility Conference on *Multinational Companies and Human Resources*, Barcelona, 19–21 November.

Erickson, C. and Kuruvilla, S. 1995: Labor cost incentives for capital mobility in the European Community, in S. Jacoby (ed.) *The Workers of Nations. Industrial Relations in a Global Economy*, New York/Oxford: OUP, 35–53.

Ferner, A. 1997: Country of origin effects and HRM in multinational companies, *Human Resource Management Journal*, 7(1), 19–38.

Ferner, A. and Hyman, R. 1992: Introduction. Industrial Relations in the New Europe, Oxford: Blackwell Publishers, xvi–xlix.

Golden, M. and J. Pontusson (eds) 1992: *Bargaining for Change: Union Politics in North America and Europe*, Ithaca: Cornell UP.

Hege, A. and Dufour, C. 1995: Decentralization and legitimacy in employee representation, *European Journal of Industrial Relations*, 1(1), 83–99.

Hirst, P. and Thompson, G. 1996: *Globalization in Question*, Cambridge: Polity.

Jones, G. 1996: *The Evolution of International Business*. London: Routledge.

Katz, H. 1993: Decentralization of collective bargaining, *Industrial and Labor Relations Review* 47, 3–22.

Köhler, C. and Woodard, J. 1997: Systems of work and socio-economic structures: a comparison of Germany, Spain, France and Japan, *European Journal of Industrial Relations*, 3(1), March, 59–82.

Leisink, P., Van Leemput, J. and Vilrokx, J. (eds) 1995: *The Challenges to Trade Unions in Europe*, Aldershot: Edward Elgar.

Locke, R. 1995: The transformation of industrial relations? A cross-national review, in K. Wever and L. Turner (eds) *The Comparative Political Economy of Industrial Relations*, Madison: IIRA, 9–32.

Locke, R. and Thelen, K. 1995: Apples and oranges revisited: contextualized comparisons and the study of comparative labor politics, *Politics & Society*, 23(3), September, 337–67.

MacDuffie, J.P. 1995: International trends in work organization in the auto industry: national-level vs. company-level perspectives, in K. Wever and L. Turner (eds) *The Comparative Political Economy of Industrial Relations*, Madison: IRRA, 71–113.

Marginson, P. and Sisson, K. 1994: The structure of transnational capital in Europe: the emerging Euro-company and its implications for industrial relations, in Hyman, R. and Ferner, A. (eds) *New Frontiers in European Industrial Relations*, Oxford: Blackwell Publishers, 15–51.

Mueller, F. 1996: National stakeholders in the global contest for corporate investment, *European Journal of Industrial Relations*, 2(3), 345–68.

Mueller, M. 1997: Human resource and industrial relations practices of UK and US multinationals in Germany. University of Innsbruck: mimeo.

Olson, M. 1982: *The Rise and Decline of Nations*. New Haven: Yale University Press.

Regini, M. 1997: Still engaging in corporatism? Recent Italian experience on comparative perspective, *European Journal of Industrial Relations*, 3, 3.

Reich, R. 1991: *The Work of Nations. Preparing ourselves for 21st century capitalism*. New York: Alfred Knopf.

Ruigrok, W. and van Tulder, R. 1995: *The Logic of International Restructuring*, London/New York: Routledge.

Standing, G. 1997: Globalization, Labour flexibility and insecurity, *European Journal of Industrial Relations*, 3(1), 7–37.

Streeck, W. 1992: National diversity, regime competition and institutional deadlock, *Journal of Public Policy*, 12, 301–30.

Streeck, W. 1996: Public power beyond the nation-state in Boyer, R. and Drache, D. (eds) *States Against Markets: the Limits of Globalization*, London: Routledge, 299–315.

Traxler, F. 1995: Farewell to labour market associations? Organized versus disorganized decentralization as a map for industrial relations, in C. Crouch and F. Traxler (eds) *Organized Industrial Relations in Europe: What Future?*, Aldershot: Avebury: 3–19.

UNCTAD 1994: *World Investment Report (1994) Transnational Corporations, Employment and the Workplace*. New York/Geneva: UN.

Visser, J. 1994: European trade unions: the transition years in R. Hyman and A. Ferner (eds) *New Frontiers in European Industrial Relations*, Oxford: Blackwell, 323–56.

Visser, J. 1995: Trade unions from a comparative perspective, in J. Van Ruysseveldt, J. Visser and J. van Hoof (eds) *Comparative Industrial and Employment Relations*, London: Sage, 37–67.

Whitley, R. (ed.) 1992: *European Business Systems: Firms and Markets in their National Contexts*. London: Sage.

Whitley, R. and Kristensen, P.H. (eds) 1995: *The Changing European Firm. Limits to Convergence*. London/New York: Routledge.

1 Great Britain: From Partial Collectivism to Neo-liberalism to Where?

PAUL EDWARDS • MARK HALL • RICHARD HYMAN • PAUL MARGINSON • KEITH SISSON • JEREMY WADDINGTON • DAVID WINCHESTER

Introduction

The period since the election of the Conservative government under Mrs Thatcher in May 1979 has seen major changes in observable features of the British industrial relations landscape and in their underlying nature. The features include the longest recorded decline in trade union membership and a fall in strike rates to their lowest ever levels. Underlying developments include a decline in the role of collective bargaining and the growth of new management practices which often go under the label of human resource management (HRM).

Four issues need to be addressed in understanding these developments. First, how far have new forms of managing the employment relationship taken root and, to the extent that they have, what explains them? For example, some observers have argued that employment legislation had direct effects on such things as union membership and strikes, while others focus on the indirect effects of free market policies and privatization and yet others deny any effects at all. Second, does the period since 1979 mark a watershed? Though change is undeniable, two elements of continuity are crucial. On the one hand, many of the developments of the period have been slow and patchy; in particular, the take-up of HRM has been limited and there is little evidence that it is directly replacing trade unions. On the other hand, the pre-1979 period was much less firmly institutionalized as a system than is now often suggested. There was never a single system, for there were marked differences between the public and private sectors in the nature of collective bargaining, and significant groups of employees, notably the low-paid and those in small firms, were never covered by it. It was thus not a matter of a shift from a fully institutionalized system to an equally clearly deregulated one. Third, what have been the effects of new systems on economic performance? Finally, what are the prospects? A notable trend during the 1980s and 1990s was the growing impact of European Community legislation, for example in the areas of European Works Councils, consultation on redundancies and equal opportunities. What, then, are the links between European regulation and the British model, and how far does that model itself contain regulatory as well as free market tendencies?

It was commonly argued up to the mid-1980s that, though there had been changes in the conduct of industrial relations, the main institutions of collective bargaining remained in place. From the vantage point of the 1990s, it is apparent that change gathered pace from about 1987. Such developments have led some observers to speak of the end of institutional industrial relations (Purcell 1993). But claims by the government that a fully flexible and high-skill economy had been created, and arguments by critics that change has meant only low-skill jobs and a growth in exploitation, are too simple. In some parts of the economy there has been up-skilling and a growth in commitment from workers. But they are a small part. Divisions between those in 'good' jobs and those in 'bad' jobs or with no jobs at all have widened. In between these extremes is a wide range of situations in which pre-existing assumptions have disappeared but in which there is no clear new model.

The chapter draws on an earlier textbook (Edwards 1995) which contains discussion of important issues, such as industrial relations in small firms, which are not considered in any detail here. As well as updating some material, the chapter gives particular attention to the 'outcomes' issues and to where Britain stands in the European context. The focus is on Great Britain, with its workforce of about 22.5 million, as distinct from the whole of the United Kingdom, which also includes Northern Ireland (with around 0.5 million workers). Northern Ireland is distinctive in some respects – notably labour law, a relatively high level of union membership (attributable in part to a large public sector) and the pattern of trade union organization – though it shares many of the broader features of the British situation.[1]

The chapter begins with an outline of the distinctive historical evolution of British industrial relations. It then outlines key changes in the operation of the labour market. Government policy, in particular in the field of labour law, is then described. The three following sections turn to employers in the private and public sectors (including the take-up of HRM) and then to trade unions. The final substantive section examines change at workplace level including strikes and economic performance.

Capital, Labour and the State

Origins of the System

Three characteristics mark Britain out from other countries: the continuity of experience, the centrality of the workplace, and the role of the state. First, in no other country do contemporary developments reflect as strongly deep historical origins. There have been few decisive turning points, such as the agreements of 1909 and 1938 in Sweden or post-war reconstruction in Germany, and many contemporary themes, such as the lack of legally enforceable collective agreements, reflect the legacy of history. By the 1880s, when Beatrice Webb coined the term 'collective bargaining', the practice that she identified was already well established in British industrial relations; and by the end of the nineteenth century, support for 'free collective bargaining' was an accepted element in British public policy.

Second, this legacy involved the handling of industrial relations at the level of the workplace. As described below, the alternative of legal regulation was never a serious possibility. The other alternative, of comprehensive industry-level agreements, existed in certain sectors such as clothing and building, but in the key industry of engineering there was no such system (Sisson 1987). There was no framework defining the rights and obligations of the parties. The rules of employment were settled on a day-to-day basis within the workplace. A major source of authority was 'custom and practice': the unwritten norms and understandings which established in a particular workplace the rules of work. Workplaces developed their own sets of custom and practice rules, which naturally had some family resemblance with each other but which stemmed from negotiation at the point of production and not from any higher-level authority.

A key juncture was the 1897–8 dispute in the engineering industry. The employers won the strike but failed to use their victory to root out craft practices from the shop floor. They certainly did not welcome such practices, and they tried to tackle them aggressively when they had the chance; but this tactical toughness was not matched by any strategic vision, and the practices were able to re-emerge. The alternative, of a co-operative approach, was rejected because it was felt to undermine the cherished 'right to manage' (Zeitlin 1990). The result was two-fold: space was left for workers to develop their own shop floor practices, and the oscillation between toughness and distancing from the shop floor promoted distrust of management which allowed workers, when conditions permitted, to build on these practices an institutional challenge to managerial authority.

Considerable attention has been given to the role of the shop steward – a member of a work group elected to represent the group in dealings with management – in the conduct of workplace bargaining. By the 1960s stewards had come to prominence in large parts of engineering and, in large factories in particular, their organizations operated largely independently of official union hierarchies (Terry 1995). Yet, before then, large sectors of engineering had stewards only for limited numbers of craft workers, while, outside engineering, they were even less common. Workplace bargaining should not be equated with the specific presence of a shop steward. The general situation was one in which managers and workers reached an accommodation within the workplace without a framework of rules laid down either by the state or by industry-wide agreements.

The reasons for this state of affairs can be located in the structural conditions faced by employers and workers, and in the choices made at key junctures. The timing and pace of industrialization discouraged radical breaks with the past: the early start meant that factories grew up when craft skills were still crucial, whereas in Germany, for example, industrial growth occurred after these skills became less central; a slow pace of change permitted craft systems to remain. By the key period of the late nineteenth century, British firms were small and they produced for specialized markets, not for mass consumption. Compared with their American counterparts, their size made them less able to take on craft unions, while their market structure reduced the incentive to do so (Lazonick 1990). Moreover, the craft system brought considerable benefits, notably the use of skilled workers to supervise and discipline the less skilled. As Hyman (1995: 32) puts it, there was a tradition of 'unscientific' management, as opposed to the model of rationalized scientific management developed in the United States.

It is often assumed that British firms failed to take up new techniques such as assembly line production. Yet in the leading case of the car industry innovation did take place (Williams et al. 1994). As Whitston (1996) shows, in the engineering sector as a whole British firms did take a clear interest in new production techniques. What was 'unscientific' was, first, a relative absence of formal education, which meant that attempts to be scientific were largely the shop floor activities of 'practical men' (Aldcroft 1992: 117). Hobsbawm (1977: 58–9) notes high illiteracy rates in England (but not Scotland) in 1875 and the fact that until 1898 the only way into the engineering profession was through apprenticeship. Second was a lack of integration of production with product design and marketing, so that production innovations never led to the capture of new markets. British firms, it is often argued, were good at designing new products but not at developing mass markets or exploiting economies of scale. Employers also received no encouragement from the state to develop detailed, legally enforceable, collective agreements. This brings us to the third distinctive feature of Britain, the role of the state.

The State and the Tradition of Voluntarism

The approach adopted by organized labour – of a resistance to change and an adversarial posture in the workplace, combined with little wider political militancy – had parallels in the behaviour of the state. At various critical junctures from the late eighteenth century onwards the ruling classes could have chosen an authoritarian response to challenges from below. But at each point they rejected this route, fearing that it might so disrupt the political fabric that it would provoke even stronger challenges. Instead, they relied on a long tradition of the 'rule of law' (Fox 1985: 39–41). Their own political power had been forged in opposition to royal absolutism, and there was a strong commitment to due process and to the rights of 'free-born Englishmen', a situation which they contrasted with Continental tyranny. There was a strong distrust of statist solutions, and a preference for compromise and a search for social stability based on traditional methods. A reluctance to use the full weight of the state's powers allowed space for workers' organizations to build up a tenacious, if shadowy, existence. As Fox (1985: 168) argues, this grudging toleration of working class organization might have collapsed without the position of Britain in the world economy: foreign trade and imperialism provided the resources which allowed opposition at home to be accommodated. Early industrialization thus helped to reinforce the tradition of limited state intervention.

This approach to the management of class conflict was reflected in labour law. The voluntary regulation of employment was more important than the law. This did not mean a complete absence of legislation, but its role was limited to protecting those outside the framework of collective bargaining, as in the regulation of the employment of women and children, and to supporting collective bargaining, for example the provision of conciliation and arbitration machinery. This tradition of voluntarism was supported by both sides of industry: unions wished to avoid what they saw as hostile intervention of the courts in industrial disputes, while employers were keen to avoid legislation which constrained their freedom to manage. Moreover, the state upheld the tradition of the rule of law, which meant that the law was not just an instrument of ruling class power but contained an element of justice; there was little sense among unions of the need to mount a class project in the political arena. Voluntarism thus sustained a narrow view among unions of their political role.

The era of voluntarism has its roots in the 1870s. Its fullest expression was the Trade Disputes Act of 1906. This act removed the ability of employers to take legal action against trade unions and protected the organizers of industrial action from common law liabilities, notably for inducing a breach of employment contracts, provided that they were acting 'in contemplation or furtherance of a trade dispute'. This was the famous 'golden formula': a negative immunity from common law liability, in contrast to other countries' positive right to strike (Wedderburn 1986). Other key aspects of the voluntary system were the absence of any obligation on employers to bargain with unions and the fact that collective agreements were not legally enforceable.

As the role of the state became increasingly defined as that of maintaining the rule of law, the state was not available to employers to help them to resolve their problems. It would certainly act to try to contain union activity within legitimate bounds, but it could not be relied on to give any consistent support to a long-term policy of rationalizing control of the workplace. Employers, unions, and the state were all strong enough to maintain defensive positions while too weak to organize radical departures from the tradition of compromise and muddling through.

State and Economy in the Post-war Period

These tensions continued into the period after 1945. Employers maintained their wish to manage the shop floor as they saw fit. Unlike their counterparts in Germany, who had suffered a major crisis of legitimacy and had to think carefully about their own authority, they could pursue a policy of business as usual, which meant that they neither rooted out the shop floor challenge nor created a way of accommodating it. The Labour government was more concerned with macro-economic policy than with detailed institutional reconstruction. It is true that there were worries about productivity, illustrated by a number of joint employer–union bodies which visited America to study production methods. But there were relatively few such bodies and their findings were not implemented. The reasons were that employers were hostile to a joint approach, fearing that it would undermine their legitimacy and seeing little need to worry about productivity in a sellers' market, and that the Labour government lacked any understanding of the role of management and was unable to make itself an agency of modernization

(Tiratsoo and Tomlinson 1994). This episode illustrates a key point: it was not a lack of information or will which constrained, and arguably continues to constrain, the actors in Britain but a set of structures and relationships in which no party could take a lead.

While Britain's economic position remained powerful, these problems did not matter very much. After 1945, however, competition from overseas grew dramatically. In 1953, the UK held 21 per cent of world exports of manufactures (the percentage for Germany was 13, for France 9, and for Japan 4). By 1980 the British share had halved to 10 per cent, while Germany's had gone up to 20 per cent, France's was steady at 10 per cent while Japan's had grown to 15 per cent (Williams et al. 1983: 116). During the 1980s, Britain's share fell to 8.6 per cent, and manufacturing imports grew much faster than exports. A symbolic turning point came in 1983, when for the first time since the Industrial Revolution more manufactured goods were imported than were exported. A slow rate of economic growth was associated with unit labour costs that grew fast by international standards and continuing low levels of labour productivity. From the 1950s to the 1970s economic policy was characterized by a series of 'stop-go' cycles, that is economic expansion, producing inflation and a balance of payments crisis, which in turn led to a sharp recession. Some industries, notably the car industry, were used as macro-economic regulators, making long-term investment and production planning very difficult.

Difficulties of economic management were perhaps most apparent in attempts to establish incomes policies. The post-war Labour government made the first effort in 1948. The attempt set the pattern for the more ambitious efforts of the 1960s and 1970s (Crouch 1977). An economic crisis, in particular a severe balance of payments problem, led to demands for wage restraint. The government secured the compliance of union leaders for a time but it proved impossible to regulate the chaotic wage bargaining system, and the policy fell apart in acrimony.

It was not only Labour administrations which used tripartite mechanisms to try to promote industrial regeneration. A Conservative government created, in 1962, one of the major institutions of British efforts at corporatist solutions, the National Economic Development Council. The Council brought together representatives of employers, unions, and the government to discuss economic policy. It was abruptly abolished in 1992 at the end of a long attack on corporatism by a very different Conservative administration.

In 1966 another Labour government instituted a more rigorous pay policy. It included statutory penalties for breaches of the policy and it established a new body, the National Board for Prices and Incomes, to review not just pay increases but also prices. The policy had some immediate success, but by 1969 it was beginning to decay (Clegg 1979: 345–77). In the private sector, some managements found ways round the policy, while some groups of workers pursued their own sectional interests. In the public sector, pay restraint provoked discontent and hitherto quiescent groups began to use strikes, a development which accelerated during the 1970s.

The third major phase of incomes policy was the 'Social Contract' of 1975–79, so-called because it avoided the compulsion of the earlier policy, being based instead on a quasi-contractual exchange between government and the Trades Union Congress; wage moderation was exchanged for tax concessions and other benefits in the field of labour legislation. It received strong support from the leaders of some unions, notably Jack Jones of the Transport and General Workers' Union. Yet it again proved impossible to regulate settlements in the private sector, and the collapse of the policy was symbolized by the defeat of Jones at his own union conference on the issue of whether to continue to co-operate with it. But particularly damaging was a series of highly visible disputes in the public sector which culminated in the 'winter of discontent' of 1978–9. The government appeared to have lost control of the economy, and the image of strikes in essential services seriously damaged its credibility.

In retrospect, British corporatism can be seen to have been a very partial and ramshackle affair. Its practices emerged out of attempts to manage economic crises, and not out of any deeper commitment to long-standing structural change. Not only were employer and union sides fragmented and divided, but the British state also lacked the structures to engage in long-term industrial and economic planning (P. Hall 1986). Its whole tradition of intervention had been to manage the economy rather than actively to regulate it. During the depression of the 1930s, for example, British state planners were far less willing to embrace Keynesian solutions than their counterparts in Sweden (Weir and Skocpol 1985).

Debate up to the 1970s turned on the possibilities of reforming the system. The 1980s showed that a non- and in fact avowedly anti-corporatist approach was politically feasible. The reason why it did not produce turmoil is two-fold. First, British workers have long had a limited view of politics and class action. Studies comparing Britain with Sweden (Scase 1974) and with France (Gallie 1978) have shown that British workers had a low level of resentment at economic inequality and saw the role of unions as restricted to the economic sphere. Second, there was a gap between beliefs about equality and the means available to pursue them. From their survey of social class in Britain, Marshall et al. (1988) conclude that Britons are characterized by an 'informed fatalism': fatalist because they tolerate what happens to them and informed because they are cynical about the ability of political parties to effect lasting change. The 1980s did not see any widespread move to accept individualism – ideas that Thatcherism had attained an ideological hegemony were seriously at odds with the evidence (Gamble 1988: 174–207) – and concern about class inequality remained largely as it had been. But people did not believe that there was any real means of dealing with this problem, and mass protest about unemployment seemed out of place.

▍ Structure of the Labour Force

▍ Decline of Manufacturing

The 1980s were marked by a dramatic shift of employment away from manufacturing. This was caused in particular by the deep recession of the early part of the decade: between 1979 and 1981 manufacturing output and employment both dropped by 14 per cent, but a subsequent slow recovery of output contrasted with a continued decline in employment. This sharp decline was an indirect and probably unintended effect of government policy, in that the first Conservative administration allowed the exchange rate to rise; this put sudden pressure on manufacturing competitiveness.

By 1990, manufacturing accounted for only 23 per cent of all employment, compared with 30 per cent in 1980 and 38 per cent in 1960. The rate of decline between 1960 and 1990 was more rapid than that in most industrialized countries: manufacturing's share fell by 41 per cent, compared to 22 per cent in France and 8 per cent in Germany (Nolan and Walsh 1995: 67). This led some observers to argue that Britain was suffering a marked 'de-industrialization', as the manufacturing sector lost competitiveness and as output stagnated. Kitson and Michie (1996) stress a continuous decline in new capital investment in manufacturing from 1960 to 1980, with stagnation thereafter. There was also a decline in the average size of manufacturing plants that strengthened the tendency away from large concentrations of workers.

Unemployment and Labour Market Participation

As in other OECD countries, unemployment rose during the 1980s. What marked Britain out was a particularly rapid increase between 1979 and 1983. Because of numerous changes in definition consistent data are not available. But the peak of unemployment came in 1986, when 3.2 million people, representing 11.7 per cent of the workforce, were included in the figures. This national average concealed wide regional variations, with rates much higher in Scotland, Wales, and the north of England, and consistently the highest in Northern Ireland. Even previously prosperous areas such as the West Midlands experienced increases in unemployment to above the national average. After 1986 unemployment fell consistently, but it increased sharply again after 1990 as the economy entered a further steep recession. Job losses and employment insecurity increasingly affected white-collar and managerial, as well as manual, employees.

By the mid-1990s, a sense of job insecurity was widespread. As Gregg and Wadsworth (1995) show, this was not due to a decline in the time for which the average job lasts, for there was little overall change between 1975 and 1993. What was critical was a growth of insecurity in entry-level jobs, together with a fall in wages; such jobs offer half the wages of the average job. As these authors stress, the split between primary and secondary labour markets has deepened. Temporary employment, for example, grew from 6 to 11 per cent of the workforce during the first half of the 1990s.

This tendency was reinforced by the structure of unemployment. In 1988, 45 per cent of the unemployed had been out of work over a year (Anderton and Mayhew, 1994: 18). Permanent removal from the active workforce also became more common. In 1981, 75 per cent of people ending a period of unemployment entered jobs (the remainder leaving the labour market completely); by 1993, the figure had fallen to 60 per cent (Gregg and Wadsworth 1995: 88).

There were associated developments in the composition of the workforce. As in other countries, the proportion of women rose: from 33 per cent in 1951 to 48 per cent in 1990. The proportion of economically active married women increased particularly rapidly: from 26 per cent in 1951 to 57 per cent thirty years later (Walker 1988: 220). What was particularly marked, however, was the growth in part-time employment: female full-time employment remained relatively constant from 1971 to 1986, while the number of part-timers increased by 45 per cent (Rubery and Tarling 1988: 101). Virtually all part-timers were women. Such trends led to concerns that part-time married women would be used as a secondary labour force, being drawn in to employment during prosperity and being expelled during recessions. In fact, it was male unemployment which rose the more rapidly during the 1980s, reflecting the decline in staple industries such as manufacturing and mining. Britain is unusual in having a female unemployment rate lower than that for men. Women found jobs in services and the expanding sections of manufacturing such as electronics.

A Flexible Labour Market?

Wage inequality. A notable trend in many countries from about 1980 was a widening gap between the top and bottom of the pay distribution. In Britain, in 1979 a male manual worker at the highest decile of the income distribution earned 2.4 times as much as a worker at the lowest decile; by 1993 the figure was 3.5. Machin (1996) shows that the increase in inequality was, compared to other OECD countries, particularly sharp in Britain and the US. This could be a statistical artefact in that different people might be at different points of the earnings distribution, with there being no lasting rise in the gap between individuals. In fact, Machin shows that around three-quarters of the growth of inequality related to the same people, as opposed to an instability of earnings across individuals.

Leslie and Pu (1996) show that such developments were not the result of an increase in demand for skilled relative to unskilled labour: there was no correlation between measures of skill shortages and the movement of inequality. Nor was global competition forcing down the wages of the unskilled – most trade is with developed countries (and the proportion is rising). The most likely explanation lies in the structure of collective bargaining. As discussed below, bargaining coverage has declined, and the sole statutory means to regulate wages, the Wages Councils, were weakened in 1986 and abolished in 1993. Reductions in the powers of the Councils were associated with a widening of the gap between the low-paid under the scope of Councils and average wages; while, as in the US, declining unionization was associated with increased pay inequality (Machin 1996).

Thus inequality was the result, not of inexorable market forces, but of changes in the pattern of bargaining, reflecting employer choices and changes in the legal framework of pay determination.

Table 1.1 Trends in pay, 1979–1995 (percentage change on previous year)

	Money earnings	Real earnings		Money earnings	Real earnings
1979	15.9	2.4	1988	8.7	3.7
1980	24.4	2.0	1989	9.1	1.2
1981	13.0	1.4	1990	9.8	0.3
1982	9.3	0.6	1991	16.8	10.3
1983	8.5	3.8	1992	−2.3	−5.3
1984	6.1	0.9	1993	3.3	1.7
1985	8.5	4.0	1994	4.0	0.9
1986	7.5	4.0	1995	3.4	−0.3
1987	7.2	3.4			

Source: Calculated from data on indices of average earnings and inflation published in the *National Institute Economic Review*, various issues.

Pay and jobs. One of the most notable features of the 1980s was that, despite unemployment and widening pay inequality, the overall level of pay increases remained high. Table 1.1 gives figures for money and real earnings. In only one year in the 1980s did the rate of growth of money earnings drop below 7 per cent. There was always some growth of real earnings. It was also notable that pay increases in the non-union sector outstripped those in unionized firms (Ingram 1991). Such facts were explained in terms of the need for managers to buy consent: new working practices were being widely introduced, and pay increases were an important way of gaining acceptance. Even non-union firms seemed to be caught in this situation.

As the table shows, during the 1990s the situation changed. Money earnings growth declined in response to falling inflation. But real growth was also contained and was sometimes negative. During the recession of the early 1990s pay freezes were introduced by some firms.

A central issue is how far labour market deregulation together with the re-organization of managerial control has addressed a long-standing problem in the British economy, namely, a tendency for wages to rise faster than productivity. Metcalf (1994: 142–3) and Dunn and Metcalf (1996: 91) summarize research showing that the union 'mark-up' (the extent to which a union worker is paid more than a similar non-union worker) declined during the 1980s. They also show that it is in firms with some monopoly power that a union mark-up is observed. But equivalent non-union firms also have the same tendency to pay relatively high wages (termed efficiency wages: Stewart 1990). In more competitive conditions, there is no space for unions to exert bargaining power or for employers to pay efficiency wages.

How should we interpret such results? First, in competitive conditions, unions can have little effect on relative wages, and hence ideas that the economy as a whole was constrained by union power are incorrect. Second, the fact that unions can gain some of the extra profits accruing to oligopolies does not necessarily restrict efficiency. In the absence of this effect, employers could simply take a greater level of profit. As noted below, there is indeed evidence that British firms as a whole distribute to shareholders a larger proportion of their profits than do their counterparts in other countries. Third, what of non-union firms? The assumption in economists' models of pay is that such firms pay market rates, with unions introducing restraints. But there is no strong evidence to support this. They also pay efficiency wages and, as shown below, it was the union rather than the non-union sector that was taking the lead on the path to a high commitment system. Finally, McCarthy (1993) has argued powerfully that during the 1980s pressure on wages from 'below' (a pressure which was expressed by unions but was not exclusive to them) was replaced by a new force from 'above': the highly publicized pay increases of top executives. These, he argues, tended to pull up other wages.

Despite all these points, it did seem that by the early 1990s pay pressures had been reduced. It is impossible to say whether they had been eliminated. On the one hand, bargaining decentralization will have made co-ordinated pay campaigns harder. On the other, many groups of workers, particularly in the public sector, have experienced pay restraint together with increasing workloads. It remains to be seen whether British managements have established the means to manage such pressures more effectively than they did in the 1980s.

Employment flexibility. Blanchflower and Freeman (1994) have investigated whether the Thatcher reforms achieved their goal of making labour markets more flexible. They show that cuts in unemployment benefits made work attractive compared to non-work but that this did not improve the rate of transition of men from unemployment into jobs, though there may have been some effect for women. Blanchflower and Freeman also show that there is little evidence that the responsiveness of employment at the level of the firm to changing market conditions improved. They conclude that there was little change in labour market flexibility.

The Legal Framework

The law was a major instrument in the Conservative government's efforts to effect change during the 1980s. To place these efforts in context, the development of labour law up to 1979 needs to be understood. The origins of the Conservative government's project may then be considered before the details of the legislation are outlined. A key question concerns the effects of the law; these cannot be understood in isolation from other developments, and they are considered at the end of the section.

Regulation in the 1960s and 1970s

As noted above, the voluntary system came under increasing strain from the 1960s. The imposition of incomes policies was the most obvious break with the tradition. Intervention was also proposed in labour law. As early as the 1950s, some Conservative lawyers were proposing tighter control of unions and restrictions on the right to strike. In 1965, the Labour government appointed the Donovan Royal Commission to investigate industrial relations. When the Commission reported in 1968, it focused on the voluntary reform of collective bargaining, as discussed below; but it left open the possibility of more legalistic approaches. One such approach was attempted by the government when it proposed, towards the end of its period of office, laws to regulate unconstitutional strikes (that is, those in breach of procedure), but strong opposition from the unions forced the abandonment of the proposals. Some significant legislation was passed, notably the Redundancy Payments Act 1964, which for the first time required compensation to be paid to workers losing their jobs for economic reasons. But the voluntarist approach largely survived the challenges to it.

In 1971, however, the new Conservative government introduced the Industrial Relations Act, which proposed a comprehensive legal framework. Closely modelled on American legislation, the Act replaced the unions' traditional legal immunities with restrictions on industrial action; tightly regulated arrangements for closed shops (that is, the practice that workers must be or become union members as a condition of employment); and endeavoured to make collective agreements legally enforceable. The Act was resisted by the unions, and it had only a very limited effect on day-to-day industrial relations, largely because employers did not put its provisions into practice (Hyman, 1995: 46). Where it was invoked, it provoked some major clashes with the unions, in which its provisions seemed unworkable or counter-productive. The Act lost credibility, and the incoming Labour government returned the law on trade disputes and the status of unions broadly to what it had been before 1971 (Weekes et al. 1975).

One significant feature was retained, namely, provisions against unfair dismissal. The 1971 Act included the first laws in Britain restricting employers' freedom to dismiss; cases could now be taken to industrial tribunals. Though modified in the 1980s, these laws have not been fundamentally altered. Important new individual rights, notably for women employees to return to their jobs after maternity leave, were included in the Employment Protection Act 1975; other legislation strengthened laws against sex and race discrimination.

Origins and Basis of the 1980s and 1990s Legislation

The 'Thatcher project' was neither a completely pre-planned strategy nor an opportunistic reaction to events. There were strong elements of opportunism: specific legal provisions were 'greatly influenced by the immediate experience of contemporary disputes' (Brown and Wadhwani 1990: 58). But there was a broad set of ideas guiding opportunistic action. The governments of the 1980s were 'the first . . . since the war to pursue a policy on industrial relations which [was] integrally geared into [their] overall economic policies' (Wedderburn 1985: 36). These policies had their intellectual origins in the New Right, with its emphasis on the free working of markets and the need to minimize state interference. During its period of opposition from 1974 to 1979 the Conservative Party reflected on the lessons of the 1971–4 Heath government, in two ways. Strategically, it developed a more coherent statement of free market principles, and it thus criticized the interventions to rescue failing private sector firms which that government had made. Tactically, rather than seek a once and for all change, it consciously adopted a 'step by step' approach to legal reform. This explains the large number of Acts under Conservative administrations.

As union bargaining strength was considered to stem from immunities in relation to industrial action and the 'coercive power' of the closed shop, these became central targets of the government's legislative programme. The government also saw union leaderships as being unrepresentative of the views of their (implicitly more 'moderate') members, and so legislated to prescribe the internal democratic procedures unions should adopt. A policy of 'enterprise confinement' (Wedderburn 1989: 27) was pursued in restricting the scope of lawful industrial action. The government also viewed employment protection provisions not as essential minimum standards but as 'burdens on business' (particularly in respect of small employers). This led to a sustained emphasis on the need to 'deregulate' the labour market.

In addition to laws on unions and collective bargaining, deregulation was applied in areas such as training. Before 1979, there were moves, albeit limited, to establish a statutory basis of training. In 1964, the Industrial Training Act allowed for Industrial Training Boards which could impose training levies on firms in their industries. In 1973, a Conservative government established the Manpower Services Commission to oversee labour force planning and manage government training schemes. In 1981, most ITBs were abolished, as was the MSC in 1988. Training was now to be employer-led with no statutory underpinning (Keep and Rainbird 1995).

The Legislative Programme: Restriction and Deregulation

Against this background, the Conservatives introduced a series of Acts of Parliament – most notably the Employment Acts of 1980, 1982, 1988, 1989 and 1990, the Trade Union Act 1984, the Wages Act 1986 and the Trade Union Reform and Employment Rights Act 1993 – and backed them up with a number of statutory Codes of Practice. The key provisions of these complex and interlocking measures can be seen as having a number of complementary objectives: the legal restriction of industrial action; the eradication of the closed shop; the regulation of internal union government; the dismantling of statutory support for collective bargaining; and the curtailment of individual employment rights.

During the 1980s, legal restrictions were increasingly placed on industrial action. Despite the fact that the statutory immunities from common law liabilities were merely the functional equivalent of the positive right to strike enjoyed by workers in other countries, they were seen by the government as unique 'privileges' putting trade unions 'above the law', and were narrowed significantly by successive pieces of legislation. Picketing away from the pickets' own workplace, and 'secondary' industrial action (i.e. that by workers whose employer is not party to the dispute) other than in certain tightly defined circumstances, were made unlawful by the 1980 Act. More fundamentally, the 1982 Act introduced a narrower, enterprise-specific definition of what constituted a trade dispute and exposed unions as organizations to injunctions and damages in cases of unlawful industrial action, whereas previously only individuals organizing the action were so liable. The 1984 Act made it unlawful for unions to authorize or endorse industrial action called without a secret ballot. The 1990 Act made all secondary industrial action unlawful, extended the scope of union liability to include industrial action organized by shop stewards, and enabled employers to dismiss selectively any employee taking unofficial industrial action.

Repeated changes were made to the law concerning the operation of 'union membership agreements or arrangements'. The 1980 Act, for example, gave statutory exemption from a requirement to belong to a trade union to 'conscientious objectors' and to those who were non-members at the time such a requirement was introduced. The dismissal of such employees for non-membership thus became unfair. The 1988 Act made the dismissal of any employee on grounds of non-membership of a union automatically unfair. With the passage of the 1990 Act, all forms of the closed shop became unlawful. These successive steps were backed up by provisions outlawing commercial arrangements and industrial action to ensure that work would be done only by unionized labour.

On union democracy, the government at first confined itself to providing public funds to encourage unions to use secret ballots. However, the measures introduced by the Trade Union Act 1984 and the Employment Act 1988 represented the most detailed statutory regulation of internal union affairs yet attempted in Britain, based on a highly individualist model of the rights and obligations associated with trade union membership (McKendrick 1988: 141). The 1984 Act required five-yearly secret ballots of union members for the election of union executive committees and presidents and general secretaries with voting rights on such committees. The 1988 Act extended these requirements to all union presidents and general secretaries, and stipulated that election ballots should be fully postal and independently scrutinized. It also provided a range of statutory rights for individual union members enforceable against their union with the assistance of the new 'Commissioner for the Rights of Trade Union Members', including the right not to be 'unjustifiably disciplined' by a union for refusing to take part in industrial action.

Much of the existing statutory support for collective bargaining was also dismantled during the 1980s. In 1980, the statutory recognition procedure introduced in 1975 was abolished, as was Schedule 11 of the Employment Protection Act, which had provided procedures to extend collectively-bargained rates of pay to comparable groups of workers (see Rubery 1995: 555). The statutory regulation of pay was addressed through changes to the Wages Councils. The councils had been established in 1909 to provide statutory minimum wages and conditions for workers in certain industries where collective bargaining was weak; by 1986 they covered about 2.5 million workers. In the 1986 Act all protection for workers aged under 21 was removed, and other powers of the councils were reduced. In 1993, the councils were abolished, with only the agricultural industry retaining any statutory regulation of pay.

Several steps were taken to curtail individual employment rights, notably the adjustment of the qualifying period of employment (from 6 months to 2 years) and of the procedural rules relating to unfair dismissal, and the erosion of working women's maternity rights. The 1989 Act continued the emphasis on 'deregulation' by repealing a range of laws which restricted the employment of women and regulated young people's hours of work (Deakin 1990).

Countervailing Pressures from Europe

In carrying through its legislative programme, the government has had to act within the constraints imposed by the UK's membership of the European Union. Although key aspects of the government's agenda – especially the restriction of the freedom to take industrial action and the statutory regulation of trade union government – have essentially been unrestrained by EU requirements, the need to conform to EU law has placed limits on the extent to which the government has been able to pursue its deregulatory ambitions. In a succession of instances, the UK government has been forced, by EU directives and rulings of the European Court of Justice (ECJ), to take legislative steps it would rather have avoided. Examples include the EU transfer of undertakings directive of 1977 which the government transposed into national law in 1991 with a self-confessed 'remarkable lack of enthusiasm' (Davies and Freedland 1993: 577); the relevant regulations require that, when an undertaking is taken over by another, existing contracts of employment continue in force, a provision which has been significant when public sector work has been contracted out to the private sector. A second illustration is the ECJ ruling in 1984 that the Sex Discrimination Act 1975 failed to comply with the EU equal treatment directive; the result was the Sex Discrimination Act 1986 which extended the coverage of sex discrimination legislation and made discriminatory clauses in collective agreements void.

The clear tension between the government's domestic labour market policies and an EU social agenda which reflects mainstream, continental regulatory models has resulted in the UK attempting to extricate itself from the EU social policy framework. In 1989, the UK government refused to sign the Community Charter of the Fundamental Social Rights of Workers (the 'social charter'). More significantly, in 1991, it negotiated an 'opt-out' from the proposed 'social chapter' of the Maastricht Treaty on European Union, fearing that the extension of qualified majority voting procedures to a range of EU social policy measures would undermine the UK's ability to block legislation it opposed (M. Hall 1994).

Nevertheless, EU measures originating before the UK's 'opt-out' have continued to influence domestic labour law. In 1994, the ECJ ruled that the UK's implementation of the collective redundancies and transfer of undertakings directives was deficient because the requirement to consult employee representatives about impending redundancies and transfers was limited under UK law to employers who recognized trade unions. This ruling highlights the tension between the traditional legal framework of employee representation in this country based on the voluntary recognition of trade unions by employers and the universal approach to employee information and consultation rights embodied in EU legislation. As a result, the UK was obliged to introduce new regulations concerning consultation in situations where there are no recognized unions: employers must now consult either representatives of recognized unions or representatives elected by the employees affected. The prospect of further EU intervention in this areas seems likely to mean that UK law and practice will eventually have to accommodate the predominant European model of universal employee representation rights more generally (M. Hall 1996). In addition, the EU working time directive – the UK's legal challenge to which was dismissed by the ECJ in November 1996 – requires the introduction of a new statutory framework regulating a range of working time issues. This constitutes a direct reversal of the deregulatory thrust of government policy over the 1980s which saw the repeal of what little UK working time legislation previously existed (Hall and Sisson 1997).

Moreover, even where the UK has successfully opted out of EU social measures, the effect may be more formal than real. The European Works Councils directive, for example, though formally not applying to the UK because it was adopted under the Maastricht social policy procedures, has still had a major impact in the UK. UK-based multinational companies with the required number of employees elsewhere in the European Economic Area are obliged to establish EWCs in the respect of those employees. To date, none has chosen to exclude their UK workforce.

Effects of Legal Changes

It is hard to isolate the effects of the law, for two reasons. First, many other developments were occurring at the same time. Second, through what mechanism does a change in the law affect behaviour? For example, in what ways do laws governing the conduct of strikes affect people's willingness to go on strike? Some specific effects of the law are considered in this section. In some areas, direct effects for the law can be discerned but in others the effects are much more uncertain.

Employment rights. The restriction of employment protection and the ending of the Wages Councils were intended to promote employment levels. There is certainly evidence that the end of the Councils allowed some employers to cut pay (Lucas and Radiven 1996). But much research (summarized by L. Dickens and Hall 1995: 272) found that employment protection laws did not discourage firms from hiring new workers. Research on Wages Councils (R. Dickens et al. 1993) found that employment growth was greatest where council regulation was tough rather than weak.

The closed shop. One area where fairly direct effects can be discerned is the closed shop. There has clearly been a substantial decline in the number of employees covered by closed shops, from a peak of 5.2 million in 1978 to between 0.3 and 0.5 million in 1990 (Millward et al. 1992: 96). As Dunn and Metcalf (1996: 79) argue, the early fall reflected 'compositional effects' (that is, the decline in employment in sectors where the closed shop was prominent) but later developments may have reflected the law. In the public sector, for example, the institution had become widespread, and the evident pressure on managers to be law-abiding hastened its demise. There is also evidence, however, that in some cases the closed shop continues to exist, but in a more informal manner than in the past. One can also question the benefits of the demise of many forms of closed shop arrangements. As Dunn and Wright (1993: 52) conclude, the closed shop was often not seen by managers as a major problem and its 'managers are prone to see neither great gains nor losses from the practice's disappearance'.

Unionization. Freeman and Pelletier (1990) construct an index of the favourableness of labour laws to unions and conclude that, for the period 1980–86, increasing legal hostility accounted for almost the whole of the decline in density. However, Disney (1990) shows that the decline began before the key legal changes. Moreover, if the law is the only factor, one would expect, with the further tightening of legal controls, an accelerating decline in density since 1986; this has not occurred. One would also expect fairly uniform decline across industries; again, this has not occurred (Waddington 1992). The effect of the law has occurred in combination with the effects of adverse economic conditions and new management policies. The failure to organize newly opened establishments was particularly important (Marginson et al. 1993). It may be that the legal climate was one factor encouraging employers to resist unionization after 1987; its effects have been indirect rather than direct.

As discussed below, unions have accepted the requirement to hold ballots to elect their officers. The law has probably had a clear effect here. As Dickens and Hall (1995: 292) conclude, the whole tenor of the debate on union democracy has changed, and it is now 'firmly equated with a requirement for individual balloting'.

Strikes. Dickens and Hall (1995: 283–7) identify four forms of impact of the law on the nature and extent of strikes. First, employers could be encouraged to use new legal rights. Though in most strikes such rights were not deployed, there were several significant disputes (for example Messenger Newspapers and the National Graphical Association in 1983 and P&O and the National Union of Seamen in 1988) in which they played a central role. This readiness to use the law reflected the simplicity of procedures requiring ballots in strikes but also an economic and political situation in which employers did not fear a significant union reaction.

Second, union procedures in industrial action have been transformed. By 1990, strike ballots had become more or less universally employed. The Labour Party also now accepts this part of the Conservatives' labour law reforms. There does seem to have been a clear effect on the procedures for handling industrial action, which have become more formalized.

Third, has the conduct of collective bargaining changed and in particular is there any evidence that alleged excessive wage claims have been moderated? Evidence shows that the great majority of ballots support strike action and that the ballot can usefully be used by union bargainers to demonstrate the strength of membership feelings. Against this must be set the legal weapons open to employers, and the fact that about a quarter of union negotiators questioned report some kind of legal threat from the employer (Dunn and Metcalf 1996: 85). As the leading research concludes, the overall effect has been 'ambivalent' (Martin et al. 1991: 206).

Fourth, has the level of strike action been reduced? The fall in strikes evidently reflects many other forces, of which two may be highlighted. First, compositional effects have been particularly clear: strikes used to be concentrated in the coal industry, the docks and certain parts of manufacturing, notably the car industry. All of these saw sharp falls in employment levels and often a more assertive management style. Second, unemployment and labour market uncertainty have long tended to reduce workers' willingness to strike, and this effect is also likely to have been strong after 1979. Dunn and Metcalf (1996: 86–7) summarize econometric models which try to take account of such facts. Some do find that a measure of legislative action is correlated with a fall in the level of strikes. But the authors stress that, as with the measures of union decline discussed above, the measure of 'the law' may be picking up a range of economic and political trends.

Perhaps the safest conclusion, in relation to strikes and other matters, is that the law was part of a much wider set of changes. It is unlikely that specific enactments had a direct effect on the number of strikes, but the law certainly symbolized a determination to act against what was perceived as the inappropriate use of industrial power, and the numerous legal restrictions made the use of action a more considered activity than it had been in the 1970s. The law helped to change the conduct of industrial relations, and the reduction in employment protection plainly gave employers more power. As noted above, there seems little evidence, however, that job creation was enhanced. To understand why, we need to consider the behaviour of employers.

Employers and Collective Bargaining

The focus in this section is on the large companies who have been the engine of most recent developments. These employers are unusual within Europe in having so fully turned their backs on multi-employer bargaining as the means of regulating basic terms and conditions. From the 1960s there was a trend in many industries for single-employer bargaining, at company or unit level, to replace multi-employer bargaining at industry or district level. Industrial relations have become increasingly enterprise-specific: jobs have come to be defined in terms of the internal requirements of companies, and pay systems have been oriented towards rewarding individual and collective contribution to company performance. Both employer and trade union solidarity across companies have been weakened.

Employers' Associations

Like the other countries considered in this collection, Britain has a large number of employers' organizations to which individual companies belong. In addition to the 'peak' organization or employers' confederation, the Confederation of British Industry, the Certification Officer for Trade Unions and Employers' Associations reports the existence of more than 250 such organizations. Their structure and government are also very similar to those of employers' organizations in other countries (Sisson 1987: 45–80).

The membership of these organizations is, however, low compared to that in most of the other countries, and in many sectors it fails to reach 50 per cent of eligible companies (though membership details are often kept secret, and it is hard to produce exact figures). Significantly, many of the large multinational companies, which are members of employers' organizations in other countries, are not members in Britain. For example, none of the large car manufacturers – Ford, Peugeot–Talbot, and Vauxhall (General Motors) – are members of the Engineering Employers' Federation. GEC, which is the largest employer in the engineering industry, is no longer a member. Many of the large companies in the chemical industry, including ICI, are 'non-conforming' members of the Chemical Industries' Association: they belong to it but do not follow the terms of the multi-employer agreement that it negotiates. Paradoxically, it is the CBI which has the most representative membership, because it is essentially a pressure group and individual companies are eligible to join direct.

The Changing Structure of Collective Bargaining

The explanation for the low membership of employers' organizations is inextricably bound up with distinguishing trends in the structure of collective bargaining in Britain when compared to other countries in Western Europe. One is the move away from multi-employer bargaining and the other the declining coverage of collective bargaining.

In Britain, most leading firms have abandoned industry-wide agreements. The move towards single-employer bargaining, which had always covered important substantive matters, began in the 1960s rather than the 1980s. The reasons for it were two-fold (Brown et al. 1995: 138): the negative factors of a lack of employer solidarity, which meant that there were few forces tying firms into industry-wide agreements; and the positive reason that it allowed employers to cultivate internal labour markets and to link pay to the performance of the firm itself. As Brown et al. stress, this decentralization does not mean that pay bargaining is now in the hands of managers in individual establishments. In many cases, in service industries in particular, pay is set at the level of the whole company rather than the operating establishment. In other cases of plant bargaining, it is generally the case that plant bargainers are constrained to operate within parameters determined by corporate or divisional management (Marginson et al. 1993).

Table 1.2 Estimated private sector bargaining structure, Great Britain, 1950–1990

	1950	*1960*	*1970*	*1980*	*1984*	*1990*
Per cent of private sector employees whose:						
Pay not fixed by collective bargaining	20	25	30	30	40	50
Pay fixed by collective bargaining:	80	75	70	70	60	50
of which:						
multi-employer	60	45	35	30	20	10
single employer	20	30	35	40	40	40

Source: Brown et al. (1995: 137), drawing on various sources for 1950–70 and the Workplace Industrial Relations Surveys thereafter.

The second main trend has been the abandonment of collective bargaining altogether. Table 1.2 summarizes trends in private sector pay bargaining since 1950. As the table shows, there was a steady decline in multi-employer bargaining, which covered 60 per cent of private sector employees in 1950 but only 10 per cent by 1990; the coverage of single-employer bargaining doubled. As for non-bargaining, up to 1970 it remained quite small (though, in contrast to the stereotype of the 1970s as a period of total collectivism, it covered 30 per cent of employees). From 1980, its prevalence grew, to cover half the private sector workforce by 1990.

This withdrawal from collective bargaining marks a major change from the past. It reflects several developments as well as the disappearance of multi-employer agreements in sectors of substantial employment such as engineering and multiple food retailing. First, numerous surveys have shown that new workplaces tend to have characteristics, such as small size, location in the service sector and a part-time work force, which have made union organization difficult. Many of these new workplaces belong to large organizations which continue to recognize unions at other sites. Second, there is the removal of union recognition and bargaining rights in existing workplaces.

Up to the mid-1980s, surveys indicated that this union derecognition was rare and that it tended to be concentrated in a few sectors such as newspaper publishing. More recent evidence paints a different picture (Claydon 1996). First, the extent of derecognition increased sharply in 1987, though this appears to be a step change and not a continuous trend. Second, the process appears to have a more purposive and planned character. Claydon shows how employers in industries such as chemicals started with some opportunistic derecognition in certain plants but gradually developed a more general and deliberate approach. At firms such as Esso and BP collective bargaining was progressively dismantled. Findlay (1993), in a study of electronics firms in Scotland, underlines the absence of unions in new plants and argues that in non-union firms managerial hostility to unions ran deep and was expressed either through the use of high wages to deter unionization or through direct and open hostility.

From Collective Bargaining to Where?

A major issue of debate has been whether the move away from collective bargaining has led to a new model of industrial relations based on the direct relationship between employer and employee. From the mid-1980s, there was increasing debate about 'human resource management' which was initially discussed as an alternative to collectivism. HRM was supposedly associated with a more strategic approach to employee relations, in the double sense that managerial policies were chosen and coherent (rather than short-term expedients) and were more closely related to the business aims of the organization. Two closely related debates concerned flexibility and Japanization. Flexibility, both numerical (the use of part-time and temporary workers to respond to demand fluctuations) and functional (a reduction in demarcations and an increase in the range of tasks performed by each worker), was claimed to permit firms to respond to business needs by using labour in a more flexible way. As for Japanization, this was seen as one of the mechanisms which encouraged a more coherent approach to labour management as British firms emulated the Japanese firms setting up in the country.

Human Resource Management

The definition of HRM remains controversial. But, in addition to the point about strategic integration, HRM is widely taken to include: an emphasis on direct communication with the workforce; harmonization of conditions between white-collar and manual workers; the linking of pay to performance; and an emphasis on employee training and development. We look at the overall take-up of HRM and then at each of these four themes. (A fifth, increasing employee autonomy, is considered later.)

Studies of HRM point to the rarity of integrated approaches. Storey (1992) examined 15 firms in depth and identified 27 practices associated with the HRM model. He found that these practices were in operation in a wide variety of combinations. Wood and Albanese (1995) surveyed firms for evidence of the 'high commitment' systems often associated with HRM. They found a normal distribution (i.e. a few firms had no practices, most had a middling number and few had them all). This is consistent with the absence of distinct clusters of high commitment systems. Wood and Albanese (1995) identify only a small minority of employers adopting an integrated set of 'high commitment' practices.

On communication, studies have distinguished between three forms: downward (from managers to workers, as in newsletters or videos); upward (where worker opinions can be expressed, as in employee surveys); and two-way (where there is discussion, for example in problem-solving groups). Surveys show more use of the first than the second or third. What WIRS calls 'systematic use of the management chain' was reported in 60 per cent of establishments whereas surveys or ballots were used in only 17 per cent (Millward et al. 1992: 167).

On harmonization, Price and Price (1994) summarize evidence pointing to a significant narrowing of the gap between manual and white-collar workers in areas such as holidays, sick pay, and pensions, but less progress regarding hours of work and payment systems. Some companies, such as the Rover Group, have moved a long way towards 'single status', and many of these use terms such as 'associate' in place of 'employee'. However, these authors conclude, much of the evidence is limited to manufacturing, and the growth of service employment and an increasing number of workers in insecure jobs means that, though the old 'works and staff' distinction may be declining, new forms of divide are replacing it.

On pay and performance, surveys (summarized by Kessler and Purcell 1995) point to a growing use of schemes linking pay to appraisals of individual merit or performance. They are particularly common for managerial or white-collar staff, though they also extend to manual workers, particularly where 'single status' has been introduced. It is now very common for managers to have a substantial part of their pay determined by individual performance. Studies also suggest, however, that the practice of performance-related pay (PRP) is a long way from the model of commitment. Richardson and Marsden (1991) show that PRP has little effect on motivation, one reason being that, as Kessler and Purcell argue, it is often linked to 'hard' targets for achieving specific goals and not to 'soft' developmental targets. PRP has been part of a move towards 'individualizing' the employment relationship, but this is very different from the claims of HRM.

Finally, training has, as noted above, been increasingly left to the individual employer. As Keep and Rainbird (1995: 515) note, nowhere has change been more dramatic than in the field of training. A statutory tripartite system has been replaced by a voluntary, employer-led one. Numerous initiatives have been introduced in the area of youth training but a central issue is the demand by employers for trained workers. There is survey evidence that the volume of training may have increased from the early 1980s (Rainbird 1994). A 1993 survey of employers estimated that 45 per cent of employees attended a training course during the year (Employee Development Bulletin 1996). Some large UK firms, such as Ford and British Steel, made training central to their activities. However, 60 per cent of firms surveyed in 1990 had no training budget. The 1993 survey contained no evidence on the quality of training provided, and it is widely argued that only a minority of firms have anything approaching an integrated training policy. A series of comparative studies with Germany shows that much training in Britain remains focused on relatively low-skilled activities (e.g. Steedman and Wagner 1989). Many commentators stress the danger of Britain becoming locked in a low-wage, low-skill equilibrium (Keep and Rainbird 1995).

In conclusion, much of the above evidence on HRM comes from relatively large firms, where particular HRM practices have been adopted, albeit sporadically. As Sisson and Marginson (1995: 111–12) stress, when we consider the economy as a whole there is even less support for the view that HRM has taken root. In many small firms, employee relations systems remain rudimentary; from the mid-1980s there has been a growth of individual workers' complaints of unfair dismissal and other actions, and, as discussed below, work intensification has been widespread.

US experience suggested that HRM would replace union-based systems. Growing evidence shows that HRM practices are in fact concentrated in the union sector. The evidence from WIRS (Millward et al. 1992: 168) and other surveys (Guest and Hoque 1996) shows clearly that the use of, for example, workforce communication is higher in union than non-union establishments. Moreover, unions shape the form of HRM practice: two-way communication is much more widespread where unions are present, whereas in the absence of unions, managements tend to use only downward communication. The implication is that there is no clear non-union model that is replacing collectivism. Indeed, it becomes difficult to distinguish in meaningful terms between those companies which claim to apply such a model and those which say they are pursuing a social partnership approach with trade unions.

Flexibility

Early accounts of flexibility posited a model of a flexible firm in which various forms of flexibility were linked together. The first wave of critical reaction showed that there was considerably more evidence of numerical than functional flexibility and that the reasons for numerical flexibility were often the traditional ones of meeting seasonal fluctuations rather than any new approach to labour relations (Pollert 1988). Subsequent evidence showed that decisions over labour use were rarely part of a coherent employer strategy, with the use of different forms of labour growing up in an ad hoc manner (Hunter et al. 1993).

Such evidence does not imply a complete dismissal of the flexibility model. As Procter et al. (1994) point out, there has been substantial growth in atypical forms of work, and there has been a clear move towards the widening of tasks. In particular, demarcations between different groups of craft workers have been extensively relaxed.

In Britain's highly decentralized arrangements, however, it is numerical flexibility which poses the biggest challenge. This is rarely the subject of collective bargaining. Especially important has been the increase in the practice of putting out to tender such activities as cleaning, catering, maintenance and transport. Although considerable controversy surrounds the strategic significance of these developments, the practical implications are clear enough. Where the activity is subcontracted, it very often means that the group falls out of the coverage of collective bargaining. As discussed below in relation to privatization, where the activity remains 'in house', the tendering process may be used to drive down the pay or conditions of the groups involved.

Japanization

In 1993, there were only 167 Japanese manufacturing firms, employing 50,000 workers, in the UK (Grant 1996: 203). But their significance has been greater than the numbers imply, for they have been seen as in the forefront of new forms of work organization. New inward investment has been hailed by Conservative ministers as evidence of the attractiveness of Britain's deregulated labour market.

Early accounts of Japanization suggested that, through team working, complete task flexibility and devices such as quality circles, employee commitment could be won and productivity improved. A wave of more critical studies noted an intense work pace and the very close monitoring of worker performance (Garrahan and Stewart 1992), often using electronic means to identify faults and trace them back to the individual operator (Sewell and Wilkinson 1993). The limitations of Japanization have also been stressed. It soon became clear that Japanese firms were not transposing their own labour relations practices; in Britain, two of the 'pillars' of the Japanese system, lifetime employment and enterprise unions, are largely absent. It has been argued that there has also been a tendency for firms to lose their distinctiveness as time goes on (Broad 1994; Palmer 1996), and for workplace discipline to become 'British' in style.

As for the impact on British companies, Japanese firms do seem to have encouraged genuine improvements in the technical organization of production, stimulating, for example, the adoption of new production techniques such as improved plant layout and quality control (Bratton 1992). In the case of Rover, Scarbrough and Terry (1996) show how the alliance with the Honda company encouraged new ways of thinking. Scarbrough and Terry also stress, however, that there was no simple direct transfer of Japanese techniques. Developments in Britain were varied and uncertain: a further example of ad hoc adaptation.

▌ Assessment

Employers have been a major driving force for change in UK industrial relations. It is not just that, as in other countries, they have promoted new pay systems, direct communications and more flexible ways of working. Uniquely so far among EU member states, they have shifted the focus of collective bargaining from the sector to the individual unit and, in many cases, have abandoned collective bargaining altogether. There is little evidence of employers developing a coherent model to take the place of collective bargaining, however. The approach remains largely 'opportunistic' and 'pragmatic'. Even the rhetoric of HRM, so powerful in the late 1980s and early 1990s, is in decline. 'Downsizing' and 'delayering', rather than increased job security, became the leading managerial messages; while the 'flexibility' promised by a deregulated labour market did not lead to serious job creation.

The most plausible explanation for this state of affairs links the institutions of industrial relations to the wider organizational context. The inability (and, in some cases, the unwillingness) of trade unions to maintain the effectiveness of multi-employer bargaining, coupled with the lack of legal support for employee representation at company or workplace level, has reinforced the *laissez-faire* approach to standard-setting in the areas of pay, training and development, and employment rights. In these circumstances, key features of the organizational context have been allowed to become dominant. The ability of employers to develop a coherent approach to employment depends on relatively predictable conditions. In fact, take-overs were a growing threat. Research shows that firms involved in acquisitions had less integrated industrial relations policies than others (Marginson et al. 1993). In the highly diversified firms that became common during the 1980s, it made sense to relate labour policy to the position of each business unit, rather than operate at the level of the whole company, still less an industry.

There was also pressure for short-term financial returns. Short-termism became an acknowledged problem for British firms, encouraged by the ease of take-over and the primacy of pension funds and investment trusts in the structure of share ownership. It has been found that British firms distribute relatively high proportions of profits to shareholders, which indicates a low retention of profit for long-term investment (Lloyd 1991). Doyle et al.'s (1992) survey of British, American and Japanese firms found that the British firms had strategies which were the least directed towards long-term market share and the most oriented towards 'down market' customers and low prices. In such a climate, any kind of strategic approach to industrial relations is hard to achieve. There has been little pressure on UK employers to take their human resources seriously and every reason to be ad hoc and pragmatic in approach.

In this context, models of social dialogue have little place. Small wonder, then, that there is so much fear and misunderstanding of the EU's social charter. As noted above, however, several British-based firms affected by the European Works Councils Directive have set up councils voluntarily. There remains scepticism about other European measures, notably in the field of working time, and many British firms were wedded to models of deregulation and labour market flexibility.

Trade Unions

British trade unions can trace their origins back two centuries; the predecessors of some modern unions were created at the time of the industrial revolution. Historical continuity is thus a major consideration in the understanding of trade unionism in Britain. Particular organizations may over the years have fallen victim to recession, industrial restructuring, employer resistance, internal fragmentation or insolvency; but the movement as a whole, though experiencing periods of defeat and numerical decline, has never had to face a crisis so serious as to threaten its very existence. This long stability clearly differentiates Britain from many other European countries.

The four decades from the outbreak of the Second World War saw a development of unions' place in industry: there was an unprecedented growth of membership; the scope of collective bargaining steadily expanded; and unions became increasingly involved in the formulation and implementation of government social and economic policy. But in the 1980s and 1990s these advances were rapidly reversed.

Membership

In contrast to most European countries, the right to belong to a trade union is only recent. Traditionally, the employer was free in law to obstruct a union's

Table 1.3 Trade union membership, Great Britain, 1948–1995

	Total membership (000s)	Labour force density (%)	Employment density (%)
1948	9,102	44.9	45.5
1968	9,739	42.9	43.9
1979	12,639	53.4	55.8
1987	9,874	41.0	46.3
1995	7,275	not available	32.1

Note: 1995 data are calculated on a different basis from those for earlier years, and are not directly comparable.
Source: 1948–87: Waddington, 1992. 1995: Labour Force Survey, reported in *Labour Market Trends*, May 1996, 215–25.

efforts to recruit. The Industrial Relations Act 1971 introduced the right to join a union, and this was re-enacted in the Social Contract legislation. But there was still only a series of individual rights, and no explicit guarantee of freedom of association. By the same token, there are few legal restrictions on membership. Unionism of military personnel is illegal, and there are major restrictions on collective organization and action in the police force; however the Police Federation, while debarred from affiliation to the TUC, is officially registered as a trade union and its membership is included in the aggregate statistics given in table 1.3. In general, civil servants (including civilian employees of the armed forces) are subject to no special restrictions.

For most purposes union density – the ratio of actual to potential membership – is the most useful measure of unionization. Most definitions of potential membership exclude the armed forces and the self-employed (who in Britain are unionized only in exceptional cases). Some measures only cover those in employment; others include the unemployed, who in Britain rarely join trade unions or retain membership which they may previously have held, even though some unions have recently made serious efforts to organize those out of work. In periods of high unemployment, such as the 1980s, different definitions of potential membership will entail very different density figures. We therefore present two sets of density statistics: the first basing potential membership on the labour force in employment or seeking employment (Labour Force Density); the second based only on those in employment (Employment Density).

As can be seen from table 1.3, in the post-war period there were three main phases of development. The years between 1949 and 1968 were a period of stagnation, when membership failed to keep pace with the expansion of employment. Then followed a decade of pronounced expansion: between 1969 and 1979 Labour Force Density grew from 43 to 53 per cent, and Employment Density from 44 to 57 per cent. During the 1980s both measures, in particular the former, show a sharp decline. This was the longest continuous decline on record. In the latter part of the decade Employment Density declined faster than the labour force measure, an indication that unions were failing to make significant inroads in those areas of the economy where employment was expanding. During the 1990s,

Table 1.4 Trade union employment density (%), selected industries (Great Britain)

	1989	1995
Agriculture, forestry, fishing	13	7
Manufacturing	41	32
Food, drink, tobacco	47	38
Vehicle manufacturing	63	53
Chemicals	38	28
Construction	30	26
Services		
Wholesale trade	16	9
Hotels and restaurants	11	8
Postal services	84	66
Telecommunications	80	55
Rail transport	94	80
Insurance	36	34
Water supply	82	53
Education		
Schools	63	59
Higher education	56	49
Hospitals	67[a]	56
All employees	**39**	**32**

[a] Including nursing homes.
Source: Labour Force Survey.

these trends continued, so that by 1995 fewer than a third of the workforce belonged to a trade union.

Disaggregated data reveal how the composition of trade union membership has altered with the changing structure of employment. The proportion of union members who are women doubled in 40 years (18 per cent in 1948, 35 per cent in 1987) as did the proportion of white-collar workers (23 per cent in 1951, 48 per cent in 1987).

Many explanations have been offered for trends in union density, involving some combination of such factors as shifts in the composition of employment, the business cycle, the changing environment of industrial relations, and characteristics of unions themselves. The changing structure of employment, in particular a decline in traditional manufacturing industry, tends to weaken unions (Waddington 1992); but this alone does not explain the severity of the decline in the 1980s. As table 1.4 shows, it was not just that the number of manufacturing jobs fell; density within manufacturing also fell. Nor can it account for the rapid growth of the 1970s, achieved despite adverse shifts in employment composition (Kelly 1990). Business cycle indicators – movements in unemployment, retail prices and wages – explain much of the short-term fluctuation in union membership (Carruth and Disney 1988; Disney 1990). Because some sectors and occupations are more vulnerable than others to unemployment, this explanation is linked to the compositional one.

Table 1.4, showing density data for a selection of industries, reveals three

Table 1.5 Trade union employment density (%), by workplace size and employment status (Great Britain)

	1989	*1995*
Workplace size		
Up to 24 employees	18	16
25 or more employees	48	40
Employment status		
Part-time	22	21
Full-time	43	36

Source: Labour Force Survey.

patterns. First, in some sectors such as rail transport and to a lesser extent schools, density levels remain high; even here, however, declines are apparent. Many of these sectors have a large representation of public enterprises. Union density in the public sector as a whole in 1995 was 61 per cent, as against only 21 per cent in the private sector. Continuing trends towards privatization, discussed below, have important implications for unions. Second, there have been steady declines in some sectors with traditionally strong organization (vehicles) as well as those where unions have always been weaker (chemicals). Third, many sectors such as distribution and hotels have always been weakly organized.

Table 1.5 underlines low union organization in small firms and among part-time workers. The growing importance of both is likely further to weaken unions. However, the table also suggests that the decline in unionization was concentrated among large establishments and full-time employees, reinforcing the above argu-ment that employers in 'core' parts of the economy were moving away from collective bargaining.

As Waddington and Whitston (1995: 172) conclude, recession and the collapse of manufacturing were central to the decline of unions in the early 1980s. From the middle of the decade, legal and employer hostility became more important. The role of law is discussed above. As for employers, derecognition and, in particular, the absence of unionism in new plants, grew after 1987. Significant parts of the private sector were becoming 'union free'; by 1995, four unionists in seven worked in the public sector.

Trade Union Structure

In one respect, the pattern of British trade union organization is simpler than in many other European countries: there is only one central confederation in Britain, the TUC. This unitary characteristic reflects the facts that British unions have never been radically differentiated on ideological grounds and that the unioniza-tion of public employees and white-collar grades has largely evolved out of the traditional union structure. Some relatively large unions (for example the largest teachers' union, the NUT) were originally outside the TUC, but joined during the

1960s in order to gain a voice in the developing machinery of tripartism. By the end of the 1970s, 90 per cent of all trade unionists were members of TUC affiliates. Though the proportion has now fallen to 80 per cent, there have been no serious attempts to create a rival federation to the TUC.

The structure of contemporary British trade unions reflects their slow historical evolution and displays a complex pattern with no underlying organizational logic. In 1992 there were 268 trade unions in Britain with an aggregate membership of just over 9 million. However, the distribution of membership was very uneven. The ten largest unions contained almost half of all trade unionists. This uneven pattern has always been characteristic of British unions. In 1948 the proportion of members in the ten largest unions was almost the same as today. However, the composition of the numerically dominant unions has changed as the sectoral and occupational composition of employment has altered. Formerly prominent unions like those of coalminers and railway workers have declined rapidly in numbers. Those representing workers in education, the health services and other public services have replaced them in the 'league table'.

The number of unions continued to fall during the 1980s. However, the large TUC-affiliated unions are no longer the beneficiaries of change. The TGWU and AEU, the two largest unions in 1980, each lost some 40 per cent of their membership during the decade. The main success stories were outside the TUC: some large organizations such as the Royal College of Nursing and the Police Federation, and also many smaller professional and staff associations.

The principal reason for the declining number of small unions is a 'merger wave' (Waddington 1995) since 1966 in which a total of 347 unions have been absorbed by amalgamation; 84 per cent of these had less than 5,000 members. This reflects company restructuring and tougher employer policies; a rise in the threshold of union solvency with the diversification of the range of services which unions sought to provide; and, in some cases, numerical decline resulting from the contraction of a union's recruitment base. Such mergers, which may allow the junior partner to function as a semi-autonomous section of the larger union, have reflected no obvious industrial relations logic, but rather have stemmed from the political allegiances of the leaderships involved or from a simple desire to extend recruitment bases.

Today, most significant unions are to some extent general unions: multi-occupational and often multi-industrial. Former craft unions have opened their membership in one direction to lower-skilled workers, in another to white-collar staff. In the face of the overall decline in membership in the 1980s, recruitment strategies have become increasingly opportunistic, and inter-union conflict has inevitably resulted.

Finance

The internal organization of unions in Britain is also distinctive. By comparison with most Northern European countries, membership contributions are relatively low (on average, roughly 0.5 per cent of members' income), and union bureaucracy is undeveloped. The ratio of full-time officials to members is low (in general, ranging between 1:100 and 1:500); most unions depend heavily on 'lay' rank-and-file activists to recruit new members, undertake local administrative tasks, and perform workplace-level collective bargaining. Specialist functions at national level, such as research, education and communications, have traditionally been very poorly resourced. As shown below, however, since the 1960s some unions have significantly increased their staffing in these areas in an attempt to become more 'professional'.

For most of the post-war period, the proportion of income received directly from members in subscriptions has declined. Only in the 1980s were most unions forced to introduce substantial increases in real subscription levels in order to remain solvent in the face of declining membership. With rising expenditure and static subscriptions during much of the past quarter-century, unions have been sustained to an important extent by income from property and other investments. This in turn has tended to erode the 'real net worth' of British unions, that is the real value of assets minus liabilities (Willman et al. 1993: 13). Though unions remained solvent, their financial health weakened as members were lost.

▌Union Structures

Union Governance

Underlying the 1984 Act was the view that in many unions the traditional forms of collective decision-making allowed policy to be dictated by 'militant' leaders or shop stewards. By requiring secret individual ballots as the central mechanism of union democracy, it was assumed that 'moderate' policies would prevail (Undy et al. 1996).

A major administrative burden has been placed on unions by legislation requiring elections of officers by secret postal ballot. In some unions, membership records in the past were notoriously unreliable, and the spur to greater efficiency might perhaps be welcomed. But the absolute requirement to maintain up-to-date registers of members eligible to vote, together with current home addresses, is difficult for any union to satisfy, particularly where membership turnover is high.

Most unions have been forced to transform their electoral systems. In many unions, notably white-collar organizations in the public sector, general secretaries were not elected but appointed by the executive committee or the conference. In other unions national officers were initially elected by a membership ballot, but were not subject to re-election (as in the Railwaymen, now merged with the Seamen to form the National Union of Rail, Maritime and Transport Workers). It was also common for executive committee members representing specific occupational interests to be appointed by the relevant union committee rather than directly elected by the membership (for example, trade group representatives in the TGWU).

With varying degrees of reluctance, unions have been forced to comply with the new legal requirements. The consequences have probably been less marked than the government anticipated. In few unions have the new election methods brought radical changes in the political disposition of the executive. However, because postal balloting often seems to result in far lower voting figures than other methods, the outcome can be greater unpredictability and fluctuation.

The second area in which the 1984 Act introduced new balloting requirements, political funds, resulted in a clear defeat for the government. Under the 1913 Trade Union Act, unions undertaking political activities (including affiliation to the Labour Party) were required to ballot members to establish a separate fund. The 1984 Act required new ballots to confirm support for existing funds. An effective campaign resulted in confirmation of all existing political funds, usually by very large majorities. Some unions which had not previously had political funds also held successful ballots to establish them.

Unions have responded to the environment in various ways. First, as Willman et al. (1993) show, they have improved their financial disciplines. They have also, partly in response to legislative requirements, improved their membership records and means of communicating with members. Second, in response to laws on strikes, they have tightened the authorization of industrial action. In many respects, they have become more organized and also more centralized.

Although the legislation may have failed to transform the political characteristics of British unionism, many critics would argue that it has helped encourage a more individualistic conception of trade union democracy, and thus subvert the collective character of trade union organization and action. However, opinion polls suggest that the principle of secret ballots is very popular among union members, many of whom are receptive to the argument that leaders and activists are out of touch with the opinions of the majority, even though they have shown no marked disposition to vote these leaders out of office.

Relations with Members

In the face of this change in the character of unions' links with their members, the TUC has attempted to co-ordinate the responses of its affiliates. To the extent, however, that the internal authority of Congress depends on the status derived from dealing with the government, its ability to exert effective leadership in policy formulation has if anything diminished. In 1987, Congress established a Special Review Body (SRB) to consider future policy for the movement. Its deliberations concentrated on two problems: recruitment and retention of members, and inter-union relations. Its reports emphasized the need for more targeted recruitment methods, encouraging increased attention in membership campaigns and in bargaining priorities to vulnerable groups with distinctive needs, such as women, young workers, and ethnic minorities.

A notable TUC initiative was to commission studies of union membership in local labour markets where employment had recently expanded. On the basis of the findings, the SRB attempted to co-ordinate the recruitment efforts of its members in such areas, on the grounds that unrestricted competition among affiliates for new members would prove counterproductive. However, some of the larger TUC unions effectively vetoed such intervention, since they felt able to gain more from a recruitment 'free-for-all' than smaller and less well-resourced competitors. Highly publicized efforts were also made to recruit members in two specific localities; the results were very limited and further similar recruitment drives were abandoned.

A perceived interest among potential members in specific services rather than traditional collective bargaining functions led the TUC to encourage affiliates to offer a wide range of financial services, including credit cards and mortgage facilities. However, fewer than 3 per cent of new members cite financial services as one of the two most important reasons for joining. Traditional services such as 'support if a problem arises at work' (cited by 72 per cent as one of the two main reasons for joining) remain central (Waddington and Whitston 1997).

Despite a substantial effort to come to terms with the changes of the 1980s, unions have yet to present an agenda that appeals to many potential members. Workers in such areas as private sector services, where traditions of collectivism have been weak and where employer hostility and high labour turnover militate against unionism, have proved hard to attract.

▌ Trade Unions and Politics

Most of the larger unions affiliate to the Labour Party (though the TUC itself does not); Party membership via national trade unions is one of the many unique features of the British system. However, the relationship between unions' 'political' and 'industrial relations involvements is complex and often contradictory. Traditionally a tacit division of labour existed between Party and unions. Although affiliated unions provided most of the Party's funds, and potentially had the decisive vote at its conference, the parliamentary leadership was allowed a virtually free hand on policy issues except where these affected the conduct of collective bargaining (Minkin 1991). Conversely, the Party did not seek to interfere in industrial relations.

In the 1970s, this relationship came under strain as Labour governments strove to operate incomes policies and as left-wingers in some unions questioned the split between 'industrial relations and 'politics'. Labour's links with the unions were an important part of Conservative rhetoric, and after the general election defeat of 1987 Labour Party and union leaderships considered that a looser relationship was desirable. The Party has accepted many of the labour law changes of the Conservatives, notably on strike ballots and union elections, a move in which unions have acquiesced. During the 1990s, the Party reduced the voting power of the unions at its conference while still relying heavily on their financial support.

In terms of substantive political programmes, union policies developed in two main areas. First, most unions endorsed some statutory support for collective bargaining, and in the 1990s this was buttressed by calls for a framework of individual employment rights, including the right to call in a union representative in the case of a grievance. Where significant membership support could be demonstrated, unions would have the right to recognition. Second, unions' allegiance to free collective bargaining extended to opposition to statutory minimum wages, which were felt to undermine collective bargaining. A major change occurred during the 1980s, as unions responded to attacks on Wages Councils and the difficulty of protecting low-wage workers. All major unions came to endorse a policy of a national minimum wage (NMW) based on half the male median wage. Commitment to an NMW was a distinctive Labour election commitment, though the Party declined to specify any exact figure.

A marked development of the late 1980s was the transformation in union attitudes towards the European Union. Ever since the issue of UK membership was first debated, most unions were hostile. During the referendum of 1975, the TUC called for British withdrawal. In the 1980s, however, with their strength in collective bargaining reduced, and with their aspirations to represent a new and more vulnerable constituency, British unions have come increasingly to see legislation as a necessary and desirable method of achieving employee rights. Given the hostility of the government towards such legislation, unions have looked to Brussels for what Westminster denies. The TUC became an enthusiastic supporter of European integration, in particular of a 'social dimension' to the single market. Unions have supported keenly the development of European Works Councils and have been active in pursuing claims through the European Court.

Assessment

During the 1980s unions made considerable efforts to re-orient their policies and methods in the light of the changing structure of the workforce, employer attempts to redefine the employment relationship, and legal and political challenges. As yet there is little consensus on the responses to be adopted, and the effectiveness of new policy initiatives remains unclear. Unions have certainly survived, and there is no evidence that most workers have abandoned collectivism as a general principle (Gallie 1996). Yet the meanings and constituencies of collectivism may well have altered. Some recent policy initiatives may be seen as adaptations to increasing differentiation among trade unionists and within the labour force more generally. At one level, it can involve increased attention to the needs of those whose labour market position is weak. At the other extreme, though, a concern of many unions in the 1980s was how to appeal to relatively advantaged groups with scarce skills or secure careers. Allowing such groups scope for policy-making autonomy has become, in particular, an important feature of the trade union merger process. The implications of such sectionalization – particularly when allied to more bureaucratic modes of union organization and administration – are deeply ambiguous. Unions have survived, but they have not created a new identity, and the idea of a labour 'movement' is perhaps more distant than ever.

Public Sector Industrial Relations

Britain is unusual in the very limited extent to which employment legislation differentiates between the public and private sectors. However, the character of public sector industrial relations has been profoundly shaped by government policies. These include the strategic decisions that determine the scope of public ownership; the legal and administrative rules and informal political pressures that limit the discretion of local service managers; and government expenditure policies that exert a crucial influence on pay determination because salaries consume up to 70 per cent of current expenditure in public services.

In 1993, the state was directly or indirectly responsible for 5.5 million employees, 22 per cent of the labour force in employment (Winchester and Bach 1995: 305). Public sector employment fell from a peak of nearly 30 per cent of the work force in 1977. This was caused by a gradual reduction in central government staff, and the rationalization and privatization policies that halved employment in nationalized industries in the 1980s. Much of the decline reflected the reclassification of some sectors, and, government claims notwithstanding, the size of the state sector did not diminish very much during the Thatcher period.

▌ The Traditional Pattern

Until the late 1960s, public sector industrial relations attracted very little academic and political interest. A broad consensus supported the continued public ownership of major power, transport and other industries, and the expansion of education, health, and social services within the welfare state. In this favourable environment, public sector industrial relations were fairly stable. Centralized collective bargaining, and a commitment to the principle of 'fair comparison', led to pay movements broadly in line with those of the private sector. When pay and conditions grievances arose, potential conflicts were settled mainly through arbitration procedures. Trade union membership density was high, union policy-making was centralized, and most of the unions representing non-manual employees had modest policy objectives which they pursued cautiously. There was little incentive to develop management expertise in industrial relations; various forms of 'consensus management' were based on formal consultation with staff representatives and a bureaucratic style of decision-making. The ideology and rhetoric of 'public service' values encouraged a tacit understanding that if government and public sector managers sustained a long-established obligation to be 'model employers', then staff and their unions would accept a reciprocal obligation to preserve industrial peace.

During the 1970s, far more conflictual patterns of industrial relations emerged. In most countries, high and fluctuating levels of inflation threatened existing methods of pay determination and expenditure planning and control in the public sector. In the British context of weak economic performance and volatile electoral politics, however, public sector disputes generated unpredictable and dramatic political consequences. The general elections of 1974 and 1979 were influenced decisively by industrial disputes in the public sector.

At the beginning of the 1970s, at a time of relatively low unemployment and weak public expenditure control, trade unions embarked on radically new strategies. Those representing low-paid manual workers organized pay campaigns that succeeded in mobilizing a previously quiescent membership and won a remarkable degree of public support during disputes with public sector employers such as local authorities and the health service. In traditionally hierarchic and moderate non-manual public service unions, national leaderships were often challenged by a form of 'radical professionalism'; and school teachers, social workers, and civil servants engaged in selective strike action for the first time.

Public service values and the limited management expertise of employers left them quite unprepared for such conflict. The strategy of the 1970–4 Conservative government fluctuated uncertainly between corporatist and coercive approaches to union leaders in implementing incomes policies and industrial relations legislation. On several occasions, it misjudged public opinion, and the ultimate political miscalculation was made by the prime minister when he chose to call a general election in 1974 during the second miners' strike.

In the late 1970s, the form and consequences of public sector wage conflict were quite different. There were few disputes during the early years of the Labour government because most public sector workers received large pay settlements – the classic 'catching-up' phase of the cycle. This contributed substantially to the public expenditure crisis of 1975, and paved the way for the introduction of cuts and cash limits that would have profound consequences in later years. Active trade union support for the incomes policies was undermined by declining real incomes and the deterioration in pay relativities with the private sector. Despite union opposition, the government tried to sustain a pay limit of 5 per cent in the autumn of 1978. Government ministers refused to sanction public service settlements above the pay norm, and widespread industrial disruption took place in the early months of 1979. The strikes of the 'winter of discontent' exposed severe inter-union conflict, and tensions between the leadership, activists and members within some unions. Unlike the conflicts of the early 1970s, there was widespread public hostility to the disruption of essential services.

Conservative Government Policies in the 1980s and 1990s

The disruption of public services contributed significantly to the Conservative Party's election victory in 1979 and legitimized the policies it had developed during 5 years of opposition. Its general commitment to confront trade union power included a specific hostility to public sector unions. Strict controls on public expenditure, leading to job losses and pay restraint, were central.

The government soon abolished the Pay Comparability Commission established under the Labour government and systematically attacked the principle of comparability, by substituting the 'ability to pay' as the key criterion for public sector pay determination. Cash limits and other financial controls defined this 'ability to pay'. The government virtually abandoned the previous system of volume planning of public services in favour of cash planning, implying that the volume of public services emerged as a residual after taking account of pay increases and other costs. The collective bargaining implications of cash limits were equally significant.

First, in contrast to the fixed pay norms of previous policies, where a single publicized breach often undermined the credibility of the whole policy, cash limits allowed unequal pay awards to reflect the potential industrial power or labour market position of different groups. Second, cash limits forced union and employer negotiators to confront income–employment trade-offs more explicitly; they could exceed the pay assumption of the cash limits, but only if the extra cost could be recovered by job losses, efficiency savings, or service reductions. Thirdly, cash limits encouraged public sector managers to seek a more direct influence on negotiations.

The imposition of tight cash limits in the early 1980s led to a number of protracted disputes in the steel industry, civil service, health service, schools, and water supply industry. All of these disputes revealed that the Conservative government had recalculated the political costs of public sector conflict and had developed a more strategic approach to conflict management. First, government ministers rejected traditional methods of conciliation and mediation; opportunities for compromise were repeatedly scorned as a sign of weakness. Second, the government was willing to pay substantial financial costs to defeat public sector unions. A key example was the coal miners' strike in 1984–5 against pit closures. A combination of determined employer and government strategy and divisions among the miners (which meant that one-third of coal capacity remained operational) led to the defeat of the strike. The estimated £5 billion cost of defeating the miners was merely the most dramatic example of the government's determination to win (Adeney and Lloyd 1986). Third, public sector employers were encouraged to adopt a more abrasive and confrontational style of management in negotiations and disputes.

For most of the 1980s, this strategy seemed to be successful. Many public sector unions adopted a version of 'new realism' based on the recognition that militancy was unlikely to be rewarded. While the frequency of nationally co-ordinated strikes over pay declined, especially in the middle of the decade when most workers' real incomes rose, public sector conflict did not disappear altogether. For instance, ambulance staff sustained an effective programme of non-strike sanctions in their pay dispute of 1989–90. More generally, a number of disputes arose from defensive union action to preserve bargaining procedures or conditions of service.

Conservative governments also promoted more decentralized methods of pay determination that would be more sensitive to local labour market conditions and individual employees' performance. The government can claim some success in undermining national bargaining structures. Throughout the public sector, senior managers have been removed from the coverage of collective bargaining; national agreements are now less prescriptive than in the past; and some local authorities have withdrawn from the national machinery. Legal and administrative changes have been introduced to allow a devolution of pay and personnel policies to separate 'executive agencies' in central government, separate 'businesses' in nationalized industries, 'self-governing trusts' in the health service, and 'locally-managed' schools and colleges in education. These changes reflect the substantial devolution of managerial authority in all parts of the public sector.

More than 1.5 million employees, including nurses (since 1983) and schoolteachers (since 1991), are covered by Pay Review Bodies. While the pay review system formally ends 'free collective bargaining', permitting the government to accept, modify or reject the review bodies' recommendations, it sustains a 'quasi-bargaining' process in practice. Trade unions, employers, and government departments submit evidence and arguments covering the usual pay determination criteria, and the possibility that the government might reject the review bodies' recommendations is minimized by the potential political costs involved. Although the pay awards for nurses have been deferred or staged on several occasions, their relative pay has improved under the pay review procedure during the 1980s.

What has happened to public sector pay? Elliott and Duffus (1996) show that overall public sector groups lost out relative to the private sector during the 1980s but that by 1992 there had been a notable recovery. They, and more pointedly Bailey (1996), also show that groups covered by collective bargaining fared relatively badly while those subject to pay review, notably the police and nurses, have done relatively well. This was accompanied by increasing variation in the treatment of different services and occupational groups. In general, pay differentials between staff with professional qualifications and their administrative, clerical, and ancillary support staff widened. Police prospered more than teachers, and teachers in schools were treated more favourably than their colleagues in further education or universities.

Privatization

From the mid-1980s the government embarked on a policy of privatizing (i.e. selling shares in and establishing as private companies) many public sector organizations including those supplying telecommunications, electricity, gas and water as well as British Steel and British Coal and, most recently, the railways. The rationale of this policy was to stimulate competition but, in practice, monopoly power remained intact in several instances. Similar motives spurred the introduction of Compulsory Competitive Tendering (CCT) in many parts of the public sector, which required organizations such as health and education authorities to put out services such as cleaning and laundry services to tender.

The effects of these processes have been profound (Colling and Ferner 1995). Employment levels have fallen. As for collective bargaining, in many industries such as electricity several new companies replaced the former integrated structure, and national bargaining has been replaced by company-level arrangements. Union derecognition, however, remained rare, though some managers and relatively small unions lost their recognition rights. Developments such as CCT severely weakened unions as workers were taken out of the coverage of collective agreements, often by non-union private contractors. Where activities stayed 'in house', union structures were too weak to handle the new demands placed on them (Colling 1995).

Within the workplace, Colling and Ferner (1995: 505–6) conclude, privatization has encouraged the tighter control of attendance standards and has allowed the introduction of new work patterns, such as extended response in the gas and electricity industries to customer requests. Cost pressures have also required many workers to work harder. This is a theme to which we now turn.

Change in the Workplace

Shop Stewards and Employee Representation

The shop steward emerged in parts of the engineering industry in the nineteenth century. It was not until the 1960s that the steward's role was given much attention (see Terry 1995). This interest reflected the growing role of stewards, especially in the car industry, in negotiating many key issues of pay levels, work allocation and discipline. During the 1970s steward organization in manufacturing was promoted by many managements which sought to reform workplace industrial relations through new payments and discipline and grievance procedures and which saw the steward as the means to negotiate such changes. In the public sector, the moves towards managerialism discussed above promoted, for the first time, activity at local level. From the late 1970s the influence of the steward was eroded. Significantly, the process began before 1979 as some firms with strong steward bodies (such as the car firm then called BL, later the Rover Group) and others with relatively quiescent stewards (such as Cadbury's) began to question the influence of stewards. The process accelerated in the 1980s.

On the causes of this decline, Terry (1995) identifies four factors. First, unemployment and the changing industrial distribution of employment had effects here, as in areas such as union membership. A specific influence was the decline in plant size, for steward organization was closely linked to the size of the plant. Second, employers were increasingly hostile to shop stewards' authority, and it was hard for stewards to respond to the new managerial agenda of HRM. The case study evidence assembled by Terry shows that the managerial agenda was very different from that of negotiated agreement and that few stewards' organizations could exert any major influence over such initiatives as team working. Third, there were internal weaknesses of steward organization. The benefit of hindsight shows that the strength of stewards was often more apparent than real. Managerially sponsored bodies lacked much independent influence, while more autonomous bodies drew their strength from the workplace itself and found it hard to respond to more strategic initiatives. Finally, the absence of any legal underpinning to workplace representation meant that there was no institutional barrier to the operation of these forces.

The outcome of declining union presence, of a diminished role for stewards where unions remain, and of the rarity (noted above) of two-way channels of communication is a 'representation gap' at the workplace. Workers often lack an effective means of expressing their views to employers.

Table 1.6 Strikes in the UK, 1946–1995 (annual averages)

	ALL INDUSTRIES			NON-COAL INDUSTRIES		
	Strikes	Workers involved (000s)	Days lost (000s)	Strikes	Workers involved (000s)	Days lost (000s)
1946–52	1,698	444	1,888	625	228	1,318
1953–59	2,340	790	3,950	608	551	3,407
1960–68	2,372	1,323	3,189	1,451	1,189	2,872
1969–73	2,974	1,581	12,497	2,723	1,447	9,881
1974–79	2,412	1,653	12,178	2,141	1,555	11,147
1980–85	1,276	1,213	9,806	1,022	1,046	5,830
1986–89	893	781	3,324	656	705	3,166
1990–93	366	252	960	333	242	929
1994	205	107	278	205	107	278
1995	235	174	415	231	174	415

Source: 1946–73: Durcan et al. (1983); subsequent years, annual article on stoppages of work due to industrial disputes in *Employment Gazette*.

Strikes

Table 1.6 gives some indices of the strike pattern. Figures are given separately for coal mining and for other industries because of the domination of the overall figures by coal: in 1957, as many as three-quarters of all strikes occurred in this one industry. Because trends here often ran in a different direction from those in the rest of industry, the overall strike figures obscure what was happening outside coal.

All the main strike indicators fell sharply from 1980. The number of strikes recorded in 1995, 235, was a mere 6 per cent of the number in the peak year (1970). As the table shows, the decline in strikes is particularly steep compared to the 1960s and 1970s. In a longer-term context, the reduction is much less dramatic, for the 1950s were relatively quiescent. None the less, when changes in the size of the labour force are taken into account, the strike propensity of British workers is probably at an all-time low. As well as becoming less common, strikes have become shorter. From 1977, there was a steady decline in the proportion lasting 3 days or more. By the mid-1990s, over three-quarters of strikes lasted less than 3 days, compared to two-fifths in the late 1970s.

The pattern of strikes also changed. As noted above, the coal industry used to dominate the figures, with the docks and parts of manufacturing also being relatively strike-prone. Coal also accounted for many of the most prominent disputes, most importantly the national strike of 1984–5. Thereafter, the industry was rapidly run down. At first, strike activity per worker remained above national levels but with the further shrinkage of the industry and its eventual privatization strikes virtually disappeared; there were none in 1994 and four in 1995. Manufacturing, too, saw a reduction in strike rates, both absolutely and relatively, so that days lost per worker fell from levels well above the national average to around the average.

The place of traditional strikers was taken by public sector workers. Some, such as postal employees, had had some record of militancy. Others, such as employees in education and public administration (each of which groups accounted for more strike-days in 1995 than did the whole of manufacturing), had been relatively quiescent. The decline in strikes in the traditional sectors is likely to have reflected the new management policies, such as more communication with workers, analysed above and the workplace changes discussed below. It is worth stressing a simple but important factor. Most British strikes were small and related to immediate workplace grievances. They stemmed from a lack of trust in management, and when a specific grievance arose workers had the confidence to pursue it. Change from the 1980s improved the technical organization of work and reduced some of the sources of grievance. A climate of uncertainty also reduced workers' willingness to walk out on strike. The decline in strikes did not necessarily mean that there was more trust but it certainly suggested that some of the specific sources of dispute had been removed.

The other feature of the past was the large national strike. Its decline reflects the fragmentation of bargaining and the privatization of large parts of the public sector as well as high unemployment. The groups that remained relatively strike-prone were often employed in relatively large bargaining units, so that they retained a collective base on which to organize action. Some strikes were seen as union gains, such as some of the public sector disputes discussed above. In the private sector, the most significant dispute involved demands in 1989 for shorter working hours in the engineering industry. The unions marked out certain key employers for industrial action, and claimed widespread success. They were able to exploit the lack of solidarity among British employers and, on this occasion at least, to turn the decentralization of bargaining to their own advantage.

Overall however, the decline in strikes is one of the more dramatic developments of the 1980s and 1990s. Its link to workplace relations is illustrated by Darlington's (1994) study of the Ford plant on Merseyside, which had long had a militant reputation. The number of strikes recorded by management fell from 310 in 1976 to about 15 a year in the late 1980s. Whether such trends reflect a wider improvement in the quality of workplace relations we now consider.

Work Effort

A series of surveys from the mid-1980s (some across the working population and some focused in specific firms) consistently found that employees reported an increase in their work effort. Table 1.7 summarizes five of them. This rise in effort could simply be a perception. But, as noted above, in sectors such as privatized firms there is objective evidence of the same tasks being carried out with fewer workers. The situation is not limited to manual and clerical workers. There is growing evidence that managers report working longer hours and a growth in pressure to achieve targets or face sanctions (Scase and Goffee 1989). There is, moreover, one objective indicator for manufacturing, the Percentage Utilization of Labour index. This is compiled from reports by work study engineers from 171 factories and attempts to measure the intensity of labour; the index shows cycles during the 1970s, a sharp increase from 1980 to 1984, and stability to 1990 (Nichols 1991). Finally, Waddington and Whitston (1996) report a large survey of trade union activists. This shows that members' grievances focused on issues to do with work organization (such as staffing levels) and the working environment (e.g. health and safety); they interpret this as evidence of work intensification.

Within this overall picture, two points are important. First, the pattern is likely to have varied between industries. There is very clear evidence of work intensification in parts of the public sector and in privatized firms; evidence from the coal industry is given by Nolan and O'Donnell (1995). Second, some writers suggested that work intensification meant an unacceptable increase in pressure on employees. Some of the surveys address this. Thus Batstone and Gourlay found that shop stewards reported that effort levels were often still reasonable. Over half the sample studied by Collinson and Edwards (1996) were working harder but were satisfied with their level of effort. This is important in suggesting that change was far from being a zero-sum development. Collinson et al. speak of a disciplined worker model: they show that there was more work effort and closer managerial monitoring of performance but also that such closer monitoring went along with favourable views of management.

▌ Distrust or Commitment?

Studies suggest that change has not generally led to the creation of a high level of trust in management or high commitment to organizational goals. Reviewing a range of studies of the 1980s, Kelly and Kelly (1991) conclude that 'them and us' attitudes were still prevalent. Hedges (1994: 48), reporting a general population survey, found that only 26 per cent of people felt that their workplace was 'very well managed' Kessler and Undy (1996) say that 40 per cent of their sample felt 'a lot' of loyalty to their organization but they also argue that widespread insecurity undermines a sense of commitment. Collinson and Edwards (1996) found rather low levels of trust even though their organizations were adopting advanced HRM techniques. Some studies of the workplace paint a picture of intensification and others of high commitment. Which is right?

On the 'intensification' side, Sewell and Wilkinson (1993) report, in a Japanese-owned electronics firm, very strict control of work through electronic surveillance. McArdle et al. (1995) describe total quality management initiatives in another electronics firm and they argue that these initiatives reduced any genuine worker autonomy and tightened managerial control of the work process. Pollert (1996: 201) shows that team working in a chocolate company involved tighter budgetary controls which in many ways reduced rather than enhanced the autonomy of shop floor managers; as for workers' attitudes, 'there was no indication of a change from a primarily instrumental orientation to labour'.

Table 1.7 Surveys of changing effort levels

Source	Date of study	Sample	Results	(%)
Batstone and Gourlay (1986: 125)	1984	1,023 shop stewards from 13 groups (reporting on workers they represent)	Increase in effort levels to very high levels	23
			Increase, reasonable levels	50
			Little change	20
			Fall	6
Rose et al. (1994: 35)	1986	6,111 employees from 6 towns or cities	Increase in effort	55
			Increase in pace of work	38
Edwards and Whitston (1993: 249)	1987–90	197 employees in 4 case study firms	Work is harder	38
			Work is not harder	14
Collinson and Edwards (1996)	1995	300 employees in 6 case study organizations	Work is: a lot harder	25
			Work is: a little harder	50
			Work is: no harder/less hard	25
			Working harder and like this	57
			Working same or harder and dislike this	19
			No change or less effort and like this	24
Kessler and Undy (1996: 7, 9)	1995	1000 employees	Working harder	63
			No change	29
			Working less hard	6
			Look forward to going to work	57
			Mixed feelings/don't care one way or other	28
			Wish didn't have to go	14

On the 'commitment' side, a leading study is Clark's (1995) analysis of the greenfield site in South Wales opened by the Pirelli company. The HRM strategy included a high level of workforce flexibility, pay linked to the learning of new skills, and self-supervision. Clark argues that worker satisfaction was high and that the plant attained a high position in the Pirelli world-wide league of performance measures. The plant's total quality programme 'created a sense of involvement and empowerment' (p. 235). Clark is, however, very clear that change was a complex process with limits and contradictions. Workers felt powerless in relation to such issues as pay and staffing levels. Like other studies, Clark's points to a weakening of the influence of the trade union. Ambitions of attaining complete flexibility were also abandoned. As for self-supervision, this increased job satisfaction even though it was often accompanied by 'intensified work effort over a shift' (p. 154). The picture, then, is not simply one of benefits for all. Workers generally value the new system but it meant more work effort, in line with the disciplined worker model mentioned above. The problems for unions in playing an effective role also stand out.

Research has yet to identify the conditions under which intensification or commitment is the more likely outcome. Some features can, however, be suggested. Cases like Clark's often occur in sectors where labour represents a small proportion of costs and where skills are important. Studies stressing intensification often come from sectors with assembly line operations using semi-skilled workers. A second set of influences is management choice. Managers at Pirelli consciously sought a new form of employee relations, and there were (as in the HRM model discussed above) clear connections with business strategy.

Three conclusions are suggested. First, it is possible in Britain for some form of high commitment systems to be introduced, though the limits of these are also important. Second, the conditions promoting them are unusual. As discussed above, most managements in large firms have embraced the HRM model in only a very partial way, and at the same time the growth of insecure employment in smaller firms suggests that most employees will not be exposed to any coherent HRM strategy. Third, evidence in support of greater work effort is persuasive. Some accounts of this have implied a straight degradation of labour, but this neglects evidence on the use of new technology and on workers' acceptance of the need to work harder. Managers also need some degree of worker compliance and, as we saw in relation to Japanization, there is evidence of their making of concessions and tolerating some worker means to regulate work effort.

It seems likely that some workers, particularly those in the competitive parts of the economy, were subjected to demands that they found excessive. In other cases, there will have been a resigned acceptance of the need for change: recognition that competitive forces required more effort, and acceptance of the need for this but without any wider commitment to managerial goals. A third group of cases comprises situations where there is genuinely better communication from management and where workers feel that their jobs, though harder, are more adequately managed. Commitment here is likely to remain fairly pragmatic. Finally, there are the relatively few situations such as the case described by Clark in which a fuller sense of participation has been achieved.

Change in the workplace, then, has involved what Geary (1995) terms the re-regulation of labour: a reorganization of control in which more effort and the tighter measurement of performance are common but in which there may also be an improved technical division of labour and in some cases greater skill and responsibility.

Productivity

Debates on productivity turn on three issues: how far productivity really improved; the role of labour relations in any change; and the nature of that role. The third is particularly important. It is common for writers to claim that change in industrial relations made a difference, but to be unclear whether the change implies a harsh reassertion of managerial prerogative, the ending of previous restraints on productivity, or a shift towards some genuine high commitment route.

Consider the example provided by Oulton (1995). He argues that the trend growth rate of productivity, compared to other countries, improved during the 1980s. He suggests that unions of a British kind (but not necessarily all unions) will restrict productivity because of such factors as multi-unionism (which reduces the speed of change) and the length and uncertainty of shop floor negotiation. He then cites various studies (e.g. Gregg et al. 1993) which indicate that productivity growth in the union sector was faster than in the non-union sector. Oulton and others argue that this is consistent with the removal or reduction of unions' ability to restrain productivity improvements. The argument also fits the evidence, reviewed above, concerning a reduction in the union mark-up.

Oulton is not suggesting that there has been any transformation of industrial relations towards a high commitment system. He is merely arguing that a blockage on productivity was removed. Metcalf (1994: 153) makes the point explicitly: '[changed productivity performance] is surely not a "transformation". The changed outcomes seem to be mainly the result of compliance by labour in the conduct of workplace relations. What is still needed for a transformation is a change of gear by management – greater emphasis on co-operation and more investment in physical and human capital.' As we have seen, evidence for a widespread change in workplace attitudes remains limited to a few sectors.

But Oulton's account needs severe qualification. First, it says nothing about the nature of productivity as measured, which is output per worker hour. As we have seen, there is evidence that workers may be working harder. More work effort means an increase in labour input. Measured productivity may mean that, in part, workers are simply working harder rather than that productivity has improved in the strict sense of the efficiency with which inputs are transformed into outputs. Second, Oulton equates industrial relations effects on productivity with trade unions. But unions differ greatly in their degree of organization and their ability to influence the work process. Multi-unionism was a feature of only part of the British economy, and not all unions were able to have any influence over the pace of technical change, those in sectors like footwear and clothing being good examples.

Third, even where unions are strong, their impact cannot be isolated from management choices. A case study of a very strongly unionized plant in the late 1970s, when union influence was at its peak, illustrates the point (Scullion and Edwards 1988). The plant had two unions, and there were significant demarcation disputes between them. In addition, the larger union exerted numerous controls over the work pace and manning levels. Yet even in this extreme case, the unions favoured technical innovation. It was not that they disliked new practices but that they distrusted the ways in which managers would introduce them. Managers, for their part, seemed to treat union controls as an excuse for inaction. The controls, moreover, had grown up over many years in which managers were willing to concede power to shop stewards. The undoubted poor productivity of this plant reflected its whole industrial relations climate and not the policies of the unions in isolation. It may be contrasted with the case of Cadbury (Smith et al. 1990). Here, there was a traditionally moderate and indeed quiescent shop floor union, and it is hard to see how restrictions prevented new investment. Managers certainly came to believe that their systems of consultation and negotiation held back change, and in 1977 they introduced a more unilateral and assertive style. This was a case of managerial rather than worker responsibility for the initial situation.

Nolan and O'Donnell (1995) provide further arguments against the view that it was the removal of 'restrictions' which stimulated productivity. They show, first, that large numbers of plants made no organizational or technical change at all. Second, they note the common finding that union firms outperformed non-union ones throughout the Thatcher period, which would scarcely suggest that it was industrial relations institutions which were retarding productivity. Using evidence from the coal industry and elsewhere, Nolan and O'Donnell underline the importance of managerial unwillingness to innovate and the importance of the wider competitive environment. In the case of coal, for example, government policy from the 1950s discouraged new investment, even though the miners' unions had a long-standing policy of co-operating with technical change.

Assessment

The emerging workplace system was not a leap forward to a new age of flexibility or sophisticated human resource management: firms adopting advanced styles of personnel management remained very much in the minority, even in sectors such as electronics. Yet neither was there a simple return to the past. The use of communications systems, merit pay, and performance appraisal has no close parallels in the past, and new forms of work organization reshaped jobs and how workers were expected to perform them. Cadbury is again a good example: under old technology, workers used a mix of craft skill and informal knowledge to operate machines, whereas the new computerized system not only eliminated jobs but also controlled and monitored the production process so that the worker was less of a machine operator and more of a general adjunct to a technically driven process.

At least four patterns of change can be identified. First, there were the few cases where high commitment took root. Second came a variant of this in which worker–manager differences remained but in which there was sufficient job security to encourage workers to accept the disciplines of new work practices such as team work. It is here that workers are likely to be working harder but also being reasonably happy to do so. A third, and probably much more common pattern involved firms making piecemeal use of HRM techniques, often alongside technical and organizational innovation. Here, there were at best limited moves to increased employee involvement; any increases in efficiency will have reflected a better technical organization of work, perhaps stimulated by Japanese examples, but not necessarily any increased worker satisfaction. Finally, there were cases where work effort was intensified, unions were possibly derecognized and stress and insecurity increased.

Only in the first of these patterns is any serious social partnership likely to have been practised. In a context of deregulation and union weakness, the British workplace was shaped by employers' needs. In some cases, economic survival was feasible. But in others low levels of investment and the economy's position as a low-wage, low-skill producer left large questions over the future.

▌ Conclusions: Future Prospects

We have argued that Britain has not shifted from a collectivist to an individualist system. First, collectivism was never fully established in the 1970s, and private services in particular remained a domain of unilateral management regulation. Second, it has not disappeared. Unions continue to be recognized in most of the largest firms in the economy. Third, 'individualism' is often poorly specified. If it means a system of well-developed and two-way communication between manager and individual worker, pay linked to individual merit, and the ability of individuals to pursue their own training needs, it is a very rare feature. Yet individualism is often taken to mean no more than the re-establishment of employers' discretion in areas such as pay. Only in this sense does the collapse of wage regulating institutions imply individualization. And it often involves, not the free exchange of individuals in the market place, but control by the employer. Fourth, many recent trends, such as the move towards teamworking, entail an orientation to the work group rather than pure individual activity. A central issue in many organizations is not the promotion of individualism but the balance between individual and group goals.

The dominant influence has been the extension of market-based regulation, most obviously in the privatization of public sector bodies but also in employers' growing use of non-standard forms of employment. By their nature, markets are variable and uncertain. Systems of industrial relations reflect similar variability: in place of collective bargaining which lay at the heart of the system up to the 1970s, there is an array of practices. A minority of firms, often those with relatively stable markets, have moved towards the 'high commitment' model. At the other extreme are those which have abandoned collective bargaining but have put little in its place. In between come those struggling to piece together an employment policy from aspects of HRM and managerial prerogative.

How far is the move away from collective bargaining likely to continue? The decline in trade union influence was shaped by employment shifts away from traditionally unionized sectors, employers' policies of by-passing or avoiding unions and of decentralizing bargaining, and restrictive legislation. Many of these forces seem likely to continue. Some economic trends, such as the move towards private services, are well-established. Shifts in the composition of the economy also suggest that the closed shop and the strike are unlikely to attain anything like their significance of the 1970s. Employers' confidence in their ability to manage with no or minimal union involvement is becoming increasingly entrenched. As for the law, many aspects of the Conservatives' industrial relations programme, notably the requirement of strike ballots, have been accepted by the other main political parties. Wider policy changes also have industrial relations implications; for example, the setting of performance standards for schools and the use of budgets at the level of the individual school influence recruitment, pay levels and staff workloads. Many of these changes have also been accepted by other parties.

Yet there are some counter-trends. As noted above, European regulation has already had a direct impact on issues as varied as equal opportunities, working time, and the consultation procedures on redundancies. There has also been an indirect impact, as where, despite the UK's 'opt-out', British-based firms include their UK employees in the consultation arrangements required under the European Works Councils Directive. The Labour Party's commitment to sign up to the 'social chapter' means, in addition, that this directive will in due course apply to all UK firms of the relevant size, and not just to those which are covered in respect of their employees in other EU states. In the future, there may be an agreement between the social partners under the Maastricht social policy protocol or even a directive requiring national-level works councils, for information and consultation, in undertakings with more than 50 employees. Such a development would take Britain further along the path from its voluntarist tradition. Finally, the directive on working time will now be applied in the UK by the incoming Labour government.

Turning to Labour's 'home grown' industrial relations programme, perhaps the most dramatic commitment is to a National Minimum Wage, which would, in contrast to the old Wages Councils, cover all employees. Trade unions have campaigned for a rate equivalent to half of male median earnings, estimated at around £4.25 per hour in 1997. About 2 million workers would be covered by a minimum set at £3.50 per hour; the figure is about 3.8 million for a minimum at £4.00. The party refused to commit itself to any specific figure. Prior to the 1997 election, it did, however, make clear that the NMW would apply to workers aged 18 and over; younger workers would probably be excluded, rather than be paid a proportion of the adult minimum. A Low Pay Commission, with representation from a wide range of bodies, will recommend the initial level of the NMW and advise on future progress. Labour sees the NMW as important not only in promoting social justice but also in contributing to economic development through a high-wage, high-skill route. The greatest uncertainty concerns how far employers will follow this logic, and how far they will simply see a NMW as increasing costs and thus dismiss workers or try to recoup the costs by increased labour intensification.

Labour also proposes a statutory obligation on employers to recognize a union for collective bargaining where a majority of the workforce vote for union representation. Experience in North America has shown that such a 'duty to bargain' does not prevent employers from opposing unions or a continuing decline in unionization. Much will depend on the details of the provisions (for example, whether they specifically address situations in which an employer is trying to derecognize a union). The large number of non-union establishments suggests that achieving majority support may in many cases prove difficult for unions. Labour will also have to address an underlying tension between two approaches to representation: the traditional 'single channel' system based on trade unions; and a universal 'works council' model, which underlies European Works Councils, possible national-level works councils, and also the 1995 regulations on consultation on redundancies (which require non-union firms to consult employee representatives elected for the purpose).

Labour proposes a range of other measures, including allowing workers sacked for taking part in industrial action to pursue a claim for unfair dismissal and providing certain minimum employment standards. As with Conservative laws, these may be more important in changing the climate of industrial relations than for their specific effects. Labour's aim is to develop a model of social partnership, which embraces improvements in training and inducements to invest. There is some basis for such a model. For example, the Commission on Public Policy and British Businesses (set up by a centre-left think tank with a predominance of business leaders), which reported in January 1997, endorsed the minimum wage and the acceptance of the 'social chapter' as well as the need for investment.

Yet one major constraint may be Labour's commitment to avoid increasing taxes: very tight macro-economic policy could leave little space for spending on investment or education and training. Such a policy also implies strict control of public sector pay, which was one of the major problems for Labour governments in the 1970s. It may be that privatization and union weakness have taken the sting out of this issue. But remaining discontent together with new expectations of what a Labour government would promise could also fuel significant disputes on the issue.

A reasonable expectation is that there will be a move from the extremes of marketization. To some extent, this is in train as companies realize that decentralization can go too far and as influential employers' bodies oppose such Conservative suggestions as the removal of small firms from unfair dismissal legislation. New employment laws would also alter general assumptions and expectations. But the tone is likely to involve a softening of market principles rather than the development of a complete new model of social partnership. Within this broad pattern there is likely to be wide variation. Some commentators speak of a development of the low-wage, low-skill model while others hope for social partnership and a skills-based economy. The thesis of this chapter is that, because of the absence of a strong regulatory framework, both tendencies can be observed.

Social partnership may operate in some specific circumstances but in others competitive pressures will make it hard to sustain a long-term view of employee relations.

▌Abbreviations

AEU   Amalgamated Engineering Union
CBI   Confederation of British Industry
CCT   Compulsory competitive tendering
HRM   Human resource management
ITB   Industrial Training Board
MSC   Manpower Services Commission
NMW   Statutory minimum wage
NUT   National Union of Teachers
PRP   Performance related pay
SRB   (TUC's) Special Review Body
TGWU   Transport and General Workers' Union
TUC   Trades Union Congress
WIRS   Workplace Industrial Relations Surveys

▌Notes

1 The main legal differences from Great Britain are that statutory procedures for union recognition remain in force and that a Fair Employment Agency aims to promote equal opportunities for members of the two religious communities (see Cradden 1993). Data are presented for Great Britain wherever possible, though some are available only for the UK as a whole.

▌References and Further Reading

Adeney, M. and Lloyd, J. 1986: *The Miners' Strike, 1984–5*. London: Routledge.
Aldcroft, D.H. 1992: *Education, Training and Economic Performance, 1944–90*. Manchester: Manchester University Press.
Anderton, R. and Mayhew, K. 1994: A Comparative Analysis of the UK Labour Market. In Barrell 1994. *The UK Labour Market*. Cambridge: Cambridge University Press.
Barrell, R. (ed.) 1994: *The UK Labour Market*. Cambridge: Cambridge University Press.
Bailey, R. 1996: Public Sector Industrial Relations. In Beardwell 1996. *Contemporary Industrial Relations*. Oxford: Oxford University Press.
Batstone, E.V. and Gourlay, S. 1986: *Unions, Unemployment and Innovation*. Oxford: Blackwell Publishers.
Beardwell, I.J. (ed.) 1996: *Contemporary Industrial Relations*. Oxford: Oxford University Press.

Blanchflower, D. and Freeman, R. 1994: Did the Thatcher Reforms Change British Labour Market Performance? In Barrell, 1994. *The UK Labour Market*. Cambridge: Cambridge University Press.

Bratton, J. 1992: *Japanisation at Work*. Basingstoke: Macmillan.

Broad, G. 1994: The Managerial Limits to Japanisation. *Human Resource Management Journal*, 4(3), 39–51.

Brown W. and Wadhwani, S. 1990: The Economic Effects of Industrial Relations Legislation since 1979. *National Institute Economic Review*, 131, 57–70.

Brown, W., Marginson, P. and Walsh, J. 1995: Management: Pay Determination and Collective Bargaining. In Edwards, 1995 *Industrial Relations*. Oxford: Blackwell Publishers.

Carruth, A., and Disney, R. 1988: Where Have Two Million Members Gone?, *Economica*, 55(1), 1–19.

Clark, J. 1995: *Managing Innovation and Change*. London: Sage.

Claydon, T. 1996: Union Derecognition. In Beardwell 1996. *Contemporary Industrial Relations*. Oxford: Oxford University Press.

Clegg, H.A. 1979: *The Changing System of Industrial Relations in Great Britain*. Oxford: Blackwell.

Coleman, D.C. 1988: Book Review. *Business History*, 30(1), 130–31.

Colling, T. 1995: Renewal or Rigor Mortis? *Industrial Relations Journal*, 26(2), 134–45.

Colling, T. and Ferner, A. 1995: Privatisation and Marketisation. In Edwards, 1995. *Industrial Relations*. Oxford: Blackwell Publishers.

Collinson, M., and Edwards, P. 1996: Empowerment or Constrained Involvement? Paper to International Labour Process Conference, Aston University, March.

Cradden, T. 1993: The Tories and Employment Law in Northern Ireland. *Industrial Relations Journal*, 24(1), 59–71.

Crouch, C. 1977: *Class Conflict and the Industrial Relations Crisis*. London: Heinemann.

Darlington, R. 1994: Shop Stewards' Organisation in Ford Halewood. *Industrial Relations Journal*, 25(2), 136–49.

Davies, P., and Freedland, M. 1993: *Labour Legislation and Public Policy*. Oxford: Clarendon.

Deakin, S. 1990: Equality under a Market Order: the Employment Act 1989. *Industrial Law Journal*, 19(1), 1–19.

Dickens, L., and Hall, M. 1995: The State: Labour Law and Industrial Relations. In Edwards, 1995. *Industrial Relations*. Oxford: Blackwell Publishers.

Dickens, R., Gregg, P., Machin, S., Manning, A. and Wadsworth, J. 1993: Wages Councils. *British Journal of Industrial Relations*, 31(4), 515–30.

Disney, R. 1990: Explanations of the Decline in Trade Union Density in Britain: An Appraisal, *British Journal of Industrial Relations*, 28(2), 165–78.

Doyle, P., Saunders, J., and Wong, V. 1992: Competition in Global Markets. *Journal of International Business Studies*, 23(3), 419–34.

Dunn, S., and Metcalf, D. 1996: Trade Union Law since 1979. In Beardwell, 1996. *Contemporary Industrial Relations*. Oxford: Oxford University Press.

Dunn, S. and Wright, M. 1993: Managing without the Closed Shop. In D. Metcalf and S. Milner (eds), *New Perspectives on Industrial Disputes*. London: Routledge.

Durcan, J.W., McCarthy, W.E.J., and Redman, G.P. 1983. *Strikes in Post-war Britain*. London: Allen and Unwin.

Edwards, P.K. (ed.) 1995: *Industrial Relations*. Oxford: Blackwell Publishers.

Edwards, P.K., and Whitston, C. 1993: *Attending to Work*. Oxford: Blackwell Publishers.

Elliott, R.F. and Duffus, K. 1996: What Has Been Happening to Pay in the Public-Service Sector of the British Economy? *British Journal of Industrial Relations*, 34(1), 51–86.

Employee Development Bulletin. 1996. Getting the Measure of Training in the UK, *EDB*, 84, 6–8.

Findlay, P. 1993: Union Recognition and Non-unionism. *Industrial Relations Journal*, 24(1), 28–43.

Fox, A. 1985: *History and Heritage*. London: Allen and Unwin.

Freeman, R. and Pelletier, J. 1990: The Impact of Industrial Relations Legislation on British Union Density, *British Journal of Industrial Relations*, 28(2), 141–64.

Gallie, D. 1978: *In Search of the New Working Class*. Cambridge: Cambridge University Press.

Gallie, D. 1996: Trade Union Allegiance and Decline in British Urban Labour Markets. In D. Gallie, R. Penn and M. Rose (ed.), *Trade Unionism in Recession*. Oxford: OUP.

Gamble, A. 1988: *The Free Economy and the Strong State*. London: Macmillan.

Garrahan, P. and Stewart, P. 1992: *The Nissan Enigma*. London: Mansell.

Geary, J. 1995: Work Practices. In Edwards, 1995. *Industrial Relations*. Oxford: Blackwell Publishers.

Grant, D. 1996: Japanisation and New Industrial Relations. In Beardwell 1996. *Contemporary Industrial Relations*. Oxford: Oxford University Press.

Gregg, P. and Wadsworth, J. 1995: A Short History of Labour Turnover, Job Tenure and Job Security, 1975–93. *Oxford Review of Economic Policy*, 11(1), 73–90.

Gregg, P., Machin, S. and Metcalf, D. 1993: Signals and Cycles? *Economic Journal*, 103(4), 894–907.

Guest, D. and Hoque, K. 1996: Human Resource Management and the New Industrial Relations. In Beardwell 1996. *Contemporary Industrial Relations*. Oxford: Oxford University Press.

Hall, M. 1994: Industrial Relations and the Social Dimension of European Integration. In R. Hyman and A. Ferner (eds), *New Frontiers in European Industrial Relations*. Oxford: Blackwell Publishers.

Hall, M. 1996: Beyond Recognition? *Industrial Law Journal*, 25(1), 15–27.

Hall, M., and Sisson, K. 1997: *Time for Change?* London: Eclipse.

Hall, P.A. 1986: The State and Economic Decline. In B. Elbaum and W. Lazonick (ed.), *The Decline of the British Economy*. Oxford: Clarendon.

Hedges, B. 1994: Work in a Changing Climate. In R. Jowell et al. (eds), *British Social Attitudes: the Eleventh Report*. Aldershot: Dartmouth.

Hobsbawm, E. 1977: *The Age of Capital, 1984–1875*. London: Abacus.

Hunter, L., McGregor, A., MacInnes, J. and Sproull, A. 1993: The 'Flexible Firm'. *British Journal of Industrial Relations*, 31(3), 383–408.

Hyman, R. 1995: The Historical Evolution of British Industrial Relations. In Edwards 1995. *Industrial Relations*. Oxford: Blackwell Publishers.

Ingram, P. 1991: Ten Years of Manufacturing Wage Settlements. *Oxford Review of Economic Policy*, 7(1), 93–106.

Keep, E. and Rainbird, H. 1995: Training. In Edwards, 1995. *Industrial Relations*. Oxford: Blackwell Publishers.

Kelly, J. 1990: British Trade Unionism, 1979–89: Change, Continuity and Contradictions. *Work, Employment and Society*, Additional Special Issue, May, 29–66.

Kelly, J. and Kelly, C. 1991: 'Them and Us'. *British Journal of Industrial Relations*, 29(1), 25–48.

Kessler, I. and Purcell, J. 1995: Individualism and Collectivism in Theory and Practice. In Edwards, 1995. *Industrial Relations*. Oxford: Blackwell Publishers.

Kessler, I. and Undy, R. 1996: *The New Employment Relationship*. London: Institute of Personnel and Development.

Kitson, M. and Michie, J. 1996: Does Manufacturing Matter? Paper to Employment Research Unit Conference, Cardiff Business School, September.

Lazonick, W. 1990: *Competitive Advantage on the Shop Floor*. Cambridge, Mass.: Harvard University Press.

Leslie, D., and Pu, Y. 1996: What Caused Rising Earnings Inequality in Britain? *British Journal of Industrial Relations*, 34(1), 111–30.

Lloyd, T. 1991: Anatomy of the Corporate Community Heavyweights. *International Management*, April: 26–66.

Lucas, R. and Radiven, N. 1996: Minimum Wages and Pay Determination in the Non-union Sector. Paper to British Universities Industrial Relations Association Annual Conference.

McArdle, L., Rowlinson, M., Procter, S., Hassard, J. and Forrester, P. 1995: Total Quality Management and Participation. In A. Wilkinson and H. Willmott (eds), *Making Quality Critical*. London: Routledge.

McCarthy, W.E.J. 1993: From Donovan Till Now. *Employee Relations*, 15(6), 3–20.

McKendrick, E. 1988: The Rights of Trade Union Members. *Industrial Law Journal*, 17(3), 141–61.

Machin, S. 1996: Wage Inequality in the UK. *Oxford Review of Economic Policy*, 12(1), 47–64.

Marginson, P., Armstrong, P., Edwards, P., and Purcell, J. 1993: The Control of Industrial Relations in Large Companies. *Warwick Papers in Industrial Relations*, 45. Coventry: IRRU.

Martin, R., Fosh, P., Morris, H., Smith, P. and Undy, R. 1991: The Decollectivisation of Trade Unions? *Industrial Relations Journal*, 22(3), 197–208.

Marshall, G., Newby, H., Rose, D. and Vogler, C. 1988: *Social Class in Modern Britain*. London: Hutchinson.

Metcalf, D. 1994: Transformation of British Industrial Relations? In Barrell, 1994. *The UK Labour Market*. Cambridge: Cambridge University Press.

Millward, N., Stevens, M., Smart, D. and Hawes, W. 1992. *Workplace Industrial Relations in Transition*. Aldershot: Dartmouth.

Minkin, L. 1991: *The Contentious Alliance, Trade Unions and the Labour Party*. Edinburgh: Edinburgh University Press.

Nichols, T. 1991: Labour Intensification, Work Injuries and the Measurement of Percentage Utilisation of Labour. *British Journal of Industrial Relations*, 29(4), 569–92.

Nolan, P. and O'Donnell, K. 1995. Industrial Relations and Productivity. In Edwards, 1995. *Industrial Relations*. Oxford: Blackwell.

Nolan, P. and Walsh, J. 1995: The Structure of the Economy and Labour Market. In Edwards 1995. *Industrial Relations*. Oxford: Blackwell.

Oulton, N. 1995: Supply Side Reform and UK Economic Growth. *National Institute Economic Review*, 154, 53–70.

Palmer, G. 1996: Reviving Resistance. *Industrial Relations Journal*, 27(2), 129–42.

Pollert, A., 1988: The Flexible Firm: Fixation or Fact? *Work, Employment and Society*, 2(3), 281–316.

Pollert, A. 1996: 'Team Work' on the Assembly Line. In P. Ackers, C. Smith and P. Smith (eds), *The New Workplace and Trade Unionism*. London: Routledge.

Price, L. and Price, R. 1994: Change and Continuity in the Status Divide. In K. Sisson (ed.), *Personnel Management*. Oxford: Blackwell Publishers.

Procter, S., Rowlinson, M., McArdle, L., Hassard, J. and Forrester, P. 1994: Flexibility, Politics and Strategy. *Work, Employment and Society*, 8(2), 221–42.

Purcell, J. 1993: The End of Institutional Industrial Relations. *Political Quarterly*, 64(1), 6–23.

Rainbird, H. 1994: Continuing Training. In K. Sisson (ed.), *Personnel Management*. Oxford: Blackwell Publishers.

Richardson, R. and Marsden, D. 1991: Does Performance Pay Motivate? London: LSE.

Rose, M., Penn, R., and Rubery, J. 1994: Introduction. In R. Penn et al. (eds), *Skill and Occupational Change*. Oxford: Oxford University Press.

Rubery, J. 1995: The Low-paid and the Unorganised. In Edwards 1995. *Industrial Relations*. Oxford: Blackwell Publishers.

Rubery, J. and Tarling, R. 1988: Women's Employment in Declining Britain. In J. Rubery (ed.), *Women and Recession*. London: Routledge, 100–34.

Scarbrough, H. and Terry, M. 1996: Industrial Relations and the Reorganization of Production in the UK Motor Vehicle Industry. *Warwick Papers in Industrial Relations*, 58. Coventry: IRRU.

Scase, R. 1974: Relative Deprivation: a Comparison of English and Swedish Manual Workers. In D. Wedderburn (ed.), *Poverty, Inequality and Class Structure*. Cambridge: Cambridge University Press, 197–216.

Scase, R. and Goffee, R. 1989: *Reluctant Managers*. London: Unwin Hyman.

Scullion, H. and Edwards, P. 1988: Craft Unionism, Job Controls and Management Strategy. In M. Terry and P. Edwards (eds), *Shopfloor Politics and Job Controls*. Oxford: Blackwell Publishers.

Sewell, G. and Wilkinson, B. 1993: Human Resource Management in 'Surveillance' Companies. In J. Clark (ed.), *Human Resource Management and Technical Change*. London: Sage.

Sisson, K. 1987: *The Management of Collective Bargaining: An International Comparison*, Oxford: Blackwell Publishers.

Sisson, K., and Marginson, P. 1995: Management: Systems, Structure and Strategy. In Edwards 1995. *Industrial Relations*. Oxford: Blackwell Publishers.

Smith, C., Child, J. and Rowlinson, M. 1990: *Reshaping Work: the Cadbury Experience*. Cambridge: Cambridge University Press.

Steedman, H., and Wagner, K. 1989: Productivity, Machinery and Skills in Britain and Germany. *National Institute Economic Review*, 28, 40–57.

Stewart, M. 1990: Union Wage Differentials, Product Market Influences and the Division of Rents. *Economic Journal*, 100(6), 1122–37.

Storey, J. 1992: *Developments in the Management of Human Resources*. Oxford: Blackwell Publishers.

Terry, M. 1995: Trade Unions: Shop Stewards and the Workplace. In Edwards 1995. *Industrial Relations*. Oxford: Blackwell Publishers.

Terry, M. and Edwards, P.K. (eds) 1988: *Shopfloor Politics and Job Controls*. Oxford: Blackwell Publishers.

Tiratsoo, N., and Tomlinson, J. 1994: Restrictive Practices on the Shopfloor in Britain, 1945–60. *Business History*, 36(2), 65–84.

Undy, R., Fosh, P., Morris, H., Smith, P. and Martin, R. 1996: *Managing the Unions*. Oxford: Clarendon.

Waddington, J. 1992: Trade Union Membership in Britain, 1980–1987, *British Journal of Industrial Relations*, 30(2), 287–324.

Waddington, J. 1995: *The Politics of Bargaining*. London: Mansell.

Waddington, J., and Whitston, C. 1995: Trade Unions: Growth, Structure and Policy. In Edwards 1995. *Industrial Relations*. Oxford: Blackwell Publishers.

Waddington, J., and Whitston, C. 1996: Empowerment versus Intensification. In P. Ackers,

C. Smith and P. Smith (eds), *The New Workplace and Trade Unionism*. London: Routledge.

Waddington, J. and Whitston, C. 1997. Why Do People Join Unions in a Period of Membership Decline? *British Journal of Industrial Relations*, 35.

Walker, J. 1988: Women, the State and the Family in Britain. In J. Rubery (ed.), *Women and Recession*. London: Routledge, 218–52.

Wedderburn, K.W. (Lord). 1985: The New Policies in Industrial Relations. In P. Fosh and C. Littler (eds), *Industrial Relations and the Law in the 1980s*. Gower: Aldershot, 22–65.

Wedderburn, K.W. (Lord). 1986: *The Worker and the Law*. 3rd edn. Harmondsworth: Penguin.

Wedderburn, K.W. (Lord). 1989: Freedom of Association and Philosophies of Labour Law. *Industrial Law Journal*, 18(1), 1–38.

Weekes, B., Mellish, M., Dickens, L. and Lloyd, J. 1975: *Industrial Relations and the Limits of the Law*. Oxford: Blackwell.

Weir, M. and Skocpol, T. 1985: State Structure and the Possibilities for 'Keynesian' Response to the Great Depression in Sweden, Britain and the US. In P.B. Evans et al. (eds), *Bringing the State Back In*. Cambridge: Cambridge University Press, 107–68.

Whitston, K. 1996: Scientific Management and Production Management Practice in Britain between the Wars. *Historical Studies in Industrial Relations*, 1(1), 47–76.

Williams, K., Williams, J. and Thomas, D. 1983: *Why Are the British Bad at Manufacturing?* London: Routledge.

Williams, K., Haslam, C., Williams, J., and Johal, S. 1994: *Cars*. Providence: Berghahn.

Willman, P., Morris, T. and Aston, B. 1993: *Union Business*. Cambridge: Cambridge University Press.

Winchester, D., and Bach S. 1995: The State: the Public Sector. In Edwards, 1995. *Industrial Relations*. Oxford: Blackwell Publishers.

Wood, S. and Albanese, M.T. 1995: Can we Speak of High Commitment Management on the Shop Floor? *Journal of Management Studies*, 32(2), 215–47.

Zeitlin, J. 1990: The Triumph of Adversarial Bargaining. *Politics and Society*, 18(3), 405–26.

2 | Ireland: Corporatism Revived

FERDINAND VON PRONDZYNSKI

▌Introduction

In late 1996, the trade unions and the main employers' associations were engaged in negotiations to agree on a national agreement between the social partners which would determine a range of issues, including pay and conditions for the national workforce. The agreement, to be known as 'Partnership 2000', materialized eventually in mid-December, and like its predecessor agreements consisted of a programme of economic and social policy, with an appended pay agreement between the employers and the trade unions of a more traditional kind. The agreement, which was ratified after difficult discussions within the trade union movement, is the latest in a series of agreements which began in 1987 with the Programme for National Recovery (PNR) and which led to the last agreement in force, the Programme for Competitiveness and Work (PCW) concluded in 1994; this series is itself to some extent modelled on the National Wages Agreements and National Understandings of the 1970s.

The process described above – despite occasional problems in the negotiations to which we shall return – confirms Ireland as a country in which industrial relations are still influenced by corporatist tendencies. For a while, and in particular in the light of the previous two national agreements, it looked as if the basic corporatist framework was being eroded by the increasing force of market-driven provisions within the agreements; thus the PCW was very different from those negotiated in the early 1970s in particular. During the 1980s the various industrial relations actors were searching for an opportunity to return to central-ized, national bargaining, but at the same time Ireland was affected by the trends of recession and free-market politics which were in evidence in other countries. The result was a system of centralization which is, nevertheless, much more local in many of its aspects, and much more market-driven in many of its rules. But the 1997 agreement appears to mark a return to some of the 1970s tendencies, with a much greater emphasis on social policy as a focus of the programme; we return to this below.

Irish industrial relations are therefore interesting in that they exhibit characteristics associated with a variety of quite different systems in other countries. These characteristics betray the diverse strands of Irish political and social history, as well as the growing importance of new political structures. However, the Irish system is still in many of its characteristics derived from the British model of industrial relations, even if current trends are moving it away from this source. The traditional features of the Irish system owe much to its origins in the United Kingdom before Ireland[1] achieved independence in 1922; the British characteristics were kept alive after independence by geographical proximity, by the close cultural relations between Ireland and Britain, and by the fact that British trade unions continued to organize a substantial minority of workers in Ireland (McCarthy 1977).

Before we go on therefore to consider the current trends of Irish industrial relations, it may be useful to list the main characteristics of what we may call the 'traditional' model, and to indicate the effects they have had on industrial relations practice over the years.

The Traditional Features of Irish Industrial Relations

The main features of the Irish industrial relations framework could be described as follows:

Voluntaristic. The Irish system of industrial relations is built on the premise that it will, for the most part, be regulated by the voluntary collective bargaining of the social partners. To put this another way, there is, as the Commission of Inquiry on Industrial Relations remarked in its 1981 Report, an assumption by all parties that legal regulation should be avoided (Commission of Inquiry 1981: 114; von Prondzynski 1985a). This tradition, usually described as voluntarism, grew out of the evident hostility towards organized labour which lawyers and judges exhibited in the nineteenth century; it still tends to influence trade union thinking (Kerr 1989). The idea of voluntarism, however, not only led trade unions to avoid the law, it also persuaded successive governments to avoid legal intervention where possible, and most employers were also willing to accept an alternative regulatory framework based on collective bargaining.

Antagonistic. The Irish system of industrial relations is based strongly on the pluralist assumption that the interests of employers and organized labour are in constant conflict. This conflict can be temporarily resolved by means of collective bargaining, and such bargaining may indeed make possible stable and extensive co-operation between the social partners, but the basic relationship between the two sides of industry is an antagonistic one. This is further made possible by relatively high trade union density which has not suffered the sharp decline experienced elsewhere in the 1980s and 1990s (see below). Despite the continuing success of Irish unions in protecting their membership levels, there have been incursions into the adversarial model, particularly through the human resource management practices of certain multinational enterprises (Roche and Geary 1996).

Non-participative. In Ireland the post-war movements towards various experiments with industrial democracy were not followed, and both employers and trade unions tended to be suspicious of any formalized worker participation schemes. There is still no general legal provision for participative or consultative machinery which gives employees a formal say in the organizational decision-making processes of the bodies which employ them. The sole exception relates to certain public sector organizations under the Worker Participation (State Enterprises) Acts of 1977 and 1988. Under these Acts one-third of the directors of the organizations concerned are elected for a fixed period by the employees from candidates nominated by trade unions or other representative bodies. The experience of some of the elected worker directors has demonstrated the limited extent to which the idea of participation has taken root in Ireland – they were in some organizations largely excluded from the real decisions, and in return they felt more motivated by solidarity with fellow workers than management concerns (Kelly 1989). It has generally been felt that worker participation has not readily become part of the Irish industrial relations culture, but the transposition of the provisions of the European Works Council Directive into Irish law through the Transnational Information and Consultation of Employees Act 1996 may have an impact on this in the future.

Centralized. A very strong feature of Irish industrial relations is the tendency to deal with issues in a centralized way. For example, from the early 1970s almost all pay agreements for the entire national workforce were either centrally negotiated (in the 1970s under the aegis of a body known as the Employer–Labour Conference), or followed a general pay norm, often established as a result of agreements between the government and public service employees. Local pay bargaining either has not taken place at all, or has tended to follow the general trend set elsewhere. This tendency to centralize comes naturally in a country like Ireland where there are almost no devolved political or economic powers. It shares this characteristic with countries such as Austria, and this is one important context in which the British tradition is of no importance.

Non-flexible. Irish employment was, in the past at any rate, usually centred around a number of restrictive practices. Jobs were constructed on the basis of rigid demarcation lines, with job descriptions which excluded the possibility of flexible work practices (von Prondzynski 1989). It could of course be said that this only mirrored the wider social traditions of what one might call a demarcation society, with restrictive practices carried on by the various professional bodies in areas such as legal practice, medicine, and accountancy.

Institutionalized. All the parties to the industrial relations process rely to a large extent on the ability of various institutions to solve their problems, not only trade unions and employers' associations, but also state-sponsored dispute resolution agencies, government departments, and so forth. This, as has been noted by some writers, is a typical feature of a pluralistic industrial relations system (Crouch 1982). In Ireland this reliance on institutions such as the Labour Relations Commission or the Labour Court (see below) continues, particularly in the case of intractable industrial relations problems in which the parties often tend to look to outside agencies for a solution.

The picture here presented of the traditional industrial relations model is one of a conservative, rigid, pluralistic and antagonistic system, characterized by powerful institutions and widespread restrictive practices. Perhaps its most significant feature, particularly from the perspective of some outside observers, is the degree of centralism which it exhibits. This partly reflects the small size of the country. It also owes something to the fact that, when the institutional framework matured to something like its present status in the late 1940s, Ireland was still in the grip of a particular form of corporatism which was derived in part from Roman catholic social teaching and in part from some continental European models, including Salazar's Portugal and Franco's Spain. The first chairman of the Labour Court (see below), R.J.P. Mortished, also attempted to use the Court to install a centralized form of pay bargaining in the national economy. This historical legacy has been much modified in practice, but continues to have an influence on general structures and expectations.

Although today it could be argued that severe pressures on the traditional industrial relations model have significantly altered the picture, and changes are presently taking place, nevertheless this model suited the generally conservative social partners in Ireland for many decades.

However, the effect of a severe economic recession during the 1980s, a more hostile attitude by governments towards the traditional industrial relations pattern of conduct, and the arrival of often anti-union multinational companies in greater numbers, called this traditional model into question (von Prondzynski 1987). These enterprises have frequently come expecting to import their human resources practices, often built on preferences for a non-union environment (Roche and Geary 1996). Also, Ireland has not escaped entirely the deregulation trend which has swept European labour markets. It is probably true to say that the secondary labour market in Ireland has experienced a less dramatic growth than in some other countries, but there has been some increase in atypical forms of employment, and this has had at least some impact on industrial relations practice (Roche 1994). An interesting feature of Irish industrial relations has therefore been that while many of the same trends are visible as elsewhere in Europe, they have not necessarily led to a fundamental overhaul of the characteristics of the system, but have merely exposed it to certain tensions.

The Economic Context and the Labour Market

The total labour force in Ireland is almost 1.4 million, out of a population of 3.5 million. Ireland still has one of the largest agricultural sectors in Europe, employing 13.2 per cent of the labour force, compared with 27.2 per cent in industry and 59.6 per cent in services in 1994; even as recently as the late 1960s, about 30 per cent of the labour force were engaged in agriculture, twice the OECD average at the time. The large service sector continues to grow as a proportion of the overall economy. The public sector is important, not only in public services, but in energy, transport and communications and the financial sector, although privatization is also beginning to make (so far relatively small) inroads into state employment in Ireland.

Foreign capital, especially from North America and Japan, has been playing an increasingly important role in the Irish economy. Attracted by favourable tax incentives and substantial capital grants, many multinational companies have established subsidiaries in pharmaceuticals, electronics and the food industry, and most notably in advanced sectors such as consumer electronics, often on 'green-field' sites in non-traditional industrial areas.

Employment and unemployment have had a major and persistent influence on industrial relations developments in Ireland. Compared with other European countries, the unemployment rate has tended to be high. For decades the seriousness of the problem was masked by high emigration rates, but when emigration became more difficult in the 1980s, unemployment rates were found to rise even at times when total employment also increased. By 1985, unemployment in Ireland had reached nearly 17 per cent of the total workforce, a figure exceeded in the European Community only by Greece. The unemployment rate peaked in 1992 at 21 per cent, but then began to drop, reaching 15.2 per cent in 1994. Although there are monthly fluctuations, the general trend is still downwards. The most recent reliable figures available at the time of writing were the Labour Force Survey figures for April 1996, which showed a total of 190,000 unemployed, compared with 279,200 in 1992.[2] It may however be worth noting that in Ireland, as in other European countries, those in employment are now increasingly in less secure or less well paid jobs, including jobs which are part-time or fixed-term or based on contracts described as something other than employment (Gunnigle and Roche 1995).

As we have noted, potentially higher rates of unemployment have usually been avoided by the existence of the outlet of emigration, especially to the United Kingdom. In periods when Britain was itself in recession the emigration option was not so readily available: with renewed economic difficulties in Britain and the US at the beginning of the 1990s, net emigration for the twelve months to April 1991 fell to just 1,000, compared with 31,000 in the previous twelve-month period (EIRR 212, September 1991: 6). Periods of high unemployment have often been accompanied by greater management insistence on new work practices (von Prondzynski 1989).

Irish Trade Unions and Employers' Associations

Ireland is by international standards fairly highly unionized. In 1981, it was estimated that 85 trade unions organized a total membership of 499,000, a figure which represented almost exactly half of the national workforce. Of these trade unions, 72 were affiliated to the Irish Congress of Trade Unions (the central umbrella body for the trade union movement), representing a total of 464,000 members. By 1989 the number of trade unions had shrunk to 60 (mainly as a result of mergers), with a total membership of 471,700; of these 54 were ICTU-affiliated, with a total membership of 441,000. This drop in membership was not as marked as might have been expected at the end of a decade of recession, growing employer militancy, and political ambivalence towards trade unions. Moreover, in the 1990s, membership has risen again. In 1996, according to ICTU figures, there were 52 ICTU-affiliated unions, with a total membership of 491,164. It may be that the status of the trade union movement, and of the Irish Congress of Trade Unions in particular, in a centralized, corporatist state has cushioned them from the trends visible elsewhere in recent times. This may also account for the greater willingness of some multinational employers investing in Ireland to recognize trade unions when, in other countries, they have a record of refusing to do so.

Trade unionism in Ireland has been marked, since almost the beginning of the century, by the dominant position of large general unions. As in Britain, this reflects in part the strongly entrenched position of craft unionism in the formative stages of modern Irish trade unionism – effectively precluding continental patterns of industrial unionism. But it may also be attributed to the powerful impact, in the early decades of this century, of ideas of the 'one big union' as a vehicle for working-class interests.

From the foundation of an independent Irish state, trade unionism was dominated by the Irish Transport and General Workers' Union (ITGWU) – not to be confused with its British near namesake (which organizes in Ireland under the name Amalgamated TGWU). In 1924 a split occurred, and the Workers' Union of Ireland (WUI – later the Federated WUI) was for much of the subsequent period the country's second largest union. In 1990, the two organizations came together in the Services, Industrial, Professional and Technical Union (SIPTU). Amalgamations in the 1980s reinforced the traditional skewed distribution of Irish union membership. Both the former general unions had merged with a number of smaller organizations, and the new SIPTU now claims around 190,000 members – around 40 per cent of the total membership of unions affiliated to the ICTU. The next largest unions are much smaller – the Irish Municipal, Public and Civil Trade Union (IMPACT) formed by amalgamation in 1991 has some 27,000 members, as does the public sector union MANDATE. Other important unions, with around 20,000 each, are the teachers' union (INTO), the Irish Distributive and Administrative Trade Union (IDATU), Manufacturing Science and Finance (MSF) and the Communication Workers' Union (CWU); the Amalgamated Transport and General Workers' Union has 18,000. At the other extreme are numerous small organizations: until recently, three-quarters of Irish unions had fewer than 3000 members, though many of these have been absorbed in the amalgamation movement of the 1980s.

It has already been noted that a number of trade unions in Ireland have their headquarters in Great Britain. There are currently twelve unions with members in Ireland which have their head office outside the jurisdiction, with a total membership of 63,700, including the fourth and sixth largest unions in Ireland (MSF and ATGWU). The proportion of Irish trade union members represented by British-based unions is in fact growing slightly. All of the British-based trade unions are affiliated to the Irish Congress of Trade Unions. These unions now have a secure place in Irish industrial relations, but historically their role has been controversial, and their presence contributed to a split in the Irish trade union movement (McCarthy 1977). During the 1940s special legislative provisions were introduced (Part III of the Trade Union Act 1941) to make it difficult for British-based unions to represent Irish workers; however, the provisions were eventually declared to be unconstitutional by the Supreme Court in 1947. The hostility on the part of some Irish unions to the British presence has now largely evaporated.

As in Britain, the basic administrative unit of trade union organization is the local branch, while shop stewards act as union representatives within the workplace. However, stewards in Ireland have traditionally been more integrated into the official union structure, and hence enjoyed less autonomy, than has often been the case in Britain.

The central umbrella body for Irish trade unions is the Irish Congress of Trade Unions (ICTU). The ICTU is the product of the merger between the Irish Trades Union Congress (ITUC) and the Congress of Irish Unions (CIU) in 1959, as a result of which the ICTU is the central trade union body for both the Republic of Ireland and Northern Ireland; in Northern Ireland a separate committee provides a forum for local discussions and negotiations. Most of the affiliated unions in Northern Ireland are British-based. The ICTU regulates various aspects of inter-union relations, including transfer of membership (von Prondzynski 1987), and nominates trade union members on various official bodies and agencies.

Irish employers are also well organized (O'Brien 1989). When legislation was passed in 1941 requiring all bodies engaged in collective bargaining to have trade union status with so-called 'negotiation licences' (an aspect of the move to corporatist structures at the time), a large number of employers set up the Federated Union of Employers. Conceived initially as a private sector association, the FUE eventually also admitted into membership various state bodies and public sector employers. In 1989 it changed its name to Federation of Irish Employers, largely in response to the changing patterns of industrial relations, and the growth of multinational enterprises for whom the designation 'union' was suspect. In 1993 the FIE merged with the Confederation of Irish Industry (which was a pressure group lobbying for member companies in all matters other than industrial relations) to become the Irish Business and Employers' Confederation (IBEC). IBEC organizes employers with a total workforce of approximately 250,000.

Other employers' associations organize companies in specific sectors of the economy; the most influential of these is the Construction Industry Federation.

▎ Institutions of the 'Middle Ground'

The Irish system of industrial relations is, as already noted, a highly institutionalized one. Most public interest is focused on the activities of the main organizations and institutions. Amongst these institutions are what the late Irish academic and trade union leader, Charles McCarthy, described as the 'institutions ... which take up the middle ground and which the public authority may have an interest in providing', particularly 'in the case of intractability' (von Prondzynski and McCarthy 1989). The 'institutions of the middle ground' are those bodies, usually (but not always) set up by the state, which provide dispute resolution facilities and which can offer advice to the social partners. Such institutions have always been heavily relied upon in Ireland to calm the waters in cases of industrial conflict, and their successes and failures have tended to contribute to or reflect the ups and downs of national industrial relations performance.

Broadly speaking, one may classify these institutions as, first, those which have adjudicatory functions, particularly where they declare the legal rights and obligations of the parties; second, those whose task it is to provide dispute resolution facilities or give advice on good industrial relations; and, third, those which provide a forum for general discussion or negotiation. In Ireland the first type can be seen in the form of the Employment Appeals Tribunal, which interprets and applies a number of employment protection statutes, and the Labour Court in its role as the tribunal to which sex discrimination cases are taken under the Anti-Discrimination (Pay) Act 1974 and the Employment Equality Act 1977; the second type is represented by the Labour Relations Commission and the Labour Court (in its other role); and the third by the Employer–Labour Conference. Of these bodies, the Labour Court, the Labour Relations Commission and the Employer–Labour Conference need to be explained a little further.

The Labour Court is a tripartite body originally created under the Industrial Relations Act 1946 to provide some direction for wage bargaining after the lifting of the pay freeze imposed during the Second World War. Its main function was to support the system of collective bargaining through conciliation and mediation, offered on a voluntary basis. Since 1990, some of these functions have been removed from the Court and transferred to the new Labour Relations Commission, to which we return. Before that, in 1974 and again in 1977, the Labour Court had also been given juridical functions under the sex discrimination legislation; these functions remain. But otherwise the Labour Court is not a 'court' at all, but rather a body which uses its good offices to persuade and cajole parties in dispute to achieve a peaceful settlement. In this function it has been largely successful, in that a large proportion of disputes taken to the Court are resolved either at the conciliation stage or through mediation (called 'investigation' in the Court's terminology). However, the Court's task is not always easy, and in particular at times when the government has attempted to influence pay bargaining the Court has been subjected to apparent government pressure, often prejudicing its standing in the eyes of unions and employers. Experience indicates that the Court works well in what one might call 'average' disputes, but less effectively when the system comes under major pressure, as in the case of, say, disputes in public utilities such as energy and transport.

The Labour Relations Commission was set up under Part III of the Industrial Relations Act 1990. The Act gave the Commission the functions *inter alia* of providing a conciliation service and an industrial relations advisory service, preparing codes of practice, and conducting or commissioning research. The Commission is broadly modelled on the Northern Ireland Labour Relations Agency, or the British Advisory Conciliation and Arbitration Service; however, given the tendency to centralize industrial relations issues in Ireland, the Commission arguably has a greater role in setting norms than these two bodies. The Commission had been heralded in a number of discussion documents in the late 1980s. The creation of the Commission initially provoked a hostile response from the Labour Court, which saw it as diminishing the Court's effectiveness by divorcing it from the conciliation service that had always been a central part of its activity. Eventually, however, the reform was largely accepted by all industrial relations practitioners.

The Employer–Labour Conference was set up in its present form in 1970. It is an ad hoc body, with no statutory foundation. Its original purpose was to rationalize pay bargaining after a period of great industrial relations turbulence in the late 1960s, and to remove the then government's threat to introduce a statutory incomes policy (McCarthy 1973). The Conference is bipartite or tripartite in nature: members are nominated in equal numbers by the ICTU and various employer bodies, but the employer nominees include government representatives; in any case, its conduct since the mid-1970s has been clearly tripartite, with the government taking a distinct line in its deliberations. During the 1970s the Conference was responsible for negotiating the succession of 'National Wages Agreements' (to which we return below), but since around 1980 it has merely been a forum for union–employer discussions: recent national bargaining has taken place elsewhere.

| Collective Bargaining

As already noted, the voluntaristic nature of the Irish system of industrial relations has put collective bargaining at the centre of all activity. Most workers have their terms and conditions of employment settled by collective agreements, and it has been long-term public policy to support this process. However, support for collective bargaining, particularly on the part of the government, is not unqualified.

Governments tend still to approve of voluntary bargaining and industrial relations self-regulation, but not in every context and at any price; in particular, recent years have seen the growth of a widespread belief that the inflationary effects of collective bargaining must be reined in, and that this is easier in the context of centrally determined pay norms. How to set these pay norms is, however, another matter. The FitzGerald government of the mid-1980s appeared to prefer a norm set by the government and backed up, if necessary, by the threat of retribution against employers minded to exceed the figure; the Fianna Fail administrations from 1987 appeared to prefer the notion of a centralized, national agreement between the government and the social partners, and for the moment this approach appears to be favoured also by the Fine Gael-led coalition government of the mid-1990s.

Historically, collective bargaining in Ireland has proceeded on several levels. General pay increases have tended to be determined at the most centralized level available; so-called 'special' increases – i.e. all those pay increases justified by something other than inflation, such as productivity, changes in working practices, relativities, and so forth – have tended to be settled at the level of the firm or, sometimes, the plant; other terms and conditions of employment, and matters of local procedure, have been the subject of lower-level bargaining. Industry-wide bargaining, common in other countries, is rare in Ireland, although in evidence in certain sectors such as printing. Overall, there is no doubt that the main emphasis has always been on the centre.

Before 1970 there had been a number of attempts to reach national collective agreements covering the entire workforce, but in each case the arrangement was beset by problems, and the outcome was invariably that a central, national agreement was not replaced by a similar arrangement on its expiry. The first centralized agreement was the 'National Wages Policy' of 1948; later attempts were made in 1952, 1957 and 1964. The last of these led directly to the major round of strikes of the late 1960s (McCarthy 1973). In this setting, when the government published a Prices and Incomes Bill in 1970, in which it threatened to exercise statutory control over wage and price increases, the employers and unions were sufficiently jolted to set up the Employer–Labour Conference, where they then negotiated a 'national wages agreement' to run from January 1971. This time the exercise worked, and the first national wages agreement (NWA) was followed by others in 1972, 1974, 1975, 1976 and 1978 (O'Brien 1981).

These agreements, which set the agreed rate of pay increase for the entire national workforce in all industries and sectors, were initially deemed a success: they contributed to industrial peace, adopted recognizable principles of equity (including special provisions for the lower paid and for women), were generally non-inflationary, and stabilized what had previously been a chaotic picture. However, they coincided with the economic problems associated with the first oil crisis in the aftermath of the 1973 Yom Kippur war, and by 1975 the government was no longer prepared to let employers and unions fix pay increases which were unrelated to the needs of macro-economic policy. This led to tripartite negotiations: following the conclusion of the 1975 NWA, the government offered employers and unions budgetary concessions if they agreed the specified pay increases. The significance of this development was that a precedent had been set for a bargaining round between the government and interest groups, in which the subject matter for negotiation included aspects of government policy and parliamentary initiative. Economic recession had pushed Ireland further down the road to corporatism, and established a tendency which has persisted since.

The NWAs continued for the next few pay rounds, but were beginning to run into problems. The trade unions found it increasingly difficult to persuade local officials and activists of the merits of a system where decisions were taken centrally, without much local input; furthermore, some unions had always taken the view that national agreements robbed them of the opportunity to realize their full bargaining potential, particularly in the case of craft workers and employees of the financial institutions. Many employers felt that centrally-fixed pay norms were not appropriate, particularly for those with trading difficulties, and that too many trade unions or their officials breached the terms of the agreements. When the 1978 agreement was due to expire, a Special Delegate Conference of the ICTU voted not to negotiate a replacement agreement, and the NWAs thus came to an end.

Once again, the emergence of a problem tended to reinforce the corporatist trend. In 1979 the government was determined to secure industrial growth through centralized collective bargaining, and when the proposal for an NWA was rejected, it offered the social partners a new concept, described as a 'National Understanding'. This was to involve a moderate pay agreement, combined with a social-contract-style agreement on economic and social policy. For the first time, the government became directly involved in national negotiations with the social partners in its own right, rather than simply in its capacity as an employer represented on the Employer–Labour Conference. The arrangement was, after some difficulties, duly initiated: the 'National Understanding for Economic and Social Development' involved an NWA-type pay agreement, but with an added section covering such issues as employment, taxation, pay, industrial relations, social welfare and health. A second National Understanding was agreed in 1980 (O'Brien 1981). However, the concept did not survive beyond that, partly because the employers in particular were now determined to have local pay bargaining, and partly because the government had been almost completely unable – or in some cases unwilling – to deliver almost any of the commitments entered into in the areas of economic and social policy; job creation targets in particular were not met.

Following the second National Understanding, from 1981 until 1987, there was no centralized or national agreement. That does not mean however that collective bargaining was conducted on a local, 'free-for-all' basis; rather, during each pay round a 'trend' or 'norm' emerged which set the standard for local negotiators. During the first two years or so of this period the norm was set by agreements between the government and the Public Services Committee of the Irish Congress of Trade Unions (of which the present author was at the time a member) for the public service; the pay increase reached there was almost invariably adopted in other negotiations. During later pay rounds the trend was set in the private sector, usually by those companies or sectors which were the first to conclude agreements.

The government attempted at times to impose a norm through pay guidelines, but these guidelines were largely ignored in the private sector, and should more realistically have been seen as opening shots in the public service pay negotiations (von Prondzynski 1985b).

It is clear that the FitzGerald coalition government of 1982–7 failed to establish the level of pay increase that was economically appropriate. When the government was urging employers to concede either no pay increases at all, or only very low ones, the actual statistics for the '26th Pay Round' in 1986–7 showed average increases of around 6 per cent. However, the government's attempt to re-model industrial relations practice in other respects bore more fruit, and the complicated framework of special pay awards based on productivity (often bogus) or relativity was largely dismantled during this period, with pay awards being related to what the employer could afford, rather than the market rate. This important structural change has been reinforced further in the subsequent period.

It has been stated by one writer that 'market control' in industrial relations has never been a strategic objective of the Irish state (Roche 1989). Nevertheless, market control came to dominate government thinking by 1982 at the latest, when the then Haughey administration unilaterally announced that it was proposing not to honour its commitments under a public service pay agreement because of macro-economic considerations; and has been the primary objective of public policy towards collective bargaining ever since. The policy was manifestly unsuccessful until 1987, but none the less real.

In 1987, however, the new Fianna Fail minority administration embarked on a new attempt to enter into a national agreement, at the prompting of the ICTU, and in October of that year the government, unions, employers, and a small number of other interest groups (including a farmers' organization) entered into an agreement entitled the 'Programme for National Recovery' (PNR). This agreement might have indicated that monetarist economics was once again giving way to corporatist tendencies, but in reality the PNR was merely a different vehicle for achieving market control. Covering the period to the end of 1990, the Programme expressed the parties' commitment to providing an economic climate conducive to growth, constructing a more equitable tax system, reducing social inequalities, and creating employment. Pay rises were not to exceed 2.5 per cent in each of the three years 1988–90, and special provision was made for the low paid: there was a higher percentage increase for the first £120[3] of weekly pay, and a flat rate minimum increase.

The basic similarity between the PNR and the National Understandings of the late 1970s lay in the fact that both dealt with pay and terms of employment on the one hand, and issues of social and economic policy on the other. There, however, the similarity largely ends. The PNR was an agreement covering three years; the pay terms of the PNR were not fixed norms, but guidelines which had, in the private sector at least, to be converted into agreed rates through local bargaining (thus meeting a major employer demand); and the terms on economic and social policy were to a much lesser extent government commitments, but rather targets for all relevant parties to the continuing corporatist process – for example, the job creation targets were largely for the private sector, particularly manufacturing. In summary, the PNR was an agreed framework of general guidelines, rather than a document of binding commitments. Furthermore, as it turned out, the PNR was to run side-by-side with a government programme of massive cost-cutting in the public sector, as well as a number of other measures to reduce inflation and cut the budget deficit which might, in earlier times, have met stiff trade union resistance. While a delegate to the 1988 Annual Conference of the ICTU might complain that 'we do not believe that the way the economy has been managed is in accordance with the letter or the spirit of the agreement', in practice the PNR locked the trade union movement into an alliance with the government which made difficult any serious opposition to other aspects of government policy.

The PNR was remarkably successful. Pay bargaining at a local level, which was to continue under the Programme, produced results which were almost invariably those suggested by the PNR; over the 3-year period, these rates in turn were more or less in line with inflation, which fell steadily to under 3 per cent in early 1991. With strong manufacturing and export performance, job creation targets were also generally met in the private sector, although the jobs gained were partly lost again in redundancies elsewhere. Economic growth averaging more than 4 per cent a year between 1987 and 1990 helped reduce the gap between Ireland and the stronger EC economies: GDP per head rose from 64 per cent of EC average in 1987 to 68 per cent in 1990. One other aspect of the PNR, the general agreement that negotiations should take place on reductions in working hours, led to a framework agreement and local negotiations which have resulted in the shortening of the working week for most workers by one hour to 39 hours.

However, while the FIE described the PNR as an 'unprecedented success', the agreement did not meet with much enthusiasm on the union side. At the 1988 Annual Conference of the ICTU three motions were submitted on the PNR, all largely critical; two were carried, and one was remitted. Furthermore, for the duration of the PNR's terms Congress in particular was constantly engaged in soul-searching over its role in the agreement, and over whether it should continue to operate it. In the end the PNR held together, and furthermore was followed by a similar arrangement, the 'Programme for Economic and Social Progress' (PESP). This described as its core objective the development of 'a modern, efficient market economy with innate capacity for satisfactory and sustainable growth and discharge of the obligations of a developed social conscience'. Again, this agreement was described by a senior trade union official as one which demonstrated that 'issues like taxation, inflation and economic growth are a legitimate and necessary part of the trade union agenda, since they all have bearings on the standard of living'.

As with the PNR, the PESP set targets for job creation – 20,000 new jobs each year in manufacturing and a similar number in the international services sector. It also acknowledged the need for special measures to help the long-term unemployed, and the government committed itself to implementing specific measures – for example, enacting legislation to protect part-time workers, and amending equal opportunities and unfair dismissals law – and to reviewing other aspects such as conditions of employment, holidays and the control of employment agencies. As also was the case with the PNR, the PESP contained a pay policy set out in the form of a separate agreement between the ICTU and employers' organizations. A final aspect of industrial relations covered by the PESP was employee participation. A joint declaration of the FIE and the ICTU encouraged increased 'employee involvement' in firms, in the form of communication and consultation arrangements, financial participation schemes, quality of working life programmes and quality circles.

During the final months of the PESP, the trade unions and employers went through what has become a standard ritual, involving the expression of serious reservations with the national bargaining process and with the idea of another centralized agreement. In the event, however, the same parties entered into a new agreement, the Programme for Competitiveness and Work (PCW) in February 1994. This was another three-year agreement, the pay provisions of which, for the first time, differentiated between public service employees and other workers. The rate of increase over three years was to be 8 per cent for all groups, but phased differently for the public services. As with previous agreements, there were special provisions for low-paid workers, who were to benefit from minimum levels of increases in pay.

The period preceding the expiry of the PCW were characterized by the usual uncertainties and posturing on the part of all the parties. Nevertheless, early in 1996, the main trigger for another set of negotiations – the decision by the ICTU to enter into discussions on a new agreement – was followed by a period of bargaining and analysis, in which this time there was a much larger role for bodies representing socially disadvantaged groups, such as the Irish National Organization of the Unemployed (INOU) and the Community Platform (representing a number of voluntary organizations). These latter bodies took an increasingly assertive approach in defending the interests of the disadvantaged or the socially excluded; indeed, in opening the negotiations between the parties, the Taoiseach (Prime Minister), John Bruton, listed 'the fostering of increased social inclusion' as the second of six objectives of the new programme (Government press release, 23 October 1996).

After a fair degree of uncertainty, the parties to the talks finally agreed on a new programme in mid-December 1996, 'Partnership 2000 for Inclusion, Employment and Competitiveness'. Despite strong opposition from some trade unions (including the large public sector trade union MANDATE), the ICTU ratified the agreement early in 1997.

'Partnership 2000' represents something of a change of direction when compared with the national agreements since 1987. Unlike the previous programmes, its emphasis is not as single-mindedly on economic competitiveness: the reference to 'inclusion' and 'employment' before 'competitiveness' in the title is significant. In its introduction, the programme lists three challenges to which the programme is intended to be a strategic response: first, 'maintaining an effective and consistent policy approach in a period of high economic growth'; second, 'significantly reducing social disparities and exclusion, especially by reducing long-term unemployment'; and, third, 'responding effectively ... to global competition and the information society'. There then follows a detailed programme of social, economic and fiscal policies, accompanied, as has become the custom, by a separate pay agreement between the employers' organizations, and the ICTU in an appendix to the programme. This is to last for three years, with phased increases in pay during that period; as before, the low paid are given special protection through minimum amounts of increases for each phase. Public service pay is dealt with in an additional annex to the main pay agreement, and involves the same basic phased increases, but subject to a later implementation of the first full phase.

It can be seen that 'Partnership 2000' will both continue the established pattern of agreed national programmes for social and economic policies, and will extend this pattern significantly. At a time of an increasingly optimistic outlook for the Irish economy, the emphasis has shifted, at least slightly, from containing costs and combating inflation to protecting livelihoods and promoting employment. In that setting, the corporatist instincts of the Irish system have been given a significant boost after the ambiguities of previous agreements.

▌ Industrial Conflict

For much of the post-war era, Ireland was regarded – by both foreign and domestic observers – as a strike-prone country. Whether this view of Irish industrial relations was ever entirely accurate could be a matter of some debate, but in any case there is no reason to suppose that it is accurate now. High strike levels in the late 1940s were followed by relative peace in the 1950s, but the 1960s were a 'decade of upheaval' (McCarthy 1973), and this turbulence was to continue through the 1970s. Conflict was reflected in the large numbers of strikes – with a peak of 219 recorded stoppages in 1974 – and high figures of days lost – over 1.4 million in 1979. For much of the period, some two-thirds of strikes were unofficial; but there were also many protracted disputes – for example, the national stoppage which closed down the Irish banking system for six months in 1970.

In the 1970s, Ireland ranked consistently near the top of the European strike league table (as measured by the ratio of days lost to employment). But Irish strike-proneness declined consistently during the 1980s, and particularly rapidly from the latter part of the decade: an indication of the growing impact of centralized concertation. In 1980, a total of 404,000 working days were lost in 132 strikes; by 1988 days lost were down to 130,000, and in 1989, the number of recorded strikes fell to 38, and days lost to 50,000 – placing Ireland near the bottom of the European league table. During the 1990s, this trend has largely continued. In 1994 there were 32 strikes, with 24,000 days lost (Department of Enterprise and Employment); this figure rose again in 1995, mainly due to a small number of public sector disputes. In fact, it is possible to say that the trend has been consistently downwards, with only occasional bouts of public sector unrest tending to disturb the trend in certain years.

It could be argued that the incidence of industrial conflict in recent years has been so low that it is not a serious feature of Irish industrial relations. Unofficial industrial action, which was once considered to be a major industrial relations problem (von Prondzynski 1982), is no longer seen as significant. Disputes do still occur, but the pattern they set and follow is no longer one indicating a strike-prone system of industrial relations.

Irish industrial relations, when put under stress by industrial conflict, rely heavily on state-run mechanisms to provide resolution facilities. The natural tendency of employers or trade unions is to turn to the Labour Court – or, now, the Labour Relations Commission – to offer a way out. A very large proportion of disputes are taken to these institutions, and many are settled there. Equally, however, when the institutions temporarily lose the confidence of the parties – as happened in the mid-1980s when the trade unions felt that the Labour Court was being put under pressure by the government to apply its pay guidelines – the ability of the system to relieve the stress is seriously compromised. In a major dispute in 1991 in the electricity service, the institutions failed to deliver a quick resolution, and the parties seemed at a loss to find one elsewhere.

Irish industrial relations law is still built on the basic notion of immunities first introduced under the (British) Trade Disputes Act 1906. That Act has now been replaced by the Industrial Relations Act 1990, which retains the principle of immunities available to trade union officials and members who are acting 'in contemplation or furtherance of a trade dispute'; the idea which had been floated by the government in 1986 of creating a system based on the 'right to strike' (Department of Labour 1986) was subsequently abandoned. However, some of these immunities are now more tightly drawn than under the 1906 Act: for example, under the 1990 Act, unions failing to hold secret pre-strike ballots risk losing their negotiation licence, and restrictions are also placed on picketing. Another development encouraged by the Act is the widespread use of strike codes of practice. The Labour Relations Commission was granted powers to prepare industrial relations codes of practice, a power of which it has made use, for example in setting out guidelines on disputes procedures.

Conclusion

From the perspective of the 1990s, there are a number of influences at work in Irish industrial relations. First, there are the British origins of the system, visible in the trade union structures and traditions, employer preferences, bargaining tactics, industrial relations terminology, and so forth; these origins continue to have an impact, reinforced by such matters as the presence of British-based trade unions, and the strong cultural ties between these islands. Second, there is the now well-established Irish trend to seek corporatist solutions to problems of an economic and social nature. Third, there is the influence of the (often American) multinational enterprises, with their sophisticated personnel management tactics and, frequently, their preference for a non-union environment (Roche and Geary 1996). Fourth, there are the effects of economic cycles, with a weakened trade union presence and a more confident management during periods of recession (as in much of the 1980s), and a more confident expression of trade unionism during periods of economic growth (as in the mid-1990s). And finally, there is the influence of the European Union, and its moves not only towards economic integration but also towards a stronger social policy in the context of what one might describe as a more 'Germanic' system of industrial relations (von Prondzynski 1990).

The above influences are largely at odds with each other. So for example, the British industrial relations tradition is not comfortable with a move towards formal worker participation, or tripartite arrangements coming from the centre, or non-union personnel management, or minimum wage legislation; the Irish corporatist tendency does not sit easily with a tradition of grassroots union activism, or the recession-inspired management preference for local solutions and negotiations. And yet, the Irish genius for 'muddling through' has kept an industrial relations framework on the road which has apparently been able to absorb these contradictions and retain much greater levels of stability than those enjoyed by more homogeneous systems elsewhere. Every so often the stresses grow to where they appear to place the future of the established patterns in doubt – as during periods of public sector unrest, or major private sector disputes, or the closure of undertakings employing large numbers of workers (such as the closure of Packard Electric in Tallaght in 1996); but these doubts are invariably overcome when the system settles down again.

The 1980s undoubtedly added new dimensions to the Irish model of industrial relations, partly through recessionary conditions and partly as a result of changes in government policy. The 1990s have added a more dynamic European dimension. However, these developments seem certain merely to add new layers, rather than to create an entirely different system. If one looks at the characteristics of the traditional model of industrial relations listed earlier, then one can be confident in predicting that some of these will change: more flexibility and more participation, for example, seem likely. But the essence of the Irish system overall, rooted in a small society increasingly confident of its status internationally, is secure.

▌Abbreviations

CII	Confederation of Irish Industry
CIU	Congress of Irish Unions
EAT	Employment Appeals Tribunal
ELC	Employer–Labour Conference
FIE	Federation of Irish Employers (see IBEC)
FUE	Federated Union of Employers (see IBEC)
IBEC	Irish Business and Employers' Confederation
ICTU	Irish Congress of Trade Unions
ITGWU	Irish Transport and General Workers' Union (see SIPTU)
ITUC	Irish Trades Union Congress
LRC	Labour Relations Commission
NU	National Understanding
NWA	National Wages Agreement

PCW   Programme for Competitiveness and Work
PESP   Programme for Economic and Social Progress
PNR   Programme for National Recovery
PSPA   Public Sector Pay Agreement
SIPTU   Services, Industrial, Professional and Technical Union

Notes

1 When the term 'Ireland' is used in this chapter it must be taken to be a reference to the state of that name established by the 1937 Constitution (*Bunreacht na hEireann*), or where appropriate, the Irish Free State of the period 1922–1937. In other words, this chapter concerns itself solely with the 26 counties of the Republic of Ireland, and it does not deal with Northern Ireland.
2 The alternative source of statistical information, the 'Live Register' (of persons unemployed and in receipt of welfare benefits), showed a figure higher by 91,000 for the same date. The Labour Force Survey, published by the Central Statistic Office is generally accepted as more accurate.
3 References in this chapter are to the Irish pound (or punt), the value of which, at the time of writing, was slightly below that of sterling.

References and Further Reading

Cassells, P. 1989: The Organisation of Trade Unions. In Murphy, T. et al. (eds), *Industrial Relations in Ireland: Contemporary Issues and Developments*. Dublin: University College Dublin, 13–20.

Commission of Inquiry on Industrial Relations 1981: *Report*. Dublin: Stationery Office.

Crouch, C. 1982: *Trade Unions: The Logic of Collective Action*. London: Fontana.

Department of Labour 1986: *Outline of Principal Provisions of Proposed New Trade Disputes and Industrial Relations Legislation*. Dublin.

Department of Labour 1980: *Discussion Paper on Worker Participation*. Dublin.

Gunnigle P., and Roche, W.K., 1995: *New Challenges to Irish Industrial Relations*. Oak Tree Press, Dublin: Labour Relations Commission.

Gunnigle, P., McMahon, G. and Fitzgerald, G., 1995: *Industrial Relations in Ireland: Theory and Practice*. London: Sweet & Maxwell Ltd.

Kelly, A. 1989: The Worker Director in Irish Industrial Relations. In *Industrial Relations in Ireland: Contemporary Issues and Developments*. Dublin: University College Dublin, 305–310.

Kerr, T. 1989: Trade Unions and the Law. In Murphy, T. et al. (eds), *Industrial Relations in Ireland: Contemporary Issues and Developments*. Dublin: University College Dublin, 217–34.

McCarthy, C. 1973: *The Decade of Upheaval: Irish Trade Unions in the Nineteen Sixties*. Dublin: Institute of Public Administration.

McCarthy, C. 1977: *Trade Unions in Ireland: 1894–1960*. Dublin: Institute of Public Administration.

Murphy, T., Hillery, B. and Kelly, A. (eds) 1989: *Industrial Relations in Ireland: Contemporary Issues and Developments*. Dublin: University College Dublin.

O'Brien, J.F. 1981: *A Study of National Wage Agreements in Ireland*. Dublin: Economic and Social Research Institute.

O'Brien, J.F. 1989: The Role of Employer Organisations in Ireland. In Murphy, T. et al. (eds), *Industrial Relations in Ireland: Contemporary Issues and Developments*. Dublin: University College Dublin, 73–82.

OECD (Organisation for Economic Co-operation and Development) 1988: *Economic Surveys. Ireland 1987/1988*. Paris: OECD.

OECD 1991: *Economic Surveys. Ireland 1990/1991*. Paris: OECD.

Roche, W.K. 1989: State strategies and the politics of industrial relations in Ireland. In Murphy, T. et al. (eds), *Industrial Relations in Ireland: Contemporary Issues and Developments*. Dublin: University College Dublin, 115–31.

Roche, W.K. 1994: Pay Determination and the Politics of Industrial Relations. In T.V. Murphy, T.V. and Roche, W.K. *Irish Industrial Relations in Practice*, Oak Tree Press, Dublin.

Roche, W.K. and Geary, J. 1996: Multinational Companies in Ireland: Adapting to or Diverging from National Industrial Relations Practices and Traditions? *Journal of Irish Business and Administrative Research*, 17, 14–31.

Von Prondzynski, F. 1982: Unofficial Strikes: Myth and Reality. *Administration*, 29, 400.

Von Prondzynski, F. 1985a: The Changing Functions of Labour Law. In P. Fosh and C.R. Littler, *Industrial Relations and the Law in the 1980s*. Aldershot: Gower, 176–193.

Von Prondzynski, F. 1985b: The Death of the Pay Round. *IRN Report*, 7(11), 16.

Von Prondzynski, F. 1987: The Changing Face of Irish Industrial Relations. *IRN Report*, 9(24), 16–20.

Von Prondzynski, F. 1989: Flexibility and New Work Practices. *IPM News*, 4, 2.

Von Prondzynski, F. 1990: Irish Labour Law and the European Community. *Comparative Labor Law Journal*, 11(4), 498–510.

Von Prondzynski, F. and McCarthy, C. 1989 (2nd edn): *Employment Law in Ireland*. London: Sweet & Maxwell.

Von Prondzynski, F and Richards, W.R. 1994: *European Employment and Industrial Relations Glossary: Ireland*. London: Sweet & Maxwell.

3 | Sweden: Restoring the Model?[1]

ANDERS KJELLBERG

Introduction: The 'Nordic Model' of Industrial Relations

Since the mid-1960s Swedish industrial relations have undergone such fundamental changes that the very existence of a 'Swedish model' is now questioned. Nevertheless, given the continuing similarities between Nordic countries,[2] and the differences between them as a group and other European countries, the notion of a 'Nordic model' of industrial relations still has descriptive and analytic value. First, therefore, the broad outlines of the 'Nordic model' will be presented. The main focus of the chapter, however, is on Swedish industrial relations: the roots of the 'historic compromise' between capital and labour in the 1930s, and the erosion of the Swedish model of 'self-regulation' and centralized bargaining by increased state intervention and pressures to decentralization.

Nordic industrial relations characteristically reflect a relative balance of power between capital and labour: compromises between employers' associations and unions were concluded at an early stage in the three Scandinavian countries, although Finland lagged behind. Cross-class deals – notably with farmers' parties – allowed Scandinavian labour movements represented by strong social-democratic parties to extend their already considerable industrial and political strength to the political sphere (Therborn 1984; Katzenstein 1985). This occurred in the 1930s in Norway and Sweden, and considerably earlier in Denmark. Important legislation on union balloting rules, with centralizing effects on industrial relations, was passed in Denmark as well as Norway in the 1930s.

In the long run, however, the coalitions of the 1930s were of lesser significance. They were succeeded by a long era of 'bloc policy' with social-democratic parties as leaders of a 'socialist bloc' competing with a 'bourgeois bloc'. Since the early 1930s, governments led by social democrats have been in power for all but 9 years in Sweden and for all but a dozen or so in Norway. Denmark has had somewhat longer periods of centre-right rule, notably from 1982 to 1993, but social-democratic governments have again predominated, ruling with only short breaks between 1929 and 1982. In Finland there have been periods of social-democratic-led governments since the late 1940s, although their dominance has been much less striking than in the Scandinavian countries. In contrast to other Nordic countries, Finnish governments have generally consisted of coalitions bridging socialist and non-socialist blocs. Thus the agrarian/centre party has been a major component of governments for more than 50 years. In the 1990s, however, co-operation between social democrats and centre parties broke down in Finland but was established in the other Nordic countries. Another distinct feature of Finnish governments is the participation of communists during the 'popular front' governments of 1945–8, in 1966–70, and finally in a 'third wave' in 1975–9.

The crucial element in Scandinavian compromises between capital and labour was the development of co-operation in the industrial arena. The Danish September Compromise of 1899 was the first basic agreement in the world. In Norway and Sweden basic agreements were reached in 1935 and 1938 respectively, although there were important precursors: the 1907 Metal Agreement in Norway, the 1905 Engineering Agreement and the 1906 'December Compromise' in Sweden. Employer prerogative was accepted by the unions in exchange for recognition of basic trade union rights. Under Sweden's 'historic compromise' of the 1930s, it was agreed that the efforts of social democratic governments to bring about economic growth should not challenge the capitalist nature of production (Korpi 1978; 1983). Class compromise in Finland was delayed by the civil war from which the bourgeois forces emerged victorious, and by the absence of a unified labour movement.

In the Scandinavian countries, social-democratic hegemony within the labour movements was an essential precondition for capital–labour compromises. Their subsequent strategy has been based on strengthening the position of workers and unions through economic growth, permitting 'full employment' and social reforms. The close links between manual workers' unions and social-democratic parties have facilitated the implementation of this strategy.

The basic agreements promoted another distinctive feature of Nordic union movements and industrial relations: the combination of centralization and decentralization (Kjellberg 1983). The decentralized element already existed from an early stage in the form of union workplace organizations, which still represent the national unions at workplace level and have important functions including recruitment and bargaining. This has favoured high union density: mutual recognition at central level has curbed the fragmentation of trade unionism, while granting basic union rights that have facilitated the unions' presence at the workplace and allowed direct contact with workers.

The basic agreements, together with political initiatives, paved the way for the introduction of a three-tier system of collective bargaining. The traditional system of collective contracts concluded by national unions and their workplace organizations was supplemented by a third level of centralized agreements on wages and related issues (in Denmark from the 1930s, Norway from the 1940s and Sweden from the 1950s).

The introduction of centralized bargaining presupposed a certain centralization of the parties themselves. Almost from the start, the threat from powerful unions drove Scandinavian employers towards centralized organization and their confederations were given extensive powers over affiliated bodies. Large dispute funds were built up and had to be co-ordinated centrally, especially as extensive lockouts came to be the favourite weapon of Scandinavian employers. (In Finland a similar centralization of employers did not occur until the 1950s.) The centralization of Scandinavian union confederations took place later. In the 1940s, the Swedish LO (Federation of Trade Unions) was given considerably increased powers over affiliated unions, within which the authority of the leadership was strengthened at the expense of the members. Balloting on collective bargaining outcomes was abolished.

The regular use of membership ballots on draft agreements in Denmark and Norway puts intense pressure on union negotiators to win concessions. This makes centralized bargaining a much more complicated affair than in Sweden and helps explain the greater state intervention in collective bargaining in Denmark and Norway. In Denmark (and in Norway until 1982), state mediators are given the right to aggregate ballot results from different unions and sectors, and mediation proposals have in Denmark often been transformed into law. The extensive use of compulsory arbitration in Norway should also be mentioned. In addition, there have in both countries been periods with wage laws.

The traditional three-tier system of collective bargaining corresponds to a four-level system of union organization: the workplace; local union branches; national unions; and union confederations and bargaining cartels. Where workplace organizations are absent – particularly in small enterprises – local union branches take care of bargaining at this level. In other cases they assist workplace organizations if required.

From an international perspective, the Nordic union systems are both comparatively centralized and decentralized. Nordic union confederations have long had an important role in centralized bargaining for manual workers in the private sector; however, this role has been undermined by the expansion of public-sector and white-collar employment which has strengthened the role of bargaining cartels. At the same time, union workplace organizations have important decentralized bargaining functions – in contrast to many European countries where bodies other than unions, such as works councils, are assigned these tasks. (Works councils in Nordic countries are exclusively union mechanisms.)

The absence of political and religious divisions in the Nordic unions (with the exception of Finland in the late 1950s and 1960s) and their success in avoiding dual systems of representation have facilitated the recruitment of members. Labour legislation in the 1970s further extended the role of union workplace organization. Furthermore, the collective character of Nordic labour law implies that unions and their workplace organizations – not individual workers – are legal entities. Together with the combined centralization and decentralization, these circumstances explain why union densities in the Nordic countries are very high from an international perspective: 83–85 per cent in Sweden, 82–88 in Denmark, 79 in Finland, and 56 in Norway (1994–5). In contrast to the first three countries, Norway has no union unemployment funds, which might explain the lower Norwegian density.

Nordic countries are also distinguished by high rates of affiliation to employers' associations. In the private sector the aggregate density of employers' associations (the proportion of the workforce in affiliated firms) is 75 per cent in Sweden (author's calculation), 55 per cent in Norway (Dølvik and Stokke in this volume), and 51 per cent in Denmark (Scheuer 1996: 84, 256). Despite the absence of procedures for extension, the coverage of collective agreements is impressive, ranging from 69 per cent of workers in Denmark to 94 per cent in Sweden. In Sweden it is only slightly lower in the private sector (90 per cent), in contrast to Denmark and Norway whose lower private sector coverage (52 and 50–55 per cent respectively) seems to be related to the lower density of employers' associations and to the fact that some contracts are valid only if a majority of workers at a workplace are union members.

The characterization of Nordic unions as both centralized and decentralized does not imply that intermediate levels – the national unions and their local branches – are less important than elsewhere. Bargaining by national unions at industry level has increasingly replaced centralized agreements, and even where central agreements exist (as in Norway), sectoral bargaining is important in adapting their provisions to each industry. Without the consent of major national unions, no centralized negotiations will take place. The prominence of Nordic national unions is emphasized by the fact that union workplace representatives – in contrast to British shop stewards – are wholly integrated into the national unions and their branches.

Since the 1980s there has been a tendency to decentralization of collective bargaining, above all in Sweden and Denmark; Finland and Norway have tended to remain more centralized. The objective of Swedish employers has been to decentralize bargaining down to workplace level. The unions have successfully defended national bargaining, although the concrete substance of the agreements is increasingly being displaced to workplaces. In Norway at the end of the 1980s and in Finland in the mid-1990s, tripartite recentralization occurred in response to the economic recession. In Sweden similar developments took place in the first half of the 1990s, but they were considerably more fragile and without direct participation of union and employer confederations. Economy-wide tripartite co-ordination on wage increases in Sweden did not preclude continued decentralization.

Structural Changes Generating Tensions in the Swedish Model: The Economy and Labour Market

Few if any economies are so concentrated and internationalized as the Swedish. Despite its small population – 8.8 million – a surprisingly large proportion of big companies are based in Sweden. Out of the top 500 European firms by capitalization, 32 were Swedish in 1996 (*Financial Times* 1997). Among the other Nordic countries, Denmark and Norway accounted for nine each and Finland for seven. There is obviously a close correlation between the size of firms and the degree of internationalization in a small country like Sweden: only by selling the greater part of production in foreign markets (through exports and production abroad) has the impressive expansion of the largest Swedish firms been possible. Many of them employ far more workers abroad than in Sweden. A recent trend is an explosive growth in foreign investments in Sweden.

The size and internationalization of leading Swedish firms, combined with the smallness of the country, have given them a strategic position among the country's social forces. There is, however, an increasing discrepancy between the growing economic significance of the 'C-sector' (the sector competing on international markets) and its declining share of labour force. In 1963 the sector accounted for 30 per cent of the total number of working hours; by 1992 the figure had fallen to 18 per cent.

For decades social-democratic policy favoured the big, export-oriented enterprises as a motor of economic growth. The historic compromise at the end of the 1930s was based on a common aspiration for economic growth and efficiency. However, tensions were to be generated by the rapid expansion of the welfare state – another aspect of the Swedish model – where productivity failed to keep pace with that of the private sector. The central role of the relationship between LO and the peak employers' body has been undermined by the massive growth of the public sector. The number of public employees has outstripped those represented by LO in centralized wage negotiations with SAF (the Swedish Employers' Confederation); in 1995, the public sector accounted for 39 per cent of employed workers. The overwhelming majority (73 per cent) were women and as many as 55 per cent of all female workers were employed in the public sector in 1995, but only one in five male workers. By international standards the activity rate of women in the Swedish labour force is very high: 74 per cent in 1994, compared to 78 per cent for men.

The LO–SAF axis was also undermined by the increasing proportion of white-collar workers, in particular as the manual–white-collar division is very marked in Swedish union structure. Almost all national unions affiliated to LO are manual workers' unions. TCO (the Swedish Confederation of Professional Employees, founded in 1944) and SACO (the Swedish Confederation of Professional Associations, established in 1947) are composed exclusively of white-collar unions. In 1996 LO had 1,890,000 'active' members (i.e. excluding pensioners, students, etc.), of whom about 800,000 were in the public sector. TCO had 1,122,000 and SACO 310,000 (see table 3.5).

With the accelerating internationalization of the Swedish economy, the introduction of new production concepts and an increasingly fragmented union structure, centralized bargaining has gradually been dismantled in line with a new, militant strategy on the part of employers. The transition from co-operation to confrontation between the 'labour market parties' in both the industrial and state arenas can be traced back to the extensive labour legislation of the 1970s, which responded to union and worker concerns at the negative implications of the Swedish model: a one-sided emphasis on economic growth and structural rationalization, and the persistence of employer prerogative as a result of the historical compromise. The radicalization of the union agenda prompted a more militant approach by the employers. In the 1990s they withdrew from corporatist representation, but ironically were forced to participate in the corporatist concertation of collective bargaining under the auspices of the state. Despite rising unemployment, no other formula could be found to combat inflationary wage settlements in an increasingly fragmented bargaining system. Consequently, the classical Swedish model of 'self-regulation' (see below), was partly replaced by 'state regulation'.

Until the early 1990s, low unemployment was a distinctive feature of the Swedish labour market, with a low point of 1.5 per cent in 1989, when the OECD–Europe average was 8.3 per cent. Since 1991 a profound change has occurred. Unemployment rose sharply, reaching 8.2 per cent in 1993 before dropping back to 7.7 in 1995. In contrast to earlier recessions in which the expansion of public services offset falling employment elsewhere, the public sector has itself been hit by redundancies.

The traditional Swedish policy of full employment has gradually come into conflict with pressures from international capital markets, especially given the dominance of large multinational exporters in the Swedish economy. The deregulation of credit and foreign exchange at the end of the 1980s has starkly revealed the narrowing confines of national economic policy. It was not by chance that Sweden announced plans to join the EU in a (social democratic) crisis package in 1990. Addressed primarily to the (financial) 'markets', this step was taken without prior public debate.

The internationalized character of big Swedish firms is also increasingly restricting the scope for national collective bargaining. With the structure of wage negotiations increasingly fragmented and the Swedish unions' capacity to take industrial action still intact, co-ordination by the state is on the agenda. So too is new labour legislation – this time on the initiative of the employers. The outcome seems to be a tripartite compromise over a new Swedish model of collective bargaining.

The Establishment of the Swedish Model of Industrial Relations: Centralized 'Self-regulation'

The Swedish variant of the 'Nordic Model' of industrial relations was long distinguished by remarkably limited state regulation. This changed in the 1970s when labour legislation was introduced on a massive scale. Since the 1980s the frequency of government intervention in collective bargaining has accelerated, culminating in tripartite co-ordination in 1991–5. As a result, Swedish industrial relations have become more similar to those of other Nordic countries.

From the end of the 1930s up to the 1980s the Swedish model could be labelled centralized 'self-regulation'. Even at the beginning of the twentieth century the balance of power in the industrial arena, reflected in the fundamental compromises between unions and employers' associations, made extensive labour legislation less urgent (Kjellberg 1992). Labour law did not play a significant role until the end of the 1920s. In the 1930s both LO and SAF preferred self-regulation –

through the 1938 'Saltsjöbaden Agreement' – to the extension of labour law threatened by the social-democratic government if the 'labour market parties' failed to reach agreement. Self-regulation allowed the unions to retain a function in the eyes of their members, while employers could avoid regulation of industrial relations by a social-democratic government. Finally, the government believed that union members were more likely to accept 'labour peace' and pay restraint if the unions preserved a degree of autonomy.

Social democracy's attainment of political power encouraged a co-operative strategy by the unions. In exchange for social reforms and improved material conditions, they were prepared to show 'social responsibility'. One aspect of this was the reduction of the very high, albeit declining, levels of industrial conflict (see table 3.1). This was seen by all parties as essential for economic recovery and, in particular, to combat high unemployment. To foster labour peace the powers of LO over affiliated national unions were strengthened under the new LO constitution of 1941.

Despite self-regulation, the state intervened informally in several aspects of Swedish industrial relations. The intimate links between the social-democratic party and the union movement provided a two-way channel of influence between government and LO. As a consequence of the 'historic compromise' the employers also came to use informal channels, influencing government policy through 'non-political' experts and through representation on government agencies and commissions, rather than attempting to support the bourgeois parties and mounting a political challenge to social democracy. Confrontation thus gave way to co-operation and corporatism.

The basic agreement of 1938 and the subsequent centralization of LO were complemented by a third step, the introduction of centralized bargaining in the 1950s. For almost three decades centralized bargaining was a successful alternative to open government intervention and enabled LO to implement a 'solidaristic wage policy'. The initiative, however, came from the employers who wanted to overcome a lack of discipline and to improve co-ordination between SAF associations, as well as between individual employers.

The solidaristic wage policy functioned as an extra-governmental form of incomes policy and accelerated structural transformation by forcing up wages in low-paid industries, while export industries benefited from relatively low wage increases. The 'active labour market policy' managed by the Labour Market Board played an important supplementary role by encouraging geographical and occupational mobility of workers.

The Swedish Model under Growing Pressure

By the 1960s, the classic Swedish model was already under pressure from both structural change and growing internal contradictions. Public sector expansion, technological development, new areas of competition and accelerating internation-

Table 3.1 Strikes and lockouts

Period	(1)	(2)	(3)	(4)	(5)	Per million employees***
A. Average number of strikes and lockouts per year						
1920–29	–	–	–	–	271	148
1930–39	–	–	–	–	124	63
1940–49	3	102	–	–	105	48
1950–59	1	21	–	–	22	9
1960–69	<1	14	9*	23*	14	5
1970–79	<1	10	131	142	11	3
1980–89	1	12	108	121	13	4
1981–89**	1	11	99	111	12	3
1990–95	4	11	27	42	15	4
						Per thousand employees***
B. Average number of participating employees per year (000s)						
1920–29	–	–	–	–	68	37
1930–39	–	–	–	–	24	12
1940–49	–	–	–	–	22	10
1950–59	–	–	–	–	6	3
1960–69	–	–	2*	5*	4	2
1970–79	4	3	18	25	7	2
1980–89	82	43	14	122	108	30
1981–89**	15	25	13	53	40	11
1990–95	22	24	3	45	42	11
						Per thousand employees***
C. Average number of days lost per year (000s)						
1920–29	–	–	–	–	3.256	1.780
1930–39	–	–	–	–	1.446	736
1940–49	–	–	–	–	1.219	558
1950–59	–	–	–	–	151	59
1960–69	–	–	7*	54*	47	16
1970–79	28	72	65	165	100	30
1980–89	454	252	14	717	702	194
1981–89**	47	244	12	299	287	79
1990–95	170	140	4	282	278	76

(1) Legal lockouts, (2) Legal strikes, (3) Illegal strikes, (4) All strikes and lockouts, (5) Legal strikes and lockouts.
* Illegal strikes only 1965–69.
** 1981–89 is shown separately to exclude the big lockout and strike of 1980.
*** Only legal strikes and lockouts.
Note: Employees simultaneously covered by strike and lockout are shown in each of columns (1) and (2), while columns (4) and (5) and the last column are cleared of double-counting.
Source: Calculations of data from Statens förlikningsmannaexpedition and SCB.

alization of the economy caused substantial shifts in the employment structure and changed power relations. Gradually, the negative effects of the model were becoming evident. In the late 1960s and early 1970s, with unions relatively weak at the workplace (reflecting the historical compromise), rapid structural transformation and the intensification of work provoked worker discontent. In addition, the solidaristic wage policy was disadvantageous to some groups, such as the traditionally well-paid miners of northern Sweden. Worker unrest, manifested in wildcat strikes, stimulated a radicalization of the union movement. In the face of employer resistance, collective bargaining was an inadequate means of solving these problems.

The principle of self-regulation was abandoned and extensive labour legislation was introduced in the 1970s to increase union influence over employment and production matters. Measures were passed on job security (1974), union workplace representatives (1974) and co-determination (1976); the Co-determination Act was a framework agreement to be implemented through subsequent collective agreement. Taken together with LO's subsequent campaign for wage-earners funds, this represented the replacement of the spirit of co-operation of the Saltsjöbaden agreement by confrontation. The employers, encouraged by the social democrats' loss of office after 44 years (1932–76), launched a strong ideological and political counter-offensive. SAF refused to conclude an agreement under the Co-determination Act until 1982; the agreement reinforced negotiating rights in the event of major changes within enterprises, but beyond that it contained no substantive rules of co-determination. In contrast to the 1930s, the balance of power gradually shifted in the employers' favour and SAF later saw the dismantling of the corporatist system of representation as a way of further reducing union influence (see below).

Although the labour legislation of the 1970s left the system of wage negotiations untouched it influenced the employers' bargaining strategy by calling into question important parts of the 'historic compromise'. Structural shifts within the employers' camp were also of importance. Even in the 1930s, big export-oriented industrialists had initially opposed the policy of co-operation, while home market industries had been more favourable. In the 1960s, a pressure group of big exporters unsuccessfully called for SAF to reconsider the policy of centralized bargaining. By the 1980s, however, the growth of the export sector and accelerated internationalization paved the way for a profound shift of policy within SAF in favour of decentralization.

The changing structure of employment, reflected in new and more complicated union constellations, was a further important impetus for dismantling the centralized system of bargaining. The privileged position of the LO–SAF axis in the system of centralized wage negotiations was eroded by the expansion of public sector and white-collar employment. As a consequence of the 'segregated' Swedish union structure, the growing proportion of white-collar workers favoured TCO and SACO at the expense of LO, an effect reinforced by white-collar union density that was very high by international standards (about 85 per cent). LO public sector unions, who were not part of LO–SAF negotiations, increased their weight within the organization: the rapidly-growing Municipal Workers' Union (Kommunal) replaced Metall as the largest LO union in 1977.

LO–SAF wage negotiations therefore covered a shrinking proportion of workers. Instead powerful bargaining cartels emerged, i.e. federations of national unions performing common negotiating tasks. In 1973, TCO and SACO unions founded the PTK cartel to bargain with SAF. Despite the strong centralizing ambitions of the government a more complex pattern emerged among public sector workers, with the foundation of a number of unions and cartels: TCO-S (1967), and the LO union SF (1970; SEKO since 1995) in the central state sector; the TCO cartel KTK (1976), and Kommunal in the municipal sector.

Public sector white-collar unions and bargaining cartels did not hesitate to follow a militant approach. New union alliances arose from the profound shifts in employment structure and bargaining strength. In the 'great conflict' of 1980 these trends were clearly manifested. The LO and TCO public sector organizations (known as the 'Gang of Four') co-ordinated wage negotiations and seized the initiative. Their high wage demands forced LO to raise its own demands, triggering the 'great conflict'. Two contrary but parallel processes underlay this development: the centralization of white-collar and public sector unions, and the fragmentation of the union system as a whole into blocs of relatively equal strength – LO (manual workers, private sector), PTK (white-collar workers, private sector) and the 'Gang of Four' (LO and TCO public sector unions).

In the 1980s, the success of LO's solidaristic wage policy generated considerable tensions between LO and TCO/SACO unions. White-collar unions other than SACO were influenced by solidaristic norms, but applied them only *within* their ranks and firmly opposed diminished wage differentials between white-collar and manual workers. Consequently wage differentials declined within the LO and TCO spheres but not between manual and white-collar workers. Furthermore, in the mid-1970s, clauses had been introduced in agreements to compensate white-collar and public sector workers for the fact that manual workers in manufacturing had greater opportunities to benefit from wage drift, i.e. increases in earnings beyond those negotiated in collective agreements. On the whole, pay increases have developed in parallel between manual and white-collar workers (see table 3.2).

Continuing differentials between union blocs made it difficult for LO to urge wage restraint and 'social responsibility'. With more militant groups demanding substantial wage increases, LO was forced to revise its claims upwards. Solidaristic wage policy, based upon the privileged position of the LO–SAF axis, lost its role as an alternative to incomes policy. Accelerating pay competition between competing union blocs, combined with declining economic growth, resulted in a divergence between real and money wages, further sharpening conflicts between the blocs. Between 1970 and 1992 total wage costs rose 700 per cent, productivity 45 per cent and real wages only 10–20 per cent (SAF annual report 1992: 18).

Table 3.2 Contractual wage increases and wage drift in manufacturing industry, 1975–96 (yearly averages)

Year	Manual workers			White-collar workers		
	(A)	(B)	(C)	(A)	(B)	(C)
1975–82	5.9	4.3	10.2	7.3	2.4	9.7
1983–86	4.4	3.6	8.0	3.3	4.0	7.3
1987	–	–	6.4	2.0	4.1	6.1
1988–90	3.6	5.8	9.3	3.1	5.8	9.0
1991–95	2.0	2.3	4.3	1.6	2.5	4.1
1996	3.9	3.0	6.9	3.4	5.1	8.5

(A) = contractual wage increase.
(B) = wage drift.
(C) = (A) + (B) = total wage increase.
Source: Konjunkturinstitutet.

Decentralization as an Employer Strategy in the 1980s and 1990s

Since the beginning of the 1980s, Swedish employers have increasingly challenged centralized bargaining (Martin 1995). Having forced the unions to accept centralized bargaining in the 1950s, they now argued that central agreements failed in their objective of restraining wages, functioning as a 'floor' for wage increases, rather than as a 'ceiling'. Additional wage increases at the lower levels of the three-tier system therefore threatened the competitiveness of Swedish industry, temporarily restored by repeated devaluations. The introduction of compensation clauses and intensified efforts to raise wages of low-paid groups meant that wage drift in profitable export firms spread to the whole economy, making it difficult for employers to use wages to recruit and retain skilled labour. In the period of central SAF–LO agreements, 1956–82, wage drift among manual private sector workers on average accounted for almost 50 per cent of total wage increases (Edin and Holmlund 1992: 7).

As international competition intensified, employers increasingly saw decentralization as a means of securing greater wage flexibility at local level. Workplace bargaining has long had a prominent role in Sweden, but it has taken place within a framework established by centralized bargaining, allowing central principles and norms to be transmitted to local level, and imposing uniform and, according to employers, inflexible provisions across a wide variety of different local conditions. The erosion of wage differentials diminished employers' ability to use pay as a tool for promoting productivity, flexibility and quality in a period when traditional piece-work declined and many employers felt compelled to pursue flexible work organization based upon teamwork and multiskilling (Pontusson and Swenson 1996: 236–7).

The great conflict of 1980 clearly demonstrated the limitations of centralization for the employers under the prevailing power relations in the Swedish labour market. SAF called a massive lockout of its 750,000 members, but it completely failed to come up to the expectations of the organization's new militant leadership. Not surprisingly, strategy soon shifted in favour of decentralization (de Geer 1992: 142–43), which employers believed would minimize the risk of large labour conflicts (Elvander 92: 13). (In practice, the 1990s have shown that employers may be vulnerable even to relatively limited strikes – see below.) Engineering employers were in the forefront of the call for decentralization. They were particularly exposed to rising wage costs because of high export shares, relatively labour-intensive production and local pay systems promoting wage drift. The engineering employers' organization VF, the dominant body within SAF, threatened to leave the organization unless it changed its statutes to facilitate decentralized bargaining; and, in 1983, it broke away from economy-wide negotiations.

However, the path to the ultimate goal of completely decentralized pay determination has been far from smooth. Externally, employers have faced resistance from union confederations and social-democratic governments. Internally, they have been undecided over objectives. The collective employer interest in wage restraint, implying a degree of central co-ordination of pay determination, appears to be incompatible with a full-blooded decentralization strategy – at least in countries like Sweden with high union density and (until the 1990s) low unemployment (Elvander 1988). Uncertainties and divisions over strategy also reflected differences between companies competing in international markets, led by VF (but excluding the capital-intensive process-based forest industries), and those oriented to the domestic market, for example retail trade (de Geer 1992: 131; Pontusson and Swenson 1996: 239–42). However, most associations favoured some co-ordination of bargaining when decentralized negotiation failed to deliver moderate pay settlements (as in 1984 and 1988). As a result, they have followed a 'zigzag' path towards decentralization, with bargaining rounds oscillating between centralization and decentralization (see table 3.3).

Union positions were also complex. In the export sector, for example, unions were joined with employers in a 'cross-class coalition' of interests (Iversen 1996) which saw decentralization as necessary for the promotion of international competitiveness through more flexible wages and production systems. Thus, the largest private sector union, Metall, supported VF's initiative: centralized bargaining had opened a widening gap between skilled workers and lower-level white-collar workers; this prompted many skilled workers to leave Metall and join the TCO union, SIF, in order to benefit from more favourable contracts. Metalworkers were also irritated by compensation clauses favouring workers in the protected sector, and failed to see why others should benefit from their increased productivity and wage drift.

Several steps may be identified in the gradual decentralization of bargaining. First, the three-tier system was replaced by a two-tier system by the removal of the top level (see table 3.4). Second, the contents of national collective agreements have become less detailed, and their pay provisions may be superseded by local agreements between companies and union workplace organizations. Third, these tendencies have paved the way for new pay systems at workplace level: pay-setting

Table 3.3 Collective agreements, 1980–98

Duration	Sector			
	LO–SAF	PTK–SAF	National Government	Local Government
One year 1980	x	x	x	x
Two years 1980–1982	x	x	x	x
One year 1983	x[a]		x	x
Two and a half years (1983/85)		x		
Two years 1984/85			x	x
Varying lengths 1984– (10–27 months)	x[b]			
One year supplementary contract 1984/85		x		
Recommendation one year 1985[c]	x			
Half a year 1985		x		
Two years 1986/87		x		
Recommendation two years 1986/87[c]	x			
Two years 1986/87			x	x
One year 1988	x[b]	x[b]	x	
Two years 1988/89	x[a]	x	x	
One year 1990				x
Renegotiations[d]		x	x	x
Two years 1991/93[e,f]	x[b]	x[b]	x	x
Two years 1993/95[f]	x[b]	x[b]	x	x
Three years 1995/98[g]	x[b]	x[b]	x	x

Source: Konjunkturinstitutet.
[a] Excl. Metall-VF.
[b] No private sector central agreements, decentralized negotiations between national unions and employers' associations.
[c] LO–SAF recommendations to national unions/employers' associations.
[d] Price clause 1990.
[e] One and three quarters of a year: 1 July 1991 to 31 March 1993.
[f] Economy-wide co-ordination of agreements by the Rehnberg Commission (1991) and state mediators (1993).
[g] Some agreements 2 years (paper and pulp), others 5 years (nurses, teachers).

and new forms of work organization are increasingly co-ordinated to promote productivity, flexibility and quality. Manual workers are, like white-collar employees, increasingly paid according to task and individual performance. Profit-sharing bonuses and other alternative pay systems have also expanded as devices for increasing employee commitment and retaining workers in tight labour markets. At the beginning of the 1990s, about one in eight manual workers and one in seven white-collar workers in the private sector were covered by profit-sharing (LO 1994a/part 3: 97–8). The rapid introduction of new wage systems at the workplace has represented a breakthrough for the employers in their strategy of decentralization.

The growth of new pay systems for manual workers is illustrated by a Metall survey (1995a) showing that in 1994, 60 per cent of metalworkers received some

Table 3.4 Levels of negotiations and agreements in the mid-1990s

Type of agreement etc.	Employers	Unions
A. Basic agreements		
(1) private sector	central: SAF	central: LO, PTK
(2) public sector	central: public employers*	national unions and cartels**
B. Agreements on insurance schemes, co-determination and other non-wage issues		
(1) private sector	central: SAF	central: LO, PTK
(2) public sector	central: public employers*	national unions and cartels**
C. Collective agreements		
(1) private sector	SAF associations: VF, Almega, etc.	national unions: LO unions, PTK unions
(2) public sector	central: public employers*	national unions and cartels**
D. Collective agreements (implementation at local level)	local: public agencies, enterprises/plants	local: union workplace organizations***

  * Arbetsgivarverket (National Agency for Government Employers), Kommunförbundet (Swedish Association of Local Authorities) and Landstingsförbundet (Federation of County Councils).

 ** National government: Arbetsgivarverket and each of SEKO, TCO–OF-S-P-O and SACO–S (but with similar contents of basic agreements). Local government: Kommunförbundet and Landstingsförbundet on one hand and national unions of LO (Kommunal), TCO (SKTF, nurses, teachers etc.) and SACO (teachers etc.) on the other.

*** At small workplaces assisted or replaced by officials from union branches.

form of payment by results. The fixed basic component, related to the type of job and the tasks mastered, was typically supplemented by a personal element depending on qualifications, co-operativeness, and so on, and by a variable bonus related to performance, often on a team basis. By 1989–90, wage dispersion was back to the levels of the mid-1970s, reversing the substantial wage compression up to 1982–3 (Hibbs 1991).

However, the progress to decentralization has been uneven. Unions in private services and public sector (Handels and Kommunal the most prominent) lag behind Metall in introducing new wage systems (*LO-tidningen* 5, 7 1995). (However, the removal of compensation clauses in national agreements has promoted interest in new wage systems, not least among public sector unions like Kommunal (LO) and the nurses' union (TCO).) Moreover, the weight of the fixed task-related component has grown in the 1990s, reducing the relative weight of the individual and performance-related elements. Thus manual and white-collar wage systems are converging, but not as envisaged in the original employer concept of 'co-worker agreements' (*medarbetaravtal*; Mahon 1994). Under such agreements, white-collar workers' job controls would be weakened and employers would have greater flexibility to move white-collar workers freely between tasks; at the same time wages for manual workers would be individualized. This was seen as 'the best of both worlds, blue-collar job flexibility and white-collar pay flexibility' (Martin 1995: 281). However, common pay agreements for manual and white-collar employees at local level are rare owing to union resistance, and in the private sector there are still no industry-level co-worker wage agreements – which the unions have insisted as a prerequisite for local agreements.

Thus it appears that the unions' insistence on 'objective' wage systems has not been without effect. In contrast to the employers' stress on 'subjective' individual-centred measures (individual performance, co-operative ability etc.), unions prefer clear and task-oriented criteria to avoid unfair or arbitrary wage differences (on the importance of fair pay standards, see Swenson 1989: 15–19). They also argue that clear and fair wage norms stimulate 'competence development'. Unions and employers agree on differentiated wages as an incentive, but differ as to how this may best be done. Furthermore, unions strongly emphasize that all workers, not just the core, should be given the opportunity for continuous training, a career with respect to pay and skills, and developing jobs ('solidaristic work policy').

The erosion of centralized bargaining was followed by a substantial shift from inflation caused by wage compression to market-driven wage inflation (Hibbs and Locking 1996: 134–5). It is not surprising, therefore, that since the beginning of the 1990s and the decision to join the EU, austerity policy has been given higher priority than full employment – particularly given the political aspiration to avoid further devaluations (Åberg 1994: 87–8; Glyn 1995: 52–3). A policy of fixed exchange rates and budget cuts, by social democratic and bourgeois governments alike, transformed a situation of excess demand, high inflation and extremely tight labour market into the opposite: unemployment, which had been less than 2 per cent in 1988–90, increased to 8 per cent by 1994.

Developments in the 1990s suggest that union opposition will prevent a complete shift to decentralized bargaining for the foreseeable future. Indeed, the bargaining rounds of the early 1990s have been highly co-ordinated within a framework of tripartite negotiations. As the 1990s draw to a close, the two key polarities of the Swedish system of wage formation – centralization *versus* decentralization and state- *versus* self-regulation – are under renewed scrutiny.

▍ From Self-regulation to State Regulation

Paradoxically, while the government as employer had taken significant steps towards decentralized bargaining in the 1980s, government intervention became a further recentralizing force. Intervention was motivated, as in the formative period of the 'Swedish model', by a concern for economic stabilization.

The escalation of direct government intervention in collective bargaining in the 1980s reflected the factors undermining the foundations of the classical Swedish model: the emergence of powerful new organizations of white-collar and public sector workers; accelerating wage competition between the blocs, and the consequent rapid rise in wages (more rapid than in other European countries in the early 1980s); the increasingly transnational character of large Swedish enterprises, magnifying the impact of even moderate wage increases; and the increasing potential for multiple conflicts with the decline in LO–SAF dominance. All these developments heightened the pressures on government to intervene.

When the social democrats returned to power following the bourgeois interregnum of 1976–82, they were determined to reject the austerity policies that were causing high unemployment elsewhere. Traditional Keynesian demand management was also rejected as increasingly inappropriate for an internationalized economy. Instead they opted for the 'third way', based on the promotion of investments by high profits and low nominal wage increases. The principal means of transferring resources from wages to profits was a 16 per cent devaluation in 1982. Supported by LO and subsequently also by TCO, this devaluation proved to be the only substantial success of social-democratic 'incomes policy' in the 1980s (Elvander 1990: 16). Government intervention in the 1985 pay negotiations marked the high point of 'negotiated incomes policy': in return for a 5 per cent norm for pay increases the government offered tax concessions favouring low-paid workers (Elvander 1990: 14). This integration of wage negotiations and political decision-making challenged the principle of self-regulation. LO feared that unions would appear superfluous if state intervention were required at top level and low nominal wage increases were combined with relatively high wage drift (Elvander 1988: 181). In 1986–7, therefore, although centralized bargaining was restored, the parties agreed to return to the Swedish model of 'free collective bargaining', and government action was less pronounced.

Despite the failure of both decentralization (as in 1988) and centralization (as in 1989–90) to slow wage drift in these years of low unemployment, the government's role was relatively passive towards the end of the 1980s. At the beginning of the 1990s, however, the picture changed completely. Early in 1990, it became clear that price rises would exceed the rate of 4 per cent at which the unions' right to renegotiate the 1989–90 contracts was triggered. The government called for a return to centralized bargaining and a restrictive 2-year agreement. But VF, and SAF, refused. The social democrats then prepared the most far-reaching intervention in the history of Swedish industrial relations. In concert with top leaders of LO and affiliated unions (except Kommunal), in February 1990 the government announced a 2-year general pay freeze and strike ban, with increased fines for wildcat strikes, and ceilings on prices and dividends. The proposal, widely regarded as a violation of basic trade union rights, aroused a wave of protests from rank-and-file members and from many local union branches and workplace organizations. This forced union leaders to dissociate themselves from the initiative, leading the government to resign (though a new social-democratic government was formed).

The collapse of its proposal forced the government to look for more consensual methods to contain the wage-price spiral. A tripartite 'national mediation commission', the Rehnberg Commission, composed of a national mediator and one former official each from SAF, LO, TCO and SACO, was appointed. The commission was given a mandate to persuade unions and employers to accept a 2-year 'stabilization agreement' (1991–2) for the whole labour market. Faced with a wage-price spiral and the looming prospect of economic crisis and mass unemployment, most organizations approved the 'Rehnberg agreement' setting out the framework of industry bargaining. It prohibited local negotiations in 1991, and stipulated that any wage drift would be subtracted from 1992 increases. Efforts of the workplace clubs of some PTK unions to conclude local deals exceeding the Rehnberg terms were thwarted by strong employer discipline and the downward turn in the economy.

At first sight, SAF's role in encouraging the Rehnberg agreement was ironic in view of its fervent adherence to decentralized bargaining. In practice, the Rehnberg agreement could be seen as encouraging a form of 'super-decentralization' since by avoiding local negotiations, local pay determination would be a matter for individual employer prerogative. In the breadth of its coverage, however, the Rehnberg agreement represented a 'super-centralization': almost all unions concluded agreements within its terms. But this, too, was in SAF's favour, since pay competition was reduced and a non-fragmented bargaining model temporarily restored, removing a major SAF objection to central negotiations. Private and public employers formed a close alliance to support the agreement, which they saw as a way of containing the high nominal wage rises of previous years.

The Rehnberg agreement represented a new type of centralized industrial relations in Sweden. The multitude of bargaining centres following upon the changed composition of the labour force meant that centralization could only be restored under the auspices of the state. The role of the commission was not in the first instance to engage in political exchange (although the effect of the tax reform was to be taken into account), but above all to co-ordinate a large number of collective bargaining actors (about 110 employers' associations, national unions and bargaining cartels).

The opening of negotiations on the basis of a pre-established consensus on the desirability of both wage restraint and co-ordination was an innovation in Swedish collective bargaining (*Stabiliseringsavtal 1991–92*: 112). The commission sounded out the views of unions and employers before presenting its final proposals, but concertation was backed up by threats of more far-reaching state intervention should the parties fail to comply with the commission's demands. Thus collective bargaining in the early 1990s became more 'corporatist' than ever before, even though the implementation of the Rehnberg agreement was left to the parties themselves, through contracts at industry level. In the background, LO and SAF played an important supporting role, in close co-operation with public employers and the government.

The agreement did succeed in slowing down wage drift in 1991–2 (helped by rising unemployment), co-ordinating the length of contracts, and dampening labour conflicts; but it failed to halt the rapid deterioration of the Swedish economy. With the financial system close to collapse, the budget deficit and interest rates rising dramatically, and unemployment climbing to levels unknown since the 1930s, 1992 was aptly called 'the year of crises'. A succession of 'crisis packages' failed to preserve the unilateral link between the Swedish krona and the ecu. The depreciation at the end of 1992 aided the recovery of exports, but came too late to prevent the massive loss in manufacturing employment: over 20 per cent of engineering sectors jobs were lost between 1989 and 1993. For the first time, the public sector did not expand during a recession.

The abnormal depth of the recession, coupled with deadlock between employers and unions over bargaining levels, created considerable uncertainty when the Rehnberg agreement expired in 1993. The continued strength of Swedish unions made the SAF model of completely decentralized bargaining unrealistic. Confronted with a wave of industrial action, even VF, the most fervent advocate of enterprise agreements, had to abandon its initial refusal to grant wage concessions to national unions. In contrast to Denmark, unions also rejected industry agreements setting minimum wages only.

Again tripartite bargaining provided a way out of deadlock. And once again the state – this time in the form of state mediators – successfully appealed for co-operation between national unions and employer associations to avoid inflationary wage increases at a time of economic crisis. A co-ordinated series of agreements, covering almost all key industries and sectors, was concluded in accordance with principles laid down early on by the group of mediators (*Rapport om 1993 års avtalsrörelse*). In effect the Rehnberg agreement was prolonged for a further 2 years by a series of stabilization agreements.

It is remarkable that the voluntary and informal Swedish mediation machinery, so weak by Nordic standards, succeeded in co-ordinating the 1993 bargaining round. Without the determination of the labour market parties to avoid a return to the pre-Rehnberg situation of inflationary wage competition, such an 'informal centralization' under state auspices would hardly have been possible. As with the Rehnberg Commission, the mediators' starting point for each settlement was to gain acceptance of a number of basic principles: co-ordination, wage restraint in the context of economic crisis, 2-year contracts without compensation clauses, wage drift to be offset against contractual increases, increased wage determination at workplace level, etc. The work of the mediators was facilitated by co-ordination between LO unions. The Commercial Employees' Union was allowed by LO to take the initiative as deep divisions between VF and Metall/SIF/CF brought engineering negotiations to a deadlock (Elvander 1996: 4–5). The settlement for the distribution sector became a model for almost all subsequent contracts – including the engineering agreement (*Rapport om 1995 års avtalsrörelse*). The existence of a common negotiating body for Metall and the white-collar unions SIF and CF in the engineering industry provided a platform for extending the stabilization agreements to other white-collar unions.

Although the Swedish economy was still in crisis when the 1993 contracts expired 2 years later, the state mediators were not as successful in reaching a further series of agreements. The underlying obstacle was the sharply diverging economic performance between industries and sectors. The export sector was booming in wake of the depreciation of the krona, the home market was stagnating, and the public sector was hit by cuts. The resulting centrifugal forces were simply too strong for a replication of the 1993 bargaining round. In the engineering sector, for example, following the collapse of negotiations between VF and Metall/SIF/CF the state mediators aimed to secure a three-year contract compatible with the 3.5 per cent per annum 'Edin norm'. This was a norm, corresponding to the expected European average rate of wage growth, proposed by the Edin Group of economists representing leading unions and employer associations, in a report, *I takt med Europa* (In step with Europe). Ironically, with mediation in engineering in a delicate phase, VF was hit by a 'decentralized' move by the paper and pulp employers' association, which concluded an agreement exceeding the Edin norm in response to its members' booming export market. In addition, union members were demanding substantial improvements after several years of wage restraint and cuts in welfare benefits. The militant demands of engineering employers for decentralized bargaining and more flexible labour law also contributed to making the 1995 bargaining round the most conflictual for many years, with an overtime ban in engineering, strikes in retail trade, transport, hospitals, etc. Each agreement tended to be considered a floor for subsequent wage negotiations.

The efforts of the state mediators were not altogether in vain. Most national agreements were concluded for a period of three years (1995–8). In general the Edin norm was exceeded, but without the efforts of the mediators and the existence of the norm, rises would probably have been considerably higher. The design of contracts, high unemployment and low inflation were expected to keep wage drift within reasonable bounds, although recent data indicate the opposite (table 3.2). As in the preceding bargaining round, demands of both employers and unions were to an extent satisfied. Thus while the former gained long contract periods and increased scope for workplace negotiations, the latter managed to keep the system of national wage agreements intact, and secured relatively high increases for unions (such as Handels, Kommunal and the TCO nurses' union) dominated by women. Unions like Metall clearly preferred co-operation with white-collar unions to LO co-ordination. The increasing similarity of manual and white-collar contracts may pave the way for 'co-worker agreements' in the future, not only at workplace level (the policy of employers), but also at national level (a union objective).

To sum up: two tendencies have dominated collective bargaining in the 1990s, both already evident in the 1980s. One is the continued advance of 'decentraliza-tion', in the sense of the extension of the scope for workplace negotiation within the framework of national industry agreements. The second is the increased activity of the state in co-ordinating national agreements and in making them compatible with low inflation and other economic policy goals. This 'centralization by state regulation' does not, however, entail a return to the traditional three-tier system abandoned in the 1980s, but signals a new model of economy-wide co-ordination (implying centralization at a higher level than ever) on the basis of the current two-tier system. Growing exposure to international financial markets and the ambition of qualifying for membership of the EMU mean that the long tradition of compensating for wage inflation by devaluation has had to be relinquished.

▌The Decline of Tripartite Corporatism

The growth of corporatist representation had occurred in parallel with the expansion of the welfare state and national crisis management (Hägglund and Degerblad 1994: 235). It was logical therefore that, as the fissures in the Swedish model became more apparent, corporatism too should go into decline. Internationalization and European integration have also made corporatist representation less important by diminishing the significance of nation states, especially in small countries dominated by large firms, like Sweden.

The shift in the political climate to one more friendly to the employers encouraged SAF to work for a profound 'change of system'. From the mid-1980s, SAF increasingly called into question the corporatist system (de Geer 1992:155–7), partly as a way of decreasing the power of the unions. It mounted intense public campaigns to spread the market ideology and to improve the electoral prospects of liberal and conservative parties. SAF's ideas on privatization and deregulation have influenced not only bourgeois but also social-democratic governments. It has also been intensely hostile to the social dimension of European regulation. This almost 'British' stance reflects its concern that the benefits of deregulation at national level might be nullified by increased social regulation at EU level. Thus the former SAF chairman Ulf Laurin, now chair of the social affairs committee of UNICE, considered it his most important task to 'put some gravel into the social EU machinery so it does not run too fast' (*Näringsliv* 13, 1996).

In 1992, SAF withdrew from almost all government bodies at central as well as regional and local level. Withdrawal has given SAF more freedom to pursue its aims, particularly since one of its targets is the state apparatus itself. The decline of corporatism has meant that other means of influence, such as political campaigns, lobbying, and participation in informal advisory groups and expert commissions, have achieved greater prominence (Pestoff 1995). The increased emphasis on influencing governments directly, rather than through state agencies, is closely related to SAF's new 'political' strategy. Its central principle is to intervene at a relatively early stage of the decision-making process in order to influence the policy agenda and avoid becoming a 'hostage' to policies devised elsewhere; in short, to move from a defensive to an offensive posture.

In 1992, as a direct result of SAF's initiative, parliament adopted a proposal from the bourgeois government to end corporatist representation (with the exceptions specified by SAF). In consequence, tripartite government bodies no longer exist at central, regional or local level, apart from the Labour Court and the Pension Insurance Funds. The formal representatives of employers and unions have been replaced by members of parliament and individuals from different parts of society. These include both business people and unionists, but none is nominated by employers' associations or unions. The change in the composition of the Labour Market Board (AMS) is particularly notable: until 1992 it had seven union and five employer representatives; in 1996 it included one union official from each of LO and TCO, two business representatives and two members of parliament.

However, while the formal tripartite character of Swedish government agencies has been ended, there are still elements of tripartism at national level. Thus, paradoxically, at about the same time as SAF withdrew its representatives from government agencies, SAF associations were entering into the most corporatist wage negotiations in Swedish history, leading to the tripartite Rehnberg agreement. In 1996–7, there were also tripartite talks on reforming job security legislation (which ended in failure) and on future pay determination. Unions and employer associations are still represented in some government commissions (for example the Working-Hours Commission). Mechanisms of tripartite consultation have also been introduced in some government agencies. The AMS and the Occupational Health and Safety Board established advisory councils, consisting of an equal number of representatives of unions and employers' associations (among them SAF), which are consulted prior to decisions being made. This procedure may reflect the traditionally strong influence of the labour market parties (particularly unions) in the AMS, as well as the prominent role in Sweden of bipartite bodies for improving the working environment, including safety committees at workplace level (Hägglund and Degerblad 1994: 138–43, 206–8, 218). In addition, unions and employers are represented on several working groups and committees attached to AMS and the Occupational Health and Safety Board.

Moreover, despite the absence of a spirit of co-operation between employers and unions at top level, many bipartite bodies, representing the classical policy of self-regulation, still remain. Some are related to the 1938 basic agreement between SAF–LO and the subsequent agreements of co-operation. Two such bodies are the SAF–LO Labour Market Council, which deals with labour conflicts (although SAF is now demanding a tripartite body to assess conflicts dangerous to society); and the Joint Occupational Safety Council involving SAF and LO/PTK. A special category of bipartite bodies deals with supplementary insurance and job security schemes. However, the SAF–LO Joint Committee on Statistics was dissolved when SAF withdraw from centralized collective bargaining.

▌A New Swedish Model?

The construction of a new model of wage determination is widely regarded as a key to future economic performance. The labour market parties agree that wages must not rise faster in Sweden than among her competitors, but they appear incapable of creating an appropriate model of self-regulation. As demonstrated by the fate of the 'Edin norm' in 1995, the crucial problem is not one of defining an upper limit for wage increases, but of implementing such a norm. SAF argues that the present semi-decentralized bargaining system is the worst of all worlds, a position supported by leading economists. By shifting the centre of gravity away from peak organizations and bargaining cartels to industry level, the advantages of centralized negotiations have been lost while the benefits of a decentralization to workplace level have still not been attained. Given the continued strength of Swedish unions, completely decentralized pay determination seems unrealistic without a profound change in the wage policy of unions.

The outcome of this bargaining dilemma has been a partial recentralization under state guidance in the 1990s, albeit with less success in 1995 (see above). Tripartite bargaining, as a more realistic alternative to complete decentralization, may in the future play an important role as a complement to semi-decentralized negotiations in a context of entrenched bargaining positions, a proliferation of bargaining organizations, and a relatively high level of labour conflict.

The parallel to the 1930s is obvious. Now as then, the ambition is to construct a model of collective bargaining which minimizes labour conflicts and promotes economic growth in a context of profound crisis and societal change. In contrast to the 1930s, however, up to 1997 the prospects for co-operation and self-regulation appeared gloomy. While in the 1930s the threat of state intervention was used above all to spur the parties to regulate their dealings themselves, the 1990s have made decisive steps in the direction of state regulation in the proposed wage freeze and strike ban of 1990, the Rehnberg agreement, and its de facto successor.

In recent years employer representatives have been concerned to reduce the unions' capacity to engage in industrial conflict which remains intact despite high unemployment. Employers have repeatedly called for the implementation of proposals presented in a 1991 government report, especially the right of state mediators to postpone or freeze labour conflicts, compulsory mediation, considerably higher fines for wildcat strikes (partly achieved), and a new economy-wide council for 'conflicts dangerous to society' in place of the procedural rules contained in the basic agreements. SAF is also demanding further measures to restrict the use of strikes and other forms of conflict (particularly in public sector), including the introduction of pre-strike ballots among union members (*SAF-tidningen* 29, 1995; SAF 1996).

The employers' concern with the restriction of industrial conflict reflects the high level of strike action. The numbers of participating workers and days lost in *legal* strikes have been considerably higher in the 1980s and 1990s than in the 1970s (known as the decade of wildcat strikes) or the 1960s (see table 3.1). The 1995–6 bargaining round was more fraught with conflict than any since the great 1980 confrontation (Elvander 1996: 20). Wage negotiations as well as mediation are often accompanied by conflict or the threat of it. Moreover, modern production concepts such as lean production, just-in-time and outsourcing make employers more vulnerable (cf. Alasoini 1993: 135–6). This applies not only to strikes and overtime bans, but also to lockouts, which Swedish employers have consequently declared to be 'obsolete'; this has not stopped their organizations resorting increasingly to such measures in the 1990s (see table 3.1). Employers are also concerned that, should completely decentralized bargaining be achieved, the increase in the number of actors involved is likely to increase the frequency of conflict. Under decentralization, the right to call sympathy strikes and blockades (called into question by SAF) may be of crucial importance. Furthermore, it is often sufficient for national unions to select a number of strategic workplaces for strikes. (Lockouts, by contrast, are usually applied widely to maximize the cost to the unions and to avoid disturbing the terms of competition.) Another tendency is the increased use of overtime bans. They have an obvious cost advantage for unions, as no strike benefits have to be paid, while in companies with low stock levels overtime bans hit production almost immediately, and enterprises risk losing orders.

In marked contrast to the 1970s, the employers have seized the initiative for change in the 1990s. In contrast to the 1930s when the parties agreed to the Saltsjöbaden agreement in order to forestall state intervention, SAF now appears to prefer state regulation. The former bargaining director of SAF, L.-G. Albåge, now a prominent state mediator, argues that employers should abandon this approach and come to an agreement with the unions on a new Swedish model of wage determination (Albåge 1996).

In view of the reduced bargaining role of SAF and LO it is unsurprising that other actors have taken the initiative. Early in 1997, a group of eight unions ('the 8-group') representing manual and white-collar workers in manufacturing concluded a co-operation agreement with their employer counterparts, among them VF. The agreement comprises procedural rules for wage negotiations, and a policy statement on co-operation based on common views concerning the competitive position of manufacturing industry, skills development and national energy policy. A joint 'industrial committee', composed of leading representatives of national unions and employers' associations, will appoint an economic council of four independent economists, and a group of 'impartial chairs' who will act as mediators in wage negotiations and have the right to 'freeze' conflicts for two weeks. In addition, the committee itself may temporarily suspend conflicts. The agreement thus contains several mechanisms to foster labour peace, and meet the demands of employers. However, it also represents a union victory in that the idea of completely decentralized wage determination is abandoned; at the same time, the industrial committee's co-ordinating role in manufacturing industry introduces an element of centralization.

In a sign of the times, the bargaining alliance between Metall (LO), SIF (TCO) and CF (SACO) forms the core of the union group. In the public sector, LO, TCO and SACO unions continue their co-operation, manifested in the 1995 bargaining round, over the issue of future pay determination. At confederal level (between and within confederations), unity appears more remote than between cross-confederal groups of national unions in the same economic sector. Only after much agonizing did LO unions succeed in adopting a common stance on future wage determination in 1997. When strengthening of state mediators was proposed, to ensure co-ordinated bargaining and to restrain individual unions from taking advantage of moderate wage increases of others, some unions were less willing than others to give up their individual freedom.

Several factors explain the willingness of many union leaders to accept a degree of state regulation of collective bargaining and enter compromises with employers. First, the experience of the 1990s has demonstrated that economy-wide tripartite co-ordination may be the only way to attain co-ordinated bargaining. LO even failed to co-ordinate its affiliated unions in the 1995–6 bargaining round (in contrast to 1993), which also demonstrated that voluntary, informal co-ordination under the auspices of state mediators had its weaknesses. Second, by initiating accommodations on future wage determination, important aspects of self-regulation may be restored and more far-reaching proposals for state regulation prevented (for example, in response to employers' demands for controls on industrial conflict, decreased job security, cuts in unemployment benefits, etc.). Third, low nominal wage increases are sufficient to improve real wages, given current low levels of inflation. More important, they are considered necessary to fight mass unemployment in a country extremely dependent upon big transnational companies. This emphasis is understandable given that the large majority of unemployed are union members and that the policy of 'full employment' was a cornerstone of the classical Swedish welfare model. Moderate wage increases are also a prerequisite for political exchange, facilitating government efforts to stimulate the economy.

All in all, therefore, the unions are prepared to make concessions to restore such essential aspects of the Swedish model as self-regulation, co-ordinated bargaining and full employment, although co-ordinated wage negotiations now may require a more active role of the state, as in other Nordic countries. However, LO's advocacy of economy-wide centralization with the assistance of state mediators is opposed by TCO and SACO, which prefer agreements on wages, procedures and conflict rules within each industry or sector (as with the manufacturing agreement).

As in the 1930s the social-democratic government prefers agreement between the labour market parties to state regulation, but has announced that it will intervene should the parties fail to agree by spring 1997. In any event, compared with the 1930s a new Swedish model will probably comprise a different mix of self-regulation and state regulation.

In the 1990s structural developments such as the internationalization of leading Swedish firms, the increasing mobility of capital and the restricted scope for national economic and employment policy have encouraged many Swedish unions to turn to European solutions, including international union co-operation and Swedish membership of the EU. It has been argued that the Swedish model of welfare and employment can only be defended by influencing European bodies. In addition, union leaders in export sectors have taken a positive stance towards EU membership on the grounds that it was likely to bolster the international competitiveness of Swedish firms. The Metall president has been one of the foremost Swedish proponents of EMU. By contrast, the president of the Commercial Employees' Union (a union in a sector oriented to the domestic market) was one of leaders of the campaign 'no to EU'. Only a narrow majority of Swedes voted 'yes' in the referendum, and most rank-and-file members are today sceptical about EU membership. A positive effect of EU (or rather of EEA) membership is the directive on European works councils: Swedish employers had generally refused to conclude international group agreements with their unions in the past.

Swedish Unions facing the Twenty-first Century

Inter-union Tensions in the 1980s followed by New Alliances in the 1990s

The union movement experienced serious tensions in the 1980s. The rise of the public sector 'Gang of Four' symbolized the end of private sector hegemony, while the divisions among private sector unions were demonstrated by the collapse of the LO–PTK alliance. This reflected conflict over whether white-collar workers should be fully compensated for the wage drift of manual workers in manufacturing. Closer relations in the mid-1980s reflected PTK's attempts to strengthen its own internal cohesion by giving priority to low-paid members. But this did not suppress the conflict of interests between PTK unions over pay equalization policies and local union influence on pay determination. With all the PTK unions advocating the extension of negotiating rights at local level, PTK has more or less been dissolved as a bargaining organization since the end of the 1980s.

In the public sector, cleavages began to appear particularly between the more militant TCO cartels and the LO unions SF and Kommunal. Decentralization, and the transfer of teachers from the state sector to local government, led TCO–S and KTK to combine in 1991 in a co-ordinating body, TCO–OF, comprising six 'areas of national unions' (civil servants, military officers, police, SKTF, teachers and nurses), each with bargaining rights and the authority to take industrial action. Similar decentralization has occurred in SACO, but the cartel SACO–S has been retained.

While the 1980s may be characterized as a period of growing inter-union tension, the 1990s have seen the birth of new alliances across old dividing lines. Decentralization has shifted power to national industry unions and paved the way for 'co-operation from below', which appears much more viable than the old formula of 'co-operation from above'. There have been several examples of close sector-based co-operation between LO, TCO and SACO unions in wage negotiations: Metall, SIF and CF in the engineering industry; Kommunal, SKTF and 19 SACO unions in the municipal sector; SEKO, TCO–OF and SACO–S in central government; and the TCO and SACO unions in schools. TCO and SACO unions of military officers have even merged to form a new independent union. A broader form of co-operation is the '8-group' of manufacturing unions (see above). New patterns of co-operation have also been established between white-collar workers previously organized separately on the basis of their level of education. Traditional TCO–SACO rivalry has been superseded by a co-operation agreement, a precondition for SACO's entrance into the European trade union organization, ETUC. In short, the Swedish union map is being remodelled into new co-operative constellations by the forces of decentralization and internationalization.

Table 3.5 Membership of union confederations (in thousands), 1980–96

	LO		TCO		SACO		All unions	
1980	1,889	(61%)	959	(31%)	171	(5%)	3,115	(100%)
1985	2,002	(60%)	1,108	(33%)	218	(6%)	3,350	(100%)
1990	1,962	(58%)	1,144	(34%)	260	(8%)	3,388	(100%)
1995	1,927	(57%)	1,131	(33%)	299	(9%)	3,392	(100%)
1996	1,890	(56%)	1,122	(33%)	310	(9%)	3,358	(100%)

Wage and salary earners including unemployed, but excluding pensioners, students and self-employed.

Table 3.6 Union density (% membership/employed workers) in Sweden 1975–95

	1975	1980/1	1986/7	1990	1995
Manual workers					
Men	84	86	86	81	83
Women	67	80	87	81	85
Both sexes	78	83	87	81	84
Private sector	78	82	84	78	80
Public sector	76	86	91	87	92
White-collar workers					
Men	79	84	82	78	79
Women	78	84	85	83	85
Both sexes	79	84	84	81	82
Private sector	72	77	75	70	73
Public sector	88	91	93	94	94
All workers					
Men	82	84	84	80	81
Women	67	79	83	82	85
Both sexes	75	82	84	81	83
Private sector	73	78	78	74	77
Public sector	79	87	91	91	93

Sources: ULF (Surveys on Living Conditions 1975–86/87, SCB) and AKU (Labour Force Surveys 1990–95, SCB). AKU include all part-time workers, ULF most of them. This means that union density is somewhat exaggerated for 1975–87, especially for women. Correspondingly the decline of density between 1986–7 and 1990 is in reality smaller than appears from the table, again especially with respect to women. Note also that in the first three columns there is an apparent discrepancy because in the separate figures for manual and non-manual workers, but not in the totals for all workers, part-timers working less than 16 hours a week are excluded.

Extremely High but Increasingly Unstable Union Density

Swedish union density is among the highest in the world, having grown almost continuously since the mid-1920s (Kjellberg 1983; 1997). White-collar density at first lagged behind manual, but by the 1970s the gap had been eliminated. It is also notable that the female unionization rate, until the 1980s significantly below the male rate, has now overtaken it (see tables 3.5 and 3.6). This partly reflects the fact that most women are employed in the public sector, but unionization of female manual workers in the private sector has also been rising.

Since its peak of 86 per cent in the mid-1980s, Swedish union density has experienced greater fluctuations that at any time over the past 60 years. By 1990–1 density had declined to 81 per cent before recovering slightly. From an international perspective these changes may appear small, but the average figures conceal relatively large swings among both manual and white-collar workers in the private sector, especially among young workers in big cities. The basic cause is the abrupt shifts in the employment situation in recent years. Union density declined in the period of extremely tight labour markets at the end of the 1980s and the beginning of the 1990s. With exceptionally low unemployment – only about 1 per cent in Greater Stockholm – few people feared losing their jobs, while employers tended to outbid each other to offer favourable terms of employment to individual workers. The tight labour market, the decentralization of wage determination and the expansion of individualized wages for manual workers generated very high levels of wage drift (see table 3.2), an increasing proportion of it outside union control. Under these circumstances many workers felt that they had little need of unions. Within a few years, however, the labour market situation had changed dramatically. From 1991 unemployment rose to levels unknown in Sweden since the 1930s; among young workers it reached 17–18 per cent in 1993–4. Declining union density was reversed, particularly among groups where membership loss had been heavy in the preceding period. Density among young private-sector workers in big cities, which had declined by 10 percentage points in 1987–91, recovered by 7 points between 1991 and 1995.

A closer inspection reveals that the apparent short-term swings in union density may partly be resolved into two different long-term waves. For male manual workers in big cities declining density in 1987–91 fits within a pattern of protracted stagnation and decline (of about 10 percentage points in the private sector between 1975 and 1991). On the other hand, there has been a remarkable long-term growth in union membership among female manual workers which has outstripped all other groups (see table 3.6). (The temporary decline of female density between 1986–7 and 1991 is reduced to 2 percentage points when one allows for the fact that the series starting in 1990 contains far more part-time workers than the preceding one.) As a consequence, the substantial lag in female density in 1975 compared to male manual workers had been replaced 20 years later by a small lead. Among white-collar workers, unionization rates for men and women were already roughly the same by the mid-1970s; in 1995 the female rate clearly outstripped the male.

Union growth among female manual workers is all the more remarkable given that large groups, such as shop assistants and nurse assistants, are regarded as manual workers in Sweden. Moreover, about half of all women classified as manual have a part-time job. The union density of part-timers has been almost as high as that of full-timers. The introduction of union unemployment benefits for part-time workers in the mid-1970s was an important incentive for women to become union members (Bergqvist 1994: 117), but density also rose significantly among full-timers in the subsequent ten years (Kjellberg 1997). Another incentive for unionization was that the casual character of female employment declined with rising female employment. Women's relative wages improved as a result of the increasing demand for labour and solidaristic wage policy. But women's position in the labour market was still weaker than that of men. This probably constituted a third impetus to rising female unionization from the mid-1970s.

While the downward swing at the end of the 1980s was strongest among men, rising female membership was the principal element in the subsequent recovery. The combined effect of increased female employment rates and rising density has profoundly influenced the gender composition of unions. Today a majority – 52 per cent – of 'active' union members (excluding students, pensioners, etc.) in Sweden are women. In LO the proportion is 48 per cent, in TCO 60 per cent and in SACO 48 per cent.

The rise in female unionization was paralleled by political developments. While the swing to the right in the 1980s was stronger among young men than among young women, support for 'socialist' parties (including the social democrats) in the 1990s grew fastest among young female manual workers (SOU 1994: 73). Young women had the most positive attitudes towards wage equalization and the public sector. Women constitute the majority of public-sector employees and are the major beneficiaries of the welfare state; they thus have a clear interest in defending this aspect of the Swedish model (Jenson and Mahon 1993: 95). Strong sex segregation in the Swedish labour market means that women still tend to occupy the most routine and low-paid jobs with least access to training; thus the transformation of work organization towards more enriching jobs is to a large extent an issue of sex equality. This is underlined by increasing pay differentiation following the decentralization of bargaining. As a result of such factors, LO women are increasingly considered to be 'among the most radical and potentially active members of the labour movement' (Jenson and Mahon 1993: 97).

Two socio-political trends are conspicuous: first, a growing instability both of union membership and of voting patterns suggests a more critical stance towards union leaders, politicians, and institutions; second, a radicalization of female manual workers, manifested in rising union density and a growing awareness of women as a radical force within the labour movement. These tendencies pose a profound challenge to the unions, which have to develop new, more flexible forms of organization and methods of working to satisfy the demands of individuals and different groups of members.

The issue of union renewal has also been highlighted by the rapidly rising rate of individual affiliation to unemployment funds. In Sweden, as in Denmark, Finland and Belgium, unemployment funds are administered by the unions. Joining a union automatically brings membership of a union unemployment fund. As the funds are almost completely financed by the government, they are best character-ized as semi-public institutions, over which the government exerts a significant degree of control. Thus it is possible to join a union unemployment fund without being a union member. The fee for direct affiliation is considerably lower than the union membership fee.

Widespread individual affiliation to union unemployment funds is a recent phenomenon. Towards the end of the 1980s, it spread rapidly among white-collar workers in the private sector (Kjellberg 1997). In a tight labour market, these workers saw union unemployment funds as an alternative to, rather than a benefit of, union membership. As the labour market deteriorated, individual affiliation became even more attractive. The highest levels are found in private services. Among LO unions, the highest level is in Handels (14 per cent); among TCO unions, it reaches 28 per cent in HTF. The rate of individual affiliation to the largest TCO fund, that of SIF, was 16 per cent in 1996. In the biggest cities the rate of individual membership is substantially higher. On the other hand, it is still low in the public sector and among manual manufacturing workers.

Union density in the 1990s grew in parallel with the increase in individual affiliation. This reflects the fact that in times of recession Swedish unions have important functions other than administering unemployment benefits. In accordance with the Law on Job Security employers have to negotiate with unions in the event of redundancies. The law allows exceptions to the principle 'last hired – first fired' if the parties conclude a special agreement. This gives employers the flexibility to avoid laying-off key workers, but at the same time it is likely to give union members an advantage over non-members, providing an additional incentive for union membership. Moreover, in times of recession, the demand for collective action probably will be reinforced because of the impaired market position of the individual. The progressive decentralization of bargaining, combined with decreasing standardization of wages, also tends to make the individual worker more dependent upon the union workplace organization. The goods provided by Swedish unions are increasingly non-standardized, as with integration of wage setting with the development of 'competences' and 'rewarding jobs'. Although unions may stress equality of access to such benefits for members and non-members alike, it is natural that in the first instance they should look after the interests of their members. Several factors suggest, therefore, that free-riding is becoming more difficult in the 1990s.

A basic characteristic of Swedish unions, promoting their ability to recruit and retain members, is the role played by the union workplace organization (see below), which represents a decentralized and small-scale feature in the otherwise centralized Swedish union system. At workplaces with no union representation, social and instrumental reasons for joining are often lacking and rates of individual affiliation to unemployment funds considerably higher.

To explain the very high union density in Sweden the combined effects of decentralized and centralized aspects of the industrial relations system must be taken into account. As a consequence of the early development of centralized industrial relations and the rising density of employers' associations, agreements confirming the right to organize cover almost all workers. Many small workplaces however have no union representatives or clubs, in some cases because of anti-union employers (not affiliated to employers' associations), but mostly because of the lack of potential activists. Another effect of centralization is that closed shops never gained ground in Sweden: as early as 1905–06, the unions acknowledged the employers' right to hire and fire workers freely.

In the absence of closed shop agreements Swedish unions have to rely on the readiness of the individual to join. Collective pressure for union membership may exist at some workplaces, but nowadays only a small minority of workers give this as reason for joining (Kjellberg 1997). Nor are many rank-and-file members any longer motivated by an ideological commitment. Instead most have instrumental motives for belonging to a union. This does not mean, however, that they act as isolated individuals. A substantial proportion are strongly influenced by fellow-workers, union representatives, parents and so on in deciding to join a union. Instrumental incentives may themselves include a collective aspect both with regard to ends – the promotion of common interests – and means – united action against the employer.

Efforts to Bring Unions Closer to Rank-and-file Members

The decline of ideological motivation has increased the pressure on unions to respond to members' demands. Most unions lay heavy stress on improving communication with rank-and-file members. The decentralization of industrial relations and the increasingly critical stance of workers towards established institutions have intensified efforts to create 'unions close to the members' (*medlemsnära fack*). The growing proportion of women members, the rising educational levels of young workers, and the spread of non-Taylorist forms of work organization have all encouraged unions to give higher priority to the individual member – and to groups of members. At the same time, however, they have to continue to demonstrate the advantages of collective action. Otherwise, there is a risk that growing numbers of members will prefer purely individual solutions, and that the expectations of women and other groups will be frustrated.

Union workplace organizations play a double role in the unions' response to the new challenges. First, their tasks have been enlarged by the decentralization of collective bargaining and the introduction of new wage systems linked to changes in work organization. Second, they are central to the search for more flexible and participative work methods within the unions themselves. Informal meetings have been introduced to complement large, formal meetings dominated by union representatives; temporary work groups have been set up to break down the Taylorist division of labour within the unions and to produce more rapid results. The aim is, above all, to make unions more accessible to rank-and-file members and to encourage their initiatives. A prominent example is the *Kom An* (Come On) project of Kommunal (Swedish Municipal Workers' Union) (Higgins 1996; *Kom An!* 1995). About 150,000 members, mostly women, have taken part in local *Kom An* projects aimed at improving the quality and efficiency of work through changes in work organization and new wage systems. This is intended to increase the scope for local pay increases in a sector traditionally characterized by centralized bargaining. Interest in union matters has increased significantly in the workplaces concerned.

The new emphasis is on working *with* the members rather than *for* them, and on rediscovering the spirit of unionism as a popular movement. Today most members conceive unions as centralized institutions in which formal structures of representation predominate (Kjellberg 1997). At the same time, there have been calls for unions to turn themselves into service organizations, working *for* (serving) members. The outcome will probably be unions that work *with* as well as *for* members, involving them in the setting and implementation of union objectives, but also providing support and services for individual members.

One of the intentions of union renewal is to develop work methods and organizational forms more suitable for the growing numbers of female members and young workers. Although every second LO member is a woman, men account for nine out of ten officials of LO and its affiliated unions (LO 1996a: 8, 39), and the ratio of union representatives among LO women fell between 1988 and 1993 while that for men rose (LO 1989: 86; LO 1994a/part4: 60). Women are most seriously under-represented at higher levels (LO 1996b: 17–18). The proportion of women in the decision-making bodies of union confederations (particularly LO and TCO) is far below their share of membership (Bergqvist 1994: 126–30). However, parity of representation has been given high priority in important unions like Metall and Kommunal (Mahon 1996: 562). In 1991 an informal network of LO women (*Tjejligan* – 'the women's gang') was created to improve the self-esteem of women and act as a forum for exchanging ideas and experiences. The overall efforts to bring unions closer to rank-and-file members are probably even more important for increasing female participation in union affairs.

Workplace Organization

Tasks of Union Workplace Organizations

In Sweden, as in other Nordic countries, union workplace organizations are the dominant form of representation at workplace level. This contrasts with the continental European model of works councils, which are formally separate from union organization in Germany, the Netherlands and elsewhere. Workplace 'clubs' were completely integrated at an early stage with national unions and their local branches. Following the establishment of industry-wide bargaining at the beginning of the twentieth century, union workplace organizations retained important negotiating tasks. National contracts had to be adjusted to local conditions, and the widespread use of piece-work required more or less continuous activity.

Distribution functions continue to be important. Union clubs negotiate workplace contracts on pay, working hours, and so on within industry agreements. (In those, mainly small, workplaces without union clubs, negotiations are carried out by officials from the local union branch, which also provides assistance where necessary to union clubs.) They also negotiate the introduction of new pay systems, profit-sharing arrangements, and (under the 1974 Law on Job Security) redundancies. Under the MBL (Law on Co-determination) they have competence in the settlement of conflicts over the interpretation and application of laws and agreements. In recent decades production issues have been given higher priority. The production role of union clubs covers the election of health and safety representatives; participation in project groups, joint committees and company boards; and influencing the working environment, the design of work organization, and new technology. A final set of functions concerns the representation of members in the workplace, handling individual grievances and problems. In large workplace clubs, 'representative assemblies' are organized for elected representatives, but smaller clubs, and sub-units of large clubs, arrange their own meetings of union members. Clubs also organize study circles. In large firms they elect representatives to union group organizations and European works councils.

Since the 1970s, the tasks of union workplace organizations have grown in scope and complexity. This reflects the expansion of labour legislation in the 1970s, the decentralization of collective bargaining from the 1980s, and growing union aspirations to influence production issues. According to a survey, however, the average LO, TCO and SACO member still considers that the most important tasks are, for the most part, the traditional ones of pay, job security, and protection against loss of income in case of sickness and unemployment (LO 1993: 14–9). Two other issues – sex equality (a recent development) and the working environment – are given the same high priority. However, when work environment is narrowed down to particular issues such as 'influence over one's own work' and 'development of job content', its importance drops sharply (although in an earlier survey respondents emphasize the importance of jobs that promote personal development – LO 1991b: 279).

Despite the extensive network of union workplace organizations, Swedish workers see relatively little scope for influencing the actions of the local union (an average of 3 points on a scale of 1–10 in 1992–3), and have little confidence in the union's ability to influence workplace conditions (3.7 points). (The estimations of manufacturing workers were 3.3 and 4.1 respectively – SCB 1996: 255–6.) In general, survey findings reveal declining membership confidence in unions, among manual as well as white-collar workers; between 1980 and 1990 the proportion of members who were 'fairly' or 'very confident' in trade unions fell by about 10 percentage points (LO 1991b: 279).

Union workplace organization is widespread, and requires a large number of union representatives. In 1993, every seventh LO member performed some task for the union. For the white-collar members of TCO and SACO unions, this proportion was somewhat higher (LO 1994a/part 4: 60–2). The proportion of union representatives was significantly lower among LO women (8 per cent) than among men (19 per cent) (pp. 64–6). A similar cleavage existed among TCO members (13 and 19 per cent respectively) and SACO members (14 and 21 per cent).

The facilities of union clubs tended to improve in the 1980s. Employer resistance to union activities during working time was at least partly overcome, as a result of the 1974 Law on Shop Stewards. In 1993, about 40 per cent of LO members attending meetings were able to do so during working time; the figure rose to 60 per cent in the metal-working sector, but was only 25 per cent in local government (p. 39). The availability of paid time off may contribute to the relatively high level of attendance at meetings, but may also conceal a lack of membership interest in union matters. An indication of increasing passivity is the declining participation in study circles arranged by unions. Calculations for LO show that one in seven members attended such circles in 1980–1, and fewer than one in eleven in 1995–6.

Unions in the Workplace: Co-determination of Change

In the 1970s, great hopes were invested in the MBL law as a means of increasing the influence of union workplace organizations. The law recommended that employers and unions conclude agreements on 'co-determination' and it required employers to negotiate over major changes in operations, working conditions or terms of employment affecting union members.

There was a contradiction in the legislation between the legal requirements on employers to negotiate, and the recommendation to regulate co-determination by agreements. Although unions had a right to participate in the decision-making process, the employers were free to act as they thought best, provided that they had first informed the unions and given them an opportunity to present their views. The unions faced the obvious risk that employers would refuse to negotiate seriously. The impact of the law therefore depended on the attitudes of employers, and ultimately on power relations in society.

While central co-determination agreements were concluded fairly quickly in the public sector, the negative stance of private sector employers delayed agreement until 1982. The profound shift in the political and ideological climate was reflected in the 1982 'Development Agreement' on co-determination (UVA), concluded between SAF and LO/PTK after 6 years of negotiations. The agreement stressed the common endeavour to improve the efficiency, profitability and competitiveness of enterprises, rather than specific rights of co-determination. Thus the unions were obliged to abandon their radical positions of the 1970s and return to the earlier policy of co-operation.

The UVA nevertheless implied some change of approach on the part of employers. They accepted the need to involve union workplace organizations in order to increase productivity. The UVA provided for co-determination through negotiations at different levels and through participation in joint bodies and projects, allowing considerably more flexibility and adjustment to local conditions than the procedures established by the MBL law. The approach was largely based on ideas originally drawn up by SAF's technical department in the mid-1970s. From the unions' perspective, the UVA could be seen as an instrument for adapting the co-determination system to the employers' strategies of decentralization, while maximizing union influence on the process. The agreement acknowledged the right of unions to participate in the planning of work organization, with the aim of enriching and enlarging the jobs of individual workers, and in improving the work environment. In addition, workers 'should be given opportunities to participate in planning their own work'. While employers' aspirations for decentralized industrial relations have been one force for change, workplace unions have also promoted new forms of work organization, and improvements in the working environment.

In many cases, both parties prefer informal solutions going beyond the scope of the UVA. Edlund et al. (1989: 30) concluded that there had been 'a genuine shift in favour of more bipartite decision-making' at workplace level. At the Volvo plant in Olofström, for example, co-determination takes place largely through joint bodies rather than through traditional negotiations. This reflects the decentralized and flexible character of the UVA, compared with the state sector agreement, which emphasizes the role of negotiations between local union and management. At Volvo there are a number of 'partnership and co-determination groups' parallel to the lower levels of line management, but in the 1980s, management already considered them too slow for communicating important information to employees. Information was therefore increasingly given directly to workers. Thus direct employee participation tended to replace union participation at this level. According to a more recent study (1992) management and unions consider these forms of co-determination unsatisfactory. The decisive contact between management and unions has shifted to the top co-determination body in the plant. Above plant level, there are also co-determination arrangements at international level (through the European works council), at the level of the Volvo group in Sweden, and in individual companies within the Volvo group.

Surveys of the development of co-determination indicate a trend break about 1982, the year the UVA was concluded (Hart and Hörte 1989). A period in which co-determination became 'established' (1977–82) was followed by a new phase implying a change in employer strategy: negotiation and information functions were increasingly performed through 'integrated' arrangements, i.e. by joint negotiating committees established by management in co-operation with unions – for budgets and finance, personnel administration, etc. Unions also participated increasingly in project groups, a manifestation of the employers' aspirations, expressed in the 1982 UVA agreement, to increased flexibility.

The system of co-determination has become more complex as a result of the growing number of decision-making bodies. This has widened the scope for local union participation and influence, but may also have led to increasingly heterogeneous union policies across workplaces. The study by Levinson (1997) confirms the variety of co-determination methods across companies and at different decision-making levels. It also demonstrates considerable variation in union activity and methods according to the different phases of the decision-making process: initiation, preparation, decision-taking, and implementation. The unions' weak point appears to be their passivity in the early phases of decision-making. Their participation and influence is highest in the phase of formal decision-taking, but by then management is often already committed. Since the mid-1980s, however, union initiatives at earlier stages have increased. Consequently 'mixed' forms of co-determination – in which union participation in the decision-making process is combined with negotiation – have become more common, especially with the increased influence of production teams, while the pure negotiation model has declined. This has put pressure on unions to renew their own work methods. Unions are especially active on issues directly affecting their members: workforce reductions, relocations, changes in work organization and the introduction of new technology. Three out of four managers (nine out of ten in large companies) in Levinson's survey see union participation as positive.

The Transformation of Work Organization: The Car Industry as a Pioneer

Swedish employers had several motives for changing work organization. First, in a small export-oriented economy highly exposed to international competition, employers were under increased pressure to achieve flexibility and reduce costs, while at the same time harnessing workers' skills and commitment; in this context, fordist and Taylorist concepts appeared increasingly ineffective. Second, low unemployment up to the 1990s, small wage differentials and generous social welfare policies created recruitment and retention difficulties, high sickness absence and added to pressures on labour costs.

Berggren, in his study of the Swedish car industry since 1970 (1993: chs 4, 9), emphasizes such social and labour market factors as important agents of change. Volvo's efforts to apply 'small-scale manual technologies', with long cycle times, autonomous work groups with voluntary membership, and no traditional first-line supervisors, most notably at the Uddevalla plant (1989–93), have been confined to its plants in Sweden. It was the specific combination of top management 'philosophy' (different from that in the other two Swedish motor vehicle manufacturers, Saab and Scania), co-operative labour-management relations and the 'open' technological culture of the enterprise, as well as the social and labour market conditions in Sweden, that made the Udevalla concept possible. Auer and Riegler (1990) likewise attribute the change in production concepts in the Swedish car industry in the 1980s to a combination of social and labour market conditions favourable to workers and unions, changing product demand, and employers' decentralization strategies.

The principal reason for the closure of the Udevalla plant in 1993, followed by the Kalmar plant in 1994, was not changing labour market conditions, or inefficiency – both these plants had good performance records – but their small size compared to Volvo's main plants (Torslanda in Gothenburg and Ghent in Belgium). The large Torslanda union clubs dominated the weaker ones at Uddevalla and Kalmar. When drastically falling demand for cars forced Volvo to cut production, Uddevalla and Kalmar lost out to an 'unholy' alliance between mass-production managers and Torslanda unionists defending traditional Gothenburg jobs rather than humanized jobs elsewhere (Berggren 1995: 118–20). Moreover, Renault (which at the time was Volvo's major shareholder although the planned merger fell through) demanded that excess capacity should be eliminated by closing the smaller plants.

The closure of the Uddevalla plant was a major setback for the policy of 'solidaristic work' advocated by the Metalworkers' Union (see below). The plant was seen as a model both for the implementation of this concept, with strong union participation during the planning process, and for changes in work organization, with skilled workers building whole cars. Nevertheless, despite a radically different labour market situation in the 1990s, there are some indications that the Uddevalla concept may have a future. Like lean production, it gives a high priority to customer orientation, flexibility, and worker involvement and learning; by contrast with lean production, it presupposes a greater confidence in workers' capacity to accommodate to long production cycles (Sandberg 1995). Uddevalla was superior to the Torslanda plant in model changes and in small series: it is significant that Volvo, in co-operation with the British company TWR, has re-opened the plant (called AutoNova) to produce limited-series cabriolet and coupé models. Humanized concepts have also survived in Volvo's engine and truck plants and some aspects have been introduced at Torslanda and Ghent (cars), although mixed with Japanese-inspired productions systems (Fröhlich and Pekruhl 1996: 88–91).

Other leading employers seem prepared to continue their efforts to transform work organization. In the motor vehicle sector, Scania has introduced changes in work organization in close co-operation with the unions at its truck plant in Södertälje; a representative of the Södertälje metal club described the new systems as '90 per cent of Metall's "good job"' (*Metallarbetaren* 11, 1995). The Swiss–Swedish electrical engineering company ABB has introduced 'self-governing groups' as a way of drastically reducing delivery times. At ABB Distribution, the groups are responsible for the whole cycle of operations, from orders to delivery. The new system means more varied jobs, increased responsibility, fewer supervisors, and greater co-operation between manual and white-collar workers. A number of 'co-worker agreements' with harmonized conditions for manual and white-collar employees have been concluded at ABB subsidiaries.

Efforts of Employers and Unions to Integrate Work Organization and Pay Determination

The introduction of common local wage systems for different types of workers could be seen as a logical complement to new forms of work organization. With the decentralization and individualization of pay, individual and group performance will be more important in determining remuneration than membership of broad categories such as manual or white-collar employees. However, the views of employers and unions differ in some respects. LO has accepted the introduction of flexible, individualized wage systems among manual workers as a means of encouraging workers to enlarge their skills and open the way for more integrated and varied jobs (LO 1991a). But the unions wish to relate wages exclusively to systematic job evaluation, and reject the 'subjective' appraisal of individual qualities which would turn pay into an instrument of managerial control. Moreover, the unions are not prepared to abandon the two-tier system of bargaining. This stance also applies to co-worker agreements. The Metall, SIF and CF clubs at ABB, Ericsson and Volvo have jointly stated their opposition to local co-worker agreements in the absence of a common national agreement. However, given increasingly co-ordinated bargaining across the manual/white-collar divide in the 1990s (see above), national co-worker agreements providing a framework for subsequent local deals seem likely to be introduced in the not too distant future. With respect to general terms of employment (working hours, etc.) public sector unions already have co-worker agreements, as do workers in the paper and pulp sector.

In the Metall report 'Good Work' (1985), a strategy had been outlined for the 'Development of Work' on the basis of group-based work organization, integral job training, and the encouragement of job enlargement through payment systems. The 1989 Metall report 'Solidaristic Work Policy for Good Jobs', elaborated further the connection between work organization and wage issues. Squeezed between the dismantling of centralized bargaining and employers' efforts to transform pay into an instrument of management, the union concept of solidarity was reformulated to cover 'production' as well as 'distribution' issues. Through continuous training and a gradual expansion of tasks, the individual worker would benefit from enlarged job content as well as economic rewards. Thus pay differentials could be used as incentives to encourage workers to climb a skills 'ladder', developing their competence in the performance of an increasing number of tasks within a more flexible and democratic work organization. Work groups in which tasks were horizontally and vertically integrated were recommended as a way of achieving 'rewarding jobs' (cf. Mahon 1991: 306–11).

The accelerated integration of pay determination and work organization, as well as the continued decentralization of bargaining and the introduction of European Works Councils, imply a shift in power within unions from national wage negotiators to workplace and company- or group-level organizations. Whether or not this will create fragmented 'company unions' will depend on the national unions' success in co-ordinating and supporting the development of local union expertise to meet the new demands.

Another challenge for the unions is to encourage active membership participation, without which they are unlikely to be able to propose local pay systems, new work organization and training facilities that respond to members' views and aspirations. For example, the problem of individualized wage-setting ('subjective' versus 'objective' criteria, individual versus collective aspects) is likely to be best resolved at the level of the workers themselves, by the members of each work team, although wage principles might be an issue for the workplace club or higher union levels (cf. Fägerborg 1996: 158, 226–27, 243–45). Both LO and TCO unions are today energetically attempting to develop appropriate forms of workplace union activity that go beyond traditional wage negotiations.

A third challenge is to deal with conflicting interests at workplace level between manual and white-collar workers. This problem is aggravated by the almost complete separation of manual and white-collar workers into different national unions and confederations in Sweden. At the Alfa Laval plants in Lund, the dominant white-collar union, SIF, resisted the development of work groups for fear of losing additional jobs to manual metalworkers (LO 1990). At the Volvo Torslanda plant, a similar move by white-collar workers was prevented by a coalition between the company and the Metall club (Ahlstrand 1996: 31–6, 41–2, 66–7). In the long run, the solution to this dilemma would be a merger of manual and white-collar unions. In the meantime, co-worker agreements may be a practicable means of easing tensions, but the entrenched positions of employers and unions have first to be overcome. At the new AutoNova plant in Uddevalla, a co-worker agreement was concluded, even before production started; this required the white-collar union SIF to abandon the traditional job control system (*SIF-tidningen* 19, 1995).

Fourth, unions are confronted with the task of making 'good jobs' accessible to all workers and of preventing a polarization of jobs between and within work-places. Until the 1990s there was a pronounced polarization between a relatively small proportion of stimulating jobs and a growing number of monotonous and physically stressful jobs, often occupied by women. Sizeable devaluations of the currency tended to conserve an obsolete industrial structure, but polarization was also a consequence of the decline of 'basic industries' (pulp and paper, mining) and the expansion of the 'industries of the future' (electronics, transport equip-ment, pharmaceuticals) with a low proportion of skilled manual jobs and a high proportion of less-skilled manual jobs and of qualified white-collar employment (Landell and Victorsson 1991: 9, 113–16). In the 1990s, however, there has been a shift in favour of skilled jobs, with the deep recession of 1992–4 above all affecting unskilled workers in manufacturing and the public sector (LU 1994: 94–5). This is confirmed by a Metall report (Metall 1995a), which points to structural transformation and changes in work organization as causal factors. The turning-point occurred at the end of the 1980s: between 1988 and 1994 the proportion of metalworkers in 'intensive' jobs with short cycle times declined from one in two to one in three. However, by no means all jobs requiring increased skill and flexibility can be seen as 'good jobs'. Changes were followed in most cases by increasing intensity of work (60 per cent of men and women) and stress (35 per cent of men, 42 per cent of women). In all, around 80 per cent of metalworkers were affected by changes in work organization (mostly including teamwork) in 1994, twice as many as in 1988. As many as 58 per cent were involved in teamwork combined with pay systems promoting learning. But only 36 per cent also had individual training plans. The figure was reduced to 26 per cent of workers who experienced these innovations and reported the existence of a representative elected by the team, and to 10 per cent where there were self-governing teams with planning tasks. No more than 4 per cent of jobs fulfilled the strict union definition of a 'good job'.

The introduction of new work organization is, at best, a process of compromise between the enterprise's objectives of increased productivity and profits and the unions' demands for good jobs. Not surprisingly, lean production methods combined with group bonuses tend to encourage the exclusion of slower workers from teams operating an intense pace of work. At Volvo's Torslanda plant, all workers were in principle offered 'developing' jobs on the assembly line, but many of them were not considered to have suitable attitudes or physical ability (Ahlstrand 1996: 68–71). Moreover, the new wage system, designed to promote quality, short lead times and learning, in practice excluded a relatively high number of workers, who were given other tasks or offered early retirement (pp. 72–7).

A related tendency in engineering companies is to recruit young well-educated male workers at the expense of unemployed, female and older workers (*Metallarbetaren* 1, 1996). The clamour by employers for changes in the Law on Job Security may partly be explained by their preference for recruiting young well-educated workers rather than developing the competences of more senior employees. (The Metalworkers' union has for years demanded a 'competence agreement' guaranteeing training for all its members – so far without success.) In addition to changes in labour law, employers have pushed for increased wage differentials to retain the minority of workers in whom substantial educational resources have been invested. A further problem is that new wage systems have not always been introduced to accompany changes in work organization (LO 1994b: 45).

To sum up, there are several difficulties restricting the implementation of the union concept of 'good work'. First, mass unemployment in the 1990s put the focus on job security, and union efforts to change work organization lost momentum, at least in the private sector. At the same time, employers accelerated the introduction of lean production methods. Second, the implementation of the Metall reports on 'Good Work' (1985) and 'Solidaristic Work Policy' (1989) was hampered by shortcomings in union organization and methods of working. A 1995 Metall report criticized the union for lacking a consistent overall policy for implementing 'Good Work': for example, the new wage system accepted under the 1988 Engineering agreement was at odds with the union's policy of 'Solidaristic Work' (Metall 1995b). Moreover, the union failure to elaborate a coherent strategy on job enrichment and competence development reflected, according to the report, the persistence of a Taylorist division of labour at union headquarters. Although a range of courses and conferences were provided, a study circle aimed at rank-and-file members was never set up. Likewise, few of the workers affected by changes in work organization seem to have participated in shaping the changes.

The failure of the union to involve officials and rank-and-file members in broad discussions about these issues is contrasted with Kommunal's successful 'Come On' project (previously mentioned in this chapter). Local government employers frequently use Kommunal's educational package on changes in work organization and the development of public services. Again the conclusion is that to have an impact on 'production' issues, unions have to adopt a participative model and mobilize their members. After all, new work organization can only be implemented by rank-and-file members themselves, even if support from higher levels is of crucial importance. The transition from an organization whose function is wage bargaining to one dealing with integrated distribution and production issues at workplace level requires what might be called 're-articulated' unions (cf. Crouch 1994), that is a revised, but still close, relationship between different union levels.

Nevertheless, the concept of 'good work' is now firmly established in public awareness as a result of the activities of the Metalworkers' Union. Despite high unemployment there are several examples of the successful implementation of 'good work', indicated by the relatively high percentage of metalworkers involved in team work combined with pay systems promoting learning. Of crucial importance is the strength of union workplace organizations and their ability to shape lean production and flexibility initiatives in order to make the requirements of competitiveness compatible with the ideas of 'good work'.

Conclusions

In recent decades, the Swedish model of industrial relations has undergone profound change. First, private sector employers, headed by the big transnational engineering firms that dominate the Swedish economy, lost confidence in the centralized bargaining system following the abortive 1980 lockout and have since pursued a strategy of decentralization. The 1980 conflict also signalled the decline of the traditional LO–SAF axis. These employers have seized the initiative in the 1980s and 1990s. On co-determination, a compromise was reached largely on their terms in the Development Agreement of 1982, acknowledging demands for flexibility and decentralization. At the workplace, management took the lead in integrating production and wage issues, but the unions soon elaborated their own 'solidaristic' version of 'good' and 'rewarding' jobs. Tight labour markets, generous social welfare provisions, high union density, relatively powerful union workplace organizations, strong and co-operative local relations, and changing product markets paved the way for local compromises on humanized work organization and new wage systems, culminating in such post-Fordist experiments as the Volvo Uddevalla plant. At national level, the unions have accepted the continuous decentralization of bargaining and a greater spread of wages, provided that the two-tier negotiation system is not abandoned and that individual workers are given the chance to develop their jobs and perform increasingly complex tasks. 'Solidaristic work policy' is replacing 'solidaristic wage policy' as the unions' slogan.

Despite the transition from 'full employment' to mass unemployment in the 1990s, the strike capacity of national unions appear intact, at the same time as lean production makes employers increasingly vulnerable to labour conflicts. Tight labour markets in the early 1990s and a rising strike frequency subsequently have demonstrated the weak points of a relatively decentralized bargaining structure. With the old formula of centralized self-regulation apparently no longer applicable, the state has increasingly intervened since the 1980s to restore co-ordinated bargaining, a development reaching its climax in the tripartite Rehnberg Stabilization Agreement and its successor. These interventions might be described as economy-wide centralization through state regulation, and in the latter case through informal and voluntary processes co-ordinated by state mediators. However, increasingly centrifugal forces in the 1995 bargaining round exposed the fragility of this arrangement. The employers demand a strengthening of the powers of state mediators and tighter regulation of labour conflicts.

Compared with the 1970s, therefore, the objective of state regulation has shifted. Legislation introduced in that decade, in such areas as co-determination and job security, responded to union demands for restrictions on the power of employers on production issues. This agenda has been replaced by employer demands for a weakening of the role of unions: at the political level, through the ending of corporatist representation; at the workplace, through the loosening of job security regulations and so on; and in pay determination in general. In both phases, the traditional emphasis on co-operation and agreement through central-ized self-regulation has been abandoned in favour of legislation.

In recent decades, the cohesion of the labour movement has been weakened by the emergence of new conflicts between different groups of workers – manual and white-collar, public and private. In the 1990s, however, the employers' militant decentralization strategy has brought manual and white-collar unions closer together, especially in engineering. The unanimous union response to employers' demands for completely decentralized wage determination and co-worker agree-ments has been to defend the two-tier bargaining system. Consequently, any local co-worker agreements introduced in the future will have – on union insistence – to be preceded by national ones.

Another consequence of decentralization is the intense efforts of unions to renew their working methods in order to come closer to their members. Declining union density at the end of the 1980s and the increasing proportion of female members have also put union renewal high on the agenda. Finally, the integration of pay and production issues at the local level has meant that issues of justice and solidarity have increasingly to be dealt with by rank-and-file members themselves. While Swedish unions, with their extensive network of workplace organizations, may appear well able to adapt to such challenges, further decentralization and reorganization appear inevitable.

The formation of strong new union constellations across confederal and blue-collar/white-collar lines will certainly be an important element if the co-operative features associated with the traditional Swedish model are to be restored. There are currently indications that the labour market parties are prepared to come to agreements on future pay determination. However, given the large number of bargaining partners, the state will be required to play a relatively active role in the co-ordination and regulation of procedures. In short, there is likely to be a mix of self-regulation and state regulation.

| Abbreviations

AMS   *Arbetsmarknadsstyrelsen* – Labour Market Board
CF   *Civilingenjörsförbundet* – Swedish Association of Graduate Engineers
Handels   *Handelsanställdas förbund* – The Commercial Employees' Union
HTF   *Handelstjänstemannaförbundet* – Union of Commercial Salaried Employees
Kommunal   *Svenska Kommunalarbetareförbundet* (SKAF) – Swedish Municipal Workers' Union
KTK   *Kommunaltjänstemannakartellen* – Federation of Salaried Local Government Employees
LO   *Landsorganisationen* – Swedish Federation of Trade Unions
MBL   *Medbestämmandelagen* – Act on Co-determination at Work
Metall   *Svenska Metallindustriarbetareförbundet* – Swedish Metalworkers' Union
PTK   *Privattjänstemannakartellen* – Federation of Salaried Employees in Industry and Services

SACO	*Sveriges Akademikers Centralorganisation* – Swedish Confederation of Professional Associations
SACO–S	*SACOs statliga förhandlingskartell* – SACO Section for State Employees
SAF	*Svenska Arbetsgivareföreningen* – Swedish Employers' Confederation
SF/SEKO	*Statsanställdas förbund* – Swedish State Employees' Union (since 1995 SEKO – Union of Service and Communication)
SIF	*Svenska Industritjänstemannaförbundet* – Swedish Union of Clerical and Technical Employees
SKTF	*Sveriges Kommunaltjänstemannaförbund* – Swedish Union Local Government Officers
TCO	*Tjänstemännens Centralorganisation* – Swedish Confederation of Professional Employees
TCO–OF	*TCOs förhandlingsråd för offentliganställda* – Negotiating Council of TCO for Public Employees
TCO–S	TCO Section for State Employees
UVA	*Utvecklingsavtalet* – Development Agreement
VF/VI	*Verkstadsföreningen (Sveriges Verkstadsindustrier)* – Swedish Engineering Employers' Association (Association of Swedish Engineering Industries)

Notes

1 This chapter was written with financial support from the Swedish Council For Work Life Research.
2 The Nordic countries covered in this volume are Denmark, Finland, Norway and Sweden. 'Scandinavia' excludes Finland.

References and Further Reading

Åberg, R. 1994: Wage Control and Cost-push Inflation in Sweden since 1960. In R. Dore et al. (eds.), *The Return to Incomes Policy*. London: Pinter.

Ahlstrand, R. 1996: *En tid av förändring*. Lund: Department of Sociology. Research Report 1996:1.

Alasoini, T. 1993: Strikes in a changing technological context. In P. Kettunen (ed.), *Strike and Social Change*. Turku: Turku Provincial Museum.

Albåge, L.-G. 1996: En medlares tankar inför 2000-talet. In *Verkstadsindustrin, lönebildningen och framtiden*. Stockholm: Industrilitteratur.

Auer, P. and Riegler, C. 1990: *Post-Taylorism*. Stockholm: Arbetsmiljöfonden.

Berggren, C. 1993: *The Volvo Experience*. London: Macmillan.

Berggren, C. 1995: The Fate of Branch Plants – Performance Versus Power. In Å. Sandberg (ed.) 1995. *Enriching Production. Perspectives on Volvo's Uddevalla plant as an alternative to lean production*. Aldershot: Avebury.

Bergqvist, C. 1994: *Mäns makt och kvinnors intressen*, Uppsala: Statsvetenskapliga föreningen.

Crouch, C. 1994: *Industrial Relations and European State Traditions*. Oxford: Clarendon.

de Geer, H. 1992: *The Rise and Fall of the Swedish Model*. Chichester: Garden Publications.

Edin, P.-A. & Holmlund, B. 1992: *The Swedish Wage Structure: The Rise and Fall of Solidarity Policy?* Uppsala: Department of Economics.

Edlund, S. et al. 1989: *Views on Co-determination in Swedish Working Life.* Lund: Juristförlaget.

Elvander, N. 1988: *Den svenska modellen.* Stockholm: Almänna förlaget.

Elvander, N. 1990: Income policies in the Nordic countries. *International Labour Review,* 129(1), 1–21.

Elvander, N. 1992: *Lönepolitik och förhandlingssystem i Sverige.* Uppsala: Department of Economics.

Elvander, N. 1996: *1995 års avtalsrörelse.* Stockholm: Arbetslivsinstitutet 1996: 27.

Fägerborg, E. 1996: *Miljoner och my.* Stockholm: Nordiska museet.

Financial Times 1997: European Top 500. 24 January 1997.

Frölich, D. & Pekruhl, U. 1996: *Direct Participation and Organisational Change.* Dublin: European Foundation.

Glyn, A. 1995: Social democracy and full employment. *New Left Review* 211, 33–55.

Hägglund S. & Degerblad J.-E. 1994: *Att bygga Europa. Arbetsmiljön och det korporativa samhället.* Stockholm: Carlssons.

Hart, H. and Hörte, S.-Å. 1989: *Medbestämmandets stagnation.* Göteborg: Arbetsvet. Kollegiet.

Hibbs, D.-A. 1991: Market forces, trade union ideology and trends in Swedish wage dispersion. *Acta Sociologica,* 34(2), 89–102.

Hibbs, D.-A. & Locking H. 1996: Wage compression, wage drift and wage inflation in Sweden. *Labour Economics,* 3, 109–41.

Higgins, W. 1996: The Swedish Municipal Workers' Union – a study in the new political unionism. *Economic and Industrial Democracy* 17(2), 167–95.

I takt med Europa (1995). Stockholm: LO, SAF etc.

Iversen, T. 1996: Power, flexibility, and the breakdown of centralised wage bargaining. *Comparative Politics,* 4, 399–436.

Jenson, J. & Mahon, R. 1993: Representing solidarity: Class, gender and the crisis in social-democratic Sweden. *New Left Review,* 201, 76–100.

Katzenstein, P.-J. 1985: *Small States in World Markets.* Ithaca and London: Cornell University Press.

Kjellberg, A. 1983: *Facklig organisering i tolv länder.* Lund: Arkiv.

Kjellberg, A. 1992: Sweden: Can the model survive. In Ferner, A. & Hyman, R. (eds) *Industrial Relations in the New Europe.* Oxford: Blackwell.

Kjellberg, A. 1997: *Fackliga organisationer och medlemmar i dagens Sverige.* Lund: Arkiv.

Kom An! Teoriboken. Stockholm: Komanco 1995.

Korpi, W. 1978: *The Working Class in Welfare Capitalism.* London: Routledge & Kegan Paul.

Korpi, W. 1983: *The Democratic Class Struggle.* London: Routledge & Kegan Paul.

Landell, E. and Victorsson, J. 1991: *Långt kvar till kunskapssamhället.* Stockholm: SIND.

Levinson, K. 1997: Medbestämmande i förändring. *Arbetsmarknad & Arbetsliv* 3(2), 109–21.

LO 1989: *Röster om facket och jobbet* part 4. Stockholm: LO.

LO 1990: *Demokrati och inflytande i arbetslivet.* Stockholm: LO/Tiden.

LO 1991a: *Det utvecklande arbetet.* Stockholm: LO.

LO 1991b: *Rättvisa i vågskålen.* Stockholm: LO.

LO 1993: *Röster om facket och jobbet* part 1. Stockholm: LO.

LO 1994a: *Röster om facket och jobbet* part 3, 4. Stockholm: LO.

LO 1994b: *Utveckling i arbetet.* Stockholm: LO.

LO 1996a: *Kvinnor i facket.* Stockholm: LO.

LO 1996b: *Klass och kön.* Stockholm: LO.

LU 1994: *Näringslivets tillväxtförutsättningar till 2010.* Stockholm: Nutek.

Mahon, R. 1991: From solidaristic wages to solidaristic work. *Economic and Industrial Democracy,* **12**(3), 195–325.

Mahon, R. 1994: Wage-earners and/or co-workers. *Economic and Industrial Democracy,* **15**(3), 355–83.

Mahon, R. 1996: Women wage earners and the future of Swedish unions. *Economic and Industrial Democracy,* **17**(4), 545–86.

Martin, A. 1995: The Swedish Model: Demise or Reconfiguration? In R. Locke, R.T. Kochan and M. Piore (eds), *Employment Relations in a Changing World Economy.* Cambridge Mass.: MIT Press.

Metall 1985: *Det goda arbetet.* Stockholm: Metall.

Metall 1995a: *Metallarbetet och metallönen.* Stockholm: Metall.

Metall 1995b: *Rapportbok.* Stockholm: Metall.

Pestoff, V. 1995: Towards a new Swedish model of collective bargaining and politics. In C. Crouch and F. Traxler (eds), *Organised Industrial Relations in Europe: What Future?* Aldershot: Avebury.

Pontusson, J. & Swenson, P. 1996: Labor markets, production strategies, and wage bargaining institutions. *Comparative Political Studies,* **29**(2), 223–50.

Rapport om 1993 års avtalsrörelse på den svenska arbetsmarknaden. Ibid 1995 (unpublished reports of state mediators) Stockholm: Statens förlikningsmannaexpedition 1994, 1996.

SAF 1996: *Från krig till fred på arbetsmarknaden.* Stockholm: SAF.

Sandberg, Å. (ed.) 1995: *Enriching Production. Perspectives on Volvo's Uddevalla plant as an alternative to lean production.* Aldershot: Avebury.

SCB 1996: *Politiska resurser och aktiviteter 1978–94.* Stockholm: SCB.

Scheuer, S. 1996: *Fælles aftale eller egen kontrakt i arbejdslivet.* Copenhagen: Nyt fra Samfundsvidenskaberne.

SOU 1994: *Ungdomars välfärd och värderingar.* Stockholm: SOU 1994:73.

Stabiliseringsavtal 1991–92. Stockholm: Arbetsmarknadsdep. Ds 1933:23.

Swenson, P. 1989: *Fair Shares. Unions, Pay, and Politics in Sweden and West Germany.* London: Adamantine Press.

Therborn, G. 1984: The Coming of Swedish Social Democracy. *Annali della Fondazione Giangiacomo Feltrinelli,* 1983/84, 527–93.

4 | Norway: The Revival of Centralized Concertation[1]

JON ERIK DØLVIK • TORGEIR AARVAAG STOKKE

Introduction

The Norwegian system of industrial relations represents a variant of the Nordic model. Broad class compromises were established during the 1930s and in the immediate post-war period, initiating a long-lasting co-operative partnership between capital, labour and the state within a political order dominated by social-democratic governments.

Powerful confederations of trade unions (LO) and employers (NHO, before 1989 NAF) have been key actors in a multi-tiered bargaining system in which centralized concertation has been complemented by workplace structures of co-operation and negotiation (Dølvik and Stokland 1992). Solidaristic wage policies have been maintained, wage differentials reduced, and after a spell of neo-liberal experiments and crisis in the mid-1980s, centralized incomes policies were revitalized, seemingly with favourable effects on economic performance (Freeman 1997).

The revival of tripartite concertation in Norway has been formalized in the so-called 'Solidarity Alternative', a 5-year social pact agreed in 1992 between the Labour government and the main organizations of capital and labour. Within this framework of generalized political exchange, monetary policy and supply-side reforms have been in line with international trends, while the commitment to egalitarian wage and welfare polices has diverged from patterns elsewhere. This dual picture of market modernization and labour traditionalism was accentuated by the Norwegian decision to enter the single market through the EEA agreement, but to stay out of the European Union, unlike Sweden and Finland. Norway is thus a deviant case among the Nordic countries and in the broader European context. This raises the question as to whether a nationally-based corporatism[2] can represent a viable strategy for coping with international market integration (Dølvik et al. 1997).

Even though the Norwegian system of industrial relations has proved quite efficient in handling economic crisis and providing collective goods, uncertainty remains about its ability to adapt to social and labour market transformations in a period of growing affluence and expectations. The egalitarian legacy may be subject to erosion from three directions: from 'above', owing to the reduced scope for ensuring full employment, given the constraints imposed on macro-economic policy-making by internationalized capital markets; from 'below', as a result of increasing pressures from market competition, both nationally and internationally; and from 'within', owing to changes in the social and occupational structure which have altered the balance of power and the perceptions of group interests, (class) identification, justice and solidarity. Faced with such pressures, the revitalization of the solidaristic Norwegian model over recent years may seem a paradox, underlining questions about its sustainability.

In this chapter, the historical, economic and political frameworks of Norwegian industrial relations are first outlined. Second, the main actors and institutions of collective bargaining are described. Third, developments over recent decades are summarized, and, fourth, some conclusions are presented about continuity and change in industrial relations in Norway, and about the factors accounting for the divergent developments in Norway, Sweden and Denmark.

| Historical Background and Economic– Political Overview

The main features of the Norwegian system of industrial relations were largely shaped in the immediate pre- and post-war periods. After a turbulent period of economic crisis, mass unemployment and industrial conflict in the early 1930s, a co-operative system of industrial relations gradually became institutionalized after the first Basic Agreement was signed by NAF and LO in 1935. The same year, a crisis pact between the Labour party and the agrarian party brought organized labour into government. This cross-cutting coalition between labour, small farmers and fishermen, between centre, periphery and the nation state, has been a persistent feature of the political configuration in which Norwegian industrial relations have been embedded (Rokkan 1967). Accounting for the long-lasting hegemony of social democracy, it has also been at the heart of the repeated outbursts of revolt against the centre, most prominently expressed by the successful anti-EC/EU movements in 1972 and 1994, which affirmed the identification of organized labour with the nation state.

Labour party hegemony has helped shape power relations between capital, labour and the state in a way markedly different from Sweden. Since 1961, Labour have never had a majority, relying on parliamentary support either from the political centre or the socialist left. This has encouraged co-operation and compromise in politics as well as in industrial relations. Accordingly, the Norwegian labour movement has never challenged employer prerogatives in the way that organized labour did in Sweden in the 1970s (see Kjellberg in this volume). The weaker position of labour and the absence of antagonistic politicization of industrial relations in Norway have helped to prolong social-democratic rule and centralized concertation, even after labour hegemony started to decline. Thus traditional class compromises have been maintained, in sharp contrast to Sweden where political polarization led to the withdrawal of employers from central co-operation in the 1980s.

The impact of this political legacy on industrial relations has been reinforced by the nature of economic activity in Norway. The economy is small and open, with an import ratio around 40 per cent. Industrialization was late and limited: exports have predominantly been derived from natural resources such as fisheries, forestry, the utilization of cheap hydro-power to produce semi-finished metals and chemicals, and lately on North Sea oil. Since the early 1970s, the petroleum sector has gained increasing economic importance, and currently accounts for more than 30 per cent of total exports. Norway is today the third largest oil exporter in the world with petroleum production providing more than 5 per cent of GDP and a substantial proportion of government income.

The government's prominent role in the petroleum sector has reinforced the state-capitalist features of the Norwegian political economy (Mjøset et al. 1994: 63). In 1990, the newly deregulated private banking system was brought to the verge of collapse, but was rescued by a government bail-out. As a result the state again became a leading actor in the financial system – an ironic example of socialism by default – and currently controls about a quarter of the shares on the Oslo stock exchange. An extensive system of public transfers at industry and regional levels, well-developed public infrastructure, and an extensive welfare state, have reinforced the pivotal role of the state in governance of the economy and, hence, also in industrial relations.

The 'manna from heaven', as the oil revenues are known, is often used as a single-factor explanation of Norway's favourable economic performance in recent years. A closer examination, however, suggests a more nuanced interpretation taking into account the institutional features of the Norwegian model (Freeman 1997). While other countries, benefiting from large 'windfall' profits, have suffered from economic stagnation and the crowding-out of industrial activity (the so-called 'Dutch disease'), Norway has experienced the opposite (Eika 1996). On the one hand, the oil sector has boosted related industries; on the other, the system of collective bargaining has helped prevent the effects of high oil industry wage costs from spilling over into the mainland economy. In an economy based to a large degree on ground rents and the exploitation of natural resources, market-based wage-setting is always likely to generate prohibitive pay costs. The implication is that the system of centralized incomes policy and state intervention has been a strategic prerequisite for the governance of the Norwegian oil economy.

Complementing centralist concertation, workplace participation and co-operation in productivity growth and industrial restructuring have been key features of Norwegian industrial relations throughout the post-war period. Under the Co-operation Agreement of 1966 (part of the Basic Agreement between NAF/NHO and LO), co-operation committees, or works councils, were established. Later, structures for consultation in corporate groups were introduced, alongside joint management–labour plans for industrial and company restructuring (Bosch 1997). Board-level participation, giving employees one third of the seats, was established under the Joint Stock Company Act in 1973. The Work Environment Act of 1977 extended existing schemes of employee participation through the activities of work environment committees and safety delegates. Norwegian unions, unlike those in other Nordic countries, have not given priority to economic democracy through worker ownership or wage-earner funds.

Major reforms of the welfare state were undertaken in the 1960s and 1970s. A universal, tax-based public pension and (unlike the other Nordic countries) unemployment benefit system were established. While retirement age is still among the highest in Europe (67 years), a sick pay system, providing 100 per cent compensation from day one, was introduced in 1977. The expansion of services contributed to an unprecedented growth in female employment, especially in the public sector, where employment nearly doubled between 1973 and 1993 and now accounts for one third of the working population. More than 70 per cent of women of working age are economically active, roughly half of them part-time.

In the post-war period the governing Labour party advocated Keynesian stabilization policies, but in practice fiscal policies were kept tight, whereas credit policies and the state banks were used for counter-cyclical purposes within a regime of low interest rates, a fixed exchange rate and low inflation (Mjøset et al. 1994: 60). Wage determination was centrally co-ordinated with economic policies, giving priority to the competitiveness of exposed sectors. During the international crisis of the 1970s, however, expansionary Keynesian policies were used to combat recession, but rising inflation and economic imbalances triggered devaluation, austerity policies and wage and price laws in 1978–9.

In the 1980s, the Norwegian economy experienced a strong recovery along with substantial policy shifts, followed by dramatic economic fluctuations. Extensive deregulation of credit and the housing market was pursued by a conservative government in the early 1980s, leading to an extraordinary growth in credit-financed private consumption, services and employment. In 1986, falling oil-prices and external imbalances triggered the collapse of the bonanza. In a situation aggravated by large-scale industrial conflict and the fall of the conservative government, a major shift in economic strategy was initiated. The incoming Labour government devalued and introduced a hard currency regime, underpinned by austerity policies and high interest rates. There was also a change in the approach to collective bargaining: the two sides of industry played a key role in securing wage moderation, and pay legislation was introduced making excessive pay increases unlawful in 1988–9.

The change was successful in redressing external imbalances and squeezing out inflation, but the consequence was domestic recession and a debt crisis. While unemployment had been almost negligible in the post-war period until the mid-1970s, and grew only slowly in the early 1980s, it rose dramatically from 1988. Within a few years, employment had fallen by 6 per cent and the proportion of the labour force out of work reached nearly 9 per cent (including 3 per cent participating in active labour market schemes) (Rødseth 1997). To combat unemployment, expansionary Keynesian policies were reintroduced in the early 1990s, accompanied by active labour market policies and the expansion of higher education. In response to turbulence in the financial markets in 1992, the Norwegian currency was unpegged from the ecu, leading to falling interest rates.

From 1993 the domestic economy recovered, exports increased and the economy entered a phase of accelerating growth in production and employment. By autumn 1997, unemployment had been brought down to below 4 per cent (including those participating in active labour market schemes).

The change of approach in the 1980s led to the scrapping of a central pillar of the traditional macro-economic Norwegian model, state control over credit policy and capital movements. However, another feature of the traditional model was revived: the commitment to low inflation and a stable exchange rate as 'anchors' for centralized incomes policies. A crucial precondition for this shift was the active participation of labour and capital. This was formalized in 1992 in the official 'National strategy for increased employment in the 1990s', the so-called 'Solidarity Alternative' (see below).

The Norwegian System of Industrial Relations

The evolution of industrial relations and collective bargaining in Norway conforms strongly to Sisson's (1987) thesis that historical compromises shape structures, attitudes and habits that are not easily changed. The Norwegian Confederation of Trade Unions (LO), founded in 1899, was joined by the Norwegian Employers' Confederation (NAF) in 1900. The first industry-wide collective agreement was concluded in the metal industry in 1907. The metal agreement still plays an important role in Norwegian bargaining rounds. A long debate on legal frameworks culminated in 1915 with the passing of the Labour Disputes Act, which built largely on tacit agreements and compromises between the parties. The principles laid down in the law and large parts of its substantive provisions are still in force today.

The first decade of functioning of the Labour Disputes Act was marked by high levels of conflict and state intervention through compulsory arbitration in bargaining rounds (Knutsen 1993). The resolution of major conflicts in 1928 and 1931 contributed to the building of strong trust relationships between the leadership of LO and NAF, and the signing of the Basic Agreement in 1935 can be viewed as formalizing this new era (Seim 1972). LO and NAF have since been joined by other organizations, and industrial relations in the public sector developed rapidly from the 1950s. Nevertheless, Norwegian industrial relations continue to bear the strong imprint of both the institutions and the compromises of the founding phase.

Employer Organizations

While private sector employers in Norway are today represented by more than 50 associations, the Confederation of Norwegian Business and Industry (NHO, a product of the merger in 1989 between NAF and two industry and craft associations), is the only employers' confederation in the private sector. NHO comprises more than 13,500 firms with approximately 430,000 employees in 1996. The firms are members both of NHO and one of the 28 branch associations, which combine the roles of employers' associations and industrial interest organizations. NHO exerts strong central authority over member associations on bargaining strategies, industrial action and the conclusion of collective agreements. Manufacturing, construction, craft trades and the service sector are all defined as areas of recruitment for NHO, but the confederation is strongest in manufacturing. Its density is particularly high in chemicals and metals, and density – measured as proportion of employment – is approximately 70 per cent in manufacturing as a whole (Stokke 1996b). Density increases sharply with firm size.

The other major employer organization in the private sector is HSH (the Federation of Norwegian Commercial and Service Enterprises). In addition, there are significant employer organizations in financial services, insurance, private health and welfare services, agriculture and the co-operative movement. In the 1990s, organized enterprises in total covered about 55 per cent of private sector employment (Stokke 1996a).

In the public sector, there are separate employer organizations for state and local government. In addition, a new employer organization (NAVO) for semi-autonomous state enterprises was founded in 1993. The government is formally the employer in the state sector, and the main negotiation rounds, covering roughly 250,000 employees, are the responsibility of the Ministry of Planning and Co-ordination. The local public sector is covered by the Norwegian Association of Local Authorities (KS). The main negotiations in the municipal sector covered roughly 300,000 employees in 1991–2 (Nergaard 1993: 142).[3] The revision of the main collective agreement requires approval by a ballot among KS's members. Since 1964, both the state and local government sector have used the same salary scale, although actual pay for specific occupations may vary somewhat. The main bargaining rounds for the local government sector and the semi-autonomous state enterprises are regulated by the Labour Disputes Act, while bargaining in the state sector is regulated by the Public Service Disputes Act. In the state sector, agreements are settled with bargaining cartels of unions from the three union confederations and an independent teachers' union. The central bargaining partners of KS are usually also cartels of unions from the main confederations LO, YS and AF, but individual unions may in principle be entitled to bargain independently, while cartels in the state sector can commit the individual unions.

In summary, employer organization in Norway is marked by a high degree of centralized power and fairly high density. The clear demarcation of bargaining territories moderates rivalry and competition, even though some tension exists both within and between private and public sector. Nonetheless, the dominant role of private manufacturing associations, co-ordinating their policies under the auspices of NHO, has contributed to institutionalization of an encompassing bargaining structure based on mutual high-trust relations, especially with LO and its unions. NHO is, unlike its Swedish sister organization, SAF, still both willing and able to play a dominant role in collective bargaining. And unlike its Danish sister organization, DA, it has not (yet) experienced severe symptoms of internal tension between manufacturing industry and other parts of the private sector.

▍Trade Unions

Trade union density has stabilized at around 56–7 per cent since 1980. This is lower than in other Nordic countries, partly reflecting the fact that unemployment insurance in Norway is organized by the state and not by the unions (Rothstein 1990).

The Norwegian Confederation of Trade Unions (LO) is still the dominant union force. This dominance is due both to its traditional hegemony among blue-collar workers in core manufacturing industries, and to its organization of a substantial proportion of employees in the growing public sector. LO-affiliated unions covered roughly 54 per cent of unionized workers in 1994. LO consists of 28 different unions with a total membership of 800,000 members in the mid-1990s. Some 73 per cent of LO members are economically active (Stokke 1995). Approximately 55 per cent of active LO members are located in the private sector, but the proportion of membership in the public sector is steadily increasing, as is the percentage of women members.

Industrial unionism has been the main organizing principle of LO unions in the private sector since the 1920s. Tension between unskilled and skilled workers, as in the Danish LO (Scheuer in this volume), has thus never been an important factor. Industrial unionism is also a key principle in the local government sector. In the state sector, LO structure reflects the organization of the state into different departments. LO has recently begun to create cartels in the private sector, one for manufacturing and one for services. (The unions in the state and local government sectors are already organized more or less as cartels.)

The two other confederations, the Federation of Norwegian Professional Associations (AF) and the Confederation of Vocational Unions (YS), were established in the late 1970s out of pre-existing confederations and independent unions. The 36 unions in AF represented almost 250,000 members in 1995. YS consists of 18 unions with 215,000 members. About 77 per cent of AF's and 84 per cent of YS's members are in active employment (Stokke 1995 and union data). About two-thirds of the active members of AF and YS are employed in the public sector. AF mainly recruits graduates and well-educated professionals, whereas YS membership is concentrated in female-dominated, semi-skilled occupations in the public sector with low to average rates of pay. YS unions also predominate in banking and insurance. LO and AF largely organize different segments of the labour market, thus competition is muted. In 1993, they signed a collaboration agreement covering industrial policies, the protection of employee rights, research and education, equal rights and family issues. By contrast, the boundaries between LO and YS are blurred in the public and large parts of the private sector, often leading to competition and rivalry; YS also actively opposes the links between LO and the Labour party.

A substantial but decreasing number of unions are not members of any confederation. The most important organize teachers, journalists, shipmasters and mates, employees in aviation and (until recently) in oil production. The majority of the many independent unions have fewer than 5000 members. The largest

Table 4.1 Total union density and density by confederation

Year	Total	LO	YS	AF	Independent
1960	52	41			11
1970	50	38			13
1980	55	37	5	5	8
1990	56	33	9	9	5
1994	56	30	10	10	6

Note: YS and AF were both formed in the late 1970s, earlier confederations outside LO are grouped together with independent unions.
Source: Fennefoss (1988); Stokke (1995).

independent union, the teachers union, has a collaboration agreement with LO and often co-ordinates collective bargaining demands with LO unions. Nonetheless, union fragmentation is much greater in Norway than in Sweden and somewhat greater than in Denmark (cf. Fennefoss and Stokke 1991).

Although union density in Norway has been relatively stable over the whole post-war period, fluctuating between 50 and 57 per cent, LO's share of members has fallen. The broad picture is shown in table 4.1. Union density varies considerably between sectors and industries, from 22–4 per cent in trade and in hotels and restaurants to 86 per cent in public administration (Nergaard 1996).

Despite the relative decline in membership, LO unions are still the largest in both the private and public sectors, and are able to dominate the bargaining rounds. Formally and in practice, LO exerts strong central authority over member unions. It plays a decisive role in determining union policy on collective bargaining and industrial action. The strength of central authority has always differentiated Norwegian LO from its Danish and (since the early 1980s) Swedish counterparts (Elvander 1989). In contrast to Sweden in particular, the close collaboration and consultation between the LO and the Labour Party on most policy areas have continued in Norway. This privileged access to the decision-making centres of the governing party has bolstered LO's power and has been a prerequisite for the maintenance of centralized collective bargaining and economic policy concertation. However, the central role of LO has been increasingly questioned by unions and by political forces on the margins of corporatist networks.

Strong central power in Norway is combined with a significant decentralization of trade union functions. These include local bargaining at company level, which is integrated into the overall bargaining system; the approval of collective agreements in a ballot of union members covered by the agreement; and the significant role of local unions in co-determination and health and safety activities at firm level. Thus union structure, as in the other Nordic countries, is both more centralized and more decentralized than is the case in most other European countries.

▌Regulatory Frameworks of Collective Bargaining

As in all Nordic and most European countries, the distinction between disputes of rights and disputes of interest is applied in Norway (cf. ILO 1980: 6–9). The Labour Court, dealing with disputes of rights, and the Office of the state mediator, dealing with disputes of interest, are regulated by collective labour law. Both institutions were established by the first Labour Disputes Act of 1915; with the Public Sector Labour Disputes Act of 1958, the two institutions cover the whole labour market (Evju 1991: 128). After a period of compulsory arbitration in the first post-war years, a National Wage Board was set up in 1952 for voluntary arbitration of disputes of interests. The Board has five permanent members: three neutrals, one representing employers (usually NHO or the state as employer) and one representing trade unions (usually LO). In addition, each party to a dispute designates a representative to the Board. These two representatives have voting rights while the permanent members from the employer and union sides do not. Requests for voluntary arbitration have been rather rare, and the Board has in practice been used more frequently for ad hoc compulsory arbitration (Evju 1991: 135–6). Between 1952 and 1996, 91 special Acts and Decrees have resulted in the submission of more than 130 disputes to compulsory arbitration (Stokke 1996c).

Basic agreements in the main sectors complement legislation by defining overall aims, principles and procedural rules. They regulate sympathy action, amplify the peace obligation, and contain provisions on a broad set of issues such as rights of shop stewards, working time, work organization, employee participation, information and consultation, the introduction of new technology, and training. They often expand on minimum standards set by legislation. Collective bargaining covers not only pay and working conditions, but also broader issues of social policy, including pension rights, sickness absence, and training.

Although there is no statutory minimum wage, nor *erga omnes* procedures for the extension of collective agreements, private employers are bound to apply the terms of a collective agreement to their unorganized employees also (Evju 1991: 57–8). Employers not bound by any collective agreements are also generally assumed to apply the provision of the appropriate settlement, although little research has been conducted on the subject. In the state sector, parliament has determined that the terms of collective agreements should cover all employees, while in the municipal sector norms of equal treatment imply that derogations from collective bargaining outcomes are unacceptable. Survey data from employees indicate a level of coverage of collective agreements in the private sector of 50–55 per cent. Coverage is substantially higher in private manufacturing and lower in private services (Hippe and Nergaard 1992; Traxler 1994; Olsen 1995).[4] Comparison of survey data from Denmark and Norway indicates a surprising similarity in the coverage of collective agreements, despite the higher union density in Denmark (Olsen 1995, Scheuer 1997).

The Norwegian case illustrates that a centralized system of collective bargaining is not dependent upon the use of extension procedures such as exist in countries like Austria, Belgium, France and Portugal (cf. Traxler 1994: 178–9). This does not imply, however, that Norway's collective bargaining system is 'voluntarist'. The balance between labour law and collective agreements in terms of frameworks for bargaining and of the handling of substantive issues such as working time, holidays, or dismissal protection, leans more heavily towards labour law than in Denmark and Sweden (Evju 1995:328–32).

The Institutional Embeddedness of Collective Bargaining

In international comparison, Norway is usually ranked highly on measures of centralization, encompassment and the articulation of collective bargaining (Visser and Ebbinghaus 1992: 212–13; Traxler 1994: 175). Different models of collective bargaining have been used over the past 50 years, but the general picture is of an alternation between the peak intersectoral level and the industry level in the private sector. In addition, however, local or workplace bargaining is widespread, especially in private sector manufacturing. Strikes are prohibited in local bargaining. The pay of most private sector white-collar workers is determined on an individual basis, with the union sometimes acting as co-ordinator or advisor. In the public sector, local bargaining has increased, especially in the 1990s (see Barth and Yin 1995; Ellingsæter and Rubery 1997).

Since 1964, the duration of collective agreements in Norway, both in the private and public sector, has been 2 years. The stability created by taking the duration of agreements out of bargaining should not be underestimated: a glance at the Swedish situation since the late 1960s (Elvander 1988, Kjellberg in this volume) illustrates how bargaining over duration encourages leap-frogging. During the 2-yearly main bargaining rounds, the entire content of a collective agreement is open for revision. At industry level in the private sector, the respective LO-affiliated unions and NHO-affiliated employers' branch organizations negotiate some 150 collective agreements. At the intersectoral level, bargaining takes place between the peak organizations and covers broader issues. Combinations of intersectoral and industry-level bargaining have also occurred (see table 4.2). Intermediate or mid-term bargaining rounds are always centrally co-ordinated, and focus on pay. The outcome of main bargaining rounds is usually subject to ratification in a ballot of union members covered by the collective agreement, while the results of intermediate bargaining rounds are subject to approval by LO's general council.

Pay rounds in the 1950s and 1960s followed a pattern which was later formalized in the so-called 'Aukrust model', in which a 'responsible' rate of wage growth was determined by the growth of world market prices and productivity in the exposed sectors of the economy (Aukrust 1977). (The Aukrust model was an important source for the later Swedish EFO model.) Thus national bargainers had to take account of the competitiveness of exposed sectors. In mid-term bargaining rounds or in centrally co-ordinated bargaining rounds the results of the LO–NAF agreement would set the standards for the rest of the labour market. In bargaining rounds at industry level, the export-based iron- and metalworkers set the pattern for subsequent agreements.

Table 4.2 Type and level of negotiations in LO – NAF (NHO) bargaining rounds, and forms of state intervention

Year	Type of negotiation LO–NAF (NHO)	Level of negotiation LO–NAF (NHO)	Major conflicts LO–NAF (NHO)	Instances of compulsory arbitration			Wage laws etc.
				LO–NAF (NHO)	Other private sector	Public sector	
1964	Main	C		x	x	x	
1965	Mid term	C			x		
1966	Main	C		x	x	(x)	
1967	(No bargaining)						
1968	Main	I/C				x	
1969	(No bargaining)					x	
1970	Main	C			x		
1971	(No bargaining)						
1972	Main	C			x	x	
1973	Mid term	C					
1974	Main	I	Electr. instal.	Electr. instal.		x	
1975	Mid term	C					
1976	Main	C			x		
1977	Mid term	C			x		
1978	Main	C		x	x	x	(x)
1979	(No bargaining)						x
1980	Main	C/I			x	x	
1981	Mid term	C		x	x	x	
1982	Main	I	Transport	Transport	x		
1983	Mid term	C					
1984	Main	I			x	x	
1985	Mid term	C			x		
1986	Main	I	Major lockout/strike		x	x	
1987	Mid term	C					
1988	Main	C				x	x
1989	Mid term	C					x
1990	Main	C/I			x		
1991	Mid term	C					
1992	Main	C			x	x	
1993	Mid term	C					
1994	Main	I	Transport		x	x	
1995	Mid term	C				x	
1996	Main	I	Manufacturing				

Note: 'C' = centrally co-ordinated; 'I' = industry level. The number of workers or employers covered by compulsory arbitration may vary considerably, especially between the LO–NAF area and the rest of the private sector. The wage and price freeze in 1978 is in brackets because it did not affect the 1978 bargaining round.
Source: Stokke, unpublished material.

The high point of Norwegian incomes policies was reached with the so-called 'combined' settlements of 1975–7. The Labour government participated directly in the negotiations and provided tax concessions, transfers, pension contributions and price subsidies. Real pay increased by an average of 5 per cent per annum, a figure not achieved before or since, and according to Dahl (1989: 28), the state in effect paid between 40 and 60 per cent of the cost of the 1975–7 settlements. This peak era of concertation culminated in compulsory arbitration and a wage and price freeze in 1978.

Dispute resolution relies heavily on mediation, which is, in practice, compulsory in Norway. The effects of mediation on bargaining between LO and NAF/NHO are difficult to disentangle. More visible is the mediator's right to treat several settlements as one entity. In the main centrally co-ordinated bargaining rounds between LO and NAF, this has been of great importance in gagging militant unions or minimizing the effects of workplace rebellion against settlements (Frøland 1992).[5] Mediators in Norway are careful to put forward more favourable solutions to groups which are not content with the pattern set by previous agreements, a mediator strategy also found in Denmark, but not in Sweden (Stokke 1996c). The strategies and rights of Norwegian state mediators might be said to challenge the traditional Anglo-American understanding of the mediator's role (cf. ILO 1980; Kochan and Katz 1988). Nevertheless, the institution is highly respected, and NAF/NHO and LO have always supported a strong mediation body. Norwegian dispute resolution resembles the Danish mode of compulsory mediation, in which the mediators have even greater powers. In Sweden, by contrast, mediation is essentially voluntary and since the 1970s has generally been manipulated by the organizations in their bargaining strategies (Elvander 1988; Stokke 1996c; Kjellberg in this volume).

Compulsory arbitration has also been an important factor in ensuring discipline and compliance with the model. However, its use in disputes of interest has always been a matter of great controversy in Norway. Introduced as early as 1916 through ad hoc legislation, compulsory arbitration has had three main purposes in the post-war period. First, both LO and NAF, and their affiliates, have on occasion allowed disputes to drag on in the confident expectation that this will eventually result in state intervention through compulsory arbitration. This tactic has played an important role where one or other of the parties wishes to save face, where it is feared that LO members will vote down a mediator's proposal, or where this has already happened (Elvander 1989: 128; Frøland 1992). These ingredients characterized the centrally co-ordinated bargaining rounds between LO and NAF in 1951, 1958, 1964, 1966, 1978 and 1981. In the 1986 round, tense relations between the parties made a peaceful conclusion unlikely (see below). Nevertheless, compulsory arbitration has never been the main way of settling disputes between LO and NAF/NHO. Most bargaining rounds (see table 4.2) have been resolved on the basis of a proposal from the state mediator, either voted on and accepted by union members or accepted by LO's general council.

Second, compulsory arbitration has been an important mechanism in containing militant unions both inside and outside LO. For example, the three largest strikes in the municipal sectors during the 1980s and 1990s were all led by the Norwegian

Union of Municipal Employees (the largest LO union), and halted by the use of compulsory arbitration. Both historically and more recently, compulsory arbitration has been most frequently used to gag independent unions, or YS unions competing with LO unions in the private sector. Sanctions have sometimes been imposed on groups initiating conflicts, suggesting that the use of compulsory arbitration has tended to preserve the solidaristic legacy of co-ordinated pattern bargaining (Evju 1991:136). Until the 1970s, sea and coastal water transport were plagued by union rivalries, and two independent unions in particular were frequent guests at the National Wage Board. Subsequently, the use of compulsory arbitration has been essential to prevent workers from exploiting ground-rents in the oil production sector, especially given the industry's fragmented union structure (Stokke 1996c). In 1982, after a turbulent bargaining round the previous year and an intervention by the prime minister compelling the oil companies to act in concert with NAF, the National Wage Board established a new pay system for workers on oil production platforms. The system, comprising an onshore manufacturing wage element and an offshore compensation element, has had the intended effect of reducing the spill-over of wages from the oil industry (Høgsnes 1994: 651–86). Strikes, and oil company defections from NAF, have been avoided through the use of compulsory arbitration.

Third, compulsory arbitration has always had a role in preventing labour conflicts from disrupting essential services. However, this has allowed both unions and employers to manipulate conflicts so as to provoke compulsory arbitration – a strategy used, for example, by nurses in the municipal sector in 1994, and by the AF unions in the state and municipal sectors in 1995 (Stokke 1996c).

The most evident impact of both mediation and arbitration is their role in the preservation of 'social order', by preventing external groups from undermining the bargaining framework set by the principal LO–NHO actors. Functional equivalents to Norwegian institutions of dispute resolution can be found in Denmark; in Sweden, by contrast, the doctrine of 'freedom of the labour market from state intervention' (Elvander 1989: 128) has been very strong. Consequently, temporary breakdowns of centralized collective bargaining can be reversed or at least stabilized in Norway and Denmark, while the Swedish bargaining structures are much more fragile (Stokke 1996c). However, since the early 1980s, the use of compulsory arbitration in Norway has come under pressure. The International Labour Organization has repeatedly criticized intervention in disputes that do not threaten essential services, a practice that ILO regards as incompatible with conventions 87 and 98 (see Evju 1991: 212–21, NOU 1993: 18). Such criticism has recently lead to a review of Norwegian collective labour law (see below).

Collective Bargaining in Transition – Recent Developments

During the 1980s the Norwegian system of collective bargaining came under increasing pressure. In 1980, following the compulsory arbitration and wage and price freeze of 1978–9, LO and NAF agreed on a 'low-wage-guarantee', co-financed by employees and affected employers. This brought the upward levelling of wages across sectors by means of specific pay increases for groups earning less than 85 per cent of the average in manufacturing. In return, LO accepted a ceiling on wage drift.

During the neo-liberal phase under conservative governments (1982–6), the state withdrew from tripartite concertation. The main pay rounds were decentralized to industry level, local wage drift accounted for as much as 70 per cent of pay increases, inflation rose and the central actors appeared to lose control. Employers demanded deregulation and market-based wage determination. They also tried to get rid of the 'low-wage guarantee', which sparked a major conflict in the 1986 pay round. NAF pursued a strategy of confrontation and rejected trade union demands for the equalization of blue- and white-collar working time. Negotiations quickly reached deadlock and the employers imposed a general lockout. However, they were organizationally and politically unprepared for a large-scale conflict. Facing internal division, the employers suffered a humiliating defeat. As a result of mediation they were forced to accept high wage increases (averaging 11.5 per cent, with a further 8.5 per cent in wage drift), the retention of the 'low-wage guarantee' (with some modifications) and a reduction of the normal working week to 37.5 hours. This was against a background of overheated labour markets and an economy on the verge of collapse.

The virtual breakdown of central co-ordination and the inability to take account of changing economic circumstances in 1986 was a formative experience, particularly for the employers. It paved the way for profound changes over the subsequent years.

From Crisis to Solidarity Pact – The Revival of Concertation

In response to the onset of recession in 1987, trade union and employer leaders played a key role in the reintroduction of incomes policies and the recentralization of collective bargaining. Following a change of leadership in NAF and LO, and in the government, the main actors agreed in informal high-level consultations to break the inflationary wage-price spiral; competitiveness had been eroded and jobs lost, while there had been only minor real wage increases.

The interim pay round in 1987 ended in a LO–NAF agreement that there should be no wage increases, but local wage drift was still significant (8.5 per cent in manufacturing). In 1988 unemployment was accelerating and LO offered pay moderation, on condition that no other groups should gain higher settlements. Acting in concert with LO and NAF, the social-democratic government passed a regulation, approved by Parliament, prohibiting wage increases beyond the terms of the central LO–NAF settlement. When the income regulation expired in 1990, LO and NHO agreed centrally on a limited across-the-board pay increase. In addition, local and industry-level bargaining was allowed within strict guidelines based on a company's economic situation, results, productivity, prospects and competitiveness (NHO/LO 1992: 20), a formula which has been followed since. Following an initial grassroots rejection, LO members finally voted for the settlement after mediation. The 1990 pay round thus marked a cautious return to normality, based on a joint commitment to solidaristic wage moderation, formalized in 1992 in the 'Solidarity Alternative'.

▎ The 'Solidarity Alternative'

In 1991 the Labour government appointed an Employment Commission chaired by Per Kleppe, former Norwegian Minister of Finance, and composed of representatives of all political parties, LO and NHO. The Commission submitted its report, entitled 'A national strategy for increased employment in the 1990s', the following year (NOU 1992: 26; Norwegian Employment Commission 1992).

In order to bring unemployment down to 3–3.5 per cent in the 1990s, a five-year social pact, the 'solidarity alternative', was proposed, comprising the following main elements. First, there would be a programme of wage determination and incomes policy co-operation that would secure an improvement in cost competitiveness of around about 10 per cent and a growth in real wages of at least 0.5 per cent per year between 1993 and 1997. Second, the proposals included a review of the composition of public expenditure with a view to reducing transfer payments and creating scope for active measures to increase employment. Third, structural policy measures would be implemented, including an examination of the regulatory framework of industrial policy, labour markets, social security and education, aimed at reducing the equilibrium rate of unemployment. Fourth, an active labour market policy would be pursued to reduce unemployment and enhance skill formation. Finally, a macro-economic formula was proposed under which monetary policy would aim to achieve a stable exchange rate, fiscal policy to stabilize the growth of demand, and incomes policies to control inflation. Supplementary reports argued for cuts in transfers and a strengthening of the so-called 'working-line', aimed at increasing labour market participation among recipients of social benefits.

Following the policy shift of the late 1980s, the gap in manufacturing wage costs between Norway and its main trading partners decreased steadily, from 25 per cent in 1988 to 7 per cent in 1994 (NOU 1996/4: 44). As indirect labour costs are comparatively low in Norway and international comparison of relative wage costs usually do not include wages of white-collar workers – which are also low in Norway – it may be assumed that total labour costs in Norwegian manufacturing have largely been brought in line with the country's main trading partners (p. 68). Weak productivity growth and currency appreciation meant that unit labour costs improved less rapidly (falling by 2.5 per cent between 1988 and 1994), and they rose again in 1995–6 (p. 43). Nevertheless, measured in terms of export market share, which rose by some 10 per cent between 1988 and 1994 (and has increased further since), Norwegian competitiveness has improved significantly (pp. 38–9).

Although the double figure nominal wage increases (roughly on a par with inflation) of the early- to mid-1980s were brought down to around 3 per cent in the first half of the 1990s, an even stronger drop in inflation (to an average of 2.5 per cent per annum since 1992) and interest rates, has brought a significant growth in real wages.

The 'solidarity alternative' expressed broad political consensus and the commitment of the social partners to continued concertation. This could be seen as a concrete example of the concept of 'generalized political exchange' (Traxler 1990). The attractiveness to employers and government of the unions' capacity to deliver wage restraint was skilfully exploited by LO to obtain ambitious employment and labour market policies, together with a guarantee that major welfare schemes (e.g. the sick pay system) would be maintained. The main partners have largely kept to their commitments, and employment objectives have been fulfilled, facilitated by growth rates far beyond the Commission's assumptions.

Compared to developments in other European and Nordic countries these results are noteworthy. Tripartite concertation and solidaristic policies in Norway have been essential elements in what may be seen as a self-imposed convergence programme, akin to that imposed on EU countries under the EMU criteria. Oil revenues have eased the transition, but have also had a potentially inflationary impact; this makes the contribution of centralized wage determination to containing inflation all the more striking. While Norway has experienced much higher growth than Sweden in recent years, the increase in nominal wages has been substantially lower. A central feature of the Norwegian turnaround was the use of trade union influence to secure a pattern of distribution and a policy mix that enhanced legitimacy and popular consent. This was facilitated by a climate of economic emergency. The active participation of the social partners from the late 1980s was in striking contrast to the interventionism and wage laws of the 1970s, which had little lasting impact on wage setting. The trade unions in particular have been able to influence the broad parameters of state policy within an institutionalized social compromise.

Denmark pursued a similar strategy in the early 1980s – the so-called 'Cartofflecure'. The Danish government actively intervened in collective bargaining and suspended (and eventually abolished) the index-linking of wages. Sweden tried to copy the Norwegian example in early 1990 by calling for wage laws, but the social-democratic government was constrained by the lack of support from the two sides of industry. The politicized Swedish employers had previously withdrawn from all corporatist bodies and denounced central bargaining, while several trade unions actively opposed interventionist incomes policies. Thus there were striking differences between Sweden and the other Scandinavian countries. In Sweden there were no established traditions of compulsory arbitration or other forms of public intervention, by means of which the state could ensure general compliance with a centrally agreed package of crisis measures. Thus compliance had to be secured by the parties themselves, a task which proved impossible. As shown by Kjellberg in this volume, the arrangements for co-ordinating Swedish wage determination have proved fragile. The employers' association's weak central authority, the segmented structure of union confederations and the erosion of LO authority, the absence of a tradition of state intervention, and the more polarized political situation all inhibited the emergence of an overall 'social deal' as in Norway.

The 1996 Pay Round – The Crumbling of Solidaristic Concertation?

A striking feature of the mid-1970s and mid-1980s was the inability of the Norwegian industrial relations system to cope with economic boom, prompting decentralization, wage inflation and economic crisis, followed by austerity and interventionist wage regulation. The key question is thus whether history is about to repeat itself, or whether the dominant actors have learned from past experience. The issue has been highlighted by the 1996 pay round. As a result of rank-and-file impatience in the metalworkers' union (Fellesforbundet), the pay round was conducted at industry level, though within a centrally co-ordinated framework. Negotiations brought a real wage increase of around 3 per cent, a clear departure from past policies of moderation.

In the pace-setting metal sector, a relatively favourable agreement reached by mediation and recommended by the parties, was rejected by union members, prompting the most far-reaching private sector strike since the 1930s. This reflected mounting disaffection with wage moderation. In the period of centralized incomes policies they had on several occasions voted against agreements that were accepted by the majority of private sector LO union members. Discontent was fuelled by a call for higher management pay during the conflict, and by generous settlements in the state and municipal sectors.

The 1996 pay round thus deviated from past policies of centralized wage moderation. By co-ordinating claims across sectors, the unions achieved objectives such as a reduced flexible retirement age and recognition of the principle of life-long training, on top of substantial real wage growth, especially for low-paid groups. The main private sector strikes were resolved without state intervention, and the government also appeared to acknowledge the need for dissatisfied public sector unions and employees to let off steam: this could be seen as a prerequisite for the stability of an overly rigid centralized bargaining system (Frøland 1996). In the context of economic growth and rising profits over recent years, a one-off 4.5 per cent pay rise should not represent major problems. Some have argued, however, that the 1996 pay round confirms the inability of trade unions to sustain wage moderation in times of recovery, suggesting that the 'solidarity alternative' will break down in the coming years (Skånland 1996). In the light of tight labour markets and falling interest rates, the government has made clear that continued wage moderation and fiscal restraint will be required to prevent a resurgence of inflation.

▍The EU and European Labour Regulations

The 'No-coalition' against EU membership won a three-vote victory at the LO Congress in September 1994. In a situation in which the pro-EU Labour government and employers were being vigorously challenged by a broad coalition of forces (including the primary sector, the districts, environmentalists, and various radical and centrist parties), the narrow vote in LO may have had a decisive influence on the final outcome (a vote of 52 per cent against EU membership). Union opponents of membership argued that EU labour regulations would entail the undue juridification and individualization of Norwegian industrial relations, and would possibly result in downward harmonization and the erosion of collective bargaining (Stueland et al. 1994). It was also argued that the EU (and EMU in particular) would have a negative impact on the Norwegian welfare state and employment policies, and this brought strong support for the No-coalition among women and public sector employees.

Through the EEA agreement Norway is supposed to implement EU directives on labour standards, although it has a right of veto. It has been assumed that the Norwegian level of employee protection is more stringent than EU/EEA minimum standards, but Community regulations imply an improvement in protection on issues such as employee consultation over collective redundancies, the right to a written employment contract, working-time regulation, the transfer of undertakings, information and consultation in transnational companies, and certain health and safety measures (see Dølvik and Olsen 1994). EU social policy has mainly taken the form of statutory regulation, even in areas previously regulated by collective bargaining alone. One exception is the European Works Councils directive: in 1995 NHO and LO signed a collective agreement (incorporated into the Basic Agreement) on transposition, which was subsequently underpinned by statutory regulation. European Works Councils have been established voluntarily in most Norwegian transnational companies covered by the directive (Berg et al. 1997).

In general, it is fair to say that adjustment to EU regulation has been smooth and has not brought major change in Norwegian industrial relations. One crucial reform has been implemented. Legislation was passed in 1993 to inhibit 'social dumping' by foreign companies. The law provides for the imposed extension of collective agreements, allowing the signatories to an agreement to claim that all employees within a given area or industry should be covered by its provisions (Holo and Dølvik 1994: 430). The final decision is taken by a Collective Agreement Board appointed by the government and constituted in much the same way as the National Wage Board. So far the provisions have not been tested in practice, but it represents an interesting example of international deregulation causing national re-regulation of labour markets (cf. Traxler and Schmitter 1994).

▌A Changing Industrial Relations Agenda?

New 'trends' in industrial relations are not easily detectable in Norway. Performance-related pay schemes exist in roughly 10 per cent of private companies (Langeland 1995), although employer sources claim they are spreading. In the public sector, greater scope for local wage-setting has been introduced in recent years, partly based on individual appraisal, but it has not yet had a significant effect on wage dispersion (Barth and Yin 1995). (In the 1996 pay round, however, a potentially significant minimum pay system was introduced in the municipal sector.)

Flexible working-time schemes, such as the annualization of hours, are reported to be poorly developed. The most important source of flexibility in private firms is overtime (Bosch 1997), while part-time work dominates in the public sector. In some areas, such as temporary work where more stringent rules were adopted in 1995, the trend has been to reregulation rather than deregulation. Nevertheless, 14 per cent of all employees, and over 20 per cent in the municipal sector, were reported to have temporary contracts in 1995 (Nergaard and Stokke 1996).

Functional flexibility has been the subject of a long tradition of joint union–management programmes on work organization, rooted in the provisions of the Basic Agreement. Even though new production concepts such as just-in-time, more direct employee participation and teamworking are spreading (Olberg 1995), such innovations appear generally to be integrated with existing structures of corporate organization and employee participation (Bosch 1997: 222). In addition to the LO–NHO Joint Enterprise Development Programme (HFB) (in which 15 per cent of metalworking and engineering firms had participated by 1995), the state-supported action research programme 'Enterprise Development 2000' aims to improve competitiveness 'by utilizing Norwegian traditions of co-operation'. There are few signs that new management styles are seriously challenging established patterns of co-operation. On the contrary, it has been suggested that the weak decision-making powers of management, the poor training of supervisors, and the complex system of workplace representation have contributed to a consensual, easy-going culture in many Norwegian companies, inhibiting innovative work reorganization (p. 229).

In the area of the relationship between work and family life, quite radical reforms of parental leave have been introduced, giving parents up to one year's leave on 80 per cent of pay; this can be stretched to 3 years using a time-account scheme (Ellingsæter and Rubery 1997). On the other hand, eligibility criteria for several welfare provisions have been tightened, including unemployment benefits and support for single mothers, as a way of increasing labour force participation among vulnerable groups.

Important reforms have been implemented in education and vocational training, including the right to twelve years' schooling, and the strengthening of a dual system of apprenticeship and theoretical training (Dølvik et al. 1997). In response to rising profits and economic performance, LO has given priority to qualitative demands over real wage increases. It has emphasized issues such as reduced working time, flexible retirement age and life-long training; its proposal for individuals to have the right to spend 10 per cent of working time on education, using a time-account system, prompted the government to set up a tripartite commission to examine ways forward. Unions of well-educated, professional groups feel, however, they are hostages of the solidaristic legacy, and have tried to focus on redressing declining returns to education and an overly compressed wage structure, suggesting new lines of cleavage may gain prominence in the years ahead.

Nevertheless, in contrast to other countries, industrial relations change in Norway has not been dominated in recent years by an employer-driven deregulatory agenda. Instead, new issues have derived from the logic of central concertation, with trade unions and the state as principal agents.

Conclusion – Continuity and Change in Norwegian Industrial Relations

Economic recovery and the revival of centralized concertation in Norway since the late 1980s have parallels with post-war national reconstruction. Despite shrinking constituencies, the labour movement took responsibility for handling a national crisis and demonstrated its capacity to govern and generate loyalty. This implied the revitalization of a traditional facet of the Norwegian model, the primacy of internationally exposed traded goods sectors within a framework of solidaristic incomes policies.

The policy shift lends support to Katzenstein's thesis that 'small states' with corporatist systems of governance derive comparative advantage from their flexibility in tackling external imbalances and competitive pressures in an internationalized economy (Katzenstein 1985). It also fits with comparative research showing that economic adjustment and performance is better in countries with either highly decentralized or highly centralized bargaining systems (Calmfors and Driffill 1988; Traxler 1996). In the Norwegian case, it seems that the capacity of the corporatist bargaining system to contain wage–price inflation has served as a functional alternative to more restrictive economic policies and labour market deregulation.

Contrary to the widespread assumption that internationalization and monetary integration will undermine national corporatism (Streeck 1993), the Norwegian example suggests that 'renationalized' co-operative practices can be a viable strategy for coping with such pressures (Traxler and Schmitter 1994). While market integration is generally assumed to weaken unions, the increased attractiveness of wage restraint may, under certain conditions, as in Norway, improve union bargaining power in political exchange. Such mechanisms may encourage diversity, rather than the convergence of European industrial relations. However, a logic of social partnership increasingly entrenched within the confines of the nation state may encourage beggar-your-neighbour policies, reinforcing international constraints on collective bargaining. Hence solidaristic national strategies may intensify international competition (Dølvik 1993; Mahnkopf and Altvater 1995).

It could be argued that, in an era of decentralization and deregulation of industrial relations, internationalization will make national corporatist practices more difficult to sustain. Recent comparative research, however, does not lend support to the thesis that decentralization is a universal trend (e.g. Traxler 1994; Wallerstein and Golden 1996). Centralized bargaining prevails in most OECD countries other than the UK, the USA and New Zealand, and has become more entrenched in some (Wallerstein and Golden 1996: 4). It seems that the radical decentralization taking place in some Anglo-Saxon countries was the outcome of strong political agendas, rather than reflections of structural change in the working life (p. 31).

In the Nordic context, where pressures towards the abolition of central bargaining should presumably be most visible, substantial decentralization has occurred only in Sweden. Since the Norwegian LO, unlike its Swedish counterpart, has never seriously challenged managerial prerogatives, there has not been any strong employer desire to undermine the political strength of LO in Norway. On the contrary, it can be argued that employers have been dependent on a strong LO to promote the interests of manufacturing within the oil economy and to curb fragmentation of the bargaining system. Moreover, while the powerful Swedish multinationals were the driving force behind SAF's withdrawal from centralized bargaining, there are few such companies in Norway, and they are often partly state-owned. Finally, in some important respects Sweden represents a deviant case in Scandinavia, due to the absence of a tradition of state intervention and of dispute management institutions with the authority to fashion central solutions covering the whole labour market. While the hegemony of Swedish LO was undermined by the growth of strong white-collar confederations from the 1970s, the relative fragmentation of white-collar unions in Norway has enabled LO to maintain its dominance. Thus it is misconceived to see the decline of central bargaining in Sweden as the pattern for what is going to happen in Norway and the other Nordic countries.

A number of factors encourage the continuity of established institutions and practices in Norway. First, the Norwegian economy has long been highly internationalized. The export/import ratio has been fairly stable since the 1950s, and it is questionable how far the single market has added to existing competition. Given the adjustments pursued since 1986, it is plausible to argue that the Norwegian industrial relations system is already well accustomed to coping with changing international circumstances.

Second, the Norwegian system of collective bargaining is embedded in a dense web of formal and informal relations between the main actors and institutions (Høgsnes 1995: 3). The mutual interdependence, trust and personal attachments of key organized actors reinforce continuity rather than change, so that none of the main organizations has strong incentives to defect from current co-operation, and indeed the costs of withdrawal might be considerable. Furthermore, the corporatist legacy and the institutions of dispute resolution effectively constrain free-riding or exit from the existing order by groups benefiting from market-based power (Stokke 1996c).

Third, despite Norway's comparatively compressed wage structures (Freeman 1997), opinion polls suggest that the legacy of solidaristic wage moderation enjoys broad public acceptance. Even the wage laws of the late 1980s gained popular support, and in recent surveys around 80 per cent have supported continued wage moderation (*Arbeiderbladet* 28 December 1996). Contrary to what might be expected, the level of unlawful conflicts has also been low in comparative perspective.

Finally, strong public finances and soaring oil revenues provide incentives for organized actors to continue co-operative political exchange with the state, which still appears capable of delivering desired collective goods. Moreover, the predominance of industries based on natural resources, and the oil sector in particular, inhibits market-based wage setting and reinforces the central actors' interest in interventionist incomes policies.

There are, however, factors that might point in other directions. First, in recent pay rounds professional groups have campaigned for a realignment of relative pay structures, claiming that they disadvantage semi-skilled and skilled occupations in the public sector. AF and YS have frequently accused LO of invoking the 'solidarity alternative' to constrain the outside unions' right to bargain freely. This suggests that the legitimacy of solidaristic wage policies and LO–NHO's lead in wage determination may come under increasing pressure in the years ahead, especially as LO and NHO cover a shrinking proportion of the labour market.

The pursuit of wage moderation in recent years has required some use of force to discipline outside unions, and LO and NHO have recently called for stricter rules on who is allowed to take industrial action. In this connection, a 1996 report of the government-appointed Labour Law Commission proposes a reform of the Labour Disputes Act in order to reduce the need for compulsory arbitration, and so comply with ILO conventions (NOU 1996: 14). One suggestion is to make it harder for independent unions to depart from agreements signed by one of the main trade union confederations. In addition, stricter criteria for recognition of confederations may strengthen central authority over collective bargaining and industrial action in AF and YS, presumably reducing the scope for independent union action in areas with a confederal presence. In the municipal sector, it is proposed that the votes of individual unions can be aggregated within each confederation, as happens in the state sector. If implemented, the reform could curb independent free-riders, but it is harder to see how it could resolve the more pressing issue of the conflicting settlements concluded by the main confederations, especially in the public sector. On the contrary, it has been suggested that the Commission's proposals, combined with the scrapping of compulsory arbitration, could open the way to a 'Swedish' situation of three competing union confederations (Stokke 1996c). However, with strong opposition from several political parties and from unions outside LO, it is difficult to judge whether the proposals will be enacted.

A second factor of uncertainty is the loyalty of business in supporting its leadership's commitment to the 'solidarity alternative'. Employers face a dilemma in that, on the one hand they have an interest in taking wages out of competition and controlling costs by means of centralized agreements; on the other hand, they wish greater wage differentiation in order to attract scarce skilled labour and to increase flexibility in the context of corporate human resource strategies. This may strengthen pressures within the employers' camp for a less rigid framework and more decentralized bargaining. Rising profitability and the growth of exports in recent years may also reduce employers' concern with labour costs and increase their focus on stable production and the elimination of regulatory obstacles to labour utilization.

In this context the 'solidarity alternative' may come to be seen as an uncomfortable straight-jacket. In recent years, employers have repeatedly, but unsuccessfully, called for the abolition of low-wage guarantees, looser regulations on shedding of labour, and greater working-time flexibility. Following their defeat and loss of credibility in 1986, employers had an obvious interest in joining forces with the Labour government and union leaderships during the turbulent period of economic adjustment and the struggle over EU membership. However, in the current phase of recovery, it seems uncertain whether they still have equally strong incentives to continue along this path.

A recent NHO discussion document on future labour relations in the era of internationalization is severely critical of the Norwegian system (NHO 1995). The current collective bargaining system is seen as 'an inherently conservative force', inhibiting adequate human resource policies, encouraging free-riding, constraining working-time flexibility and raising costs. In general, it is claimed to promote compromise and industrial peace to the detriment of necessary change that might involve conflict. Accordingly, a fundamental overhaul of the system is recommended, with thorough decentralization to enterprise level, more individualized pay systems, and increased scope for negotiated derogations from agreements. Although it sees a place for centrally negotiated frameworks, sectoral and confederal bodies should limit their role to establishing broad principles and providing support to actors at enterprise level. It does not seem likely that such a radical approach will gain support in NHO executive bodies in the short to medium term, but the document clearly signals that diverging views are developing inside the employers' camp and that, in the longer term, employers seek more latitude.

A third cause of uncertainty is the impact of the strong recovery of the Norwegian economy. The acceptance of wage moderation in recent years was facilitated by economic downturn and unacceptable levels of unemployment. From 1988 to 1995, however, capital's share of GDP has increased substantially. With a prospering economy, soaring company profits, lucrative share option deals for top-leaders, rising public budget surpluses and buoyant labour markets, the willingness of unions to persist with wage moderation might easily evaporate. LO unions seem committed to their current strategy, but faced with growing pressures from membership and outside unions to achieve a larger share of the pie, their task will not be easy. With concern rising that the Norwegian economy may overheat, the industrial relations system is in for a strong test of its robustness; not least because – in contrast to the 1970s and 1980s, when economic bonanzas ended with devaluations and wage laws – the use of the exchange rate for stabilization purposes has now been abandoned (Rødseth 1997).

A fourth cause of uncertainty is the resignation of the Labour government after the election in September 1997, paving the way for a minority coalition led by Christian-Democrats. Composed of centrist parties that were against EU member-ship, the new government is more reluctant to accept further EU adjustment; while the position of the nationalist Progress party has also been radically strengthened. Although the government has signalled a positive attitude to continued incomes–political co-operation, it is less devoted to the macro-economic formula of the 'solidarity alternative' and wants to use more oil revenues on welfare expenditure. This could entail the use of interest rates to prevent economic overheating, causing concern among the social partners. NHO has received the new government without enthusiasm. LO has declared that it will continue its co-operative approach, but has also made clear that any attempts to encroach on labour rights will provoke conflict with the unions. In view of the fragile parliamentary basis of the new government, the critical question is whether it can develop and muster support for an economic policy that prevents the booming economy from veering out of control and provides a basis for continued wage restraint from the unions.

Thus, even though Norwegian industrial relations have achieved stability in recent years, there are clear signs of strain. Tensions are visible between traded and non-traded goods sectors, well-educated and poorly-qualified groups, men and women, public and private sector, and production-oriented and distribution-oriented union sectors. The class configuration emerging out of the growth of the welfare state does not easily fit with the post-war 'productionist' class compromise. Such tensions are not limited to relations between LO, YS and AF but also affect unions within LO. Strains are also generated between employer associations in different sectors. Thus controversies over principles of legitimacy, justice and distribution seem likely to grow. A key question for the future is whether unions can succeed in bridging the cleavages between sectoral interests, occupational identification and class solidarity, and establish a new and more comprehensive social compromise (Dølvik et al. 1997).

If they fail to do so, one scenario is an upsurge in inter-union rivalry and the disruption of centralized co-operation, unleashing a dynamic of competing wage claims, inflation and distributional conflict. This would probably give renewed encouragement to employer demands for labour market deregulation and govern-ment intervention. At present, however, radical change or the dismantling of the Norwegian system of industrial relations do not appear likely. The high degree of integration and close ties between central, industrial and local levels characteristic of the Norwegian model have enabled it to display considerable adaptability. Despite employer misgivings, the solid local foundation of co-operation, encom-passing qualitative, supply-side issues, suggests that a relaxation of the centralized grip of recent years will not necessarily disrupt the system and might, if necessary, be subsequently reversed. Even if employers were to turn to a more autonomous approach, it seems improbable that they would break with the co-operative tradition by adopting a radical, unilateral agenda for decentralization and conflict, as in Sweden. In conclusion, therefore, the most likely scenario seems to be a process of cautious adjustment and decentralization, closely controlled by the central actors.

Abbreviations

AF   *Akademikernes Fellesorganisasjon* – Federation of Norwegian Professional Associations
HSH   *Handels- og Servicenæringens Hovedorganisasjon* – The Federation of Norwegian Commercial and Service Enterprises
KS   *Kommunenes Sentralforbund* – The Norwegian Association of Local Authorities
LO   *Landsorganisasjonen i Norge* – The Norwegian Confederation of Trade Unions
NAF   *Norges Arbeidsgiverforening* – Norwegian Employers' Confederation, merged in 1989 with two industry and craft associations to form NHO
NHO   *Næringslivets Hovedorganisasjon* – Confederation of Norwegian Business and Industry
YS   *Yrkesorganisasjonenes Sentralforbund* – The Confederation of Vocational Unions

Notes

1 Parts of this chapter build on previous work financed by the Research Council of Norway. The final version was written in the course of a research project on labour relations and collective agreements, financed by the Norwegian Ministry of Local Government and Labour. We wish to thank Kristine Nergaard and the editors for their comments.
2 As many authors have noted, a genuine corporatist mode of governance implies indirect, rather than direct, state intervention (e.g. Grant 1985). Patterns of implicit and indirect concertation are well-established in Norway, but the dominant actors have not provided sufficiently inclusive representation to avoid direct state intervention playing an indispensable role in the evolving concertation on incomes policy.
3 The figures include Oslo municipal authority which conducts its own bargaining.
4 These surveys are not fully representative, mainly because groups of part-time workers are excluded. They indicate a coverage rate of around 60 per cent, while other sources suggest that the true level is closer to 50 per cent (Stokke 1996a).
5 A surprising Labour Court decision in 1982 (cf. Høgsnes 1994: 634–42) made the mediator's right to combine votes somewhat uncertain, and today LO fulfils this task itself.

References and Further Reading

Aukrust, Odd 1977: Inflation in the open economy: A Norwegian model, in L. B. Krause and W. S. Salent (eds), *Worldwide Inflation: Theory and Recent Experience*, Washington DC: Brookings Institution.

Barth, Erling and Yin, H. 1995: Lønnsforskjeller og lønnsssystem i staten, in *Søkelys på arbeidsmarkedet* 2, 1995.

Berg, N., Grove, K., Grytli, T. and Olsen, T. 1997: *Håndbok for tillitsvalgte i konsern*. FAFO, Oslo: FAFO.

Bosch, G. 1997: Norwegian labour market flexibility in comparative perspective, in Dølvik and Steen (eds), *Making Solidarity Work? The Norwegian Labour Market Model in Transition*. Oslo: Scandinavian University Press.

Calmfors, Lars, and Driffil, J. 1988: Bargaining structure, corporativism and macroeconomic performance, *Economic Policy*, 6.

Dahl, Svein 1989: *Kleppepakkene – feilgrep eller sunn fornuft?* Solum, Oslo.

Dølvik, Jon Erik 1993: *Nordic Trade Unions and the Social Dimension of European Integration. Towards Europeanization or Renationalization of Trade Union Strategies?* Fafo, Oslo.

Dølvik, Jon Erik, Bråten, M., Longva, F. and Steen, A. H. 1997: Norwegian labour market institutions and regulations, in Dølvik and Steen (eds), *Making Solidarity Work? The Norwegian Labour Market Model in Transition*, Scandinavian University Press, Oslo.

Dølvik, Jon Erik and Olsen, Torunn 1994: *Arbeidslivspolitikk og fagorganisering i EØS og EU*, Fafo, Oslo.

Dølvik, Jon Erik and Stokland, Dag 1992: The Norwegian model in transition, in Ferner and Hyman, *Industrial relations in the New Europe*, Basil Blackwell, Oxford.

Eika, T. 1996: Petroleumsvirksomheten og norsk økonomi, in *Økonomiske Analyser*, 15.

Ellingsæter, A.L. and Rubery, J. 1997: Gender relations and the Norwegian labour market, in Dølvik and Steen (eds), *Making Solidarity Work? The Norwegian Labour Market Model in Transition*, Scandinavian University Press, Oslo.

Elvander, Nils 1988: *Den svenska modellen*, Publica, Stockholm.

Elvander, Nils 1989: Bargaining systems, incomes policies and conflict in the Nordic countries, in ILO: *Current Approaches to Collective Bargaining*, Geneva, ILO.

Evju, Stein 1991: *Aspects of Norwegian Labour Law*, Institutt for offentlig rett, Oslo.

Evju, Stein 1995: European labour law from a Norwegian perspective, in *Comparative Labour Law and Industrial Relations*, 11, 4.

Fennefoss, Arvid 1988: *Lønnstaker-organisering*, Fafo, Oslo.

Fennefoss, Arvid and Stokke, Torgeir Aarvaag 1991: Norske lønnstakeres organisering, in *Søkelys på arbeidsmarkedet*, 2, 1991.

Freeman, R.B. 1997: Are Norway's solidaristic and welfare state policies viable in the modern global economy?, in Dølvik and Steen (eds), *Making Solidarity Work? The Norwegian Labour Market Model in Transition*, Scandinavian University Press, Oslo.

Frøland, Hans Otto 1992: *Korporativt kompromiss gjennom korporativ konsert*, Historisk institutt (doctoral dissertation), Trondheim.

Frøland, Hans Otto 1996: *Lønnsforhandlinger gjennom korporative kompromiss*, Paper presented at LOS-conference 31 October 1996, Oslo.

Grant, W. 1985: Introduction, in Grant, W. (ed.), *The Political Economy of Corporatism*, Macmillan, London.

Hippe, Jon M. and Nergaard, Kristine 1992: *Collective Agreements Coverage in Norway*, Fafo (mimeo), Oslo.

Høgsnes, Geir 1994: *Collective Wage Bargaining and the Impact of Norms of Fairness*, Institutt for samfunnsforskning, Oslo.

Høgsnes, Geir 1995: Nyliberalisme og fleksibilitet i lønnsdannelsen, *Sosiologi i dag*, 4.

Holo, Lars and Dølvik, Jon Erik 1994: Rapport Norvégien, in *Social Policies in the Community Legal Order and the European Economic Area*, XIVth Congress, International Federation for European Law, Rome.

ILO 1980: *Conciliation and Arbitration Procedures in Labour Disputes*, ILO, Geneva.

Katzenstein, Peter J. 1985: *Small States in World Markets*. Cornell University Press, Ithaca.

Kjellberg, Anders 1992: Sweden: Can the model survive?, in Ferner and Hyman, *Industrial Relations in the New Europe*, Basil Blackwell, Oxford.

Knutsen, Paul 1993: *Korporatisme og klassekamp. Studier i forholdet mellom Norsk Arbeidsgiverforening, fagbevegelsen og statsmakten, 1915–1928*, University of Oslo (doctoral dissertation).

Kochan, Thomas and Katz, Harry C. 1988: *Collective Bargaining and Industrial Relations*, Homewood, IL: Irwin.

Langeland, Ove 1995: Alternative belønningsformer og incentivstrukturer i arbeidslivet, in Olberg, D. (ed.), *Endringer i arbeidslivets organisering*, Fafo, Oslo.

Mahnkopf, Birgit and Altvater, Elmer 1995: Transmission belts of transnational competition? Trade unions and collective bargaining in the context of European integration, *European Journal of Industrial Relations*, 1, 1.

Martin, A. 1994: The transformation of employment relations in Sweden, in Kochan, Locke and Piore (eds), *Employment Relations in a Changing World Economy*, MIT Press, Boston.

Mjøset, Lars, Cappelen, Ådne, Fagerberg, Jan and Tranøy, Bent Sofus 1994: Norway: Changing the model, in Anderson. P. and P. Camiller (eds), *Mapping the European Left*, Verso, London.

Nergaard, Kristine 1993: *Samarbeid og selvstendighet*, Fafo, Oslo.

Nergaard, Kristine 1996: *Organisasjonsgraden målt gjennom AKU 2. kvartal 1995*, Fafo, Oslo.

Nergaard, Kristine and Stokke, Torgeir Aarvaag 1996: *Midlertidige ansettelser i norsk arbeidsliv. Hvor mange, hvem, hvor og hvorfor?* Fafo, Oslo.

NHO/LO 1992: *Utredning av visse tariffspørsmål*, NHO, Oslo.

NHO 1995: *Nye driftsformer og tariffpolitikk. Fremtidens system for lønns- og arbeidsvilkår*, NHO, Oslo.

Norwegian Employment Commission 1992: *A national strategy for increased employment in the 1990s*, Ministry of Finance, Oslo.

NOU 1992:26: *En nasjonal strategi for økt sysselsetting i 90-årene.*

NOU 1993:18: *Lovgivning om menneskerettigheter .*

NOU 1996:14: *Prinsipper for ny arbeidstvistlov.*

NOU 1996:4: *Om grunnlaget for inntektsoppgjørene 1996.*

OECD 1995: *Economic Surveys – Norway*, OECD, Paris.

Olberg, D. 1995: Endringer i arbeidslivets organisering – en introduksjon, i Olberg (ed.), *Endringer i arbeidslivets organisering*, Fafo, Oslo.

Olsen, Torunn 1995 EUs arbeidslivspolitikk: Nasjonale og europeiske utfordringer, in *Tidsskrift for Samfunnsforskning*, 36, 4.

Rødseth, A. 1997: Why has unemployment been so low in Norway?, in Dølvik and Steen (eds), *Making Solidarity Work? The Norwegian Labour Market Model in Transition*, Scandinavian University Press, Oslo.

Rokkan, Stein 1967: Geography, religion and social class: Crosscutting cleavages in Norwegian politics, in Lipset and Rokkan (eds) *Party Systems and Voter Alignments. Cross-national Perspectives*, The Free Press, New York.

Rothstein, Bo 1990: Marxism, institutional analysis, and working-class power: The Swedish case, in *Politics and Society*, 18, 3.

Scheuer, Steen 1997: Collective bargaining coverage and the status divide: Denmark, Norway and the United Kingdom compared, *European Journal of Industrial Relations*, 3, 1.

Seim, Jardar 1972: *Hvordan Hovedavtalen av 1935 ble til*, Tiden, Oslo.

Sisson, K. 1987: *The Management of Collective Bargaining*. Oxford: Blackwell Publishers.

Skånland, Hermod 1996: Solidaritetsalternativets fall og fremtid, Aftenposten, 8/6–1996.

Stokke, Torgeir Aarvaag 1995: *Organisasjonsgraden på arbeidstakersiden 1956–1994*, Fafo, Oslo.

Stokke, Torgeir Aarvaag 1996a: *Estimering av tariffavtaledekningen i Norge – strategier og foreløpige makrotall*, Fafo, Oslo.

Stokke, Torgeir Aarvaag 1996b: *NHO: Medlemmer, organisasjonsgrader og tariffavtaler*, Fafo, Oslo.

Stokke, Torgeir Aarvaag 1996c: *Konfliktløsning og lønnsforhandlinger i Skandinavia*, Paper presented at LOS conference, 1 November, Oslo.

Streeck, Wolfgang 1993: The rise and decline of neocorporatism, in Ulman, Lloyd et al. (eds) *Labor and an Integrated Europe*, The Brookings Institution, Washington DC.

Stueland, Einar, Thoresen, Finn E. and Østvold, Per 1994: *Norsk fagbevegelse og den europeiske unionen*, SME/NTEU, Oslo.

Traxler, Franz 1990: Political exchange, collective action and interest governance. Towards a theory of the genesis of industrial relations and corporatism, in Marin, B. (ed.) *Governance and Generalized Exchange. Self-Organizing Policy Networks in Action*, Campus – Westview, Frankfurt/Boulder.

Traxler, Franz 1994: Collective bargaining: levels and coverage, *OECD Employment Outlook*, Paris.

Traxler, Franz 1996: Collective bargaining and industrial change: A case of disorganization? A comparative analysis of eighteen OECD countries, *European Sociological Review*, 12, 3.

Traxler, Franz and Schmitter, P.C. 1994: *Prospective Thoughts on Regional Integration, Interest Politics and Policy Formulation in the EC/EU*, Paper for the International Political Science Association XIVth Congress, Berlin.

Visser, J. and Ebbinghaus, B. 1992: Making the most of diversity? European integration and transnational organization of labour, in Greenwood, Justin, Grote, Jürgen and Ronit, Karsten (eds), *Organized Interests and the European Community*, Sage, London.

Wallerstein, M. and Golden, M. 1996: *The Fragmentation of the Bargaining Society? Changes in the Centralization of Wage-Setting in the Nordic Countries 1950–1992*, UCLA (paper), Los Angeles.

5 | Denmark: A Less Regulated Model

STEEN SCHEUER

Introduction

'Decentralization' and 'flexibility' have been the industrial relations watchwords of the 1980s and 1990s. Denmark is no exception to the general trend towards more decentralized pay bargaining. This has involved two distinct elements: first, the settlement of general terms and conditions in collective bargaining agreements has been transferred increasingly from national, multi-industry bargaining to national single-industry bargaining; second, the determination of actual earnings has been devolved from the national, industry-wide level to local workplace bargaining.

Many observers regard decentralization as a symptom of a serious crisis in the Scandinavian model of industrial relations, particularly in Sweden but also in Denmark (e.g. Amoroso 1990), while others have emphasized the in-built stability and strength of the 'Danish Model' (e.g. Due et al. 1994). Is decentralization in Denmark really something new, or are actors merely rediscovering 'lost patterns' from the period before the strong centralization of bargaining in the 1960s and especially the 1970s? What impact have bargaining changes had on the institutional framework that is an important part of the 'Scandinavian model'? Has this framework been dismantled since the end of the centralized bargaining and incomes policies of the 1970s, or has it been revitalized?

Industrial relations actors have faced other challenges in the 1990s. Their strength is partly a reflection of their membership density. Denmark, like Sweden, experienced high and increasing union densities in the 1980s and 1990s. As in other Scandinavian countries, however, the dominant position of the major union confederation, LO, has been undermined, with growing numbers of employees joining unions outside LO. This poses a serious challenge to the Scandinavian model and to the ability of LO unions to make their influence felt.

Another challenge is the imposition of EU directives. There is continuing debate as to whether this threatens to weaken the Danish system of industrial relations, and whether implementation should be through collective agreements rather than legislation.

One issue raised by the decentralization of bargaining is the role of collective industrial relations actors at the workplace level. There is not a great deal of research into local workplace bargaining over pay and related issues in Denmark, but some recent studies have cast new light on the local roles of industrial relations actors. It appears that the workplace is in many cases much less well-regulated than previously thought, and that industrial relations actors face a major challenge in responding to tendencies that may weaken their role.

The answers to these questions will provide clues to the future direction of Danish industrial relations and the fate of the broader Scandinavian model. The next section sets the scene by outlining the nature of the Danish economy and labour market. The origins of Danish industrial relations in the historic agreement of 1899 are then described, and the key institutional dynamics of the system examined. This section also summarizes the main features of union structure. The fourth section turns to developments in the last couple of decades. It deals with the impact of the 1970s crises in the world economy on the development of Danish industrial relations, looking in turn at the subsequent evolution of union density, organization and strategies; the changing policies of the conservative–liberal governments of the 1980s and 1990s; and the trend towards decentralization in bargaining. In particular, it assesses the role of unemployment insurance funds in explaining the persistence of high union density. The section also examines the strategies of employers in response to the challenge of flexibility.

The Danish Economy and the Labour Market

Denmark is a small, open, exporting economy. It is thus very dependent on fluctuations in the world economy and has an interest in minimizing trade barriers in the world market. Thirty-eight per cent of industrial production is exported, the major exports being agricultural (butter, bacon, canned ham) and related products, such as agricultural machinery, beer, and insulin (formerly derived from pigs' pancreases).

Though there are some large manufacturing companies (e.g. B&O, Lego, Monberg & Thorsen) and important transport and shipping firms (such as A.P. Møller [Maersk] and ØK [EAC]), Denmark has a large proportion of small and medium-sized enterprises. During the 1980s, there was a marked shift of employment from large to small and medium-sized firms. By the early 1990s, little more than a fifth of employees in Danish industry were employed in firms with 500 employees or more compared with over a quarter in 1978. Half of all employees in industry work for firms with between 50 and 500 employees, and a further quarter in firms of between 10 and 50 employees (*Statistical Ten-Year Review* 1989 and 1992).

Important changes have taken place in the structure of firms. These include a wave of company mergers, notably in food and drink, pharmaceuticals, and banking. For example, Novo and Nordisk Centofte combined to form the new

Novo Nordisk, controlling almost half the world market in insulin; De Danske Spritfabrikker (Danish strong spirits), Danske Sukkerfabrikker (sugar industry) and Danisco merged to become the largest food-processing company in Denmark (no small achievement); and two new 'mega-banks' were created, Den Danske Bank and UniBank Danmark. While mergers peaked in 1989, merger activity in the 1990s has been higher than in the 1980s (Molin and Pedersen 1996: 52). These mergers are indications of a process of concentration among the very largest Danish firms. Between 1974 and 1987, the 30 largest manufacturing companies increased their share of manufacturing employment from 21 to 27 per cent, although this was far below the comparable figures for the other Nordic countries (Pestoff 1991: 31–2).

Some observers consider the rather small size of Danish firms a weakness. Small firms tend to spend relatively less on R&D, and there is evidence that Denmark spends less in this field than comparable competitors. The fear is, therefore, that it will become progressively more difficult for Danish firms to maintain their international position in areas where research efforts are an important part of competitiveness, in high-tech industries and in biotechnology, for example. However, others claim that competitive industrial performance is possible not only in large, capital-intensive corporations but also in small companies operating in networks (Kristensen 1996). While such firms may not be able to mass-produce at a competitive price compared to Germany or Sweden (or countries with lower wage costs), they are characterized by greater dynamism and the ability to innovate rapidly, enabling them to be the first to enter new markets or to launch new products, such as wind generators (cf. Karnøe 1991).

Since small and medium-sized firms form the backbone of the Danish economy, laws regulating the labour market have, to a large extent, aimed to facilitate employment mobility, providing relatively generous unemployment benefits, rather than to impose rigid job security rules on the individual firm (Jensen et al. 1987). With high and persistent unemployment in the 1970s and 1980s, this system came under increasing pressure, since it placed a substantial burden on public expenditure. Almost 6 per cent of GDP was spent on these measures in 1989, by far the highest level in Europe and more than double that of Britain, France, Germany, and the other Nordic countries (OECD 1991: 240–8). Unemployment increased from the middle of the 1970s, reaching 10 per cent of the dependent workforce in 1983 before slowly falling again. Since 1993, there has been a marked decrease in unemployment, due to a general economic upturn, changes in legislation on unemployment benefit, and increased possibilities for employees to take temporary leave from work (see below).

Denmark has a labour force of 2.7 million, of whom almost 90 per cent are employees. The labour force has grown significantly faster than the population as a whole, mainly because of higher participation by women. For every 100 men in the labour force there are 84 women, compared with 48 in 1958. This trend is common to all western countries, but nowhere so marked as in Scandinavia. Thus, while labour force participation has been declining somewhat for men, it has increased for women from 39 per cent in 1960, to 71 per cent in 1980 and 76 per cent in 1990 (Brüniche-Olsen 1996: 34). The category of 'housewife' has virtually

Table 5.1 The relative distribution of the labour force in Denmark by sector (%), 1960–1995

	Primary	Secondary	Tertiary private sector	Tertiary public sector
1960	21	33	32	14
1970	11	34	33	21
1980	8	27	32	33
1990	6	26	33	35
1995	5	25	37	33

Source: Statistical Yearbook of Denmark and Statistical ten-year review, various years.

disappeared in Denmark. In 1965, 66 per cent of mothers with children up to 6 years of age were full-time housewives, in 1987 the figure was 5 per cent (Christoffersen 1993: 113–15).

A related development has been the growth of the tertiary sector: accounting for just under half the labour force in 1960, it now employs more than 70 per cent. Two areas of employment stand out in this growth: public services and private financial services. Both sectors have more than doubled their employment in the period from 1960 to 1995, finance from 3 to 9 per cent, and public services from 14 to 33 per cent of the total labour force (see table 5.1).

The public sector has thus been the main field of employment expansion, and also the area where most women currently in employment have taken up work. Private services other than finance have not shown the same growth: their workforce has grown in absolute but not relative terms. In Denmark, the transition from 'industrial society' to 'service society' has to a very great extent been a transition to a 'public service society'. This has had some clear implications for industrial relations and for the unions.

The Basic Features of Danish Industrial Relations

The Making of the Institutional Setting

The origins of the Danish industrial relations system can be traced back to the 'September Compromise' of 1899. This followed a bitter conflict, subsequently known as the 'Hundred Days' War', between the newly formed Employers' Association (DA) and the union confederation, LO (then DsF), established in 1896 and 1898, respectively. Following a series of minor strikes, the employers launched an all-out confrontation in an attempt to impose a permanent framework of industrial relations upon the unions. Their aims included a greater centralization of bargaining and union recognition of management prerogative. They also wanted the unions and DsF to accept the principle that collective bargaining agreements should be observed until they expired (usually after 2 years): in effect, a 'peace obligation'.

The employers did achieve many of their aims, but the unions imposed a price which proved valuable in the long run. Managerial prerogative was recognized, and written into the collective agreement. Some observers, including recently Due and colleagues, have seen this as a major defeat (Due et al. 1994: 92), while others have argued that the agreement merely formalized an issue that the unions had never really contested. Indeed, some have regarded the concession of managerial prerogative as a fig leaf for the employers. The unions also accepted responsibility for enforcing collective agreements – with the centralization of bargaining that this implied. It was, however, national unions rather than DsF that became responsible for agreements, since DsF was not in general the bargaining partner. DA's aim of a complete centralization of responsibility for bargaining and for enforcing collective agreements was not achieved.

It is important to note in this connection that collective responsibility for policing agreements was (and is) two-way. The peace obligation extended also to employers. Lockouts were prohibited while collective agreements were in force, and individual employers who did not adhere to agreements (on pay, working hours, notice of dismissal, etc.) would certainly be held to account. In subsequent decades this became, and remains, a major source of union power, since unions were able to enforce agreements even if their members in a specific area were unwilling or unable to fight for their implementation. Thus the formal working of the system made union power to a large extent independent of membership militancy and much less sensitive to unemployment.

An important element of the September compromise was the recognition by each party of the other's right to organize. The recognition of unions as legitimate bargaining partners was no small matter in the Denmark of 1899, some two years before the introduction of parliamentary democracy. Following the agreement, an industrial court and arbitration tribunals were established, where anti-union activities of individual employers were repeatedly challenged. In Sweden, by contrast, workers only gained these rights in the 1930s. As a consequence of these arrangements, union membership grew steadily in the following decades.

In the years after 1899, employers and unions called on parliament to give legal backing to the industrial court system *(Arbejdsretten)*, together with the various arbitration arrangements and the procedures for the renegotiation of expiring agreements. The system has been written into law (generally on the basis of the joint proposals of the two parties) and is also codified in the so-called Main Agreement *(Hovedaftalen)*. This agreement was revised in 1960, in 1973 and most recently in 1993, introducing rules on the protection of the union shop-floor representative (the *tillidsmand*), co-operative committees in the enterprise *(Samarbejdsudvalg)*, the working environment, and the introduction of new technology. However, its basic planks are essentially those established in 1899, and in the main, the workings of the Danish system of industrial relations date back to this compromise.

In general, the early emergence of relatively strong collective actors has meant that several areas of working life, which in other countries would be governed by legislation, are regulated by collective bargaining (OECD 1994: 154). Thus collective agreements determine rules on overtime, shift work, notice of redundancy or lay-offs, and maximum and minimum working hours (for example, the agreements for some groups of manual workers prohibit part-time working). Minimum wage rates (at 74.80 DKK [£6.82] per hour in September 1997) have always been regulated by collective bargaining.

The advantage of this system is that it is seen as more flexible than one based on legislation. Collective labour market actors can adjust rules more quickly and flexibly to changing demands, or to specific sectoral or local conditions, without the rigidity and inertia of legal regulation (cf. e.g. Due et al. 1994: 12). Furthermore, the Industrial Court provides individuals and organizations covered by collective agreements with a mechanism for resolving conflicts that is quicker and more convenient than systems based on the use of civil courts, as in the USA. The disadvantage of the Danish system is that not all private-sector employees are employed under a collective agreement, and thus do not enjoy the rights and minima contained in these agreements. This traditional pattern of limited legal intervention may of course be affected by developments in European social regulation, as is discussed below.

A key issue in Danish industrial relations is the problem of reaching a new settlement when existing agreements expire. The existence of a bargaining agreement is crucial for industrial peace. This is because the peace obligation on the parties (including individual employees and unions, but not LO) ceases to exist when agreements run out. Both employers and unions have a strong tradition of threatening industrial action (in accordance with the procedural rules) when expiry approaches, and strikes and lockouts commonly occur in the context of contract renewal. Given the synchronized and co-ordinated nature of bargaining, industrial action on a very large scale may occur if negotiations break down. The state mediator has an important role in avoiding open conflict by calling upon the parties to take part in bargaining, and by exercising the power to postpone conflicts (if there is hope of agreement) twice for a fortnight. The mediator may also put forward his or her own proposal for a new agreement, and require the parties to hold a ballot on this proposal. But these attempts – though often successful – may also fail.

In such cases, a tradition has developed in Denmark (as in Norway) of parliamentary intervention to end the conflict. Parliament may prolong existing agreements for a two-year period unchanged, or it may adopt the state mediator's proposal after it has been rejected by negotiators or by a ballot of the membership. Alternatively, parliament may devise its own new agreement, usually on the basis of existing agreements and possibly incorporating proposals from the state mediator. In all cases the effect is to introduce a new and binding collective 'agreement' for the following two years, together with a built-in peace obligation on the parties. The tradition of parliamentary intervention to resolve a deadlock in collective bargaining dates back to 1933. In the wake of the world-wide economic crisis, Danish employers threatened a general lockout to impose substantial pay reductions. The social-democratic government intervened through parliament, prolonging existing agreements with some minor modifications, and also devalued the Danish krone, causing a reduction in real pay. Since the war, there has been a series of interventions, many of them when special groups outside the scope of LO–DA negotiations have been unable to reach agreement. It has generally been considered unacceptable for such groups to engage in conflict, with major repercussions for the rest of the labour market, when all other groups have already reached a settlement. Such 'lagging' behaviour is seen as an attempt to hold the rest of the labour market to ransom, and great efforts are made (especially by the state mediator – see below) to make potential 'laggards' fall into line (Scheuer 1991).

But there have also been interventions in general bargaining, as for example in the 1956 round, when a ballot of union members rejected the negotiated settlement which was then enforced by parliament, and again in the 1963 round, when parliament created the so-called 'aggregate solution' *(Helhedsløsningen)*, and prolonged existing agreements – in effect an early attempt at incomes policy (see Auken and Buksti 1975).

The positive side of such intervention (and the rationale for it) is that, in the short run, industrial peace is secured and major conflict avoided. There is, however, also a negative side: the peace obligation in collective agreements has generally been justified by trade union leaders (especially when confronted with left-wing criticism) on the grounds that agreements are subject to endorsement by the membership in union ballots. This legitimacy is lost if settlements are repeatedly imposed by parliament, as they were in the 1970s. Thus, from a long-term perspective, intervention by parliament in collective bargaining must be minimized if the system is to work.

Trade Union Structure

In international comparisons, Danish union structure is often seen as among the most heavily influenced by craft unionism (e.g. Visser 1990, Kjellberg 1983). The structure is sometimes simply described as being 'predominantly based on crafts' (Amoroso 1990: 78). The latter statement is, however, an exaggeration: only 12 per cent of the dependent workforce are classified as skilled workers, and membership in craft unions accounted for 12.5 per cent of aggregate union membership in 1995. Thus well over 80 per cent of union members are in unions not 'based on crafts'. The following types of unions exist.

Craft Unions and General Unions

The labour movement in Denmark, as in Britain, has developed along craft and general union lines, rather than in the form of industrial unionism as in Sweden or Germany. General unions, once established as a response by unskilled workers to a craft unionism that has little to offer them, often stand in the way of subsequent attempts to create industrial unionism. In Denmark, the establishment of general unions followed a very distinct pattern. Unskilled workers reacted to the creation of unions for skilled workers by attempting to form their own local unions. The first was established in 1873. But it was not until 1897 that a national general workers' union, *Dansk Arbejdsmandsforbund*, was formed (Lund 1972: 39). Excluded from what was eventually to become the *Specialarbejderforbundet*, SiD, unskilled female workers were forced to create their own women-only union, KAD (Union of Female Workers in Denmark). This union still exists and it has 93,000 members, all women. Chief among the general unions is the white-collar union, HK (Union of Commercial and Clerical Employees). With 360,000 members, it is today the biggest single Danish union. HK organizes 'across the board', in the private as well as the public sector. Most craft and general unions are members of LO.

Industrial Unions – Vertical and Non-vertical

Not all Danish unions are craft or general. In some industries, for example food processing and wood, industrial unionism has been established. Some industrial unions are not comprehensive in their recruitment. Those mentioned above do not organize supervisors or other salaried employees. Others recruit members at all levels of the organizational hierarchy. Such comprehensive industrial unions exist in the finance sector and for civil servants in the traditional occupations of the public sector. Blue-collar industrial unions are members of LO, while the comprehensive ones are mostly members of FTF (Central Confederation of Salaried Employees).

Professional Unions

Associations of professional groups have increasingly adopted union-like behaviour and must today be counted as unions. This category includes all unions of professionals, but also a whole range of semi-professional groups, such as schoolteachers, nurses, librarians and social workers. University graduates' unions are members of AC (Central Confederation of Professional Associations), while the semi-professionals' unions are mostly members of FTF.

Status Unions

Finally, there are bodies that could be labelled 'service' or 'status' unions. These are unions for groups attempting to defend their position in the face of strong unions of the categories mentioned above. One example is the Supervisors' Union, defending not only supervisors' pay differentials, but also the 'status differential' of those who have risen from the shop-floor either into management (as supervisors) or into technical jobs (e.g. in the drawing office). The resulting typology is shown in table 5.2.

Professional and craft unions together account for 29 per cent of Danish union members. General unions on the other hand command 46 per cent of aggregate membership, while industrial unions cover 14 per cent. Finally, status and others form 10 per cent of union membership. The overall impression is one of stability over the past decade or so, although the decline of craft and the increase of professional unionism are worthy of note.

Table 5.2 Typology of unions in Denmark, with estimates of membership distribution

	Total membership (000s)		Share of union members (%)	
	1985	*1995*	*1985*	*1995*
Craft	276	270	14	12
General	947	1,002	48	46
Professional	294	357	15	17
Industrial				
vertical	101	129	5	6
non-vertical	163	176	8	8
Status	155	162	8	7
Other	35	67	2	3
Aggregate membership	1,971	2,163	100	99

Source: Statistical Yearbook of Denmark,1986 and 1996.

The 'craft and general' nature of Danish union structure is substantial and undeniable. However, with the decentralized bargaining of the 1980s and 1990s taking place mainly along industrial lines, there is an apparent contradiction between 'membership structure', which is craft and general, and 'bargaining structure', which is in the main industrial (Scheuer 1990: 44–77). This has prompted repeated attempts to build bargaining cartels of unions with substantial member groups in major sectors of the Danish economy. Grandiose plans were drawn up by the LO at the end of the 1980s, but they have had only limited success. In the public sector, two bargaining cartels do exist (one for state employees, one for regional and local employees), and in manufacturing, the traditionally strong cartel of metalworkers (skilled and unskilled) has broadened its scope to encompass manufacturing generally, and it includes the lower tiers of salaried employees. In the rest of the private sector, however, the established cartels have so far proved very weak, and collective bargaining is still the responsibility of the national unions. The reason for this lack of success of the attempted 'rationalization' of union structure lies primarily in the opposition of SiD, the powerful general workers' union. Not only has it resisted attempts to break it up, it has even counteracted the cartel structure by absorbing several smaller unions, such as those for bricklayers, seamen, and textile workers. Industrial unionism as a general organizing principle seems farther away than ever in Denmark.

Despite the complexity of union structure in Denmark, demarcation disputes and poaching are relatively rare. This is because the recruitment boundaries of union unemployment insurance funds (closely related to union membership) have to be approved by the Ministry of Labour, and thus a union cannot recruit members in what is clearly another union's domain since it cannot legally pay such a member unemployment benefit. Existing demarcations are therefore institutionalized and maverick behaviour restrained.

A further feature of union structure is the changing balance between individual

Table 5.3 The development of union confederations' share of union members (%) 1945–1995

Year	LO	FTF	AC	FR	Outside
1945	96	*	*	.	4
1950	95	*	*	.	5
1955	81	10	*	2	5
1960	79	12	*	3	5
1965	79	12	*	3	5
1970	78	14	*	3	4
1975	73	16	3	2	5
1980	72	16	4	1	7
1985	71	16	4	1	8
1990	68	15	5	3	6
1995	70	15	6	3	5

* Union confederation not in existence.
Source: Statistical Yearbook of Denmark, various years.

unions and union confederations. Not surprisingly, unions with a mainly blue-collar membership have been in gradual decline. Table 5.3 shows the overall share of union membership by union confederation. LO unions have been able to recruit many of the new white-collar groups, especially lower-level salaried employees. Nevertheless, they are losing ground, especially to unions within the FTF (middle-level salaried employees and semi-professional groups, mainly in the public and in the finance sectors) and also to some independent unions. Today, 70 per cent of union members are members of an LO union, a figure which shows a very slow decline, from 78 per cent in 1970 (see also table 5.4); FTF has around 15 per cent. LO has tried to counteract the downward trend by attracting FTF unions or those which have not hitherto belonged to a union confederation. LO is thus gradually losing its status as 'sole representative' of the employee side of industrial relations (although the rate of decline has slowed since the 1970s).

Table 5.4 Aggregate union membership, number of employees in labour force and union densities in Denmark, 1960–1995 (000's)

Year	Number of union members (1)	LO membership (2)	Number of employees (3)	Union density (4) (= 3/1) (%)
1960	932.5	739.5	1,533.5	60.8
1965	1,061.5	834.0	1,714.3	61.9
1970	1,140.2	894.4	1,856.1	61.4
1975	1,303.5	953.3	2,052.7	63.5
1980	1,747.1	1,249.6	2,245.8	77.8
1985	1,963.7	1,399.1	2,434.0	80.7
1990	2,106.8	1,423.0	2,629.1	80.1
1995	2,162.8	1,509.7	2,648.4	81.7

Source: Statistical Yearbook of Denmark, various years.

In addition, the character of LO itself is changing. In 1970, around a quarter of its membership were salaried employees; by 1995 this figure had grown to around 45 per cent. The General Workers' Union, SiD, had almost 40 per cent of LO membership in the late 1940s, but this share has declined sharply, and today SiD has little more than a fifth of the total (316,000 members). At the same time, HK – the main LO union for white-collar employees, which affiliated in 1932 – has increased its share from under 10 per cent in the 1940s and 1950s to 24 per cent (361,000 members) today, making it the biggest LO union. It organizes lower-level clerical employees in both private and public sectors (unlike the situation in Norway and Sweden, where clerical employees are mostly unionized outside LO). The largely white-collar Union of Public Employees, FOA, has also increased its share of LO membership, and is now bigger than the blue-collar skilled metal workers' union (Dansk Metal).

Although LO has succeeded in expanding its organizational territory well beyond the traditional blue-collar sectors, most semi-professionals (teachers, nurses, finance employees) still seem out of reach. The LO's ability to halt the downward trend of its share of union membership will depend mainly on the strategies of co-operation or competition that it pursues with regard to FTF and its member unions. The rationalization of LO's membership structure has been a priority for many years. Mergers reduced the 72 member unions in LO in 1946 to 57 by 1971 and to 24 today.

▎ Employer Organization

Membership in the employers' association, DA, has been stable through the 1980s and 1990s, when measured by the number of employees in firms which are members of the DA. DA's 'share' of private sector employees is approximately 525,000 out of 1.3 million, i.e. 40 per cent. If one also includes other minor employers' associations, the aggregate 'coverage' by these organizations is 675,000 employees, or 51 per cent of the private labour market. No reliable time series of employer organization exists, but available data suggest that this level has been stable for a number of years. It must be noted that, despite its modest share of the workforce compared with union density of employees, the DA has maintained a dominant role as the 'trendsetter' for pay developments in the private and (therefore also) in the public sector.

In recent years there has been a major restructuring of DA's member associations. Until around 1990, DA had both individual firms and industrial or local employers' associations as members. The number of affiliated organizations had remained stable at around 150 for many years. As a result of extensive restructuring and mergers between smaller units, the number of member organizations had been reduced to 28 by the end of 1996, and the process is continuing (information from DA). One of the more important mergers was between the employers' associations in the metal industry and in general manufacturing. The resulting association, Dansk Industri (DI), covers a little more than half of all employees employed by DA members, and it therefore presents an implicit threat to the central authority of DA. There is no doubt that these organizational changes have reinforced the decentralizing trend in collective bargaining.

In the Danish finance sector – outside the scope of LO and DA – the move to industry bargaining has been encouraged by mergers on both the employer and union sides. The previously separate employers' associations for clearing and savings banks have merged, and the four minor unions for employees in clearing and savings banks, insurance companies and property institutions, agreed to amalgamate into a single finance union (Andersen 1995).

While structural change both in the employers' associations and the unions has generally been planned and carried out under the central direction of DA and LO, the outcome may be to accelerate a limited process of decentralization. New structures have, in practice, weakened the authority of the central confederations and increased the emphasis on industry-level bargaining in the 1990s.

The Crises: Intervention in the 1970s, 'De-intervention' in the 1980s

With its high degree of dependence on exports and foreign trade, Denmark was hard hit by the oil crises. After a period (lasting from 1959 to 1973) of virtually full employment, unemployment rose to 7–10 per cent of the dependent workforce. Inflation rose, balance of payments deficits grew, and the problems of public expenditure worsened. These factors were interrelated: for example, public employment was used to stem the rise in unemployment, exacerbating the problem of public sector deficits already under strain from the burden of rising unemployment benefit payments. (The level of unemployment benefit had been increased substantially in the days of full employment.) Such developments created pressures for change, not only in the political arena, but in industrial relations as well. There were moves towards new patterns of negotiation and industrial relations problem-solving. These new patterns did not prove durable, however, and they were partly reversed in the 1980s and 1990s.

Implications of the Crises (I): Union Densities and Unemployment Insurance

Union strength – whether measured by membership numbers or by union density – increased slightly in the 1950s. With the substantial rise in labour force participation in the 1960s, density stagnated, although absolute numbers of members increased. But the period from 1973 to the beginning of the 1980s was marked by a very substantial increase both in the number of union members and in union density. Aggregate union membership rose from 932,000 in 1960 to 1.1 million in 1970, and to 1.7 million in 1980; density was constant at 61 per cent in the period from 1960 to 1970, but increased to 78 per cent in 1980, rising by almost three percentage points every year between 1975 and 1980 (see tables 5.4

Table 5.5 Aggregate union membership, number of employees in labour force and union densities in Denmark. 1960–1995

	Yearly changes in membership (000s)	Yearly changes in union densities (%)
1960–65	25.8	0.22
1965–70	15.7	−0.10
1970–75	32.7	0.42
1975–80	88.7	2.86
1980–85	43.3	0.58
1985–90	28.6	−0.12
1990–95	11.2	0.32

Source: Table 5.3.

and 5.5). Membership and density have also been increasing since 1980, but much more slowly The number of members passed 2 million in 1989 – having doubled over the previous 25 years, and density reached 81.7 per cent in 1995.

One consequence is that traditional variations in union organization have more or less disappeared in Denmark. It is no longer true that blue-collar workers are much better unionized than salaried employees, men than women, public-sector employees than private sector employees, employees from large enterprises than employees from small enterprises, and so on. This is borne out by available survey evidence (see table 5.6). Although there are still slight differences in union density between workers and salaried employees, with workers a little over and salaried employees a little below the 90 per cent mark, these represent only minor variations in a general picture of virtually total unionization.

Table 5.6 Union densities of male and female, and of manual and non-manual employees according to omnibus survey data. Percentage of employees in union. 1966–1995

Year	Employees				
	Male	Female	Manual	Non-manual	All
1966	79	53	77	67	71
1972	77	53	72	62	67
1976	81	65	78	71	74
1979	85	75	84	77	80
1982	89	84	88	85	86
1985	89	88	90	87	88
1987	89	87	91	87	88
1991	–	–	87	88	88
1994	88	88	94	84	88
1995	–	–	93	86	88

Source: Living Conditions in Denmark – compendium of Statistics by the Danish National Institute of Social Research (1992), and Scheuer (1996).

Why is it that union density in Denmark has risen with rising unemployment, when the opposite is the case in many other Western market economies?

The Role of Unemployment Insurance and of Individual Services

Some writers have argued that the way in which unemployment insurance is organized in Denmark amounts to a state-financed system of union recruitment (e.g. Pedersen 1989; Neumann et al. 1991). From the early days of Danish trade unionism, unemployment insurance funds (UIFs) were established alongside the unions, together with strike funds, sickness insurance funds, etc. UIFs have increasingly been financed by the state and as a result have formally become financially and legally separated from the unions. In practice, however, a close link remains, since virtually every LO union has its own UIF, and the elected officials are mostly union leaders. With increasing unemployment in the 1970s, many white-collar and professional unions established their own UIFs. Formally, one may be a UIF member without being a union member. In practice this is difficult, especially in manual unions where norms of solidarity with the unemployed are dominant and the funds are seen as an integral part of union organization. Unemployment benefit rates were higher than in many other western European countries in the 1970s (about 70 per cent of a manual worker's mean annual wage), while members' contributions were moderate. The state bore almost 90 per cent of the costs of unemployment benefit.

The argument that UIFs encourage union membership finds support in the early-retirement scheme – the so-called 'post-employment wage' – introduced by the social-democratic and liberal coalition government in 1979. Designed to make room for more young people in the workforce, it provided pensions from the age of 60 (normal age of retirement in Denmark is 67) for workers who had been UIF members for 5 of the last 10 years (amended in 1980 to 10 of the last 15 years). The programme was a great success, in terms of the number of those eligible who took early retirement. For the unions, this scheme had the advantage of deterring older members from leaving the union (and the UIF), since it would disqualify them from the scheme. It was in effect an early retirement scheme for union members only (or more strictly, for UIF members only).

The role of the UIF system in encouraging union membership has, however, been questioned. Assumptions about the system that seemed obvious 10 years ago seem questionable today. From 1982, compensation levels were cut in real terms and employees' contributions tripled. But even though unemployment insurance is formally voluntary in Denmark (like Sweden but unlike most other European countries), these changes had absolutely no effect on union densities (Arbejdsmin-isteriet et al. 1989: 87; Scheuer 1989: 34–5); membership of UIFs actually increased remarkably, from 66 per cent of the labour force in 1982 to 78.5 per cent in 1995 (*Statistical Ten-Year Review*).

Government policies towards UIFs in the 1980s reflected two objectives. One was to reduce unemployment. There was indeed some fall in unemployment in the early years of the new government, but from 1986 the figure rose again; in 1991 it surpassed the previous peak reached in 1983. The other objective was to reduce the substantial financial burden on the state budget, and the government had some success in shifting the costs of unemployment benefit to the labour market actors. The tripling of employees' contributions and quadrupling of those of employers reduced the share financed by the state from 88 per cent in 1982 to 65 per cent in 1989 (Arbejdsministeriet et al. 1989). At the same time, the value of unemployment benefit fell from 71 per cent of mean annual income in 1982 to 64 per cent in 1988, primarily as a result of the government's decision to freeze the level of benefit.

Following the election of a social-democrat-led government in 1993, with a social-democrat minister of labour, rules concerning unemployment benefit underwent substantial changes. The government rejected a neo-liberal approach of cutting unemployment benefit levels and shortening the duration of benefit. Instead it introduced major reforms of the system. First, 'active' demands on claimants were increased. This meant that unemployment benefit claimants would have to take up jobs or training offers, but these offers did not give them access to renewed periods of unemployment benefit, as had previously been the case. If the claimant was unable to find gainful employment within 7 years, he or she would then drop out of the UIF and lose entitlement to unemployment benefit. This regime is still much less strict than in most other OECD countries. Another perhaps more significant tightening of policies was to make it harder for people under 25 years of age to claim unemployment benefit. People under 25 are given job offers immediately (at reduced pay). This has led to a sharp fall in unemployment in this particular group. Second, a successful cornerstone of the labour market reform has been a policy of fighting 'bottle-necks' by means of an active training policy under which decentralized Labour Market Councils respond to shortages of specialized skills in the local workforce by running programmes at local public training centres. Third, the reform increased the scope for individuals to take leave on a lower level of benefit. Employees could take educational leave to improve their qualifications; extended parental leave; or employment 'sabbaticals'. The last of these had the lowest level of benefit of the three. All three forms proved popular.

There has been debate over how far government policies have contributed to the fall in unemployment since 1993. Some observers (and the conservative–liberal opposition in parliament) attribute the fall to the enormously popularity of the leave schemes. Although this is undoubtedly part of the explanation, the labour market reforms, both of training and of policies for the younger unemployed, appear to have had independent positive effects. Although some unions, especially the General Workers' Union (SiD) have protested against parts of the reform, it does not appear to have had any detrimental effects on unions.

Union Services

Whether or not unions can grow in a weak labour market partly depends on the range of services on offer to potential members. Some of the specific traits of Danish industrial relations seem to assist unions in this respect. The first may be called bargaining implementation. As mentioned earlier, collective agreements are binding on the parties: unions can be fined if their members break the rules, but this goes for individual employers and their associations as well. Thus employers who try to exploit high unemployment to pay below the contract rates (or who dismiss employees without observing notice periods) can be taken to the industrial court and fined. In this way, unions do not have to rely on membership militancy to enforce agreements. This is particularly important in times of unemployment. The rights of the employees under collective agreements are collective rights, so that complaints can only be taken to the industrial court by the union (or rather, the union confederation, LO). In other words, the unions have in some cases a monopoly in defending workers' rights through the industrial court, a power that they exercise effectively. As a result, union membership is imperative for workers needing help in protecting their rights under collective agreements.

In the 1980s and 1990s, there has been a slight tendency for these principles to be eroded. Civil courts have increasingly allowed individual employees who are not union members to bring cases on legally regulated matters of employment protection. But these are exceptions, and even for groups of employees, the cost of access to the civil courts (for example on matters of equal pay) is prohibitive. This tendency has to do with the increased role of EU regulation and the European Court. Increasingly, the supra-national institutions demand that employee rights are given at the level of the individual, and some unions are trying to exploit the new rights of employees by taking cases to civil courts on behalf of individuals, e.g. equal pay claims.

The unions provide other important services to members. For example, many manual unions operate their own labour exchange. Formally, this service should be provided for all members of a UIF, even if they are not union members, but in practice such 'yellow' members are not normally catered for. Another service is the system of vocational training, financed by the state but run jointly by unions and employers' associations, for union members only. This system reflects the importance of craft unions in Denmark. By offering union members the opportunity to obtain job qualifications, it encourages the most able sections of the workforce to remain within unions. Taken together, these services help explain why Danish unions experience membership stability in times of low unemployment, and high recruitment in times of high unemployment.

Implications of the Crises (II): Centralization and Decentralization of Collective Bargaining

Collective Bargaining in the 1980s and 1990s

Denmark's entry into the European Community in 1973 had at first little impact on industrial relations. For the first 20 years, it was very much 'business as usual', and neither the employers' associations nor the unions appear to have ascribed any role in collective bargaining to decision-makers in Brussels. The only major change resulting from EC membership was that bargaining over state support for agriculture, which traditionally was closely tied to collective bargaining in the food processing industry, now took place within a broader European context.

However, the passing of the Single European Act (following a referendum in Denmark in 1986) had a major impact as large companies, unions, and employers' associations adjusted their policies and their organizational structures in readiness for the completion of the single market in 1993. Thus the 1980s and 1990s may be seen as the last period where Danish industrial relations were basically unaffected by international regulation and obligations. This view is confirmed in a roundabout way by the fact that in some respects the 1980s and 1990s brought a return to the traditional post-war pattern of collective bargaining.

In 1982, the social-democratic minority government of Anker Jørgensen was replaced by the four-party, conservative–liberal government of Poul Schlüter, and the political climate turned less union-friendly. The new government introduced labour market policies clearly aimed at diminishing union influence and membership. Union leaders lost their close contacts with ministers, and the real value of unemployment insurance was lowered by the government's suspension of the price indexation of pay – a measure long demanded by DA – and of public transfers (except old age pensions). However, as discussed earlier, these measures failed to have any impact on union density, and while some unions experienced slight falls in membership, nowhere was it on the scale experienced in the UK and elsewhere in Europe.

Unexpectedly perhaps, the suspension of price indexation seems to have helped the unions. High inflation and frequent parliamentary intervention had meant that wage drift and price indexation, rather than national bargaining agreements, had become the major factors in pay determination in the 1970s. Following the suspension of indexation in 1982, however, collective bargaining again became the key determinant of pay increases, accounting for well over half the total in some years (OECD 1990: 78; Ibsen 1990: 173). This was a striking recovery in the influence of union bargainers, helped – albeit unintentionally – by the conservative–liberal government.

The desire to avoid the deadlocks and political intervention of the 1970s led to decentralized bargaining in 1981, but in 1983 there was a return to centralization in the absence of industry-level agreement. In 1985, parliament had to break the deadlock again. This was partly due to the increased politicization of collective bargaining: some major unions, especially SiD, saw industrial confrontation as a way of bringing down the Schlüter government. This was not, however, the strategy of most unions and union leaders, and in 1987 a major breakthrough was achieved. A four-year contract (with a provision for adjustments after 2 years if prices rose more than expected) was agreed in decentralized negotiations. This helped confirm the move to single-industry bargaining.

Collective bargaining thus regained its significance from the second half of the 1980s, and it became possible to resolve problems without resorting to politicians and parliament. The 1987 solution stands out, not only because it was agreed much faster than expected, but also because it provided significant increases in pay and a phased reduction of the working week from 39 to 37 hours, which is now standard in Denmark. (The 39-hour week had been introduced by parliamentary intervention in 1985.) The 1987 agreement was reached in a series of negotiations between major unions or cartels, with the CO Metal cartel and the employers' association for the metal industry, JA, making the initial breakthrough.

Although the 1987 negotiations were ostensibly decentralized (within the general LO–DA framework), the CO Metal–JA settlement was virtually 'carbon copied' by the other bargaining units. This highlights several important aspects of Danish collective bargaining. First, collective bargaining is highly synchronized. It takes place every second year, over a relatively limited period of time, roughly from December until March. Thus for the rest of the 2-year period, agreements are implemented, not bargained over. There may of course be local adjustments, but such bargaining takes place under the peace obligation.

Second, some unions (and employers) seem to be able to 'set the pace' and establish the pattern for increases in pay, reductions in working hours and so on for all employees, private or public. No substantial differences in bargaining outcomes between sectors are normally tolerated, even though trends in actual earnings may be quite different from pay rates agreed upon in collective bargaining. So not only do employers outside DA follow agreements and pay levels agreed upon by LO and DA or their members, but the results of decentralized bargaining are also standardized. When one talks of decentralized solutions in Danish collective bargaining it is decentralization of processes rather than of outcomes.

From the end of the 1970s, bargaining cartels were established for groups of public employees. Today two cartels exist, the CFU – for state employees – and the KTO – for employees in regional and local government and institutions (hospitals, schools etc.). The remarkable thing about these cartels is that they have been able to cross several boundaries that earlier seemed insurmountable: they represent both civil servants (that is, state employees with special pension rights and enhanced security of employment) and the majority of employees on normal contracts of employment. They also represent groups of manual workers and include LO unions as well as members of FTF and AC. Thus between them they cover virtually all public employees, accounting for a third of the total Danish workforce. The cartels are able to co-ordinate their bargaining efforts relatively closely. They are, therefore, heavyweight participants in the bargaining process. In recent years, however, this unity has come under strain, especially in the KTO area. Nurses, in particular, have felt that their pay has fallen behind, but their demands for additional increases to make up lost ground were met with great animosity from other unions in the KTO, especially the school teachers' union and FOA. Public employees have secured for themselves a share in any private sector wage drift through a long-standing regulation mechanism which gives them 80 per cent of private sector pay increases above the agreed levels.

The leading role of the public sector was demonstrated in the 1989 round which for the first time provided lower-paid employees in the public sector with general employment-related pension schemes, schemes enjoyed by semi-professionals and academics for many years. This breakthrough was followed in the 1991 round by the establishment of similar pension schemes in significant parts of the private sector, including the engineering industry. This may be considered a step towards European integration, since such earnings-related schemes are similar to those in continental Europe, and thus a step away from the traditional Scandinavian model in which pensions were financed out of general taxation and did not depend on former labour market status (a step which Denmark is the last of the Scandinavian countries to take, see Andersen 1991: 13).

The establishment of strong bargaining cartels in the public sector and the willingness of the conservative–liberal government as employer to negotiate at this level has strengthened the move towards decentralization. By including non-LO unions, these cartels have probably weakened the power of the central LO leadership to determine bargaining outcomes. In general, the role of bargainers at industry or sector level has been reinforced, while the influence of the national level leaderships of DA and LO has been reduced. In the private sector, however, only the CO Industri cartel has established itself reasonably strongly. In the other sectors, cartels are quite weak, and collective bargaining takes place under the auspices of the national unions.

Increasing Flexibility in the Workplace

There have been profound changes in the framework of rules governing bargaining over pay and working time at different levels of the system. Rules have become more flexible. One aspect of this is the regulation of working hours and overtime. Earlier agreements laid down very precisely the number of working hours per week, overtime rates, and, in many cases, the maximum overtime allowable. The rules have been undermined by local practices, and have been formally relaxed. For example, the 1987 agreements merely prescribe average monthly or even yearly working hours. In building and construction, working hours may thus be shorter in winter and longer in summer, without employers having to pay overtime. Thus the details of the working time of the individual employee are today settled at the workplace, and central regulations have been reduced to a minimum. Other areas of employment regulation have been similarly affected.

Flexibility has also increased in the area of pay. Traditionally, pay bargaining in Denmark has taken place under two types of system, one centralized, the other more decentralized. Under the first, the so-called 'normal pay system', pay and conditions are basically bargained over at the sectoral level, i.e. between national unions and sectoral employers' associations. Pay scales are based on level, qualifications and length of service. Wages and salaries established in sectoral bargaining cannot be supplemented through local pay bargaining. This system is prevalent in the finance sector, transport (for manual workers) and of course the public sector, where it reigns supreme. The role of the shop steward (*tillids-repræsentant*) in such sectors is largely to monitor adherence to established agreements.

Under the second system, the so-called 'minimum pay system', only minimum pay levels are regulated through sectoral bargaining. Actual pay levels are settled by local pay bargaining at workplace level. Local negotiations take place every year (following the conclusion of the sectoral bargaining round in years in which there are sectoral negotiations). Bargaining may be for all manual employees together, or group by group. Workers have no right to strike over local pay bargaining issues, but it is not unusual for minor strikes to occur. There is little

Table 5.7 Percentage of employees in the private sector who are covered by collective bargaining agreements, 1985 and 1995

	1985	1995
All employees	57	52
Salaried employees	40	39
Workers	71	72
Men	56	50
Women	59	56

Source: Scheuer (1996: 86).

research on how local bargaining actually works, but the shop steward plays a significant role. Local pay bargaining often takes the form of 'pay-sum bargaining'. This means that the shop steward will bargain with management over the aggregate size of the pay rise for the group of workers he or she represents. It is then up to management (or supervisor) to allocate the award to employees; pay increases for individual workers may vary widely. Under this system, management thus retains the ability to link pay to individual performance or qualifications. Little is known about the power of shop stewards and employees to restrict management's discretion to award differential pay increases in practice. However, it is apparent that the shop steward's role under this system is much more important and strategic than under the normal pay system.

In recent years, the normal pay system has been increasingly replaced by the minimum pay system and by arrangements containing no pay clauses at all. In the area covered by DA and LO, normal pay systems covered 34 per cent of employees in 1989, but only 16 per cent in 1997, according to DA figures (*Agenda*, 17 April 1997: 6). This indicates that decisions about actual pay are being moved from the sectoral to the workplace level and sometimes to the level of the individual. In the part of the private sector covered by collective agreements, minimum pay systems today cover around 67 per cent of employees, against 62 per cent in the mid-1980s. The rest – mainly salaried employees – are covered by collective agreements which have no pay clauses at all (17 per cent of employees). This implies quite a significant decentralization of decisions over pay.

The unions are naturally wary of the implications of this trend. Together with employers' associations, unions in industry have therefore attempted to establish systems which, while allowing pay differentiation, are based on objective measures of qualifications or performance and hence avoid favouritism or discrimination. This system has been implemented by a number of major Danish industrial firms, but its prevalence is unknown (cf. Ibsen and Stamhus 1993).

In the private sector, almost half the workforce (48 per cent) is employed solely on individual contracts (cf. table 5.7). Available evidence indicates that there are considerable 'spill-over' effects for groups of employees not covered by collective agreements. That is, pay and conditions tend to follow those of comparable groups of employees covered by agreements, although the protection afforded is by no means complete. Annual personnel reviews – 'status interviews' – are used both to evaluate and plan individual employees' activities and to review their pay and conditions. There appears to be a strong tradition of yearly reviews of pay, but the form and more precise contents of these reviews are unknown.

EU Regulation and the Danish Collective Bargaining Tradition

In recent years, the debate over the impact of the EU 'social dimension' and EU directives on the Danish labour market has increased the interest in the scope and coverage of Danish collective agreements. Traditionally, it has been said that in Denmark labour law plays a relatively modest role in regulating the labour market, while collective agreements more than make up for the absence of legal protection for the employee. As mentioned earlier, this is seen by many observers as a more flexible system, because it allows collective actors to adjust labour market rules in the light of changing circumstances. It is feared that, if EU directives increase legal protection and regulation in the labour market, the function of collective agreements will be undermined and so, consequently, will the role of unions.

For this reason, EU social directives have been implemented in Denmark through collective agreements rather than legislation. The main consequence is that if the rules are broken, unions can take the offender to the industrial court, instead of going to the civil courts. This is the case for the directive on written employment contracts, and it has been used in relation to several directives. Recent EU directives have been implemented through collective agreements, supplemented with legislation for those parts of the labour market not covered by collective bargaining. In 1996, however, the Danish government decided for the first time – in agreement with LO and DA and all parties in parliament – to implement a directive (the working time directive) through collective agreements alone. This is done on the assumption that the spill-over effects of these agreements will be sufficiently strong to ensure that the directive is also applied in areas not covered by collective agreements.

This has drawn the attention of labour market observers to the question of collective bargaining coverage more generally. As noted earlier, the coverage by DA and the other employers' associations in the private sector is modest, around 50 per cent. Not all of these are covered by a collective agreement, however, because salaried employees from non-LO unions may in many instances be employed on individual contracts. The extent both of spill-over effects and of so-called adherence agreements (collective agreements signed between a union and an individual unorganized employer) was until recently unknown, but a recent survey of private sector employees has established that private sector coverage is probably no higher than 52 per cent, 72 per cent for workers and 39 per cent for salaried employees (see table 5.7). Public sector coverage is 100 per cent, so aggregate coverage is around 70 per cent (Scheuer 1996: 138; 1997). Coverage appears to have declined slightly since 1985, although this cannot be certain owing to the small size of the 1985 survey. What is certain, though, is that coverage has not been increasing, and any increase is unlikely without either legislation or a significant stepping up of union efforts.

The level of coverage is a great deal lower than was usually assumed, and it gives renewed impetus to the debate on the balance between legislation and collective bargaining in the regulation of the labour market. As long as the Danish system of industrial relations is voluntary, without legal extension mechanisms (cf. Traxler 1994: 172), a substantial proportion of employees remain outside the collective bargaining system. Since most of these employees are nevertheless union members, unions have to consider how to provide for them. This debate is still unresolved.

Conclusions

The Danish economy suffered from continuing imbalances in the 1980s which governments were unable to correct. These problems were partly connected to structural and institutional aspects of the labour market, placing a heavy burden on industrial relations actors. Some problems have been alleviated, but there is general agreement that basic flaws remain. The 1980s and 1990s saw a weakening of the corporatist system of consultation following the change of government in 1982, and this trend was not reversed by the return to a social-democrat-led government in 1993. But Denmark still has a system with strong corporatist traits. For example, representatives of major organizations continue to sit on many important public committees.

Important changes have been taking place in collective bargaining procedures and in the structures of the industrial relations actors, mostly in the direction of a slow but sure decentralization. This has certainly not weakened the 'Scandinavian' or 'Danish model'. On the contrary, the 'Scandinavian way' of handling industrial conflict and collective bargaining in a highly institutionalized manner has been strengthened in Denmark. Attempts in the 1970s to establish a model closer to the Swedish pattern – based on high-trust relationships between leaders of (social-democratic) governments, LO and the employers' confederation, acting partly independently of their 'constituencies' – have failed utterly in Denmark.

Danish unions and employers face great changes in the 1990s. How should they handle the risk that they will be increasingly marginalized, and the growing role of non-manual employees in collective bargaining? For the employers, DA is restructuring extensively, but its legitimacy is constrained by competition from employers' associations in agriculture and in the finance sector, and from a great number of individual employers outside any association. DA's problem is how to improve relations with other employers' associations, and – most importantly – how to increase its membership 'density' so as to become comparable with its generally stronger Scandinavian counterparts.

LO has had some success in enticing minor unions away from FTF. It has been trying without much success to make its structure more 'industrial', via the new cartel proposal. However, it might also try to exploit the strength of craft-based unionism (and of its white-collar professional counterpart) by giving greater emphasis to professional qualifications and training in the 1990s. Such a strategy would probably require closer co-operation between LO and non-LO unions, something that is already taking place in the public sector. Formal co-operation, including mergers, would probably require LO to play down its affiliation to social democracy, perhaps introducing the kind of 'political levy' system which exists in Britain, where members have a formal right to opt out. If this were done, the justification for staying outside LO would disappear, and for many of the smaller status and professional unions, closer co-operation would become possible.

Finally, the LO unions and other major unions will have increasingly to consider the problem of regulation and protection of the employee in connection with the collective bargaining coverage issue. It can no longer be taken for granted that virtually all employees have this coverage, and this shows that Danish industrial relations are in fact much less regulated than was generally believed. Danish unions and other actors in this area will need to consider how to avoid this less regulated system becoming a totally deregulated one. Although the threat is not imminent, there does seem to be a long-term trend in this direction.

▎Abbreviations

AC	*Akademikernes Centralorganisation* – Central Confederation of Professional Associations
CFU	*Centrale Forhandlingsudvalg* – The Central Bargaining Committee (for state employees' unions)
CO Industri	*Centralorganisationen af Industriansatte* – Union cartel of employees in industry (formerly *CO Metal*)
CO Metal	*Centralorganisationen af Metalarbejdere* – Union cartel of workers in metal engineering (now *CO Industri*)
DA	*Dansk Arbejdsgiverforening* – Danish Employers' Federation
Dansk Metal	*Dansk Metalarbejderforbund* – Union of Danish Metal Workers (skilled)
DI	*Dansk Industri* – Danish Industry (employers' association)
DsF	*De samvirkende Fagforbund* – Danish Union Confederation (now *LO*)
FOA	*Forbundet af Offentligt Ansatte* – Union of Public Employees
FTF	*Funktionærernes og Tjenestemændenes Fællesråd* – Central Confederation of Salaried Employees
HK	*Handels- og Kontorfunktionærernes Forbund i Danmark* – Union of Commercial and Clerical Employees in Denmark
JA	*Jernets Arbejdsgiverforening* – Federation of Employers in Metal industry (now *DI*)
KAD	*Kvindeligt Arbejderforbund i Danmark* – Union of Female Workers in Denmark
KTO	*Kommunale Tjenestemænd og Overenskomstansatte* – (Union bargaining cartel for) Municipal civil servants and salaried employees
LO	*Landsorganisationen i Danmark* – Danish Federation of Trade Unions
SiD	*Specialarbejderforbundet i Danmark* – General Workers' Union in Denmark
UIF	Unemployment Insurance Fund

References and Further References

Amoroso, B. 1990: Development and crisis of the Scandinavian model of labour relations in Denmark. In Baglioni, G. and Crouch, C. (eds), *European Industrial Relations – The Challenge of Flexibility*, London: Sage, 71–96.

Andersen, B. R. 1991: Den danske model i EF's indre marked. *Samfundsøkonomen*, 1, 13–23, Copenhagen: DJØF.

Andersen T. 1995: The deregulation of the Danish banking industry. In Crouch, C. and Traxler, F. (eds), *Organized Industrial Relations in Europe*, Avebury: Aldershot, 249–68.

Arbejdsministeriet 1989: *Hvidbog om arbejdsmarkedets strukturproblemer*. Copenhagen: Arbejdsministeriet Ministry of Labour.

Auken, S. and Buksti, J. 1975: Den indkomstpolitiske problematik i Danmark. *Økonomi og politik*, 49(3), 241–73, Copenhagen.

Brüniche-Olsen, P. 1996: *Arbejdsmarkedspolitik*. Copenhagen: Copenhagen Business School.

Christoffersen, M.N. 1993: *Familiens ændring – en statistisk belysning af familieforholdene*. Copenhagen: Danish National Institute of Social Research.

Danish National Institute of Social Research 1992: *Living Conditions in Denmark – Compendium of Statistics*. Copenhagen: by the Danish National Institute of Social Research.

Due, J., Madsen, J.S., Jensen, Carsten Strøby and Petersen, Lars Kjerulf 1994: *The Survival of the Danish Model*. Copenhagen: DJØF.

Elvander, N. 1989: Bargaining systems, incomes policies and conflict in the Nordic countries. *Current approaches to collective bargaining*. Geneva: International Labour Office, 127–37.

Ibsen, F. 1990: Lokale lønforhandlinger – omfang, muligheder og problemer. In *Årbog for Arbejderbevægelsens Historie*, 20, 167–85. Copenhagen: Selskabet til Forskning i Arbejderbevægelsens Historie.

Ibsen, F. and Stamhus, J. 1993: *Fra central til decentral lønfastsættelse – muligheder og konsekvenser*. Copenhagen: DJØF.

Jensen, P. H., Larsen, J. E. and Olofsson, G. 1987: Labour movement and unemployment policies. In Lund, R., Pedersen, P.J. and Schmidt-Sørensen, J.B. (eds), *Studies in Unemployment*, Copenhagen: New Social Science Monographs, 123–61.

Karnøe, P. 1991: *Dansk vindmølleindustri*. Copenhagen: Samfundslitteratur.

Kjellberg, A. 1983: *Facklig organisering i tolv länder*. Lund: Arkiv.

Kristensen, P.H. 1996: *Denmark: An experimental laboratory of industrial organization*. Copenhagen: Samfundslitteratur.

Lund, R. 1972: *Sammenslutningen og Centralorganisationen. Tilblivelse og udvikling*. Copenhagen: Danish National Institute of Social research.

Molin, J. and Pedersen, J.S. 1996: *Fusioner i Danmark. Organisation og ledelse*. Copenhagen: Copenhagen Business School.

Neumann, G., Pedersen, P.J. and Westergård-Nielsen, N. 1991: Long-run international trends in aggregate unionization. *European Journal of Political Economy*, 7(3), 249–74, North-Holland: Elsevier Science.

OECD 1990: *Denmark*. OECD Economic Surveys. Paris: OECD.

OECD 1991: *Employment Outlook*. July. Paris: OECD.

OECD 1994: *Employment Outlook*. July. Paris: OECD.

Pedersen, P.J. 1989: Langsigtede internationale tendenser i den faglige organisering og i den politiske venstrefløj. *Økonomi og politik* 62(2), 91–101. Copenhagen: DJØF.

Pestoff, V.A. 1991: *The demise of the Swedish model and the resurgence of organized business as a major political actor.* Paper presented at 10th EGOS conference in Vienna Stockholm: University of Stockholm.

Scheuer, S. 1989: Faglig organisering 1966 til 1987 – Del 1: Betydningen af a-kasser og af kvindernes stigende erhvervsdeltagelse. *Økonomi og politik* 62(1), 30–38. Copenhagen: DJØF.

Scheuer, S .1990: Struktur og forhandling. In *Årbog for Arbejderbevægelsens Historie*, 20, 17–79. Copenhagen: Selskabet til Forskning i Arbejderbevægelsens Historie.

Scheuer, S. 1991: *Leaders and laggards: Who goes first in bargaining rounds?* Leverhulme Public Lecture, Coventry: Warwick Papers in Industrial Relations. [Also published in Boje, T. and Olsson-Hort, S.E. (eds) 1993: *Scandinavia in the New Europe.* Oslo: Scandinavian UP, 239–70.]

Scheuer, S. 1996: *Fælles aftale eller egen kontrakt i arbejdslivet?* Copenhagen: New Social Science Monographs.

Scheuer, S. 1997: Collective bargaining coverage and the status divide: Denmark, Norway and the United Kingdom compared. *European Journal of Industrial Relations*, 3(1), 39–57. London: Sage.

Traxler, F. 1994: Collective bargaining: Levels and coverage. OECD *Employment Outlook* chapter 5, 167–194 Paris: OECD.

Turner, H.A. 1962: *Trade Union Growth, Structure and Policy.* London: Allen and Unwin.

Visser, J. 1990: In search of inclusive unionism. In *Bulletin of Comparative Labour Relations*, 18. Boston: Kluwer.

6 Finland: Continuity and Modest Moves Towards Company-level Corporatism

KARI LILJA

Introduction

The Finnish industrial relations system increasingly resembled the Scandinavian model current at the end of the 1960s. In international comparison, the most notable feature of the Finnish system is the importance of centralized national agreements between the confederations of employers and the unions. A very extensive neo-corporatist system for negotiating incomes policies has grown up, involving the government and the key interest organizations. During the 1980s, the role of incomes policy in macro-economic regulation diminished. The agenda and dynamics of Finnish society became increasingly moulded by the internationalization of Finnish firms and the deregulation of the financial markets. This change provoked a discussion on the needs to reform negotiation procedures, but it was not until the start of the deep recession in the 1990s that the debate became urgent. In the depths of the recession in 1993, almost 20 per cent of the labour force were unemployed as all sectors of the economy suffered cutbacks.

Commentators on the Finnish industrial relations system have predicted the collapse of centralized collective bargaining and its replacement by more company- and workplace-based arrangements. Though this prediction reflects a significant trend, it ignores the fact that the role of industry-level bargaining has not been challenged by employers. Moreover, the strong corporatist tradition in Finland over the last 30 years has constituted an arena of political exchange between political parties, interest groups and the government, providing an important complement to the normal legislative process in parliament. In addition to explicit agreements between the actors on pay norms, labour peace, fiscal policy and other parameters of macro-economic regulation, more implicit political exchanges are co-ordinated through the medium of participatory conferences, consultative committees, party political connections and social networks.

This chapter first describes the institutional structures and major actors of the Finnish industrial relations system. It then analyses developments in the predicted transformation of the institutional system, in particular the nature of decentralization trends. The chapter also examines the prospects for institutionalizing new

Table 6.1 Membership of Finnish Union Confederations, 1944–1995

Year	SAK	SAJ	TVK	STTK	AKAVA	All unionized employees
1944	106,000		25,800			167,200
1945	299,600		70,300			371,300
1950	269,100		70,800	8,500	12,000	381,900
1955	269,400		780,000	11,800	19,000	405,500
1960	228,500	53,500	114,400	11,300	22,400	468,000
1965	248,000	105,400	152,200	16,100	28,700	642,900
1970	650,200		210,800	27,200	42,400	946,300
1975	920,600		286,000	83,700	103,500	1,399,200
1980	1,032,100		324,600	105,400	162,200	1,646,000
1985	1,054,900		369,800	130,100	213,900	1,783,900
1990	1,071,300		387,500	155,500	278,400	1,915,500
1991	1,086,600		424,000	166,100	296,300	1,997,000
1992	1,112,900			174,900	312,100	1,996,300
1993	1,136,300			619,100	318,400	2,118,800
1994	1,114,700			623,100	324,700	2,107,500
1995	1,111,350			635,400	329,500	2,124,250

Source: Yli-Pietilä et al. (1990); Statistical Year Book of Finland, 1991–1996.

forms of work and employment regulation, and speculates on the possible emergence of a weakly regulated low-cost segment of the labour market.

Actors, Structures and Outcomes of the Finnish Industrial Relations System

Union Structure and Density

The largest and most influential union confederation is the Central Organization of Finnish Trade Unions, SAK (see table 6.1). It covers the manufacturing, construction and transport unions, and several large unions representing public sector workers (state and local authority). The principle of organization has long been industrial unionism. No significant craft unions remain. The last such union of note was the electrical workers' union, which has largely become an industrial union in energy and electrical construction. The percentage of white-collar workers in SAK is about 30 per cent. The second largest federation, the Confederation of Salaried Employees (TVK), grew steadily until its bankruptcy in 1992 as a result of speculative investments in property and shares. Its member unions, which mainly represented female white-collar employees, subsequently joined the Finnish Confederation of Technical Employees (STTK). This formerly male-dominated confederation was thus abruptly transformed into a significant representative body, under the new name of the Finnish Confederation of Salaried Employees –

Table 6.2 Union density in Finland 1944–1994

Year	All employees (%)
1944	17
1945	37
1950	35
1955	33
1960	34
1965	42
1970	57
1971	62
1975	74
1980	82
1985	80
1989	87
1994	96

Source: Yli-Pietilä et al. (1990) Sandqvist (1996: 48).

STTK. The third confederation (AKAVA) is composed of the unions of professional employees, mainly organized according to the educational background of their members. The largest union in this confederation is the teachers' union.

It is difficult to compute reliable figures on union density: figures include retired members and unions have also accepted students as members. Thus in 1994 the number of union members was equivalent to 96 per cent of the total number labour force. Table 6.2 presents figures for union density based on the percentage of union members in relation to the total labour force. However, according to a careful statistical study by Sandqvist (1996), the real figure for union density in 1994 was 79 per cent. This represents the number of union members covered by collective bargaining contracts as a percentage of all employees in the labour force. According to her study, Finnish union density has been growing in recent years, especially in the private sector, and has never been as high as in the mid-1990s. The main reason for this growth has been the threat of unemployment. The unions administer unemployment funds, paid for by the state and to a lesser extent by employers and employees themselves. Unemployment benefits are linked to the level of wages and salaries of those who are members of the unemployment funds. Employee contributions to unemployment funds are collected together with the membership subscriptions to the unions. This check-off system, administered by the employers, helps maintain a high level of union membership.

The Structure and Membership Density of Employers' Organizations

Like the unions, the employers are also highly organized, both in the private and public sector. With an emphasis on retrenchment and cost reduction during the

1990s recession, the level of contributions to interest organizations has come under scrutiny. As a result, there have been a series of mergers of trade associations and employers' associations, both at industry and confederal level. The metal industry was the first to implement a merger between associations, followed by the forest industry. The merger between the two peak organizations, the Finnish Confederation of Employers (STK) and the Confederation of Industry (TKL), created the Confederation of Industry and Employers (TT) at the beginning of 1993.

There are currently three main groups of employers' organizations: the confederation of employers' associations representing manufacturing, construction and transport industries (TT), the confederation for commerce and service industries (PT), and the public sector employers who are organized into two associations – one for the state administration (VTML) and one for local authorities (KT). There is a separate association for small businesses (SYKL), but it does not negotiate collective agreements.

The great majority of large and medium-sized firms are members of trade and employers' associations, although it is difficult to compute accurate figures for organizational density. In 1995, the 5,863 firms which were members of TT had about 490,500 employees. According to its own statistics, TT estimates that in manufacturing its member firms cover 75 per cent of employees whose terms of employment are regulated by the collective bargaining contract. In construction the figure is considerably lower. Similarly in 1995, the 6,071 member firms of PT had 250,500 employees (SYBF 1996: 349) representing around 50 per cent of the sector's employees whose terms are regulated by a collective bargaining contract.

▌ Delivering the Agreements

The high density of unions and employers' associations has made it possible to centralize collective bargaining and to link incomes policies with other macro-economic policy issues. Both employer and union confederations negotiate deals with the government, a tradition established in 1968, with some earlier precedents. Initially, the main partners in centralized agreements were STK for the employers and SAK from the union side. But since the mid-1970s, the other confederations have become officially incorporated into the centralized system of negotiations. Since 1968 there have been six bargaining rounds (in 1973, 1977, 1982, 1988, 1994, 1995) which have failed to reach a centrally agreed contract or guidelines (Vartia and Ylä-Anttila 1996: 305).

In practice, however, centralized confederal agreements have become diluted. For instance, contracts made are not binding on the member unions of SAK, which have two weeks in which to accept or reject the agreement. In the course of every bargaining round a number of unions withdraw to try to get a better agreement at industry level. In many cases this is possible only by resorting to strike action. The peaks in the statistics for days lost in strikes (see table 6.3) are due to unions breaking away from the centralized agreements.

There is a strong political element in the system of collective bargaining.

Governments have facilitated agreements by promising measures such as tax reforms, changes in labour laws and improvements in social security. From the point of view of macro-economic regulation, the Finnish tradition has been criticized for being biased towards political compromise and consensus, rather than being focused on adjustments to fluctuations in the business cycle. For decades, labour costs have risen faster than in competing countries. This has created pressure on the Finnish currency, leading to periodic devaluations to bring the price competitiveness of Finnish firms in line with those of their competitors (cf. Lilja et al. 1992). Thus, Finnish corporatism has been called 'fair weather corporatism' because it has been successful in booms but unable to cope with economic crises (Rehn 1996: 271).

Informal personal ties between the top leaders of the four power blocs – employers, farmers, unions and the government – have played an important role in making neo-corporatist negotiations work. It has also proved necessary to have political ties between the unions and the political parties in government. In the Finnish case, this linkage has been carried out mainly through the social-democratic party since 1966. But the party has not held such a hegemonic position in Finland as in Sweden: the Finnish communist party and its successor, the Left Wing League, have played an important role in the trade union movement, in the co-operative movement, in parliament, and even in coalition governments. The labour movement has had to deal with the problem of the divided loyalties of its constituents at all levels of the organization.

Workplace and Company-level Participation

One of the main areas of reform covered by incomes policy agreements has been employee participation. The approach which was finally adopted in 1979 (the Law of Co-operation within Companies) was based on strengthening the position of shop stewards. Thus negotiation rights have been extended from wages and conditions of employment to issues of managerial prerogative. Though the right of final decision still rests with management, the new generation of professional managers has involved workers' representatives in investment planning and other areas of management. This development was strengthened by an amendment to the 1979 law: in 1991 board-level participation was introduced in firms with more than 150 employees. A related reform made it possible to establish employee funds. Firms can pay bonuses to company-specific funds according to jointly agreed rules. The rules emphasize economic performance indicators and the intention is to motivate employees by providing a stake in improved company performance.

Reforms relating to employee participation have clearly lagged behind developments in Sweden. Finnish managers in Swedish companies tend to complain at the delays in decision-making caused by the extended negotiating process.

Table 6.3 Strikes in Finland 1945–1995

Year	Frequency	Number of employees involved	Working days lost
1945	102	37,000	358,000
1950	78	118,000	4,644,000
1955	72	42,000	344,000
1960	44	19,000	96,000
1965	29	7,000	16,000
1970	240	201,600	233,200
1971	838	403,300	2,711,100
1972	849	239,700	473,100
1973	1,009	678,200	2,496,900
1974	1,788	370,700	434,800
1975	1,530	215,100	284,200
1976	3,282	512,700	1,325,500
1977	1,673	743,800	2,374,700
1978	1,237	164,600	132,400
1979	1,753	229,000	243,400
1980	2,238	413,100	1,605,600
1981	1,612	492,960	659,100
1982	1,240	167,500	207,600
1983	1,940	421,840	719,700
1984	1,710	562,480	1,526,900
1985	848	171,350	174,300
1986	1,225	602,730	2,787,600
1987	802	99,290	130,890
1988	1,353	244,070	179,820
1989	629	158,480	204,210
1990	455	244,760	935,150
1991	284	166,770	458,340
1992	168	103,510	76,090
1993	126	23,190	17,310
1994	171	70,540	525,700
1995	112	127,039	869,422

Source: Yli-Pietilä et al. (1990) Statistical Year Book of Finland 1996, Table 335.

▎ High Propensity to Strike

Compared with the Scandinavian countries, the Finnish system has one distinctive feature: the high level of industrial disputes (see Korpi and Shalev 1980; Poole 1986). The number of strikes increased sharply at the end of 1960s (see table 6.3). The peak year was 1976 when the number of industrial disputes reached 3,200. While the number of strikes also increased in Sweden in the 1970s and in Denmark especially in the 1980s, the Finnish case is still qualitatively different. The annual number of strikes in Sweden has not risen above 250, and in Denmark the peak figure has been about 850 (Yli-Pietilä et al. 1990: 141). There was thus a positive correlation in Finland in the 1970s and the 1980s between the trend towards centralization in the system of collective bargaining and the increase of strikes. However, in the 1990s there has been a conspicuous decline in the strike trend.

There are several institutional factors which explain the high propensity to strike in the 1970s and 1980s. The first is the strong local organization of workers based on the shop steward system. Second, the political rivalry in the trade union movement tends to lead to bargaining demands which cannot be accommodated within the framework agreed in centralized contracts. Third, there is significant inter-union and inter-confederation competition. The declining trend in strike statistics since the mid-1980s is based on changes in all three areas. First, the shop steward mechanism has been linked with new areas of workplace regulation and employee representatives are provided with accurate economic information and with opportunities for consultation on a wide range of issues. Employee representatives have learned new ways of signalling discontent, as they now have constant access to management. Second, tensions between the political parties within the trade union movement have decreased. The social-democrat leadership of SAK is no longer openly challenged from the radical left. This makes unions' elections less politicized, and political differences no longer have the same resonance for collective bargaining agendas. Third, inter-confederal tensions have also been dampened, since all confederations now have a legitimate status in centralized negotiations. However, inter-union competition has remained strong. Moreover, the recession has highlighted wide variations in economic conditions between sectors and industries. As a result, there are equally wide variations in the approach of employers in different sectors to labour costs and pay levels. This development is bound to have a deep impact on the structure and outcomes of collective bargaining in Finland.

Pressures for Change

Growing sectoral differentiation is only one of several 'drivers' of change in the Finnish industrial relations system. The main 'exogenous' drivers are the high level of unemployment, the internationalization of Finnish firms and the globalization of competition, and, the decreasing importance of the national polity in the wider European framework of policy-making. While it is evident that the industrial relations system has only limited autonomy with respect to changes in the economy and polity, it is important to stress that there is no 'visible hand' or power structure capable of engineering 'from the top down' a new design for industrial relations. The constellation of forces and interests is different from the period in which the highly centralized system of incomes policy was created. In the 1960s and the 1970s, developments were supported by employer and union confederations, the governments (based mainly on centre-left party coalitions) and a strong president (Lilja 1983). The role of the state as an autonomous arena for policy-making was decisive. Moreover, the state was also an important economic actor in Finland. It was a large employer, the owner of major manufacturing and banking concerns, and the regulator of bilateral trade with the Soviet Union – at its peak, this trade amounted to 25 per cent of Finnish foreign trade. The privatization of most of the state-owned corporations, the collapse of the Soviet trade, and Finnish membership of the European Union, have thus significantly changed the co-ordinates of industrial relations.

For an understanding of the change process in the Finnish industrial relations system, it is useful first to describe the programmes and strategies of the major actors. The impact of tensions in the change programmes will then be assessed.

The Employers' Stance on Industrial Relations Reform

The Finnish case neatly fits Clegg's (1976) conclusion that it is the employers' associations which select the structural level for collective bargaining (see Lilja 1992). The strategic objective of a more decentralized model of collective bargaining was clearly formulated by the Confederation of Employers (STK) in 1991 (Köykkä 1994: 90–1). It was preceded by several official statements exploring alternatives to the tradition of centralized incomes policy agreements. A similar interest in greater local leeway has also been expressed by the bodies representing employers in the public sector.

The change in the strategic aims of employers' associations in the manufacturing sector is not only rhetorical. The mergers of trade and employers' associations, mentioned above, have been used as levers for radical organizational reform. The number of officials has been cut and their functions partly contracted out to professional service firms in the areas of training, consulting, research, publishing, legal services, public relations, and so on. This has allowed employers' associations to prepare themselves for a new role in the design and implementation of distinctive company and workplace level human resource management programmes. The professional services of the new units are often offered on a competitive market basis.

The other element of employer strategy has been support for wide-ranging experiments with local agreements at company and workplace level. The same experimental approach was used by the employers' organizations in the 1970s to introduce systems of employee participation in large companies prior to the Law on Co-operation at the end of the 1970s (cf. Lilja 1977). The breakthrough for the local experiment approach was made in the collective bargaining rounds of 1993 and 1994. The new industry-level agreements allowed for company agreements, on working time, holiday pay and special holiday arrangements, that differed from the provisions of the industry agreement. This gave a new twist to the concept of the local agreement: unlike earlier industry and local bargaining, which had been a means for the unions to improve on the provisions of agreements signed at the central level, the new arrangements made it possible for the provisions of local deals to be less favourable to employees than higher-level agreements. The main argument for the increased local flexibility is that win–win solutions can be found. Employers are keen to develop forms of work organization which are responsive to customer needs. There is scope for such innovation because individual employees have different preferences with regards to ways of organizing work and allocating working time.

In some pioneering companies, experimentation has gone well beyond the areas that are jointly regulated by the collective bargaining contract. There has been a willingness on the part of the management to conclude comprehensive packages covering not only the terms of employment but also work organization, forms of reward beyond those stipulated in the collective bargaining contract, and ways of creating employee commitment to business objectives and corporate visions of the future. This proactive style of human resource management is one model for 'company-level corporatism'.

Difficulties between union and employer confederations in national collective bargaining and the collapse of consensus in the national polity have also been taken as indicators of a change in the employers' stance towards incomes policy. Representatives of the employers' confederation have emphasized that participation in centralized agreement is decided according to the situation. The track record of centralized agreements has, indeed, been mixed during the 1990s. Moreover, the employers' confederations were unenthusiastic about a comprehensive tripartite programme for paving the way out of recession: the programme was prepared under the leadership of Mr Pekkanen, a key figure in the history of Finnish incomes policies and a former director of the employers' association for the forest industries (see Rehn 1996: 265–7). The employer and union confederations have also been unable to agree at central level on a large number of issues concerning the content and application of laws. This lack of consensus has forced the government to act unilaterally.

Though there have been considerable difficulties at national level in conducting incomes policies, employers' associations have expressed no desire to move away from industry-level collective bargaining. Under the present legal framework, employers gain considerable advantages from multi-employer bargaining: labour peace is quickly established at industry level once contracts have been signed. Employers' organizations are demanding flexibility at the workplace under the labour peace proviso. From the employees' point of view this would amount to a system of concession bargaining. The Confederation of Industry and Employers has outlined an increased flexibility programme in several booklets (e.g. TT 1994; 1996). One objective is to allow local agreements on the terms of employment to differ from the currently binding industry contracts. Another target is to remove the contractual differences between the blue- and white-collar workers, which would facilitate the adoption of new types of work organization.

Reasons for the Change in the Employers' Stance

The principal reasons for the change in the employers' attitude towards the level and scope of collective bargaining, and to the role of centralized incomes policy, include: the precedents set in the Scandinavian countries; the increasing diversity of firms and their market conditions; and the need to prepare for the impact of Economic and Monetary Union.

The Scandinavian Precedent

The change in employers' attitudes to centralized bargaining took place in the other Nordic countries before they occurred in Finland. These changes have been well documented (see e.g. Kjellberg in this volume; Scheuer 1992; Due et al. 1995; Pestoff 1995; Köykkä 1994). The practice of comparing policies and learning from each others' experiences has been a common feature of Nordic industrial relations as well as of other spheres of society. The employers' active role in the centralization of the collective bargaining system in Finland was strongly influenced by the Swedish model and the advice of the Swedish Confederation of Employers (SAF). Similarly, the commitment to decentralization of collective bargaining was influenced by SAF's withdrawal from centralized negotiations, and from state consultative bodies, in 1991 (Pestoff 1995).

The relationships between interest organizations and the government in Sweden and Finland have not been identical, however. In Sweden, the strong links between the trade union movement and the social-democratic party have allowed the labour movement to exert a strong influence on government policies and working-life reforms. This has not been the case in Finland, where governments have been based on party coalitions in which the left has not had a majority. Employers' organizations in Finland also adopt a much more pragmatic stance towards policy-making than their Swedish counterparts. This makes it difficult to forecast how rapidly a more decentralized model of bargaining will be introduced in Finland.

The Increasing Diversity of Firms

During the last 20 years, Finnish firms have experienced several waves of mergers and acquisitions, leading to considerable concentration. In 1995, for instance, the five largest firms accounted for 48 per cent of Finnish exports (Lehtinen 1995). At the same time, the operations of large firms have become more international: a third of the capacity of Finnish paper producers is now located beyond Finnish borders. This change has not been driven by 'workplace regime shopping', in other words by the desire of companies to locate production in countries with lower standards of labour regulation; nor have Finnish firms been active in shaping the local industrial relations cultures in host countries. Nevertheless, the increased complexity of large Finnish corporations, as well as the current diversity of the national industrial relations cultures to which they are exposed, have encouraged them to explore company-specific, innovative human resource policies as one source of competitive advantage. This is especially the case of Finnish firms in the forest products and telecommunication sectors, because they are now competing in the opening global markets.

Large manufacturing enterprises have been preparing themselves for the decentralization of collective bargaining for a considerable time. Firms in the pulp and paper industry had already largely decentralized wages bargaining to the mills in the late 1960s. But local negotiation still occurs in the context of industry-level bargaining, since the relatively small number of establishments, and the homogene-ity of their operations and mentality, make it is easy to co-ordinate bargaining across mills. Workers' participation has been extensive in the pulp and paper industry, and the disclosure of detailed economic information on a monthly basis to shop stewards has been common practice. Participation in divisional manage-ment groups was also introduced in this sector prior to the 1991 amendment to the Law on Co-operation. This high degree of involvement by employee represen-tatives has had a noticeable impact on the bargaining climate at local level. For instance, while 10 years ago over 100 formal grievances were being sent to industry-level conciliation annually, the figure is now around 20 (Niemi 1996). The main reason for this change is the commitment of mill-level management to finding local solutions. External bodies are not able to come up with social innovations in situations where local knowledge is essential. The increased openness of the management has enabled employees' representatives to assess the impact of rapidly changing economic conditions on the profitability of the mills, and to offer more considered suggestions for change.

Though the Finnish pulp and paper industry has been a pattern-setter in widening the system of employee participation, the most extensive change pro-grammes for human resource development have been in more labour-intensive firms, as in the electronics and service industries. Such companies have had a greater incentive to implement programmes such as total quality management, business process re-engineering or 'learning organization' schemes. Their introduc-tion has been supported by systematic training programmes for all levels of employees. Organizational transformation processes have also been supported by external management consultancy firms. The involvement of employees in these innovations has meant that conventional issues of working hours and pay for increased effort have not been tackled with the collective bargaining process, but in a much more implicit way.

These developments suggest that a new cohort of Finnish top management has closed the competence gap in human resource management at the Nordic level (cf. Kettunen 1996). It has gained the confidence to address personnel issues within companies through an approach based on dialogue. Within a collectively con-structed vision of change, such companies have created participatory mechanisms that allow the emergence of bottom-up solutions.

Given the complexity of corporate decision-making structures, the involvement of staff in operational or even business management decisions does not threaten managerial prerogative in strategic areas. This is clearly demonstrated by the way in which most of the major Finnish corporations have restructured their portfolios, reducing the diversity of businesses. Such changes have been motivated by global benchmarking to meet the profitability, size and growth targets set by the major competitors in each business area. This phase of restructuring has raised concerns even among top managers about the continuity of their employment, since each new business structure is often accompanied by the formation of a new managerial team (Kosonen 1994). At lower levels of the corporation, restructuring processes are initiated not only to adapt to changes in market demand but also in response to signals from centralized management information systems. The use of 'coercive comparisons' within the corporation, between establishments and production lines producing similar products in different countries, has become an important source of managerial intervention.

The programmatic changes in the strategy of employers' associations are clearly related to the increased heterogeneity of member firms, both within industry-specific associations and in the federations. The employers' associations are not in a position to intervene in the management of large Europe-wide corporations. They are, therefore, trying to create a new role for themselves as the facilitators of change.

European Economic and Monetary Union

A further impetus to the reform of centralized collective bargaining has resulted from the linking of the Finnish currency to the European Monetary System. In the summer of 1991, the mark was linked to the ecu for the first time. The term 'internal devaluation' subsequently came into use, by which employers meant that Finnish firms should be able to adjust to changes in the price competitiveness of their products through lower labour costs rather than through changes in the exchange rate. Such externally-driven imperatives have intensified since Finland linked its currency to the European Exchange Rate Mechanism (ERM) in October 1996, in fulfilment of one of the criteria for becoming a founding member of EMU.

The Competence Trap of the Finnish Trade Union Movement

The changing stance of employer interest organizations on centralized negotiations has not escaped the attention of the Finnish trade union movement. However, it has been unable to develop a counter-strategy, trapped by its achievements over the last 25 years as part of the centralized system of political exchange. This corporatist mechanism generated high economic growth in comparison with the OECD average from the beginning of the 1960s until the end of the 1980s. The centralized agreements transformed Finland into a welfare society. At the same time, union density grew from a level that was very low by Scandinavian standards to one of the highest in the world.

The agendas of union officials at different levels, and the rewards resulting from their work, have little overlap. For leaders and officials at the confederal level, the abolition of central agreements would imply a complete change in their role. The chairmen of union federations have been instrumental in setting a unified agenda for centralized negotiations. They have been active in getting the member unions to agree the terms of centralized agreements by extracting benefits (tax cuts, social reforms, price controls, etc.) from the government in exchange for support for the agreement. In the negotiation phase of central agreements, confederal leaders have had a high public profile which has promoted the importance and legitimacy of the trade union movement in society. The prospect of losing this significant role does not appear attractive. Top leaders would have few other functions if centralized negotiations were abandoned: the main industry unions are strong, and capable of taking care of industry-level collective bargaining by themselves.

To bolster their role as part of the national political elite, the leaders of the union confederations have demanded negotiations with the government over the terms on which the union movement would support Finland's membership of EMU. SAK has demanded the establishment of funds to buffer employees' earnings level in future recessions. A system of training insurance, paid by the state, has also been on the agenda for negotiations. The theme of life-long learning offers major advantages for the trade union movement if it can be developed into a solution to the politically sensitive problem of wide-scale unemployment as well as enhancing competence-based corporate strategies in R&D-intensive industries. However, especially in the blue-collar unions, the problems of skill development and new forms of work organization have not had a high priority.

For union officials, the logic of action during the last 30 years has been to conquer new areas of working life for joint regulation, or to bring them under the control of the union movement, as in the case of unemployment benefits. This logic of action is reflected in the unions' organizational structure, with separate sections for wage bargaining, labour protection, workers' participation and for various specialist services covering legal advice, research, management of the environment, international relations, and so on. The successive regulatory reforms that have institutionalized this machinery have been compromises with the employers and/or the state. As a result, each reform has left union ambitions partially unfulfilled, creating targets for future reforms within the specialism. There is also a constant need to increase the number of officials in each specialism in order to provide a better service to members at the workplace.

The reason why this logic of union action is leading to a competence trap is that there are no mechanisms at the industry collective bargaining level to intervene in the actual world of work and skill development in a proactive way. Union members are increasingly wanting to improve their skills. They are facing organizational changes which require multiple skills, inter-craft flexibility and participation in work teams with collective responsibility for results. These new forms of work organization are also the main source of increased productivity of work and thus a condition for increased pay and other benefits. At the same time, employees experience directly the constant struggles for survival of establishments, divisions or whole companies. However, the unions' internal organization and the specialized experience of their officials are not well suited to handling these types of 'holistic' managerial problems, which can less and less be solved by invoking state support. Only the large unions have research sections capable of supporting local union representatives in complex change programmes initiated by management in response to market forces.

A third group of actors, local activists, has also been created by the various reforms linked to incomes policy agreements. This group is larger than that of the officials at the union level. Several hundred, including for example senior shop stewards in large workplaces, work full-time on representative duties. Key local activists typically carry out a very wide range of representative work. They handle all kinds of negotiations at the workplace and are consulted about many kinds of issues at the workplace and in the local community (cf. Lilja 1997). Local activists thus have intrinsically satisfying working lives; training provided by the union movement and the employer, and participation in a broad range of issues, bring symbolic and material rewards far exceeding those available in ordinary jobs. However, the 'privatization' of the lifestyles of employees and alternative uses of spare time will make it increasingly difficult to attract employees to perform unpaid work as part of the workplace representative system of the unions. Thus there are clear limits to the scope for further participatory reforms.

The final group of actors, the ordinary trade union members, have always had weak links to the everyday activities of the union movement. In the past, however, differences in lifestyles among workers of the same socio-economic status were rather small; the locality provided a common focus and shared leisure activities. With increased prosperity, workers' identity outside work is defined more by their role as consumers, and as the practitioners of different leisure activities. An earlier class-based worker identity has thus fragmented and it no longer functions as a source of mobilization for the trade union movement (cf. Zoll 1993). When virtually the whole of the adult population belongs to the unions, unions are faced with conflicting interests and preferences which cannot be reconciled through collective bargaining alone. High unemployment divides the labour force into two distinct groups whose interests are very difficult to contain within the policy-making processes of the trade union movement; yet unions cannot be turned into political parties.

Many of these generalizations about the different actors within the union movement are not of course unique to Finland. Nor is the main lesson for the actors unique to Finland: that it is not possible to respond to changes in the national system of industrial relations by resorting to patterns of action developed in the past. Continuing high unemployment, the globalization of markets, the spread of the operations of Finnish firms throughout the member countries of the European Union, and changing managerial approaches to corporate restructuring and working life have combined to put the trade union movement on the defensive.

The Way Ahead: Multiple Models within the System, Fragmentation, and Gaining Employee Commitment

Three separate trends may be identified for the future of the Finnish industrial relations system (Bruun 1994: 26–38). The most dominant builds on the legacy of the three-tier system of collective bargaining, although there are significant modifications with respect to the past, best described by the concept of 'centralized decentralization' (Due et al. 1995; Traxler 1995: 7–8). The other developments cannot be analysed in terms of the traditional system of industrial relations. The first arises from the need to adapt to, and act upon, high levels of unemployment and to the gradual erosion of competitiveness in some sheltered nationally based sectors and industries. The second builds on the success of some internationalized corporations and smaller innovative firms which are able to secure the commitment of their employees and institutionalize systems of company-level corporatism. What are the building blocks of these complementary trends?

As a result of the cyclical nature of the Finnish economy, labour markets have never matched the levels of stability found in the other Nordic countries. During recessions, unemployment has risen well above that in the Scandinavian countries. In the 1990s, this divergence from the Scandinavian model has again become visible. With persistently high levels of unemployment – about 15 per cent at the end of 1996 – new labour market features are bound to emerge. One is the growth of atypical forms of employment. In 1992, for example, 13 per cent of all employees had temporary employment contracts (OECD 1996: 22). The weakened negotiating power of individual employees can be seen in the fact that, for the period 1994–6, 60–70 per cent of all new employment contracts were temporary (Ylöstalo et al. 1997: 151–2). Second, there has been a growth of the black economy, especially in such industries as construction and some services, creating problems of unfair competition and lost tax revenues. Third, the debate on the relationship between paid and unpaid work has again become heated. Finland has the most equal distribution of incomes after tax in the OECD countries (Atkinson et al. 1995; Pohjola 1996: 134–6). As a result, the demand for personal services is very low and opportunities for creating jobs in this sector are meagre without radical changes in the system of taxation. Fourth, the unemployed are covered by unemployment benefits paid mainly by the state. In 1993 Finland devoted almost 7 per cent of its gross domestic product to such benefits, the highest proportion of any OECD country (OECD 1996: 28).

With high budgetary deficits, there are great pressures to reduce barriers to increasing the level of employment. This is also a demand put forward by small and medium-sized firms and their interest organization. They claim that it is impossible for entrepreneurs to be aware of and comply with all the regulations imposed upon them by labour legislation and collective contracts. The rationales of the actors who have been excluded from the centralized system of collective bargaining are very different from those of the key players in the tripartite system. But it is clear the conditions exist for new issue-based coalitions which would upset the existing balance of power, to the detriment of the trade union movement. Small and medium-sized firms are not competing with internationalized corporations but function as suppliers and sub-contractors for them. Thus a reduction in costs throughout the value chain would be of interest to the core firms within the system of inter-firm networks and 'clusters'.

The critique of the centralized and highly unified system of industrial relations is an inherent element in the demands of the employers' associations, and is also reflected in the work of the two committees set up by the government to reform the rules of the employment contract and of collective bargaining. A critical issue being examined is the role of individual employment contracts. Employers are seeking the right to draw up individual employment contracts containing weaker terms than those stipulated in industry-level collective agreement, which currently are binding on all employers, whether or not they are members of employers' associations.

The second new dimension derives from innovative human resource policies in well-managed corporations and business units. The diffusion of share ownership and other forms of capital income to lower levels of the corporate hierarchy represents the newest method for establishing company-level corporatism. Such schemes can be seen as an extension of collective bonus payment schemes and company-wide employee fund systems, and as a logical step following the introduction of employee participation at board level. Thus Nokia – the Finnish-based telecommunication firm – has announced that it will extend its share option scheme from top management to about 1,700 of its experts. This can be seen as a way of tying key personnel into longer-term employment with the firm, and of discouraging the poaching of key employees by rivals. In addition, all the 30,000 of Nokia's employees will also get a bonus payment of from 2.5 to 5 per cent of annual earnings depending on corporate profitability (HS 1997). If Nokia employees benefit from rising share prices in the future, as top management have over the last three years, this scheme is likely to represent an important milestone in the institutionalization of enterprise-level corporatism in Finland. Nokia's share option and bonus payment schemes are only one example of a changed ideological climate in Finland which tolerates greater income differentials than in the past. The main mechanism for the widening of differentials has been the relatively low tax rate on capital income, currently 28 per cent.

There is a further reason why company-level reorganization programmes are growing beyond the traditional system of industrial relations. In 1996, the government launched a national programme to support organizational innovations at the workplace and their diffusion through research and development, the first time that the state in Finland has committed investment to such innovation. The programme resembles similar efforts in Germany, Norway and Sweden (Alasoini 1996), but with more modest resources. Its symbolic effect is considerable, however, since it specifies and legitimizes a new form of investment. Incentives for investing in organizational development are very important in a country with a long history of over-investing in capital goods (Pohjola 1996), a pattern reflecting the strong position of managers with engineering backgrounds in Finnish firms (Lilja and Tainio 1996).

Conclusion: The Future of Institutional Industrial Relations

The Finnish system of industrial relations is experiencing many types of friction. There is a clear disparity in the reform programmes of employers' organizations and the trade union movement. Neo-liberal labour market rhetoric has received much attention in the media. At the same time, however, the representativeness of the trade union movement has never been as extensive as it is at present. This gives Finnish unions a high level of legitimacy within the political system. In particular, it makes it more difficult for the government, led by the social democrats, to ignore the demands of the union movement. Faced with these conflicting pressures, the government and the state machinery are undecided as to how to mediate the alternatives proposed by employers and unions for regulating employment contracts and collective bargaining.

Despite the tensions, continuity is still the strongest feature of the Finnish industrial relations system. The decentralization pursued by employers' associations is occurring to a large extent through industry-level agreements. The employers' demands for increased flexibility at the workplace cannot be interpreted merely as an attempt to weaken employees' conditions of employment. Wide-scale experiments have been initiated in the reorganization of work and in training workers to assume more responsibility collectively for work organization and for supplier and customer relations. Some of these experiments clearly go beyond the scope of the traditional industrial relations system.

Though employers' associations have intensified their critique of centralized agreements, and of unified incomes policy, the heritage of the last 30 years is also influencing the future shape of neo-corporatist relations. Central national agreements are still possible. Policy-making at EU level is creating new functions for the social partners which require national co-ordination. The need to harmonize national institutions of collective bargaining, labour law and social welfare with those of other European countries maintains the government's interest in involving the social partners in joint policy-making. These contacts and implicit understandings, especially in a country where the political elite is small, can be used as the social 'infrastructure' for consensual policy-making at national level.

▌ Acknowledgement

I am indebted to Niklas Bruun and Heikki Niemi for their comments on the earlier versions of this chapter.

▌ Abbreviations

AKAVA   *Akateeminen Yhteisvaltuuskunta* – the Confederation of Unions for Academic Professionals, Finland
KT   *Kunnallinen työmarkkinalaitos* – Employer Organization of Local Authorities
PT   *Palvelutyönantajat* – Employers' Confederation of Service Industries
SAK   *Suomen Ammattiliittojen Keskusjärjestö* – Central Organization of Finnish Trade Unions
STK   *Suomen Työnantajain Keskusliitto* – the Confederation of Finnish Employers (1907–92)
STTK   *Suomen Teknisten Toimihenkilöiden Keskusliitto* – the Finnish Confederation of Technical Employees until 1993

STTK   *Toimihenkilökeskusliitto STTK* – the Finnish Confederation of Salaried Employees – STTK, since 1993

SYKL   *Suomen Yrittäjäin Keskusliitto* – the Finnish Confederation of Entrepreneurs

TKL   *Teollisuuden Keskusliitto* (1976–92) – the Confederation of Industry, Finland

TT   *Teollisuus ja Työnantajat* (1993–) – the Confederation of Industry and Employers

TVK   *Toimihenkilöiden Keskusliitto* (1924–92) – the Finnish Confederation of Salaried Employees

VTML   *Valtion työmarkkinalaitos* – Employer Organization of the State

▌References

Alasoini, T. 1996: *Työelämän tutkimusavusteinen kehittäminen oppivassa yhteiskunnassa. Kansallinen työelämän kehittämisohjelma.* Työpapereita 1. Työministeriö.

Atkinson, A.B., Rainwater, L. and Smeeding, T.M. 1995: Income distribution in the OECD countries. *Social Policy Studies*, 18. Paris: OECD.

Bruun, Niklas 1994: The transformation of Nordic industrial relations. *Swedish Institute for Work Life Research*. Reprint No 4.

Clegg, H.A. 1976: *Trade Unionism under Collective Bargaining*. Oxford: Blackwell Publishers.

Due, J., Madsen, J.S., Petersen, L.K., and Jensen, C.S. 1995: Adjusting the Danish model: towards centralised decentralisation. In Crouch, C. and Traxler, F. (eds), *Organised Industrial Relations in Europe: What Future?* Aldershot: Avebury, 121–50.

HS 1997: Nokian kannattavuus pysyi loppuvuonna huipputasolla. Helsingin Sanomat, 14th February.

Kettunen, Pauli 1996: The Nordic model and the making of the competitive 'us'. A paper presented at the workshop The Globalization of Production and the Regulation of Labour, University of Warwick, 11–13 September.

Korpi, W. and Shalev, M. 1980: Strikes, power, and politics in western nations, 1900–1976. *Political Power and Social Theory* 1, 301–34.

Kosonen, P. 1994: *Corporate Transformation and Management*. Helsinki: Helsinki School of Economics. Series A–98.

Köykkä V. 1994: *Työnantajien muuttuvat strategiat*. Helsinki: Työministeriö.

Lehtinen, J. 1995: Vienti on viiden varassa. *Talouselämä* 39, 28–30.

Lilja, K. 1977: Työntekijöiden osallistuminen hallintoon teollisuusyrityksissä. Helsinki: Helsingin kauppakorkeakoulu B–22.

Lilja, K. 1983: *Workers' Workplace Organisations*. Helsinki: HSE, A:39.

Lilja, K. 1992: Finland: No longer the Nordic exception. In Ferner, A. and Hyman, R. (eds), *Industrial Relations in the New Europe*, Oxford: Blackwell Publishers, 198–217.

Lilja, K. 1997: Bargaining for the future. In Whitley, R. and Kristensen, P.H. (eds), *Governance at Work*, Oxford University Press, 123–36.

Lilja, K. and Tainio, R. 1996: The nature of the typical Finnish firm. In Whitley, R. and Kristensen, P.H. (eds). *The Changing European Firm*. London: Routledge. 159–91.

Lilja, K., Räsänen, K. and Tainio, R. 1992: A dominant business recipe: the forest sector in Finland. In Whitley, R. (ed.), *European Business Systems*, London: Sage, 137–54.

Niemi, H. 1996: Personal communication.

OECD 1996: *The OECD Job Study*. Paris: OECD.

Pestoff, V. 1995: Towards a new Swedish model of collective bargaining and politics. In Crouch, C. and Traxler F. (eds), *Organised Industrial Relations in Europe: What Future?* Aldershot: Avebury, 151–82.

Pohjola, M. 1996: *Tehoton pääoma.* Porvoo: WSOY.

Poole, M. 1986: *Industrial Relations.* London: Routledge.

Rehn, O. 1996: Corporatism and Industrial Competitiveness in Small European States: Austria, Finland and Sweden, 1945–95. Thesis, University of Oxford.

Sandqvist, L. 1996 Palkansaajien järjestäytyminen Suomessa 1994. Helsinki: Työministeriö. Työpoliittinen tutkimus Nro 138.

Scheuer, S. 1992 Return to decentralisation. In A. Ferner and R. Hyman (eds.), *Industrial Relations in the New Europe.* Oxford: Blackwell Publishers. 168–97.

SYBF 1996: *Statistical Yearbook of Finland.* Vol. 91. Jyväskylä: Statistics Finland.

Traxler, F. 1995 Farewell to labour market associations? Organised versus disorganised decentralisation as a map for industrial relations. In Crouch, C. and Traxler, F. (eds), *Organised Industrial Relations in Europe: What Future?* Aldershot: Avebury, 3–19.

TT (Teollisuuden ja Työnantain Keskusliitto) 1994: 'Paikallinen sopiminen – käänne joustavuuteen'. Maaliskuu.

TT 1996: Muuttuva toimintaympäristö. Paikallinen sopiminen toimintatavaksi. Teollisuustieto 5/1996. Liite.

Vartia, P. and Ylä-Anttila, P. 1996: *Kansantalous 2021.* Helsinki: ETLA.

Yli-Pietilä, P., Alasoini, T., Kauppinen, T., and Mikola-Lahnalammi, T. 1990: Työelämän suhteet. Aikasarjoja 1907–1988. Helsinki: Työvoimaministeriö. Työpoliittinen tutkimus Nro 2.

Ylöstalo, P., Kauppinen, T. and Heikkälä, A. 1997: *Työolobarometri.* Lokakuu 1996. Helsinki: Työministeriö.

Zoll, R. 1993: *Alltagssolidarität und Individualismus.* Frankfurt: Suhrkamp.

7 | Germany: Facing New Challenges

OTTO JACOBI • BERNDT KELLER • WALTHER MÜLLER-JENTSCH

| Introduction: Continuity and Change in the 'German Model'

For most of the past half-century, the German economy has been one of the most successful in Europe. Most observers, both within the country and outside, have regarded the German industrial relations system as an important element in a virtuous circle: the distinctive institutions and traditions in industrial relations contained industrial conflict and encouraged workplace co-operation in high-quality production, while the resulting economic prosperity in turn contributed to peaceful and collaborative industrial relations. There is now increasing doubt whether this virtuous relationship can persist. Since the late 1980s the German economy has faltered, and many observers argue that institutional inflexibility has been at least in part responsible. Attempts by government and employers to initiate significant changes in industrial relations practices have in turn provoked a much tenser and more volatile climate than in previous decades.

The 'German model' is based on five principles (Müller-Jentsch 1995a). The most important is the dual structure of interest representation, originating in the early years of the Weimar Republic: workers' representation at workplace level is formally separated from the collective bargaining system. Hence structural conflicts between labour and capital are dealt with in two arenas separated according to interests, actors and modes of enforcement. In collective bargaining, interests are generalized and basically quantitative (especially wages and hours); in the workplace they are specialized and more qualitative. Unions and employers' associations are responsible for collective bargaining, usually at sectoral and regional level; works councils and managements for relations at company level. Strikes and lockouts are a legitimate means of applying pressure in collective bargaining, but not in the exercise of co-determination, consultation and information rights in the workplace, where only peaceful negotiations and labour court proceedings are permitted.

Within this dual system both sets of actors are, in strictly legal or formal terms, independent. In reality, however, they are mutually dependent, have a close and elaborate division of labour, and are reliable partners within a network of stable co-operation. Unions train members of the works councils, and provide them with information and legal advice; while works councillors are in most cases trade unionists, often actively involved in policy-making and recruiting members for their union. Employers and management, too, see advantages in being relieved of some of their responsibilities by employers' associations which, for example, take wages out of competition.

A second notable feature of German industrial relations is the importance of the law (*Verrechtlichung*). The dual system has an elaborate legal basis, and there is detailed legal regulation of labour conflicts and of industrial relations at the workplace. The works council has no right to strike; and a system of labour courts at local, regional and national levels adjudicates disputed issues. Extensive juridification helps to channel and depoliticize industrial conflict and also encourages the professionalization of conflict management. Since the penalties for breaches of the law are severe, legal experts, especially on the workers' side, gain importance and influence.

Third, of special importance for German industrial relations is the degree to which the institutions of collective representation encompass their constituencies. The institutions of worker representation, unions and works councils, can make decisions in the name of the entire workforce, with little obligation to seek endorsement. The law requires unions to represent the interests of all employees, and not just those of their members; the works council is not subject to any mandate from its constituency (save for the need to seek re-election every four years). Employers' associations also effectively represent all employers in their industry, or even (in the case of the peak confederation) the whole economy, not by law but by virtue of their strength of organization.

A fourth important feature is the 'intermediary' character of these institutions (Müller-Jentsch 1985). The works council through its legal constitution must explicitly consider the company's economic goals. Trade unions too, more than in many other European countries, have followed an evolutionary path to become 'mediators' between the interests of labour and capital and bulwarks of the tradition of 'social partnership'.

A final characteristic is the relative centralization of collective bargaining and the co-ordinated policies of the bargaining parties at sectoral level. Towards the end of the nineteenth century, unions adopted the principle of central authority rather than local autonomy, and later they chose industrial unionism in preference to craft or occupational organization. After 1945, the unions' former political divisions were replaced by the principle of unitary trade unions (*Einheitsgewerkschaften*). Since then, the main German unions have faced little organizational competition. The employers also tended to organize in central confederations from an early date. Each side promoted the concentration and centralization of the other; the result was a relatively centralized bargaining system with large bargaining territories.

During the 1960s and early 1970s academic socialists and union activists condemned the dual system for stifling industrial militancy and suppressing class conflict. They argued for an increased role for shopfloor union delegates (*Ver-*

trauensleute) and for a shopfloor bargaining system as ways of strengthening the rank and file and reducing the control of union officials. However, unionists and academic experts of the political mainstream of social democracy viewed the 'dual system' much more positively, arguing that it provided benefits for both unions and works councils. This controversy has now died down. In many European countries, unions suffered defeats and serious loss of membership as a result of economic crisis and the strategies of conservative governments. The relative resilience of German union membership and bargaining power has made the advantages of the dual system self-evident. It is now almost universally agreed that the system allows flexible adjustment to change, without weakening the representational strength of unions.

Economic and Legal Framework

Economic and Political Background

Created in 1949, the Federal Republic of Germany (BRD) has achieved a dominant position in world trade and the leading economic role within the EU. The establishment of a stable democratic order is an element of this (West) German success story; an order based on the model of the 'social market economy' underpinned by legal regulation, free collective bargaining and co-determination. With the accession of the former German Democratic Republic (DDR) in 1990 and the growing internationalization of the economy, Germany has entered a new stage of development.

The history of the BRD can be divided into five main phases, roughly corresponding to the decades since the foundation of the Republic. The 1950s were marked by the reconstruction of the productive base as well as public administration and infrastructure. GNP doubled in real terms; inflation was kept to an annual rate of 2 per cent. At the same time, the number of wage- and salary-earners rose to 20 million. These trends continued in the 1960s: industrial production, exports and investment continued to increase rapidly, and the value of the deutsche mark (DM) rose in relation to foreign currencies. The most important innovation in economic policy was the formulation of sophisticated Keynesian instruments for managing the economy, including tripartite consultation (*Konzertierte Aktion*) over economic policy and wage negotiation. This change in part reflected a major political shift: the Christian Democrats (CDU/CSU), who had governed (usually in coalition with the Free Democrats, FDP) since the formation of the BRD, lost ground electorally and in 1966 brought the Social Democrats (SPD) into a 'grand coalition', with an SPD Economics Minister.

After 1969, the SPD governed in coalition with the FDP. But economic circumstances soon conspired against the social democrats. All western economies were shaken by the collapse of the Bretton Woods system of fixed exchange rates and by the oil price rises of the early 1970s. Germany experienced recessions with troughs in 1974–5 and 1981–2, reflected in a fall in investment and a steep rise in unemployment. Keynesian-based efforts to stimulate growth and employment proved futile in the face of the policy of the *Bundesbank*: its constitutional autonomy from the political authorities allows it to pursue tight monetary policies that can negate the expansionary preferences of governments. The unions were put on the defensive and were unable to maintain workers' share of national income. Foreign trade continued to expand, however. The shock of both recessions triggered a wave of modernization. The Council of Economic Advisers (*Sachverständigenrat*), the government's most influential advisory body, had already indicated in 1981 that sustained competitiveness required new products and technical solutions. The unions opposed only certain measures for implementing the modernization process, in particular the government's supply-side economics and the *Bundesbank*'s tight money policy; for these policies implied the deliberate creation of unemployment to penalize wage increases which were considered excessive.

The SPD lost office in 1982, when their coalition partners switched support to the CDU. Labour's share of national income, which had been stable at around 68 to 71 per cent in the 1970s, declined from 72 per cent in 1981 to 69 per cent in 1985 and 66 per cent in 1994 (Müller-Jentsch 1997). Real wages fell continuously in the first half of the 1980s, before starting to rise once more until the early 1990s. However, deregulation and cuts in social services were limited; and during the 1980s there was a new phase of growth, based again on industrial production and exports.

A broad consensus exists that the German economy depends on success within a prosperous and expanding world economy. This export orientation explains the interest of government and business in the completion of the Single European Market and the development of Monetary and Political Union. European integration has sparked a wave of capital concentration in which German enterprises have been leading participants. Mergers and take-overs have created powerful German transnational firms in the manufacturing sector; during the 1990s these have mainly expanded internationally and have often reduced their domestic workforce (table 7.1). Multinational concerns have also developed in banking and insurance: for example, *Deutsche Bank* with approximately 75,000 employees and *Allianzversicherung* with about 70,000 are Europe's biggest financial companies with world-wide activities. Many medium-sized enterprises have also undertaken foreign direct investment, which reached a total of DM 50 billion in 1995.

Since the early 1990s the German economy, though still successful in terms of exports, has been threatened by growing international competition. The export volume in 1995 was in excess of DM 800 billion, second only to the USA; but market shares are declining in the face of competition both from other advanced countries and from economies with low wages, inferior social and environmental standards, or low tax rates. Adding to this problem is the upward revaluation of the German currency; industrialists (and unions) are therefore strongly in favour of European Monetary Union. Employers argue that Germany's locational advantages (*Standort Deutschland*) can be sustained only by reducing production costs through wage curbs, cuts in taxes and social benefits, and relaxation of environmental controls. Between 1990 and 1995, nominal wages in western Germany

Table 7.1 The largest German private employers (1995)

Firm	Sector	World Employment
Siemens	Elec./engineering	375,000
Daimler-Benz	Vehicles/technology	310,000
Deutsche Post*	Post	310,000
Deutsche Bahn*	Rail	300,000
Volkswagen	Vehicles	250,000
Deutsche Telecom*	Communications	210,000
Bosch	Electrical	160,000
Hoechst	Chemicals	160,000
Bayer	Chemicals	145,000
RWE	Energy	140,000
Thyssen	Steel/engineering	125,000
VEBA	Chemicals	125,000
Mannesmann	Steel/engineering	120,000
BMW	Vehicles	115,000
BASF	Chemicals	110,000

* Privatized companies

rose by approximately 20 per cent; real net wages, on the other hand, fell slightly as a result of higher taxes and social security contributions and price inflation. Income distribution therefore shifted in favour of profits. Given that the public debt has doubled since unification and now amounts to 60 per cent of GDP, curbing public expenditure has become a top priority.

As in other countries, there have been significant changes in the structure of employment. In the 1990s part-time work has increased to about 20 per cent of the labour force, and other 'atypical' forms of work have also expanded. White-collar employment has risen consistently, overtaking the manual labour force in 1986 (see Table 7.2). The service sector has continued to increase in importance. The centres of economic activity are shifting to high-tech regions such as the Munich and Stuttgart areas, or to service-oriented centres such as Frankfurt. Nevertheless, it should be noted that 'de-industrialization' has been far less a feature of (west) Germany than of other European economies. Manufacturing continues to employ a far higher proportion of the labour force than in the other major EC countries (see table 7.3).

Another aspect of modernization in the 1980s was the improvement in employment, which in 1992 reached a record level of 26 million in the original BRD (35.8 million in unified Germany as a whole). Though the rate of unemployment was also high, there were some regional and sectoral shortages of skilled workers. The unions found themselves in a strong position to push for wage increases, sometimes through special additional earnings in areas where labour was especially scarce. The *Bundesbank* reacted with a tight money policy and announced it was willing to run the risk of higher unemployment. This policy reinforced the effects of employer efforts to curb labour costs in the west and the collapse of employment

Table 7.2 Dependent labour force in Western Germany, 1950–1995 and all Germany, 1996

Year	Employed[a] (000)	Manual	White-collar	Beamte	Women	(000)	Unemployed[b] (%)
1950	13,674	70.9	23.0	6.11		580	10.4
1955	16,840	68.7	24.9	6.4		928	5.2
1960	20,257	62.3	30.4	7.2	33.6	271	1.3
1965	21,757	59.7	32.1	8.2	33.8	147	0.7
1970	22,246	56.2	35.1	8.7	34.0	149	0.7
1975	22,467	50.1	39.9	10.0	36.1	1,074	4.6
1980	23,897	48.0	41.9	10.1	37.0	889	3.6
1985	23,559	45.2	44.0	10.8	38.2	2,304	8.9
1990	25,460	43.0	46.5	10.5	39.0	1,883	6.9
1995	25,022	39.1	52.0	8.9	39.2	2,565	9.3
1996	30,375					4,024	11.6

[a] Employed wage and salary earners, including civil servants (*Beamte*)
[b] Officially registered unemployed
[c] Unemployed persons in relation to the entire dependent labour force (employed + unemployed)
  Source: *Sachverständigenrat, Statistisches Bundesamt* and *Bundesanstalt für Arbeit.*

Table 7.3 Employment by sector (% of dependent labour force), 1960–1995

Year	Agriculture, energy, construction	Manufacturing	Services
1960	15.7	44.1	40.2
1965	15.0	43.6	41.4
1970	13.2	43.3	43.5
1975	11.5	38.7	49.8
1980	11.3	36.6	52.1
1985	10.3	34.5	55.2
1990[a]	9.5	33.7	56.8
1995[a]	9.4	29.1	61.5
1995[b]	11.9	26.7	61.4

[a] West only
[b] Unified Germany
  Source: *Sachverständigenrat.*

in the east: by 1997 unemployment had reached 4.5 million or 12 per cent of the workforce (10 per cent in the west, almost double in the east).

The impact of unemployment is occupationally as well as regionally uneven. Nearly three-quarters of all unemployed workers have only basic education. Women are disproportionately unemployed. Special employment measures have been unable to correct structural unemployment, characterized by shortages of some skilled workers and a surplus of those with few if any qualifications. The unions have been weakened by high unemployment; and their offer at the end of 1995 to accept wage restraint as part of a tripartite pact to achieve employment stability (*Bündnis für Arbeit*) failed to gain employer support. The government too, while initially favourable, has embraced many of the employers' demands for cuts in social expenditure.

The Impact of Unification

On 3 October 1990 the former *Deutsche Demokratische Republik* (DDR) became part of the *Bundesrepublik*. The entire West German state and constitutional system was extended into eastern Germany, as was the framework of industrial relations. The economic and social structures of the east were adapted to the West German model, transforming a command economy into a social market economy. This has involved the modernization of production technology and infrastructure, changes in the organization of the labour process and industrial relations, and the development of the service sector. A process which required several decades in the BRD is currently being compressed into a few years in eastern Germany.

Efforts to integrate eastern Germany have turned out to be unexpectedly difficult and expensive. In stark contrast to the economic dynamism of western Germany, the DDR was marked by technological backwardness and low productivity, antiquated infrastructure, inefficient administration and extreme ecological damage – the full extent of which became apparent only after unification.

The introduction of the *Deutschmark* into the DDR shortly before unification symbolized the political downfall of the communist regime and triggered economic consequences which are still being felt. With the removal of state subsidies, most East German products became uncompetitive in the west. There was a similar collapse in eastern European markets, because currency shortages in those countries led to drastic reductions in imports. The economic consequences were concentrated in what was once the backbone of the DDR economy: the manufacturing sector. Entire branches, such as motor vehicles, collapsed because the products no longer found a market. In chemicals, additionally burdened by disastrous environmental damage, the number of jobs fell from 330,000 to 30,000 in 1996. Expansion is taking place only in those sectors which were neglected by the old government: construction, printing, banking and insurance.

This transformation crisis has been accompanied by a massive overall decline in jobs. Statistics for 1989 put the number of employed at 9.5 million; by the end of 1995 the figure had dropped to 6 million. Since 1989, the eastern German economy has lost about 2.5 million jobs in manufacturing, 800,000 in agriculture, and 700,000 in public administration; only the private service sector experienced an increase (of 500,000 jobs). According to an estimate of the Council of Economic Advisers, the 'deficit in normal employment' amounts to 25 per cent. Beyond the economic centres of Berlin, Dresden, and Leipzig, the level of unemployment is significantly higher, especially in traditional industrial areas. The impact of job loss has been cushioned by relatively generous unemployment benefits, early retirement allowances and financial grants for retraining. Following trade union pressure, publicly subsidized employment agencies have been launched to train or upgrade unemployed workers. Thus enormous financial resources (up to 50 billion DM per year) were used to subsidize labour market policies in the east, though these transfers have been reduced since 1993, despite the desolate state of labour markets (Keller 1997).

Despite broad consensus between government and opposition parties, as well as employers' associations and trade unions, on the integration of the *neue Bundesländer* within the western system, there have been disputes over the speed and the extent to which market forces should prevail. Significant conflicts between government, employers and unions were triggered by the privatization of East German operations formerly owned and operated by the state. The *Treuhand* institute set up to undertake this task followed a policy of selling off companies which could be restructured and made immediately viable, and shutting down those which it considered unsalvageable; the unions (and many eastern politicians) argued for a longer-term perspective of support and restructuring.

Integration of the two economies has required massive support from the west. Subsidies to the *neue Bundesländer* to stimulate investment, to establish modern infrastructure and administration, and to support the victims of labour market collapse amounted to DM 1,000 billion between 1991 and 1996. Despite the economic and social problems, all observers (including the unions) agree that the standard of living has risen. First, the conversion of East German savings into western marks (at the very favourable ratio of 2:1) allowed East Germans to acquire high-value consumer goods. Second, the infusion of unemployment benefits has meant that the majority of workers in eastern Germany who lost their jobs have been able to maintain their standard of living. Finally, the wage increases negotiated by the unions have improved the living standards of those workers who still have jobs. While union demands for rapid wage equalization between east and west (initially supported by the government and by western employers) have not been realized – eastern wages are still on average only 85 per cent of the western level – this is a considerable improvement on the situation at unification and also contrasts with productivity levels in the east of only slightly above 50 per cent of western standards. There is vehement conflict over the fact that East German wages are outstripping productivity. Politicians, employers and most economic experts tend to attribute the modest success of employment policies to the high wage levels. Unit labour costs are 30 per cent higher than in western Germany.

A double dilemma has arisen which will take some time to resolve. The high wage levels in eastern Germany are politically as well as socially justified, but they inhibit the competitiveness of East German businesses. Massive transfers have doubled the public debt for all of Germany, without, however, achieving stable and self-sustaining growth in East Germany. GDP per head of population was DM 12,900 in the east in 1991 as against DM 41,300 in the west; by 1994 the figures were DM 22,100 and DM 45,200; the gap between east and west remains substantial but is closing. It has become clear that the costs of reconstructing the East German economy will be higher, and the process more protracted, than was widely imagined in the euphoric days of the collapse of the Berlin Wall and the old DDR regime.

The Legal Framework: The State and Law

The high degree of juridification of German industrial relations has already been emphasized. The Works Constitution Act (*BetrVG*) requires the election of a works council (*Betriebsrat*) in all but the smallest private firms and defines precisely the questions on which councils possess rights of information, consultation or co-determination. There is provision for combine works councils (*Gesamt*- or *Konzernbetriebsräte*) in multi-plant companies. The operation of this pivotal institution is discussed in detail in a later section. There is parallel legislation in the public sector, the Federal Staff Representation Act (*Bundespersonalvertretungsgesetz*) with supplementary Acts in the various *Länder*. These provide for staff councils with somewhat fewer powers than works councils. Their operation is also examined below.

The other main level of employee representation is on company boards, which in Germany have a two-tier structure: a small management board which reports to and is appointed by a supervisory board. There are three different types of legal provision. The *BetrVG* of 1952 provides for one-third employee representation on the supervisory boards of all companies with over 500 employees. The Co-Determination Act 1976 provides notional parity in firms with more than 2,000 employees, though in practice the shareholders' representatives retain a majority in the event of disagreement. In the 1980s about 500 enterprises were covered by this provision; the number increased to 750 after unification.

Finally there is a special law (the *MontanMitbG* of 1951, amended several times) which applies to the coal and steel industry. This provides genuine parity on the supervisory board; and the employee representatives have a veto over the appointment of the labour director who acts as a de facto representative of the employees and their interests on the management board. The *MontanMitbG* guarantees the most far-reaching opportunities for co-determination ever established in Germany and is therefore of enormous symbolic significance. Nowadays, it is only of limited practical importance because of the decline of the coal and steel industries: only about 30 companies in the west and fewer than 20 in the east operate under the Act.

Perhaps surprisingly, collective bargaining is not subject to detailed legal regulation. The right to bargain is assigned to trade unions on one side and employers' organizations or single employers on the other (the peak confederations are not directly involved). The Collective Agreement Act (TVG of 1949, amended in 1969) guarantees free collective bargaining: the right of the parties to negotiate pay and other working conditions without state intervention. Once an agreement is adopted, however, it is legally binding and there is a strict peace obligation during its currency. There is a clear legal distinction between disputes of right over the interpretation of existing agreements, which must be settled by company-level arbitration committees or by reference to the labour courts; and disputes of interest concerning the terms of new agreements. Collective agreements are in practice, though not in legal terms, applicable to all employees and not just to union members. Under the TVG a declaration of general applicability can be made by the federal or *Land* Minister of Labour if either party so requests and a special committee of the social partners agrees. This provision is rarely used. An important instance however was in 1996 when minimum wages for the construction industry were set for the first time and declared generally binding, following concerns that cheap foreign labour was being used to undercut standards.

There is no legislation directly related to union recognition, which is rarely a problem in Germany; but indirectly, as will be shown below, the law provides very strong support for collective representation. Nor is there legislation regulating the internal affairs of trade unions, which are free to determine their own rules and constitutions.

As well as the dense network of statute law, German industrial relations are subject to a considerable body of case law. In particular, the conduct of strikes and lockouts (which as noted above, are permissible only between the expiry of an existing agreement and the conclusion of a new one) is regulated by a series of judgments of the Federal Labour Court and the Federal Constitutional Court. Two key principles of case law are 'social adequacy' and 'proportionality'. A strike or lockout must relate to the agenda of collective bargaining – hence political and sympathy strikes are illegal – and be called only after the breakdown of bargaining. Industrial action is legitimate only if it is not excessive in comparison to the issue provoking it. Only trade unions can call strikes; 'wildcat' action is illegal. Strikes suspend, rather than terminate, contracts of employment. Lockouts have been judged lawful – a contentious issue – but only in response to a (selective) strike; and the numbers locked out must not substantially exceed those on strike.

The Work Promotion Act (AFG) of 1969 introduced an 'active and preventive' labour market policy, and has become increasingly important since the mid-1970s when unemployment started to rise dramatically. It has not been particularly effective, although expenditure on labour market policies has increased considerably since the mid-1970s, and especially in the early 1990s after unification. Most of its instruments were designed for a context of full employment, and are difficult to adapt to conditions of structural, long-term mass unemployment and especially the disastrous labour market situation in the east. As in other European countries, many employment-related conditions and benefits (retirement pensions, health insurance, maternity benefits, maximum hours of work, minimum holiday periods, unemployment insurance) are the subject of legislation.

Germany is exceptional in having a formal national system of vocational training with trade unions directly involved in its tripartite administrative structure. Participation for a period of some three years is compulsory for all school-leavers who do not proceed to higher education. The system eases the transition from school to labour market, counteracting youth unemployment (which in Germany, in contrast to most other European countries, is no higher than the overall rate). There is a dual system which blends general training in specialized, independent public vocational schools with specific training within companies. The system guarantees the acquisition of standardized qualifications which are both practical and theoretical and creates opportunities for internal mobility and functional flexibility, reducing the significance of job demarcations and avoiding over-specialization (Sengenberger 1987). There exist more than 400 detailed curricula, many of which have in recent years been adapted through tripartite negotiations to new technological requirements, introducing new 'key qualifica-tions'. It is often argued that this system of vocational training creates a competitive advantage for German industry (Timmermann 1990).

In the 1990s the system has been facing two interrelated problems. There has been a sharp fall in the number of apprenticeship places because of the more difficult economic climate; training opportunities are thus significantly below the number of young people seeking apprenticeships. At the same time, there is an over-supply of places for mechanics and hairdressers and a shortage of training for high-technology qualifications.

Up to the 1970s, it was common to criticize the high degree of juridification of Germany industrial relations (Erd 1978, 1979); but the positive effects have since become more evident. Legalization now appears not so much a restriction on collective action as a relatively effective institutional buffer against attempts to change the system drastically. It places a brake on aggressive moves by employers when capital has the upper hand; and on major changes initiated by conservative or liberal governments (cf. Katzenstein 1989). All these rules create a legal, institutionalized framework for the voluntary interaction of the actors at different levels. Individual and collective actions and their consequences can be predicted by the other side, leading to an iterated game of mutual interdependence, co-operation and compromise.

Trade Unions

When trade unionism was rebuilt after 1945, a single peak association, the German Trade Union Confederation (DGB), transcended the movement's former ideological divisions and combined in a single organizational structure for workers of different social status – blue- and white-collar and *Beamte* ('civil servants'). The DGB originally had sixteen affiliated unions, each responsible for one industry or economic sector. In 1978 the Police Union joined as the seventeenth affiliate; and in 1989 the unions of printers and the arts amalgamated (see table 7.4). Otherwise the structure remained unaltered until the early 1990s.

The corollary of a 'unitary' trade union movement is that German unions are not formally affiliated to any political party. Nevertheless the DGB maintains close links with the SPD, most full-time union officials are party members, and the majority of members vote for the social democrats. However the DGB, and almost all industry unions, reserve a minority of executive seats for CDU members. Traditional patterns of political alignment have been weakened in the last decade or so by the rise of new social movements on the left, and in particular the emergence of the Green Party as a significant force.

There are two other significant confederations: the German Salaried Employees'

Table 7.4 Deutscher Gewerkschaftsbund (DGB) membership (000) 1995

Sector	Manual	White-collar	Beamte	Women	Total
Metal industry	2,363,947	505,522	–	511,735	2,869,469
Public service	779,727	919,322	71,740	814,385	1,770,789
Chemicals	573,915	149,325	–	168,296	723,240
Construction	575,382	64,469	–	61,961	639,851
Posts	196,297	76,721	256,215	224,657	529,233
Commerce, banking, insurance	59,711	460,455	–	350,459	520,166
Rail	205,960	60,165	132,279	75,730	398,404
Mining and energy	289,924	86,210	232	27,932	376,366
Food, drink, tobacco	252,401	69,618	–	128,131	322,019
Education, science		143,454	119,666	207,868	306,448
Textile, clothing	107,750	17,704	–	128,900	216,288
Media	88,932	48,464	–	67,644	206,786
Police	10,745	22,729	165,423	27,854	198,897
Wood, plastics	134,306	12,532	–	31,734	170,908
Agriculture	67,556	12,573	2,596	23,389	82,725
Leather	20,842	2,239	–	10,779	23,081
Total DGB	5,727,395	2,651,502	748,151	2,861,454	9,354,670

Source: DGB.

Union (DAG) and the German Civil Servants' Federation (DBB). In contrast to the position during the Weimar Republic – and in some European countries today – these two rival confederations represent fewer white-collar employees and civil servants than does the DGB. From the early 1990s there has been a rapprochement between the DAG and the DGB-affiliated unions, and a merger is possible. A fourth confederation, the Christian Federation of Trade Unions (CGB), has fewer than 300,000 members. Eighty-three per cent of all union members belong to the DGB.

In the period of unification the West German unions expanded their organizational domains to the east. The old, communist-dominated FDGB was transformed in 1990 into a somewhat similar structure of industrial unions. These eventually decided to dissolve and recommended their members to join the trade unions affiliated to the DGB. Initially this was remarkably successful: DGB membership increased by nearly 50 per cent, from 8 million in 1990 to 12 million the following year. However the processes of merger and take-over were accompanied by a number of fairly serious demarcation disputes between individual unions. Of the other three confederations – DAG, DBB and CGB – which also expanded their organizations to the east, only the DBB made considerable gains in membership.

These gains were short-lived: in the following 4 years the unions lost 1.8 million members in the new *Bundesländer* and another 600,000 in the old. Overall, the density ratio of DGB membership fell below 30 per cent. The main reasons why East Germans left the unions were the dramatic losses of jobs, and the disappointment of workers' unrealistically high expectations of their new unions. In the old

Table 7.5 Union membership and density 1950–1995

Year	DGB (000s)	DGB Density (%)	DBB (000s)	DAG (000s)	CGB (000s)	All confederations (DGB. DBB, DAG, CGB) (000s)	All confederations (DGB. DBB, DAG, CGB) Density (%)	Potential membership (employed and unemployed)
1950	5,450	35.7	234	344	–	6,028	39.5	15,254
1955	6,105	34.4	517	421	–	7,043	39.6	17,768
1960	6,379	31.0	650	450	200	7,679	37.4	20,528
1965	6,574	30.0	703	476	235	7,988	36.5	21,904
1970	6,713	30.0	721	461	199	8,094	36.1	22,395
1975	7,365	31.3	727	470	224	8,786	37.3	23,541
1980	7,883	31.8	821	495	288	9,487	38.3	24,786
1985	7,719	29.8	796	500	307	9,322	36.0	25,863
1990	7,938	29.0	799	508	309	9,554	34.9	27,343
1995[a]	9,355	26.9	1.076	507	304	11,242	32.3	34,812

Source: Union figures.
Note: [a] East and West combined.

Länder the fall of membership was mainly due to job losses, and only marginally to withdrawals by those still in employment.

These membership fluctuations caused disastrous financial problems for some unions. Shortly after increasing their personnel to cater for the new members, the loss of income made cutbacks inevitable. The loss of members and the demarcation disputes have given rise to new mergers and discussions on a far-reaching reorganization of the DGB, whose affiliates will decrease to eleven by 1999. In 1996 the union of construction workers amalgamated with the union of agricultural workers (now IG Bauen – Agrar – Umwelt); in 1997 the mining and leather industry unions joined IG Chemie (now IG Bergbau, Chemie, Energie); and in 1998–9 IG Metall will absorb the two unions of employees in textiles and clothing and in wood and plastics. Further mergers are expected, perhaps ultimately leaving only five to eight big unions. One obvious consequence is that the organizational pattern of industrial unionism is likely to be watered down in favour of general unionism, even though the principle of 'one enterprise – one union' will remain. The future role of the DGB is more uncertain than ever.

Union density in Germany is not high. Membership density in DGB unions fluctuated around 30 per cent for most of the post-war decades. After a brief increase following unification, the figure has now fallen to 27 per cent. But since the groups with high density rates (blue-collar workers in manufacturing and public employees) occupy strategic positions, their unions are in a position to negotiate pace-setting agreements. In addition, the system of industrial unionism and sectoral collective bargaining has up to now left little room for a non-union sector. Only very small employers could pay below union rates without provoking their employees to join a union. Union density is also an inadequate measure of union strength because it tells us nothing about the intensity and quality of the membership bond. A large membership – perhaps recruited on the basis of individual incentives – may not provide real collective strength. Smaller numbers, but a greater commitment to collective interests, may make for stronger unionism. In this respect the German unions, despite relatively low density, have from time to time demonstrated their ability to mobilize their members in disciplined, protracted and effective strike action.

In the past decades the composition of DGB membership has shown a shift from industry to the service sector, and from blue-collar to white-collar work. Between 1950 and 1995 the percentage of blue-collar workers in DGB unions fell from 83 to 63, while that of white-collar staff rose from 11 to 29 and of *Beamte* from 6 to 8. But although white-collar and female employees constitute an increasing proportion of union membership (with higher density rates in the east than in the west), their unionization has not kept pace with their growing numbers in the labour force. Nearly half of all blue-collar workers (46.3 per cent) are members of a DGB union, but only 16.5 per cent of *Angestellte* and 30.9 per cent of *Beamte*. Male workers are 36.5 per cent organized in DGB unions, women only 21.8 per cent. Thus membership composition is more in line with the labour force of 1950 than that of today. The very low density rate among younger workers (17 per cent) is particularly worrying (see table 7.5).

Union democracy is based on a delegate system with representative and executive bodies at local, regional and national levels. Ordinary members are directly involved – apart from elections for local representatives – only when ballots on industrial action are held. Such ballots are called by national executive committees, and require a 75 per cent vote before a strike can be declared, according to the unions' own rules. On the same principle, a strike can be ended by a vote of 25 per cent. The logic behind these rules is that strikes need to have the support of a large majority of members to be effective.

The national trade union conference is the most important policy-making body. As a rule, it takes place every 4 years (though in the past, conferences were held more frequently) and elects the national executive committee, which is the most important body for policy implementation.

The segmentation of the labour market into relatively privileged and underprivileged groups is clearly reflected in unions' representational structures. Male skilled or professional employees are generally over-represented. To counteract this tendency, most unions now have provisions regarding proportional representation of their female membership in union committees and conferences. There are also clear signs of professionalization: most elected bodies have a high proportion of full-time officers. There have been parallel tendencies towards bureaucratic structures, centralization of decision-making and concentration of control over personnel and financial resources in the national executive committee that co-ordinates wage policy, selects full-time officers and controls the union press. Restrictions on the influence of the rank and file are an expression of oligarchical tendencies in labour organizations, present since before the First World War, as shown in Michels' famous study. Some authors (Weitbrecht 1969; Bergmann et al. 1975; Müller-Jentsch 1985) have argued that the neutralization of direct member influence on union policy is a prerequisite for the unions to perform their intermediary functions of negotiating and dealing with employers and the state in a co-operative and authoritative way.

In the course of its history, the DGB has formulated four basic policy declarations: the Munich Programme of 1949, the Düsseldorf Programmes of 1963 and 1981, and the Dresden Programme of 1996. The programme formulated at the founding congress was anti-capitalist, arguing for the 'reorganization of the economy and society' with the socialization of key industries, economic planning, and co-determination. The second programme (1963) revised the anti-capitalist goals and followed the neo-Keynesian line of the 1959 Godesberg Programme of the SPD. The third programme (1981) was primarily an extension of the second. Both Düsseldorf programmes combined socialist rhetoric with pragmatic accommodation to a Keynesian model of capitalism: offering, in effect, a compromise between the right and left wings of the DGB.

In the late 1980s and early 1990s, unions initiated an open debate on their role in a changing economic and social environment. The microelectronic revolution and the globalization of economic relations, the death of traditional working-class cultures and the decline of socialist ideology, the crisis of the Keynesian welfare state and the 'silent revolution' of value systems, the increasing tertiarization and feminization of the occupational structure, the political cleavages caused by the emergence of new social movements and parties, all these challenges and their consequences for unionism formed the agenda of union conferences and workshops. In response to these pressures, the DGB has now formulated a new basic programme which abandons any idea of a socialist economic order, but rejects 'pure-and-simple capitalism' and supports a 'socially regulated market economy'.

▌ The Representation of Business Interests

German business has long been highly organized, and despite some loss of cohesion during the 1990s, most companies remain loyal to their associations. Three basic types of organization can be distinguished (Bunn 1984; Keller 1997): Chambers of Industry and Commerce, Business Associations, and Employers' Associations.

The Chambers of Industry and Commerce are local organizations with a formal legal status which makes membership compulsory for all eligible firms. They perform a variety of public or semi-governmental tasks: licensing and regulating trade practices and managing occupational training programmes, in particular apprenticeship training. They also offer a broad range of market-related services, including advice on current business issues. Their national organization, the German Association of Chambers of Commerce (DIHT), represents about 100 regional and local chambers on questions of economic policy and foreign trade.

Business (or trade) associations are organized by industry, in local associations affiliated to sectoral peak organizations. They are concerned with such matters as technology, production, marketing and research. The Association of German Machine and System Builders (VDMA) is a good example of the structure and functioning of these business organizations: with approximately 3,000 member companies (1994) it represents about 55 per cent of the eligible firms and more than 80 per cent of the sales in this key industry. It has separate *Länder* associations, and sub-divisions for mechanical engineering, printing equipment and other specialist products. The main economy-wide peak association is the Federation of German Industries (BDI), which comprises the business associations of the entire industrial sector. In 1994 it consisted of 35 business associations with provincial subdivisions and some 350 specialized industrial sub-units.

Employers' associations are the third type, responsible for negotiating the sectoral and multi-employer collective agreements which cover the vast majority of employees. It is legally possible for a single employer to negotiate a collective agreement, and Volkswagen is a well-known example; but it is very much an exception. Although in most industries bargaining takes place at regional level, the national employers' associations exercise tight co-ordination and control over the process. Member companies may not independently conclude company agreements and must observe collective agreements reached by their employers' association; breach of these principles is grounds for expulsion. The Federation of Employers' Associations of the Metalworking Industry (*Gesamtmetall*) far exceeds all others in influence, representing employers in the motor, machine-tool and electrical industries. It is a multi-sectoral federation of employers' associations, which – like its union counterpart, IG Metall – has to reconcile diverse interests as well as handling collective bargaining for four million workers.

The sectoral employers' associations are combined in the Confederation of German Employers' Associations (BDA). Like the DGB, it plays no direct role in collective bargaining, but has a co-ordinating and mediating function. The BDA represents German employers in the field of social policy and industrial relations to the government, the public and international organizations. The BDA is an association of associations and, unlike the BDI, extends far beyond manufacturing industry, covering almost all private-sector employers' associations. The Employers' Association of the Iron and Steel Industry is the only significant organization outside the BDA network. In 1995 the BDA consisted of 46 national industry associations and 15 regional associations; altogether, there are approximately 1,000 different employers' associations at the sectoral, regional and local level. It is estimated that around 70 per cent of employees in the private sector are covered by the BDA's member associations. *Gesamtmetall* (with 7,500 member companies) covered 43 per cent of eligible firms in 1994; these companies employ nearly 2.5 million workers, about 65 per cent of the labour force in the metalworking industries. In some other sectors – the chemical industry or the financial services sector, for example – the degree of representation is higher, and occasionally reaches 100 per cent. The sectoral peak associations such as *Gesamtmetall* have substantial financial resources, including dispute funds to support member companies that are the target of strikes.

The BDA and its member associations are governed by executive and management boards elected by member firms with votes proportional to company size; hence the leadership and the policy of the employers' associations are determined by the largest firms. Positions on the BDA management board are filled by full-time staff; the praesidium is the central policy-making body and is composed of senior representatives of the member companies. Great importance is attached to about 20 committees and working groups which deal with such questions as wage policy, labour law, training programmes, the Single European Market, and overall policy co-ordination.

For most of the post-war era, employers generally have valued multi-employer bargaining as a source of orderly labour relations and a guarantee of industrial peace during the currency of the industry-wide agreement. During the 1990s, however, employers' associations have experienced increasingly severe internal criticism. Numerous member firms (mostly medium-sized companies with fewer than 500 workers) representing 4 per cent of the dependent labour force left their ranks, while many new businesses – in particular in Eastern Germany – refused to join. In addition, more and more member firms fail to comply with the terms of sectoral agreements. The employers' associations in metalworking, printing, and construction suffer most from these developments; other sectors like the chemical industry or the public sector are not affected.

Divisions within employers' associations have been accompanied by growing tensions between the different business organizations. For the first time in post-war history, in 1996 the DIHT and BDI publicly challenged the policy of the BDA and its member associations; and they caused a great sensation when they prevented the BDA president from running for the presidency of the European employers' association. The reason for these controversies is the inability of the employers to develop a common bargaining strategy. This in turn may be attributed to intensified international competition over products, location factors, technologies and costs. The DIHT and BDI, which primarily represent the interests of the German export sector, consider it essential to reduce unit labour costs through wage restraint and a cut in non-wage costs (such as sick pay). They complain that Germany has the highest wages and shortest working time in the world, and that the uniformity and standardization of sectoral agreements prevent individual companies from adapting flexibly to their particular economic circumstances. The BDI has called for a shift to single-employer negotiations at company level and an amendment to the Works Constitution Act enabling works councils as well as trade unions to negotiate collective agreements.

The BDA rejects such ideas, though it seeks substantial reform of the sectoral bargaining system. It regards multi-employer agreements as still necessary to underpin social peace; a move to purely company bargaining would allow unions and works councils to divide employers. However, it wishes to change the industry-wide settlements into broad framework agreements allowing employers greater flexibility to adapt their working conditions to their particular circumstances. It also favours 'opening clauses' permitting temporary non-compliance for businesses facing an economic crisis if they guarantee employment stability in return. Sectoral collective agreements would still be reached between employers' associations and unions, while the supplementary company-specific regulations would be defined in single-plant agreements between management and works council.

In essence, the position of the BDA is that procedural changes should be pursued 'better with the unions and works councils than against them'. The unions for their part have agreed to take part in negotiations about the future of a reformed collective bargaining system. A new balance between a sectorally centralized and a company-level decentralized bargaining pattern, perhaps a new model of regulated decentralization and controlled flexibility of industrial relations, is emerging.

The State

Moderate Macrocorporatism in the 1960s and 1970s

As in other western market economies, the state in Germany has played a gradually increasing role in economic affairs and industrial relations. In the 1960s, as previously conservative economic policies shifted towards Keynesian macro-economic management, two initiatives were taken which remain important. First, the Council of Economic Advisers (*Sachverständigenrat*) was created in 1963. Its role is to report regularly on the state of the economy and likely developments. Although it has no formal powers and is not authorized to offer detailed policy recommendations, its informal influence – usually in favour of some form of wage restraint – has been considerable. Second, the Act on the Promotion of Stability and Growth of 1967 obliges the state and *Bundesländer* to adopt economic and financial policies consistent with such macro-economic goals as price stability, full employment, foreign trade balance and economic growth.

In the late 1960s and 1970s, when active labour market policies and expansionary macro-economic strategies were part of the political agenda, tripartite concertation between the state and national leaderships of unions and employers' associations was an important feature of German industrial relations. Unions became a powerful partner within a system of voluntary political exchange with SPD-led governments between 1969 and 1982. An essential part of the German version of corporatism was the *Konzertierte Aktion* (concerted action) which lasted from 1967 to 1977 and was intended to achieve relative stability of prices and of income distribution, including some sort of voluntary wage restraint, and steady economic growth. The results of the more or less informal meetings were not binding, but had an important influence on public discussion and the internal and external decision-making processes of the parties involved. Union leaders hoped to gain increased organizational strength, improved rights of co-determination and participation, expansion of the welfare state and more influence within the political process. But they could not vigorously pursue their members' immediate economic interests because of the constraints of consensual wage policies and came under heavy pressure from the rank and file, who could see no positive benefits in exchange for their voluntary wage restraint. *Konzertierte Aktion* came to an official end in 1977 after the employers' associations raised a constitutional challenge to the legality of the new Co-determination Act; the unions took the opportunity to withdraw from formal concertation.

Nevertheless the idea of concertation is not dead. In the mid-1990s the unions launched an initiative to establish a so-called 'alliance for jobs' (*Bündnis für Arbeit*). They offered to abandon their traditional demand for productivity-based wage increases in exchange for increased employment and training opportunities. The ambitious goal of halving unemployment by the year 2000 helped unions to mobilize broad public support. Trilateral talks came to an end in the spring of 1996 when the employers' organizations were unable to offer new jobs and the conservative government announced major cutbacks in public expenditure. For the time being it seems that the whole idea of macroconcertation has been political symbolism only; though some agreements along the lines proposed have been concluded in chemicals and at enterprise level in other sectors.

▌ Moderate Deregulation in the 1980s and 1990s

The formation of the neo-conservative CDU/CSU government in 1982 did not cause a complete or abrupt change of policy as in some other western countries. Its orientation to supply-side monetarist strategies had been anticipated in the later stages of its SPD-led predecessor, while political regulation has only partially been replaced by market forces. In practice, there are clear continuities in economic, social and industrial relations policies.

There have indeed been efforts to deregulate aspects of social and labour law. A highly contentious change was Paragraph 116 of the Work Promotion Act of 1986, which ended the entitlement to unemployment and short-time working benefit for employees indirectly affected by industrial action in another bargaining district in the same industry. Such payments had been a valuable resource for the unions since, while negotiations – and hence also strikes – are normally conducted at regional level, it was possible to choose strike tactics which affected an industry across the whole economy. Selective strikes, aimed at focal points of integrated production chains and 'just in time' production, had been developed to a fine art by IG Metall in the 1970s and early 1980s. This intensified the pressure on employers to settle, while the union had only to give financial support to workers striking or laid off in a single district.

In 1995 the Federal Constitutional Court decided that this legal change does not (yet) violate constitutional rights: the unions' ability to perform their functions had 'been impaired, but not radically weakened'. So far, the one empirical test of the consequences of this legal change was in 1995 when IG Metall tried to adapt its strike strategy by avoiding all large enterprises integrated into long production chains (like car plants) and targeting medium-sized establishments. Thereby the traditional, and fairly successful, policy of regionalized but centrally co-ordinated bargaining policy could be preserved.

The Employment Promotion Act of 1985, extended in 1989 and 1994, dilutes previous labour legislation giving protection against dismissal. For new recruits, fixed-term contracts for up to 24 months (the previous maximum was six months) were legalized. The law accelerated the trend towards precarious employment without, however, achieving the government's proclaimed aim of a significant increase in employment. It has however had a significant structural effect, increasing labour market segmentation (Büchtemann and Höland 1989). Yet to the surprise of most labour market experts the number of fixed-term contracts has remained fairly stable (Bielenski and Kohler 1995). From 1996, firms with under 10 employees have been exempted from employment protection legislation (the previous limit was 5), in the hope of creating additional job opportunities in small establishments.

The 1989 amendment to the Works Constitution Act brought various detailed changes. Most were fairly technical, but the main contentious innovations were the creation of special representative bodies for managerial staff (*leitende Angestellte*), and the strengthening of representation rights for other minority groups. The unions interpreted these changes as steps towards deregulation and feared that they would lead to fragmentation; but it is clear from the results of the works councils elections of 1990 and 1994 that there has been no such effect.

The Working Time Act of 1994 replaced the one of 1938 and some even older regulations. It is supposed 'to guarantee the safety and protect the health of employees' but also 'to improve the conditions for more flexibility of working time' and 'to adjust the length of working time to changed economic and social conditions'. The Act allows increased flexibility: the normal 40-hour week maximum (an eight-hour day and five-day week) may be averaged over a six-month period. Within this so-called compensation period employers may operate a 10-hour per day (or 60-hour week) without special justification. Even longer periods of work are possible if the social partners agree. The Act contains a general prohibition of work on Sundays and holidays but also specifies a long catalogue of exceptions. The most controversial is that purely industrial production work can be allowed 'to avoid considerable losses', 'to safeguard employment' and 'to preserve the ability to compete with foreign countries'. In addition the Act greatly extends the legal possibilities for night-work (removing the special restrictions previously applying to women) and for shift-work.

The practical relevance of the changed regulations is limited, since collective agreements (which are in fact quite differentiated and flexible) normally define a working week as well below 40 hours. Empirical research shows that the percentage of employees involved in night- and shift-work has been fairly stable (at about 9 per cent) over a long period and has even decreased in the early 1990s (Seifert 1995). Thus the urgent necessity for legislative change is difficult to understand. Furthermore, in this Act the government has not seriously attempted to deal with the pressing problem of overtime by defining a strict limit on the permissible amount.

Another contentious area of deregulation concerns employment agencies. For many years the Work Promotion Act prescribed a public monopoly of placement services. Following criticism of the low 'acceptance' and decreasing 'efficiency' of these services, since 1994 private employment agencies have been allowed without any legal restrictions, but their impact has so far been marginal.

Important consequences may result from the accumulation of individual measures of deregulation, and the elimination of individual protective rights. Current employer moves towards more flexibility coincide with high unemployment, which has significantly reduced the bargaining power of the unions. The danger of a more severe segmentation of the labour market cannot be dismissed. Nevertheless, deregulation in Germany cannot plausibly be viewed as a coherent long-term political strategy and is likely to have only limited effects; it is more important as an expression of conservative political ideology than in practice. Existing institutions, formal and informal mechanisms of regulation and strategies of the actors function as important stabilizers.

Why has deregulation in Germany been so half-hearted? One important factor is the role of christian-democrat trade unionists, who exercise a two-way mediating role in German industrial relations. One of the bases of the post-war construction of a unitary trade union movement was the guarantee of institutionalized representation (albeit as a small minority) for christian democrats in the unions' governing bodies – inhibiting too unqualified a commitment by the unions to the SPD. But conversely, important CDU politicians possess a strong trade union identity, and are organized in a long-established 'social committee' within the party. This group has strongly opposed deregulation, causing friction within the CDU. The influence of this friction should not be exaggerated, but it has undoubtedly placed a brake on deregulation. In addition, it should be noted that the FDP – the minority governing party – is more committed to deregulation than the CDU/CSU majority.

Another important explanation of the limited extent of deregulation is that the majority of German employers' associations are not seeking the complete deregulation of the collective bargaining system or the destruction of institutions of workers' representation. Their interest in deregulation is limited and specific. They see the advantages of the present system, which they want to reform but not to destroy.

Workplace Institutions and Relations

Works Councils

Works councils are mandatory in all private firms with five or more employees. They possess rights of information, consultation and co-determination. Co-determination (which implies at least a provisional right of veto) applies to 'social' matters such as principles of remuneration and the introduction of new payment methods, bonus rates and performance-related pay, daily and weekly work schedules, regulation of overtime and short-time working, holiday arrangements and the use of technical devices to monitor employees' performance. It also covers such personnel matters as policies for recruitment, transfer, regrading and dismissal. In specific circumstances there is a right of veto over individual cases of hiring, grading, transfer and dismissal. Information and consultation rights apply to personnel planning and changes in work processes, the working environment, new technology and job content. Finally, there is a right to information on financial matters. A standing committee of the works council, the economic

Table 7.6 Works council elections

Year	No. of establish-ments	Councillors elected	Members of works councils				
			Female (%)	Foreign (%)	DGB (%)	DAG & others (%)	Non-union (%)
1965	23,813	149,672	11.0		82.7	4.3	13.1
1968	24,902	142,412	11.4		83.1	3.5	13.4
1972	29,298	173,670	13.5	2.2	77.6	3.5	18.9
1975	34,059	191,015	15.7	2.6	77.5	3.5	18.8
1978	35,294	194,455	17.1	3.1	78.1	3.8	18.1
1981	36,307	194,125	19.3	3.3	77.5	3.9	18.6
1984	35,343	190,193	20.0	3.1	77.4	3.6	19.0
1987	34,807	189,292	20.5	4.5	76.6	3.4	20.0
1990	33,012	183,680	23.5	4.6	76.3	3.1	20.6
1994	40,039	220,245	23.4	4.2	75.2	2.9	21.0

Source: Deutscher Gewerkschaftsbund, Institut der Deutschen Wirtschaft.

committee, must be informed by the employer 'in full and good time of the financial affairs of the establishment'; the same applies in case of planned changes 'which may significantly disadvantage employees'.

In general, participation rights are strong in relation to social policy; weaker in the case of personnel issues; and weaker still in financial and economic matters. In other words, the potential for works council intervention in managerial decision-making decreases the more closely it impinges on business policy. The participation rights are linked to the legal obligation to work with management 'in a spirit of mutual trust for the good of the employees and of the establishment'. The works council is required to negotiate 'with a serious desire to reach agreement'; 'acts of industrial warfare' as well as 'activities that interfere with operations or imperil the peace of the establishment' are prohibited. In addition, information defined by the employer as commercial secrets may not be shared with the workforce.

Works councillors are elected for a 4-year term of office. By law they are formally independent of the unions and represent the entire workforce of an establishment. There are no official statistics on the coverage of works councils, but the DGB collects data for all establishments where affiliated unions are represented, and these are regarded by Ministry of Labour officials as a fairly accurate picture of the overall situation. The DGB figures for 1994 cover more than 40,000 establishments with works councils, in which some 220,000 council-lors were elected (see table 7.6).

In spite of the legal provisions, in many small and medium-sized companies no works council exists. Frick and Sadowski (1995) have estimated that only 24 per cent of all eligible private enterprises, covering 60 per cent of the private sector workforce, have a works council. The proportion is only 10 per cent in the smallest establishments with 5 to 20 employees, and about 30 per cent in plants with 20 to 50; whereas virtually every establishment with more than 300 employees has one.

The size of works councils varies according to the number of employees. In larger establishments a specified number of works councillors can act as full-time employee representatives: one in plants with 300 employees, more in bigger firms. In large establishments they have their own offices and secretaries. The works council cannot be mandated by the workforce, but is required to call a quarterly works meeting of all employees, when it reports on its activities. All costs arising out of the activities of the works council have to be paid by the employer.

Most works councillors are loyal unionists with close ties to their union. There is a relationship of mutual dependence: the union supplies the council with information and expertise through educational courses or direct advice by full-time officials; while works councillors usually sustain union organization by recruiting new members and in general functioning – despite the legal distinction between the two institutions – as the arm of the union in the workplace. This dependence of the unions on the works councils gives the latter significant autonomy in relation to union officialdom; their power is, however, constrained by the fact that election and re-election usually depend on being nominated on an official union list.

In the 1960s and 1970s, it was common in large establishments for works councils to negotiate informally with management for additional wage increases after the settlement of the industry-wide wage agreement. Technically this practice was usually illegal, since matters which form part of the agenda of collective bargaining can be regulated by works agreements only if the collective agreement authorizes this step by a so-called opening clause. In the 1970s, some important collective agreements on working conditions and new technology introduced such a clause and prescribed supplementary works agreements to permit the flexible implementation of general rules. This move towards negotiation at establishment level, as a complement to union collective bargaining at industry level, was strengthened in the 1980s with agreements on flexible working time. Thus more than 10,000 works agreements were negotiated in the engineering industry after the 1984 strike for the shorter working week (see below). Today, some works councils complain about the burden of negotiations.

The stable coalition that has developed requires a sufficient number of unionists elected as works councillors. For this reason the results of works council elections are of primary importance for unions. Challenges are possible, first from competing unions and unorganized groups mobilizing protest votes, and second from oppositional groups within the union itself demanding a more militant policy of interest representation.

DGB-affiliated unions have been fairly successful in warding off the first type of competition; according to union sources more than three-quarters, and according to an employers' survey (Niedenhoff 1995) more than two-thirds of all elected works councillors belong to DGB unions. Hence union dominance in the councils is far in excess of union density among the workforce. The exceptions to this pattern are the management staff committees set up under the 1989 legislation: nearly 50 per cent of those elected in the last elections, held in 1994, were non-unionists; another 47 per cent belong to the ULA, an independent management association with some 40,000 members.

The second type of challenge was quite common in the 1970s, when workplace activists (*Vertrauensleute*) or militant dissenters in many large companies challenged established works councillors. In several cases, oppositional unionists submitted their own list, sometimes with spectacular success. In a few establishments, foreign workers also challenged the official union lists following complaints about under-representation. Overall, however, such oppositional initiatives in works council elections have become very exceptional, even after the amendment of the Works Constitution Act in 1988 which was designed to strengthen the representation rights of minority groups.

While the trade unions have been weakened, the status and functions of the councils have gained in strength over the past decades (Müller-Jentsch 1995b). Their competences have been extended by the devolution of bargaining from sectoral to company level; and their growing involvement in companies' modernization and rationalization processes has at times given them a function of co-management. Managers quite frequently take advantage of the works councils' authority over the workforce to make them share responsibility not only for awkward personnel matters but also for more strategic goals. In general, works councils positively support rationalization of the production system if they are convinced that the establishment's economic position will benefit, and providing two preconditions are met: no dismissals and no fall in wages for employees transferred to other jobs. There is also a broad understanding that work reorganization should serve a dual goal: increased productivity and product quality on the one hand and extended participation rights on the other.

Studies (Eberwein and Tholen 1990; Kotthoff 1994) have shown that employers have increasingly accepted works councils and their functions after the uncertainties and reservations which accompanied the substantial amendment of the Works Constitution Act in 1972. Today no other industrial relations institution is as unquestioned as the works council. Even the most radical advocates of deregulation envisage a continuing and indeed enhanced role for works councils: in some blueprints they would even replace the unions as bargaining agents.

Union Delegates

Most, though not all, German unions have their own representatives alongside the works council, the *Vertrauensleute*. These are union stewards, each of whom usually represents between 30 and 50 workers and is elected by union members in a department or group. Their functions are limited, but include recruitment of members, distribution of union material and serving as a channel of information. They are also expected to support the (unionized) works councillors in fulfilling their tasks. In many cases, *Vertrauensleute* are both messengers of the works council and the mouthpiece of their work groups. In the event of open conflict, such as token or unofficial strikes, they function as informal organizers of industrial action.

Conflict may sometimes arise between *Vertrauensleute* and works councils. Rivalry was fostered in the late 1960s and early 1970s, when IG Metall and some other unions adopted the aim of increasing the powers and functions of the *Vertrauensleute* to make them a counterweight to the works councils. Some activist union delegates adopted an explicit oppositional stance, and became the mouthpiece of discontented groups among the membership. The rivalry ended in victory for the works councillors, a reflection of the legally established position of the councils and their strategic role in recruiting union members. Today *Vertrauensleute* are expected to support the works councils' activities. Most unions have made the unionized works councillors *ex officio* members of the *Vertrauensleute* organization, which in most establishments they are able to dominate.

Quality Circles and Teamworking

As in several other countries, new forms of employee involvement have been introduced as part of a human resource management policy by many German companies, but in a distinctive manner. In Germany 'participatory management', the term preferred to HRM, is intended to complement institutionalized employee representation rather than to displace it. Quality circles and teamwork are the two main models of direct participation.

Some unions and works councils at first opposed such initiatives, especially quality circles, but in most cases they have now accepted them, and some representatives of the unions and works councils regard them as a first step towards their goal of 'co-determination at the workplace'. Since the mid-1980s several works agreements have been signed in individual establishments, mainly large companies in the motor and chemical industries, regulating the formation and functioning of quality circles and guaranteeing works council participation in the process (Breisig 1991). In some other firms, circles have been unilaterally established by management. The latest trend is to move on to establishing procedures of total quality management.

Estimates suggest that quality circles have expanded greatly in recent years. Before the 1980s they were almost unknown in Germany; by the latter part of the decade there were well over a thousand, and more than half of the hundred largest companies have now introduced them. According to a recent study (Dreher et al. 1995: 147) 15 per cent of all manufacturing companies have introduced quality circles and 14 per cent teamworking.

Teamworking has been introduced principally in car firms, as part of a process of restructuring production and work organization stimulated by the large productivity lead of Japanese and American car producers. A survey conducted by IG Metall shows that 22 per cent of production workers in the car industry work in teams (Sperling 1997: 28). In most cases, management and works councils have signed agreements on teamworking, providing for extra time for team discussions, the right to elect team leaders, and better pay for the more integrated and flexible work tasks. In the chemical industry, the union and the employers' association have signed a framework agreement with guidelines and recommendations for works agreements on teamworking. There is debate over the need for new wage systems for employees working in flexible teams, but so far only a few companies (among them Volkswagen) have developed these.

Increasing Diversity in Labour–Management Relations

There is considerable evidence of diversity in labour–management relations. Industry-wide collective bargaining no longer entails (if it ever did) a common pattern of labour relations at company and workplace level within each industry. As has been seen, though sectoral multi-employer bargaining still prevails, the scope of negotiations between management and works councils has increased. This can result in undercutting the minimum standards prescribed in the collective agreement, either with the agreement of the works council or at least its tacit acquiescence. Such 'wildcat co-operation' is a growing problem for the unions, especially in the east.

At one extreme there is a large sector of small and medium-sized establishments with rather informal labour relations. Many are sweat-shops, but the more dynamic estabishments work on the basis of an implicit reciprocity and a kind of 'tacit participation' by the workforce, mostly without an elected works council (Hilbert and Sperling 1990). At the other extreme are large enterprises with company-specific patterns of labour relations. For example Bertelsmann, the biggest European company in the media industry, established a far-reaching participative culture long before 'corporate identity' came into vogue. The scheme of employee participation, introduced in co-operation with the works council, includes semi-autonomous groups, quality circles, employee reviews of their supervisors and profit-sharing. The Media Union (IG Medien) initially opposed this management initiative, which is why it is very poorly represented among the workforce (about 12 per cent) and its influence on the central and combine works councils is severely limited. Although Bertelsmann is subject to the terms of the collective agreements for the printing and media industries, these do not have a great impact on labour relations in practice.

Another case is Volkswagen, which is not a member of the employers' association and bargains directly with IG Metall, generating company collective agreements and a host of works agreements. The union's bargaining committee is almost entirely composed of works councillors. Very high density rate blue- and white-collar workers, and the close collaboration between the union and works council, allow IG Metall to use Volkswagen to pioneer socially progressive policies. While the origins of this special case lie in the history of Volkswagen as a nationalized company, the relationship has continued since partial privatization. The early agreement to establish a European Works Council, which first met in March 1992, and guarantees of employment security in exchange for a (largely uncompensated) reduction in working time from 35 to 28.8 hours (with a four-day week) are examples of innovatory industrial relations.

Collective Bargaining and Industrial Disputes

Types and Mechanisms of Agreement

According to the Collective Agreement Act (TVG) the parties to a collective agreement must be unions on the workers' side and single employers or employers' associations on the other. There are many company collective agreements but they are mainly found in smaller firms (Volkswagen and the oil companies are the obvious exceptions) and they cover only a small minority of employees. Industry-wide or sectoral agreements contribute to a high degree of standardization of wages and other working conditions, as does state regulation. Though in many cases (such as metalworking and chemicals) sectoral bargaining is formally undertaken at regional level, it is centrally directed by the national organizations on each side. So-called pilot agreements reached in key areas of the engineering industry (usually Baden–Württemberg) are the model for the rest of this sector and exert influence on all other industries. This creates a specific German form of 'pattern bargaining' with IG Metall as pace-setter: other wage agreements are generally within a narrow margin of the engineering settlement.

Three different kinds of collective agreements are commonly distinguished: wage agreements fix the level of wages and periodic alterations; framework agreements specify wage-payment systems; and 'umbrella' agreements regulate all other conditions of employment (working time, overtime, holidays, dismissals).

The collective bargaining process follows a characteristic sequence. A more or less extended period of negotiation leads to agreement in the majority of cases; but if negotiations fail, both parties try to resolve the conflict through mediation procedures. These are established by voluntary union–employer agreement, not by government intervention – in clear contrast to the Weimar Republic, when compulsory state arbitration existed. In the vast majority of cases mediation proves successful. However, if it fails, a collective labour conflict becomes possible, in the form of a strike and possibly also a lockout (Kalbitz 1979; Keller 1997).

Such a centralized bargaining system needs mechanisms for adapting the general conditions of collective agreements to the circumstances of individual establishments. Works agreements, negotiated between works councils and management, may not violate or contradict the provisions of the industry-wide collective agreement but are important supplements. They are almost universal in larger firms with over 200 employees; the largest establishments have hundreds of works agreements which are sometimes extensive documents. In general these are restricted to 'social' and 'personnel' questions on which co-determination rights exist. They are less common in small firms with weaker works councils.

▍Collective Bargaining Outcomes

Collective Agreements in Western Germany

Collective agreements now regulate a vast and complex range of issues affecting wages, working time and working conditions, and the negotiating parties employ large staffs of experts to keep abreast of collective agreements within the branches they represent. A recent study (WSI 1996) found that in 1995, there were about 43,600 valid collective agreements (approximately 37,700 in the west, and 5,900 in the east). Each year between 7,000 and 8,000 new contracts are concluded. About one third of them were negotiated at the enterprise level, but the vast majority of employees were covered by sectoral agreements. Only a rather small fraction (about 600) were declared generally binding (most of them in the construction industry). All these figures exclude works agreements negotiated between managements and works councils.

Agreements involving the two largest unions – IGM and the public-sector union ÖTV – cover the largest number of workers, though HBV, with a smaller membership, covers almost as many as ÖTV. This indicates an important feature of German industrial relations: the scope of collective regulation is not closely related to union membership, i.e. a decline in membership has no direct or immediate consequences. Roughly 80 per cent of all employees are covered by collective agreements – three times the number of union members. This figure has, in contrast to some other countries, hardly changed over the years (Traxler 1996). The majority of negotiations concern pay, since these agreements usually have only a twelve- to fifteen-month lifespan; but non-pay agreements are normally of longer duration and comprise the majority of agreements currently in force. The 1.7 million civil servants are excluded. As indicated below, their conditions of employment are set not by collective bargaining but by legislation, though after consultation with the relevant unions.

Within the collective bargaining system, both parties have been able to change priorities from 'quantitative' to 'qualitative' issues, and to adapt their collectively created institutions and regulatory methods. Unions in particular have had to adapt to new circumstances. Since the 1970s, with severely reduced scope for real wage increases, pay has had a lower priority and non-wage issues have received enhanced attention. In the late 1970s, bargaining in many industries focused on protection against rationalization. Working-time arrangements have dominated 'qualitative' union demands since the mid-1980s, in part as a strategy for job-creation. Perhaps surprisingly, most studies suggest that the effect of shorter hours – as the unions claimed, and employers disputed – has indeed been to increase employment (Keller 1997). Since 1992, conflict over wages has returned to the agenda. The costs of German unification, the efforts to fulfil the convergence criteria for the European Monetary Union and the requirement to limit public deficits have led the government and the *Bundesbank* to press for rigid pay restraint. Union efforts to protect real wages have not been successful, but led to strikes in some industries.

In much of the private sector, actual wages are higher than the contractually agreed pay-scales. Multi-employer agreements are based on the economic situation of the average enterprise; in more profitable companies, the works council may succeed in securing higher wages through a works agreement. This gap between the contractually agreed wage and actual rates differs greatly from sector to sector and from region to region as a result of varying conditions in product and labour markets. Earnings drift, which has been important in some countries, is not a significant phenomenon in Germany. The evidence is that the decisions of the collective bargainers actually follow the labour market.

Collective bargaining seems to have had only a limited impact on income differentials. German unions have not regarded egalitarian pay policies as a priority. The 1970s did indeed see a narrowing of differentials, but these have widened again since the 1980s. Pay differentials are greater for white-collar than for manual employees, though the gap between the average rates for the two groups has been closing – a trend which has encouraged the development of common pay scales. Geographical differences in pay have increased recently. It should also be noted that women tend to be concentrated in the lowest pay grades.

Annual holidays have increased progressively, from two weeks in the early 1950s to six weeks in 1990. As in many other areas of collective bargaining, there were pace-setting agreements which then stimulated a wave of matching settlements in other sectors of the economy.

From the founding of the BRD until well into the 1950s the working week was contractually fixed at 48 hours. This was followed by a long phase of step-by-step reductions, leading to the 40-hour week in printing in 1965, followed by metalworking in 1967, chemicals in 1970 and the public sector in 1974. The 40-hour week remained in force until 1984 when IG Metall conducted a successful strike, defeating the employers' 'taboo' against a shorter week, and the movement towards reduced working hours has continued. At the end of 1995, fewer than 4 per cent of the labour force still worked a 40-hour week. About a quarter – as in metalworking, printing and steel – were covered by 35-hour-week agreements. By the end of 1995 the average working time was 37.5 hours per week (WSI 1996). The future development of working time is uncertain. In 1997 the IG Metall and ÖTV called for a 32-hour week, without full pay compensation, to reduce unemployment; conversely, some employers have pressed demands for longer hours, and some groups of employees are more interested in working overtime than in shorter hours and additional jobs.

The price which the trade unions had to pay for their successes in working-time policy was the flexible regulation of working time, with a diversity of models in different sectors and companies. Some trend-setting agreements were negotiated by unions and employers' associations, but many others by works councils and managements under so-called opening clauses which authorize them to conclude enterprise-level working-time agreements. Trade unions' earlier fears of losing control over this sphere of labour relations have given way to the view that flexible working hours serve not only the employers but also the unions themselves, by satisfying employee demands for individual variability of working time. In the 1990s, the so-called compensation periods for reaching the average working-time have been extended, working-time corridors have been negotiated, and the idea of working-time accounts has been introduced (though not often implemented). Some individual employers have pressed for even more flexible arrangements.

'Umbrella' or general framework agreements have undergone significant changes. The unions' earlier preoccupation with defensive, protective measures has given way to a more active attempt to shape the bargaining agenda on such issues as job descriptions and working conditions. Several new types of agreement deserve special attention. First are those relating pay to the individual's training and qualifications, rather than to the job currently performed. Second are collective agreements which regulate and promote vocational training and education. IG Metall, for example, has managed to achieve a more closely defined regulation of continuing education within the metal industry of Baden-Württemberg. The construction union, to give another example, has developed the occupational profile of a 'high-tech' construction worker in order to protect skilled workers from competition from low-paid immigrant workers from Eastern Europe. These contracts are however difficult to implement since they require a capacity for planning manpower and human resources that hardly exists in small and medium-sized companies, and create additional responsibilities and new tasks for the work councils (Bahnmüller et al. 1992).

Third, some collective agreements provide for a common pay structure for blue- and white-collar workers. Innovations in technology and the organization of the labour process have blurred the differences between the two categories and have led the unions to demand unified wage and salary scales. Fourth, unions also seek to extend collective bargaining to include questions of work organization (group work) and to cover all employees with the exception of senior executives. One aspect is the inclusion in collective agreements of the precariously employed as well as those in more secure and highly paid occupations: for example, a recent agreement in construction includes building cleaners, a group of poorly paid temporary employees who are usually unskilled women or foreign workers.

Fifth, a relatively new type consists of collective agreements to secure employment. Unions have made major concessions in wages in exchange for temporary employment guarantees by management; working time has been reduced without fully compensating increases in hourly wages. Volkswagen is probably the best known example; others include mining where additional free shifts have been introduced. The majority of sectoral agreements leave the decision to implement these solutions to management and works councils.

Bargaining Outcomes in Eastern Germany

The key feature of labour relations in eastern Germany is the continuing, but rather slow adaptation of wages, working time and other working conditions to west German standards. The initial consensus between all actors on the need for a rapid equalization of wages led to a series of short-term contracts giving significant improvements, but conflict broke out in the autumn of 1991 over the speed of this process. In their desire for a slower tempo, the government and employers' associations have been supported by the reports and recommendations of the *Bundesbank* and the *Sachverständigenrat* (the Council of Economic Advisers), which have consistently argued that wages are already too high in relation to productivity. The trade unions, on the other hand, insist that it is essential to close the gap between workers in the east and west in order to guarantee social peace and justice, prevent the growth of political radicalization and stem the migration of skilled labour to the west. The fact that prices have been quickly rising to the western German level also tends to support the union position.

In 1990 and 1991 so-called 'political bargaining rounds' brought fairly high wage increases, not matched by corresponding increases in productivity. In the spring of 1991 it was agreed to equalize wages in the engineering industry by 1994. In 1993 this contract was terminated without notice by *Gesamtmetall*, the employers' federation: the first time in the history of German collective bargaining that this had occurred. After a two-week strike, the first large labour conflict in the new *Länder*, the period of adaptation was extended until 1996; and a so-called hardship clause was introduced allowing the payment of wages below the collectively agreed standards if enterprises faced the risk of bankruptcy and if jobs could be saved. This hardship clause is different from a frequently demanded general opening clause because the explicit approval of both union and employers' association, and not only of management and the works council, is required. This explains why the hardship clause has not often been used. Later, in 1996, the construction industry employers also terminated their contract without notice. The crucial question for the future is whether such action will remain an exceptional response to the specific economic conditions in the east rather than presaging a general shift of employers' strategies with consequences also in the west.

The current ratio of collectively agreed wages (excluding supplements, which in the west may be more than 10 per cent of basic pay) in east Germany to those in the west varies according to industry: 100 per cent in printing and the metal industry, only about 70 per cent in private transport, clothing and textiles. Full equalization should be reached in all sectors in a few years. Working time in the east is still longer, in most sectors between 38 and 40 hours, but paid holidays have been virtually equalized. For many areas regulated by framework or umbrella agreements (pay classification schemes, overtime or shift-work bonuses, vocational training and retraining) the standard provisions of the west have been introduced (WSI 1996). But all in all, it will take much longer than first expected before all working conditions are the same.

One problem of growing importance, formerly almost unknown in the west, is that an increasing number of companies (particularly small and medium-sized enterprises and unorganized firms) do not pay the collectively agreed wages. Only 60 per cent of east German enterprises (with about 83 per cent of all employees) pay the contractually prescribed rates (DIW et al. 1994). Frequently underpayment reflects an attempt to save jobs and involves not only a tacit agreement between management and the works council, but also with the union. Thus collectively agreements no longer 'take wages out of competition'.

▌ Trends to Decentralization

As has been seen, moves towards employment deregulation by the German state have been relatively modest. However, employers and their associations have pursued flexibility in other ways. A central priority has been to increase productivity by detaching individual working time from the operating hours of the establishment (through shift systems, variable weekly working hours or other devices) so that production time can increase even as the individual working week is reduced. The typical 'exchange' between unions and employers' associations since the mid-1980s has been a staged reduction of the working week and guarantees of employment security for a defined period in return for more flexibility in the organization of working time.

There is no necessary interconnection between deregulation (initiated by neo-conservative governments) and flexibility (pursued by assertive employers); but in practice they coincide and both contribute to an obvious process of decentralization of labour relations. The actors at plant level gain in importance whereas the actors at sectoral level, unions and employers' associations, lose some of their former power. Microcorporatist arrangements or productivity coalitions (Streeck 1984, Windolf 1989) have developed at establishment level between works councils and management which further the complementary interests of both sides, although often to the disadvantage of those outside the firm's internal labour market. The goal of these 'high trust–low conflict relations' is, above all, a stabilization of the company product and labour markets and an internalization of advantages – accompanied by strong tendencies towards increasing labour market segmentation.

Within this general shift of competence and influence a new institutionalized balance of power will have to be found. The associations on both sides will need to provide new kinds of services to their constituents at establishment level, while seeking to contain the more disruptive aspects of 'company egoism'. The most serious example of 'wildcat co-operation' between management and some works councils has already been mentioned: the explicit or tacit agreement on lower wage rates and higher working hours than the industry-wide collective agreement stipulates in response to a crisis of competitiveness. There are less dramatic but still serious examples of 'wildcat co-operation' which are more common. Works councils often agree to overtime working, which enhances the earnings of their constituents while allowing the company to increase production without the long-term commitments involved in taking on new workers. This contradicts the policy to which the unions are strongly committed, to restrict overtime and encourage additional recruitment in order to reduce unemployment. Both unions and employers' associations have an obvious interest in retaining the multi-employer collective bargaining system, even though opinions to the contrary are sometimes voiced on the employers' side. Decentralization is inevitable; the question is whether it will involve the displacement of state and institutional control by market forces, or whether new regulatory structures will emerge that are compatible with the increased autonomy at lower levels of the system.

▌Industrial Disputes: Strikes and Lockouts

By international standards, Germany has a very low level of industrial conflict. There are few strikes; and while there is a pattern of major disputes every few years, the aggregate economic impact is small. Post-war experience has however been somewhat uneven.

The 1950s, a decade of reconstruction and economic growth, saw a relatively high intensity of conflict because collective bargaining still had to be re-institutionalized; once this was achieved, the early and mid-1960s were years of low conflict marked by co-operative wage policies. In the late 1960s and early 1970s, a period of full employment after the first, short post-war recession of 1966–7, conflict returned: there were waves of wildcat and spontaneous strikes in a period of general political unrest. Working conditions, as well as pay, were central issues. The mid and late 1970s were a phase of comparatively high and intense conflict, mainly about new 'qualitative' demands (protection against rationalization, introduction of new technologies and new forms of work organization) even though unemployment had reached levels not experienced for several decades. In the 1980s, a period of economic modernization was accompanied by mass unemployment (despite considerable growth of employment), but there was a marked decline in conflict, with the exception of the protracted disputes over the shortening of the working week in the metalworking and printing industries in 1984.

This recent development of 'high-trust, low-conflict relations', which matches international trends towards fewer disputes, has, however, been interrupted by several large-scale pay strikes: in the public sector in 1992 (the first for 18 years); in east Germany in 1993 after the metal industry employers' association terminated the collective agreement on pay parity (see above); and in the Bavarian metal industry in 1995. In 1996, conflict erupted over the government's amendment to the law on sick pay (reducing the benefit during the first six weeks from 100 to 80 per cent of regular pay). Since IG Metall had achieved the principle of full pay in a protracted sixteen-week strike in the 1950s, this was a powerful symbolic issue; and when individual employers in several industries took measures to apply the new provisions (even though existing collective agreements provided for full pay), they provoked stiff opposition. Large-scale demonstrations and token strikes forced the metal industry employers, among them Germany's biggest company Daimler-Benz, to retreat. In several industries, unions succeeded in negotiating agreements maintaining 100 per cent sick pay in return for moderate concessions on other issues, without needing to strike. Only in two industries – food, drink and tobacco, and banking – did unions have to call an official strike.

The sectoral distribution of strikes has undergone significant changes since the 1950s. The decline of such traditionally strike-prone sectors as mining, textiles, iron and steel and construction is mirrored in their decreasing strike activity, whereas the significance of engineering, and also printing and paper, has consistently increased. Thus strikes today are concentrated in a few industries, whose unions tend to exercise wage leadership; and even here, the system of 'pilot agreements' means that disputes are concentrated in particular bargaining districts.

Table 7.7 Strikes and lockouts (annual average) 1950–1994

Years	Strikes			Strikes and lockouts	
	Establishments affected	Workers involved	Days lost	Workers involved	Days lost
1950–54	1,467	100,843	1,098,126	100,843	1,098,126
1955–59	552	178,392	868,089	178,392	868,089
1960–64	113	44,755	289,773	87,864	483,333
1965–69	218	75,321	147,924	75,329	148,117
1970–74	486	195,376	874,600	235,768	1,251,466
1975–79	376	109,798	691,414	160,788	1,078,085
1980–84	321	166,403	632,799	193,962	1,172,065
1985–89	123	85,222	47,617	85,222	47,617
1990–94	934	296,233	472,682	296,236	472,684

Note: Geman official statistics do not indicate the number of strikes.
Source: Own calculations based on data from *Statistisches Bundesamt* and *Bundesanstalt für Arbeit*.

From the mid 1970s there was a change in strike strategies, initiated by IG Metall. The so-called 'new mobility' replaced the one big, expensive strike of indefinite length *after* a breakdown in negotiations by a series of more or less unpredictable, smaller, shorter, and therefore inexpensive walk-outs in different establishments *during* the negotiations. These served to increase the pressure on employers and accelerate the negotiations. The legality of these so-called warning-strikes was confirmed by decisions of the Federal Labour Court in the 1970s and 1980s.

A related, rather sophisticated innovation was the 'pinpoint strike' which hits a selected number of suppliers whose products are of crucial importance for the production process of a whole industry (notably the car industry, as in the 1984 strike). This proved very effective because of the increasing interdependence of different establishments and their suppliers (particularly those using 'just-in-time' production); hence the introduction of paragraph 116 of the AFG, discussed earlier. Wildcat strikes are illegal because of the unions' strike monopoly but have occurred throughout the history of the Federal Republic: especially in the late 1960s and early 1970s, when frequent spontaneous walk-outs caused public concern. Nevertheless, such strikes are far less significant in Germany than in many other countries.

Lockouts are more frequent than in most other western nations where they are either illegal or – because of decentralized bargaining systems – insignificant in practice. Their use increased in the 1970s in response to unions' selective strike tactics: key instances have been in metalworking (1963, 1971, 1978, 1984); printing (1976, 1978); and steel (1978–9). Lockouts affect more employees and last longer than strikes, because their main purpose is to increase the financial pressure on the union which has to pay strike benefits to its locked-out members. On both sides, those affected by disputes are financially supported from funds maintained if necessary by special levies. Unions have long demanded the prohibition of lockouts, which they consider unconstitutional; but the courts have backed the employers' contention that the 'parity of weapons' is necessary in order to preserve the balance of bargaining power.

Public-sector Labour Relations

Trends and Structure of Public Employment

Public agencies, including the federal, *Land*, and local governments, employ about 5.4 million workers. The postal service and the railways are no longer part of the public sector because of privatization. In international terms, Germany has a medium-sized public sector. Employment expanded steadily until the end of the 1970s; the rate of increase slowed in the early 1980s, and came to a virtual standstill in the late 1980s. In the 1980s, a steady rise in the number of part-time jobs (now more than 1.1 million) offset a reduction in full-time jobs (now about 4.3 million). Sharp increases in the very early 1990s were caused by German unification, when the over-staffed public sector of the former DDR had to be adjusted to the West German pattern (see below). This apart, differences in the labour market behaviour of public and private employers are diminishing as both pursue greater flexibility; public employers are no longer 'model' employers guaranteeing stable and life-long employment. The number of fixed-term contracts has also increased within a system of otherwise stable employment conditions; they now cover about 10 per cent of public employees (mostly in education).

Of fundamental significance is the differing legal status of the three employee groups: the conventional contractual position of salaried staff (*Angestellte*) and wage-earners as against the public law status of *Beamte*. The so-called 'customary principle of officialdom' dating back at least to the Bismarck Constitution and maintained in the Basic Law establishing the modern Federal Republic applies such rules as employment for life to a wide range of public employees (mainly skilled or professional) such as teachers and train-drivers, as well as civil servants narrowly defined. *Beamte* are not permitted to strike, and their conditions of employment are determined by law rather than by collective bargaining (see below). This special status can hardly be justified on functional grounds in a modern democratic state, since there are many contexts (including the postal service or education) where salaried employees and *Beamte* perform exactly the same jobs. It is notable that the changing nature of public employment in recent times has brought a decline in the proportion of *Arbeiter* (now just over 20 per cent) and a corresponding increase in *Angestellte* (to about 37 per cent); yet the proportion of *Beamte*, at about 40 per cent, has remained almost unchanged.

Within the German political system there is a clear and stable division of responsibilities between federal, *Land* and local authorities influencing, among other things, the number and qualifications of personnel. The *Länder* do not differ significantly in their public employment legislation, despite some variations in practices. Some public employers have tried to increase the number and proportion of their *Beamte* in order to bypass collective bargaining and prevent strikes. But again, this has not been a general trend. Employment policies are neither horizontally nor vertically co-ordinated between different public authorities, who tend to intensify general labour market fluctuations by acting in a pro-cyclical fashion.

Two Related Systems of Regulation

The system of labour relations in the public sector has a comparatively long history which can be traced back to the early days of the Weimar Republic. All public employees have the same right as private-sector workers to join unions or other interest organizations. The degree of organization is high, about 60 per cent, significantly above that in private industry. In both sectors, unions have similar difficulties in organizing such categories as women, part-time employees and young workers.

For historical reasons (which have often been questioned), employee participation in decision-making in the public sector is governed by a distinct body of legislation. At 'establishment' level the Federal Staff Representation Act (1955, 1974, 1989) and supplementary legislation in each of the *Länder* correspond to the *BetrVG* in private industry. The functional equivalent of the works council is the staff council, on which the different employment groups (blue- and white-collar workers and *Beamte*) have proportional representation. Government departments and staff councils work together, 'in a spirit of mutual trust', according to the Act, 'for the benefit of the employees and in fulfilment of the obligatory functions of the government departments'. Like their counterparts in private industry they have a whole range of precisely defined rights, from strict co-determination and veto power to mere consultation and information. In general, the allocation of rights – which most staff councils exercise actively – is on the same basis as in the private sector: co-determination over 'social' issues, consultation over personnel policy. However, there is no equivalent to the (weak) private-sector right to information on 'economic' questions.

The legal basis for the collective bargaining system is the *TVG* of 1949, which guarantees free collective bargaining throughout the economy and does not differentiate between the private and the public sectors. Unions and employers' associations negotiate for wage-earners and salaried employees; there are no special restrictions on industrial conflict. But the Act applies to *Arbeiter* and *Angestellte* only; *Beamte* are covered by special legislation. According to statute and court judgments, *Beamte* have no rights to collective bargaining or to strike. While such rights are restricted in some other western countries for categories of public employment, in Germany the restriction is defined by the collective status of all *Beamte* and not by the performance of particular essential jobs. Furthermore, it applies at every level, from local authority to federal government. This does not mean that the organizations representing *Beamte* are ineffectual. Pay and conditions are determined by legislation; but the laws defining the status of *Beamte* also specify that their representative associations must be consulted during the parliamentary process (Keller 1983).

The completion of the Single European Market in 1992 forced a change in the law on *Beamte* status. The principle that most areas of public sector employment in all member states should be open to all Community citizens contradicted the requirement that *Beamte* should (with very few exceptions) be German nationals. In practice, however, the removal of this provision does not drastically affect either the status of *Beamte* or the actual recruitment practices of public employers. Given financial stringencies and cutbacks, the number of new *Beamte* appointments is limited; language competence remains a legitimate basis for rejecting foreign applicants; and almost inevitably, informal discrimination still occurs (Keller and Henneberger 1992).

The most important public-sector union is the Union for Public Services, Transport and Communication (ÖTV), which with about 1.8 million members is Germany's second largest union. There are two other, smaller unions, which unlike ÖTV are occupationally specific but are also affiliated to the DGB: the teachers' union, GEW (with about 300,000 members), and the Police Union (with almost 200,000 members). The DAG also organizes in the public sector. In the past there has been friction between ÖTV and DAG, but a co-operation agreement was signed in 1994 and the two organizations now negotiate jointly.

National employers' associations exist for municipalities and *Länder*, the Federation of Local Government Employers' Association and the Bargaining Association of German Länder (Keller 1993). At federal level the Minister of the Interior is responsible for employment issues, co-ordinates the interests of all public employers, and leads all negotiations on their behalf. The centralization of collective bargaining, which is a general feature of German industrial relations, is particularly marked in the public sector; normally a single set of negotiations covers all wage-earners and salaried employees in federal, *Land*, and local government. Even though there may be conflicts of interest between public employers at different levels (for example local authorities, with a high proportion of low-paid workers, find flat-rate pay settlements particularly expensive), all public employers know that it is in their own long-term interest to maintain their coalition. Centralization leads to uniform regulations and procedures as well as to an increasing standardization of pay and working conditions for the different groups of employees. This avoids problems which occur in some other countries, such as the definition of bargaining units. Collective bargaining in the public sector – over both wages and other conditions of employment – tends to follow the pattern of settlements in private industry. In particular, the agreements negotiated by IG Metall normally serve as a model.

For *Beamte*, collective organization is divided almost equally between two confederations. The DGB has seven member unions recruiting in the public sector which together represent over 760,000 *Beamte*. The DBB, which almost exclusively covers *Beamte*, claims 1.1 million members in more than 50 affiliated associations. As well as utilizing their formal rights of consultation, these associations are adept at parliamentary lobbying. Some 40 per cent of members of parliament at federal and *Land* levels are themselves *Beamte* and are susceptible to appeals for *Beamte* to be treated no less favourably than groups which bargain collectively. If necessary, campaigns can be organized to win public sympathy, and the threat to mobilize the votes of *Beamte* and their families against unsympathetic legislators can also prove potent. Hence the restricted rights of *Beamte* are not necessarily a handicap (Keller 1983).

Both forms of interest representation usually lead to identical results which are implemented simultaneously. Thus the legal differences in employment status and models of interest representation do not lead to significant differences in pay or other working conditions, though recently the employers have used short delays in applying pay increases in order to save money.

After unification the reorganization of the public sector of the former DDR turned out to be a long-term political and administrative problem. Dismissals for such reasons as political identification with the old communist regime, or the dissolution or privatization of former public agencies were the main short-term means of cutting public employment and re-modelling it on the West German pattern. The former East German public sector, with about 2.2 million employees including the secret service, was considerably over-staffed; the strict introduction of western standards would have meant a cut of 50 per cent. Employment decreased gradually to 1.3 million by the mid-1990s. Retraining of public employees turned out to be a major long-term task. Another major problem was that some parts of the new public sector (like employment offices and administration of the new *Länder*, neither of which existed in the DDR) had to be built from scratch. Western *Beamte* were drafted in (and paid special bonuses) in order to reproduce in the east the administrative structure of the BRD.

In the east, *Beamte* status, unknown in the DDR, was introduced rather cautiously: a highly contentious and politically motivated step, since this status is now widely regarded as an anachronism. It is limited to some core groups such as police and tax officials, and excludes teachers; only about one in seven public employees are covered.

In the former DDR, the public sector was affected by the general process whereby West German unions and interest associations expanded their domains into the east; public employers also formed associations and copied the West German model (Rosdücher 1994). As in private industry, the first collective agreements attempted to adjust wages and all other conditions of employment by stages to West German standards. The aim was to prevent a further mass exodus from the territory of the former GDR and to create 'equal living conditions' in both parts of the country. In the mid-1990s, pay levels had reached 84 per cent of those in the west (Bispinck/WSI-Tarifarchiv 1996: 407).

Strikes and Mediation Procedures

Though public employees (apart from *Beamte*) enjoy the same right to strike as their private-sector counterparts, disputes are very rare. Only two significant strikes have occurred in the history of the BRD, in 1974 and 1992. The absence of the public-sector militancy evident in other European countries in the 1980s may be attributed to the continuing efficacy of disciplined, centralized bargaining procedures. When strikes do occur in public services it is always at local level.

Bargaining pressure is directed selectively by groups – such as refuse collectors or public transport staff – whose action will achieve an immediate impact. Such tactics can be very effective in winning gains for the groups involved; and because of the centralized bargaining system the improvements in pay and other working conditions achieved by these groups are automatically extended to all other groups. This pattern has been evident in a whole series of bargaining rounds since the mid-1950s. Strikes in the public sector are on average shorter than those in private industry, and protracted stoppages never occur. Employers are strike-sensitive and are therefore prepared to make quick concessions, above all because of their limited experience in responding to strikes. More common than strikes have been such actions as go-slows by wage-earners and salaried employees and working-to-rule by *Beamte*. These protests are limited to a few departments and are shorter than strikes, but can be just as effective.

Because conflict is rare, there is no elaborate system for dispute resolution in the public sector. Only after the 1974 strike were mediation procedures introduced. In contrast to many other countries, arbitration is never used in the German public sector if the parties to collective bargaining fail to reach agreement.

Privatization and Flexibility

Privatization has been on the political agenda since the 1970s, when employers' representatives and conservatives started to demand a 'roll-back of the state'. Some moves were made at local level (privatizing refuse collection, slaughterhouses, public transport, cleaning of public buildings), but hardly any at *Land* and federal levels. Until recently the overall impact was insignificant.

Why did German governments give privatization such low priority? The SPD, in power (with the FDP) until 1982, resisted privatization on grounds of political principle. Within the CDU–FDP coalition which replaced it, many different interests and political positions are represented; this makes any radical shift of policy difficult to accomplish. Moreover, the federal constitution gives considerable autonomy to the *Länder*, many of which are controlled by the SPD. In contrast to Britain, it is impossible for central government to impose a general policy of privatization (König 1988). There are other practical obstacles: all public-sector unions and major interest organizations have offered strong and co-ordinated resistance to privatization, and a more vigorous policy would cause serious social conflicts. Moreover, the German public sector contains few easily disposable units. The majority of public-sector jobs created in the late 1960s and early 1970s were in areas unsuitable for privatization (education, social services, health care, police). Substantial reductions in public personnel in the period of high unemployment since the mid-1970s would have created additional labour market problems and incurred serious political costs for the government. Finally, the limited exercises in privatization which were undertaken have not been clearly successful in reducing costs or improving the quality of service (Sturm 1990).

In the 1990s there has been a certain acceleration with the privatization and restructuring of the federal railway system and the postal service. The Deutsche

Bahn AG Holding has three business units: track, passenger transport and freight. After two reforms, in 1989 (deregulation as the first step), and 1995 (privatization as the goal), the formerly unitary postal service now consists of three parts: Deutsche Post AG (the postal service in the narrow sense), Deutsche Telekom AG, whose monopoly will be abolished by the beginning of 1998, and Deutsche Postbank AG.

This politically motivated 'marketization' has created significant problems, including the very complicated transition of former public employees into the completely different employment patterns and principles of private industry: especially *Beamte*, who constituted more than 50 per cent of all employees in these privatized sections of the public sector. Difficult legal questions included the comprehensive job security attached to their former special status and other statutorily defined rights. These complicated legal questions did not affect white- and blue-collar employees, but there was still a problem in adapting their collectively agreed terms of employment to private-sector mechanisms for the determination of pay and other working conditions. Massive redundancies were considered necessary, various programmes of continuous retraining and further training had to be developed, new 'flexible' forms of work organization were implemented, and favourable early retirement terms were offered (and widely accepted).

All these problems of transformation and transition have created threats to the former stable co-operative pattern of industrial relations. The relevant DGB unions which have traditionally enjoyed very high density rates (about 85 per cent in the postal serice) will have to adapt to the competitive environment of private industry while confronting new problems of interest representation. They will face representatives of three different employers instead of just one, and probably new competition from other unions in parts of their former organizational domains.

Though privatization has been less significant in Germany than in many other countries – except of course in the east, where wholesale privatization followed unification – as elsewhere there have been important changes in employment practices within the core public sector. As in private industry, managements are seeking more flexibility and adaptability. Above all, there have been moves towards more or less systematic use of part-time work (especially for *Angestellte* and *Arbeiter*), fixed-term contracts and other forms of 'contingent' or 'atypical' employment in place of the old pattern of full-time, life-long employment with tenure from the very beginning of the employment relationship. A frequent complaint has been that the rigidity of the *Beamte* status prevents urgently needed numerical and functional flexibility.

The new patterns of employment do not necessarily entail a high degree of insecurity; but the obvious result is further segmentation within the employment structure, between 'good' and 'bad' jobs. Public employment has traditionally been based on archetypal internal labour markets with a limited number of 'ports of entry', internal promotion to senior positions rather than external recruitment, and protection against market forces (Brandes et al. 1990). The 'insiders' still enjoy considerable security in terms of their salaries and other working conditions; the 'outsiders' face more difficulties than ever before, first in finding jobs and later in achieving job security and promotion. Public authorities are no longer the 'model employers' who formerly set an example to private industry (Keller and Henneberger 1993). Nowadays the state and all other public agencies act more or less like any other employer, taking advantage of the present labour market conditions.

▌European Integration

Unions and employers are in broad agreement on the need for rapid European integration. They endorse the current schedule for completing the Single European Market, argue for the rapid establishment of European Monetary Union, and support further and irreversible steps towards Political Union. The German economy is more dependent on a flourishing world market than that of any other large European country, and this limits support for parochial nationalistic positions.

German employers view the Single European Market and monetary union as necessary responses to intensified competition with the US and Japan. However they often complain of what they consider the pro-union attitude of EU bodies and single out for criticism the so-called 'social dimension complex' of the European trade unions, the Economic and Social Committee, the EU Commission and especially the broad consensus on social policy between the large socialist and christian-democratic blocs in the European Parliament. The employers have repeatedly confirmed their qualified commitment to a social Europe, but object to what they regard as excessive social intervention and bureaucratic over-regulation. They accept the Social Charter, which is a 'solemn declaration without legal effect'; but the Action Programme and the Commission's 'far-reaching policy of social regulation' come in for heavy criticism. They insist with regard to the Maastricht Social Protocol that priority must be given to the principle of subsidiarity at the national level and to agreements between the two parties involved in collective bargaining. Many of the Commission's (draft) directives are viewed by German employers as violations of the principle of subsidiarity and rejected on that basis.

Unlike the employers, the trade unions were slow to recognize the new dynamic of European integration in the mid-1980s and long underestimated the powerful economic thrust and political attractiveness of the Single European Market project. In the early 1990s, European issues were largely neglected because the organizational capacities of the trade unions were fully absorbed by the unification problems. Two concerns have, however, forced them to take European integration seriously. First, the likely introduction on schedule of the single currency has caused intense discussion of the unions' response to the powerful European Central Bank and the need to develop a European employment strategy. Second, the erosion of national capacities to regulate wages and working conditions has raised the question of compensatory EU regulations. Leading union representatives recognize that the German trade unions and the German system of co-determination enjoy growing prestige in other countries. Their self-confidence and their readiness to assume greater responsibility for Europe's social dimension have increased.

German trade unions have welcomed the Social Charter, the social dialogue and most of the directives (especially those on working time, European works councils and posted workers) as steps in the right direction. Despite criticisms that the planned measures are insufficient, they increasingly accept the Commission's strategy that Euro-legislation should be used only to secure basic minimum conditions, with superior provisions negotiated by the bargaining parties themselves. According to IG Metall, the transnational co-ordination of the unions' collective bargaining policies and the creation of a European collective bargaining culture are crucial goals. The conviction is growing that the construction of a social Europe is a trade union task and that negotiations with the employers' associations are an appropriate means to shape industrial relations at the European level. The joint opinions within the framework of the ongoing social dialogue (especially the agreement reached by the ETUC, UNICE and CEEP at the end of 1991 on the revision of Article 118 of the EC Treaty, and those on parental leave and part-time work) have been greeted as milestones on the road to the European-ization of labour relations.

The German unions attach great importance to agreements with transnational firms on the establishment of European Works Councils, even though the rights to consultation and information are clearly below the standards of co-determination provided by German law. By 1996, such agreements had been concluded with around 100 out of approximately 300 German-based multinationals. Most of these agreements were in the metal and the chemical industries, though in 1996 there was a breakthrough in the financial sector at Deutsche Bank. In general (the main exception is the chemical industry), EWCs in German-based transnationals are exclusively composed of workers' representatives, following the German model of works councils.

▌The Future of German Industrial Relations

Five years ago we gave our contribution to the first edition of this text the subtitle 'Co-Determining the Future'. This reflected a widespread confidence – both within Germany and beyond – that the distinctive institutions of interest representation and the traditions of 'social partnership' provided a robust basis for continued economic success and social stability, whatever challenges the 1990s might bring. As we indicated, it was common in the past to regard German industrial relations as rigid, formalistic and over-legalized; but in recent decades the system had proved markedly adaptable in the face of economic fluctuations and political changes.

While more pessimistic views indeed existed, they were very much a minority. We expressed the predominant informed opinion in arguing that the most important pillars of the 'dual system' of interest representation had proved their resilience, despite in particular the enormous test of German unification and the immense strains of political, economic and social transformation which this entailed – strains which in the rest of the former Soviet bloc had proved traumatic.

Hence despite qualifications, our conclusions were positive and guardedly optimistic. While elsewhere in Europe there was talk of a 'crisis of trade unionism', in Germany the unions had largely maintained their membership throughout the 1980s and had made unexpected increases following unification. As for employers' organizations, their cohesion and representativeness were not in doubt. On each side the 'social partners' had made peace with their counterparts and were fully committed to sustaining the established framework of industrial relations.

The system of collective bargaining had also proved far more stable than in many other European countries. The coverage of collective agreements remained very high, ensuring that virtually all employees received at least the minimal standards defined in collective negotiations. The multi-employer sectoral agreement remained the principal instrument of regulation. There had indeed been some devolution to enterprise level, particularly in respect of the regulation of working time. However, the close co-operation between most works councils and 'their' trade unions ensured that the sectoral and enterprise levels were effectively articulated: decentralization was taking place in a regulated manner, indicating the flexibility and adaptability of the German system.

The 'employer offensive' evident in some European countries seemed less significant in Germany. Certainly there were demands for greater flexibility and for a relaxation of statutory controls over the labour market, to allow firms greater scope to respond to competitive pressures. However, the moves towards deregulation on the part of the conservative government had been limited and hesitant; the juridification of the institutional framework, and the inbuilt checks and balances of the political system, seemed to provide a secure buffer against dramatic and abrupt deregulatory initiatives. Within individual companies, new forms of 'direct participation' were being introduced, and posed some problems for the existing system of co-determination; but initial suspicion and even resistance on the part of trade unions and works councils were giving way to a more positive evaluation of these changes.

More generally, though the 'economic miracle' of previous decades was no longer untarnished, the German economy remained dominant within Europe and had successfully absorbed the initial costs of unification. Unemployment, at around two million, had been unusually high throughout the 1980s; but 'de-industrialization' had been modest and there had also been an impressive process of job creation in new sectors of employment.

Today the future seems far less certain. Trade unions have lost members in both parts of the country, in consequence facing considerable financial difficulties; many consider that their power and influence have declined correspondingly. In addition, the collaboration between unions and works councils, formerly the key ingredient in the success of the German system, today seems weaker in the face of new strains, particularly in the east.

Employers' associations have also suffered unexpected defections and have had little success in recruiting membership among newly created firms, especially in the east. The interests of their constituents seem increasingly heterogeneous, making unified strategies difficult to achieve. In some sectors, the associations seem unable to enforce the agreements negotiated and their representativeness is in question. Among business organizations the traditional structure of multi-employer bargaining has been increasingly challenged, even though the employers' associations as such reject complete decentralization. Whatever the outcome, co-ordinating industrial relations at sectoral and at company levels will be an increasingly delicate task.

Confidence in the German economy has been shaken by the debate surrounding *Standort Deutschland*. It is clear that the economic strength and vigour of firms varies considerably between sectors, and this is reflected in growing inter-sectoral differences both in the outcomes of collective bargaining and in the effectiveness of agreements. In some important sectors such as engineering and construction, the terms of collective agreements are today undercut by an unprecedented number of firms, often with the tacit agreement of their workforce representatives. Unemployment has increased dramatically in the 1990s while the number of those in employment has fallen – in contrast to the experience of the 1980s. There is talk of halving unemployment by the year 2000, but there are few grounds for expecting much improvement in the labour market; if anything, the more plausible prognosis is for further deterioration. The government response to these challenges has involved a rather less half-hearted pursuit of deregulation and privatization, together with efforts to curb public expenditure which breach the former consensus on the integrity of the 'social market'.

Finally, the ambiguous consequences of German unification are now far clearer. There have been success stories in the east, and after the initial collapse of much of the industrial base there have been some areas of expansion; but the eastern economy still has the features of islands of modernity within a sea of backwardness. It is now indisputable that the former DDR will for the foreseeable future remain a dependent transfer economy. New instabilities in industrial relations have resulted. Some western companies have used subsidiaries in the east as 'flexible' laboratories in which to develop new models of work organization and employment conditions which can then be applied in the west. Works councils in the east, often suspicious of what they see as attempts by western union officials to dictate their behaviour, have been prone to 'wildcat co-operation' with managements who themselves are not yet socialized into western norms. In turn, there appears to be feedback effects within the west which threaten the industrial relations system of the country as a whole (Hyman 1996).

The forces of destabilization should not be exaggerated: but they are far stronger than a few years ago. There is little prospect that the post-war German industrial relations system will simply collapse or disintegrate, but its foundations are in some respects being eroded. The system seems to be undergoing a gradual but cumulative change of character; in the new century it is likely to be more decentralized, more fragmented, less legalized, less cohesive, and more internally differentiated. The virtuous circle of stable industrial relations institutions and economic success is no longer the obvious starting point for students of the German model.

▌ List of Terms and Abbreviations

Angestellter – Salaried employee
Arbeiter – Wage earner
Arbeitsgericht – Labour Court
AFG – *Arbeitsförderungsgesetz* – Work Promotion Act
Aufsichtsrat – Supervisory Board
Beamter – Civil servant with special status
BeschFG – *Beschäftigungsförderungsgesetz* – Employment Promotion Act
Betriebsrat – Works council
BetrVG – *Betriebsverfassungsgesetz* – Works Constitution Act
Bundesbank – Federal Bank
Bundesland – See *Land*
BPersVG – *Bundespersonalvertretungsgesetz* – Federal Staff Representation Act
BRD – *Bundesrepublik Deutschland* – Federal Republic of Germany
BDI – *Bundesverband der Deutschen Industrie* – Federation of German Industries
BDA – *Bundesvereinigung der Deutschen Arbeitgeberverbände* – Confederation of German
    Employers' Associations
CDU(/CSU) – *Christlich-Demokratische Union (/Christlich-Soziale Union)* – Christian
    Democratic Union /Christian Social Union
CGB – *Christlicher Gewerkschaftsbund* – Christian Federation of Trade Unions
DAG – *Deutsche Angestelltengewerkschaft* – German Salaried Employees' Union
DDR – *Deutsche Demokratische Republik* – German Democratic Republic
DBB – *Deutscher Beamtenbund* – German Civil Servants' Federation
DGB – *Deutscher Gewerkschaftsbund* – German Trade Union Federation
DIHT – *Deutscher Industrie und Handelstag* – German Association of Chambers of
    Commerce
FDP – *Freie Demokratische Partei* – Free Democratic Party
Friedenspflicht – Peace obligation
Gesamt-/Konzernbetriebsrat – Combine Works Council
Gesamtmetall Gesamtverband der metallindustriellen Arbeitgeberverbände – Federation of
    Metal Industry Employers' Associations
IG – *Industriegewerkschaft* – Industrial Union
Konzertierte Aktion – Concerted Action
Land – Regional/provincial unit of the BRD
Leitende Angestellte – Senior Staff
MitbG *Mitbestimmungsgesetz* – Co-determination Act
MontanMitbG – Special Co-Determination Act for the Coal and Steel Industries
ÖTV *Gewerkschaft Öffentliche Dienste, Transport und Verkehr* – Union for Public
    Services, Transport and Communication
SPD – *Sozialdemokratische Partei Deutschlands* – Social-Democratic Party
Tarifautonomie – Free collective bargaining
Tarifvertrag – Collective agreement
TVG – *Tarifvertragsgesetz* – Collective Agreement Act
ULA – Union der Leitenden Angestellten
Verrechtlichung – Juridification
Vertrauensleute – Union workplace representatives

| References and Further Reading

Bahnmüller, R., Bispinck, R., and Schmidt, W. 1992: *Betriebliche Weiterbildung in der Metallindustrie. Die Rolle von Personalmanagern und Betriebsräten.* Baden-Württemberg, Tübingen.

Beisheim, M., von Eckardstein, D. and Müller, M. 1993: Partizipative Organisationsformen und industrielle Beziehungen. In W. Müller-Jentsch (ed.) *Konfliktpartnerschaft: Akteure und Institutionen der industriellen Beziehungen*, 123–38. Munich: Hampp.

Bergmann, J., Jacobi, O. and Müller-Jentsch, W. 1975: *Gewerkschaften in der Bundesrepublik. Vol 1: Gewerkschaftliche Lohnpolitik zwischen Mitgliederinteressen und ökonomischen Systemzwängen.* 3rd edn. Frankfurt: Campus.

Bielenski, H. and Kohler, B. 1995: Wie un-normal sind befristete Arbeitsverträge? Eine Positionsbestimmung auf der Grundlage empirischer Erhebungen. In B. Keller and H. Seifert (eds), *Atypische Beschäftigung. Verbieten oder gestalten?* Köln: Bund, 139–162.

Bispinck, R./WSI-Tarifarchiv 1996: Die Tarifrunde 1996 – Eine Halbjahresbilanz, *WSI-Mitteilungen* 49, 405–413.

Bollinger, D., Cornetz, W. and Pfau-Effinger, B. 1991: Atypische Beschäftigung – Betriebliche Kalküle und Arbeitnehmerinteressen. In K. Semlinger (ed.) *Flexibilisierung des Arbeitsmarktes. Interessen, Wirkungen, Perspektiven*, 177–99. Frankfurt-New York: Campus.

Brandes, W., Buttler, F., Reinicke, U. and Weinert, A. 1990: *Der Staat als Arbeitgeber. Daten und Analysen zum öffentlichen Dienst in der Bundesrepublik.* Frankfurt-New York: Campus.

Brandt, G., Jacobi, O. and Müller-Jentsch, W. 1982: *Anpassung an die Krise: Gewerkschaften in den siebziger Jahren.* Frankfurt/Main-New York: Campus.

Breisig, T. 1991: Betriebsvereinbarungen zu Qualitätszirkeln – Eine Inhaltsanalyse. *Die Betriebswirtschaft*, 51(1), 65–77.

Büchtemann, C. F. with A. Höland 1989: 'Befristete Arbeitsverträge nach dem Beschäftigungsförderungsgesetz (BeschFG 1985)'. Ergebnisse einer empirischen Untersuchung im Auftrag des Bundesministers für Arbeit und Sozialordnung. Bonn: Bundesminister für Arbeit und Sozialordnung.

Bunn, R. F. 1984: Employers' Associations in the Federal Republic of Germany. In J.P. Windmuller and A. Gladstone (eds), *Employers Associations and Industrial Relations.* Oxford: Clarendon Press, 169–201.

Dabrowski, H., Jacobi, O., Schudlich, E. and Teschner E. (eds) 1989: *Tarifpolitische Interessen der Arbeitgeber und neue Managementstrategien.* Düsseldorf: Hans-Böckler-Stiftung.

DIW 1994: Gesamtwirtschaftliche und unternehmerische Anpassungsfortschritte in Ostdeutschland, *DIW-Wochenbericht* 61 (15/1994), 209–27.

Dreher, C., Fleig, J., Harnischfeger, M. and Klimmer, M. 1995: *Neue Produktionskonzepte in der deutschen Industrie.* Berlin: Physica-Verlag.

Eberwein, W. and Tholen, J. 1990: *Managermentalität.* Frankfurt: FAZ.

Endruweit, G., Gaugler, E., Staehle, W.H. and Wilpert, B. (eds) 1985: *Handbuch der Arbeitsbeziehungen: Deutschland – Österreich – Schweiz.* Berlin: de Gruyter.

Erd, R. 1978: *Verrechtlichung industrieller Konflikte. Normative Rahmenbedingungen des dualen Systems der Interessenvertretung.* Frankfurt: Suhrkamp.

Erd, R. 1979: Verrechtlichte Gewerkschaftspolitik. Bedingungen ihrer Entwicklung und Veränderung. In J. Bergmann (ed.), *Beiträge zur Soziologie der Gewerkschaften.* Frankfurt: Suhrkamp, 143–82.

Frick, B. and Sadowski, D. 1995: 'Works Councils, Unions and Firm Performance' in F. Buttler, W. Franz, R. Schettkat and D. Soskice (eds), *Institutional Frameworks and Labour Market Performance*, London, 46–81.

Gesamtmetall 1990: *Perspektiven aus Tradition*. Cologne: Deutscher Instituts-Verlag.

Hilbert, J. and Sperling, H.J. 1990: *Die kleine Fabrik*. Munich: Hampp.

Hoffmann, R., Jacobi, O., Keller, B. and Weiss, M. (eds) 1995: *German Industrial Relations under the Impact of Structural Change, Unification and European Integration*. Düsseldorf: Hans-Boeckler-Stiftung.

Hyman, R. 1996: Institutional transfer: Industrial relations in Eastern Germany. *Work, Employment and Society*, 10(4), 601–39.

Jacobi, O. 1990: Elements of a European Community of the Future: A Trade Union View. In C. Crouch and D. Marquand (eds) *The Politics of 1992*. Oxford: Blackwell Publishers.

Jacobi, O. and Müller-Jentsch, W. 1990: West Germany: Continuity and Structural Change. In G. Baglioni and C. Crouch (eds), *European Industrial Relations*. London: Sage.

Jürgensen, H. 1991: Die Bundesrepublik Deutschland zwischen Wiedervereinigung und Binnenmarkt 1993. *Volkswirtschaftliche Korrespondenz der Adolf-Weber-Stiftung*, 30(10), 1–4.

Kalbitz, R. 1979: *Aussperrungen. Die vergessenen Konflikte*. Frankfurt: EVA.

Katzenstein, P. 1989: Industry in a changing West Germany. In P. Katzenstein (ed.) *Industry and Politics in West Germany*. Ithaca: Cornell University Press, 3–29.

Keller, B. 1983: *Arbeitsbeziehungen im öffentlichen Dienst. Tarifpolitik der Gewerkschaften und Interessenpolitik der Beamtenverbände*. Frankfurt: Campus.

Keller, B. 1993: *Arbeitspolitik des öffentlichen Sektors*, Baden-Baden.

Keller, B. 1996: Arbeitspolitik in den neuen Bundesländern. Eine Zwischenbilanz der Transformationsprozesse, *Sozialer Fortschritt* 45, 88–102.

Keller, B. 1997: *Einführung in die Arbeitspolitik. Arbeitsbeziehungen und Arbeitsmärkte in sozialwissenschaftlicher Perspektive*, Munich-Vienna: Oldenbourg.

Keller, B. and Henneberger, F. 1992: Europäische Einigung und nationaler öffentlicher Dienst. *WSI-Mitteilungen*, 45, 1.

Keller, B. and Henneberger, F. 1993: Privatwirtschaft und öffentlicher Dienst: Parallelen und Differenzen in den Arbeitspolitiken, in: Müller-Jentsch, W. (ed.), *Konfliktpartnerschaft: Akteure und Institutionen der industriellen Beziehungen*, 2nd edn. München-Mering: Hampp, 249–276.

Kern, H. and Schumann, M. 1984: *Das Ende der Arbeitsteilung?* Munich: Beck.

Kittner, M. 1974: *Streik und Aussperrung*. Frankfurt-Cologne: EVA.

Knuth, M. 1982: Nutzung betrieblicher Mitbestimmungsrechte in Betriebsvereinbarungen. *Die Mitbestimmung*, 28(6), 204–8.

König, K. 1988: Entwicklung der Privatisierung in der Bundesrepublik Deutschland – Probleme, Stand, Ausblick. *Verwaltungs-Archiv*, 79(3), 241–71.

Kotthoff, H. 1990: Arbeitsbericht zum Antrag 'Kontinuität und Wandel betrieblicher Interessenvertretungsstrukturen' (unpublished).

Kotthoff, H. 1994: *Betriebsräte und Bürgerstatus. Wandel und Kontinuität betrieblicher Mitbestimmung*. Munich: Hampp.

Kreikebaum, H. and Herbert, K.J. 1990: *Arbeitsgestaltung und Betriebsverfassung*. Berlin: Duncker & Humblot.

Malsch, T. 1989: Flexibilisierung der Massenproduktion in der Automobilindustrie und ihre arbeitspolitischen Gestaltungsperspektiven. In L. Pries, R. Schmidt and R. Trinczek (eds) *Trends betrieblicher Produktionsmodernisierung*. Opladen: Westdeutscher Verlag.

Michels, R. 1911: *Zur Soziologie des Parteiwesens* (2nd edn 1925). Stuttgart: Kröner. [In English: *Political Parties*.]

Müller-Jentsch, W. 1985: Trade unions as intermediary organizations. *Economic and Industrial Democracy*, 6(1), 3–33.

Müller-Jentsch, W. 1995a: Auf dem Prüfstand: Das deutsche Modell der industriellen Beziehungen. *Industrielle Beziehungen*, 2(1), 11–24.

Müller-Jentsch, W. 1995b: Germany: From Collective Voice to Co-management. In J. Rogers and W. Streeck (eds), *Works Councils*. Chicago and London: University of Chicago Press, 53–78.

Müller-Jentsch, W. 1997: *Soziologie der industriellen Beziehungen*. 2nd edn Frankfurt: Campus.

Niedenhoff, H.-U. 1987: *Kosten der Mitbestimmung*. Cologne: Deutscher Instituts-Verlag.

Niedenhoff, H.-U. 1995: Betriebsrats- und Sprecherausschußwahlen 1994. Cologne: Deutscher Instituts-Verlag.

OECD, *Employment outlook*, Paris 1994.

Rosdücher, J. 1994: Kommunale Arbeitgeberverbände in den neuen Bundesländern, *Zeitschrift für öffentliche und gemeinwirtschaftliche Unternehmen*, 17, 414–429.

Sadowski, D. and Jacobi, O. (eds) 1991: *Employers' Associations in Europe: Policy and Organisation*. Baden-Baden: Nomos.

Schmidt, R. and Trinczek, R. 1991: Duales System: Tarifliche und betriebliche Interessenvertretung. In W. Müller-Jentsch (ed.) *Konfliktpartnerschaft: Akteure und Institutionen der industriellen Beziehungen*. Munich: Hampp, 167–199.

Schnabel, C. 1987: Trade Union Growth and Decline in the Federal Republic of Germany. *Empirical Economics*, 12, 107–27.

Schroeder, W. 1996: Gewerkschaften und Arbeitgeberverbände. *Gewerkschaftliche Monatshefte*, 47(10), 601–615. Cologne: Bund.

Seifert, H. 1995: Rückläufige Entwicklung bei Schicht-, Nacht und Wochenendarbeit. *WSI-Mitteilungen*, 48(3), 182–8.

Sengenberger, W. 1987: *Struktur und Funktionsweise von Arbeitsmärkten. Die Bundesrepublik Deutschland im internationalen Vergleich*. Frankfurt: Campus.

Sinzheimer, H. 1907/8: *Der korperative Arbeitsnormenvertrag. Eine privatrechtliche Untersuchung*. 2 vols. Leipzig.

Sinzheimer, H. 1976: *Arbeitsrecht und Rechtssoziologie. Gesammelte Ausätze und Reden*. 2 vols. Frankfurt: EVA.

Sisson, K. 1987: *The Management of Collective Bargaining*. Oxford: Blackwell Publishers.

Sperling, H.J. 1997: *Restrukturierung von Unternehmens- und Arbeitsorganisation – eine Zwischenbilanz. Trend-Report Partizipation und Organisation II*. Marburg: Schüren.

Streeck, W. 1981: *Gewerkschaftliche Organisationsprobleme in der sozialstaatlichen Demokratie*. Königstein: Athenäum.

Streeck, W. 1984: Neo-corporatist industrial relations and the economic crisis in west Germany. In J. Goldthorpe (ed.) *Order and Conflict in Contemporary Capitalism*, 291–314. Oxford: Clarendon Press.

Streeck, W. 1991: More Uncertainties: German Unions Facing 1992. *Industrial Relations*, 30(3), 317–47.

Sturm, R. 1990: Privatisierungspolitiken im internationalen Vergleich. *Zeitschrift fur öffentliche und gemeinwirtschaftliche Unternehmen* 13(2), 170–84.

SVR (*Sachverständigenrat zur Begutachtung der gesamtwirtschaftlichen Entwicklung*) 1990: *Jahresgutachten 1990/1991*. Bonn: Bundestagsdrucksache 11/8472.

SVR 1991: *Jahresgutachten 1991/1992*. Bonn: Bundestagsdrucksache 12/1618.

SVR 1996: *Jahresgutachten 1996/1997*. Bonn: Bundestagsdrucksache 13/6200.

Timmermann, D. 1990: Zukunftsprobleme des dualen Systems unter Bedingungen verschärften Wettbewerbs. In D. Sadowski and U. Backes-Gellner (eds), *Unternehmerische*

Qualifikationsstrategien im internationalen Wettbewerb, 37–58. Berlin: Duncker & Humblot.

Traxler, F. 1986: *Interessenverbände der Unternehmer*. Frankfurt: Campus.

Traxler, F. 1989: Unternehmerinteressen, Arbeitgeberverbände und Arbeitsbeziehungen. In Dabrowski et al. (eds), *Tarifpolitische Interessen der Arbeitgeber und neue Managementstrategien*. Düsseldorf: Hans-Böckler-Stiftung.

Traxler, F. 1996: Collective Bargaining and Industrial Change: A Case of Disorganization? A Comparative Analysis of Eighteen OECD Countries, *European Sociological Review*, 12(3), 271–87.

Walwei, U. 1991: Job placement in Europe. An international comparison, *Intereconomics*, 26, 248–54.

Walwei, U. 1993: Zum Regulierungsbedarf bei Zulassung privater Arbeitsvermittlung, *MittAB*, 26, 285–93.

Weber, H. 1987: *Unternehmerverbände zwischen Markt, Staat und Gewerkschaften*. Frankfurt: Campus.

Weitbrecht, H. 1969: *Effektivität und Legitimität der Tarifautonomie*. Berlin: Duncker & Humblot.

Windolf, P. 1989: Productivity Coalitions and the Future of European Corporatism. *Industrial Relations*, 28(1), 1–20.

Womack, J.P., Jones, D. and Roos, D. 1990: *The Machine that Changed the World*. New York: Rowson.

WSI 1996: *WSI Tarifhandbuch 1996*. Cologne: Bund.

8 | Austria: Still the Country of Corporatism

FRANZ TRAXLER

▌Introduction

Austria is one of the smaller countries in the EU. In 1993 it had a population of 8 million, including a total labour force of 3.7 million and employment of 3.6 million; 7, per cent in agriculture, 35 per cent in manufacturing and 58 per cent of them in the service sector. Austria's political system is among the most corporatist of all western countries. In this system of 'social partnership' (*Sozialpartnerschaft*), based on close co-operation between the state, capital and labour, industrial relations play a key role. Capital and labour are represented by the 'big four' interest associations: the Federal Chamber of Business, the BWK; the Peak of the Chambers of Agriculture; the Austrian Trade Union Federation, ÖGB; and the Federal Chamber of Labour, BAK. Although the membership and leadership of ÖGB and BAK largely overlap, co-operation between them prevails over competition. While collective bargaining is the ÖGB's exclusive domain, the BAK works as a brains trust for ÖGB, and is entitled to advise the authorities on all matters affecting workers' interests. Hence ÖGB and BAK co-represent labour *vis-à-vis* government. Their complementary relationship is manifested in the fact that BAK's organizational structure is territorial, while the ÖGB's is mainly sectoral.

Social partnership arrangements reconcile collective bargaining with state economic policy, and in turn subject all economic and social policy matters to the influence of the principal interest associations of labour and capital. As well as being consulted on the drafting of policy regulations, the peak organizations also perform regulatory functions.

Austria's industrial relations system is exceptional, not only in its extremely corporatist form but also in its stability: it has been comparatively immune to the pressures which have challenged corporatism elsewhere in Europe over the past decade. This chapter's analytical focus is, therefore, on explaining this stability. It argues that stability rests on a unique configuration of power relations, institutional (i.e. associational and legal) arrangements and cultural patterns. However, this configuration has been weakened since the mid-1980s. Hence, the chapter concludes with some hypotheses on the future prospects for 'social partnership'.

▎Social Partnership: Origins and Properties

Although it may appear paradoxical at first glance, the same enduring properties of Austrian society gave rise both to violent class struggle in the inter-war period, culminating in the civil war of 1934, and to intimate co-operation after the Second World War. Compared with other European countries, Austria is notable for its relative weakness of capital and strength of labour. This is the product of relatively late industrialization, the negative effects of which were magnified by a political alliance between the great feudal landowners and the petit bourgeoisie during the Habsburg Empire. By protecting the agricultural and handicraft sectors from competitive pressures at the cost of big business, this alliance helped to preserve small establishments as the dominant form of production. Large enterprises were hard hit by the loss of a good part of their former home markets following the fall of the Habsburg Empire in 1918. Politically, capital was confronted by an insurgent working class, which could be pacified only by extending welfare legislation, and by a legal framework granting representational and organizational rights to labour organizations.

Though unfavourable conditions of accumulation hampered improvements in living standards, they nevertheless strengthened the labour movement organizationally. After the repeal of measures outlawing the labour movement and social democracy, unions enjoyed rapid growth in the late nineteenth century. Most importantly, social democracy succeeded in forming a cohesive network of organizations covering all aspects of workers' interests. In addition, the predominance of small firms in the Austrian economy encouraged the development of unions. In all European countries for which data is available, unionization and multi-employer collective bargaining first spread through the skilled trades, which were dispersed among a multiplicity of small and medium-sized firms. There are two main reasons for this. First, such firms tended to employ a high proportion of skilled workers, whose strong labour market position facilitated collective organization. Second, small firms found multi-employer collective bargaining a useful means of taking wages out of competition. In contrast, highly concentrated sectors such as heavy industry were much more hostile to unionization and collective bargaining.

Before the First World War, unions were at best tolerated by the state. But relations began to change when the state needed the assistance of the associations of capital and labour in implementing its wartime command economy. In exchange, the associations were granted a corporate legal status and organizational security, and their role in the formulation of aspects of public policy was formally recognized. During the brief post-war revolutionary republic, the legal status of unions and employers' associations was reinforced; and this juridification (*Verrechtlichung*) persisted. Legislation introduced in 1920 made collective agreements legally enforceable. The Works Constitution Act, passed in 1919, established works councils as the legal representatives of workers' interests within companies, at the same time restricting their activities in a well-ordered system of industrial relations. In 1920, parliament passed a law on the formation of chambers of labour. Based on compulsory membership, the chambers were granted the right to consultation on all matters of economic and social policy. The aim of the legislation was to create an equivalent to the chambers of business which had been established at the time of the bourgeois revolution of 1848.

For all these reasons, Austrian social democracy developed into a fully-fledged political camp opposed to that of the Christian–conservative bourgeoisie after the First World War, and became the strongest and most well-organized labour movement outside the Soviet Union in the inter-war period. Ideologically integrated by Austro-Marxism, the social-democrats (then called the Social Democratic Party of Labour, SDAP) remained unchallenged at the political level; communism was unable to establish itself in Austria. Although the union movement was politically and ideologically fragmented, the social democrats maintained their dominant role, representing more than 70 per cent of total union membership (Traxler 1982).

In its manifesto of 1926, the SDAP claimed that it would transform capitalism into socialism by attaining a majority in parliament, whereas the bourgeois camp intended to remove the achievements that labour had gained in the peaceful revolution of 1918–19. The conflict ended with the bourgeoisie's victory in the civil war of 1934 and the outlawing of social-democratic organizations. But the outcome was short-lived: Austria was occupied by Nazi Germany in 1938.

With the elites of both political camps exposed to persecution during the Nazi regime, the occupation of Austria was the turning point in their relationship. They unanimously perceived occupation as the consequence of the bitter conflict between them, exacerbated by a permanent economic crisis culminating in one of the highest unemployment rates in Europe. Thus with the defeat of the Nazis, both camps were determined to replace class struggle with co-operation. Concerted, consociational policy-making became the guiding principle and the promotion of economic growth and employment became the predominant goals of Austria's social partnership.

Why has corporatism been so pervasive and stable in Austria? Its strength derives, first, from specific *institutional* preconditions: favourable labour legislation, close ties between the state, the political parties and the 'big four', and encompassing and centralized associational structures. Second, corporatism has a *material* base: it rests on the unique properties of the Austrian economy, most notably the relative weakness of private capital.

This structural weakness of capital, most obviously demonstrated by the country's relatively large sheltered sector and small firm size, forces capitalists confronted with a strong labour movement to co-operate on labour market issues. In addition to this imperative, which applies to all sectors of Austrian capital, inter-class co-operation is also required to protect the specific product market interests of the export-oriented sector (Traxler 1992).

Given the weight of small firms, which tend to orient their activities towards the domestic economy, protectionist interests prevail among Austrian employers. It is estimated that, before Austria's entry into the EU, 50 per cent of domestic consumption was supplied by the sheltered sector, compared with only 15 per cent in the EC (Polt 1988). As internal decision-making is based on the 'one person, one vote' principle in Austria's main business association, the BWK, small capital is in a strong position to pursue business interests through political and associational action. As a consequence, not only has large, export-oriented industry been forced to set up a trade association of its own, but it is also extremely dependent on the support of labour's peak associations to defend its product market interests in the face of the protectionist demands of small firms.

The predominance of protectionist interests among capitalists is also the key reason for the state's greater willingness than in any other western country to share its economic and social governance responsibilities with the associations. Capital's weakness poses a persistent threat to the international competitiveness of the Austrian economy. Hence Austria faces a unique dilemma: on the one hand, as a small country, its economic prosperity is particularly dependent on foreign trade and international competitiveness; on the other hand, maintaining competitiveness through economic modernization is very difficult because of capital's weakness. This task cannot therefore be left to the free play of market forces but must be politically guided. The state's interests in achieving economic modernization and maintaining competitiveness can only be achieved if allies can be found against protectionism.

In this respect, organized labour plays a key role, given the inherent 'organizability' problems of employers: business associations are less capable than unions of unifying members' interests in pursuit of collective goals (Traxler 1993). Furthermore, ÖGB, the central labour representative, tends to support the export-oriented sector as a result of its own internal balance of power. Since union density is above average in large industrial firms, the ÖGB's policies – in stark contrast to those of the BWK – are structurally biased in favour of large firms whose interests are generally anti-protectionist. Together with BAK, ÖGB also sees itself as the consumers' representative, advocating an anti-protectionist policy in order to keep down consumer prices.

The completion of the single European market renewed the division between export-oriented and protectionist business interests. As Austrian industry has been in full competition with EC firms since the 1972 free trade agreement, the export and import-competing sectors have long since paid the price for achieving international competitiveness. The business association representing export interests took the initiative in 1987 to call for Austria to apply for Community membership. However, it was the joint recommendation of the 'big four' to join the EC which paved the way for the government's application for membership in 1989 and for the clear vote in favour of membership in the 1995 referendum (Karlhofer and Tálos 1996; Traxler 1992). The 'big four' have a legally privileged role in formulating Austria's position on EU issues. In addition each association can use its own office in Brussels and its affiliation to the corresponding Euro-confederations to channel its interests into EU policy-making. However, there is a structural problem in linking Austria's associational system to that of the EU since, owing to its principle of compulsory membership, the BWK cannot be a member of UNICE.

▌State and Law

The state plays four main roles in Austria's industrial relations, although these roles tend to overlap in practice, especially in the public sector: first, it lays down substantive rules governing working conditions; second, it defines procedural rules establishing the formal framework of industrial relations; third, it is an employer in its own right; and fourth, it is the sponsor of corporatist macro-economic management.

▌The Legislative Framework

Industrial relations are highly regulated by law. But there is no unified statute covering all dimensions of the employment relationship. Instead, there are a variety of laws, each regulating a specific aspect of employment (for example, vocational training, working hours) or the employment rights of specific groups of employees. The law makes a fundamental distinction between 'public' employment by state authorities and 'private' employment by other employers; and in the latter, between blue- and white-collar workers. While individual employment relations are based on freedom of contract, they are regulated by legal norms which define such matters as methods of payment, working hours and dismissal.

A special Works Constitution Act (ArbVG) governs collective labour relations in the private sector. As in Germany, this law distinguishes between collective employment relations within the firm and at multi-firm (i.e. associational) level. The works council is constituted as the main employee representative body within the firm. In every establishment with five or more employees, a works council must be set up if the workforce so requests. In multi-plant companies, each works council is entitled to elect a number of its members to a central (enterprise) works council. Works councils can also be established for holding companies. The works councils' role in representing employees *vis-à-vis* management is precisely defined. Like their German counterparts, councils must act in a co-operative manner.

Works councils' rights extend from information and consultation to co-determination, including the opportunity to conclude a formal plant agreement (*Betriebsvereinbarung*) with management. While information and consultation rights apply to all matters affecting the establishment's employees, co-determination is legally limited to a narrow range of social and personnel matters. Management decisions are dependent on the works council's approval for matters such as the introduction of control systems that affect human dignity, for the introduction of performance-related payment schemes, and for internal transfers that downgrade the position of employees within the firm. The scope of matters subject to settlement by plant agreement is also specified by law, while collective agreements at multi-employer level may also delegate matters for regulation by plant agreement. Plant agreements on matters such as working-time schedules, and provisions for coping with the impact of major changes within the firm, are legally enforceable, as are those of higher-level collective agreements. In firms with

Table 8.1 Unionization in Austria, 1955–1995

	Total membership[1]	Density ratio[2]
1955–59[3]	1,439,548	66.5
1960–69[3]	1,523,776	65.0
1970–79[3]	1,581,008	60.4
1980	1,660,985	59.6
1981	1,677,265	59.9
1982	1,672,509	60.5
1983	1,660,453	60.7
1984	1,672,820	61.0
1985	1,671,381	60.6
1986	1,671,217	60.1
1987	1,652,839	59.3
1988	1,643,586	58.5
1989	1,644,408	57.5
1990	1,644,841	56.2
1991	1,638,179	54.7
1992	1,633,480	53.5
1993	1,616,016	52.9
1994	1,599,135	52.1
1995	1,583,356	51.6

[1] Recorded membership.
[2] Percentage of all employees.
[3] Yearly average.
Source: *Tätigkeitsberichte des ÖGB, Hauptverband der österreichischen Sozialversicherungsträger.*

a supervisory board, one-third of the board's seats are reserved for the works council. Overall, the system of employee representation resembles the German model, the main difference being that works councils in Austria have fewer rights than in Germany.

Although based on the principle of free collective bargaining, labour relations at the multi-firm level are also governed by the ArbVG, which regulates the bargaining parties and the scope and legal effects of agreements. One of the most notable features of Austria's labour law is that – with a few exceptions – it authorizes only associations (employers' associations and unions at multi-employer level) to conclude collective agreements. In order to be licensed to conclude collective agreements, an association must be independent from its bargaining counterpart. Agreements at this level may cover all aspects of the employment relationship as well as the relationship between the bargaining parties themselves. Closed and union shop agreements are prohibited. Agreements bind not only the bargaining parties' members but also non-members within these parties' associational domain. Bargaining parties are subject to a peace obligation as long as an agreement is in force.

Despite the comprehensive regulation of other industrial relations issues, the law does not cover industrial disputes or internal union affairs. There are so few strikes in Austria (table 8.1) that the issue has never troubled the legislature or the courts. Nevertheless, the ArbVG provides voluntary public mediation or arbitration procedures for disputes over the content of collective agreements. In contrast, the resolution of disputes over rights enacted in the ArbVG can be legally enforced by either party. Depending on issues, the labour courts or special public arbitration boards are responsible for judgements on such disputes.

Overall, the ArbVG defines a highly ordered system of industrial relations in terms of both procedural rules and regulatory levels. Different types of regulation (statutes, collective agreements, plant agreements, employment contracts) generally follow the principle that the provision most favourable to labour overrides others on the same issue. The ordering of regulatory levels establishes a clear predominance of the actors at the multi-employer level over those below. The exclusive right of employers' associations to conclude collective agreements is notable, given that in other countries employers' associations regularly have trouble obtaining such authority from their members (Traxler 1995b). Unions are superior to works councils, as almost all industrial relations issues may be subject to collective bargaining by unions at multi-employer level, while the works councils' competence embraces only a narrow range of issues. Most importantly, this implies that only unions are empowered to conclude legally enforceable agreements on wage rates.

The State as Employer

In the public sector, which accounted for about 21 per cent of all employment in Austria in 1991, employee representation in the workplace is analogous to that laid down in the ArbVG. Rules vary somewhat for different public employers. Similarly, individual employment relations vary between different groups of public sector employees in terms of legal employment status and the employing authorities. In collective employment relations, this is reflected in patterns of union representation. Thus there is a separate union for employees of each of the following areas: the *Bund* (federal state) and *Länder* (provincial governments); local authorities; railways; and the postal service.

The employment conditions of almost all public employees are fixed by law. In practice, however, they are not determined unilaterally by the state but by regular bargaining rounds between the four public employees unions and the authorities. Agreements are formally embodied in legislation.

While in several other countries the growing militancy of public employees posed a particular threat to incomes policies, no comparable development has taken place in Austria. Nonetheless, the union of federal and provincial state employees accounted for the highest strike share of all unions, with 92 per cent of workers involved and 77 per cent of working hours lost for 1990–5. Conflicts are likely to intensify owing to continued cuts in public expenditure to meet the Maastricht criteria for monetary union.

Macro-level Concertation and the State

Two main arenas of macroconcertation can be distinguished. The first is incomes policy, which is formulated on a voluntary basis. During the 'classic' era of social partnership, incomes policy covered both wages and prices, which were regulated by the Parity Commission composed of the 'big four' and government representatives. Corporatist price control began to lose its effectiveness in the late 1970s as a result of growing import penetration, and in 1994 the 'big four' formally agreed to refrain from further price control (except for a few goods). While the Commission's wage control has become a purely formalistic procedure, macroeconomic concertation of wages has nevertheless been maintained on the basis of internal bargaining co-ordination by both ÖGB and the BWK in combination with sectoral pattern bargaining (Traxler 1995a).

The second arena of concertation covers all other economic and social policy issues under the formal responsibility of the state, with the big four's influence resting on devolution by the state of advisory and regulatory powers. In this context the Parity Commission also serves as a forum for developing concepts for economic and social policy. Whereas the goal of voluntary incomes policy is to avoid wage–price spirals and thus to ensure economic competitiveness in the short term, state-licensed co-operation is mainly aimed at increasing long-term competitiveness through economic restructuring. Since wage concertation is an essential precondition for Austria's hard-currency policy, its importance has increased. In contrast, 'horizontal' co-operation among the big four and the government has weakened somewhat (Tálos et al. 1993). This is mainly due to the fragmentation of the party system and the rise of populist politics.

Labour

Union Structure

The ÖGB was founded in 1945, after the overthrow of the Nazi regime and before sectoral unions were set up. Completely new union structures were then reconstructed from the top down, in line with the political aim of preventing inter-union rivalry.

Austrian unionism is the most centralized in western Europe, and, uniquely in terms of unity, ÖGB encompasses the whole of the country's union membership. It consists of fourteen affiliates which cover the whole economy. Though each has a distinct jurisdiction, industrial unionism (in the strict sense of one plant, one union) is not fully established. In the private sector, blue-collar workers are organized separately from white-collar employees: while there are eight sectoral unions of blue-collar workers, nearly all the private sector's white-collar workers are in a single union, the GPA. In addition, one union recruits both white- and blue-collar workers in the arts and the media. The remaining four affiliates each organize distinct parts of the public sector, as outlined above.

Separating blue- from white-collar workers has been important to prevent the formation of an autonomous white-collar union outside ÖGB, as happened in Sweden and to a lesser extent in Germany. Thus the principle of industrial unionism is moderated for the sake of unity. However, the distinction between white- and blue-collar workers has recently become much less clear than in the past. For example, employers seeking to increase employee involvement may classify workers performing manual tasks as white-collar employees, a status privileged by higher pay and better legal protection. This threatens to undermine the membership basis of manual unions – particularly since qualified manual workers, who tend to be those who shift from blue- to white-collar status, represent their unions' key recruiting ground for officials and works councillors. The problem is further exacerbated by the expansion of white-collar employment in the service sector. Since 1974, the GPA has been the ÖGB's largest member (Traxler 1982); since 1994, membership of the metal-workers' union GMBE, formerly the ÖGB's largest affiliate, has even fallen behind that of the largest public-sector union. In response, some manual unions have called for a stricter application of the principle of industrial unionism: in effect restricting white-collar unions to the service sector, with industrial unions embracing all types of employees within their sector of organization. A further challenge to the established structure is the ongoing privatization which in principle implies a shift of employees from the public sector unions to the GPA.

In response to the proposals of a reform commission, the 1995 ÖGB congress agreed to orientate 'co-operation between affiliates and concentration of resources towards the basic groupings of manufacturing, services and the public sector'. This rather vague conclusion reflects the continuing diversity of interests among affiliates. Taken seriously, it would mean breaking up the GPA by transferring its numerous members in manufacturing to the blue-collar unions – a solution the GPA is hardly likely to accept. Restructuring will most probably continue, therefore, through amalgamations of smaller blue-collar unions. The two unions covering textiles, clothing and leather, and chemicals, are planning to merge in 1997. As a first step towards restructuring, the 1995 conclusion recommends the synchronization of bargaining rounds within each of the three groupings.

The power relations between a federation and its affiliates are broadly determined by three resources: control over finance, control over full-time officials, and the allocation of representative functions. Under its constitution, the ÖGB exercises control over the entire system of union finances. Members' dues are collected by the unions for the ÖGB, which then receives a percentage (27.6 per cent on average for 1990–4). The ÖGB also sets the level of subscriptions (currently 1 per cent of an employee's gross income). Control over personnel is regulated in a similar fashion: the ÖGB appoints not only its own staff but also those of its member unions, although only a minority (27 per cent in 1996) work in its office.

The ÖGB is responsible for representing interests common to all employees, and member unions are responsible for matters affecting their own membership. In practice, the ÖGB is pre-eminent in formulating long-term union goals as well as in representing labour in government. Union representatives in corporatist policy-making are nominated by the ÖGB. According to the ÖGB constitution, member unions are not independent associations but subdivisions of the ÖGB; hence, they are not entitled to make binding agreements with external interlocutors. Accordingly, the ÖGB has the exclusive right to conclude collective agreements. However, power is in reality more decentralized than this suggests. For instance, the ÖGB's affiliates define the basis of calculating membership dues. Despite the uniform level of subscription this has resulted in variations in dues across the affiliates. Most importantly, wage bargaining has been delegated to the ÖGB's affiliates, which conclude collective agreements on its behalf. The ÖGB itself negotiates only on 'general' non-wage issues involving all sections of the labour force.

Organizational unity is even more developed than formal centralization. Since there is no union outside its umbrella, the ÖGB enjoys a de facto monopoly of representation. Given the politicization of Austrian society, entrenched in political camps since the late nineteenth century, this unitary structure can only be sustained by the systematic internalization of political schisms. Seven political factions (enabling the unions to maintain links to all parties in parliament excepting the liberal party) exist within the ÖGB. Although they are not explicitly recognized under the union's constitution, they have achieved a quasi-official status, and about 1 per cent of the ÖGB's revenues is allotted to them each year. As a result of these political affiliations, since 1945 union representatives have continuously held not only parliamentary seats, but also ministerial posts. Especially close ties exist with the Social Democratic Party (SPÖ), within which the union faction has formed a highly influential group. Conversely, the unions are clearly dominated by the social democrats.

The strength of political factions and representation on union bodies at all levels up to the top of the ÖGB is determined by the results of works councils elections. By nominating separate lists of candidates for these elections, the factions compete for employees' support. This electoral system is unorthodox in that the works council is formally independent of the unions. It is questionable whether the system is truly representative. Those unionists working in plants without a works council are inevitably excluded from union elections. Conversely, employees who are not unionized can influence intra-union delegations since all employees have the right to vote in the works council election. Nevertheless, unions prefer this system for three reasons. First, it is said that it ensures a higher turnout than conventional union elections in other countries, thus providing great plebiscitary legitimacy for union representatives (Lachs 1976). Second, the system gives the two main political camps some degree of freedom in distributing seats on representative bodies, because of the impossibility of ascertaining the ideological affiliation of all the works councillors elected. 'Independent' works councillors are not normally accepted as members of the unions' representative bodies. Third, the issues discussed in the context of a works council election are related to the specific problems of the establishment in which it takes place. The formulation of more general union policies can thus be separated to a considerable extent from controversial debates among union members and employees (Traxler 1982).

However, the central precondition for using works councils elections for the purpose of intra-union representation is the integration of works councils with the unions. More than 90 per cent of works councillors are estimated to be union members. Many are also union officials, and they predominate in the unions' representative bodies. Some unions have a formal rule that their representative bodies should consist exclusively of works councillors. Most importantly, the works councils perform union representative functions on the shopfloor; alternative channels of union workplace representation such as shop stewards do not exist. What makes the devolution of shopfloor representation especially attractive to the unions is that, in performing functions on the unions' behalf, works councils can make use of their legally privileged position, and their protection from discriminatory treatment by the employer. Works councils are the backbone of the unions, performing essential organizational functions such as collecting dues, explaining union policy, and supplying union officials with information on employees' opinions and morale. Above all, works councils play a key role in recruiting members: as a rule, density is notably higher in establishments which have a works council than in those which do not.

Thus there are two basic structural channels through which interests are processed and unified. The formalized one is a modified industrial unionism. According to their sector and occupational affiliation, employees are grouped in the ÖGB unions. These in turn send delegates to the ÖGB federal congress and its general executive committee. The second, informal channel, based on political differentiation by factions, cross-cuts the first, shaping policy formation in the ÖGB and its affiliates.

Union Policy and Legitimation Patterns

Austria's unions are unusual not only in their structure, but also their policy. They have adopted an extremely consistent position based on long-term co-operation with capital. The ÖGB's main goal has always been to preserve employment by promoting economic growth. This has permitted increases in incomes without generating conflict with capital over income redistribution. Accordingly, productivity is the guiding principle of Austria's wage policy. Over the last three decades, real wages have increased by 3.3 per cent and total productivity by 3.1 per cent a year on average (Guger 1993). Employment problems in the 1980s were reflected in increases in real wages below the rate of growth of total productivity, causing a shift in income distribution in favour of capital. In addition to its ability to gear real wages to productivity in the long run, wage bargaining has also been very sensitive to the short-term business cycle for employment reasons. Wage flexibility in response to fluctuations in employment is higher than in most other countries (Guger 1993). By giving employment priority over wage increases, the ÖGB succeeded in keeping the unemployment rate comparatively low – 3.3 per cent on average over 1980–93 compared with 9.6 per cent for the EU. However, this has been at the expense of a solidaristic wage policy. Intersectoral wage differentials are higher than in any other Western country with the exception of Japan, the United States and Canada (Guger 1993).

Despite considerable continuity, union policy has responded to changes in the balance of political power. The single-party social-democratic government in the 1970s shared the unions' primary commitment to full employment. Thus the ÖGB could turn to the government to achieve its employment goals, as well as other improvements in workers' living standards. Since 1983, when SPÖ lost its absolute majority and was forced to form a multi-party government, the ÖGB's influence on policy has decreased. At the same time, coalition governments have placed a lower priority on full employment. The unions have concentrated on negotiating shorter working hours as a way of combating growing unemployment. In 1992 agreements were reached in several sectors, covering 40 per cent of employees, on working weeks of under 40 hours. Since cuts in working time in other industries seem unlikely to be achieved by bargaining, given the weakness of these sectors' unions, the ÖGB has been calling for a general agreement on the 35-hour week.

All in all, the ÖGB's co-operation with capital and the state has strongly oriented it towards quantitative, macro-economic goals; qualitative goals relating to workplace issues are clearly of secondary importance. Job control scarcely figures on the collective bargaining agenda in Austria. There is only one collective agreement, in printing, regulating the introduction of new technology. When the ÖGB addresses the question of new technology, it does so mainly with reference to industrial policy and international competitiveness rather than to its workplace implications. There are several reasons for this. First, qualitative demands are more likely to provoke conflict with employers. Second, centralized unionism and collective bargaining are remote from employees' experience in the workplace. Third, the predominance of small and medium-sized companies makes it more difficult for the unions to take up workplace issues.

It would be no exaggeration to say that a 'co-operative bias' is built into unionism. Three structural elements foster inter-class co-operation. First, representational monopoly and unity make it almost impossible to externalize the costs (for example, of increased inflation and unemployment) of a conflict-oriented policy; the absence of competition for members facilitates union restraint. Second, internal political differentiation exposes decision-making to strong pressures for consensus. Third, the establishment of the works council as the union representative in the workplace has also encouraged co-operation.

All these structures support the formulation, but not necessarily the implementation, of co-operative policies. The most serious implementation problems arise over member recruitment. The more centralized policy-making becomes, the fewer the opportunities for participation; and the more union policy is oriented toward the technocratic requirements of macro-economic management, the less it can be related to the immediate interests of workers.

The ÖGB succeeded in maintaining a high union density over a long period (table 8.1). However, since the early 1990s the decline in density has accelerated. The trend is even more pronounced for employed membership, as opposed to recorded unionization. Among OECD countries, Austria experienced one of the sharpest declines in the density of employed membership – from 56.2 per cent in

Table 8.2 Industrial disputes in Austria 1955–1995

	Workers involved		Work hours lost	Share of non-union strikes in work hours lost
	Total	Per 1000 employees		
1955–59[1]	32,913	15.2	562,080	13.2
1960–69[1]	62,880	26.8	114,905	3.3[2]
1970–79[1]	11,028	4.2	135,222	17.6
1980–89[1]	3,715	4.2	51,793	1.2
1990	5,274	1.8	70,962	0.0
1991	92,707	30.9	466,731	0.0
1992	18,039	5.9	181,502	0.0
1993	7,512	2.5	131,363	0.0
1994	0	0.0	0	0.0
1995	60	0.0	894	0.0

[1] Yearly average.
[2] 1963 excluded.
Source: *Tätigkeitsberichte des ÖGB*; Traxler 1982.

1980 to 46.2 per cent in 1990 (Ebbinghaus and Visser 1996); survey data suggest a fall in the density of employed membership from 51.5 per cent in 1986 to 48.0 per cent in 1993.

There are three main reasons for this development. First, changes in the occupational structure (particularly the expansion of the service sector and white-collar employment) have made recruitment more difficult. Second, the culture of political camps, which – through their incorporation into the ÖGB – helped to integrate the employees, has been eroded. The case of young employees highlights the implications for unionization. From 1986 to 1992 their membership declined by 4.7 per cent per year. Third, the ÖGB's selective incentives (e.g. representation in labour court proceedings, individual advice and training courses) no longer have the same power to attract members. This is because BAK has significantly extended its activities to such individual services in order to assure its legitimacy in the face of the populist challenge to compulsory membership.

Employers

The Structure of Capital and the Organization of Employers' Associations

Austria's economy displays great contrasts in performance and ownership patterns. Those industrial sectors that are highly integrated into the world market achieved the same level of productivity as their West German counterparts in 1990; in the

1970s their productivity had been only 40 per cent of the Germans'. However, the productivity of the sheltered sectors is only two-thirds of the German level.

There has traditionally been a large public sector, comprising state authorities and nationalized enterprises. In 1978, about 29 per cent of employees in Austrian industry worked in enterprises where the state held a majority share; for financial institutions, the figure was 47 per cent (Ederer et al. 1985). With their large size and their subordination to government and the 'big four' (especially the ÖGB), public enterprises dominated industrial relations and for a long time set the pace in improving pay and working conditions. In the 1970s, nationalized enterprises played an important role in maintaining full employment by hoarding excess labour. During the 1980s, however, they were increasingly beset by economic problems and lost their pace-setting role in industrial relations. Massive state subsidies were necessary for their survival.

In response to this, the government decided in 1990 to embark on a privatization programme. The early focus was on public enterprises in the manufacturing sector; the first bank was sold only in 1997. From 1979 to 1994 the share of the nationalized industry in employment of Austria's 100 largest companies dropped from 42 per cent to 18 per cent. The most valuable units were sold to foreign investors, marking the failure of industrial policy to build a big multinational enterprise capable of serving as a flagship for Austria's industry (Karazman-Morawetz and Pleschiutschnig 1997). The relative weakness and fragmentation of domestic private capital is thus underscored by the fact that, in contrast to other small countries, no big multinational enterprise has its home base in Austria.

Generally, Austrian firms are very small. Among 15 OECD countries, the contribution of large enterprises (i.e. 500 and more employees) to employment in the manufacturing sector in the early 1980s was smaller only in Denmark, Ireland and Japan (OECD 1985).

The fragmentation and relative weakness of capital contrasts sharply with the unique degree of unity and organizational strength of the central employers' association. The BWK is Europe's most comprehensive, well-resourced and politically influential association (OBI 1985). It has more resources relative not only to country size, but also in absolute terms. For instance, in 1980 the BWK's office staff (4,665 employees) was 58 times higher and its total revenues (AS3.6 billion) 36 times higher than the principal West German employers' association, the BDA.

The co-existence of weak and fragmented capital and a strong, unified business association is no coincidence. The high degree of *associational* concentration and centralization compensates politically for the low degree of *economic* concentration and centralization; small firms, more than large ones, need the collective interest representation and the individual consultancy provided by associations. The centralization of business organization in Austria has also been stimulated by the extraordinarily comprehensive and centralized character of Austrian unions.

As the BWK and its subunits negotiate on behalf of nearly all sections of employers, it is worth dealing in more detail with the BWK's constituency, structures and policy. The BWK has public status in so far as it was established by a special law that regulates its coverage, organizational structure and functions.

All firms in the BWK's domain are legally required to be members. Thus it embraces all privately and publicly owned firms in industry, the artisan sector, commerce, banking and insurance, transport and tourism. Agriculture and the non-trading public sector are the main areas of the economy outside the BWK's domain. In 1990–1, the organization had 244,306 member firms which together employed 69 per cent of all Austrian employees.

The BWK is the peak of a complex chamber system with a two-dimensional, matrix organization (Traxler 1986). The first dimension is based on Austria's territorial differentiation. For each of the nine *Länder* of the Austrian federal state, a special territorial chamber exists. The second dimension focuses on sectors and branches. The BWK members are grouped by product market, which allows them to form subunits for different subsectors of activity. They are incorporated into the territorial chambers as well as into the BWK. Within the BWK nationally there are more than 130 sectoral subunits, and more than 1,200 such subunits exist within the territorial chambers. The regional organizations are the basic units of the whole chamber system, articulating and aggregating territorial as well as sectoral interests. It is in these subunits that member firms directly participate.

Members elect the representatives of their respective territorial sector subunit. Other representatives are appointed in a hierarchical process beginning with the territorial sector subunits and continuing up to leadership positions in the BWK. Lists of candidates are mainly presented by political parties; thus elections serve as the link connecting the chamber with the party system. In 1995, 58.5 per cent of the representatives directly elected by members were affiliated to the conservative party, and 6.7 per cent to the SPÖ.

Given the high degree of internal differentiation, the division of responsibilities is especially important for co-ordinated collective action. The chamber system follows the principle of subsidiarity: that matters should be dealt with at a level as close to the members as possible. However, this principle is qualified in so far as a unit is autonomous only in dealing with matters exclusively affecting the interests of its own members. If members of other units are affected, responsibility must be transferred to the higher-level body whose domain covers all members involved. As a result of the highly centralized mode of public policy, many responsibilities are concentrated at the top level of the BWK.

The BWK is both a trade association and an employers' organization, as it represents business interests in the product as well as the labour market. This is one important precondition for macro-corporatist concertation, which deals with product market and labour market interests in an integrated way. The BWK enjoys a legally guaranteed right to be consulted by government on all economic and social matters. This privileged position is further strengthened by the authorities' preference for dealing with the BWK rather than with other business associations.

The BWK also comes close to having a representational monopoly in collective bargaining. About 95 per cent of all collective agreements are signed on behalf of business under the umbrella of the BWK. Here too, the division of labour between the BWK and its subunits is based on the principle of subsidiarity. This means that the BWK itself negotiates collective agreements only when they have generalized coverage. Other collective bargaining is left to the sectoral subunits within the chamber. They sign agreements partly on behalf of particular subgroups of members, partly on behalf of their membership as a whole, and they sometimes form a common bargaining committee with other closely related sectoral subunits. Collective bargaining is conducted on behalf of both public and private firms in the same sector.

Although subunits have collective bargaining autonomy on matters relating to their specific domain, their activities are co-ordinated by the BWK by means of a continuous exchange of information. Vertical co-ordination is supplemented by horizontal co-ordinating activity among sectoral subunits negotiating on behalf of contiguous business groups, in order to prevent business groups being played off against each other.

The agreements concluded by the BWK and its subunits do not cover all their members, some 4–5 per cent of whom remain outside these agreements. The chamber acts on behalf of these members only as a trade association. Historically, their labour market interests have been represented by specialized employers' associations based on voluntary membership. Since the chamber is the representative of nearly all employers, special inter-associational co-ordination is not necessary. The other employers' organizations tend to base their policies on the collective agreements concluded by the chamber.

Employers' Strategies and Intra-Firm Labour Management

Individual employers generally have a free hand in personnel management: unions are little concerned with qualitative, workplace-related issues for the reasons outlined above. Successful firms also have considerable autonomy on pay and working hours, since unions' quantitative demands are geared to the productivity of the economy as a whole. This autonomy, which is upheld by labour law, is reflected in pay drift. In 1992, actual earnings for workers in manufacturing were 23 per cent on average above pay rates (Guger 1993). Research (Traxler 1991) suggests that the ArbVG exerts a downward ratchet effect on interest representation by the works council. On the one hand, the law confines works council activities to narrowly defined issues, which must be dealt with in a co-operative manner. On the other, the works council's ability to exploit its rights depends significantly on union strength, and particularly on a high union density in the enterprise.

Given this room for manoeuvre, it is not surprising that some multinationals have used their Austrian subsidiaries as a site for testing strategic approaches to human resource management and the restructuring of work organization. A notable example was General Motors' introduction of a new form of work organization based on integrated working teams in its plant in Aspern in the 1980s. While an anti-union objective often underlies human resource management approaches in other countries, the GMBE was able to enforce the right to be fully involved in the project through its unionized works councillors. In general, multinationals have been in the forefront of introducing human resource management in Austria, with domestic firms following suit. Co-operation with the works council is also the norm. Companies have placed special emphasis on establishing quality circles, granting white-collar status to all employees, setting up internal training programmes and introducing performance-related pay.

A long-term approach to industrial relations is the exception rather than the rule among Austrian companies. Given the small size of most firms, scarcity of resources constrains strategic planning. The high degree of juridification and the representational monopoly of the ÖGB further reduce the scope for strategic choices in industrial relations. However, although employers may not be able to affect the institutional framework of industrial relations, they can decisively influence its practical application within the firm. Employers have formal and informal ways of influencing the establishment and subsequent operation of the works council. Informally, management can attempt to prevent employees from setting up a works council. Formally, companies can avoid the legislation by dividing themselves into subunits with fewer than five employees: this has been the strategy adopted by some large retail firms. Nevertheless, as industrial relations are highly co-operative, most firms (especially large ones in the core industrial sectors) have learned to value unions and works councils as guarantors of social peace. One expression of this is management assistance in the collection of union subscriptions.

In the past, employers have never publicly questioned the basic structure of Austrian industrial relations. However, in recent years, some have called for deregulation and increased flexibility of employment relations, echoing the international trend. These demands focus on flexible pay and working hours, the easing of regulations protecting young people at work, and the removal of restrictions in the domestic labour market. In recent bargaining rounds, employers have called for increases in basic rates to be split into a fixed and a flexible (performance-related) component. With the exception of the metal industry's agreement in 1993, this has been rejected by the unions, and wage flexibility remains an issue to be dealt with at the level of the individual enterprise.

While the incidence of performance-related pay has decreased among blue-collar workers, it has increased for white-collar employees, eroding seniority as the main criterion of pay differentiation (Traxler et al. 1995). As a result, the 1996 collective agreement introduced a new pay system for white-collar workers. This weakens the seniority principle, reduces the number of grades, and provides higher starting salaries. Sectoral working-time agreements have combined cuts in the working week with increased flexibility. Within this framework, large, capital-intensive manufacturers such as BMW, Philips and Siemens have reached firm-specific arrangements with their works councils and the GMBE, meeting their requirement for the decoupling of machine operating time and employee working time.

However, employers' interests are not unequivocal. For example, the majority of small retail firms are opposed to more flexible business hours. There is also evidence that employers have failed to take full advantage of existing opportunities for increased flexibility. An investigation (Maurer et al. 1990) in printing and engineering showed that firms hardly used the scope for more flexible working hours provided in sectoral agreements but preferred conventional, rigid working-time arrangements. Likewise, a wage flexibility clause in the 1993 metal industry agreement was rarely used (Auer and Welte 1994). The clause authorized management and works council to agree a pay increase lower than that stipulated by the collective agreement in order to facilitate joint measures to secure employment.

The 'conventional' approach to personnel management and work organization in Austrian firms reflects the properties of the Austrian economy described above. Small firms often do not have the skills and resources to apply flexibility options effectively. In any case, they are generally less bureaucratic and more adaptable than large ones. Consequently, small firms are likely to be less dependent on a formalized strategy for achieving flexibility. Another important reason for the prevailing approach is labour's high level of skills, provided by a system of vocational training very similar to the German one. This enables firms to operate in a flexible and efficient way, even within a rather conventional personnel management framework. Consequently, formalized flexibility established through new forms of work organization is less important (Flecker and Krenn 1994).

Patterns of Collective Bargaining

There is widespread misunderstanding of the nature of Austria's collective bargaining system. Thus it has been wrongly classified as highly centralized, comparable with the Scandinavian systems in the heyday of corporatism (e.g. Calmfors and Driffill 1988). Some authors have then tried to explain why 'centralized' Austria is among the countries with the highest wage dispersion – in stark contrast to the Scandinavian countries (e.g. Rowthorn 1992). The puzzle simply disappears if one differentiates between the level and co-ordination of bargaining. In the early 1950s, just as bargaining switched from the central to the sectoral level in Austria, Sweden's bargaining system was moving in the opposite direction. Since then, Austria has undergone 'organized decentralization' (Traxler 1995a): that is, a step-wise shift to lower bargaining levels, while retaining macro-economic co-ordination.

For a long period, co-ordination across sectors was mainly performed by the Parity Commission and was based on the sectoral bargaining parties' obligation to apply jointly for the Commission's approval before renegotiating agreements. Co-ordination was aimed at influencing the *timing* of bargaining rounds; no attempt was made to prescribe their agenda or outcome. Since the early 1980s, the metal industry has played a pace-setting role and Parity Commission co-ordination has correspondingly declined in importance. A series of sectoral agreements in the 1980s represented a further step towards decentralization by combining a cut in working time with opening clauses allowing management and works council to negotiate over flexible working-time schedules. As mentioned above, in 1993 an opening clause on wage flexibility was agreed for the metal industry.

Collective bargaining is highly inclusive, covering more than 90 per cent of those employees with rights to bargaining (Traxler 1996). Responding to the ÖGB's and BWK's internal structure, bargaining is differentiated according to employment status (i.e. white- or blue-collar), sectors (including a distinction between 'industrial' and handicraft production in manufacturing), and even region in some cases. Overall co-ordination via pace-setting mainly rests on the GMBE's strength in terms of unionization. Since the early 1990s, the GMBE has co-operated closely with the GPA, and the two unions have conducted joint negotiations for blue- and white-collar employees in the metal industry. This in turn sets the pattern for the GPA's 'global' agreement for white-collar workers in most of the rest of manufacturing. The agreements negotiated by the GMBE and the GPA (covering around 17 per cent of all employees subject to bargaining rights) define the framework for all other bargaining rounds, including de facto negotiations in the public sector. Pace-setting by the metal industry adopts a *macro* approach to wage co-ordination, since the GMBE bases its demands on overall productivity increases rather than the metal industry's (higher) productivity growth.

There are two main reasons for this macro-orientation. First, in response to the metal industry's exposure to the world market and its economic heterogeneity, the GMBE tends to tailor its demands to the situation of the industry's weaker subsectors and firms. This brings wage policy closer to overall productivity increases. Second, in 1983 the GMBE proposed that macro-economic growth and inflation should be the main criteria for wage policy, and that the exposed sector be recognized as the pace-setter for the sheltered sector. This concept was subsequently accepted by all ÖGB affiliates. For reasons of inter-union balance, the exposed sector – for which the GMBE is the most important union – can maintain its leading role in relation to public sector unions only if the GMBE refrains from fully exploiting the metal industry's higher productivity increases.

Given that the metal industry's co-ordinating function only covers average wage increases, it is no surprise that wage differentials are comparatively high in Austria. High wage inequality and pay drift imply that the effects of macro-economic co-ordination are rather limited. However, it should be noted that labour law enables the bargaining parties to agree 'effective wage clauses', governing actual pay increases, in addition to the nominal standard rate. Such clauses cover around 25 per cent of all private-sector employment (Guger 1993). They tend to limit management's willingness to concede extra increases as these become part of the collective agreement through subsequent bargaining over effective wage clauses. However, under conditions of full employment, it has proved difficult to keep pay drift in line with macro-economic requirements. Since the hard-currency policy offered a way to suppress autonomous shopfloor bargaining it was supported by the ÖGB from the beginning, and defended even against sections of the SPÖ – including Chancellor Kreisky – in the early 1980s. Moreover, hard-currency policy is also in line with the ÖGB's concern for real wage increases rather than nominal wage policy.

Extra payment and benefits are conceded either unilaterally by management, or settled in negotiations where an effective works council exists. In large enterprises, a second bargaining round often occurs, customarily resulting in a plant agreement. Since works councils are not formally authorized to negotiate on wage increases, they can only conclude informal (i.e. legally unenforceable) plant agreements on this issue (Traxler 1982). This somewhat restricts pay drift and at the same time permits a flexible adaptation of wages to the business cycle and to company performance. Other informal arrangements most frequently concern the introduction of flexible working time and performance-related pay schemes.

This divergence between formal and informal procedures arises from two phenomena: 'plant egoism' (implying a conflict between the plant-specific interests of employees and supra-plant arrangements); and the 'ratchet effect' of co-determination outlined above, in which a works council is typically forced to tolerate a lax enforcement of the legal rules in exchange for other rights or informal concessions. Even this form of 'political exchange' demonstrates how much informal procedures are bound up with the formal framework defined by the ArbVG, since the works council's ultimate power resource is the legal enforceability of its rights. To create informal opportunities for bargaining, a works council can deliberately refrain from enforcing certain rules only to the extent that this does not generally endanger compliance with labour law as its basic power resource. Hence the room for informal negotiations is rather limited.

Prospects and Conclusions

From a comparative perspective, Austria's industrial relations look odd. Strongly centralized associations combine with rather decentralized bargaining which in turn is compatible with macro-economic co-ordination. Strong corporatism is accompanied by an extraordinary degree of flexibility and inequality of wages. There is good reason to assume that these paradoxes are crucial for the stability of Austrian corporatism. Organized decentralization has kept the BWK and the ÖGB from overextending their governance with solidaristic wage policy (as happened in Sweden). Instead, they have been able to build 'surplus capacity' for interclass compromise.

Corporatism seems to be compatible with more policy options than conventional wisdom assumes (e.g. Lash and Urry 1987). In this regard, Austria represent an interesting test of the impact of monetary union, which some have argued will bring about the 'disorganization' of industrial relations (e.g. Busch 1994). For more than a decade, Austria has formed a de facto monetary union with Germany, by pegging the schilling to the Deutschmark. Under this currency regime, pressures on wage policy have indeed been enormous but have not led to the break-up of 'social partnership' and wage concertation. Even though the schilling has been revalued by more than 60 per cent over the last two decades, the economy's competitiveness in terms of labour unit costs has not deteriorated (Traxler 1995a). Despite evidence of an erosion of class identity, corporatism and its actors have maintained their legitimacy. In response to populist pressures, the BAK and BWK each held a vote among their members on compulsory membership in 1995–6: 91 per cent of BAK's voters and 82 per cent of the BWK's supported the principle. However, success may be short-lived in a volatile world. Future challenges are likely to result from both political and economic developments.

Politically, the main source of instability is the collapse of the political camps, manifested in the dramatic rise in the proportion of floating voters in elections, accompanied by the formation of a more competitive party system in which populist, liberal and green parties confront the two traditional political camps. The 'big four' are affected by these developments through their political affiliation to the two camps. Externally, state support, and thus continuity in political exchange, has become much more uncertain for them. Internally, the main parties' contribution to legitimizing associational policies has been qualified. While the ideological challenge to social partnership in general and the unions in particular comes mainly from the Liberal Party, Haider's populist Free Party has challenged the ÖGB most directly. The composition of its electoral support has fluctuated greatly over time, but the Free Party is now trying to present itself as the 'true' party of employees. This has particularly attracted workers marginalized in the wake of economic restructuring. In the autumn 1996 elections for the European Parliament, more blue-collar workers voted for the Free Party than for the SPÖ. On the basis of this success, Haider threatened to set up a new union confederation, mainly in order to press for more influence for its faction within the ÖGB. However, the results of works councils' elections indicate little support for its faction at the workplace, other than in minor parts of the public sector. Since the costs of setting up an effective union organization are considerable and private-sector employers have signalled their lack of interest in a new interlocutor, the Free Party will presumably refrain from any serious attempt to found its own union.

Economically, there are pressures for restructuring. EU membership implies the opening up of those markets that are still sheltered. In addition, labour-intensive industry has to face strong low-wage competition from Eastern Europe. This has given rise to a *Standort* debate on how Austria's economy can be kept competitive. In contrast to its German counterpart, this debate has not led to a questioning of the established industrial relations system. However, in combination with continued immigration and restrictive fiscal policy to meet the Maastricht criteria, intensified international competition is likely to increase unemployment significantly. An even stronger imperative to curb labour costs will thus be imposed on wage policy. At the same time, an ageing population and cuts in public expenditure make a reform of the welfare state necessary.

The progressive opening up of markets to international competition and the continuing privatization of public enterprises are likely to strengthen and 'normalize' the power of capital *vis-à-vis* labour, bringing it more into line with the position in other European countries. This means that capital in Austria is likely to become more independent from labour's support in advancing its interests. Thus one central prerequisite of Austria's macro-corporatism and of labour's key role in the system may be eroded.

All these developments tend to constrain the associations' ability to reach intra- and interclass compromises. While this primarily affects peak-level negotiations it also involves sectoral bargaining, since it has become more difficult to apply standard rates across broadly defined sectors. Another question is whether the exposed sector can retain its pace-setting role in relation to the public sector. Despite its shrinking membership, the GMBE's predominance in bargaining seems to have been reinforced by its close co-operation with the GPA. However, if the ÖGB's decision to transform its affiliates into three basic groups is realized, this will create three large bargaining cartels which – as the Swedish experience shows – may raise more co-ordination problems than the *status quo*. A complicating factor is developments in Germany, owing to the high degree of economic integration between the two countries. If the present crisis of the 'German model' results in a collapse of co-operative multi-employer bargaining, Austria may face destabilizing spill-overs.

Although one cannot rule out the possibility that these problems will overstrain corporatism in Austria, future development will depend not only on the weight of problems but also on the system's adaptability. In this respect, Austria's corporatism, with its flexible mode of organized decentralization, is likely to be better able to cope with contemporary challenges than most industrial relations systems in Europe.

| Abbreviations

ArbVG   *Arbeitsverfassungsgesetz* – Labour Constitution Law
BAK   *Bundesarbeitskammer* – Federal Chamber of Labour
BDA   *Bundesvereinigung der Deutschen Arbeitgeberverbände* – Federal Confederation of the German Employers' Associations
BWK   *Bundeskammer der gewerblichen Wirtschaft* – Federal Chamber of Business
EC/EU   European Community / European Union
GMBE   *Gewerkschaft Metall-Bergbau-Energie* – Union of the Blue-collar Workers of the Metal Industry, Mining and the Power Economy
GPA   *Gewerkschaft der Privatangestellten* – Union of the Private Sector's White-collar Workers
ÖGB   *Österreichischer Gewerkschaftsbund* – Austrian Trade Union Federation
SPÖ   *Sozialdemokratische Partei Österreichs* – Austrian Social Democratic Party.

| References

Auer, M. and Welte, H. 1994: Öffnungsklauseln in der tariflichen Lohnpolitik Österreichs. *Industrielle Beziehungen* 1, 297–314.

Busch, K. 1994: *Europäische Integration und Tarifpolitik*. Köln: Bund.

Calmfors, L. and Driffill, J. 1988: Bargaining Structure, Corporatism and Macroeconomic Performance. *Economic Policy*, 6, 14–61.

Ebbinghaus, B. and Visser, J. 1996: Social Change and Unionisation. The Development of Union Membership in Western Europe, 1950–90. Paper prepared for the 1996 Annual Meeting of the American Political Science Association, San Francisco, August 29–September 1.

Ederer, B., Goldmann, W., Reiterlechner, C., Reitzner, R.N. and Wehsely, H. 1985: Eigentumsverhältnisse der österreichischen Wirtschaft. Sonderheft *Wirtschaft und Gesellschaft*.

Flecker, J. and Krenn, M. 1994: *Produktionsorganisation und Personaleinsatz im internationalen Vergleich*. Vienna: FORBA.

Guger, A. 1993: Lohnpolitik und Sozialpartnerschaft. In E. Tálos (ed.) *Sozialpartnerschaft*. Wien: Verlag für Gesellschaftskritik, 227–241.

Karazman-Morawetz, I. and Pleschiutschnig, G. 1997: Wirtschaftsmacht und politischer Einfluß. In H. Dachs et al. (eds.), *Handbuch des Politischen Systems Österreichs*. Vienna: Manz, 418–31.

Karlhofer, F. and Tálos, E. 1996: *Sozialpartnerschaft und EU*. Wien: Schriftenreihe des Zentrums für angewandte Politikforschung.

Lachs, T. 1976: *Wirtschaftspartnerschaft in Österreich*. Vienna: ÖGB.

Lash, S. and Urry, J. 1987: *The End of Organized Capitalism*. Oxford: Polity Press.

Maurer, A., Moser, U., Perchinig, B., Pirker, R. and Traxler, F. 1990: *Arbeitszeit zwischen Verkürzung und Flexibilisierung*. Vienna: BMfAS.

OBI 1985: Data-Set of the 'Organization of Business Interests' Project (MRDF). Berlin/Florence.

OECD 1985: *Employment Outlook*. Paris: OECD.

Polt, W. 1988: Einige kritische Thesen zur EG-Integration Österreichs. *Kurswechsel*, 3, 8–11.

Rowthorn, B. 1992: Corporatism and Labour Market Performance. In: J. Pekkarinen, M. Pohjola and B. Rowthorn (eds) *Social Corporatism*. Oxford: Clarendon Press, 82–131.

Tálos, E., Leichsenring, K. and Zeiner, E. 1993: Verbände und politischer Entscheidungsprozeß – am Beispiel der Sozial- und Umweltpolitik. In E. Tálos (ed.) *Sozialpartnerschaft*. Wien: Verlag für Gesellschaftskritik, 147–85.

Traxler, F. 1982: *Evolution gewerkschaftlicher Interessenvertretung. Entwicklungslogik und Organisationsdynamik gewerkschaftlichen Handelns am Beispiel Österreich*. Frankfurt/Vienna: Braumüller/Campus.

Traxler, F. 1986: *Interessenverbände der Unternehmer*. Frankfurt/New York: Campus.

Traxler, F. 1991: Mitbestimmung und ökonomisch-technischer Strukturwandel. In H. Diefenbacher and H.G. Nutzinger (eds), *Mitbestimmung in Europa*, Heidelberg: FEST, 131–58.

Traxler, F. 1992: Interests, Politics, and European Integration. *European Journal for Political Research*, 22, 193–217

Traxler, F. 1993: Business Associations and Labour Unions in Comparison: Theoretical Perspectives and Empirical Findings on Social Class. Collective Action and Associational Organisability. *British Journal of Sociology*, 44, 673–91.

Traxler, F. 1995a: From Demand-side to Supply-side Corporatism? Austria's Labour Relations and Public Policy. In C. Crouch and F. Traxler (eds) *Organized Industrial Relations in Europe: What Future?* Aldershot: Avebury, 271–86.

Traxler, F. 1995b: Two Logics of Collective Action in Industrial Relations? In C. Crouch and F. Traxler (eds) *Organized Industrial Relations in Europe: What Future?* Aldershot: Avebury, 23–44.

Traxler, F. 1996: Collective Bargaining and Industrial Change: A Case of Disorganization? A Comparative Analysis of Eighteen OECD Countries. *European Sociological Review*, 12, 271–87.

Traxler, F., Bohmann, G., Ragacs, C. and Schreckeneder, B. 1995: Labour Market Regulation in Austria. Department of Economics, Vienna University of Economics and Business Administration, Working Paper No. 38 Vienna.

9 | Switzerland: Still as Smooth as Clockwork?

ROBERT FLUDER • BEAT HOTZ-HART

Introduction

Switzerland is one of the smaller European countries, with just over 7 million inhabitants. A stable democracy, neutral in both world wars, its institutions – including those of industrial relations – have displayed few radical changes during the present century. Internal pluralism is symbolized by the confederal political system, with the 26 cantons enjoying considerable autonomy. German, French and Italian are all official languages; but German is spoken by over two-thirds of the population, and in this chapter Swiss institutions are therefore referred to only in that language.

Maintaining social and political unity despite diversity has depended on a complex pluralistic system of interest accommodation. This has certainly been true of industrial relations. In contrast to the unitary representational models of Germany and Austria, Switzerland is characterized by inter-organizational competition. Nevertheless, differences both within and between the two sides of industry are normally resolved peacefully; industrial conflict is almost non-existent.

The Swiss system of industrial relations is characterized by a structure of social partnership, which dates from the 1937 'peace accord' in the engineering industry. Neither the right of collective organization nor the right to strike (and, as a counterpart, the right to lockout) is explicitly enshrined in the Swiss constitution or legal system. Conditions of employment in the private sector are settled by negotiation between employers' associations and trade unions or employee associations. Voluntarism has been practised in Switzerland in an exemplary way and with a high sense of responsibility.

The Economic Background

Swiss prosperity is based primarily on technological know-how and skills. By international standards, manufacturing remained relatively central to the Swiss economy until the early 1990s. What is notable, however, is that Swiss industry has never rested on the mass production of a narrow range of products; and it still reflects its origins in craft traditions, remaining heterogeneous and diversified, and therefore more broadly based for instance than Swedish manufacturing. Most products are small-batch, customer-oriented specialized items of high quality and reliability, supported by prompt delivery and excellent after-sales service. The Swiss economy is, to a very high extent, internationalized and focused on foreign trade, but primarily oriented to market niches not as yet penetrated by large enterprises.

In percentage terms, the Swiss economy is one of the most research-intensive in the world, yet in absolute terms the amounts spent on R&D are relatively modest: comparable with the budgets of IBM or GM. Switzerland is therefore unable either to instigate technological developments or to achieve a leading position simultaneously in a number of key technologies. Its competitive edge lies in the role of 'first user', the intelligent first application of new technologies. It is therefore in its interest at least to have a presence in key technologies in order to spot new developments at an early stage, and to make use of their potential.

A particular strength of the Swiss economy is a workforce which is skilled but not academically qualified, technicians with considerable specialist knowledge as well as craftsmen. The associated industrial–commercial culture sustains a high degree of work discipline and morale, quality awareness, reliability and accumulated expertise. These qualities are geographically fixed and are difficult for other countries to imitate. The so-called 'skill-based' economic activities, dependent on such qualifications, represent an important competitive advantage for Switzerland.

The economic structure is dominated by small and medium-sized enterprises. Ninety-nine per cent of all companies in Switzerland (including legally independent affiliates of larger enterprises) have fewer than 250 employees and account for three-quarters of private-sector employment. These comprise a great variety of enterprises, diversified by size and also by sector. From 1985 to 1991 companies with fewer than 50 employees grew substantially faster than bigger ones, and in the stagnation years from 1991 to 1995 they lost fewer employees; more than half of all Swiss employees now work in firms of this size.

Two main areas of the economy can be distinguished. The traditionally strong export sector, in particular chemicals and pharmaceuticals, consists of a few big multinational companies and a multitude of medium-sized and small enterprises. Science-based and capital intensive, these firms reflect the typical characteristics and strengths of Swiss manufacturing.

Other areas of export manufacturing, such as clothing and textiles or shoes and leather, were formerly successful but have been losing market share; of all sectors they show the highest decrease of employment in the 1990s. Engineering (machine-building and vehicles) is the most substantial single industry in Switzerland and is structurally at risk too; from 1986 to 1996 employment in engineering decreased by 18 per cent.

In order to meet international competition, export-oriented firms pursue a number of different strategies. These can involve abandoning products which face declining markets; adoption of newer technologies; and mergers and joint ventures

– for example ABB (Brown Boveri and Asea), Ascom (a merger of all the main Swiss telecommunications companies) and Novartis (Ciba and Sandoz). Swiss companies have invested substantially outside the country, particularly in the USA; between 1990 and 1996 they created some 300,000 jobs outside Switzerland. The 108 biggest Swiss companies have 80 per cent of their total employment (over a million workers) abroad.

Activities oriented to the domestic market are, by contrast, highly regulated and protected from foreign competition. This sector consists of *Gewerbe* (small businesses), the retail trade, construction, and banking, as well as the state sector: the post office, telecommunications, railways and electricity. These organizational characteristics result in a price level which was in 1990 well above the European average: by 35 per cent for consumer goods, 18 per cent for investment goods and 60 per cent for public services. The high price of domestic goods has become a substantial cost factor for exports and a cause of conflict; export-oriented interests ask for liberalization and deregulation.

In the first half of the 1990s there was a dramatic structural change: employment in manufacturing and related activities fell from over a third of the labour force in 1991 to 27.9 per cent in1996. In the same 5 years the workforce in manufacturing, narrowly defined, decreased by 14 per cent; from 24.4 per cent of total employment to 19.6 per cent. Labour turnover has significantly increased; managers agree that it is easier to restructure companies in Switzerland than in other European countries.

The service sector is heterogeneous. Financial services (finance and insurance) and tourism are of considerable and increasing importance, but services are not universally strong in Switzerland. Instances of less competitive areas are software production, technical planning and advisory services. Recently the service sector has also undergone substantial structural changes as a result of intensive use of information and communication technologies and an active internationalization strategy. In banking and insurance, companies have combined activities and developed towards global financial trusts with substantial foreign direct investment; employees are now required to be highly mobile and flexible.

Services and manufacturing are interdependent and often complementary. Many services, such as engineering and planning, are found within manufacturing: a quarter to a third of people employed in manufacturing are engaged in such services. This reflects the complexity of many manufacturing projects: what is sold is no longer just machines or instruments but fully installed factories or hospitals or projects such as the electrification of a whole town. In a highly developed economy such as Switzerland's a separation of sectoral activities has become practically untenable. Today there is a servo-manufacturing area in which services are no longer merely supportive, but have become a principal ingredient of competitiveness; the ability of the servo-manufacturing system to find solutions to complex problems and also put them into practice has become crucial.

To sum up: the Swiss economy is characterized by a mature manufacturing sector coupled with a dynamic service sector. It operates principally by applying new technologies in traditional markets which world-wide are stagnant or even shrinking. Examples are textile machinery and machine tools, textiles and organic chemicals. Of central importance is the creative combination of high, middle and low technologies. Switzerland's strength lies in its ability to use new technologies for numerous made-to-measure solutions of a high standard, and to combine well-known products and processes with new developments. In new, technologically dynamic markets, by contrast, Swiss firms are not well represented.

Overall, the Swiss economy has proved extremely successful, and per capita GNP is among the highest in the world. But since 1991 the economy has stagnated – the longest no-growth period since the war – and has undergone severe structural change. The employment situation has changed dramatically. Although job loss was in absolute terms even more severe in earlier recessions (such as 1974–75), unemployment has now (February 1997) passed 200,000 for the first time in Swiss history – and the rate of 5.7 per cent is higher than during the world recession of the 1930s. Inflation has long been among the lowest in the world and is still below 1 per cent; long-term interest rates are at a historic low.

▌ The Labour Market

Employment in Switzerland reflects the general economic structure, described above. Industry now employs less than 28 per cent of the labour force, and this is decreasing; private services cover the largest sector of workers; while public services and public administration are relatively small by international standards but catching up quickly (see table 9.1). Some public employees (though fewer than in Germany) possess the distinctive status of *Beamte*, regulated by law, which guarantees virtual permanence of employment but prohibits strike action.

All western industrialized countries are experiencing a rise in the ratio of older people in the total population. This is particularly true of Switzerland and Germany. In Switzerland the number of young people entering the labour market is declining annually. Between 1980 and 1995 the under-20 age group diminished by about 115,000 to a share of 23.2 per cent while the 65 plus age group increased by 163,000 to a share of 14.7 per cent. This 'demographic time bomb' has dramatic long- and medium-term implications for the whole system of social welfare.

In Switzerland participation rates (full-time employment) reached a peak in 1960. During the 1970s the activity rate declined, but rose again to about 67.5 per cent in 1996. The participation rate for men (78.8 per cent in 1996) is above average, but has clearly declined over time. By contrast, the participation rate for women has steadily increased to 57 per cent in 1996, though this is still below the European average. Between 1960 and 1990, employment of middle-aged women noticeably increased while that of younger and older females declined. This is partly due to the lowering of the retirement age (or the disinclination to continue work after reaching retirement age) and partly to a change of attitude among young women towards training and education. The share of part-time employees – 28 per cent of all employees in 1995 – is one of the highest in Europe.

Despite these trends in demography and labour force participation, employment

Table 9.1 Employment by sector

Sector	1991		1996	
	Numbers employed (000s)	%	Numbers employed (000s)	%
Agriculture	197	5.5	177	4.7
Industry	1,226	34.4	1,063	27.9
Energy, water, mining	25	0.7	26	0.7
Manufacturing	869	24.4	747	19.6
Building	332	9.3	290	7.6
Services	2,137	60.1	2,567	67.4
Hotel, catering, distribution, repairs	813	22.8	791	20.8
Transport, communications	219	6.2	227	6.0
Banking, insurance, consultancy, real estate, personal services	447	12.6	576	15.1
Health	211	5.9	292	7.7
Education, R&D	173	4.9	253	6.6
Public administration	132	3.7	174	4.6
Other services	142	4.0	254	6.7
Total	**3,560**	**100.0**	**3,807**	**100.0**

Source: Statistisches Jahrbuch der Schweiz.

has been increasing consistently since 1976 (the end of the recession caused by the oil crisis), reaching a record level of 3.8 million in 1996. The expansion has been in such sectors as health, education and public administration, all mainly public funded.

Expansion has largely depended on the availability of foreign labour. After the Second World War, Switzerland became a country of high immigration, which reached a peak in the 1960s. In that period the number of foreign residents rose by nearly 50,000 (about 1 per cent of the total population) per year. The 1980s saw another rise in numbers, giving Switzerland the highest proportion of foreign workers in Europe: in 1992, in a labour force of 3,480,500, there were 976,500 foreigners. This figure declined during the recent period of stagnation to 911,000 in 1996, though foreign inhabitants increased from 17.4 per cent of the population in 1990 to 19.6 per cent in 1995, mainly through immigration of family members.

Employment of foreign workers is concentrated in particular sectors (though the dispersion has become greater in recent years): engineering, construction, retail distribution, hotels and catering and the health services. While most migrant workers once came from neighbouring countries (Italy, France, Germany, Austria), the proportion from such countries as Spain and former Yugoslavia has been steadily increasing.

Right-wing campaigns against immigration have been influential since the 1960s. Restrictions were imposed in 1963, and since 1970 have taken the form of a national ceiling on immigration, set annually by parliament. Quotas are set for different forms of work permit, all temporary – with in most cases a maximum period of nine months. Immigration is linked to social divisions within the Swiss labour force, reinforced by these legal regulations. Less skilled, unpleasant and heavy work is increasingly undertaken by foreign workers, resident in Switzerland on a temporary basis and without political rights. They are weakly placed to improve their working conditions. The availability of a vulnerable temporary workforce lowers labour costs artificially. Certain industries, in particular construction and tourism, whose value added per employee is clearly below the Swiss average, can rely on a relatively secure source of cheap labour.

If Switzerland wants any kind of co-operation with the EU, it will not be possible to maintain restrictions on the cross-border mobility of workers. Improvements in the statute covering seasonal workers, or its replacement by new forms of short-term permit, are imminent. Repeal of the statute will result in wage rises since foreign workers will be able to choose their jobs freely; this will force employers to adapt their production techniques and lead to structural improvements in the economy. Not surprisingly, representatives of the building industry, tourism, and other trades benefiting from the seasonal worker status, campaign vehemently for the retention of the statute and are extremely sceptical, if not hostile, towards European integration.

The Political System and Industrial Relations

Switzerland possesses a stable political system in which divisions of class, religion and language are accommodated. There is a bicameral parliament, with an upper chamber of two members from each canton (a system which benefits the right) and a federal assembly elected by proportional representation. Four parties have traditionally dominated: the Liberal Democrats (FDP), Christian People's Party (CVP), Social Democrats (SPS) and Swiss People's Party (SVP). Government is by a seven-member federal council, which for the past century has involved a cross-party coalition. Since 1959 the so-called 'magic formula' has prevailed, with two seats each for the three largest parties and one for the SVP. By convention, two or three members are French or Italian speakers.

Politics in Switzerland (as in Austria) relies on the mobilization of social consensus through a system of democratic corporatism. It involves an ideology of social partnership at national level, despite often intense political arguments within the individual interest groups; and voluntary and informal accommodation of interests through continuous political bargaining between interest groups, the state and the political parties (a 'collaborative policy process') (Katzenstein 1984: 27). This corporatism permits the combination of political stability and economic flexibility. It is linked to liberal capitalism based on strong, export-oriented enterprises, strong conservative political parties, few centralized political institutions, and a policy of global adaptation and private profit.

The emphasis on consensus and compromise is furthered by the mechanisms of direct democracy, the referendum and the initiative. Opponents of any Act of parliament need obtain only 50,000 signatures in order for a referendum to be held. By such means, radical economic policy initiatives are likely to end in defeat; hence moderate solutions are the rule. Consultations and negotiations between the administration and influential interest groups play a crucial role in the preparation of legislation. Another distinctive constitutional provision is the 'right of initiative' (*Initiativrecht*). On the basis of 100,000 signatures, a referendum may be demanded on any constitutional proposal. This enables new ideas and claims to be put forward. Almost without exception, measures proposed by this mechanism – regularly used in recent years – have been defeated. Yet where an initiative reveals substantial public support for reform, government and parliament have typically responded by introducing compromise legislation. Hence the consensual nature of politics is sustained.

Trade unions play a minor role within the social coalition in Switzerland, because of the structure of the Swiss economy and the unions' own political choices (Katzenstein 1984: 101). The strength of the trade union movement has been hampered by the decentralized industrial structure, the small size of enterprises, and the growing number of employees transferring from manufacturing to the service sector. The trade union movement was also weakened up to the early 1990s by economic prosperity and full employment.

In addition the unions are politically divided. There is a considerable difference between the moderate engineering workers and the more militant public service trade unions, the industrial unions of the printers, the building workers and the woodworkers, and the chemicals, textiles and paper union.

There is also a difference in approach between the trade unions and the Social Democratic Party (SPS). The unions tend towards private solutions to their problems while the social democrats look for solutions via the state. An example was the discussion of the regulation of old age pension schemes, with the trade unions (together with the bourgeois parties) supporting the existing private insurance schemes and the social democrats pleading for a national pension plan.

As for the relationship between trade unions and the political parties, the literature talks of a Dutch-style 'pillarization' (*Versäulung*) (Steiner 1970; Höpflinger 1976: 200). There are institutionalized links between unions of differing tendencies and their respective parties, from informal contacts between members of staff to an overlap of functions or mutual consultations up to formal election pacts. But, in principle, the unions are legally and financially independent of political parties. Traditionally, there are close links between the Swiss Trade Union Confederation (SGB) and the SPS and between the National Federation of Christian Trade Unions (CNG) and the Christian People's Party (CVP). These links tend to prevent state interference in the affairs of the unions or the federations and thus guarantee free collective bargaining (*Tarifautonomie*).

In the case of government measures which affect their interests, trade unions and employers participate at all levels of the so-called pre-parliamentary process. The ability of an interest group to threaten a referendum on the statute in question strengthens its position in the consultation process. In this way, inequalities of power between employers and unions are reduced, though not eliminated.

The institutionalized goal of consensus also has an effect on collective bargaining. Employers prefer regulation of working conditions by negotiation rather than by uniform and inflexible legislation. In general, negotiated solutions are faster, more progressive and more detailed than is the law. Trade unions and employees as well as employers adhere to the principle of subsidiarity: state intervention is accepted only if labour market or social policy problems can no longer be resolved by direct agreement between the parties. The principle of free collective bargaining applies in particular to wage determination: incomes policy has so far had no role in Switzerland.

Federalism, the Trade Union Movement and Industrial Relations

Unions and employers in Switzerland possess organizations at local, cantonal, regional and national level. The Swiss principle of federalism finds expression in the trade union movement and industrial relations: for example, in the delegation of functions to individual unions and the weak position of the national confederations.

The main confederation, SGB, itself possesses separate units in each canton. This is not true, however, of all affiliated unions. For example, the structure of the engineering union (SMUV) reflects the country's industrial geography, with a number of branches in cantons where the industry is concentrated, but some branches span several cantons where there is little employment in the industry. Organization by territory is stronger and institutional federalism important in the public sector with a high degree of legal regulation. Teachers' pay, for instance, is settled separately in each canton; whereas in engineering, the principles of pay are regulated in a nationally applicable agreement.

Industrial relations are indirectly affected by the federal structure of the state in a number of ways. First, there exist separate conciliation and mediation services in each canton. Second, quotas of foreign workers are allocated by canton, and in some cantons (for example, Geneva) are subject to joint negotiation between employers and unions. Third, the cantons are heavily engaged in vocational training.

The peak level of unions and employers' associations comprises central or umbrella confederations. These deal with the federal government and attempt to influence its economic and social policies to their advantage. Companies do not affiliate directly to their national confederation (although in isolated cases individual large enterprises also exert an influence on the state) but through membership of sectoral associations. Similarly, workers become members of the national confederations through specific industrial or occupational unions. Thus the national confederations are organizations of organizations. It is these sectoral associations which are primarily and directly concerned with labour market regulation.

Table 9.2 Trade Union Membership (1995)

Organization	Number of affiliates	Membership	Percentage of total
SGB	17	419,800	45
CNG	9	134,200	14
VSA	8	126,200	14
Independent	c. 34	246,900	27
Total	**c. 68**	**927,100**	**100**

| Trade Union Organization

From its origins the Swiss trade union movement has been marked by *fragmentation*: reflecting first its early development on craft and occupational lines, second the ideological division between socialists and anti-socialists. The first national confederation, the Swiss Trade Union Confederation (SGB) was linked to the social-democratic movement. Various rival catholic industrial unions were formed in the early years of this century and came together in the Christian National Trade Union Confederation (CNG), followed by the founding of a Swiss Association of Protestant Workers (SVEA) and a National Association of Free Swiss Workers (LFSA), the latter adopting a 'national-liberal' political orientation of patriotism and peaceful industrial relations (Fluder et al. 1991). In addition, separate occupational unions for white-collar staff (*Angestellte*) were established in the 1920s.

This divided structure still exists. The SGB, which remains allied to the SPS, organizes in both the public sector and the private (where its membership consists mainly of manual workers in industry). Its unions encompass almost half the total membership in Switzerland, but it has lost ground continuously in the past two decades, mainly because its traditional core membership is in declining sectors (manufacturing, public transport, postal services). The affiliates of the CNG, which is oriented politically to the CVP, organize extensively like the SGB but primarily in manufacturing industry; they have less than a third of the membership of the larger confederation. The Swiss White-Collar Federation (VSA) organizes mainly in the private sector; only one of its affiliates, the Swiss Clerical Association (SKV) covers some public employees. It maintains links with all political parties. Finally, there is a heterogeneous group of independent unions, including the LFSA, the Association of Banking Staffs (SBPV) and occupational associations such as those of teachers (LCH) and nurses (SBK). Their relative importance has increased with the growth of the public service sector; here the traditional confederations, which have been very badly affected by the recession in private industry in the 1990s, are very poorly represented. In 1995 some 40 per cent of all union members were in the public sector, as against only 31 per cent in 1980.

There are marked differences in the degree of organization between sectors and firms. In construction, engineering and printing there is a union density of 40 to

60 per cent, and collective bargaining is strongly established. By contrast, organization is almost non-existent in most private services: density is under 10 per cent in the retail sector, personal and business services and insurance. It is also under 20 per cent in hotels and catering, and in the food, textile and clothing industries. In the public sector there are also contrasts. Density is highest – about 70 per cent – in postal services, railways and central government administration, and almost as high in local government; these are the areas of most intensive collective bargaining. The best organized sectors were the growth areas of Swiss employment in the early post-war decades when the unions were most successful in recruitment; but as indicated, they are in many cases contracting today, while unionism is far weaker in the new growth areas. The two traditional confederations also suffer from their concentration among manual workers and their extremely weak representation in white-collar occupations.

Women are significantly underrepresented in both SGB and CNG, though their affiliates in public services have had some recent success in female recruitment. In 1995, 16 per cent of SGB members were women, compared with 12 per cent in much of the 1970s and 1980s. Such recruitment has prevented an even more serious loss of aggregate membership, and has been facilitated by the strong support the SGB has given to campaigns for women's rights. The age structure of union membership is also a cause for concern: the SGB in particular is strongly concentrated among older workers and includes many pensioners (18 per cent of all members), while it has had relatively little success in recruiting new entrants to the labour force. Only 8 per cent of its membership are aged below 25. It is strongly represented among foreign workers, who constitute 30 per cent of its membership.

As already indicated, Swiss unions play an important role in the political decision-making process and in most cases have close links with one or other of the main political parties, reflected in overlapping membership in the governing bodies of both. At the end of the 1980s about a fifth of all members of parliament had trade union connections; some 80 per cent of these were in the SPS (the majority of whose representatives are trade unionists). As this indicates, the bonds between the SGB and the SPS are particularly tight, but there are also close personal and institutional linkages between the CNG and the CVP. The white-collar unions also have connections with the FDP and other right-wing parties; but in the case of the independent associations, party connections are much looser.

Trade union pluralism in Switzerland is thus an expression of political divisions, and is also linked to the territorial segmentation of Swiss culture (Kerr 1987). The CNG has its strongholds in catholic cantons where the CVP dominates politically, and here the SGB is weak.

This fragmentation contributes to the overall low unionization in Switzerland, and also to the limited degree of co-ordination both between and within confederations, which possess little authority over their affiliates. There is little capacity for membership mobilization, either in strikes or in demonstrations and protests, a consequence but also a reinforcement of the tradition of peaceful reconciliation of interests. All these factors connect in turn to the absence of effective union organization at workplace level. These weaknesses did not generate major problems for most of the post-war period, when unemployment was normally below 1 per cent; but with the serious worsening of employment conditions in the 1990s, the unions need new strategies and new lines of action, and are attempting to concentrate their forces more effectively.

Thus in the 1990s, the unions have begun to reform their structures, which had remained virtually unaltered for half a century. Within the SGB, the unions in construction and the textile and chemical industries merged, followed by planned fusions between unions in the media. These reflected loss of collective bargaining effectiveness and organizational problems caused by membership decline. There have also been amalgamations among public-sector unions in response to the challenges of privatization and revisions to the *Beamte* law. Union mergers are likely in the postal service, and in the public sector more generally there are plans for increased inter-union co-operation. Meanwhile the two main SGB unions in the private sector, the engineering union SMUV and the construction and allied union GBI, have reached a mutual co-operation agreement; one outcome has been their joint support for the creation of a new organization in the private service sector – to the anger of the existing SGB union in the service sector.

The 1990s have also seen restructuring within the CNG. Its metal union has absorbed three other organizations and has become a general union covering much of the private sector – as is reflected in its new name, Christian Union for Industry, Trade and Services. Within the VSA there are also complex changes: two unions have seceded but another association has affiliated. The unions for clerical workers and bank staffs, both of which have suffered membership losses, are discussing merger. Similarly, there have recently been amalgamations and co-operation pacts among independent unions in the public sector.

Employers' Organizations

Employers' associations are not ideologically divided in the way that Swiss trade unions are. This reflects the fact that they provide a range of services (advice, training, insurance) which give firms strong practical reasons for membership; they do not need to mobilize support through the use of ideological symbolism. This also means that the degree of organization is typically more than double that of the unions.

There is only one peak employers' association, the Swiss Employers' Association (*Schweizerischer Arbeitgeberverband*, abbreviated here for convenience to SA), which was formed in 1908 and until 1996 known as ZSAO. Its aims are to represent 'the interests of employers as a whole' by supporting 'constructive social partnership' and seeking to influence parliament and the public authorities on social and industrial relations matters. SA co-operates with the central trade association, the Swiss Federation of Commerce and Industry (SHIV), which dates back to 1870 and is concerned with economic and foreign trade policy.

The powers of the central confederation are limited: it has few staff and modest financial resources. Thus considerable autonomy rests with its 72 member associations, about 30 of which are sectoral and the remainder local or regional; many are also members of SHIV. It encompasses firms employing around a million workers, implying a density rate of 40 to 50 per cent. The largest member associations are in engineering, hotels and catering and construction; those in banking and chemicals are also important. The Swiss Engineering Employers' Association (ASM) had 596 member firms in 1996, employing 146,000 workers; it has lost members in the 1990s because of the recession, and has been unsuccessful in recruiting new companies in the high-technology sector. The Association of Master Builders (SBV), which has both trade and employer association functions, claims 4,700 member firms, and an organization rate of 90 per cent.

There also exists a Swiss Association of Small Businesses (SGV), dating back to 1879, which represents both the employment and the commercial interests of its members, who mainly produce for the domestic market. By contrast, SA tends to represent the larger, export-oriented firms, and this can lead to policy differences between the two organizations – for example over European integration, competition policy or the extension of collective agreements to non-signatories (*Allgemeinverbindlichkeit*). However, they maintain close contacts and on most issues succeed in reaching a consensus. SGV has 275 member organizations, also consisting of sectoral and local bodies as well as co-operatives, and has a density of over 60 per cent in its sphere of organization. There is some dual membership between SGV and the affiliates of SA.

Neither confederation is directly involved in collective bargaining, which is the responsibility of the sectoral associations, though they do have a co-ordinating role. Before each bargaining round the SA produces a report on economic trends, and this is discussed in its management committee. The SGV organizes a discussion forum on bargaining policy in the construction sector, which can lead to the formulation of guidelines.

The confederations have few contacts with the peak trade union organizations either: perhaps one or two informal meetings a year. Their main task is representation in the political sphere. Both are represented on numerous expert committees (72 in the case of SA), most of which are advisory but a few of which have decision-making powers. These bodies also include representatives of the unions and other interest groups, the public authorities and academics. Unlike in Austria there exists no central tripartite commission to formulate macro-economic policy, though recently the government has convened tripartite meetings. Examples are the meeting on economic policy organized in the autumn of 1996, or the meeting to agree changes to unemployment insurance.

An important form of political influence is involvement in committees of experts and consultative bodies. The threat of calling a referendum gives considerable opportunities to shape the pre-legislative process (Linder 1983). Informal and semi-formal contacts with members of parliament and government officials are also important. On issues which affect their interests, they will lobby parliamentarians or make direct contact with the party organizations.

The sectoral associations have the responsibility for collective bargaining. In the main there is a clear demarcation between the sphere of competence of each, and the resulting exclusive jurisdiction means, with few exceptions, that employers' organizations escape the problems of co-ordination which affect the unions (Farago and Kriesi 1986). But employers' associations, like unions, have experienced problems in the 1990s which have encouraged structural changes. ASM and its commercial counterpart VSM co-operate increasingly closely and have merged some of their organizational functions. There have been amalgamations in the textile and clothing industries, in printing and in hotels and catering.

Collective Employment Relations

By collective employment relations we mean a system of rules, rights and obligations as well as bargaining relations, which are embodied in institutions and possess long-term stability. The relations between the organizations of employers and workers are central to these relations. We can distinguish between 'procedural' rules, which regulate the status of the organizations and the processes of accommodating conflicts of interest, and 'substantive' rules which regulate individual contracts of employment (Flanders 1965).

Katzenstein (1984) has classified collective employment relations in Switzerland as *liberal corporatism*, marked by weak unions, a weak state and a power imbalance favouring the employers. The role of interest associations in political society has expanded and intensified since the 1930s (Linder 1983); but while corporatist arrangements can be identified at sectoral level, Switzerland lacks the central corporatist structures which exist in some countries. The peak associations lack authority, and the state itself has limited functions, particularly in the regulation of employment relations, and many of the responsibilities for social security are allocated to private organizations or the individual. Employers' associations are less encompassing than their counterparts in many other countries and would have less legitimacy if they attempted to shape general public policy. This encourages a devolved form of intermediation of interests, particularly at sectoral level.

The unions are significant social organizations but are even less representative. However, they are valued as a countervailing force to the employers. Survey evidence suggests that two-thirds of the population considers that they have an important function – greater than that of the state – in reducing income inequality, and three-quarters think that employers would treat workers worse if unions did not exist (Hischier et al. 1989). This public attitude gives unions a position in the national power structure and also makes them a potential force for order.

Statutory Regulation

In Switzerland the state has an extremely limited role in industrial relations: employment regulation, and in particular wage determination, is left to the private organizations of workers and employers (Berenstein 1994). However the law defines the general framework of collective bargaining through the Collective Agreement Regulation (*Arbeitsvertragsrecht*). There is also a general Employment Act (*Arbeitsgesetz*) setting basic standards concerning health and safety, working time, rest periods and special protection for women and young workers.

Changes in this legislative framework can provoke conflict. In 1996, the employers promoted the abolition on the prohibition of night-work for women, and a relaxation of restrictions on Sunday working. After the breakdown of attempts to agree a compromise, the unions initiated a referendum which rejected the revisions by a two-thirds majority. In the same year the unions themselves were divided over revisions to the pensions system, involving the raising of the retirement age for women; this was supported by the VSA and by the social democrats because of other improvements, but opposed by both the SGB and CNG. In this case the popular vote supported the reform. Similar divisions between the unions had occurred in the 1980s (Fluder 1997).

There is a general consensus between unions and employers' associations that collective bargaining is preferable to statutory regulation. They support the principle of subsidiarity whereby state intervention should be supported only when labour market or social policy problems cannot be resolved by their own initiatives. Here too, however, there are differences: unions in the CNG and VSA assign a clear priority to collective bargaining, whereas half of those in SGB consider legislation equally valid.

Collective agreements are seen as flexible and decentralized, quicker to achieve and easier to control by those directly affected, who can influence the outcomes through participation in the internal democracy of their organizations. By comparison with other national systems, this gives Swiss industrial relations an adaptability which is regarded as one of its strengths.

Collective Bargaining and Collective Agreements in the Private Sector

The principal instrument of employment and conflict regulation is the sectoral agreement (GAV). Sectoral contracts normally last from 3 to 5 years, supplemented by usually annual negotiations to adjust wages to changes in the cost of living. Some groups such as apprentices, staff employees and temporary workers are normally excluded from the terms of a GAV. By law, agreements apply only to members of the signatory organizations; but in practice, non-union employees are treated the same as union members. However, agreements often impose a 'solidarity contribution' on non-members, so that they bear their share of the costs of negotiating and implementing the GAV. These payments are used, for example, to establish joint funds for continuing vocational education.

The parties to a GAV can apply to the national or local authorities for its extension to all firms in the sector (*Allgemeinverbindlichkeit*), so that firms outside the employers' association do not gain a competitive advantage. However, extension is subject to strict legal conditions: agreements must take account of minority interests and regional differences, a minimum representation quote, and must safeguard constitutional rights and the public interest. In 1996 there were 12 extensions at national level and 5 at canton level, affecting 52,000 employers and 358,000 employees – about a quarter of the total coverage of total agreements. Most extensions occur in the small business sector.

In 1994, collective agreements applied to about 1.3 million Swiss workers, a coverage rate of about 50 per cent: significantly below the European average (Traxler 1995). Coverage was higher in manufacturing (60 per cent) than in the tertiary sector (44 per cent) (Lopreno 1995), and for men (58 per cent) than for women (38 per cent). Though the sectoral GAV at national level is the dominant form of agreement, about 12 per cent of employees are also covered by company agreements. These are normally confined to the largest firms (Swissair, Migros, Swiss Radio-TV). There are significant gaps in coverage, coinciding with the main areas of trade union weakness. Since these are often growth sectors of employment, and since many white-collar workers are excluded from the terms of agreements, the decline in coverage (according to SGB estimates, from 54 to 50 per cent during the 1990s) is likely to continue.

Wages are regulated in a variety of ways. Some agreements, applying to about 30 per cent of employees covered, do not specify wage rates at all (BFS 1997). These include the GAV with the most extensive coverage, that in the engineering industry (where the employers' association ASM was historically strongly opposed to the whole principle of collective bargaining). This provides for company negotiations between management and the works committee; if no agreement is reached there is a three-stage procedure for mediation and arbitration (Fluder et al. 1991). The most common form of wage regulation in collective agreements is the definition of minimum rates, which may be considerably below actual wage levels. However, an increase in the minimum typically has an impact on actual pay, which may be larger or smaller according to economic conditions. Many agreements used to provide for pay to rise in line with prices, but most cost-of-living indices or guarantees have recently been abolished. All employers' associations clearly opposed automatic linkages of pay to prices, and the system of pay determination which has developed in the 1990s allows a particularly high degree of wage flexibility.

Collective bargaining covers a broad range of topics, including matters outside a narrow definition of employment conditions, for example social benefits (such as child allowances) which in most countries are legally regulated. The welfare state is less developed in Switzerland than in Germany for example, yet the social benefits obtained by a union like the metalworkers' (covering retirement, unemployment, sickness and accidents) were more extensive and more generous than those enjoyed by German metalworkers. Through negotiating such provisions, the Swiss unions have achieved a status that they value and defend: they are social partners, not just bargaining parties, and they resist any legislative initiatives such as incomes policy which might reduce their broad role in collective bargaining.

Collective employment relations in the private sector are marked by a multiplicity of joint institutions, charged with implementing and enforcing the GAV. Often they have responsibility for dispute resolution and for vocational training.

Union and employer representatives meet regularly in these joint bodies and collaborate closely, integrating the interests of their organizations and developing relations of mutual trust and loyalty.

However, the recession of the 1990s has caused an upheaval in bargaining relations. Employers want to eliminate detailed regulations from the agreements in the interests of flexibility and deregulation; the unions are concerned to maintain the regulatory strength of the GAV. In recent years there have been cases of termination of agreements or conflicts during negotiations, for example in printing and in hotels and catering. With narrower margins for compromise, negotiations have become tougher. Yet in most sectors there is still a commitment to effective social partnership. For example, in construction the unions and the employers' association agreed a 'platform for jobs' which included proposals for government incentives for new building projects. Despite disagreement on some issues such as social policy, there are attempts by the two sides to co-operate on specific questions in order to find solutions to severe economic circumstances.

Industrial Relations in the Public Sector

In contrast to the private sector, in public employment the state prescribes conditions unilaterally through statutes and ordinances. Free collective bargaining does not exist: negotiations do not result in formal agreements. Yet regular discussions do take place between employer and worker representatives, and these have the character of collective bargaining.

The central government is the largest employer in the public sector and has a leadership role in industrial relations and wage determination. Close and intensive contacts exist between top negotiators and top government officials and ministers. The union side is dominated by a federation of organizations representing some 80 per cent of membership in the federal civil service. There are regular negotiations which normally result in an agreed position which is underwritten by the government and the legislature. Parliament usually gives serious weight to the consensus between the bargaining parties, though this reciprocal understanding became weaker in the 1980s (Fluder 1996). This highly institutionalized and centralized system of negotiation between the professional elites on each side might be described as a form of corporatism.

By contrast, industrial relations for local government employees are decentralized; there is no organization on the employers' side (as exists in Germany) permitting national negotiations. Procedures therefore vary according to the institutional and political characteristics of each canton. In general, industrial relations are less institutionalized than at national government level, and contacts between the social partners are less intensive. There is also greater fragmentation of unions and associations pursuing diverse policies with little mutual co-operation; organizational density is lower, and hence interest representation is less effective.

Budgetary constraints impose strong pressures on local authorities to achieve economies. As in the private sector, they have recently tended to eliminate cost-of-living guarantees, and for the first time since the war have imposed substantial job cuts. Some have pursued organizational restructuring in line with the policies of 'New Public Management'.

For the first time since the 1940s there is now fundamental debate concerning industrial relations in the public sector. There have been demands for the removal of statutory constraints on public-sector employers (Richli 1996), linked to moves to decentralize personnel management. A parallel process is the partial privatization of public enterprises, such as Telekom. There has also been discussion of more radical changes in industrial relations: the reform of the *Beamte* law (or even the abolition of *Beamte* status) and the replacement of statutory regulation of public employment by free collective bargaining. Any such changes would pose fundamental challenges to the unions, which are already on the defensive.

Workplace Representation

In Switzerland there is a dual system of employee interest representation. The works committee (*Betriebskommission*) at company level is elected by all employees and is formally independent of the unions, as in Germany; but its powers are much more limited than in the German case. Except where union membership is particularly low, the unions normally win a majority of seats. There is an even weaker system of workplace representation in the public sector.

Co-determination is not a priority issue for the Swiss unions. Until recently there was no legal regulation of the system; in 1976, there were proposals for legislation to make works committees obligatory, but these were defeated in a referendum and the question was allowed to drop. Only with the discussions over Swiss participation in the EEA was the matter revived, and though EEA membership was rejected a Co-operation Act (*Mitwirkungsgesetz*) was approved in 1994. This authorizes the election of a co-operation committee in private firms with at least 50 employees, with rights to information and to co-determination over health and safety matters and in cases of takeover and mass redundancy.

Co-determination rights in the private sector are in part regulated by collective agreement: a third of those at sectoral level, and two-thirds of company agreements, provide for works committees (Stöckli 1990). Before the 1994 legislation, committees existed in about half of all workplaces with 50 or more employees (Jans 1991), but with considerable variation between sector. In a few sectors they play an important role: for example in engineering they have the right to negotiate over wages and working time. More generally, the decentralization of industrial relations is enhancing the importance of works committees. The most recent agreement in the chemical industry has introduced procedures similar to those in engineering for workplace wage determination, with an analogous arbitration system. However the predominance of small enterprises in Switzerland limits the scope for the spread of workplace bargaining; works committees scarcely exist in the small business sector, and this is unlikely to change.

Industrial Conflict

Swiss industrial relations are marked by institutionalized co-operation. A landmark was the 1937 agreement in the engineering and watch industry, which committed unions and employers to the peaceful resolution of disputes. This so-called peace agreement precluded any form of militant action and established a multi-stage conciliation procedure with the possibility of compulsory arbitration; it has remained in force ever since and has been elaborated over time. A strike wave in the 1940s resulted in the first collective contracts in other sectors, in most cases incorporating an absolute peace obligation during the currency of the GAV. This now applies to some two-thirds of all agreements, and is almost automatically renewed with each new agreement. In the 1970s and 1980s there was some discussion within the unions as to whether to remove the peace clause, but the employers insisted that it was a 'minimum requirement' of any bargaining relationship. Most agreements also provide for joint arbitration institutions.

In the public sector conflict is also restricted by a strike ban; the *Beamte* law at national level and in seven of the cantons explicitly prohibits strike action. Such a prohibition may more generally be derived from the 'trust obligation' of *Beamte*. Since the war, public sector unions have pursued a policy of consensual interest representation; rarely have they mobilized the rank and file or organized protest action.

The highly institutionalized regulatory system has virtually eliminated strikes in Switzerland. Industrial conflict is low even by comparison with other countries with co-operative industrial relations systems: in the 1980s there was an annual average of only 46 days lost per 100,000 employees, compared to 303 in Austria and 2,655 in Germany (Fluder 1996). Strike incidence fell in every decade from the 1940s to the 1980s. Industrial peace is encouraged by the consensual political culture, reflected by the participation of all main parties in the governing coalition. Economic growth was also important; in the post-war era of expanding production and tight labour markets the unions could win wage improvements without needing to strike. Rapid material improvement blunted distributional conflicts and encouraged societal integration.

In the 1990s a tougher bargaining environment has made conflicts more common. Recently there were several strikes in the public sector in Geneva canton. In 1996 the national government unions organized a large demonstration against wage cuts and deregulation. There have also been more strikes in the private sector. About 10,000 printing workers took part in protest strikes against a weakening of the GAV, in particular the elimination of supplementary payments, disrupting newspaper publication. There have also been strikes in the building industry. Nevertheless, such individual actions cannot be regarded as signs of a general increase in conflict or of a shift by unions to more militant strategies; co-operative relations between the social partners still predominate, reinforced by the integration of the professional representatives of each side in a network of policy-making institutions.

Conclusions

Swiss industrial relations are undergoing a minor upheaval. As indicated, there has been a certain increase in conflict, but in general there remains a strong commitment to find consensual solutions and corporatist institutions remain intact. In most areas the acceptance of social partnership remains.

There is a clear trend to the deregulation of wage determination. Yet in comparative terms the Swiss system of sectoral agreements is already very flexible, and the structure of the economy, with the predominance of small enterprises, sets limits to the decentralization of industrial relations. The room for compromise in wage bargaining is very narrow, and in some sectors there has been a reduction in real wages. The agenda of collective bargaining is embracing new issues such as vocational training, work organization and protections against technological unemployment.

Recession and higher unemployment have weakened the unions, and they are increasingly on the defensive. Their loss of membership has reduced their representative capacity, threatening the survival of a comprehensive system of employment regulation. There is a risk of a continuing erosion of the coverage of collective bargaining. To some extent there is a search for a new procedural compromise to allow union–employer co-operation to continue. The organizations on both sides are in a process of restructuring, involving concentration and the formation of new alliances. This is essential if they are to maintain and improve their effectiveness.

Abbreviations

ASM   *Arbeitgeberverband Schweizerischer Maschinen – und Metallindustrieller* – Swiss Metal and Engineering Employers' Association

CMV   *Christliche Gewerkschaft für Industrie, Handel und Dienste* – Christian Union for Industry, Trade and Services

CNG   *Christlich Nationaler Gewerkschaftsbund* – Christian National Trade Union Confederation

CVP   *Christlich Demokratische Volkspartei* – Christian Democratic People's Party

EAG   *Eidgenössisches Arbeitsgesetz* – Federal Employment Act

FDP   *Freisinnig-demokratische Partei* – Liberal Democratic Party

GAV   *Gesamtarbeitsvertrag* – collective agreement (contract)

GBH   *Gewerkschaft Bau und Holz* – Building and Woodworkers' Union

GBI   *Gewerkschaft Bau und Industrie* – Building and Industrial Union

LFSA   *Landesverband Freier Schweizer Arbeitnehmer* – National Association of Free Swiss Workers

SA   *Schweizerische Arbeitgeberverband* – Swiss Employers' Association (not an official abbreviation: until 1996 it was ZSAO)

SGB   *Schweizerischer Gewerkschaftsbund* – Swiss Trade Union Confederation

SGV   *Schweizerische Gewerbebeverband* – Swiss Small Business Association

SHIV *Schweizerischer Handels- und Industrieverein* – Swiss Federation of Commerce and Industry

SMUV *Schweizerischer Metall- und Uhrenarbeiterverband* – Swiss Metal and Watch Workers' Association

SPS *Sozialdemokratische Partei der Schweiz* – Swiss Social-democratic Party

SVP *Schweizerische Volkspartei* – Swiss People's Party

VSA *Vereinigung Schweizerischer Angestelltenverbände* – Federation of Swiss Trade Union Associations (white-collar)

ZSAO *Zentralverband Schweizerischer Arbeitgeber-Organisationen* – Central Association of Swiss Employers' Organizations

ZV *Zentralverband des Staats- und Gemeindepersonals* – Central Association of National and Local Government Staff

▌References and Further Reading

Alemann, Ulrich von (ed.) 1981: *Neokorporatismus*. Frankfurt: Campus.

Berenstein, A. 1994: *Labour Law in Switzerland*. Deventner: Kluwer.

BFS (Bundesamt für Statistik) 1995: *Statistisches Jahrbuch der Schweiz*, Bern: Erwerbsleben.

BFS 1997a: *Durée du travail et tarifs (salaires conventionnels) dans les conventions collectives de travail en vigueur en Suisse au 1er mai 1994.*

BFS 1997b: *Staitisches Jahrbuch der Schwein*. Bern: Erwersleben

Farago, P., and Kriesi, H. (eds) 1986: *Wirtschaftsverbände in der Schweiz. Organisation und Aktivitäten von Wirtschaftsverbänden in vier Sektoren der Industrie*. Grüsch: Rüegger.

Flanders, A. 1965: *Industrial Relations: what is wrong with the System?* London: Faber.

Fluder, R. 1990: Werden die Gewerkschaften vom Strukturwandel überrollt?. In: *Gewerkschaftliche Rundschau*, 82(5), 171–183.

Fluder, R. 1996: *Interessenorganisationen und kollektive Arbeitsbeziehungen im öffentlichen Dienst der Schweiz. Entstehung, Mitgliedschaft, Organisation und Politik seit 1940*. Zürich: Seismo.

Fluder, R. 1997: *Politik und Strategien der schweizerischen Arbeitnehmerorganisationen. Orientierung, Konfliktverhalten und politische Einbindung*. Zürich: Rüegger (forthcoming).

Fluder, R., Ruf, H., Schöni, W. and Wicki, M. 1991: *Gewerkschaften und Angestelltenverbände in der schweizerischen Privatwirtschaft. Entstehung, Mitgliedschaft, Organisation und Politik seit 1940*. Zürich: Seismo.

Halm, F. 1983: Entwicklung und Stärke der Sozialpartnerschaft. In: Thommen A.: *Profile der Arbeitgeberpolitik, Zentralverband schweizerischer Arbeitgeber-Organisation, 1908–1983*. Zürich 1983.

Hischier, G., Messerli-Rohrbach, V. and Zwicky H. 1989: *Die Wahrnehmung sozialer Ungleichheit in der Schweiz. Schlussbericht zu einem vom Schweizerischen Nationalfonds finanziell geförderten Forschungsprojekt.*

Höpflinger, F. 1976: *Industriegewerkschaften in der Schweiz. Eine soziologische Untersuchung*. Zürich: Limmat.

Hotz-Hart, B., Mäder, St. and Vock, P. 1996: *Volkswirtschaft der Schweiz*, Zürich: VdF.

Jans, A. 1991: Die Mitbestimmung in der Schweiz und die europäische Herausforderung. *Gewerkschaftliche Rundschau*, 83(3, 4), 58–107.

Katzenstein, P.J. 1984: *Corporatism and Change. Austria, Switzerland and the Politics of Industry*. Ithaca: Cornell University Press.

Keller, B. 1983: *Arbeitsbeziehungen im öffentlichen Dienst. Tarifpolitik der Gewerkschaften und Interessenpolitik der Beamtenverbände*. Frankfurt am Main: Campus.

Kerr, H.H. 1987: The Swiss party system: Steadfast and changing. In: Daalder, H. et al. (eds): *Party Systems in Denmark, Austria, Switzerland, the Netherlands and Belgium*. London: Frances Pinter, 107–192.

Linder, W. 1983: Entstehung, Strukturen und Funktionen des Wirtschafts- und Sozialstaates in der Schweiz. In: Riklin, A. (Hg.): *Handbuch Politisches System der Schweiz*, Vol. 1, 255–382. Bern: Haupt.

Lopreno, D. 1995: Gesamtarbeitsverträge (GAV) in der Schweiz 1994. *Die Volkswirtschaft*, 68(10), 62–68.

Naumann, J. 1984: *Der Einfluss von Interessengruppen auf die wirtschaftspolitische Willensbildung. Eine Untersuchung (nicht nur) für die Schweiz*. Zürich: Diss.

OECD 1991: *Employment Outlook 1991*. Chapter 4: Trends in Trade Union Membership, 97–134. Paris.

Offe, C. and Wiesenthal, H. 1980: Two logics of collective action. Theoretical notes on social class and organizational form. In: Zeitlin, M. (ed.): *Political Power and Social Theory*, 1, 67–115. Greenwich: Jai Press.

Parri, L. 1987: Neo-corporatist arrangements, 'Konkoranz' and direct democracy: the Swiss experience. In: Scholten, Ilja: *Political Stability and Neo-Corporatism*, 70–94.

Richli, P. 1996: *Öffentliches Dienstrecht im Zeichen des New Public Management: Staatsrechtliche Fixpunkte für die Flexibilisierung und Dynamisierung des Beamtenverhältnisses*.

Schmidt, M.-G. 1985: *Der schweizerische Weg zur Vollbeschäftigung*. Frankfurt: Campus.

Schmitter, P.C. 1981: Neokorporatismus: Überlegungen zur bisherigen Theorie und zur weiteren Praxis. In: Alemann, U. von (ed.): *Neokorporatismus*, 62–79. Frankfurt: Campus.

Steiner, J. 1970: *Gewaltlose Politik und kulturelle Vielfalt*. Bern: Haupt.

Stöckli, J.-F. 1990: *Der Inhalt des Gesamtarbeitsvertrages*. Bern: Stämpfli.

Traxler, F. 1995: Entwicklungstendenzen in den Arbeitsbeziehungen Westeuropas. Auf dem Weg zur Konvergenz?. In: M. Mesch: *Sozialpartnerschaft und Arbeitsbeziehungen in Europa*, 231–256.

Visser, J. 1989: *European Trade Unions in Figures. 1913–1985*. Denver/ Boston: Kluwer.

10 | The Netherlands: The Return of Responsive Corporatism

JELLE VISSER

Introduction

In my contribution to the first edition of this book I provided considerable historical background. On this occasion I omit this, in order to focus on recent developments. However, three key features of the past must certainly be mentioned. First, Dutch society was traditionally marked by a sharp differentiation between catholic, protestant and socialist 'pillars', all with their own associated political parties, trade unions (and in some cases employers' organizations) and social welfare funds. This system of 'pillarization' (*verzuiling*) was paradoxically a source of social cohesion: first because it prevented any simple polarization between capital and labour; but second, because the organized status of the different 'pillars' made a system of institutionalized compromises almost unavoidable. This was particularly evident in industrial relations and was epitomized by the creation of the Social-Economic Council (SER) in 1950. Second, the negotiation of interests in the industrial relations system established after the war was highly centralized and, third, it involved the state as a key actor. In particular, until 1982 there was strong state control of wage settlements.

Five years ago I chose the subtitle 'The end of an era and the end of a system'. My thesis was that Dutch industrial relations had changed substantially under the impact of such external pressures as the two oil shocks of the 1970s, intensified international competition and European integration. Unemployment, reform of social security, reduction of government spending, and moderation of wage costs had become the dominant issues. A contrast with earlier decades was also found in organizational behaviour and institutions: the 1980s had been marked by a decline in union membership and militancy, a more aggressive stance by employers, a disengagement of governments from corporatist governance, and a decline in the prestige and efficacy of tripartism as embodied in the SER.

My hypothesis was that growing international interdependence had narrowed the role of the state, reduced the effectiveness of national policies, and eroded though not erased the distinctive character of national systems of labour relations. It would be increasingly difficult to return to the type of 'responsive corporatism'

(Hemerijck 1995) which, in the Netherlands, had reached its pinnacle in the 1940s and 1950s. Classic societal corporatism, as I called it, had rested on a cross-class coalition of broadly representative organizations which had enabled the state to implement a successful policy of industrialization, based on low wages, and laying the foundations for the expansion of comprehensive social security (Visser 1990). This policy, and the coalition on which it rested, were destroyed by their own success: by the internationalization and concentration of the Dutch economy that were promoted coupled with the increased security and assertiveness of Dutch workers. Increased demands for participation in organizations and society, a decline in the autonomy and efficacy of the state, fragmentation and polarization of interests, and changes in the technology and organization of work had undermined the foundations and rationality of a centralized labour relations model. In the deep recession of the early 1980s, after a transitional decade of 'immobile corporatism' (Hemerijck 1995), 'concertation without consensus' (Zimmermann 1986) and 'income maintenance instead of jobs' (Braun 1988), the old order was disintegrating.

I was half wrong. All these changes did occur, yet corporatism has persisted and – I shall argue – returned to its responsive mode, based on 'concertation with consensus' and 'jobs before income'. An era did end but the system survived. It had been received political wisdom that sound economic policies were only politically feasible if socially acceptable, in other words if accommodated with the unions; but after 1982 the new centre–right coalition adopted a 'no nonsense' policy of reducing public spending and social security reform. The door was kept open for dialogue with the unions though the government made sure that they left empty-handed. Many firms went through a process of restructuring in which jobs were shed and labour costs reduced, yet business leaders understood that there was no need to add insult to injury: there was no significant employer initiative towards a union-free economy. Unions had no need to feel threatened in their institutional role, even though weakened, with membership under 25 per cent of all wage and salary earners in employment, and a fifth of all members on benefits. My thesis is that *the sharp curtailment of union bargaining power within an institutional and political context of unquestioned legitimacy and continued organizational security has helped the unions to adapt and re-focus their objectives towards moderation.* They have accommodated to 'hard times' (Gourevitch 1986) and the new wisdom that social policies are only politically feasible if they produce acceptable economic outcomes.

The three 'mainstays' which Windmuller (1969: 432–3) had identified in his classic study of Dutch industrial relations – a strong reliance on organized consultation, a high degree of centralization within interest organizations, and a primary role for the state in shaping social and economic policies – are recognizable still. On each of these dimensions the Netherlands is today less an exception, but still differs substantially from the major countries of Europe (van Ruysseveldt and Visser 1996). Under the influence of challenges from without (globalization, the Single European Market, Maastricht and EMU) and within (demographic and industrial change, unemployment, environmental depletion and urban congestion), the need for national policy co-ordination appears to have increased, encouraging a new version of responsive corporatism.

In this chapter I concentrate on organizational behaviour, wage moderation, collective bargaining, and the role of corporatist institutions. On the basis of various new studies I shall try to show how Dutch industrial relations have changed and how the system works. In this connection I deal briefly with labour market developments, social security and labour market reform. First, I outline the main economic and social developments in the 1980s and 1990s, then I relate these to policies and policy changes in the past 15 years. The third section discusses the organized actors, their resources, interests and preferences, and is followed by an analysis of collective bargaining, consultation and co-ordination. In the fifth and final part, the performance of Dutch industrial relations is evaluated.

❙ From Crisis to Relative Success

The Netherlands was hard hit by the second oil crisis of 1979–80, suffering its worst post-war recession. In 1981 and 1982, national income declined and the investment rate, which had already been falling in the 1970s, slumped further. Unemployment rose to a record 800,000 in 1984, more than 13 per cent of the labour force. Unions lost one in six of their members and density fell more than ten percentage points to just 25 per cent. Real wages fell by 9 per cent between 1980 and 1985, minimum wages even more. A rising public deficit, to over 8 per cent in 1982, provoked sharp austerity measures including cuts in social benefits.

There was a strong recovery after 1983, mainly thanks to the improvement of the competitive position of Dutch industry and services in an international economy which moved out of recession. Wage moderation and labour-shedding caused a sharp fall in unit labour costs, which have remained among the lowest in north-western Europe – even though the Dutch guilder has been appreciating in parallel with the German mark, to which it has been pegged since 1983 (OECD 1996; SZW 1996). Profits and investment recovered, inflation virtually disappeared. The budget deficit has been reduced, to 6 per cent of GDP in the second half of the 1980s and a mere 1.9 per cent in 1996, well within the EMU convergence criteria. At long last, the total public debt has begun to fall, to 76.2 per cent of GDP in 1996. One million new jobs have been added to the five million that existed in the mid-1980s (table 10.1). This equals an annual average growth of 1.8 per cent between 1985 and 1995, compared with 0.4 per cent in the EU and 1.5 per cent in the US. Union membership stabilized and then increased and density edged up to about 29 per cent in 1995.

Unemployment has fallen at a snail's pace. Comparison over time is hampered by changes in the basis of the official count; but a recalculation on the basis of OECD standardized rates shows that peak-to-peak unemployment in the recession years of 1983 and 1994 decreased from 11.2 to 7.6 per cent of the labour force. The 1990s recession was comparatively mild and the recovery has been strong,

Table 10.1 The labour market in 1985 and 1995

	1985		1995		
	(000)	%	(000)	%	Basis
1 Population of working age (15–64)	9,777	100.0	10,498	100	
2 Labour force	5,867	60.0	6,596	62.8	2 : 1
2a paid employment (employment ratio)	5,185	52.2	6,132	58.4	2a : 1
2b of which: part-time (under 35 hours)	1,233	23.8	2,140	34.9	2b : 2a
2c unemployment (unemployment rate)	682	11.6	464	7.0	2c : 1
3 Broad labour force (2a+4+5)	6,904	70.6	8,039	76.8	3 : 1
4 broad unemployment (a+b+c)*	1,639	23.7	1,722	21.4	4 : 3
4a unemployment (benefits)	761	11.0	789	9.8	4a : 3
4b social assistance	180	2.6	164	2.0	4b : 3
4c disability	698	10.1	769	9.6	4c : 3
5 Subsidized employment	80	1.5	185	3.0	5 : 2a
6 Not in paid employment (1−2a−5)	4,512	46.1	4,181	39.8	6 : 1
6a enrolled in day schools (15–64)	1,228	26.8	1,150	27.5	6a : 6
6b broad unemployment (see 4)	1,639	35.7	1,722	41.2	6b : 6
6c other and unpaid work (without benefits)	1,724	37.6	1,309	31.3	6c : 6

Source: own calculations from CBS, OSA and OECD data.
* In contrast to OECD calculations 'subsidised employment' (5) is not included in broad unemployment.

especially in employment terms. The current government pledged 350,000 new jobs during its term of office (1994–98), a target which will be met at least 1 year in advance. However, like most EU countries, the Netherlands has a severe problem of long-term unemployment (Layard et al. 1991); since 1984, around half of all unemployed people have remained jobless 1 year or longer, one fifth for 3 years or longer.

Most new jobs have gone to new labour market entrants with modern skills; between 1983 and 1990 fewer than 100,000 of the 700,000 newly created jobs went to benefit recipients. Labour force growth has been stronger than in most European countries, 1.5 per cent per year as against 0.5 per cent in the EU. Birth rates declined later, the overall population is relatively young (second only to Ireland) and the population of working age (15–64 years) is still growing. Women seek paid employment in far greater numbers than in the past: the participation rate has risen from only 35 per cent in 1975 to 52 per cent in 1985 and 60 per cent today, though this is still much lower than in Scandinavian and Anglo-Saxon countries.

Job creation has largely reflected the expansion of part-time work, from under 15 per cent of total employment in 1975 to 35 per cent in 1995, by far the highest proportion in the EU. Three out of four part-time jobs are held by women: only 15 per cent of all males work part-time, against 63 per cent of females. Part-time jobs are concentrated in few sectors such as retail, catering, cleaning, nursing and teaching, and cluster at the low end of the pay and skill distribution (Vermeulen and Bosselaar 1996). A minority of part-time workers would prefer to find full-time jobs (OECD 1996: 45). Preferences among both men and women incline towards jobs of between 2½ and 4 working days (OSA 1993: 16–9); a union-survey in 1993 revealed the rising popularity of the '1½ job model' among (younger) working couples, both with and without children (Pelzer and Van den Putte, 1993). This shift may be related to the pressures of 'lean production' – employee surveys show that more than half of all employees complain of the increased 'intensity and speed of work' (SCP 1994) – making it difficult to combine full-time employment with family responsibilities.

The participation rate of older workers has declined: between 1980 and 1992 the rate for men between 55 and 64 years fell from 54 to 38 per cent. Broad unemployment, which includes those who are not available for at least 12 hours a week, beneficiaries of disability and early retirement pensions and people on social assistance, went up from 7 per cent in 1970 to 17 per cent in 1980, soared to 24 per cent in 1985 and is still around 21 per cent today (table 10.1). Many of those laid off in the 1980–83 slump never found their way back into employment.

▌ Three Policy Shifts

The first key shift has been wage moderation, which resumed in the early 1980s and has continued, almost without interruption, for 15 years. The second is the reform of the social security system, which began in 1987 with the overhaul of unemployment insurance. The third is the adoption after 1990 of an 'active employment policy' combining tax rebates and employment subsidies, the creation of jobs in the public sector, the removal of 'disincentive effects' from social security, derogations from the legal minimum wage and the creation of lower 'entry' wages. There have also been moves towards privatization, deregulation and reform of the public employment services and vocational training.

All major political parties share responsibility for these painful policy reversals. Between 1982 and 1989 the Christian Democratic Party (CDA) under Ruud Lubbers was in office with the Liberal Party (VVD). Unlike previous centre–right coalitions this government no longer believed in incomes policies or striking deals with the unions, and saw reduced public spending and improved business profitability as the means of job creation. This was a true austerity coalition and for the first time deficit reduction gained primacy over full employment. After the general election of 1989 the CDA formed a coalition with the Labour Party (PvdA), which had been in almost continuous opposition since 1977. The PvdA then became jointly responsible for major cuts in the welfare state, in particular sickness and disability benefits; it almost split in the process and both government parties lost votes in the 1994 general elections. The CDA lost its position as largest party to the PvdA, allowing Wim Kok, a former union leader and Finance Minister in the previous government, to form a coalition with the Liberal Party (VVD) and the Democrats (D66), both of whom had made strong electoral gains. This Lib–Lab government is the first without a Christian party since 1918.

Wage Moderation

Between 1982 and 1997, wage determination has been the sole responsibility of employers and unions, in contrast to the practice since 1945; but the absence of statutory intervention does not mean that no 'shadow of hierarchy' (Scharpf 1993) fell over the bargaining table. The government retained instruments to influence bargaining outcomes; these are discussed in a later section.

The Accord of Wassenaar, reached in November 1982 between the central organizations of unions and employers, initiated *voluntary* wage moderation. Though real wages had already been frozen by *statutory* restraint in 1980 and 1981 (and possibly as an effect of the decline in union bargaining power), the significance of the Accord can hardly be underestimated. More than union resignation to economic hard times, it marked the victory of the moderate faction within the Dutch Federation of Trade Unions (FNV), the leading union confederation. Four years earlier, the General Industrial Union (IB), FNV's main affiliate in industry, suddenly abandoned its goal of redistributing income and power in favour of workers and adopted a 'jobs first' policy. More than any other union the IB had experienced loss of jobs and membership; between 1976 and 1986 it lost a third of its members, while a quarter of those remaining were on benefits.

In 1979, the IB had gained the support of the FNV, led by Kok, but was frustrated by the opposition of other FNV affiliates. The sharp and seemingly unstoppable rise in unemployment soon brought a change of mood. At first the central employers' federations had little enthusiasm for a central agreement; union bargaining power was no longer a problem and they opposed the reduction in working hours which the unions sought as part of a deal. They changed their mind when the new Dutch government threatened to copy the French or Belgian example and impose a general reduction of working hours as compensation for wage restraint.

In the 1982 Accord, the central organizations recommended sectoral and company negotiators to repeal cost-of-living escalator clauses in existing collective agreements and to negotiate working time reductions in an effort to reduce unemployment and improve profitability. In consequence escalator clauses, widely introduced in the 1960s, disappeared almost overnight and real wages and wage costs fell sharply; while a 5 per cent annual working time reduction, from 40 to 38 hours per week on average, was implemented between 1983 and 1986, mainly through extra holidays. In turn the Accord helped the new centre–right government to present its curbs on public sector pay and social benefits as a fair spreading of the burden.

After 1986, the movement towards shorter working time stalled. Between 1983 and 1986, working time reduction had taken place in the context of massive labour-shedding and may have saved some existing jobs, although it is hard to quantify the effect (de Lange 1989). Most workers experienced lower real wages and an increased pace of work; unemployment remained high and social security was lowered. The unions needed a success. When the economy moved out of recession they geared up for another general round of working time reduction in

Table 10.2 Percentage change of nominal wage rates in collective agreements

Years when agreements applied	Annual basis*	Level basis**	RPI
1988		0.8	0.5
1989		2.0	1.1
1990		3.5	2.5
1991		3.5	3.1
1992	4.3	4.4	3.2
1993	3.1	2.9	2.6
before 'breathing space'	*5.1*	*4.6*	
after 'breathing space'	*2.6*	*2.2*	
1994	1.5	0.8	2.7
before 'New Course'		*1.1*	
after 'New Course'		*0.5*	
1995	1.3	1.4	2.0
1996	1.6	1.8	2.4

Source: Ministry of Social Affairs and Employment; data recalculated by Dr W. Salverda.
 * change between years, taking into account the date when provisions in agreements take effect.
** change between agreements on annual basis, regardless of the date when provisions take effect.

order to create new jobs, but employers declared a reduction under 38 hours 'off limits'. Instead, they favoured flexibility and part-time employment. The unions were divided, and by the end of the decade the campaign for shorter working hours was dead and the will to continue wage restraint seemed exhausted (Visser 1989). The international economic boom between 1988 and 1991 encouraged the unions to raise their aspirations: membership growth helped them to regain confidence, even if density hardly increased. With non-affiliated unions and the federations of senior staff now focusing solely on higher wages, the mainstream unions were anxious to avoid being caught out.

A small wage rise was achieved but the party was over almost before it began. A number of major firms (such as Philips, Fokker and Daf) experienced serious difficulties and employment in manufacturing fell by 100,000, or 10 per cent, between 1992 and 1994. The government called for a 'breathing space' during which the 'new facts' of international recession could be absorbed, and, in late 1992, the unions allowed their central organizations to sign a two-month standstill on wage negotiations. Employers began a campaign for zero wage increases, most leading unions lowered their demands and many negotiated multi-year agreements in which nominal wage increases did not keep pace with price inflation (table 10.2). In late 1993 the return to wage moderation was confirmed in another central accord, the 'New Course', involving a more decentralized and less standardized model of implementing central guidelines. The impact of this Accord has been no less than that of the Wassenaar Accord 10 years earlier. Unit labour costs fell by 6 per cent in 1994, the largest single fall in 15 years.

In the 'New Course' the employers lifted their veto against a further reduction in working hours, and working time reappeared on the bargaining agenda in 1996. In a number of sectors and companies – banking, department stores, education and hospitals, Post Office, Akzo–Nobel, Unilever – experiments with shorter working hours have started, introducing corridors of 32–40 hours, relaxing constraints on unsocial hours and introducing lower overtime rates or compensation by time off rather than extra pay. In other companies and sectors – Philips, engineering, catering – employers still refuse to negotiate over shorter hours. About half of all full-time employees now have an average contractual working week of 36 hours; the unions expect that others will have moved there by the year 2000. They do not plan further reductions but now concentrate on qualitative issues, in particular training, parental leave, sabbaticals and employability.

Social Security Reform

The Netherlands spends 32 per cent of GDP on social security, fourth after Sweden, Finland and Denmark. In spite of various measures to curtail costs, this position has hardly changed since 1982 when *The Economist* (30 January 1982) wrote that 'if somewhere must be found to ride out the recession, Holland must be the nicest, comfiest place to choose'.

Measures to reduce costs first concentrated on benefit levels but later attacked the rising volume of benefits. The legal minimum wage introduced in 1969 serves as a benchmark for social benefits (such as old age pensions, disability provisions, unemployment relief or assistance). The lowest level of any benefit was set at 70 per cent of the minimum wage, the social minimum below which no citizen is supposed to fall; the level moved up to 100 per cent for those supporting families. The minimum wage was once high by international standards, since it was introduced when employment of married women was still exceptional and was thus intended to ensure a 'family wage'. From 1974, minimum wages and social benefits were linked to private sector wage increases, but this linkage was suspended in 1983; the minimum wage and benefits were cut by 3 per cent in 1984 and remained frozen until 1990 after the Labour Party joined the government.

The restoration of linkage brought renewed cost problems and calls to reintroduce statutory restraint in order to pay for solidarity between earnings and benefits. As a way out, the coalition agreed in 1992 that the legal minimum wage and related statutory social benefits should follow net real wage increases only if the latter did not exceed the anticipated growth of GDP and the number of claimants did not increase relative to the total population. The two criteria have since been combined in a sophisticated formula which presents the unions with a clear norm for wage demands. In 1993, 1994 and 1995, the government froze the legal minimum wage and benefit incomes, since the threshold was exceeded. The legal minimum wage has decreased from 63 per cent of the average wage of an adult worker to 51 per cent. It is estimated that between 4 and 11 per cent of Dutch families face dire economic conditions, 26,000 households with outright poverty (SCP 1994), and poverty has re-entered the political agenda.

In 1987 the unemployment benefit system was reformed by reducing benefit levels and tightening eligibility, at the same time removing the male (breadwinner) bias. From 1987 unemployment insurance benefits were cut from 80 per cent of last earnings to 70 per cent, falling to 70 per cent of the net minimum wage once entitlement to earnings-related benefit is exhausted.

When in 1967 a general disability insurance was introduced, it was predicted that a maximum of 200,000 people would claim benefits; but, in 1980, 660,000 and in the early 1990s, nearly 900,000 people (one-sixth of the labour force) received a full or partial disability benefit. These allowances were used on a much wider scale than in other countries, in effect to divert redundant workers from overt unemployment. This was attractive to workers (who received more generous allowances than the unemployment benefits until retirement age and did not have to be available for work) and to employers (who avoided worker resistance to restructuring and layoffs while the costs were borne by the state). In 1991 the government, horrified at the prospect of a million claimants, announced a major overhaul of the scheme including financial disincentives to employers, a reduction in benefits and more stringent controls on access. New claimants and those under 50 years of age receive lower benefits, must undergo regular medical examination, and are obliged to accept suitable jobs even at lower levels of pay. The system has been opened to private insurers, with some differentiation of premium payments between sectors or firms with high or low disability track records, and the possibility to opt out from collective schemes. Similar ideas are now being floated with respect to unemployment insurance.

The reduction in the legal minimum entitlement to less than 70 per cent of previous earnings had little impact on actual benefits, since almost all collective agreements provide for supplements to compensate; in the 1993 bargaining round employers contributed 0.6 and workers 1.4 per cent of the total wage bill. In 1993–95 this issue, together with the employers' attack on early retirement, dominated the agenda, causing the largest post-war strike in construction (Van der Meer 1996). The government insists that financing social benefits is now part of the bargaining agenda, giving both workers and employers an incentive to prevent abuse. Unions observe that their 'bargaining space' has once again narrowed and deplore the fact that they are forced to 'repair' ever more elements of the welfare state that once were taken for granted (Rojer 1996a). It is too early to evaluate the effects of the reform. The total number of beneficiaries has decreased from a peak of 925,000 in 1994 to 841,000 in 1995. Roughly half the claimants under 35 years of age who are re-examined are now disqualified or have their benefit reduced. A new problem is the lack of jobs for those who lose their benefits. This is closely related to current debate on the creation of low-paid employment.

The reform of sickness leave was implemented in two steps in 1994 and 1996, with remarkably little ado. The first change is that employers rather than sectoral funds must pay for the first six weeks of sickness leave (two in the case of small enterprises); this has apparently caused a drop in sickness absence. From 1996 the employer must pay a full year of sickness leave (the maximum duration before disability applies). There are already signs that health has become an issue in hiring decisions and that people with health problems are disadvantaged, though a new law makes it illegal for employers to ask health-related questions during job applications. Helped by the Work Environment Act, which was phased in between 1983 and 1990, health and safety at the workplace and prevention of sickness have become more prominent issues, but the current movement from rules to financial incentives as a way to control behaviour smacks of short-termism.

▌Active Employment Policies

Esping-Andersen (1990) classifies the Netherlands as a compensatory, transfer-based welfare state. In later work he argues that such regimes are easily trapped in a vicious circle of 'welfare without work': increases in labour productivity through continuous labour-shedding causing low participation rates among women, the young, older persons, and less productive workers; the high social costs which subsequently lead to high employer and employee contributions and depress net earnings. Paradoxically then, 'soft' welfare state regimes (Therborn 1986) tend to create a class of 'secondary' citizens without access to paid jobs.

In the 1990s, the problem of how to break this vicious circle has dominated the Dutch political agenda. Wage moderation cannot be the only solution, nor can it be sustained forever. Continued cutbacks in the welfare state will inevitably bring more people near the poverty line. The government's council for policy research advocated radical action to get people off benefits and into jobs (WRR 1990). It identified the low participation rate as the Achilles' heel of the Dutch welfare state and proposed a 30 per cent cut in the legal minimum wage as a means to stop the disappearance of 'simple' jobs. Despite its controversial recommendations, the report had a lasting influence.

The current Lib–Lab government has adopted 'more jobs' as its prime objective and sees deregulation as a means to encourage more economic activity, including self-employment and small firms. It has relaxed administrative restrictions on business and in 1996 adopted a Working Time Act which liberalized opening and business hours. Employers' taxes and social contributions have been reduced in order to decrease wage costs, and the government has pressed unions and employers to negotiate lower entry wages at or just above the legal minimum for inexperienced and unskilled workers.

The rationale is that wage levels are reducing employment opportunities for the less qualified. The proportion of adult workers earning the legal minimum has declined from 10 per cent in 1983 to under 3 per cent in 1995, concentrated in sectors like cleaning, hotels and catering, and personal services. The gap between the lowest rates in collective agreements and the legal minimum wage rose from 6.5 to 13.5 per cent between 1988 and 1994, but has since decreased to 8.3 per cent. The 'gap' is found mainly in industry and scarcely exists in the service sector. The widening from 1992 to 1994 coincided with the freezing of the legal minimum; in 1996 the legal minimum wage rose with average real wages. Unions have been persuaded by government pressure to introduce lower entry wages; in 1995 two-thirds of all agreements, applying to one-third of all workers, had made such changes; in particular the building industry, in which the lowest rate was

25–30 per cent above the legal minimum, has a new scale for entrants at 6 per cent above the minimum. However the lower scales need not be applied at company level; research suggests that in 1995 only 16 per cent of establishments actually used the lower scales; though incidence is higher (35 per cent) in low-skilled workplaces.

The Liberal Party has not abandoned the idea that a lower legal minimum will produce more jobs, although most economists argue that the effect would at best be very small. The Cabinet reached a compromise in January 1997, allowing a temporary one-year rate 30 per cent under the legal minimum for workers without family obligations, if offered work experience which improves the prospects of a job that pays the full minimum. The compromise has been rejected by Parliament

The scope of the various special 'employment programmes' has doubled in the decade up to 1992 to cover 3 per cent of all employees (see table 10.1). This has reduced the passive bias in Dutch labour market policies: the proportion of expenditure devoted to 'passive' measures (income maintenance) has fallen from 95 to 66 per cent, compared to 80 per cent in Austria, 50 per cent in Norway and only 20 per cent in Sweden (Allaart 1988; Hasluck 1995). There are 85,000 partly subsidized jobs in 'sheltered workplaces' for handicapped workers, another 22,000 are on waiting lists. A total of 21,500 people work in subsidized 'labour pools' in the public sector, introduced in 1990 for long-term unemployed with few opportunities in the regular labour market. The 'youth work guarantee plan' started in 1992, after experiments from 1988, and offers 22,000 work experience places to unemployed young people with the objective of a transition to permanent jobs.

These programmes are very costly and not very successful; they reach only the best placed within the target groups and few move on to regular jobs. Wages cannot be higher than 120 per cent of the legal minimum (which decreases steeply with age for people under 23 years), and jobs for young people have a maximum of 32 hours. In 1990 and again in 1995 the central employers' and union organizations pledged 60,000 additional jobs in order to raise the employment share of ethnic minorities, among whom the employment ratio (44 per cent) is far below the national average (60 per cent), while the unemployment rate is three times as high (20 per cent) (CBS 1995). Only half of all firms (mostly larger ones) employ non-native workers, whose share in the total labour force has risen to 11 per cent (CBS 1995).

Three new employment programmes target the long-term unemployed. In 1994 a start was made by creating 40,000 'simple' jobs in the public sector, aimed at meeting social needs in hospitals, homes for the elderly, child care centres and environmental protection. In a second programme which is to provide 20,000 jobs in the private sector; the government will pay the difference between actual wages and wage costs in the first year, if the employer pledges to continue employment thereafter. A third programme allows social security funds to be used for job creation.

Unions and Employers: Organization, Membership and Policy Preferences

Trade Unions

Dutch workers are not highly unionized: density was 29 per cent in 1995. Yet survey research (Klandermans and Visser 1995: 60–61) shows that most workers, both members and non-members, feel that unions make a valuable contribution. Seventy-five per cent agree that unions 'are necessary institutions for the protection of collective employee interests', only 5 per cent that they 'no longer have a function in a modern welfare state'. A majority thinks that unions should service all workers, not just their members (and most union members agree), and considers that unions do indeed 'take sufficient account of the interests of all workers'. Research 30 years ago, when Dutch society was marked by rigid 'pillarization', found that there was often pressure from colleagues, friends and family to join the union attached to one's 'pillar'. Today, *verzuiling* is weaker and so are the social pressures towards membership, while many recruits consider trade unions in instrumental terms, expecting individual services (Klandermans and Visser 1995: 76–7; Van de Vall 1963: 135).

Dutch unions have no tradition of delivering membership services in or near the workplace, which may be a major reason why their losses in the early 1980s were more severe than in comparable small countries with strong corporatist institutions (Hancké 1993; Ebbinghaus and Visser 1996). Although they play a large, but in recent years reduced role in social security boards, with minor exceptions they do not influence who gets benefits. Hence their involvement in social security administration is not an incentive to membership (in contrast to the situation in Belgium, Denmark or Sweden). Before 1940, Dutch unions did offer subsidized unemployment insurance, and membership increased with rising unemployment, but in the post-war era the relationship is negative (Van den Berg 1996). Currently, some unions are reintroducing social insurance packages for members to compensate in part for the reduced coverage and benefits in public schemes.

In the 1960s, the unions tried to obtain financial compensation for the fact that they negotiated on behalf of all employees, but compulsory membership or special levies on non-members were ruled out. Yet employers recognize that unions do provide a 'collective good' and suffer from 'free riding'; and most companies pay a financial contribution to unions which sign the collective agreement. An annual contribution of 10 guilders per member was introduced in the late 1960s and represented at the time between 10 and 15 per cent of union revenue, in some unions more. It is not possible to get an exact figure for today, but some unions would find it hard to do without this subsidy.

Table 10.3, an overview of union density data, shows that Dutch unions mainly represent full-time workers with standard contracts and are under-represented among women, young people and non-native workers. The gender difference correlates strongly with the uneven distribution of part-time employment. Those

Table 10.3   Union membership in 1995–6

Membership		Proportion (%)	Density (%)
All*	employed only	100	29
Sex*	male	77	34
	female	23	20
Age group*	15–24 years	8	15
	25–44 years	55	28
	45–64 years	37	40
Nationality*	native	94	29
	non-native	6	21
Working time*	35 hours and more	81	31
	20–34 hours	16	23
	12–19 hours	3	13
Employment contract*	standard	95	31
	flexible	5	11
Duration of employment*	long (≥5 years)	90	31
	short (<5 years)	6	13
	unknown	4	–
Sector**	manufacturing and utilities	23	32
	construction	9	43
	trade, retail and hotels, etc.	6	13
	transport and communication	10	42
	financial services	5	15
	other private services	3	5
	public administration	18	37
	education	10	39
	health	9	21
Firm size*	1–9	5	15
	10–99	23	24
	≥100	67	32
	unknown	5	–
Representation*** (private sector only)	works council	75	36
	no works council	25	18

* Spring 1996.
** 1995.
*** 1993.
Source: CBS labour force sample survey (unpublished results); of Klandermans and Visser 1995; van Rij 1997.

who work fewer than 12 hours a week (mainly women in retail and personal services) are almost completely non-unionized; in the 12–20 hours group (again mainly women) only one in eight joins a union. Density is only 15 per cent among those younger than 25 (compared to 25 per cent 15 years ago) and there is a high turnover rate: one in every three young recruits leaves the union within 2 years.

This is related to the spread of non-standard employment: in 1996 one half of new jobs were temporary or part-time. Among workers with a flexible contract the density rate in 1996 was 12 per cent, compared to 31 per cent for those with standard contracts. These developments pose a dilemma to the unions. Half of all employees (mainly males in full-time jobs who are sole breadwinners) stay more than 10 years with the same employer, and these are the unions' core constituency; but new employees, both men and women, start increasingly in temporary jobs and work less than full-time.

In the past decade, unions have tried to move away from a defensive position based on the interests of current members, surveying the characteristics and interests of workers who do *not* join and developing a more welcoming attitude towards women and those with part-time jobs and flexible working hours. They have adopted a goal of 'normalization of part-time employment', signing a 'joint opinion' with employers on improved rights for part-time workers in 1989. The same approach is applied to another Dutch speciality, agency work, which meets the flexibility needs of both employers and (particularly young) employees. Calculated in full-time equivalents, almost 150,000 employees or 3 per cent of the labour force now have such jobs. In 1996, the employers signed the first collective agreement for such workers, introducing a right of continued employment and pension insurance after 24 months of service. This led to an innovative central agreement on 'Flexibility and Security' in May 1996, paving the way for an overhaul of Dutch dismissal protection law. It is a compromise, not just between employers and unions, but also within the unions between workers with and without stable jobs, since statutory dismissal protection for regular employment has been relaxed in exchange for an improvement in the rights of temporary workers. Another example of the pragmatism with which Dutch unions currently approach the flexibility issue is an agreement in the biscuit industry providing that redundant workers will be hired by *Randstad*, the largest temporary work agency, which will train them and find new employment, preferably in the same industry.

Sectoral data show that unions are weak in private services, which currently represents 60 per cent of total employment, but are well-represented in public transport (trams and railways), communications (the now privatized PTT), public administration and public education. In banking, union density has risen from less than 10 to 25 per cent in 5 years, but organization in other financial, business, commercial and personal services is extremely weak (under 5 per cent). Perhaps surprisingly, Dutch unions are also weak in manufacturing; density is below 30 per cent in all branches except utilities (gas, water and electricity), printing (where technological and organization changes are undermining the closed shop for production workers) and building materials. The decline of unionization in engineering to 25 per cent is connected with a shift in employment from large to small firms and a growth in outsourcing; more than one-third of all Dutch private-sector employees now work in establishments with fewer than 50 employees.

Organizing requires new techniques of direct communication and expensive regional support structures, a reason why unions are now keen to merge. The works council, mandatory in firms with 35 or more employees (see below), can help; but in small firms the law is often disregarded. It appears that in every size group, union density is higher where there is a works council.

Weak in membership, Dutch unions are also divided. In January 1996 there were four federations: the Federation of Dutch Trade Unions (FNV) with 1,165,508 members; the Christian-National Union Federation (CNV) with 348,418, the Federation of White-Collar and Senior Staff (VHP) with 160,560, and the General Union Federation (AVC) with 104,885. Unaffiliated unions had an estimated membership of 110,300. About 350,000 members (18.5 per cent) were on benefits (including retirement). The FNV, with 58 per cent of total union membership, is numerically predominant. In 1997 or 1998 some AVC affiliates, representing 50,000 members in teaching and public services, will join the FNV while other occupational unions with members in central government, railways, road and air transport, nursing, financial services and engineering will form a new 'autonomous' federation. FNV, CNV, VHP and – since 1993 – AVC are represented in the major corporatist institutions. FNV, CNV and – since 1990 – VHP are members of the European Trade Union Confederation; the FNV is a member of the ICFTU and the CNV of the WCL.

Currently FNV has 19 affiliates and CNV 15, but mergers are in the offing. The dominant organizing principle is sectoral, but there is a movement from industrial via multi-sectoral towards conglomerate unions (Streeck and Visser 1997). The largest union in the private sector, the Industriebond FNV (IB, 244,587 members), resulted from a merger of three unions in 1972 and organizes blue- and white-collar workers in metal, chemicals, textiles, clothing and footwear, cleaning, and parts of the paper, food and building materials industries. It will double in size in January 1998 and dominate the private sector, through amalgamation with the largest union in private services (DiBo), with 97,324 members, and with the unions in transport and in food, dairies and agriculture. The logic of this merger is clear – IB is an asset-rich union within a declining or stagnating domain; DiBo is a poor union within a large and expanding domain of two million people working in retailing, financial and business services, social insurance and personal services. The public sector is dominated by AbvaKabo (316,726 members), which organizes civil servants and employees throughout the public, semi-public (subsidized) as well as privatized services. With 70 per cent of all FNV members in two mega-unions, the future of the federation is uncertain. In the past, the federal level has typically served to subsidize small affiliates who cannot afford full services; but the new IB and AbvaKabo will probably internalize many services and reduce their contribution – now 15 per cent of total dues income – to the federation. This will make smaller unions even less viable, except where lack of economy of scale is compensated by a strong sense of occupational identity and a high level of union security, as in the case of printers, journalists, footballers, teachers, military, and police – indeed, the most unionized groups in the Dutch labour market.

Most CNV members are in the public sector but its structure is similar. As an intermediate step to mergers, its affiliates are now increasing their co-operation through the formation of cartels and joint services, using the same offices and, in some cases, officials. There is a similar development in the VHP, which is a combination of a general white-collar union and two federations of sectoral, company, and staff unions. The trend towards union concentration is plainly a result of the rising costs of providing adequate services to members. Decentralization of collective bargaining, diversification of employment conditions, and increased membership volatility add to such costs and to the pressure to find new ways of organizing and servicing members.

Dutch unions have entered a phase of strong mutual co-operation and pragmatism, following the ideological mobilization and rivalry of the 1970s. The formation of the FNV through a federation (1975) and then merger (1982) between the social-democratic and catholic unions soured relations with the CNV, while the launch of the VHP in 1974 was an explicit reaction by lower and middle managers to the egalitarian policies of the newly formed IB. The hard times of the 1980s drew the unions closer together; but union pluralism is likely to persist for the foreseeable future, since ideological and cultural differences are deep-seated. VHP organizes a distinct clientele and its orientation is close to the liberal position in Dutch politics. CNV members are likely to be church-going protestants and CDA voters, but there are sizeable minorities of each of these categories in the FNV. Indeed FNV and CNV members, and even more so their officials, hold similar views on what unions stand for – solidarity with the unemployed, the priority of jobs above wages and income equality, though CNV members are less likely to support strike action (Klandermans and Visser 1995; Van den Toren 1996).

The principle of exclusive jurisdiction does not exist in the Netherlands; in nearly all sectors and companies there are two or more unions involved in single table bargaining. Rojer (1996b) shows that union divisions work against the union whose views deviate most strongly from the employers' initial position. Usually this is the FNV, which therefore has a strong incentive to co-ordinate the approach of the different unions. In recent years it has done so with increasing effect, in part through rebuilding the personal linkages between top officials, making good use of the corridors and meeting rooms of the various corporatist institutions. FNV and CNV have adopted more or less the same policies: wage moderation, work-sharing through working-time reduction, negotiated flexibility, more rights for part-timers, extra employment for ethnic minorities, defence of the social security system. The VHP often professes different views: it tends to favour more decentralized and even individual wage-setting and larger differentials, and is less enthusiastic about working-time reduction. VHP unions are rarely in a position to spoil the party, however; in few sectors or companies do they rival the FNV in membership, enabling employers to exploit inter-union divisions to conclude agreements without the FNV.

Low membership, weak representation and internal divisions remain the weak points of Dutch unions. Occasionally, the low density has raised doubts concerning the ability of unions to speak and act for all workers. Especially in the field of social insurance, this has been a factor in the replacement of administrative boards run by union and employer nominees by government-appointed supervisory boards. Sometimes employers publicly voice concern that unions may become too weak to continue their much-praised role of stable, reliable and reasonable bargaining partners, but there are no examples of relations being broken off.

Dutch unions are reasonably well-financed and staffed, although rising costs of services and personnel are a cause for concern, and membership dues have not risen in proportion to costs. Financial constraints have hampered union recruitment, especially in services, and the federations have been forced to adjust to leaner times. The revision of the 1982 FNV constitution, currently under debate, reflects a more sober appraisal of the objectives, tasks and instruments of union action.

The Employers

Dutch employers' associations are well-organized: their member firms employ between 60 and 70 per cent of all private-sector workers. Membership is virtually complete among firms with a hundred or more employees, including all major multinationals and many foreign firms, but density is lower in the small-firm sector. This is reflected in sectoral differences: in retail, for instance, density is probably only 25 per cent and in construction only 5,500 of the 13,000 firms are organized. In these sectors there is also considerable rivalry between associations organizing larger and smaller firms: in construction, seven associations are involved in collective bargaining for 180,000 employees, facing three unions; whereas in banking one employers' association organizes all but a handful of small foreign banks and negotiates the sector agreement for 100,000 staff with five unions. In metals and engineering the powerful FME bargains on behalf of a few hundred large firms (with a total of 187,000 employees); Philips and Hoogovens (the only steel producer) are members but negotiate their own agreements. The 30,000 small firms in this sector – the norm has fewer than 30 employees and many are no more than repair shops – negotiate one sectoral agreement for 246,000 employees through a federation of twelve employers' associations. The other main association is the General Employers' Association (AWV), which organizes throughout manufacturing and services, and includes most leading multinational firms (Shell, Unilever, Akzo–Nobel, Heineken). AWV does not usually conduct collective bargaining, but has an advisory role in the negotiation of over 500 company agreements. Like the FME it is a highly professional organization, outstripping the unions in staff and resources.

The total number of employers' associations is unknown. Fifteen years ago, De Vroom and Van Waarden (1984) counted 1,650 business associations, four to five times the number of unions existing at the time. How many of these were proper employers' associations is difficult to say. The two major peak federations, VNO and the Christian NCW, had 80–100 affiliates each, but they have now merged, removing the only remaining religious divide in employers' organizations. A major factor in the removal of this vestige of *verzuiling* was the pressure of large firms, who often held dual membership and wanted a more effective organization with a stronger presence in Europe. Similar mergers between christian and general employers' associations have occurred in the small-firm sector and in agriculture, so that there are now only three peak associations left, compared to 11 in 1965 and 7 in 1990.

The Federation of Dutch Employers VNO–NCW is the undisputed representative of Dutch business, acts as both a trade and employers' association and is a member of the European peak association, UNICE. Nearly all important sectoral associations are affiliates. NCW had a special bureau to cater for small businesses, and VNO–NCW claims to represent all firms with 10 or more employees; but it faces fierce competition from the strong and politically well-connected Dutch Federation of Small and Medium Businesses (MKB Nederland). In agriculture there is a specialized Federation of Dutch Farmers (LTO Nederland).

The three confederations work together in the Council of Central Employers' Organizations (RCO), which occasionally issues joint statements and reports. In the 1980s employers upgraded their Joint Committee for the Preparation of Wage Policies, which serves as a co-ordination platform and counterpart of the co-ordinating activities of the FNV. The Committee discusses priorities and veto points in collective bargaining. Employers have shed their traditional 'wait and see' attitude and are more assertive, often asking for concessions (more individual variation in wages, normalization of Saturday work, phasing out of early retirement) even before unions present their demands. For the purpose of bolstering solidarity, the VNO–NCW (and some affiliates, for instance FME) have created resistance funds from which firms which become the target of strikes can be reimbursed. Such funds had lapsed in the period of statutory control of collective bargaining but made their reappearance in the 1970s when the controls were lifted.

Corporatism, Collective Bargaining and Consultation

In the first post-war years, the Netherlands were regarded as a paradigm of 'neo-corporatist' tripartite regulation of industrial relations. While many elements of the 'Dutch model' were dismantled in the 1970s, others persist. Distances in the Netherlands are small. Top officials and their advisors in trade unions and employers' associations meet frequently. They have easy access to Cabinet Ministers and top civil servants. Various foundations, councils, boards and committees institutionalize mutual contact, consultation and advice.

The Institutions of Corporatism

For the purpose of wage policies the most important is the Foundation of Labour (StAr): a private foundation, created in 1945 and intended as a meeting place for employers and unions. Each have ten seats on the governing board and the chair rotates between VNO–NCW and FNV presidents. The principal accords, recommendations and joint opinions of recent times – about 70 since 1982 – have been negotiated within the StAr and its influential Wages Committee (van Bottenburg, 1995). Twice every year, in spring when the new budget is prepared, and in autumn when a new round of wage negotiations is about to begin, the Foundation meets a Cabinet delegation.

The Social–Economic Council (SER) is a tripartite organization. Employers and unions have each 11 seats, the other 11 are occupied by members appointed by the government, usually professors of economics, the President of the Central Bank, the Director of the Central Planning Bureau (CPB) and recently some ex-politicians. The SER was founded in 1950, as the apex of the three-tiered (national, sectoral, company) consultation system; it was the government's main advisory council, the reports issued by its 'Committee of Economic Experts' serving as guidelines for statutory wage policies. Until 1995, the SER had to be consulted before the government could formally introduce new legislation on social and economic matters. It also has supervisory functions, for instance over the works councils and over the bipartite Industry and Product Boards which exist in some sectors.

In the 1980s, it became fashionable to criticize the SER as a prime factor of institutional sclerosis, a means of delaying difficult decisions. Unanimity between employers and unions, which had characterized the first 20 years, had become rare. With the 1982 Accord, the prestige of the StAR increased and the continued existence of the SER seemed doubtful (Klamer, 1990). However it has displayed new life, beginning with the unanimous advice on EMU entitled *Convergence and Concertation-economy*, which was issued in record time in 1992. This proved that there was a fundamental consensus over EMU and stressed that corporatism and consultation are not liabilities but assets in a modern, internationally interdependent economy. Other influential reports have followed. Unions and employers have again discovered that if they agree, the SER can be a means to influence government policy. The most recent example is a still fragile agreement allowing workers to 'sell' five days supplementary leave, above the legal minimum of 20 days, for a 3 per cent wage increase, and to 'save' holidays over a 5-year period for the purpose of extended periods of leave. This 'advice' appears to benefit workers (currently many additional holidays remain unused and cannot be saved longer than 2 years) and goes beyond the declared intentions of the government.

In social security there has been a movement away from corporatism, with various laws removing union and employers' representatives from the governing boards, reinstalling independent supervisory boards and bringing in private providers of insurance. In the area of public employment services, tripartism is a bone of contention between the government and the social partners. In 1991, the service was privatized and the new Public Employment Board (RBA) became a tripartite forum of employers, unions and government representatives, stressing the joint responsibility for successful job placement and employment policies. At the same time the service was regionalized. Five years and a rather critical expert report later, the government has reduced its subsidy, reclaimed a direct say over how the RBA spends its considerable funds and decided to restructure the Board, side-stepping the opposition of employers and unions.

Collective Bargaining

Collective bargaining is framed by three laws. The 1927 Law on Collective Agreements requires an employer who signs a collective agreement to apply its conditions to all relevant employees, not only to union members; all agreements are legally binding. There is no obligation to bargain, nor is union recognition regulated; any union may seek to negotiate. Under the 1970 Wages Act (amended in 1988), collective agreements must be registered at the Ministry of Social Affairs and Employment. This act allows the minister, after consultation with the StAR, to order a temporary suspension of a new agreement. This happened regularly up to 1982 (seven times in 12 years) but has not occurred since, although there were threats of intervention in 1992 and 1993. The 1937 Law on Extension and Nullification of Collective Agreements allows the minister to extend a collective agreement in whole or part to employers who are not members of the signatory association(s), if the agreement covers a substantial majority of the industry (in practice interpreted as a 55 per cent coverage rate). Where this is not the case, for instance in the retail sector, the Product and Industry Boards under public law may step in and issue so-called rulings in which minimum conditions are laid down. Extension does not affect companies which already have negotiated a company agreement. Extension is routinely applied, covering 19 per cent of firms and 6 per cent of private employees; formally the minister must ask the advice of the Wages Committee of the StAR, but in practice only does so when objections are raised. The Law also allows the minister to nullify an agreement which is against public interest, but this has never occurred.

These legal principles give firms an incentive to join the relevant association and help explain the high level of collective organization among employers and the high coverage rate of collective agreements. Unions are in a more ambiguous position: on the one hand the legal system prevents competition between union and non-union firms, on the other hand it removes incentives for workers to join. Collective agreements registered with the Ministry purportedly apply to 82 per cent of the 4.8 million employees in the private sector; adding 900,000 civil servants, total coverage is 85 per cent of those employed (table 10.4). Annual establishment surveys by the Labour Inspectorate (Venema et al. 1996) show a slightly lower rate of 79 per cent in the private sector. There is considerable variation by industry: coverage is particularly high in most manufacturing industries, construction, health, banking and insurance and the retail sector, relatively low in most other private services.

There are almost 1,000 agreements, including a few hundred special company agreements, usually dealing with pensions, early retirement and similar 'single issues' in companies that are already covered by sectoral agreements. Excluding these, in 1993 there were 720 collective agreements, 198 sectoral and 522 company-level. The great majority of the latter are in very small companies. As can be seen from table 10.4, sectoral agreements are less numerous but more important in terms of coverage; they apply to 69 per cent of all employees, 59 per

Table 10.4 Collective agreements, structure and coverage

Type of agreement				Workers covered	Coverage rate (%)
Covered by company agreements				650,000	14
Covered by industry agreements				3,300,000	69
directly				2,800,000	58
through extension				500,000	10
Total coverage private sector				3,950,000	82
Not covered				800,000	17
Coverage public sector				850,000	100
Coverage total economy				4,800,000	85
	size	*no.*	*%*		*share (%)*
Company agreements	<2,000	479	67	200,000	3
	>2,000	43	6	500,000	10
Industry agreements	<10,000	133	18	400,000	9
	>10,000	65	9	3,700,000	78
All agreements		720	100	4,800,000	100

Source: based on Van den Toren 1996: tables 3.1 and 3.3.

cent directly and 10 per cent by extension; company agreements cover 14 per cent. This distribution has hardly changed in the past 20 years.

The coverage of many sectoral agreements in industry has declined, but in such services as cleaning, catering, travel agencies and surveillance, sectoral employer organizations and multi-employer agreements have expanded. In the more 'internationally exposed' business, information and financial services employer organization is less developed, unions are weak, and collective bargaining is rare. Occasionally the works councils intervene. Sometimes firms are allowed to 'step outside' the sectoral agreement; this happens infrequently and mostly when they face economic difficulties which require special 'hardship clauses'. Recent cases were Daf and Fokker, who were both allowed exemption by the FME and the unions but remain members of the employers' association.

In banking the sectoral agreement almost disintegrated in 1994. The peculiarity of this case is the oligopolistic structure of the industry: three large banks account for 80 per cent of employment and turnover, four or five medium-sized banks for 10–15 per cent, and 80 small, mostly foreign banks for the rest. Unlike most collective agreements in manufacturing, which specify only minimum rates and conditions, the banking agreement dictates standard conditions and covers all employees except top management. For the three large banks it helped keep wages out of competition, for the small banks it reduced transaction costs and protected against union interference; but the constraints on company discretion in a more competitive environment were increasingly resented. After threats to terminate the agreement, it was rescued by introducing scope for local variation and flexible application of individual working time within a corridor from 32–40 hours, with exemptions for key staff, longer opening hours, lower overtime rates for evening and weekend hours. All details were to be decided through direct consultation at the local level. This agreement was a breakthrough for the unions (an average 36-hour week) and management (flexibility and individualization), and has become a model for other sectors (Visser and Jongen 1996).

The coverage of sectoral agreements is increased by collective bargaining in the public sector. Until the 1980s, wages in the public sector (including subsidized services such as health, public transport and utilities) followed the trend in private sector wage increases; in the 1980s the government imposed cuts which put public employees 10 per cent or more behind, but at the same time a new joint consultation system was developed. Civil servants obtained the right to strike and bargain. After 10 years of transition, in 1993 public employment was divided into eight sectors (such as education and local government) with their own agreements, some of them framework agreements which allow further differentiation by category of employees or local conditions.

As elsewhere in Europe decentralization has become a watchword, but most Dutch employers have been keen to keep pay bargaining – and conflict – out of the firm. Thus sectoral bargaining has survived, though with moves towards local flexibility. Traditionally though most multinational firms, while prominent members of their employers' associations, negotiate their own agreements. In large multi-plant firms these are as significant as sectoral agreements and in some cases, as at Philips, Akzo–Nobel and Unilever, have been trend-setters. Today the largest company agreement covers 90,000 staff at the privatized PTT. Such agreements are negotiated under headquarters control, since managements are keen to prevent competitive union pressure at plant level. Hardly any employers would prefer works councils to unions as bargaining partners; they usually appreciate the professionalism and reliability of union negotiators, and fear that bargaining with the works council might jeopardize the peaceful consultation role of the latter (Teulings and Hartog, forthcoming). Fewer than 10 per cent of councils are actually involved in pay bargaining and only in firms where unions find it exceedingly hard to organize are councils involved in some kind of 'virtual bargaining', though in some cases they conclude 'covenants' or 'gentlemen agreements', the precise legal status of which is as yet untested. The FNV is today in favour of changing the law which excludes works councils from wage bargaining: if no collective agreement exists they should be allowed to bargain, a right which would be especially important in business, information and financial services (IBM, Hewlett–Packard, Coopers and Lybrand, Merrill–Lynch). Employers are not enthusiastic, the SER is divided and CNV is also opposed, so it is questionable whether this proposal will reach the statute book.

In the 1990s, public debate has concentrated on mandatory extension of collective agreements. The OECD (1995, 1996), the director of the CPB, the Ministry of Economic Affairs and various economists are in favour of abolition. They argue that extension contradicts the government policy of deregulation, handicaps small firms and protects 'insider coalitions'; without extension (and perhaps without sectoral agreements) more low-wage competition and more low-productivity jobs would be generated. The government has been sympathetic, but in 1993 employers and unions argued jointly in defence of extension, realizing that without public protection the high level of collective regulation is probably not sustainable. The current Minister of Social Affairs and Employment has indicated that he wants to keep extension on the statute book, but has seized the opportunity to make mandatory extension conditional upon 'good behaviour' by negotiators (e.g. lower entry wages and dispensation rules for new businesses). Thus far, the trick has worked.

▌ Co-ordination

Van den Toren (1996) has shown that there are various horizontal and vertical connections between the 5,000 or so officials who each year negotiate hundreds of collective agreements. In order to understand the horizontal links we must realize that 99 per cent of all agreements are reached through single-table bargaining. As was seen earlier, an agreement signed with any union applies to members of other unions as well, and this encourages inter-union co-ordination. Agreements with only one union or without the FNV are rare. Employers are generally keen to include all unions and in particular the FNV, if only because of the peace clause; though the two 1996 Philips agreements were signed by the VHP unions only; and Heineken used disagreement between CNV and FNV to exclude the latter. Established unions will try to exclude newcomers; membership does not play an important role in testing the bargaining credentials of a union, but independent unions may have to show their disruptive potential first before they are admitted (as happened in recent years with nurses' unions, and occurs frequently in transport). In one or two cases employers have reached a 'sweetheart' deal with a company union, as recently demonstrated at IKEA who needed a company agreement to avoid the risk that the more expensive collective agreement for the furniture industry would be imposed by extension. FNV and CNV failed to convince the young staff of IKEA that it was in their interest to sacrifice wages in order to subsidize the early retirement provisions for older workers elsewhere in the ailing furniture business. A similar case occurred in the port of Rotterdam.

Another contributory factor to co-ordination across bargaining settings lies in the fact that some of the larger unions, like IB or DiBo, each negotiate 150 or more agreements. All negotiations are led by appointed full-time officials supervised by headquarters; norms are strong and local defiance can be punished; voting and ratification procedures are usually across the whole membership. Vertical integration, which in multi-sectoral and conglomerate unions is vital to prevent large wage differences across sectors and firms, is further supported by centralization of strike pay: in an approved strike the FNV pays three-quarters of the strike benefits from its central fund. Consequently, there is a tendency for strikes to be organized, if at all, on issues that all unions support.

Finally, co-ordination is enhanced by the long preparation of actual bargaining in what still constitutes an annual cycle, in spite of increased variation in the length and expiry dates of agreements. Bargaining starts with the drafting of 'proposals' by the leading unions during the summer, followed by lengthy discussions in the federations and quasi-negotiations in the StAr and the SER; then there are meetings with the government in the autumn, re-statement of proposals in sectoral forums and finally the actual negotiations early in the new year. The distance between negotiators – physically, socially and ideologically – is small. Central accords are not instructions which must be applied, but guidance to lower-level negotiators with considerable 'moral' weight. Heertum-Lemmen and Wilthagen (1996) have shown that central agreements on financial matters and primary working conditions (wages, sick pay, working hours, overtime) carry more weight with local negotiators than social and qualitative issues (extra jobs for members of ethnic minorities; quality of work or industrial democracy). Publicity within employers' and union organizations is often inadequate, and sectoral and company negotiators on both sides disregard difficult and vague recommendations; their agenda is determined by their previous negotiations. These sobering conclusions support the view that the main function of the central accords and recommendations is to influence the 'bargaining climate' and create an atmosphere of goodwill.

Industrial Conflict

In the initial post-war period, statutory controls made it hard for unions to engage in official strike action. In 1970 the Netherlands moved, formally, back to the pre-war situation of freedom of collective bargaining and during the 1970s the Dutch participated in the international trend of increased worker and union militancy. However levels remained comparatively low. In the past 15 years, in line with international trends, strike levels have fallen and the Netherlands continues to be placed near the bottom of the international strike league, just in front of Switzerland and Austria. Most collective agreements contain a peace clause, and strikes are therefore illegal during their currency. While the right to strike is not otherwise regulated by law, the courts have tended to accept their legality if used as a means of last resort when contracts have expired and efforts to negotiate a new one have demonstrably failed (Rood 1991).

Consultation and Representation in Firms

The Netherlands has a dual system of employee representation. Employees are free to join a union or stay unorganized. Under the Works Council Act of 1979 (amended in 1981 and 1990) those in firms with 35 or more staff can elect a works council. In firms with 10–34 employees two consultation meetings per year are mandatory; under the Working Time Act of 1996, workers in firms with three or more staff must be consulted on working hours. The works council has three main rights: *consultation* over major decisions on investment, divestment, mergers, take-overs, relocation and restructuring; *co-determination* on HRM issues; and *monitoring* of the implementation of collective agreements and legal rights or obligations. Facilities for meetings, training and advice must be provided by the employer and the law requires a minimum of six annual consultation meetings between the council and the employer.

In half of the firms with 35 to 100 employees there was no works council in 1992; 87 per cent of larger firms did have one (van den Burgh and Kriek 1992). In our own survey in 1993, 63 per cent of all employees in private firms with 35 and more staff answered that there was an elected council; 28 per cent said there was not and 9 per cent did not know (Klandermans and Visser 1995). In the public sector – where the works councils have now also become mandatory (except in education and among military personnel) – coverage is complete. Elections for the councils take place every 3 or 4 years; unions usually present lists, but workers are free to elect non-union candidates. Nationwide, the established unions gain two-thirds of the votes, the rest goes to independent lists or non-union candidates. The FNV is represented in most councils and is often the largest faction, but an absolute majority is rare (Visser 1995). This is another reason why the FNV cannot go it alone but must seek co-operation with other unions. Electoral turnout appears to be lower than in some other countries with similar procedures: only 64 per cent of eligible workers vote, though if elections are contested turnout rises to 79 per cent (Klandermans and Visser 1995).

The rights and facilities of Dutch councils are equal to those of the German *Betriebsrat* (Streeck 1995); but in practice no more than a third of the councils fully utilize their rights. Works councils have nonetheless grown against the tide (Looise 1989); despite employers' misgivings and the criticisms of many FNV unions at the time of the 1979 reform, they have won an important place in Dutch industrial relations (Visser 1995). Employers have learned that continuous change in organization and production cannot be managed without the involvement of a competent and representative body that acts and speaks on behalf of all employees. Works councils under a strong legal regime may be demanding and lengthen the lead time of decision-making, but they also make management more accountable and implementation easier through involvement. Among workers, the councils have become an accepted phenomenon; they are seen as a complement to the unions, not a substitute (Klandermans and Visser 1995). The conflicts that characterized the early transition from 'joint' to 'employee only' councils (Teulings 1981) have disappeared. The unions have abandoned their dream of independent, union-based workplace representation and concentrate instead on co-operation with the works councils, being dependent on their detailed knowledge of organizational and technological developments in the firm. In the 'New Course' Accord there is a suggestion that employers may support decentralization by giving unions more facilities in the firm, but this is one of the recommendations which has thus far been side-stepped by local employers.

Conclusions

Recently there has been much publicity about the success of the Dutch economy. Its strong employment growth parallels the American 'jobs machine'. The quiet approach towards EMU, the absence of social unrest, the relative lack of social inequality, and the fundamental consensus between unions and employers have aroused the envy of politicians and policy-makers in neighbouring countries. So, we may well ask: Is there a 'Dutch model' behind this relative success? – relative, that is, because the threat of unemployment, inactivity and poverty has not vanished; relative, moreover, compared to the more dismal performance of the struggling German or Belgian economies. Or is it the other way round: is the 'model' nothing but the expression of success? Perhaps it is just that assumptions about how things ought to work can be as important for actual behaviour as the formal and informal structures of co-ordination, consultation and bargaining described in this chapter.

Various puzzles remain. By way of evaluating the state of play and developments in Dutch industrial relations, I mention three. First, how can 'employer-led corporatism' (Crouch 1996) be stable? What prevents employers from exploiting union weakness to create a state of disorganized capitalism? Second, how can wage moderation make a country better off? Third, is it possible to move from one 'world of capitalism' (Esping-Andersen 1990) to another?

It is fair to say that employers are the stronger party in Dutch industrial relations. A stronger party can be expected to abandon a relationship or to seek to change it if its results are consistently unsatisfactory; but this chapter has shown that since 1982 the outcomes in terms of profits, wages, investment climate and social peace have not given employers cause for complaint. As a group, they could hardly have done better. We may conclude that in this case the results produce and reproduce the model – of intensive consultation, at all levels, between relatively centralized organizations of employers and unions, facilitated by state regulation which is made contingent on 'good behaviour'. The institutions, in this view, are secondary; they facilitate the solution of co-ordination problems and discourage 'go-it-alone' strategies. Mandatory extension, for example, raises the opportunity costs for unorganized employers; and central co-ordination across unions and sectors protects wage bargaining from inter-group rivalries. The conclusion may be that corporatism works best when one party dominates but is restrained in its ambitions by public policy, institutional obligations and a high capacity for co-ordination on the part of the other party.

According to the CPB (1995: 268), wage moderation has been the country's single most important weapon in international competition. For the second half of the 1980s the Bureau estimates that two-thirds of employment growth can be attributed to wage moderation and one-third to the expansion of the world economy. The Ministry of Social Affairs and Employment estimates that wage moderation restrained increases by 1.2 per cent a year between 1983 and 1989, to which it attributes about half of the net gain of 700,000 jobs in these years (SZW, 1990). In the 1990s, the Netherlands has experienced a more labour-intensive growth pattern than for instance Belgium or Germany, contradicting the dire predictions of 'jobless growth'. The counter-argument is that wage moderation delays investment in technology and is, in essence, a 'low productivity – low wage' trajectory. Low wages do not encourage 'creative destruction' in the Schumpeterian sense and keep lazy entrepreneurs in business. Furthermore, wage moderation may create a dependency trap: if your competitors follow suit, stronger medicine will be needed.

The critical question, in my view, is how the temporary advantage of lower wage costs is used. Investment in training, research and technology is one element; public investment in services that broaden the national employment basis and reduce dependency on benefits, social charges, taxes and wage costs, is another. In the 1990s, wage moderation in the Netherlands typically presupposed lower charges and taxes, possible once public finances reached a healthier state. This increased the willingness of unions to moderate wage claims, since post-tax wages would still grow by a small amount. In exchange employers could offer minor compensation in other areas, for instance contributions for collective employee insurance provision, facilities for unions, training or extra employment opportunities. Was this successful? Yes, if judged by the 1.8 per cent job growth rate and the rising level of labour market participation. No, if the almost unchanged number of people dependent on benefits is considered. There may simply be no alternative to wage moderation in an economy in which broad unemployment is over 20 per cent, certainly not for unions who have a strongly felt preference for equality of outcomes.

The outcomes – strong job growth, yet large numbers of people who depend on benefits – suggest that it is indeed not easy to leave Esping-Andersen's world of a compensatory transfer-based welfare state. Dutch firms, unions and legislators have gone to considerable lengths to increase the flexibility of employment relations. Various disincentive effects have been removed from the social security system. But is this good enough? Not if we listen to the OECD (1994: para. 117): 'at the risk of oversimplification, it can be said that, confronted like all other industrialized countries with the problem of unemployment, the Netherlands has gone further than most of them in emphasizing equity and other social considerations rather than efficiency'. The neo-liberal message is that the next step ought to be greater wage flexibility and inequality, especially at the lower end of the labour market, even if this creates a group of working poor. In other words, in Esping-Andersen's worlds you are only allowed to move from a continental European to an Anglo-Saxon, not to a Nordic or Social-Democratic system. This, it seems to me, is the main political issue for the future of a Dutch model of industrial relations.

| Acknowledgement

In writing this chapter, I have drawn valuable data from the four reports on the Netherlands written by Dr Wiemer Salverda (Faculty of Economics, Groningen) for the European Commission's Group of Experts on the Role of the Social Partners in Implementing the Conclusions of the Essen and Madrid European Councils. In addition to Dr Salverda, I thank Dr Anton Hemerijck of the Erasmus University in Rotterdam for allowing me to read his manuscript on social security reform, Dr Marc van der Meer of the Amsterdam School of Social Science Research, and Dr Coen van Rij of the Centre for Research on European

Societies and Industrial Relations (CESAR) of the University of Amsterdam, for help with the labour market and union data. Needless to say, they cannot be held responsible for the views expressed or any errors.

▌Abbreviations

AbvaKabo	*Algemene Bond van Ambtenaren*, etc. – Union of Public Servants, Postal and Health Workers (cf FNV)
AVBB	*Algemeen Verbond Bouwbedrijf* – Federation of Building Trade and Employers' Organizations (VNO–NCW affiliate)
AVC	*Algemene Vakcentrale* – Federation of Occupational Unions
AWVN	*Algemene Werkgevers Vereniging* – General Employers' Association (VNO–NCW affiliate)
BHB	*Bouw- en Houtbond* – Building Industry Union
CBA	*Centraal Bestuur Arbeidsvoorziening* – Central Employment Board
CBS	*Centraal Bureau van de Statistiek* – Central Statistical Office
CDA	*Christen Democratisch Appèl* – Christian-Democratic Party
CNV	*Christelijk Nationaal Vakverbond* – Confederation of Christian Trade Unions
CPB	*Centraal Planbureau* – Central Planning Office
D66	*Democraten '66* – Democrats Party
DiBo	*Dienstenbond* – Private Services' Union (cf FNV)
EZ	*Economische Zaken* – Ministry of Economic Affairs
FME	*Federatie Metaal-Electro* – Federation of Metal- and Electrical Engineering (VNO–NCW affiliate)
FNV	*Federatie Nederlandse Vakbeweging* – Confederation of Dutch Trade Unions
IB	*Industriebond* – Industries' Union (cf FNV)
LTO	*Land- en Tuinbouw Nederland* – Dutch Federation of Farmers
MKB	*Midden- en Kleinbedrijf Nederland* – Dutch Federation of Small and Medium-sized Business
OSA	*Organisatie voor Strategisch Arbeidsmarktonderzoek* – Organization for Strategic Labour Market Research
OVV	*Onafhankelijk Verbond van Vakbonden* – Independent Federation of Occupational Unions
PvdA	*Partij van de Arbeid* – Labour Party
SCP	*Sociaal–Cultureel Planbureau* – Social–Cultural Planning Office
SER	*Sociaal–Ekonomische Raad* – Social–Economic Council
StAr	*Stichting van de Arbeid* – Foundation of Labour
SZW	*Sociale Zaken en Werkgelegenheid* – Ministry of Social Affairs and Employment
VHP	*Verbond van Hoger en Middelbaar Personeel* – Confederation of Senior and White-collar Staff Unions
VNO–NCW	*Vereniging van Nederlandse Ondernemers – Nederlands Christelijke Werkgeversverbond* – Confederation of Dutch Business and Employers' Associations
VVD	*Volkspartij voor Vrijheid en Democratie* – Liberal Party

WGVB   *Vereniging van Werkgevers in het Bankbedrijf* – Banking Employers' Association (VNO–NCW affiliate)

WRR   *Wetenschappelijk Raad voor het Regeringsbeleid* – Council for Scientific Advice of Government Policy

| References and Further Reading

Allaart, P.C. (ed.) 1988: *The Labour Market in Five Small Countries*. The Hague: Organisatie voor Strategisch Arbeidsmarktonderzoek.

Beer, Paul de 1996: *Het onderste kwart. Werk en werkloosheid aan de onderkant van de arbeidsmarkt*. Rijswijk: SCP.

Berg, A. van den 1996: 'Vakbeweging, economische conjunctuur en institutionele veranderingen in Nederland. Een tijdreeksstudie van tachtig jaar ledenontwikkeling'. In: Visser (ed.), 54–71.

Bottenburg, M. van 1995: *Aan den Arbeid! In de wandelgangen van de Stichting van de Arbeid, 1945–1995*. Amsterdam: Bert Bakker.

Braun, D. 1988: *Die Niederländische Weg in die Massenarbeitslosigkeit (1973–1981). Eine politisch-institutionelle Analyse*. Amsterdam: PhD thesis University of van Amsterdam.

Burgh, Y. van den and Kriek, F. 1992: *Maleving van de Wet op de Undernem Ingsraden*. The Hague: SZW-VUGA.

CBS 1995: *Enquête Beroepsbevolking* (Labour force Sample Survey). The Hague: CBS.

CPB 1995: *Centraal Economisch Plan 1996*. The Hague: CPB.

CPB 1996: *Centraal Economisch Plan 1997*. The Hague: CPB.

Crouch, C. 1996: 'Revised Diversity. From the neo-liberal decade to beyond Maastricht'. In: van Ruysseveldt and Visser (eds), 358–375.

Ebbinghaus, B. and Visser J. 1996: Social Change and Union Transformation. Convergence or Diversity? Paper presented at the 1996 Annual Meeting of the American Political Science Association (APSA), San Fransisco, August 29–September 1.

Esping-Andersen, G. 1990: *Three Worlds of Capitalism*. Princeton NJ: Princeton University Press.

Freeman, R., Hartog, J. and Teulings, C. 1996: *Pulling The Plug. An analysis of mandatory extension in the Dutch system of labour relations*. The Hague: OSA-voorstudie W144.

Gourevitch, P. 1986: *Politics in Hard Times: Comparative Responses to International Economic Crisis*. Ithaca, NY: Cornell University Press.

Hancké, R. 1993: Trade Union Membership in Europe 1960–90. Rediscovering local unions. *British Journal of Industrial Relations*, 31(4), 593–613.

Hasluck, C. 1995: *Baseline Study for the Netherlands*. Coventry: Institute for Employment Research, University of Warwick, unpublished report.

Heertum-Lemmen, A. van and Wilthagen, T. 1996: *De doorwerking van de aanbevelingen van de Stichting van de Arbeid*. The Hague: SDU.

Hemerijck, A. 1995: Corporatist Immobility in the Netherlands. In: C. Crouch and F. Traxler, *Organised Industrial Relations in Europe: What future?* Aldershot: Avebury, 183–226.

Klamer, A. 1990: *Verzuilde dromen. Veertig jaar SER*. Amsterdam: Bert Bakker.

Klandermans, B. and Visser, J. (eds), 1995: *De vakbeweging na de welvaartsstaat*. Assen: van Gorcum.

Lange, W. de 1989: *Configuratie van arbeid, vormgeven aan arbeidstijden, bedrijfstijden en arbeidstijdpatronen.* Zutphen: Thieme.

Layard, R., Nickel, S. and Jackman, R. 1991: *Unemployment, Macroeconomic Performance and the Labour Market.* Oxford: Oxford University Press.

Looise, J.-C. 1989: The Recent Growth in Employees' Representation in the Netherlands. Defying the times? In: C.J. Lammers and G. Széll (eds), *International Handbook of Participation in Organisations*, vol. 1: Organisational democracy: Taking Stock. Oxford: Oxford University Press, 268–84.

Meer, M. van der 1996: Belangenbehartiging onder druk. De langste bouwstaking na de Tweede Wereldoorlog. In: Visser (ed.), 118–43.

OECD 1994: *Economic Surveys 1993–1994: Netherlands.* Paris: Organization for Economic Co-operation and Development.

OECD 1995: *Jobs Study.* Paris: Organization for Economic Co-operation and Development.

OECD 1996: *Economic Surveys 1995–1996: Netherlands.* Paris: Organization for Economic Co-operation and Development.

OSA 1993: *Trendrapport Aanbod van arbeid 1993.* The Hague, OSA-report, 17.

OSA 1996: *Soepel geregeld. Instituties en efficiëntie van de arbeidsmarkt.* The Hague, OSA-report, 24.

Pelzer, A. and van der Putte, B. 1993: Wensen, motieven en belemmeringen ten aanyien van de arbeidsduur. *Sociaal Maandblad Arbeid*, 48(9), 488–95.

Reynaerts, W. 1985: Kantelende positie; Arbeidsverhoudingen in een keertijd. In: OSA, *Bespiegelingen over de toekomst van de sociale partners.* The Hague: SDU, OSA-voorstudie, V5.

Rij, C. van 1996: Small én breed. Een opinie onderzoek op basis van het FNV ledenpanel. Amsterdam: Centre for research of European societies and industrial relations, CESAR research paper 96/7.

Rij, C. van 1997: 'Leden en arbeidsmarkt. Een statistische verkenning van de FNV in 1996. Amsterdam: Centre for research of European societies and industrial relations, CESAR research paper 97/1.

Rojer, M. 1996a: De reparatie van de WAO-gat. Een dynamische analyse van de cao-onderhandelingen. In: Visser (ed.), 92–117.

Rojer, M. 1996b: *Cao-onderhandelingen: Een voorspelbaar, logisch en rationeel proces?* Amsterdam: Thesis publishers.

Rood, M. 1991: *Staken in Nederland.* Schoonhoven: Acadamic Service.

Rothstein, B. 1992: Labour Market Institutions and Working Class Strength. In S. Steinmo, K. Thelen, and F. Longstreth (eds), *Structuring Politics. Historical institutionalism and comparative analysis.* Cambridge Mass.: Cambridge University Press, 33–56.

Ruysseveldt, J. van and Visser J. (eds) 1996: *Industrial Relations in Europe. Traditions and transitions.* London: Sage.

Salverda, W. 1996: Is the Dutch Economy Really Short of Low-Paid Jobs?. In: C.H.A. Verhaar (ed.), *On the Challenges of Unemployment in a Regional Europe.* Avesbury: Aldershot, 221–40.

Scharpf, F. 1993: Co-ordination in hierarchies and networks. In: F.W. Scharpf (ed.), *Games in Hierarchies and Networks. Analytical and empirical approaches to the study of governance institutions.* Frankfurt a/Main and Boulder Co.: Campus and Westview.

SCP 1994: *Sociaal-Cultureel Rapport 1994.* Rijswijk: VUGA.

Streeck, W. 1995: Works Councils in Western Europe: From Consultation to Participation. In: J. Rogers and W. Streeck (eds), *Works Councils. Consultation, Representation, and Co-operation in Industrial Relations.* Chicago, Ill.: The University of Chicago Press, 313–48.

Streeck, W. and Visser, J. 1997: An Evolutionary Dynamic of Unions as Complex Organisations. The cases of Germany and the Netherlands. Cologne: Max Planck Institute for the Study of Societies, unpublished paper.

SZW 1990: *Rapportage Arbeidsmark 1990*. The Hague: Ministerie van Sociale Zaken en Werkgelegenheid (Ministry of Social Affairs and Emloyment).

SZW 1993: *Sociale Nota 1994*, The Hague: SDU.

SZW 1996: *De Nederlandse verzorgingsstaat in internationaal en economisch perspectief*. The Hague: SDU.

Teulings, A. 1981: *Ondernemingsraadspolitiek in Nederland*. Amsterdam: van Gennep.

Teulings, C. and Hartog, J. (forthcoming): *Corporatism and Competition*. Cambridge: Cambridge University Press.

Therborn, G. 1986: *Why Some People Are More Unemployed Than Others*. London: Verso.

Toren, J.-P. van den 1996: *Achter gesloten deuren? CAO-overleg in de jaren negentig*. Amsterdam: Welboom.

Vall, M. van de 1963: *De vakbeweging in de welvaartsstaat. Een macro- and microsociologische analyse*. Meppel: Boom (also published in 1970 by Cambridge University Press as *Labor Organisations: A macro- and micro-socioological analysis*).

Venema, P.M., Faas, A. and Samadhan, J.A. 1996: *Arbeidsvoorwaardenontwikkeling in 1995*. The Hague: SZW, research report Labour Inspectorate.

Vermeulen, H. and Bosselaar, H. 1996: *De onderkant belicht*. The Hague: OSA-report W145.

Visser, J. 1989: New Working Time Arrangements in the Netherlands. In: A. Gladstone, R. Lansbury, J. Stieber, T. Treu and M. Weiss (eds), *Current Issues in Labour Relations. An international Perspective*. Berlin and New York: de Gruyter, 229–50.

Visser, J. 1990: Continuity and Change in Dutch Industrial Relations. In: G. Baglioni and C. Crouch (eds), *European Industrial Relations. The challenge of flexibility*. London: Sage, 199–242.

Visser, J. 1992: The Netherlands: The end of an era and the end of a system? In: A. Ferner and R. Hyman (eds), *Industrial Relations in the New Europe*. Oxford: Basil Backwell, 1st ed., 323–356.

Visser, J. 1995: The Netherlands: From Paternalism to Representation. In: J. Rogers and W. Streeck (eds), *Works Councils. Consultation, Representation, and Co-operation in Industrial Relations*. Chicago, Ill.: The University of Chicago Press, 79–114.

Visser, J. (ed.) 1996: *De vakbeweging op de eeuwgrens*, special issue of *Mens en Maatschappij*, vol. 71, Amsterdam: Amsterdam University Press.

Visser, J., and Jongen, P.-J. 1996: Markets, Institutions, Strategies and Employment Relations in Dutch Banks. Amsterdam: Dept. of Sociology/Faculty of Economics, paper for MIT banking network.

Vogels, E. 1994: *De onderkant van de arbeidsmarkt*. The Hague: SZW, werkdocument no. 1.

Vroom, B. de, and Waarden, F. van 1984: Ondernemingsorganisaties als machtsmiddel', *Economisch-Statistische Berichten*, 25 July and 1 August.

Wellink, T. 1987: De ontwikkeling in de jaren zeventig en tachtig en enkele daaruit te trekken lessen. In: A. Knoester (ed.), *Lessen uit het verleden. 125 jaar Vereniging voor de Staathuishoudkunde*. Leiden/Antwerpen: Stenfert Kroese, 333–66.

Windmuller, J. 1969: *Labor Relations in the Netherlands*. Ithaca, NY: Cornell University Press.

WRR 1990: Een werkend perspectief. Arbeidsparticipatie in de jaren '90. The Hague: SDU, rapporten aan de regering no. 38.

Zanden, J.L. van and Griffiths, R.T. 1989: *Economische geschiedenis van Nederland in de 20e eeuw*. Utrecht: Het Spectrum.

Zimmermann, E. 1986): *Neokorporative Politikformen in den Niederlanden*. Frankfurt a/M.: Campus.

11 | Belgium: The Great Transformation

JACQUES VILROKX • JIM VAN LEEMPUT

Introduction

In the 1990s, industrial relations in Belgium have been overtaken by far-reaching changes. These have become enmeshed in what is probably the deepest institutional crisis in the country's history. In this chapter we try to show Belgian industrial relations may only be understood in relation to the peculiarities of the Belgian socio-economic and political systems. We explain how these have evolved in the post-war period, culminating in the transformation of the mid-1990s.

In our 1992 contribution to the first edition of this volume, we emphasized the resumption in 1986, after a 10-year interruption, of the pattern of 2-year national intersectoral agreements between the social partners dating back to 1960. As we anticipated, such agreements continued in the 1990s, albeit in the face of mounting obstacles. By the end of 1996, however, cumulative malfunctions had finally upset the relative stability of the industrial relations system, and the social partners failed to sign a new central agreement for 1997–8. This brought to an end the 10-year phase of central agreements, but it also marked a more profound turning-point in the Belgian model. It is unlikely that the relations between the state and social partners, or between the social partners themselves, will improve significantly over the next few years, and the chances of reaching a comprehensive new central agreement are currently slim.

Bipartite central agreements are not the only distinctive component of Belgian industrial relations, as we discuss below. However, in the post-war period they have been extremely important, both at a symbolic level and in the development of the welfare state. Successive governments have always accepted the policy and resource implications of central agreements. As such, they may be seen as the legitimatizing seal on the activities of the social partners in constructing the specifically Belgian form of the welfare state. The failure to conclude a national agreement at this crucial moment of transformation thus acquires a wider resonance.

Belgium has in some respects provided a laboratory for analysts of social transformation. At virtually all levels of socio-political exchange, established forms of regulation are being questioned. The so-called '*affaires*' of the last decade – political assassination, bribery, fraud, the opaque financing of political parties, the apparently motiveless attacks on supermarkets that killed 28 people between 1982 and 1985, and so on – have culminated in the paedophile scandal which broke in 1996, triggering the reopening of earlier unsolved cases. The Belgians' already shaky confidence in the functioning of democratic institutions was shattered completely by dramatic failures in the judicial and police investigations of the scandals. The emotional outburst that resulted, including the largest demonstration march in post-war Belgium – the White March of October 1996 – was a clear warning to the political elite that things had to change.

These events have added to the vulnerability of institutions increasingly evident since the beginning of the 1990s. This reflected, first, the gradual disintegration of the Belgian nation into a complicated federal state, with extensive political and cultural autonomy for regions and language communities, formalized in the new Constitution of 1993. Second, the political determination to comply with the Maastricht 'convergence criteria' for European Monetary Union has required such an emphasis on technical and budgetary issues that policy-making has been side-lined. Third, parliament has been bypassed by policy-makers with disturbing regularity. There is a common thread to these elements which constitutes a crucial factor in *le mal belge*: exceptionally successful economic development in the post-war period created successive generations of political élites who took personal credit for the socio-economic achievements of high growth, full employment, and a comprehensive welfare system. This was true on both the macro- and local levels. Local politicians raised to an art form the rendering of a range of personal services to actual or potential voters, from help with finding a job or housing, to completing tax forms. This system of patronage developed in parallel with the formal democratic control system, undermining the latter from within since the personnel of both systems overlapped. The party-political capture of the democratic institutions resulted in a pattern of interaction based on trade-offs between the different parties and their representatives. We refer to this style of socio-political exchange, within the context of the pillar/cleavage configuration in Belgium, as 'compensation democracy' (see Vilrokx and Van Leemput 1992); we return to this explanatory framework below.

The focus of this chapter is on the role of the government in post-war Belgium. Four distinct phases can be distinguished. The fourth, from the end of the 1980s, is a period of transition in Belgian industrial relations, marked by extensive state intervention. We argue that three distinctive features of the Belgian model – wide-ranging central agreements, an institutionalized and hierarchical negotiation structure, and the automatic linkage of wages to the cost of living – have been neutralized in the current, fourth, phase. Before turning to these developments, we first outline the nature of post-war socio-economic development in Belgium, and summarize the main institutional features of the Belgian industrial relations system.

Post-war Socio-economic Development in Belgium

An Extremely Open Economy, 'Expansion Laws', Colonial Wealth

The impact of global economic restructuring from 1973–4 was particularly dramatic in Belgium. Its traditionally open economy, colonial past, and post-war economic 'expansion laws' to encourage foreign investment, had ensured it the enviable status of one of Europe's richest countries in the 1960s. These favourable conditions proved unable to resist the shock of economic restructuring; indeed, they impeded efficient counter-measures. First, its open economy meant that economic turmoil hit Belgium earlier and harder than its neighbours. It exports some 70 per cent of its GNP to pay for its imports, compared with 30 per cent in the UK and around 25 per cent in France and Germany (OECD figures, *Bulletin van de Generale*, November 1996: 2). It has no remaining natural resources and few large industrial or financial groups. Second, the expansion laws of the 1950s and 1960s attracted foreign firms whose interests were mostly short-term. Most of them engaged in activities from which they could withdraw quite easily if better opportunities presented themselves, or simply when the time limit on fiscal and other benefits expired. One of these 'nomads', the UK-based Prestige, provoked the first post-war factory occupation, and one of the more notable experiments in 'self-production' in Belgium, by deciding in 1976 to relocate its Belgian production site to the UK (De Coninck and Vilrokx 1977). Third, the colonial past had allowed most families to share in the immense riches flowing from the former Belgian Congo. Even after the territory became independent in 1960, the transfer of wealth continued, lasting well into the 1960s. Accumulated savings shielded a large proportion of households from the effects of economic restructuring.

These features help explain why awareness of the economic situation was slow to penetrate the consciousness of most Belgians. Unemployment rose rapidly from 1974, and in 1976 the government took its first measures to provide job training for young people and to control wage levels. But it was only from the 1980s that concern about the economy and employment became generalized. This was a pivotal period: two government crises and the failure of tripartite discussions on the employment problem in 1980, the government's decision to freeze private sector wages for 1981–2, the mass 'jobless march' in 1982 and the 8.5 per cent devaluation in the same year coincided with a second sharp increase in unemployment (see table 11.1). Moreover, in many respects Belgium became in the 1980s the test bed for experiments, often by multinational firms, in working time, personnel policy, and organizational flexibility (Rosseel and Vilrokx 1992).

Table 11.1 Employment and unemployment in Belgium, 1970–1995 (000s)

| | Employment | | | Unemployment | | | | | Labour |
	Self-employed	Private	Public	Total (000s)	% Fl	Wa	Br	Belgium	force[1] (000s)
1970	679	2,266	696	71	1.4	2.7	1.0	1.9	3,769
1975	614	2,281	799	174	4.0	5.3	3.6	4.5	3,925
1980	606	2,145	949	322	7.3	9.0	7.0	7.9	4,070
1985	634	1,962	965	506	11.5	15.5	12.6	12.3	4,112
1990	675	2,118	971	365	6.4	12.5	11.4	8.7	4,179
1995	699	2,052	944	555	9.6	17.5	18.2	12.9	4,301

Fl = Flanders, Wa = Wallonia, Br = Brussels.
[1] Labour force figures include cross-border labour.
Note: From 1970–1995, the employment rate has been stable at around 37 per cent.
Source: Ministerie van Tewerkstelling en Arbeid.

The Defining Characteristics of the Belgian Model of Industrial Relations

The Belgian model of industrial relations is 'exceptional' in three respects. First there has been a pattern, from 1960, of bipartite intersectoral agreements (IPA–AIP) covering the whole of the private sector. Each of these agreements provided the framework for social and employment policy over the subsequent 2-year period (3 years at the beginning of the 1960s) and they were thus often known as 'social planning' agreements. They addressed not only direct employment issues such as the minimum wage, working time and holiday regulations, but also policies on the unemployed, pension schemes, child benefits, and so on. Indeed, the construction of the welfare state in Belgium was largely carried out through them. It is no surprise, therefore, that neo-conservatives demanding the abolition of the welfare state should launch fierce attacks on the tradition of central agreements.

The second peculiarity of the Belgian model is the highly institutionalized 'pyramid of negotiation'. The signing of an overall central agreement initiated a hierarchical sequence of negotiations at lower levels, resulting in intersectoral, sectoral and company-level collective agreements (CAO–CCT). At intersectoral level, elements of the programmatic central agreements were developed further in economy-wide collective agreements in the bipartite National Labour Council (NAR–CNT), or embodied in legislation. Other elements were the subject of bipartite negotiation at the sectoral level in the Joint Committees (PCs–CPs) and subsequently of company-specific agreements in negotiations between management and the trade union delegation (SD–DS). CAOs–CCTs are legally binding and therefore are very widely enforced. Equally, however, the trade unions have traditionally adopted a highly 'responsible' attitude to enforcement (formalized in the 1968 law on CAOs–CCTs, which includes a social peace obligation for the duration of the agreement). This institutionalized pattern of relations has promoted relatively high trust between the parties.

The third specificity of the Belgian model is the automatic linkage of wages to the price of goods and services. Under this system of 'indexation', an automatic 2 per cent rise in wages, and in most welfare benefits, is triggered by each 2 per cent rise in the cost of living. The system has had advantages as well as drawbacks for both sides of industry. The employers' increasingly urgent calls for abolition of indexation has to be understood in the context of the international economic pressures for reductions in labour costs, rather than as a wholesale rejection of the mechanism. The long-term index-linking of non-work benefits has also been called into question in the light of worsening public expenditure constraints.

Below we argue that, while none of the three elements has been formally abandoned, their ability to shape the industrial relations system has been neutralized and, as a result, the system is undergoing a radical transformation.

Actors and Institutions

Trade Unions

The structure of Belgian unionism (see Pasture 1996 for a historical account) reflects the major dividing lines of Belgian society. Thus separate confederations exist for each of the three 'pillars' or dominant ideological tendencies in Belgium – catholic, socialist and liberal. The pillars provide the institutionalized socio-cultural, economic and political mechanisms for the defence of the specific interests of each group. Each provides a comprehensive range of services for its adherents. This pillar structure is crossed by three cleavages: between capital and labour, between church and state, and between the French-speaking Walloon and the Dutch-speaking Flemish communities; each have their own institutional arrangements.

The largest union confederation is the catholic General Christian Trade Union Confederation (ACV/CSC), followed by the socialist General Belgian Trade Union Federation (ABVV/FGTB). The smallest is the liberal General Confederation of Liberal Trade Unions in Belgium (ACLVB/CGSLB). In recent decades, Belgian trade union structures have adapted to the growing autonomy of the regions (Flanders, Wallonia and Brussels). The socialist confederation has had regional structures since 1963 and the catholic body since 1978. The liberal confederation has resisted this trend, and still has a predominantly unitary character.

Despite a strong similarity in structure, internal power relations within the Christian and socialist unions are significantly different. Both have a dual industrial and geographical structure. The socialist confederation is divided into eight unions (centrals): one for white-collar workers, one for civil servants, and six organized by industrial sector. There is also an association for young workers. The centrals have considerable power and autonomy, including for example, control over their own strike funds. Each has company-level and local branches. Geographically they form sub-regional intersectoral bodies and there are three main regional organizations (Inter-Regionals) for Flanders, Wallonia and Brussels. The centrals control two-thirds of the votes at the national confederal level; the remainder are in the hands of intersectoral structures. The Christian ACV/CSC has a similar structure, with 15 centrals (nine in the private sector, two for civil servants, and four in education, as well as two associations for young workers and one for professional sportspeople) organized in three Regional Committees. But it is more centralized than its socialist counterpart. Thus in contrast to the socialist union, there is only one, centralized, strike fund. The much smaller liberal trade union (ACLVB/ CGSLB) is the most centralized. It has no industrial federations and no separate organizations for white- and blue-collar workers. Only since 1989 has it cautiously started to adapt its administrative structure to regionalism.

The first forms of workers' organization in Belgium, the corporatist *mutualités* of craftsmen, developed only in the middle of the nineteenth century, and only in the last quarter of the century were trade unions allowed to establish themselves. The socialist union has always held a dominant position in the large enterprises of Wallonia, where basic industries including coalmining and steel production were located. When economic power and employment shifted to the emerging industries and services of Flanders in the 1950s and 1960s, the Christian trade union appealed to the more instrumental, less ideological attitudes of increasingly affluent workers in the region's new small and medium-sized enterprises. Recruiting workforces mostly from the catholic hinterland, ACV/CSC's 'modern' vision contrasted sharply with the old traditional working-class image of Walloon socialist unionism. Consequently, there are considerable differences in trade union dynamics along regional lines.

Table 11.2 shows the evolution of union membership in Belgium. Union strength has been maintained even during periods of global economic restructuring. A substantial increase (11.9 per cent) took place in 1990–5. This is largely due to the fact that Belgian unions also organize the unemployed and retired workers, and play an important role in the administration of the unemployment benefit system. Thus they cannot be seen merely as organizations of and for the employed; as we have already seen, trade unions form an integral part of the Belgian socio-economic and cultural structure and they have played a large part in the development of the welfare state.

In Flanders, the minority socialist union increased membership more rapidly than the Christian union in 1990–5 (by 23.9 per cent against 7.4 per cent). Conversely, in Wallonia the minority Christian union grew by 19.8 per cent, against 12.2 per cent for the socialist union. In 1995, the Christian and socialist unions respectively recruited 66.9 and 47.8 per cent of their members in Flanders, 22.0 and 39.9 per cent in Wallonia, and 11.1 and 23.3 per cent in Brussels. Within Flanders, taking the members of the two main unions, almost two-thirds belong to the Christian union, which also has a smaller but still significant majority of members in the Brussels region. In Wallonia, the socialist union is predominant, with 57 per cent of the total.

The socialist union has a very strong presence in the public sector, where it

Table 11.2 Total membership and regional distribution of the Belgian trade unions

	Flanders			Wallonia			Brussels			Belgium		
	1985	*1990*	*1995*	*1985*	*1990*	*1995*	*1985*	*1990*	*1995*	*1985*	*1990*	*1995*
ABVV/FGTB	470,561	454,397	563,080	468,256	418,204	469,208	158,777	141,464	144,413	1,097,594	1,014,065	1,176,701
ACV/CSC	934,220	984,719	1,057,524	271,847	290,638	347,958	161,325	155,214	176,034	1,367,589	1,430,571	1,581,516
Subtotal	*1,404,781*	*1,439,116*	*1,620,604*	*740,103*	*708,842*	*817,166*	*320,102*	*296,678*	*320,447*	*2,465,183*	*2,444,636*	*2,758,217*
ACLVB/CGSLB	n.a.	n.a.	n.a.	n.a.	n.a.	n.a.	n.a.	n.a.	n.a.	210,936	213,098	216,035
Total										**2,676,119**	**2,657,734**	**2,974,252**

Source: 1985 ABVV/FGTB and ACV/CSC, Arcq and Blaise 1986; ACLVB/CGSLB figures, provided by the union; 1990 and 1995 provided by the unions.

organizes two-thirds of the members of the two main unions. Some 23 per cent of ABVV/FGTB belong to the public services central (the confederation's second largest); the comparable figure for ACV/CSC is 11 per cent. Given that the public sector has been highly strike prone in recent decades, its dominance by ABVV/ FGTB helps preserve the union's historical image as the more action-oriented and militant of the two major confederations.

Employers

On the employers' side, there are three main groups of organizations: industry and commerce, small business, and agriculture. The Federation of Belgian Enterprises (VBO/FEB) comprises 36 sectoral employers' organizations in private industry and commerce, representing some 50,000 of Belgium's 180,000 enterprises (Krzeslo 1996: 32) and 85 per cent of the workforce (Van Ruysseveldt and Visser 1995: 20). It maintains a strong 'unitary' national orientation, although it has established good working relations with the regional employers' organizations. The VBO/FEB is the main representative of the employers in intersectoral negotiation (including the bipartite central agreement negotiations) and in tripartite national concertation.

Unlike the VBO/FEB, the regional employers' organizations group individual firms rather than federations. The Flemish Economic Union (VEV), dating back to 1926, adopted a radical regionalist perspective from the start. It now actively pursues a policy of greater regional autonomy, advocating a specific industrial relations system for Flanders. Less influential regional organizations are the Walloon Union of Enterprises (UWE) formed in 1968, and the Union of Brussels Enterprises (VOB/UEB) set up in 1971.

Small and medium-sized enterprises have the possibility of affiliating to specialist organizations. The National Christian Traders' Union (NCMV/OBPME) is domi- nant in Flanders and Brussels, while its main competitor, the Union of Traders (AMV/UCM), is the the most important in Wallonia. In agriculture, employer interests are defended by the Flemish dominated Belgian Farmers' Union (BB), the Union of Agricultural Professionals (UPA) and the Belgian Agricultural Alliance (ABB). The BB is the strongest of the three organizations and is politically influential, forming the agricultural wing of the Christian Democratic Party.

Social Elections

At the level of the enterprise two consultative institutions exist: the works council (OR/CE), obligatory in companies with 100 employees and over; and the com- mittee for prevention and protection in the workplace (CPBW/CPPT, introduced under the 'Law on Well-being' of August 1996 – formerly the committee for safety, health and improvement in the workplace), obligatory in companies with 50 employees or more. Workers' representatives on these bodies are chosen by all company employees from lists of candidates drawn up by the three representative

Table 11.3 Percentage of votes for works councils 1954–1995

	ABVV/FGTB	ACV/CSC	ACLVB/CGSLB	NCK/CNC
1954	59.0	37.0	3.5	
1958	55.0	41.0	4.0	
1963	51.1	43.8	5.1	
1967	51.5	42.5	6.0	
1971	48.7	45.5	5.8	
1975	46.1	47.7	6.2	
1979	42.6	50.1	7.3	
1983	43.4	48.6	7.9	
1987	40.8	47.9	7.5	3.8
1991	37.9	51.5	7.5	3.1
1995	37.5	51.7	8.3	1.5

Source: Ministerie van Tewerkstelling en Arbeid.

trade unions (and, since 1987, by the National Confederation of Middle Management). So-called 'social elections' are held every 4 years (see tables 11.2 and 11.3). The first elections for works council were held in 1950, and for health and safety committees in 1958.

In 1995, the twelfth round of social elections took place. Safety committee elections were held in 5,376 companies covering 35 per cent of the active workforce, nearly 1.3 million employees. Works council elections took place in 3,069 companies employing around 1.1 million employees, 31 per cent of the total workforce. The results of these elections are the most important measure of the relative power positions of the different unions. The participation rate was somewhat lower for safety committees elections (63 per cent) than for works councils (65 per cent). One of the most striking features was the low participation of young workers: only half of them voted in market sector companies and even fewer (one quarter) in the non-market sector.

Works councils have only limited decision-making powers, setting annual holiday periods and organizing – under management control – so-called 'social funds'; but they are the most prominent forum for discussion of issues of mutual concern. Under the Royal Decree of August 1996, works councils were given responsibility for the drawing up of a 'social balance sheet'. From 1997, companies have to submit a detailed yearly report on the development of personnel issues, flows of staff, vocational training, and the use of government employment incentives to the Central Accounts Administration of the National Bank (where the annual accounts of companies also have to be deposited).

Table 11.4 gives the results of works council elections in terms of seats in 1991 and 1995. The general picture is of considerable stability. However, over a longer time period, the relative positions of the socialist and the Christian unions have been reversed, the turning point coming in the 1971 elections. Notable too is the decline in support for the middle management lists.

Blaise (1996: 40–1) correctly observes that the importance of the social elections should not be overestimated. They are certainly the most visible manifestation of

Table 11.4 Percentage of seats won in works councils in 1991 and 1995*

	ABVV/FGTB	ACV/CSC	ACLVB/CGSLB	NCK/CNC, etc.
Overall				
1991	33.7	59.1	4.2	3.1
1995	33.7	58.6	5.0	2.7
Sector				
Market sector				
1991	39.5	52.2	4.6	3.8
1995	39.4	51.7	5.5	3.4
Non-market sector				
1991	15.1	81.1	3.0	0.8
1995	16.3	79.7	3.3	0.7
Region				
Flanders				
1991	25.8(31.8)	68.2(60.9)	4.0(4.9)	2.0(2.5)
1995	27.0(32.6)	66.2(59.3)	5.0(5.9)	1.8(2.2)
Wallonia				
1991	46.0(55.7)	48.1(38.1)	2.7(2.2)	3.1(3.9)
1995	44.0(55.1)	50.2(38.5)	2.9(2.6)	2.9(3.8)
Brussels				
1991	41.4(43.3)	45.8(43.2)	6.7(6.3)	6.1(7.1)
1995	40.2(41.5)	47.1(45.0)	7.4(7.4)	5.3(6.2)
Category				
Blue-collar				
1991	41.8(44.1)	54.5(52.0)	3.8(3.9)	
1995	41.6(44.3)	54.1(51.3)	4.3(4.4)	
White-collar				
1991	28.6(38.4)	66.7(55.7)	4.7(5.9)	
1995	29.0(38.1)	65.6(55.1)	5.5(6.8)	
Youngsters				
1991	34.8(37.8)	62.1(59.0)	3.1(3.2)	
1995	36.2(40.2)	60.8(57.0)	3.0(2.8)	
Middle management				
1991	14.9(15.3)	32.5(29.9)	5.0(4.8)	47.6(50.0)
1995	17.1(17.3)	38.2(35.7)	7.0(7.2)	37.7(37.7)

* Figures in brackets are for the market sector only.
Source: Ministerie van Tewerkstelling en Arbeid 1992 and 1996.

competition between the unions and they receive much media attention. Their outcome largely determines the composition of trade union representation in all kinds of (semi-)public, bipartite and other bodies, and they are thus a crucial element in the smooth functioning of what we have called the 'institutional incorporation' of trade unions (Vilrokx and Van Leemput 1992). Nonetheless the results of the social elections are only a partial indicator of union influence. First, trade unions are active in companies that do not organize social elections, which form the great majority. While the electorate for social elections totals some 1.3 million workers, aggregate trade union membership is more than double (although it includes unemployed and retired members). Second, the works council electorate is not confined to trade union members but comprises all workers.

▌Negotiation, Consultation, Concertation

Mapping the relations between the social partners, Arcq (1993a) distinguishes three dimensions. The first, 'point of departure for the construction of the system of industrial relations (p. 9) is negotiation. Dedicated bipartite institutions and procedures, as well as national-intersectoral, sectoral and company-level mechanisms, are in place to deal with the negotiation aspect. The second dimension is consultation. This concerns the bipartite regulation of matters of common interest. If the first dimension implies conflicting interests, consultation favours dialogue and the exchange of information in a consensual environment. Here too institutional arrangements exist at all three levels. The third dimension is concertation. This comprises the tripartite element of relations and concerns only the national and regional levels. Contrary to the highly formalized mechanisms of negotiation and consultation, concertation is almost exclusively ad hoc. In the literature, the term 'concertation economy' (*overlegeconomie-économie de concertation*) is often used to characterize the Belgian industrial relations environment (see Beaupain 1994). This should not, however, obscure the importance of the negotiation and consultation dimensions of the Belgian model. (See figure 11.1.)

The new Constitution of 1993 gave further impetus to the strong forces (most explicitly in Flanders) seeking to reshape the dimensions of industrial relations along regional lines. The regional factor is important for an understanding of Belgian industrial relations (Vilrokx and Van Leemput 1992), but it is still too early to make a definitive evaluation of its significance. The Brussels region's extremely complicated status has prevented an institutional differentiation between the tripartite and bipartite levels. The Economic and Social Council for the Brussels Region (ESRBG/CESRB), which integrates both levels, has not played a major role. In Wallonia, the bipartite consultative Economic and Social Council of the Walloon Region (CESRW) is the main regional industrial relations forum. So far, there are few signs of pressures to develop regional industrial relations institutions at odds with national ones. In Flanders, by contrast, the tripartite Flemish Economic and Social Concertation Committee (VESOC) has concluded tripartite agreements on regional labour market policy, which nationally would be dealt with at the bipartite level. The bipartite Social and Economic Council of Flanders (SERV) advises the Flemish government on social and economic issues through its bipartite committees. There have also been increasingly urgent demands for Flanders to 'regionalize' existing social welfare mechanisms, most importantly the national social security system. Given the important role of the social partners in the management of welfare systems, 'regionalization' could entail the regionalization of industrial relations as well.

In the discussion below of the four phases of Belgian industrial relations, the different institutional settings of these three dimensions will be examined. At this point it is necessary to note that, as far as bipartite relations are concerned, conflict

Figure 11.1 Concertation, consultation and negotiation in the private sector

	Tripartite Concertation		Bipartite Consultation		Bipartite Negotiation	
	Institutional	Non-institutional	Institutional	Institutional	Institutional	Non-institutional
National	**NCEE/CNEE**	**NAC/CNT**	**NAR/CNT; CRB/CCE** **BRC/CCS** **OR/CE; CPBW/CPPT**		**NAR/CNT**	**IPA/AIP**
Sectoral					**PC/CP**	**(SD/DS)**
Company						
Regional						
Flemish region	**VESOC**			**SERV***		
Walloon region				**CESRW**		
Brussels region	**ESRBG/CESRB**			**ESRBG/CESRB**		

* The SERV has also sectoral committees since 1990.

as well as consensus has become institutionalized (figure 11.1), reflecting the divergent perspectives on industrial relations of the two main components, socialist and Christian, of the labour movement in Belgium. While conflict and consensus are, of course, integral parts of any industrial relations system, probably nowhere else are they as formally embedded in the institutional framework of industrial relations as in Belgium.

▌ Industrial Relations in the Public Sector

For some years there has been both a growing convergence in employment relations between the public and private sector, and a growing differentiation of conditions within the public sector (Vilrokx and Van Leemput 1992). In recent years, the latter trend has been reinforced by the restructuring of public administration, services and the educational system. A new element has also emerged, partly as a consequence of the recent privatization trend: the erosion of the statutory model of public sector employment relations, and the growing preference of policy-makers for a more contractual, private sector model.

Under legislation of March 1991, a number of state companies were transformed into 'autonomous public companies' providing services to the public on the basis of a 'management contract' with the government. In 1992 the national railway, telecommunications and postal services became autonomous public companies, and banking and insurance have also been affected. Private firms may buy sizeable minority, and in some cases majority, shareholdings in public enterprises and services. The most spectacular cases of such privatizations are ASLK/CGER (the largest of the publicly owned banking and insurance companies) and Belgacom (the national telecommunications company), both of which are now half owned by foreign firms. The case of ASLK/CGER is extremely significant: on privatization in 1993, all employees lost their statutory public employment status and are now governed by private sector contractual arrangements.

Notwithstanding these developments, over 900,000 civil servants (some 20 per cent of the active population) are still covered by public sector employment relations. There are similarities to private sector relations, notably in the use of negotiation, consultation and concertation, and the practice of concluding 2-year central agreements, which cover all civil servants. The first of these agreements was signed in 1962 but, as in the private sector, government pay policy contributed to the discontinuation of central agreements in the 1980s. Another element in this failure was the erosion of two features that had earlier compensated for relatively low public sector pay: life-time employment and favourable public-sector pension schemes; the latter were losing their attraction amid fears about the state's future ability to fund them.

The complex institutional arrangements of public sector industrial relations are quite different from those of the private sector (for an overview see Krzeslo 1996). However, most of the achievements of interprofessional negotiations have been extended by royal decrees to the public sector. In 1996, a government-inspired agreement on the redistribution of working time (under which employees could

Table 11.5 Strike frequency in the private sector 1976–1993

Year	NIS Belgium	Flanders	Wallonia	Brussels	Multi-region strikes	ACV/CSC TESA/VUB Belgium
1976	281	74	209	25		308
1977	220	75	175	14		264
1978	193	80	283	16		379
1979	214	101	170	12		283
1980	131	133	176	7		316
1981		74	164	14		252
1982		48	106	13		167
1983		26	99	6		131
1984		29	75	3		107
1985	64	53	123	5		181
1986		48	53	8	9	118
1987		64	45	11	1	121
1988	64	22	42	12	1	77
1989	55	57	51	7	4	114
1990	32	60	22	15	1	98
1991	62	50	42	18	5	115
1992	49	48	49	14	7	118
1993		60	52	7	15	134

Sources: National Institute for Statistics – Corrected by TESA.
ACV/CSC for 1976–8: Piret et al. 1985;: Hertogs and Piret 1986 for 1979–1985; TESA/VUB for 1986–1993.

apply for ⁴⁄₅ of a job) was reached for all public servants in state and regional administrations.

▌ Industrial Conflict

The beginning of the 1990s was marked by high profile industrial conflicts in the private as well as the (semi-)public sector. This has led to speculation that strike activity was on the increase. Our data indicate that this is not the case (see tables 11.5 and 11.6). Throughout the 1980s and the beginning of the 1990s, there was relative stability at a substantially lower level than in the second half of the 1970s. Our provisional data for the period 1994–6 suggest that this trend has continued. As table 11.5 shows, there has been no great variation in differential private sector strike behaviour between regions since the mid-1980s. The comparable numbers of strikes in Flanders and Wallonia obscure the fact that the relative strike frequency is approximately twice as high in Wallonia as in Flanders. The sectoral distribution of strikes has changed markedly: private sector strikes have more than halved since the mid-1970s peak, while those in the public sector have more than doubled (table 11.6).

Table 11.6 Strike frequency in the different sectors 1976–1993

	Private sector	Subsidized sector	Public sector	Multi-sector strikes	Total
1976	308	12	23	0	343
1977	264	n.a.	n.a.	n.a.	n.a.
1978	379	0	22	0	401
1979	283	19	32	0	334
1980	316	25	46	2	389
1981	252	13	38	0	303
1982	157	8	56	0	221
1983	131	7	29	2	169
1984	107	11	30	0	148
1985	181	8	49	0	238
1986	111	11	88	10	220
1987	121	17	81	0	219
1988	76	11	84	1	172
1989	114	21	79	4	218
1990	98	15	85	3	201
1991	115	17	74	0	206
1992	118	22	70	1	211
1993	129	18	55	11	213

Source: ACV/CSC for 1976–8: Piret et al. 1985; for 1979–1985: Hertogs and Piret 1986. TESA/VUB – for 1986–1993.

In the 1990s, perhaps surprisingly, widespread restructuring involving redundancies has not led to an increase in industrial conflict. The reason for this is that most rationalizations, closures and relocations have been accompanied by favourable packages to 'buy off' the workers affected. Within the prevailing financial–capitalist logic of the globalized economy (Vilrokx 1996) trade union action has been defensively directed at obtaining material compensation rather than preserving jobs: for example, more than 1,500,000 workers have 'benefited' from early retirement measures over the last 10 years. More recently, influenced by some spectacular cases of industrial disinvestment by companies such as Delacre, Boston Instruments, Nova, Forges de Clabecq and Renault, there has been a growing awareness among trade union leaders as well as the rank and file that the European Union is unable to curb the negative employment consequences of economic integration. The assertions of politicians that the European level is powerless to influence company strategies have led workers increasingly to blame 'Europe' for high and rising unemployment. This frustration of workers' expectations of the European Union has potentially serious consequences for Belgium's social climate.

▌Four Phases in Post-war Industrial Relations

Four phases may be distinguished in the evolution of Belgian industrial relations, each lasting roughly 15 years (see also Vilrokx 1995). This periodization may also be relevant, with adaptations, for other industrialized European countries. The role of the state, on which the periodization is based, is increasingly internationally comparable for significant aspects of labour regulation. Even if in the immediate post-war period (the first two phases in our model) the autonomy of the national states, and their potential to pursue distinct policies, was considerably greater than it is today, broad similarities are nonetheless evident.

The four phases are:
- the period 1945–59 during which the tripartite institutionalization of industrial relations took place;
- a phase of predominantly bipartite negotiation from 1960 to 1974;
- the period 1975–89 in which the negotiation process was impeded by restrictive government policies, resulting in an emphasis on bipartite consultation;
- and, finally, the current period (1990–) in which government is redefining the boundaries of negotiation and, indirectly, influencing the scope for consultation.

▌Phase 1 – Institutionalization (1945–59)

Laying the Foundations

From the signing of the Draft Agreement on Social Solidarity (the 'Social Pact'), by employers' and trade union leaders in 1944, the social partners and the state undertook an extraordinary range of activities. The explicit intention was to create a framework to facilitate post-war reconstruction. Within a couple of years a dense and subtle web of bi- and tripartite bargaining arrangements had been established.

Of crucial importance for the restructuring of labour relations during this period were the Law on the Organization of the Economy of 1948, establishing, among other things, works councils and the Central Economic Council, and the Joint Declaration on Productivity, or 'Productivity Agreement', of 1954 on the distribution of the benefits of technological and organizational innovation between workers, consumers and employers. These two events reinforced the underlying principle of Belgian industrial relations: the exclusive prerogative of employers on all matters of strategic and financial decision-making, combined with an obligation on management to negotiate and consult with workers' organizations on all social aspects of working conditions.

What distinguishes Belgium from France and the Netherlands, where quite similar developments took place in the same period, is the way in which ideological differences between the two main trade unions were addressed and how the continuity of the institutionalization of post-war industrial relations was achieved.

The ideological divide between the socialist and catholic components of the labour movement was more pronounced than today. Already in 1924, De Brouckère had developed the idea of workers' control, the main theoretical and practical reference point for the socialist union. The Walloon union leader, Renard, defined the strategic objective of workers' control in the 1950s as a 'halving of employers' power'. The doctrine of the catholic trade union was clearly opposed to such a view. Until the 1920s it was explicitly anti-socialist. Thereafter, under the influence of cardinal Cardijn, it emphasized the unique contribution of the catholic belief system to the emancipation of workers. Nonetheless, a corporatist notion of collaboration with employers, as promoted by the catholic Church through the various encyclicals, remained the dominant component of its ideology.

Probably the most important difference between the two unions was in their attitude to the crucial question of union action within the company. The socialists, still the strongest component of the labour movement at the time, advocated a union-based representative body or 'delegation' within the enterprise. This was seen as the instrument of workers' control over collective and individual matters. The trade union delegation embodied the conflictual element of industrial relations and would be responsible for negotiating company-level collective agreements. The principle of the delegation was accepted, with the backing of a government coalition of socialists, liberals and communists, in the tripartite National Labour Conference in 1947. Much later, in 1971, the National Labour Council (Collective Labour Agreement 5, last revised in 1978) formalized the status of the union delegation but left detailed arrangements to the sectoral and company levels; the delegation's composition is a matter for unions to decide. In the same period, within the framework of the 1948 Law on the Organization of the Economy, the sensitivities of the catholic trade union were accommodated through the decision to organize works councils, which were subsequently the subject of negotiations in the National Labour Council (CLA 9, 1972, modified in 1991).

The introduction of union delegations and works councils thus represents a *compromis à la belge*: instead of choosing one of the two options for workplace representation, both are implemented. As a result, a long-standing source of conflict between the two unions could be neutralized at a crucial moment in the institutionalization of industrial relations. It could be argued that this compromise at enterprise level was an essential element in the successful completion of the institutionalization process.

At other levels of bi- and tripartite interaction, similar steps toward institutionalization had already been taken. At sectoral level, bipartite joint committees had existed in some form since 1919 and their functions were progressively enlarged. The first tripartite National Labour Conference in 1936 introduced the possibility of wide-ranging concertation, legitimatizing labour movement action at the national intersectoral level. These institutional elements were consolidated in the early post-war period which saw the integration of the trade unions in the process of constructing the welfare state.

A Twofold Delegation by the State to the Social Partners

In the interrelated development of Belgian industrial relations and the welfare state, the state has delegated important functions to the social partners. First, it has transferred part of the responsibility for the conception of the welfare state to the bipartite level. This was already apparent when the state not only adopted the principles of the 1944 Social Pact on the social security system to be constructed after the War (see Vanthemsche 1994: 44), but also accepted the financial costs. The state would continue to honour this commitment during the second phase, the historically unique period of full employment from the end of the 1950s until the mid-1970s.

Second, and equally important, the state subcontracted to the social partners the implementation of several aspects of welfare state provision. Thus the unions are responsible for the administration of unemployment benefits, which is often said to be one of the reasons for high union density and the relative stability of union membership in Belgium. The administration fee that the unions receive from the state for carrying out this function is an important source of income for them. In addition, significant welfare state functions have been delegated to the bipartite level, most importantly the management of the social security system, including the National Institute of Sickness and Invalidity Insurance and the Industrial Accidents Fund. The social partners play a major role in the development of sectoral vocational training, for which central agreements since 1988 have provided funding. An elaborate sectoral system (e.g. Vilrokx and Forceville 1996; Denys 1995) of vocational training has been organized, although it is currently under pressure (Van Gramberen and Denys 1996). Government departments also fund a number of bipartite institutions, for example the Central Economic Council and the National Labour Council (for a detailed description of these two institutions, see Beaupain 1994). Finally, the Ministry of Employment and Labour has a department for collective labour relations, makes conciliators available for industrial conflicts, and provides chairpersons and logistics for sectoral Joint Committees.

The Functioning of Compensation Democracy

These interrelated elements must be analysed within the particular Belgian exchange system we have called compensation democracy (Vilrokx and Van Leemput 1992). In order to play the role allocated to them in the construction of the welfare state, the social partners, and more specifically the trade unions, had to be strong and reliable actors. But the generous allocation of resources directed to that purpose enabled the social partners to establish themselves as relatively autonomous power centres, with the capacity to destabilize the state. The state thus became, in a sense, a prisoner of the dynamic it had initiated, and was forced to maintain the involvement of the social partners in the functioning of the welfare system. This power paradox continued until the mid-1970s, when economic restructuring began to take hold.

Nevertheless, it would be wrong to isolate the evolution of relations between the state and the social partners from the broader context of socio-political, cultural and economic exchange mechanisms. It is questionable whether the first phase of post-war industrial relations can be labelled as neo-corporatist. Arcq and Marques-Pereira (1991) doubt, to our mind correctly, that the neo-corporatist frame of reference can accommodate the permanent conflicts of interest occurring within the Belgian industrial relations environment. Equally, it is doubtful whether the following 15-year period may be interpreted as 'pluralist'; although the state largely retreats from the industrial relations scene and leaves the social partners free to negotiate, it still takes responsibility for the consequences of the negotiation process. Again, the specificity of the Belgian situation makes it difficult for observers to position Belgium on the neo-corporatism–pluralism continuum (e.g. Visser 1996); the very general indicators commonly used by these models cannot convincingly account for the 'real industrial relations in Belgium. Even the highly sophisticated comparative framework offered by Crouch (1993) cannot do full justice to the complexity of the Belgian situation. This results, in our view, from the combination of, on the one hand, the specific, multi-layered structure of the industrial relations system built around negotiation, consultation, concertation, and, on the other, the institutional incorporation of the social partners in the functioning of compensation democracy in the realm of socio-economic life.

As we stressed in our contribution to the first edition, industrial relations in Belgium should not be analysed as a separate social subsystem, but in terms of the institutional and ideological incorporation of the social partners in the pillar–cleavage configuration. Conflicts of interest were resolved by acceding to the demands of one interest group while at the same time providing additional resources to compensate other groups involved. The more or less simultaneous introduction of both the works council and the trade union delegation is an illustration of this compensation mechanism within the industrial relations sphere.

The compensation principle, conceived by the élites of the different pillar and cleavage organizations, was accepted by public opinion and legitimized by the democratic institutions of the country. It explains the high level of conflicts in Belgian society, but also the specific nature of those conflicts: since they resulted in benefits for all involved, they were not seen as something to be feared and, consequently, were not systematically suppressed. An exchange system was built up in which competing demands were not eliminated but neutralized through compensation mechanisms. The state was prepared to assume the financial consequences of this positive-sum arrangement.

Phase 2 – Free Collective Bargaining (1960–74)

Bipartite Social Planning

The mechanisms created in the first 15 years after the Second World War, leading to what we have called the power paradox of relations between the state and the social actors, were perfected in the second phase. Against a background of sustained economic growth in the 1960s, the pillar and cleavage élites were able to consolidate the system of compensation democracy. A key element in this was

Table 11.7 Number of collective agreements 1970–1996

Year	NAR/CNT National level	PC/CP Sectoral level	Company level
1970	4(+0)	392	38
1971	3(+1)	453	71
1972	2(+0)	637	56
1973	5(+0)	556	50
1974	3(+0)	738	66
1975	10(+3)	500	51
1976	2(+2)	401	44
1977	2(+2)	518	46
1978	2(+3)	503	120
1979	0(+3)	400	225
1980	0(+3)	442	341
1981	4(+5)	243	480
1982	0(+2)	186	623
1983	2(+9)	277	1,861
1984	1(+1)	220	1,073
1985	0(+3)	346	3,250
1986	1(+6)	192	1,436
1987	1(+2)	512	1,985
1988	1(+4)	257	1,851
1989	2(+8)	766	2,255
1990	2(+8)	241	1,091
1991	3(+11)	879	2,146
1992	2(+6)	272	1,880
1993	5(+5)	636	2,440
1994	3(+1)	390	1,954
1995	1(+4)	834	2,038
1996	1(+1)	230	2,187

Notes: The first national level figures concern the original collective agreements; figures between brackets (in italics) are revisions to the original agreements.
Royal Decree 181 (30 December 1982) made registration of company-level agreements obligatory in practice.
Sources: Ministerie van Tewerkstelling en Arbeid Department van Collectieve Arbeidsbetrekkingen and NAR.

the series of bipartite central agreements (IPA–AIP), introduced in 1960 and continuing until 1976. Through these strongly redistributive 'social planning agreements', as they were also called, the social partners actively involved themselves in the construction of the welfare state.

In parallel with these central framework agreements, a considerable amount of bipartite negotiation also took place in the National Labour Council. Central agreements at national level and collective agreements at sectoral and company levels cover a range of issues and last for a specified period, generally 2 years (see table 11.7). By contrast, agreements arrived at in the National Labour Council cover specific issues and remain effective for an indeterminate period. They are, however, frequently revised and updated. We have already mentioned Collective Labour Agreement 5 on enterprise-level union representation. Other significant agreements are CLA 39 on technology agreements, and CLA 42 on working-time regulations (Vilrokx and Van Leemput 1992). The most important recent accord is CLA 62 (February 1996) regulating the organization of European works councils under the terms of the EU directive.

One of the subtleties of the Belgian model is that, notwithstanding the key role of central agreements, the sectoral level may be considered to lie at the heart of what we earlier termed the 'real' industrial relations. However, the data used in comparative overviews rarely include this level, and its precise significance and relationship with the national industrial relations dynamic are largely ignored. Paradoxically, it is precisely because there are central agreements that the sectoral level is so important: broad framework agreements can never address all the issues at lower levels. Moreover, it is only because the sectoral level is well structured and powerful that central agreements are possible at all. During the second phase, equilibrium was sustained between the two levels, allowing a broad degree of collective solidarity to be achieved within the system. Subsequently, however, it proved impossible to conclude central agreements and this equilibrium rapidly disappeared. The 'weak' agreements concluded between 1986 and 1994 were unable to support the objective of collective solidarity. In our conclusion we return to this issue.

It is at the sectoral level that day-to-day industrial relations activities are conducted, within the framework of minimum standards laid down by central agreements. The strong trade union presence within companies is based on the wide range of resources and support provided by the union 'centrals', from expert back-up in negotiations, through training of union representatives, to running holiday resorts for members. The dominance of the sectoral level is also reflected in the unions' overall organization structure. Decision-making powers rest largely with the 'centrals', especially in the socialist ABVV–FGTB, rather than with the regional and sub-regional multi-sector structures. At the bipartite level too, the emphasis is on sectoral activities. The organization of vocational training has already been mentioned. Most crucially, the determination of pay and other terms and conditions takes place at this level. Finally, sectoral initiatives to supplement statutory provision in the areas of pensions, financial support in the event of restructuring, redundancies, and so on, have played a significant role, helping to sustain the balance between co-operation and conflict in sectoral industrial relations and contributing greatly to the 'conviviality' that characterizes Belgian industrial relations at large (see Vilrokx and Van Leemput 1992).

The golden age of bipartism also saw the creation, in 1960, of the tripartite National Committee for Economic Expansion (NCEE/CNEE). Following the first Expansion Laws of the late 1950s, the government wished to include the social partners in institutionalized national concertation on economic planning. This may be seen as part of the institutional incorporation of the social partners, comparable to their integration in institutions such as the National Bank. Hailed by one of the former presidents of the National Labour Council as the 'prototype of tripartite concertation', the Committee's economic impact was considerable, and it overshadowed the Central Economic Council in the 1960s. However, its longer-term influence on the industrial relations system has been limited. When, at the beginning of the 1970s, the economy entered a period of restructuring, the Committee ceased to be active, although it still formally exists.

Phase 3 – Industrial Relations in Preventive Custody (1975–89)

From Social Planning to Cost Control

In 1976, the last of the seven central agreements of the series initiated in 1960 expired. The first direct government intervention on the core issue of pay took place, without concertation, in the same year. It was a sign that labour cost reduction would increasingly be on the agenda. Even such issues as working-time reduction and vocational training had financial implications that were incompatible with the deflationary thrust of government policy from the mid-1970s. Thus the tradition of social planning of the welfare state through central agreements came to an end.

We have stressed the paradoxical character of the delegation by the state to the social partners of aspects of the welfare state. When the state's capacity to bear the financial consequences of central agreements disappeared, it reassumed the responsibilities it had previously devolved, allowing it to marginalize the social partners and to adopt extremely restrictive policies. However, the state did not define its role in purely negative or passive terms during the 1980s. It intervened actively in the three issues which were seen as central to the modernization of the nation's economic performance – technological innovation, flexibility and wage determination (Vilrokx and Van Leemput 1992). The high point was the law on the Protection of Competitiveness of 1989, enabling the government to intervene systematically in the evolution of wages and in their automatic linking to the cost-of-living index. This intervention marks the end of the third period. With the competitiveness law, the government not only fashioned the instrument for achieving its goal of controlling labour costs, it also managed to involve the social partners explicitly in its operation through the bipartite Central Economic Council, which has responsibility for deciding whether the conditions for government intervention are met.

A brief summary of the first three phases can now be given. First, the state's *role* varied. It was an active facilitator in the first phase, was largely absent from the scene in the second, while in the third it created the instruments to intervene actively in industrial relations. Second, these roles followed from the state's *objectives*. In the first phase it sought to create the conditions in which the social partners could actively construct the welfare state. In the second, as a result, the state was relatively dependent on the social partners, forcing it to accept the positive-sum arrangement of compensation democracy. In the third phase, a host of pressures provoked the redefinition of the welfare state (in common with most west European countries) and the exercise of closer control over the industrial relations process. Third, the *means* employed by the state were fundamentally different in each period. In the first phase, symbolic as well as increasing material incentives were made available. The second phase was characterized by relatively unlimited resources, while in the third phase the allocation of limited resources took place within a context of fiscal crisis.

The tighter state control of 1975–89 marks this phase out as a turning-point in industrial relations. In the following phase the state goes further, and begins to remodel the existing industrial relations system in an authoritarian way.

Phase 4 – Industrial Relations under House Arrest (1990–)

From 1986 the tradition of 2-year central agreements was resumed. In contrast to the agreements of 1960–76, the five 'new-style' central agreements up to 1994 were relatively limited in content, and their impact was largely symbolic. The most important aim of the social partners appeared to be to confirm their right to negotiate autonomously. This assertion appears somewhat curious given that, for example, the 1994 central agreement only came about after the government had put heavy pressure on the social partners and had practically dictated the content of the agreement. In the 1996 negotiations, however, the government tightened the constraints on negotiation still further by imposing a 'wage norm'. With this added obstacle, it proved impossible to reach the minimal consensus necessary for an agreement. We return to this issue below, after considering evidence of the changing nature of government interference in the negotiation process, and in industrial relations in general.

The Failure of Tripartite Concertation . . .

At the end of 1993, parliament adopted the 'Global Plan' prepared by the Christian-socialist Dehaene government (see also Beaupain and Blaise 1995; Blaise and Beaupain 1995). The Global Plan followed the failure of the government's July 1993 attempt to conclude a tripartite 'social pact' (in the aftermath of the EU summit in Copenhagen and during the preparation of the Delors White Paper). The social pact was explicitly intended to reformulate the 1944 social pact, and the Belgian model of industrial relations, in the light of the challenges of unemployment, competitiveness, and the reform of the social security system. Although the failure to conclude a new pact was foreseeable (Arcq 1993b: 44) the initiative itself can be seen as a turning point in post-war industrial relations. It was the first clear indication that the implications of the budgetary policy the government had pursued for some 15 years had now to be internalized by the social partners, and in particular by the unions.

The Global Plan closely followed the aims set out by the government at the time of the abortive social pact. It reflected the budgetary preoccupations of the government's 1992 Convergence Plan drawn up to meet the Maastricht criteria (OECD 1995: 2). Most importantly, it imposed a wage freeze in the private and public sectors for 1995 and 1996, the 2 years covered by the next round of central negotiations due for 1994. The government preferred not to interfere with the 1992 central agreement (covering 1993–4) but nonetheless wanted to see an immediate impact on pay levels. A solution had thus to be found for the fiscal year 1994. Under the Global Plan, this took the form of a 'health index' which excluded petrol, tobacco and alcoholic drinks from the basket of goods used to determine the automatic adjustment of wages to the cost-of-living index (allowing the government to raise taxes on these highly 'profitable' items without any impact on wages). The explicit expectation of the government was that the health index would, in real terms, neutralize the wage increase anticipated for 1994 (Globaal Plan 1993: 8), thus removing any doubt that it was public health the government had in mind. This marked the beginning of a 3-year period of wage freeze.

The manipulation of the indexation system is not new. The government has made use of it on several occasions since 1982. This latest case is, however, more significant than previous ones, which had been mostly *ad hoc*. The 1994 episode was manifestly part of a strategy to control wages over a longer period. Given the government's concern for the country's unfavourable international competitive position (invariably ascribed to the high cost of labour), it was highly unlikely that government pay intervention would cease at the end of the 3-year period, with new central agreement negotiations due for the second half of 1996 (covering 1997–8). It was equally inconceivable, however, that the wage freeze could be reimposed. The expectations of workers and union leaders of a return to bipartite wage negotiation were too strong to be brutally frustrated by the government. Moreover, increasing tensions between the social partners, notably at company level, added to the case for caution.

The deterioration of company-level labour relations and the relatively high level of worker mobilization are illustrated by several recent cases, including the closure in 1992 of the profitable Vilvoorde biscuit plant of the long-established Belgian firm Delacre, owned by Campbell, and a subsequent two-month occupation; Sabena management's unilateral withdrawal from all collective agreements in 1995; Caterpillar's notification to 217 workers of their dismissal by telephone in 1996; the violent workers' protests in response to the restructuring of the Forges de Clabecq at the end of 1996 and beginning of 1997; and the announcement of the closure of the Renault–Vilvoorde plant near Brussels at the end of February 1997, leading to the first private sector 'Euro-strike' in Paris on 11th March 1997 and the first 'Euro-demonstration' in Brussels five days later. Another significant element has been the tendency of employers to halt strikes and occupations, and neutralize picket lines, by legal means: since the end of the 1980s, employers have commonly invoked the 'freedom to work' in this respect. The remodelling of the industrial relations system by the state unquestionably brought about the weakening of the convivial understanding between the social partners and a formalization of industrial relations. The unilateral use of the law by employers to resolve industrial conflicts must, at least partly, be seen in this context.

In the light of such developments, the government settled on a different strategy of wage regulation. In its Declaration to parliament for its second term in office following the 1995 general elections, the Christian–socialist coalition (Dehaene-II) announced its intention to link future wage developments in Belgium to pay movements in its main trading partners, France, Germany and the Netherlands. This objective has subsequently been regularly restated by the prime minister. It became the subject of tripartite concertation – even prior to the bipartite central negotiations of the second half of 1996 – when at the beginning of 1996 the government invited the social partners to agree the government-inspired 'Pact for the Future of the Employment'. This was meant to form the cornerstone of the Dehaene II policy for complying with the Maastricht criteria for EMU, and followed similar initiatives in Germany and France. Linking wage movements in Belgium to those of its three main trading partners, through what by now is called a 'wage norm', is seen as the only possible (consensual) way to restore the country's competitiveness and to halve unemployment by the end of the century. The idea of such a linkage is far from new. The 1982 Martens government introduced the idea of a 'competitiveness standard' and in 1983 asked the Central Economic Council for a study on Belgium's competitive position (Beaupain 1994: 142–3); the Council was unable to reach a conclusion. The concept was reintroduced by the law of January 1985 and confirmed in the 1989 competitiveness law. What is innovative in the case of the wage norm, however, is its anticipatory character: its predecessors were *post hoc*.

A tripartite protocol on the Pact for the Future was signed on 18th April 1996. In the two weeks that followed, the employers' organization (VBO–FEB) accepted the protocol, the Christian union (ACV–CSC) voted very narrowly in favour, but the socialist ABVV–FGTB rejected the protocol almost unanimously. The ABVV–FGTB called for a more ambitious plan for employment, arguing that long-term wage moderation in the form of a wage norm would be unacceptable if not compensated for by firmer commitments on job creation from the employers.

The government did not hesitate long. On 30th April Dehaene announced in parliament that not only would he transform the Pact for the Future into a unilateral governmental Plan for the Future, but that he would also handle three pending problems of budgetary control (including the employment and wage issue), the social security system, and the budget for 1997 through 'framework laws'. This implied asking parliament not to interfere in the legislative process, a request to which it subsequently acceded. The principle of the wage norm was given practical legal status in the first of the three framework laws, in July 1996. At the beginning of the central agreement negotiations of September 1996, the government asked the social partners to agree the level of the wage norm. It again requested the Central Economic Council to make the relevant calculations on the basis of wage movements in France, Germany and the Netherlands. The Council fixed three possible levels of wage increase (5.4, 6.0 and 6.5 per cent respectively) for the 2-year duration of the next central agreement. These figures include expected increases of the cost-of-living (3.6 per cent) and seniority-related automatic wage increases (1 per cent).

. . . and of Bipartite National Negotiation

These developments severely constrained the central agreement negotiations. It also soon became apparent there was virtually no scope for discussion on other issues, since the unions' acceptance of the wage norm was not reciprocated by any commitment on the employers' side to job creation measures. The impasse brought swift government intervention to impose a wage norm (of 6.1 per cent). After deducting cost-of-living and seniority increases, this left a mere 0.75 per cent a year for nominal wage rises. The government promised to make BF 6.3 billion available for working-time redistribution measures, but the social partners were totally at odds over the allocation of this sum, confirming their complete inability to agree common ways of addressing the employment problem. The extraordinarily rare spectacle of a general strike, organized during the negotiations by the ABVV–FGTB (without informing the ACV–CSC) is just one indication of the seriousness of the blockage, even if it did not influence the outcome of the negotiations. With the failure of negotiations, the government decided to impose its earlier proposals through legislation and extended the provisions of the previous central agreement for a further 2 years.

Why did negotiations on a new central agreement start at all? It was clear from the outset that no concessions on job creation could be expected from the employers; they had always argued that increased competitiveness depended on cutting labour costs, which would lead to economic growth and thereby generate more jobs. It was also apparent that the focus of central agreement negotiations on the wage norm was unacceptable to the unions. At the beginning of negotiations two high-level officials of ACV–CSC and ABVV–FGTB issued a common statement declaring that 'We will not sign an agreement on the wage norm *alone* – adequate proposals on employment have to be linked to it' (*Trends*, 12th September 1996; see also Serroyen and Delcroix 1996: 55).

The Belgian social partners have a long tradition of compromise, finding common ground for negotiation by treating principles pragmatically. The fact that things went wrong this time cannot be considered accidental. The social partners started negotiations convinced that, following the failure of the Global Plan and the Pact for the Future, this round of central agreement negotiations was the last chance to reach a bipartite understanding. But, with the erosion of the constituent elements of the industrial relations system becoming irreversible in the second half of the 1990s, the margins for negotiation were to prove totally inadequate.

Remodelling Industrial Relations

With no central agreement for 1997–8, the government will take any action it deems necessary to support its employment objectives. One measure is the continuation of the so-called 'company plans' which were already a key part of the Global Plan. These plans could be seen as a significant innovation in Belgian industrial relations because they confirm the relative autonomy of the company level of negotiation. While negotiation on flexibility within enterprises has been encouraged by deregulation and legislation since the early 1980s, the 'company plans' provide a new degree of legitimation for such practices. Within the framework of the battle against unemployment, company plans allow for negotiation between the social partners on the redistribution of work; the government provides financial resources to facilitate changes.

In practice, the impact of company plans (and of other measures to redistribute work) on job creation has been very modest (Ministerie van Tewerkstelling en Arbeid 1997). They run counter to the established 'negotiation pyramid', under which negotiation takes place in a hierarchical sequence. In by-passing the national and sectoral levels, the government aims, first, to legitimize the shift towards decentralized negotiation; and second, to signal its intention to restructure industrial relations, if necessary through unilateral intervention. The company plans' real significance, therefore, is that they represent a government-imposed change in the rules of the game. By its intervention, the government notified the social partners that bipartite global framework agreements had had their day and that *ad hoc* approaches were to be preferred. The government's suggestion that sectoral differences in the application of the wage norm should be possible, and its encouragement for profit-sharing schemes (not included in the wage norm) in individual firms, seems to support this conclusion.

The unions reacted negatively to company plans, but failed to convince the government to change its proposals. The employers' organization adopted an even lower profile. It welcomed the plans as an expression of support for its long-standing plea for greater enterprise-level bargaining autonomy, but at the same time it would have preferred the social partners to have come to such a conclusion without interference from government.

The second major modification to the Belgian model is the government's circumscribing of the use of the cost-of-living index through the wage norm. By incorporating the linkage to the cost-of-living as an element in wage negotiations, the government has dispensed with the previously unconditional and autonomous character of the indexation system. This appears to open the way for the link between the cost of living and wages (and perhaps also social benefits) to be questioned in the future (even if there is currently an understanding that a minimum wage norm may not be lower than the cost-of-living index).

The third set-back for the Belgian model is the failure to reach a bipartite central agreement for 1997–8; even prior to this, agreements had become relatively devoid of content, and largely dictated by government. This failure is the most visible and symbolic indication that industrial relations has entered a phase of transformation. Restructuring follows the shift in power relations between employers' and workers' organizations, and the redefinition of the role of the state in response to the pressures of the new global economy.

The earlier failures of tripartite concertation documented above (and the modest outcomes of the agreements of the mid-1970s and the 1980s) provide the backdrop to the current erosion of the Belgian model. Such developments stand in sharp contrast to the pre-war period: in 1936, influenced by the *Front Populaire* in France and by the explosive social situation in Belgium, the government finally persuaded the employers to accept national-level programmatic concertation with the trade unions. Thereafter, tripartite concertation became the indispensable backbone of the Belgian model. The decline of tripartite concertation in the third phase and its collapse in the fourth phase is, therefore, a crucial phenomenon, to which we return in the conclusion.

Conclusions

Beyond Tripartism

The increasing role of the state in industrial relations has led social partners and analysts alike to conclude that Belgian industrial relations are becoming increasingly 'tripartized'. The data provided in this chapter point to a completely different dynamic. The relative balance of power between the state, trade unions and employers' organizations was based on a considerable delegation to the social partners of the state's responsibility for the construction of the welfare state. This delegation of responsibility, which has to be seen as a necessary precondition for the Belgian variant of tripartism, has been gradually undermined from the mid-1970s. When, from the third phase on, welfare state objectives were replaced by deflationary budgetary priorities, the cement of tripartite concertation began to crumble, illustrating the vulnerability of this delegation-based tripartite concertation model. Thus, far from being 'tripartized', important elements of the industrial relations environment have been refashioned by the state, providing it with the discretionary power to impose its own agenda.

This trend is further illustrated by the establishment in November 1996 of the High Council for Employment. The Council is a political body made up of representatives of the Christian–socialist coalition partners, which will advise the government on employment issues. Chaired by the Minister of Employment and Labour, its vice-chair (and acting chair) is the secretary-general of the National Bank. The government's explicit motive for creating this body is to 'short-circuit' (*Le Soir*, 27th November 1996) the social partners' failure to agree on employment measures. This glosses over the fact that government action to curb unemployment has been highly inefficient over the past two decades. The establishment of the High Council is thus the latest step in the neutralization of the social partners.

If tripartite concertation has been the backbone of collective labour relations in Belgium, its substance has been provided by bipartite negotiation, particularly at sectoral level. Tripartite concertation and bipartite negotiation have strongly influenced each other in the post-war period: within the framework of Belgian 'compensation democracy', elaborate bipartite negotiation could only take place on the basis of tripartite understandings. The weakening of the tripartite dimension of the industrial relations system was bound to affect the dimension of bipartite negotiation as well. Underlying this transformation is a fragmentation of the industrial relations system. Several trends can be observed.

A Double 'Monopartism' . . .

There can be little doubt that, at national intersectoral level, the state has monopolized the crucial industrial relations issues of wage formation and employment. The state's strategy has been characterized by a technocratic-monetary approach to the industrial relations system in the third phase, and a strategy of reshaping the system in the current fourth phase. The latter has been dominated by the budgetary constraints of the Maastricht-convergence criteria: the formal role given to the National Bank at significant points in the remodelling of the system is revealing in this context.

In other areas of employment regulation, the state's role is less obtrusive. In the National Labour Council, collective agreements on important matters can still be concluded. Activities relating to the consultative role of the National Labour Council have also been maintained. The social partners regarded them as an important means of asserting a degree of autonomy *vis-à-vis* the government, an autonomy lost in respect of 'core' wage and employment issues at intersectoral level. We have argued that the government has been able to gain control over the three defining mechanisms of the national industrial relations system – central agreements, the negotiation pyramid and indexation. This has brought about a transformation of the Belgian model. The social partners have been neutralized at the national interprofessional level, and a 'monopartite' regime dominated by the state has been installed.

Partly as a result of this dynamic, the bipartite level of the company has also undergone quite dramatic changes. From the 1980s, the balance that had developed at enterprise level between the organization of work, the internal and external labour market, and the industrial relations system has been disturbed. The requirements of labour flexibility and employability have largely subordinated labour market objectives and industrial relations to work organization. A shift in power relations at the level of the firm has taken place in all European countries. In many respects, management now can virtually impose its own terms in the workplace, not least through the use (or merely the threat) of closure or relocation. This points towards a growing 'monopartism' at company level as well.

... and Sectoral Differentiation

The sectoral level has been subject to its own specific dynamic. On several occasions we have highlighted the importance of the sector. It is no exaggeration to claim that the sectors are the power centres of the Belgian industrial relations system. Employers' organizations and trade unions (separately or bilaterally) engage in most of their activities (e.g. internal and external education and training) within the sector, and they have considerable resources at their disposal (e.g. the bipartite Welfare Funds). Moreover, because of the frequent and intensive contacts between the social partners, much of the conviviality characterizing Belgian industrial relations is realized at sectoral level. Even severe conflicts, with major socio-economic effects, at company level have not tended to affect bipartite sectoral understanding.

In this context, and given the monopartite tendencies at national and company levels, the sectoral level may be expected to become even more central to the industrial relations system in the future and will appear as more autonomous. Increasing sectoral autonomy in industrial relations, and inter-sectoral differences in economic performance, could lead to growing differences between sector-based industrial relations systems.

Towards less Articulation?

Will the fragmentation of the industrial relations system further weaken the ability of the social partners to manage their internal relationships? The 'articulation' – to use Crouch's analytically useful concept (Crouch 1993: 54–5) – of the positions and actions of the leadership and the rank and file of both employers' organizations and trade unions can never be taken for granted. Precisely because the conflict dimension has been institutionalized within the industrial relations system, articulation is rather weak in Belgium. Thus at the end of 1960, a few months after the first central agreement was signed, the general strike of 1960–1 took place. Other examples of the fragility of articulation include the wave of wildcat strikes in the mid-1970s; the acceptance by union leaderships of government restrictions on part-time unemployment benefits in 1992 before strong protests from members forced the changes to be revised; and the rejection of the Contract for the Future in 1996.

The rejection of the Contract for the Future put a premature end to tripartite concertation. Thereafter, the government's reshaping of the industrial relations system made concertation largely redundant. Reinforcing the decline of the traditional model since the beginning of the 1990s, there has been a deterioration in bipartite relations at interprofessional level, a cooling in relations between the two main trade unions, bitter and significant conflicts at company level, open disputes within the socialist trade union between the Walloon and Flemish wings, and increasingly urgent calls from Flanders for greater regional autonomy in industrial relations, particularly in relation to the possibility (discussed in the Flemish parliament at the end of 1996) of concluding central agreements at regional level.

Belgium seems well prepared for entry to the European Monetary Union. Its industrial relations model has been transformed, and has lost much of its coherence. It remains to be seen if the expectations for the establishment of a Social Europe can curb the fragmentation to which the model is now exposed. The idea, widely accepted by the socio-political élites, that labour costs must be cut to create employment, may prove an inadequate response to the challenges facing the Belgian welfare state. In contrast to the immediate post-war period, however, no bold architecture to match the new globalized socio-economic environment has yet been proposed.

Acknowledgement

The authors would especially like to thank Jan De Schampheleire for his essential collaboration on this chapter. Thérèse Beaupain and Anthony Ferner were critical readers and provided us with many constructive remarks. Dominique Ranson gave us useful research assistance. All remaining shortcomings and errors are, as the expression goes, our sole responsibility.

Abbreviations

Note: in this list, and in the text, first Flemish and then French titles and initials are given – except for organizations which exist in only one region.

AAB	*Alliance Agricol Belge* – Belgian Agriculture Alliance
ABVV/FGTB	*Algemeen Belgisch Vakverbond/Fédération Générale du Travail de Belgique* – General Belgian Trade Union Federation
ACLVB/CGSLB	*Algemene Centrale der Liberale Vakbonden van België/Confédération Générale des Syndicats Libéraux de Belgique* – General Confederation of Liberal Trade Unions in Belgium
ACV/CSC	*Algemeen Christelijk Vakverbond/Confédération des Syndicats Chrétiens* – General Christian Trade Union Confederation
AMV/UCM	*Algemeen Middenstandsverbond/Union des Classes Moyennes* – Union of Traders
BB	*Belgische Boerenbond* – Belgian Farmers' Union
BRC/CCS	*Bijzondere Raadgevende Commissie/Commission Consultative Spéciale* – Special Advisory Commission
CAO/CCT	*Collectieve Arbeidsovereenkomst/Convention collective de travail* – Collective Agreement
CESRW	*Conseil Economique et Social de la Région Wallonne* – Economic and Social Council of the Walloon Region
CPBW/CPPT	*Comité voor Preventie en Bescherming op het Werk/Comité pour la Prévention et la Protection au Travail* – Committee for Prevention and Protection in the Workplace (called CVGV/CSHE until August 1996)
CRB/CCE	*Centrale Raad voor het Bedrijfsleven/Conseil Central de l'Economie* – Central Economic Council
CVGV/CSHE	*Comité voor Veiligheid, Gezondheid en Verfraaiing van de werkplaatsen/Comité de Sécurité, Hygiène et d'Embellissement des lieux de travail* – Committee for Safety, Health and Improvement of the Workplace
CVP/PSC	*Christelijke Volkspartij/Parti Social Chrétien* – Christian Democratic Party
ESRBG/CESRB	*Economische en Sociale Raad voor het Brussels Gewest/Conseil Economique et Social de la Région Bruxelloise* – Economic and Social Council for the Brussels Region
FBZ/TSE	*Fonds voor Bestaanszekerheid/Fonds de Sécurité d'Existence* – Welfare Fund
IPA/AIP	*Interprofessioneel Akkoord/Accord Interprofessionnel* – National Intersectoral Agreement (Central Agreement)
NAC/CNT	*Nationale Arbeidsconferentie/Conférence Nationale du Travail* – National Labour Conference
NAR/CNT	*Nationale Arbeidsraad/Conseil National du Travail* – National Labour Council

NCEE/CNEE   *Nationaal Comité voor Economische Expansie/Comité Nationale d'Expansion Economique* – National Committee for Economic Expansion

NCK/CNC   *Nationale Confederatie voor Kaderleden/Confédération Nationale des Cadres* – National Confederation of Middle Management

NCMV/OBPME   *Nationaal Christelijk Middenstandsverbond/Organisation Belge des Petites et Moyennes Entreprises* – National Christian Traders' Union

OC/CC   *Overlegcomité/Comité de Concertation* – Concertation Committee

OR/CE   *Ondernemingsraad/Conseil d'Entreprise* – Works Council

PC/CP   *Paritair Comité/Commission Paritaire* – Joint Committee

SD/DS   *Syndicale Delegatie/Délégation Syndicale* – Trade Union Delegation

SERV   *Sociaal-Economische Raad van Vlaanderen* – Social-Economic Council of Flanders

SP/PS   *Socialistische Partij/Parti Socialiste* – Socialist Party

TR   *Table Ronde* – Round Table

UPA   *Unions des Professionelles Agricoles* – Unions of Agricultural Professionals

VBO/FEB   *Verbond van Belgische Ondernemingen/Fédération des Entreprises de Belgique* – Federation of Belgian Enterprises

VESOC   *Vlaams Economisch en Sociaal Overlegcomité* – Flemish Economic and Social Concertation Committee

VEV   *Vlaams Economisch Verbond* – Flemish Economic Union

VOB/UEB   *Verbond van Ondernemingen van Brussel/ Union des Entreprises de Bruxelles* – Union of Brussels' Enterprises

▌References

Arcq, E. 1993a: *Les relations collectives du travail.* (Dossier du CRISP 39.) Brussels: CRISP.

Arcq, E. 1993b: *Du pact social au plan global.* (Courrier hebdomadaire nr. 1420–1421.) Brussels: CRISP.

Arcq, E. and Blaise, P. 1986: *Les organisations syndicales en Belgique.* Brussels: CRISP.

Arcq, E. and Marques-Pereira, B. 1991: Néo-corporatisme et concertation sociale en Belgique. *Politiques et management public,* 9(3), September, 160–79.

Beaupain, T. 1994: Belgium. In A. Trebilcock et al., *Towards Social Dialogue: Tripartite Cooperation in National Economic and Social Policy-Making,* Geneva: ILO, 121–63.

Beaupain, T. and Blaise, P. 1995: *La concertation sociale 1993–1995: I. La mise en oeuvre du plan global.* (Courrier hebdomadaire nr.1496–1497.) Brussels: CRISP.

Blaise, P. 1996: *Les élections sociales de mai 1995.* (Courrier hebdomadaire nr.1527.) Brussels: CRISP.

Blaise, P. and Beaupain, T. 1995: *La concertation sociale 1993–1995: II. L'accord interprofessionel du 7 décembre 1994.* (Courrier hebdomadaire nr.1498.) Brussels: CRISP.

Crouch, C. 1993: *Industrial Relations and European State Traditions.* Oxford: Clarendon Press.

De Coninck, P. and Vilrokx, J. 1977: Een bedrijfsbezetting: Prestige-Tessenderlo. *De Nieuwe Maand,* 20(10), December, 608–18.

De Schampheleire, J. and Vilrokx, J. 1996: Het werkgelegenheidsbeleid. In H. Matthijs and F. Naert (eds), *Sociaal-economisch beleid* (Deel 3), Brussels: Stoho, 108–33.

Denys, J. 1995: *Sectorale opleidingsinitiatieven in Vlaanderen*. Leuven: HIVA.

European Commission, 1994: *Growth, Competitiveness, Employment. The challenges and ways forward into the 21st century*. White Paper. Brussels: European Commission.

Globaal Plan, 1993: *Het globaal plan: Werkgelegenheid, concurrentievermogen, sociale zekerheid*. Brussels: Inbel.

Hertogs, B. and Piret, C. 1986: *De stakingen in 1985*. Brussels: ACV.

Hobsbawm, E. 1994: *Ages of Extremes: The Short Twentieth Century*. London: Joseph.

Krzeslo, E. 1996: *Les relations collectives du travail en Belgique: Acteurs et institutions*. (Dossier 16) Bruxelles: Point d'appui TEF.

Ministerie van Tewerkstelling en Arbeid, 1997: *Het federaal werkgelegenheidsbeleid: Evaluatierapport 1996*. Brussels: Dienst publicaties van het Ministerie van Tewerkstelling en Arbeid.

OECD, 1995: *Economic Surveys: Belgium/Luxembourg 1994–1995*. Paris: OECD.

Pasture, P. 1996: Belgium: Pragmatism in Pluralism. In Pasture, P., Verberckmoes, J. and De Witte, H. (eds), *The Lost Perspective*, Vol. 1. Aldershot: Avebury, 91–135.

Piret, C., Serroyen, C. and Hertogs, B. 1985: *De stakingen in 1983 en 1984*. Brussels: ACV.

Rosseel, E. and Vilrokx, J. 1992: *Atypisch Belgisch: Personeelsflexibiliteit in het Belgisch bedrijfsleven 1975–1990*. Leuven: Acco.

Serroyen, C. and Delcroix, J.-P. 1996: Belgium. In European Trade Union Institute (ed.), *Collective Bargaining in Western Europe: 1995–1996*, Brussels: ETUI, 33–56.

Van Gramberen, M. and Denys, J. 1996: Het sectorale opleidingsmodel bedreigd. *Nieuwsbrief van het steunpunt WAV*, 6(4), December, 134–7.

Van Ruysseveldt, J. and Visser, J. 1995: Weak corporatism going different ways? Industrial relations in the Netherlands and Belgium. In J. Van Ruysseveldt and J. Visser (eds), *Industrial Relations in Europe*, London: Sage, 205–64.

Vanthemsche, G. 1994: *La sécurité sociale: Les origines du système belge; le présent face à son passé*. Brussels: De Boeck.

Vilrokx, J. 1995: De vier stadia in de evolutie van de Belgische collectieve arbeidsverhoudingen sinds 1945. In J. Van Dijck, E. Henderickx and J. Van Hoof (eds), *Baas over de eigen (loop)baan*, Houten: Stenfert Kroese, 203–215.

Vilrokx, J. 1996: Trade unions in a postrepresentative society. In P. Leisink, J. Van Leemput and J. Vilrokx (eds), *The Challenges to Trade Unions in Europe: Innovation or Adaption*, Cheltenham: Edward Elgar, 31–51.

Vilrokx, J. and Forceville, J. 1996: Critical issues in VET in Europe: Belgium. *Training Matters*, 5, Autumn, 14–19 .

Vilrokx, J. and Van Leemput, J. 1992: Belgium: A new stability in industrial relations. In A. Ferner and R. Hyman (eds), *Industrial Relations in the New Europe*, Oxford: Blackwell Publishers, 357–92.

Visser, J. 1996: *Trends and Variations in European Collective Bargaining*, Amsterdam, University of Amsterdam-CESAR (Research Paper 96/2).

12 Luxembourg: A Small Success Story

GARY TUNSCH

Introduction

The Grand-Duchy of Luxembourg is the smallest member country of the EU, with an area of 1,000 square miles and a population of 412,000. There are three national languages: French (used for governmental business), German and Lëtzebuergesch. Luxembourg is a constitutional monarchy with three main political parties: the Social Christian Party (PCS), Luxembourg Workers' Socialist Party (POSL) and Democratic Party (PD). Government is normally by a coalition between the PCS and one of the other parties, since 1984 the POSL; at present these two parties share 38 of the 60 seats in parliament. The minor parties represented in parliament are the Greens and the Action Party for Democracy, formed in the 1980s to campaign for private-sector pensioners but now adopting a broader populist (and anti-Maastricht) stance.

Total employment in 1995 was 213,000. Only a minority of the labour force are Luxembourg citizens. Roughly a third are foreign workers, primarily Portuguese. Of growing significance are cross-frontier commuters (half of them French) whose numbers have increased from 13,000 in 1980 to 56,000 in 1995. This reflects the fact that employment is buoyant, despite the international recession, increasing at an annual rate of 5 per cent in recent years. The rate of unemployment, for many years among the lowest in Europe, fell in the early 1990s to 1 per cent of the labour force but has since risen to over 5 per cent.

The Luxembourg economy – which is heavily dependent on that of Germany – traditionally rested on the steel industry. Despite a considerable contraction in recent decades, it still employs some 9,000 workers; and the main company, ARBED, is with almost 7,000 employees by far the largest private firm in the country. Since the economic crisis of the early 1970s, Luxembourg has pursued economic diversification, encouraging such industries as tyres (Goodyear is the second largest private firm) and plastics. The main growth of employment, however, is in services, and in particular banking. Today 220 banks operate in Luxembourg, with 20,000 employees, compared with only 37 in 1970. This sectoral shift has brought some increase in female labour force participation – for

Table 12.1 Employment by sector (1995)

	(000)	%
Agriculture	5.8	2.7
Mining and manufacturing	33.4	15.6
Building and civil engineering	23.1	10.8
Energy and water	1.6	0.7
Market services	117.9	55.2
Non-market services	31.8	14.9
Total	213.5	100

Source: STATEC.

much of the 1980s, the third lowest in western Europe – but at 56 per cent the proportion is still well below the EU average. Part-time employment has also increased rapidly in recent years, although at 8 per cent of all employees is still very low.

Trade Unions

Trade unionism in Luxembourg (as in neighbouring Belgium) is marked by structural pluralism and high membership density (roughly 50 per cent). Unions have existed since the 1860s, initially based in traditional crafts, and emerging in heavy industry after the turn of the century. Schoolteachers unionized in the late nineteenth century, followed by other groups of public employees and by white-collar staff in private industry.

Before the First World War the level of union membership was very low and the structure of organization extremely fragmented. A phase of organizational consolidation then occurred, with the growth of unionization in the main industrial sectors, and the polarization of unions between socialist and catholic federations. After the suppression of trade unionism during German wartime occupation, an effort was made in 1944 to establish a unified movement; but the following year there was a communist breakaway, followed by the catholics; and in 1948 a 'neutral' occupationally-based federation was also established. In the 1960s the communist federation rejoined the socialists, but appeals for broader unification were rebuffed. Subsequent decades saw a complex pattern of alignments as individual unions switched allegiance or opted for independence from the main confederations.

Today there exist two trade union confederations with national representative status for blue- and white-collar staff. The larger, the Independent Trade Union Confederation of Luxembourg (OGB-L) comprises 14 sectoral federations with both manual and white-collar membership. While socialist in origin and orientation, OGB-L is not organizationally attached to the POSL and still aspires to unity with the other sections of the movement. The Luxembourg Confederation of

Christian Trade Unions (LCGB) is closely linked to the PCS, though it, too, is formally independent. LCGB strongly supports the principle of trade union pluralism. It contains 13 federations covering specific industries and economic sectors.

A third organization, the Federation of Private Sector Staffs/Independent Feder-ation of Workers and Managers (FEP/FITC), has national representative status on behalf of private-sector white-collar staff. Its membership is almost exclusively drawn from this group, and it is politically neutral. FEP/FITC has suffered severely in the last 12 years with breakaways by a number of sectoral associations, some joining one or other of the two main confederations and others (notably the banking and insurance union ALEBA) opting for independence. More recently an internal split, initiated by the employee committee of Goodyear, resulted in the formation of a rival federation, SNEP-R.

A variety of other unions are confined to specific sectors of the economy. The Neutral Trade Union of Luxembourg (NGL) inherits some of the traditions of craft unionism, and is associated with the 'Action Committee for Democracy'. The oldest Luxembourg trade union, the Luxembourg Book Workers' Federation (FLTL), covers printing workers, and there are two rival unions of transport workers (FNCTTFEL and FCPT). In the public sector, the Civil Service Union (CGFP) and the General Federation of Local Authority Staff (FGFC) cover national and local government respectively. Two of these organizations, FLTL and FNCTTFEL, are linked in a loose confederation with OGB-L; while FCPT is similarly associated with LCGB. The rival confederations have no negotiating functions, but serve as vehicles for political pressure and international affiliation.

▎ Employers' Organizations

The dominant representative of Luxembourg employers is the Federation of Luxembourg Industrialists (FEDIL), founded in 1917. It covers virtually every manufacturing enterprise, regardless of size, and a growing number of firms from the service sector. Currently some 350 firms are directly affiliated as well as eleven sectoral employers' associations. FEDIL is not directly involved in collective bargaining but assists member firms, particularly in cases before the National Conciliation Office (see below).

Artisan industries are represented by a national confederation established in 1905, which comprises 50 trade-based federations and occupational associations. Affiliated membership covers 3,600 firms, or 90 per cent of all registered artisan enterprises.

The first collective organization in the commercial sector was formed in 1909. After various mergers and changes of name it is now known as the Luxembourg Confederation of Commerce (CCL). The hotel and restaurant trade is separately organized, and for a long time was split between three rival associations. Since 1970, however, there has been a single organization, the National Federation of Luxembourg Hotels, Restaurants and Cafes (HORESCA).

The Luxembourg Association of Banks and Bankers (ABBL) was founded in 1939. It has 158 members, covering virtually the whole of the sector. Among other functions it represents its members in collective bargaining. The Luxembourg Association of Chartered Insurance Companies (ACA), founded in 1956, covers most firms in its sector and represents them in collective bargaining.

In agriculture there are two rival organizations: the Central Farmers' Organization (CP) founded in 1944, and the Free Federation of Luxembourg Agriculture (FLB) created in 1979. The split reflected the dissatisfaction of a section of farmers with the working of the cooperative system run by the CP.

▌Collective Agreements

Though collective agreements have been negotiated since the 1870s, they were rare before the 1930s. Greater co-ordination on the trade union side during that decade was followed by the appointment of a government arbitration committee (National Labour Council – CNT) in 1936. The current legal framework is defined in the 1965 law on collective agreements. A valid agreement must be signed between an employer or employers' association and a union or unions with representative status. This status (currently enjoyed, as indicated above, by two general confederations and one white-collar federation) is confirmed – or refused – by the Ministry of Labour when agreements are submitted for official registration. The law specifies issues which should be covered in collective agreements, and requires, in particular, rules for payments for night work and dangerous or uncongenial working conditions, for avoiding sex discrimination in pay, and for the indexation of wages to the cost of living. All workers within a company must be covered by a single agreement. There is no obligation on employers to reach an agreement, but if so requested by employee representatives, they must enter into negotiations.

Most sectors of employment in Luxembourg are currently covered by collective agreements. In wholesale and retail distribution, no general agreement has been negotiated for several years; but the provisions of the previous agreements have been maintained through enterprise bargaining. The main gap in the coverage of collective agreements is in hotels and catering, though recently the unions and HORESCA have been negotiating to introduce one. Industry-level bargaining is not particularly common in Luxembourg, though where sectoral agreements exist they can be made applicable throughout the industry. Sectors covered by multi-employer agreements include building and civil engineering, banking and insurance, petrol distribution, and road haulage. In hospitals and breweries there are also multi-employer agreements, though these have not been made generally enforceable. Elsewhere, company negotiations are the norm.

Disputes over the interpretation of collective agreements are determined by the Labour Tribunal, consisting of a judge with employer and union assessors. The Tribunal, which was established in 1989, handles individual employment disputes.

The National Conciliation Office

Established in 1945, the National Conciliation Office (ONC) is charged with the peaceful resolution of disagreements between the parties to collective bargaining. Mediation by the ONC is obligatory in the case of a breakdown in negotiations, and must precede any resort to a strike or lockout. A joint conciliation committee exists, chaired by a senior civil servant and with three representatives each of employers and workers. If conciliation fails, either party may call for the establishment of an arbitration panel chaired by a government nominee with union and employer representatives. If approved by the parties, an arbitration award acquires the status of a collective agreement.

The jurisdiction of the ONC does not extend to the public sector. However, there exist analogous procedures for conciliation and mediation.

Strikes and Lockouts

The right to strike, in the private sector, is implied in the constitution and was explicitly recognized in an interpretative motion adopted by parliament in the 1950s. In the following decade, the right to lockout was also implicitly recognized. However, neither action may be undertaken or threatened during the currency of an agreement, or before conciliation procedures have been exhausted. In the public sector, the right to strike was conceded in a law of 1979, though with the exclusion of such categories as higher civil servants, senior managers, police, and various medical and security personnel. Strikes in Luxembourg are exceptional; the level of conflict, relative to the size of the workforce, is the lowest in the EU. In the past decade there have been very few disputes involving more than 50 workers, such as the strikes of secondary teachers in 1988, postal workers in 1990, and the token strike in banking and insurance in 1991, and a three-week stoppage of tile-layers in 1994. In 1992 it seemed that this pacific record might be disrupted when OGB-L and LCGB jointly threatened a general strike against a planned law changing the health insurance system; but after discussions in the bipartite Economic and Social Council the government amended its proposals.

Individual Employment Rights

Legislation in 1989 provided for the first time an equivalent status for manual and white-collar employees, though some special conditions still apply to non-manual staff in the private sector. Every employee has the right to a written contract of employment including a job description, a statement of normal hours and pay, and any probationary period. Employment contracts should normally be permanent; fixed-term contracts are permitted only when the work to be undertaken is temporary. The law lays down detailed procedures governing dismissal, redundancy and company closure or take-over.

The legal minimum wage sets a floor to every employment contract. Every employee (except in case of physical or mental disability) is entitled to a 'minimum social wage', linked to the cost-of-living index. The level of the minimum social wage is fixed by law. Every 2 years, the government submits to parliament a report on general economic conditions and salaries, if necessary accompanied by proposals to increase the minimum social wage. Skilled workers are entitled to a minimum 20 per cent above that for unskilled, and lower rates are prescribed for juveniles. Indexation applies to all wages. Since 1963, public-sector pay has been index-linked, and this principle was legally extended to the whole of the private sector in 1975. The working week is legally prescribed, and has been set at 40 hours since 1970.

The law also provides for annual leave with pay of 25 working days for all employees, with an additional 6 days for disabled workers and for those working unsocial shift patterns. Other special leave entitlements are defined by law; while collective agreements often provide additional days. There are also ten public holidays a year.

Workplace Representation

Every employer – private or public – with 15 or more workers must provide for the election of a *délégation du personnel* (employee committee). If there are 100 or more employees, separate elections must be held for manual and white-collar delegates. The number of delegates varies according to the size of the firm: only one if there are 25 employees or fewer, up to 25 or more if there are over 5,000. Delegates can be nominated by those unions nationally recognized as representative, or by groups of workers comprising at least 5 per cent of the labour force. Election is by secret ballot, normally on the basis of proportional representation.

The function of the *délégation* is to protect employees' working conditions, job security and social rights. One delegate is designated to take specific responsibility for health and safety issues. The *délégation* has rights of information on the economic situation of the company, and of consultation over matters directly affecting employees.

In large private firms – with at least 150 employees – there also exists a *comité mixte d'entreprise* (joint works committee) composed of equal numbers of employer and employee representatives, the latter elected by the *délégation*. Either side can nominate advisers (in practice, officials of trade unions or employers' associations) to participate in committee proceedings in a consultative role. The joint committee has co-determination rights over the use of equipment to monitor employee performance; questions of health and safety; policies concerning recruitment, promotion, transfer and dismissal; employee appraisal; and company rules. Management must inform and consult the committee in advance of decisions on technical changes, working methods and the working environment, current and forecast demand for labour, and vocational education and training. Management must also provide a half-yearly written report on the economic and financial position of the company. Finally, the law of 1974 which established joint committees also provided for employee representation on the boards of companies with 1,000 or more employees. In such companies the *délégation* elects one-third of the members of the board, who enjoy the same status as other directors.

▌ Statutory National Institutions

Under legislation dating from 1924 there exists a system of chambers of labour and trade (*chambres professionnelles*) with compulsory membership, with the function of representing the interests of their constituencies, and the right to submit proposals for legislation. The members of each chamber are elected by and from their constituents. Three chambers exist for employees, catering respectively for manual workers, private-sector white-collar staff, and public officials. Each chamber has between 20 and 30 members, elected on the basis of the different industries and services which they cover. On the employers' side there are also three chambers, for industrial and commercial firms, artisan firms, and agriculture.

The Economic and Social Council (CES) is a consultative body charged with oversight of national economic, financial and social developments. It produces an annual report, and can also be asked for advice – which is normally presented unanimously – on issues of current concern, or on questions on which the *chambres professionnelles* have submitted conflicting proposals. The government is also required to consult the CES before initiating legislation on general matters of social or economic concern. It has 35 members, representing the two sides of industry and the different economic sectors, together with a number of independent experts.

The Tripartite Co-ordination Committee (CCT) is the product of a series of meetings in 1977 between government, employers and unions in response to the economic crisis which threatened to disrupt the Luxembourg labour market. These tripartite meetings expressed unanimous support for the goals of economic growth and full employment, and legislation was enacted to establish the CCT. The committee, with four members from each of the three parties, is convened when the numbers unemployed (or under notice of dismissal) exceed a specified threshold, or when other important issues relating to the labour market arise. Thus meetings have been held to discuss the single European market and immigration policy.

The Economic Committee (CC) is a similar tripartite body, created in 1975, to advise on measures to avoid dismissals caused by temporary economic fluctuations. It meets monthly, monitors developments in the economy and the labour market, and advises on job protection measures in industries threatened by job losses.

The National Employment Commission (CNE) is a tripartite advisory body, established in 1976, when the official employment department was set up. It oversees the administration of government employment policy and advises the

Minister on issues related to labour market organization and the employment services.

Prospects for Industrial Relations in Luxembourg

As in other European countries with strong traditions of consensual industrial relations, the more difficult economic circumstances since the 1980s have caused some problems in Luxembourg. In 1994, the CCT responded to the unprecedented unemployment levels by advocating some relaxation of statutory regulation and a reduction in the social security charges on employers, proposals which were adopted by the government. In the following year, additional 'active labour market' policies were implemented, including state supplements to the pay of unemployed workers who accept a new job at lower rates than their previous one. There has also been some deregulation of shop opening hours. Employers, like their counterparts in other countries, have also been considering the need for more flexibility and decentralization; FEDIL has for example proposed the ending of wage indexation, to which the unions remain strongly committed.

Nevertheless the traditions of social partnership remain strong. For example, the major restructuring of ARBED during the 1990s, involving substantial job losses, was carried through consensually. Luxembourg's distinctive framework of industrial relations still seems to be functioning successfully.

Abbreviations

ABBL *Association des Banques et Banquiers Luxembourg* – Luxembourg Association of Banks and Bankers

ACA *Association des Compagnies d'Assurances Agréés* – Luxembourg Association of Chartered Insurance Companies

ALEBA *Association Luxembourgeoise des Employés de Banques et des Assurances* – Luxembourg Banking and Insurance Workers' Union

BMIAV *Berg- Metall- und Industriearbeiterverband* – Union of Miners, Metalworkers and Industrial Workers

CC *Comité de Conjoncture* – Economic Committee

CCL *Confédération du Commerce Luxembourgeois* – Confederation of Luxembourg Commerce

CCT *Comité de Coordination Tripartite* – Tripartite Co-ordination Committee

CES *Conseil Economique et Social* – Economic and Social Council

CGFP *Confédération Générale de la Fonction Publique* – Civil Service Union

CGT *Confédération Générale du Travail* – General Confederation of Labour

CME *Comité mixte d'entreprise* – joint works committee

CNT *Conseil National du Travail* – National Arbitration Committee

CP *Centrale Paysanne/Baurenzentral* – Farmers' Central Organization

FCPT	*Fédération Chrétienne du Personnel du Transport* – Christian Transport Workers' Union
FEDIL	*Fédération des Industriels Luxembourgeois* – Federation of Luxembourg Industrialists
FEP/FITC	*Fédération des Employés Privés/Federation Indépendante des Travailleurs et Cadres* – Federation of Private-Sector Staffs/Independent Federation of Workers and Managers
FGFC	*Fédération Générale des Fonctionnaires Communaux* – Local Authority Workers' Union
FLA	*Freie Lëtzebuerger Arbechter-Verband* – Free Federation of Luxembourg Workers
FLB	*Fédération Libre des Agriculteurs du Luxembourg/Freie Lëtzebuerger Baurenverband* – Free Federation of Luxembourg Farmers
FLTL	*Fédération Luxembourgeoise des Travailleurs du Livre* – Luxembourg Printing Workers' Federation
FNCTTFEL	*Fédération Nationale des Cheminots, Travailleurs du Transport, Fonctionnaires et Employés Luxembourgeois* – National Federation of Railway and Transport Workers, Managers and White-Collar Workers
HORESCA	*Fédération Nationale des Hôteliers, Restaurateurs et Cafetiers* – National Federation of Hotel, Restaurant and Cafe Employers
LAV	*Lëtzebuerger Arbechterverband* – Luxembourg Workers' Union
LCGB	*Lëtzebuerger Chrëstleche Gewerkschafts-Bond* – Luxembourg Confederation of Christian Trade Unions
NGL	*Neutral Gewerkschaft Lëtzebuerg* – Independent Union of Luxembourg Workers
NHV	*Neutralen Handwierker Verband* – Independent Craftworkers' Association
OGB-L	*Onofhängege Gewerkschafts-Bond Lëtzebuerg* – Confederation of Independent Trade Unions
ONC	*Office National de Conciliation* – National Conciliation Office
PCS	*Parti Chrétien Social* – Social Christian Party
PD	*Parti Démocratique* – Democratic Party
POSL	*Parti Ouvrier Socialiste Luxembourgeois* – Luxembourg Workers' Socialist Party
SNEP-R	*Syndicat National des Employés Privés – Renovateurs* – Reconstructed National Union of White-Collar Workers

13 | France: The Limits of Reform

JANINE GOETSCHY

Introduction

Scholars have depicted the French system of industrial relations as atypical in several respects. First, industrial conflict and legal intervention, rather than collective bargaining, have been the traditional modes of 'rule-making' in the sphere of employment relations. Second, both unions and employers have been strongly driven by ideological considerations, and characterized by organizational weakness. Third, in recent years the French labour movement has undergone a more catastrophic decline in membership strength and influence than any other European union movement.

Explanations of the French 'anomaly' have often been sought in the ambiguous history of the links between political parties and unions. The northern European model in which a strong social–democratic party is closely linked to a strong union, with a fairly clear division of labour between the two, has been absent in France, where the links between parties, unions and politics have always been complex and their respective functions have overlapped. Thus commentators (e.g. Lange et al. 1982) argue that post-war French labour relations were indelibly marked by the existence of a strong communist party which attempted to use the trade union movement to mobilize a mass base. The result was an ideological fragmentation of the labour movement and a continuing ambivalence in party–union ties: was the union to concentrate on economic issues, or was it to be a disguised 'transmission belt', used to further the party's political objectives? Given the Communist party's long exclusion from political power, its close relationship with a major component of the union movement inevitably entailed the marginalization of the latter as well.

Historically, the role of the French state in industrial relations has been threefold. By the turn of the century, the state was already trying to reverse the emerging logic of industrial relations by encouraging some form of social dialogue between capital and labour at national level. The failure of this 'inter-class' project to gain the support of either employers or unions reflected both their ideological divisions and their organizational fragility. But the state has continued to play the role of midwife to a national dialogue between employers and unions, with rather more success in recent years. Second, since the Second World War, it has attempted to incorporate unions by treating them as a partner, albeit often in an advisory capacity, in the formulation of important social policy decisions, particularly on welfare issues. Third, the state has used legal intervention to compensate the unions for their organizational weakness. However, by granting individual rights and benefits directly to employees (for example, through the *erga omnes* provisions allowing collective agreements to be extended to employees in non-signatory firms), the state undermined the unions' role in industrial relations, and the unions' response to state intervention was thus ambivalent. Indeed, some authors (e.g. Sellier and Sylvestre 1986) have argued that the unions' weakness is state-created.

The role of historical, political, ideological and legal factors in shaping the organizational arrangements and strategic choices of French social actors, and consequently in moulding the evolution of the industrial relations system, has been analysed at length by scholars such as Mouriaux (1983) and Rosanvallon (1988). But the impact of processes of industrial and economic development since the nineteenth century on unions and employers has been much less thoroughly investigated. The historical legacy – of a productive structure highly oriented to the domestic economy, low industrial concentration, and a high proportion of the highly mobile labour force dividing its time between factory and farm – has been seen as hindering the emergence of strong and centralized unions and employers' associations.

In the post-war period, the relationship between the evolution of the economy and the industrial relations system has been better grasped, notably by the French regulationist school. Regulationists such as Boyer (1985) argue that from the end of the Second World War until the 1960s, an implicit 'Fordist' compromise characterized relations between capital, labour and the state: unions were content to leave to management issues relating to the sphere of production – work norms, job content, work organization and so on; in return, the unions were guaranteed their share of the fruits of economic progress in the sphere of distribution, as rising productivity brought higher wages. The Fordist compromise began to break down as a result of the well-known combination of economic, social and political pressures that made up the crisis of the early 1970s. The specificity of the problems faced by the French economy, and the solutions to them, have been widely analysed (e.g. Petit 1985; Lipietz 1991). One aspect is that the state in France has retained a key role in shaping responses to the crisis. Thus Crouch and Streeck (1996) identify four variants of capitalism – Rhenish, market, social-democratic, and state-oriented – which have been in competition with each other since the breakdown of the Bretton Woods system in 1971. In the state-oriented French variant, the state has continued to orchestrate the institutions of labour relations, competition rules, and the form in which France engages with the world economy.

In contrast to other European labour movements, French unions 'had very few ideas about new policies which might make French capitalism more successful in changing international economic circumstances. Instead they advocated a radical new economic order to be installed through political change' (Lange et al. 1982: 10). In recent decades, hopes for the implementation of this project were dashed by the bitter defeat of the left in 1978, then resuscitated by the election victory of the socialists in 1981. The scope for a new economic order was, however, severely constrained as economic crisis forced the socialists to abandon their attempted break with conventional economic management. Instead, developments followed a rather different path. The strengthening of the institutional framework of voluntary industrial relations in the 1980s, together with restructuring and technological innovation in French industry, encouraged the unions to turn their attention away from politics and back to the sphere of production – just as their capacity for action was being constrained by a severe drop in membership and influence.

The chapter begins by looking at French unions in a historical perspective, stressing the ideological divisions of the union movement, and the growing crisis of membership and influence occurring, paradoxically, in parallel with increasing institutional support. The following section examines the characteristics of French employers and their policy hesitations in the fight against unemployment. The role of the French state is then considered. Two key issues are the regulation of the labour market and the creation of an institutional framework of industrial relations, notably through the Auroux laws of the early 1980s and the 5-year employment law of 1993.

It is clear that the evolving legal framework of collective bargaining has encouraged the modernization and 'normalization' of French industrial relations over the last 15 years. Yet the extent of this convergence towards long-standing patterns in other European countries is still open to question. The enduring peculiarity of the French model was dramatically displayed by the massive outbreak of industrial unrest in late 1995, culminating in the December 1995 strike wave. The section on strikes and the conclusion assess the new elements in the French industrial relations system that this conflict has brought to the surface. One of the basic questions to be addressed throughout this chapter is whether these events signal an unexpected capacity within the labour movement to resist the imperatives of conventional economic rationality and to provide their own alternatives; or whether they merely reflect a despairing and fearful backlash in the face of the internationalization and liberalization of the French economy with its accompanying spectres of high unemployment and growing social exclusion.

Finally, future prospects are considered. With European integration and EMU, France is more and more influenced by the German economy, but it is not yet clear if it will follow the path of the 'Rhenish model' or of the 'market model', or a combination of both. France's exceptionalism as a form of capitalism is closely related to the exceptionalism of its industrial relations system; and changes in the economy will influence and at the same time be dependent upon changes in labour relations. One possible outcome is the end of French exceptionalism in both spheres.

Trade Unions

The French labour movement has traditionally been marked by trade union pluralism and fragmentation, inter-union rivalry, low union density, and a paucity of financial and organizational resources. Since the 1970s these structural weaknesses have become more prominent. In the mid-1990s, the French labour movement is one of the weakest in western Europe in membership terms, with barely a tenth of the workforce in unions. Some argue that 'the weakness of unionism in France is largely a state-created weakness' (Sellier and Sylvestre 1986). At first sight, the assertion appears paradoxical, since union power has been underpinned by the state in periods of social and political change – in 1936, 1945, 1968 and 1982, usually when the Left was in power.

The state has compensated for the unions' organizational weaknesses in three ways. First, it has granted special legal rights enabling unions to represent the interests of all employees and not only those of a limited membership. A good example is the quasi-monopoly granted to the five national confederations (CGT, CFDT, CGT–FO, CFTC, CGC) in collective bargaining at all levels, independent of their actual membership strength. Such measures have often proved detrimental in practice by removing the incentive for individuals to join unions, encouraging further dependence on state support. Second, social legislation has provided workers directly with benefits which unions have been unable to win through collective bargaining. This has done little to encourage unions to rely on their own resources, and has been a further disincentive for wage-earners to unionize. Third, the state has attempted to compensate for the unions' organizational deficiencies and to increase their social and political influence by granting them a substantial role in public bodies. This has tempted the unions to ground their legitimacy on a 'public service' role, defending the wider interests of employees and participating in the running of the welfare state.

The solutions adopted by the state fitted well with the unions' own early ideological preferences and organizational choices (see below). They also suited employer organizations which, in comparison with other European countries, were reluctant to recognize unions and to engage in collective bargaining, even with the more moderate unions. Though legalized in 1884, unions would have to wait until 1968 for the legally guaranteed right to establish union branches at enterprise level.

The Legacy of History

The oldest union confederation is the CGT, set up in 1895. Its founding document, the Charter of Amiens of 1906, proclaimed its autonomy from political parties and the state. Embracing the anarcho-syndicalist doctrine that real power lay in the hands of those who produced national wealth, and that the workers' direct involvement in struggle at the point of production was the path to their self-emancipation, the CGT favoured militant action and strikes at enterprise level.

From the beginning, it promoted a unionism based on the strength of a community of militants, rather than on a mass membership. This implied the early choice of a rather loose, decentralized organizational structure with minimal internal discipline.

The CGT's anarcho-syndicalist stance proved vulnerable to events. Already in 1921, the union had experienced a major split between the reformist majority and the more revolutionary minority group (CGTU). The changing relationship between union and the state was at the heart of the debate. The CGT majority turned to the state for social reforms such as the social security benefits and family allowances, which it won in the 1930s. Party politics were also to influence the union's trajectory, and the strategy of union autonomy began to be challenged. Despite the mildly reformist position of the CGT at this time, French employers failed to take the opportunity to engage in collective bargaining.

The two wings of the union reunited under the Left government of the Popular Front in 1936. This was marked by a massive spontaneous strike movement leading to labour law reforms such as the introduction of employee delegates at plant-level, industry-level collective agreements, paid holidays, and the 40-hour week. The state played an important mediating role in the agreements which ended the strike and in most of the industry collective agreements.

A new split occurred in 1939 following the Nazi–Soviet pact. Existing unions were dissolved by the Vichy government under the Nazi occupation in 1940, but underground leaders of the CGT and CGTU agreed to the formation of a united confederation, facilitated by the advent of a tripartite post-Liberation government including communists, socialists and centrists. In 1947–48, there was yet another split: the CGT–FO (including socialist, reformist and anarcho-syndicalist elements) broke off from a CGT in which the Communist Party had become increasingly dominant, taking over most official posts within the union apparatus. Opponents saw this as a betrayal of the Charter of Amiens principle of independence from political parties. Ideological divisions were heightened by the onset of the cold war, and the division was to prove permanent.

The Communist party has retained its dominance over CGT, turning the confederation into an exponent of the Leninist conception of the union as a transmission belt between the party and the workers. However, in more recent times the party has not held undivided power. Indeed, an unwritten rule says that out of the 16 members of the confederal bureau (the effective ruling body) half should be communists.

Generally speaking, CGT has been slow to react to the transformation of the political and economic context in the post-war period. At the union's 1978 congress, a less sectarian and more democratic approach was advocated, but the phase of self-criticism was short-lived and the 'reformist' communist leaders were forced to withdraw. CGT's attitude to the socialist government from 1981 to 1993 was ambiguous. Though it gave its conditional support to the government of the Left, it was bitterly critical of policies on working hours and employment flexibility, especially following the withdrawal of the communists from office and the government's abandonment of Keynesian economic policy. At its 1989 congress, it reaffirmed its faith in the confrontational model based on the centrality

Table 13.1 French union membership figures (000s) 1976–1994

	1976	1983	1986–8	1990–4
CGT	2,100	1,622	1,031	480
FO	926	1,150	1,108	400
CFDT	829	681	600	500
FEN	526	493	394	*250
CGC	326	307	241	200
CFTC	223	260	250	170
Total	4,930	4,513	3,624	2,000

Source: Bibes and Mouriaux (1990) up to 1988; Jefferys (1996a) for 1990–94.
* FEN figures include members of FSU after the 1993 split.

of the strike weapon and in which collective bargaining was regarded as a pragmatic tactic to test the balance of power between labour and capital. CGT considered itself the sole representative of the working class, opposing any idea of unity of action with other unions. It reiterated its opposition to European integration, which it sees as a socially regressive expression of ultra-liberalism, dominated by multinationals; the union supported a 'no' vote in the referendum on the ratification of the Maastricht Treaty. Such viewpoints were confirmed at its 1995 congress, held in the midst of the December unrest in which CGT was an active participant.

Nevertheless, the collapse of communism may have finally precipitated the dissolution of CGT's marxist orthodoxy. At its 1995 congress, the union's general secretary adopted a centrist line and distanced himself from more Stalinist elements. The withdrawal from the formerly Soviet-dominated WFTU was approved, opening the way to membership of the ETUC, and references to 'the suppression of capitalist exploitation' and to 'the socialization of the means of production' were suppressed in the union's new statutes.

A recurrent problem for the CGT leadership has been the drastic loss of membership over the last 20 years. Between 1976 and 1992, it lost two-thirds of its members. Numbers fell from 2.3 million to 633,000 (of whom 477,000 are in employment). (See table 13.1.) The loss is all the more dramatic as the union has always been marked by high membership turnover. Its membership allegedly renews itself completely every 5 years.

Like the other confederations, CGT is organized in industry federations (of which energy, engineering, railway, post office and telecommunications, and public services are the most important), and in geographically based local unions. Members in the public services and public enterprise are now a majority. Since 1969, the union has had an important technical, managerial and professional staff section, the UGICT.

FO, set up in 1948 in reaction to communist involvement in CGT, claims to be the true heir of CGT's old policy of political independence, and has traditionally been staunchly anti-communist. From the beginning, its basic weakness has been the diversity of its component groups – which include revolutionaries, anarcho-syndicalists and Trotskyists, as well as conservatives. This has impeded efficient organization and hampered recruitment. Despite its internal fragmentation, FO has played a major role in collective bargaining, which it sees as the main element of union action, and has secured significant benefits for its members. It opposes state intervention in private sector bargaining and thus rejects 'social compromises' involving wage restraint. It emphasizes the importance of the union's role in representing workers' interests, and distrusts direct forms of employee representation and participation.

Socialist in its inspiration, FO has nevertheless kept its distance from the socialist party and government. Its approach has been essentially pragmatic and its overall strategy sufficiently general to appeal to its different components. Its 1989 congress, however, marked a shift of emphasis towards a more confrontational strategy, and FO has since hardened its position in multi-industry negotiations (especially on employment and working hours flexibility) and in its key stronghold in the public sector. It has also become anti-European in recent years, on the grounds that the Union has benefited capital rather than labour. Thus there has been a degree of convergence with the approach of CGT, confirmed in the December 1995 strike, and this has led to some internal turmoil. The 1996 congress appears to confirm that the reformist era is over and the influence of the Trotskyists is on the increase. FO's confrontational stance contributed to the loss of the presidency of the unemployment fund (UNEDIC), and its opposition to the Juppé government's proposed reforms of social security weakened its stronghold in the sickness insurance system.

By the mid-1980s FO claimed to be the second largest confederation with nearly one million members. However, since 1988 it has lost a third of its membership. In 1994 it had 370,000 members of whom two-thirds were civil servants or in public enterprises. Its strongest federations are in public services, health, white-collar and professional work, the post office, engineering and transport. Since 1978, FO has also had a small cadre section, the UCI (*Union des cadres et ingénieurs*). At the international level, FO has been a member of the anti-communist ICFTU since 1949, as well as an affiliate of the ETUC since its creation.

Confessional unionism began in 1919 with the formation of CFTC. Its main objective was to promote peaceful collaboration between capital and labour, in line with the social doctrine of the catholic church. Two of its major principles were union share ownership and employee profit-sharing, but its plans found little favour with employers at the time.

Largely composed of white-collar employees in the early years, its membership shifted increasingly towards manual workers in engineering, chemicals and construction. Recruitment spread beyond traditional catholic regions. After the Second World War, a fraction known as the *minoritaires* called for the union to abandon its strict religious affiliation and compete directly with CGT and FO. The *minoritaires* advocated a more open, independent and democratic, though still Christian-influenced, socialist position. In its first post-war congress, the CFTC affirmed that political office was incompatible with trade union office, and in 1947, it weakened its link with the catholic church by giving up its reference to papal encyclicals. In the 1950s, it advocated a flexible economic system based on 'democratic planning'. By 1964 the reformists were in the majority, and the union split. The minority group retained the religious orientation and kept the name CFTC, while the majority severed the catholic connection and became CFDT. The CFTC currently has around 100,000 members. Its membership was quite stable for many years, but has decreased somewhat from 1986, mainly as a result of the withdrawal of the miners, traditionally its strongest base. It maintains its Christian tradition, continues to emphasize the primacy of the individual and the defence of the family, rejects class struggle and the politicization of unions, and supports the development of collective bargaining (Bevort and Labbé 1992).

CFDT was the second-largest union confederation in the mid-1970s, its membership having nearly doubled between 1948 (as the old CFTC) and 1976 to over 800,000 members; but it declined sharply from 1977 onwards and was estimated to be around 520,000 at the end of 1995. The confederation is strongest in the health sector, engineering, local government, teaching, transport. It has a small cadre section, the UCC.

Following its split from CFTC, CFDT was radicalized by its leading role in the industrial unrest accompanying the social and political crisis of 1968. At its 1970 congress, it pronounced itself in favour of class struggle and advocated a form of workers' control or self-management. The radicalization of its ideology put it in closer competition with CGT. Since 1978, however, CFDT has played down its former ideological emphasis. It embarked on a process of resyndicalization (emphasizing narrowly defined trade union issues) and *recentrage* (return to the centre), giving priority to union adaptation to economic change. Its eagerness to put forward 'constructive reforms' enabled it to obtain the presidency of the national pension system and the unemployment fund (UNEDIC) in 1992. Since 1988, CFDT has been trying to build a more united union movement among reformist unions. However, neither FO nor CFTC have shown great enthusiasm for the project.

Since the end of the 1980s, internal tensions have become sharper under the pressure of the more left-wing federations (including teaching, textiles, banking and transport) and some regional sections. These tensions were manifested in the abrupt unplanned replacement of Jean Kaspar by Nicole Notat as general secretary in 1992. In the aftermath of the December 1995 strike, dissident groups attacked Notat for her support of parts of the government's social security reform and for her apparent wish to make CFDT a privileged partner of the right-wing government and of employers. This open internal crisis has weakened CFDT and led to membership losses, compounded by splits among its railway members.

At the international level, the CFDT is a member of ETUC and has been playing an active role in the building of a Social Europe; some of its previous leaders held key posts in European institutions in the 1980s. In 1988, it left WCL – formerly with a Christian identity – and joined ICFTU.

The CGC was formed in 1944. Its 1976 membership of around 325,000 (engineers, executives, sales representatives, supervisors, technicians) had fallen to some 110,000 in 1995. It is strongest in engineering, banking, and chemical industries, and among sales representatives. The confederation has become more radical over the years with the 'routinization' of *cadres*' jobs. Its priorities are to gain greater participation for its members within the firm, to maximize their pay differentials and to protect vested interests in tax and social security matters. The fundamental issue for CGC is whether a specific union for *cadres* still has a future as the *cadres'* advantageous pension rights, and the traditional status divide between them and non-*cadres*, are increasingly called into question.

With the exception of CGC, unions from all five confederations recruit across all industries and trades and across all categories of employees. They thus compete with each other, although they each have specific sectors, occupational groups and regions in which they are traditionally best represented. The five confederations are known as 'representative unions' at national level. This is a legal attribute granted on the basis of five criteria (the most important being the ability to prove that the union is totally independent from the employer) and which confers exclusive rights, for instance in collective bargaining, in the nomination of candidates in the system of employee representation within the firm (see below) and in representation on government consultative bodies.

However, a sixth union – UNSA – is aiming to become representative; it is already recognized as representative in parts of the public sector (for state and local employees and in the hospital sector). It was created in 1993 out of seven autonomous unions and now claims 300,000 members. Its two principal federations are a teachers' union, FEN, and FGAF, a union of civil servants, most of whose members are in the police force. The union held its first congress in 1995. Although it has secured state subsidies generally granted to union confederations, it has failed for the moment to get legal 'representative' status in social elections or in state welfare bodies, and has not been party to intersectoral negotiations.

FEN has 'representative' status but only at the sectoral level, i.e. within education. FEN decided to remain independent at the time of the CGT split. With a membership of around 140,000, it is structured around different categories of teacher. The socialist-oriented primary school teachers form the major group. The defence of a non-confessional state school system was a unifying factor in the face of internal diversity. However internal tensions grew in the 1990s. One contributory factor was the failure of the Savary law which would have granted state schools exclusive rights to the detriment of confessional schools. Tensions have also resulted from the expansion of secondary schools and universities which has increased the relative weight of secondary school teachers, and strengthened communist and extreme-left tendencies. These factions were expelled from FEN in 1992 and in 1993 they founded the FSU, with some 140,000 members. FSU rejects FEN's attitude of 'collaboration' with the authorities. It condemned the 1995 Juppé plan for reform of the social security system, and joined CGT and FO in the December unrest.

Alongside these formally structured union confederations, there exists a looser gathering of unions called the 'Group of Ten'. The group was formed by ten autonomous federations in 1981 with the objective of counteracting growing inter-union rivalries through united action. It aims to function more democratically than the formal confederations: decisions, taken by the rank and file, have to be unanimous. The group aspires to defend the individual as a 'total' human being and citizen, not only as a wage-earner, and to represent 'excluded' groups such as the poor and the unemployed, as well as the employed. The 'Group of Ten' played an important role in the 1995 December strike. The group's membership remains fairly modest, at some 70,000. It currently comprises eighteen unions. Its two major unions are the tax collectors (SNUI) and post and telecommunication workers (SUD–PTT); the latter includes ex-members of CFDT who left the organization in 1989 and 1996. Individual unions have achieved some success in works committee elections, as with SUD–PTT in 1995.

▎ French Unions in Crisis

Following Caire (1990), one may identify a 'crisis of membership, a crisis of influence and a crisis of militancy' in French unions from the late 1970s (see also Bibes and Mouriaux 1990; Croisat and Labbé 1992).

The Membership Crisis

Union density has traditionally been low in France. Accurate data are hard to come by; membership figures reported by union confederations are inflated by the inclusion of members who do not pay their monthly dues regularly. (There is no equivalent of the British check-off system which is outlawed in France.) However, independent estimates suggest that density fell from around 20 per cent in the mid-1970s to 15 per cent a decade later (Mouriaux 1986), and dropped as low as 9 per cent in the late 1980s (Croisat and Labbé 1992) (see table 13.1; Jefferys 1996a).

Employees in public administration or public enterprises and older workers tend to be over-represented, while young workers and immigrants have low rates of unionization. Low union membership compounds other weaknesses. Financial resources are limited by low dues (on average less than 1 per cent of the wage) which are paid irregularly – the average member pays only six monthly dues per year (Mouriaux 1994). The formal structure of French unions is underdeveloped in comparison with other European unions, with few full-time officers.

The Crisis of Influence

Trade union support or influence (*audience*) can also be assessed on the basis of results in elections for representatives to bodies such as works committees (*comités d'entreprise*) (see below) and industrial tribunals (*Prud'hommes*). In 5-yearly industrial tribunal elections (see table 13.2), support for CGT declined continuously from 1979 to 1992, although it retains the highest level of support. The vote for CFDT remained stable, while FO's rose in the early part of the period. The independent right-wing CSL doubled its share of the vote to 4.4 per cent. But the most striking feature of the results is the abstention rate, which reached an all-time high of almost 60 per cent in 1992. This low turnout has been widely interpreted as a reflection of employee disaffection towards the unions.

In works committee elections, the five representative unions together obtained around 63 per cent of the votes in 1993 (see table 13.3). Thus the unions have a much higher degree of support in 'social' elections than might be inferred from

Table 13.2 Elections for industrial tribunals

	CGT	CFDT	FO	CFTC	CGC	Others
1979	42.3	23.2	17.3	7.2	5.2	4.8
1982	37.0	23.5	17.7	8.5	9.6	3.7
1987	36.5	23.0	20.4	8.3	7.4	4.5
1993	33.5	23.8	20.5	8.6	7.0	6.8

Source: Ministry of Labour.

their low membership. None the less, the trend indicates an increasing crisis of support. Abstention rates are rising, albeit gradually: from 28 per cent in the 1960s to 35 per cent in the 1990s. More significantly, non-union representatives have sharply increased their share of the vote, from 23 per cent in 1983 to over 30 per cent in 1993. This trend has been evident since 1966, but accelerated from the 1980s. As a result of the peculiarities of the electoral system and of the large proportion of non-unionized small firms, the trend is even more marked in terms of seats: non-unionists now occupy nearly half of all works committee seats. The major reason for the growth of the non-union share lies in the absence of union lists, which leads to non-union lists being put together: more than nine out of ten non-union lists face no competition (Labbé 1994, 1996). Within the group of representative unions, only CGT has suffered a major loss of support. Its share of the vote fell from 37 per cent in 1977 to under 20 per cent in 1993. In 1989, for the first time CGT came second in terms of votes, behind non-union representatives. Support for the other main unions has shown a fair degree of stability.

The level of union representation within enterprises continues to decline. According to the Ministry of Labour, the proportion of plants (outside the non-competitive public sector) with 50 or more employees where trade union delegates are present fell from 55 to 49 per cent between 1987 and 1993 (Ministère du Travail, *Les délégués syndicaux*, 96, June 1996). The total number of union delegates also fell slightly. This drop affected especially CGT and CGC. As regards elected workforce representatives (*délégués du personnel*), a Ministry of Labour survey (Ministère du Travail 1996) shows that their number declined from 1985,

Table 13.3 Elections for works committees (%) 1983–1993

Union	1983	1985	1987	1989	1991	1993	1995
CGT	28.5	25.9	24.6	23.0	20.4	19.6	19.7
CFDT	21.9	20.8	20.5	20.5	20.5	20.8	20.5
FO	11.1	13.0	11.7	11.6	11.7	11.5	12.3
CFE-CGC	6.5	6.7	6.5	5.9	6.5	6.5	6.4
CFTC	4.0	4.7	4.6	4.4	4.5	4.9	5.1
Others	4.7	5.1	5.2	5.6	5.6	6.3	6.2
Non-unionized	22.8	23.8	27.0	29.1	30.9	30.3	29.9

Source: Ministry of Labour.

when 48 per cent of companies which should have had employee representatives in place did so; by 1994, only 38 per cent did so.

The crisis of influence of the major unions has also been manifested in the emergence of alternative forms of representation. In the late 1980s strike wave, rank-and-file organizations (*co-ordinations*) were set up outside official union structures to pursue workforce demands (see below). Such bodies, reminiscent of the Italian *cobas* of the same period, claimed to represent all strikers and deliberately remained transitory, unstable and uninstitutionalized. In the huge December 1995 strike, unions seemed to have learnt from their experience of the *co-ordinations*, and managed to avoid their reappearance by accepting decision-making through general assemblies of workers. However, the revival during the strike of the 'Group of Ten' with its more democratic and unitary methods and its broader agenda of representation, posed a new challenge to the traditional unions.

The Crisis of Militancy and Institutional Participation

Rosanvallon (1988) argues that whereas to be a union member at the beginning of the century was automatically to be an active militant as part of the 'social community', union membership now implies varying degrees of involvement in union activities. Support for unions may range from non-membership through voting for union candidates in social elections, to being a union sympathizer, being a regular dues-paying member, and being a militant. He argues that the unions' power is essentially institutional, based on their presence and participation in state bodies rather than on their membership.

Neo-corporatist arrangements have on the whole been limited in France. Aspects of the French industrial relations system such as inter-union rivalry and the lack of internal discipline over members (for example, the lack of formal union control over the right of individuals to strike) have reduced the attractiveness of neo-corporatist solutions for the state. None the less, unions participate in around one hundred public bodies, notably the Economic and Social Council, a body which advises the government on important policy issues. Unions also participate in tripartite bodies such as the national commissions on collective bargaining, vocational training, improvement of working conditions, social security funds, and unemployment funds. About 30,000 union representatives are involved in these functions. The concentration by activists in the main unions on such activities may well have increased the attraction for employees of alternative forms of representation such as *co-ordinations* and rival unions such as the Group of Ten.

Explanations for Low Union Density

The historical pattern of low union density in France may be explained by a number of traditional features of French unions and industrial relations. First, as a legacy of their anarcho-syndicalist origins, the unions have traditionally put more emphasis on building an active core of 'militant' organizers than on recruiting a stable mass membership. This also explains why they have rarely built up strong bureaucratic organizations. This early ideological choice meant that militants tended to see their role as one of fostering strikes and political action, rather than bargaining with employers; this made it difficult to obtain concrete benefits for their members. Second, the ideological and political fragmentation of unions has hampered the recruitment and retention of members. Third, the ability of unions to organize has been affected by employer opposition to any extension of union influence, and paternalist practices were long paramount, particularly in small firms. Union organization in the workplace was especially weak, and it was only in 1968 that unions obtained the legal right to establish workplace branches. Fourth, the legal framework has constrained unionization. For example, the use of the check-off system is prohibited. The incentive for union membership is reduced by the extension of collective agreements to all employees, whether unionized or not. Finally, unlike Scandinavian countries, for example, no specific welfare benefits accrue to union members.

To these factors were added a number of new ones from the 1980s. It is a paradox of French industrial relations that the unions experienced a drastic decline in membership and influence in the 1980s, just when the political environment provided by the socialist government was apparently most favourable. A rise in membership might have been expected, as had been the case in 1936 and 1945. The accelerating weakness of the unions reflects, first, the impact of major changes in the structure of the French economy: the intensification of the shift away from traditionally well-organized industrial sectors (coal, steel, engineering, shipbuilding) to new sectors such as electronics, and from industry to the service sector. These changes meant a loss of union members (Goetschy and Linhart 1990; Visser 1990; Croisat and Labbé 1992; Mouriaux 1994).

Second, major changes in the labour market were detrimental to unionization: unemployment rose from 6.4 per cent (of the active population) in 1980 to 11.5 per cent in 1995. Changes in employment contracts and employment practices led to an increase in part-time and fixed-contract workers, groups which were difficult to unionize (see below). The rise of these precarious forms of employment contracts may be one reason why the decline in union density among women workers has been higher than that of men. The development of a multitude of schemes for youth training and employment also hindered union attempts to organize the workforce.

Third, there has been a shift in social attitudes towards trade unions. Young people have expressed increasing scepticism about the efficiency of union action and put more faith in their own individual capacity for negotiating over work matters with the employer (Linhart and Malan, 1988).

Fourth, changes in employers' personnel policies since 1977, particularly the use of direct forms of communication and participation, flexibility measures and the increased individualization of the employment relationship (Morville 1985), have tended to weaken unions within the enterprise.

Fifth, the unions' administrative capacity has been overloaded by the increase in union duties resulting from the Auroux laws and the 5-year employment law; from growing union participation in state welfare, training and employment bodies; and from the newly developing trend towards multi-industry bargaining.

The 'institutionalization' of union business also appears to have increased the isolation of the top echelons from their rank and file (Rosanvallon 1988).

A final factor in trade union decline has been increasing fragmentation and growing tensions between and within confederations. Inter-union rivalry between CGT and CFDT followed the break-up on the Union of the Left in 1977 and became even more acute in the 1980s in the face of the socialist government's austerity and modernization policies. These policies have been taken up and carried further under the governments of the right from 1993 onwards. As a result, tensions have become sharper, notably over the reform of the social welfare system. One indicator has been the redistribution of the seats on the managing boards of the various social security funds. As mentioned, FO has been ousted from its main bastion, the sickness insurance fund, and replaced by CFDT. The various social security funds are now almost all chaired by supporters of the Juppé reform plan: CFDT, CFTC and CGC. CGT holds no presidencies and has denounced the reform plans.

In short, changes in economic structure, overloaded union administration, the growing distance with rank and file, and the unions' strategic disarray and fragmentation under recent governments of both left and right, have all contributed to union decline. Attempts at reform, such as the creation of the Group of Ten, or the CFDT's strategy of *recentrage* and its periodic efforts to create an 'axis' of non-communist confederations, have had only limited impact.

Employers

The Characteristics of French Employers

The French economy has, in common with other European countries, shown a continuing shift in activity from agriculture, mining and manufacturing to the service sector. By 1995, services accounted for 47.6 per cent of the total, manufacturing industry for 39.2 per cent and the primary sector for 13.2 per cent. Small and medium firms were traditionally important in the French economy, although economic development, especially since the late 1950s, has given large companies a more dominant position in the industrial structure. None the less, family ownership continues to be more significant than say in Britain, even in large firms. As in Italy and Germany, there are extensive and complex interlinkages between industrial and financial capital. Loose 'group' structures of semi-independent companies held together through webs of financial participations (rather than by centralized financial control as in the Anglo-Saxon model) are an important feature.

French economic structure has been strongly influenced by the direct participation of the state. Public employees account for around a quarter of the total employed workforce, while the state trading sector has occupied a major role within the French economy, both in manufacturing and in service sectors such as banking. A large-scale programme of nationalization of key industrial enterprises under the socialists in the early 1980s took employment in public enterprises to a high point of 2.4 million in 1987. Thereafter, the privatization programmes of conservative governments in 1986–8 and from 1993 drastically reduced the scale of public ownership. A 1993 law authorized the privatization of 21 publicly-owned groups, some of which were among those nationalized in 1982, but others included long-standing state enterprises such as Renault, Air France, SNECMA and Usinor-Sacilor.

State enterprises have been the site of important developments in industrial relations, often serving as models of good employment practice. In the 1950s, companies such as Renault were in the vanguard in the introduction of a range of social benefits. More recently public enterprises have played a pioneering role in the development of voluntary European works committees. They have also been in the forefront of government campaigns to tackle unemployment, for example through the use of 'social plans' to cushion the impact of restructuring on the workforce. One example is the 1993 agreement at the publicly owned armaments and electronics group, Thomson–CSF, which saved 1200 jobs through worksharing.

As in other European countries, there has been a major transformation of public administration, notably through the restructuring of the rigid pay and job category systems for the 4.5 million civil servants, and through successive 'modernization' plans (the most recent in 1995) which have introduced less bureaucratic, more flexible organizational systems, the decentralization of management responsibilities, and a sharper focus on quality of service.

In recent years, major French companies have responded to the pressures of 'globalization' by embarking on a strategy of expanding abroad *à grande vitesse* (Sally 1995), raising France's share of global outward foreign direct investment from 4 per cent in 1980 to 9 per cent by 1993 (Jones 1995: 47, 53). Many of the key French corporations were nationalized by the socialist governments of the 1980s, and underwent extensive rationalization and restructuring before being reprivatized. This highlights the central, interventionist role of the state in the shaping of French industrial structure: not only as owner of key industrial and financial enterprises, but as promoter of 'national champions' through state-sponsored restructuring and the provision of secure domestic markets by way of huge public investment programmes.

French employers have traditionally been characterized as paternalist and authoritarian, rejecting worker participation in decision-making and aggressively asserting managerial prerogative (see e.g. Lane 1989). Such traits have been ascribed to the predominance of small and medium family-owned firms in the formative phase of French industrialization, reinforced by the bureaucratic ethos fostered by the elite and centralist traditions of the *grandes écoles* and by the interpenetration of state and corporate elites. Authoritarian and aggressive management was encouraged historically by the fragmentation of French unionism and the ideological rejection of capitalist enterprise by a major section of it.

Managerial control has been depicted as centralized and, in larger firms, bureaucratic and formalized, with limited delegation. Social relations within the firm have typically been marked by high 'social distance' and mutual distrust. One manifestation of such features is the high ratio of managerial, supervisory and staff employees to production workers compared with Britain or Germany (Maurice et al. 1986). French workers have tended to have narrowly defined, firm-specific skills and operate within rigid job grading structures. Lane (1989: 188–92) suggests that functional flexibility has been impeded by the pattern of low trust relationships and narrowly defined skill areas, which reduced the scope for upgrading and for the flexible use of workers' skills.

A further consequence of French industrial culture is a pattern of conflictual industrial relations and what Batstone (1978) called 'arms'-length' bargaining in which management took account of the balance of power at the workplace, granting concessions to the workforce in order to forestall workplace militancy, while preserving the appearance of unilateral managerial authority.

This picture has evolved significantly in recent years. The post-1973 economic crisis, European integration and the growth of international competition have stimulated important changes in employers' strategies and practices. Since 1977, concerned that unions should not have a monopoly on social progress, the main employers' association, CNPF, has encouraged managements to adopt an active personnel policy at plant-level, based on direct dialogue with employees. The reform of employer attitudes has been stimulated by the institutionalization of shopfloor relations as a result of the Auroux laws (see below). Some observers (e.g. Rojot 1990; Schmidt 1993) believe that there has been a 'sea change' in French business attitudes towards employees. The traditional pattern of autocracy mingled with paternalism, close supervision and limited participation has given way to a more participative style and more co-operative workforce relations. Employers have taken a wide range of measures to increase flexibility of employment contracts, moves facilitated by the relaxation of labour market regulations. Developments have included the use of more flexible, individualized and merit-based pay systems, and increased flexibility in the organization of work, for example through team-working and multi-skilling. In the words of Jean Gandois, formerly head of Rhône–Poulenc and Péchiney and currently the president of the employers' association CNPF, there was 'a century of difference' between the attitudes of late 1970s and those of the early 1990s (quoted in Schmidt 1993: 92).

These changes have been accompanied by a marked improvement in the public perceptions of business, and in employees' attitudes towards the firm (e.g. Schmidt 1993: 85–9). One of the paradoxes of the 1980s was that the recovery of business's reputation took place not only in public opinion but also among trade unions, despite their opposition to the individualization of work relationships, and that this reassessment should take place under a socialist government.

▍ Employer Organization

In contrast to the pluralism of union representation at national level, employers' organization is more unitary. The main employers' body is the CNPF, which embraces about three-quarters of all French enterprises. It is made up of 84 industry-based organizations and about 170 multi-industry groups organized into a score of regional associations. Most of its constituents are trade organizations as well as employers' associations. Ten of CNPF's sectoral affiliates provide it with more than half of its revenue. Two of the most prominent sectoral associations are in chemicals and engineering.

Early employers' organizations developed from the 1840s. They opposed free trade ideas and sought to protect the French economy against foreign competition. Resistance to trade unionism only later became a motive for employer organization. However, the national power of employer associations remained fairly weak up to the First World War. In 1919 a national confederation, the CGPF, came into existence largely at the prompting of the government which was looking to deal with a single employers' organization. CGPF was dissolved in 1940, but certain prominent employers played an active role in the organizing committees set up by the Vichy régime. In 1945, the CNPF was established to co-ordinate the various branches of trade and industry.

CNPF has often been seen as dominated by the interests of large, technocratic companies, and has had to face the hostility of rival organizations of small employers. The most important is CGPME, founded in 1944. Its history has been marked by violent hostility to taxation, technocracy, marxism, and the nationalized sector. In 1977, the more extreme SNPMI was expelled from CGPME which then became more moderate. This eased future co-operation between CGPME and CNPF in such areas as industrial tribunal elections, and helped to avoid open confrontation on official consultative and negotiating bodies. However, during the 1980s, the impact of the Auroux laws, whose provisions were costly for small and medium-sized enterprises to implement, generated further rifts between CNPF and CGPME.

Throughout its history, the heterogeneity of CNPF membership has led to tensions over its role. It has alternated uneasily between being merely a liaison body for its affiliates (as was the case in the 1950s and the 1960s) and becoming a real decision-making centre, as in the wake of the organizational reform of 1969. In the early 1980s, under a president from the medium-sized company sector, CNPF endeavoured to reduce the distance between the confederation and enterprises and to minimize the role of traditional sectoral federations. Since the mid-1980s the presidency has been in the hands of employers from large international companies who have developed the international and especially the European dimension within the Confederation – for example, encouraging the setting up of voluntary European works committees in French companies.

The role of CNPF in collective bargaining remained fairly limited until the late 1960s. Its authority to commit its powerful member federations was limited, and negotiations were carried out by them at sectoral or territorial level. It was only after 1969, following internal organizational reform and in response to governmental pressures, that multi-industry bargaining really developed under the auspices of the Confederation. Its multi-industry activity consists mostly in negotiating national framework agreements (see below). It does not play a direct role in pay bargaining, an issue reserved for its sectoral affiliates and for individual companies.

For the first time in several years CNPF declined to issue pay recommendations to its members for 1994, on the grounds that pay determination in an unpredictable economic environment had to be left to the individual company. However, UIMM, the influential metalworking employers' federation, did provide pay guidelines for its members for 1994; these encouraged companies to control their pay bill, increase productivity and develop employee profit-sharing agreements, while stressing the trade-off between employee numbers and pay levels.

The influence of CNPF and its ability to act centrally has decreased as a result of the increasing importance of the enterprise level and of its failure to develop convincing employer initiatives in the fight against unemployment. In particular, it has been unable to negotiate satisfactory national-level agreements on enhanced job creation in return for reduced social charges for business, as proposed by the Chirac government.

CNPF does not believe in work sharing and argues that the failure of job creation stems from such factors as the poor performance of the educational system, the scarcity of qualified labour, high labour costs, insufficient geographical and professional mobility, contradictory government employment policies, and underdeveloped anticipatory employment policies at enterprise and local level. In an internal document (June 1996), CNPF expressed its opposition to massive and general working time cuts as suggested by a number of politicians and trade unions. It argued that hour reductions could have a positive effect on employment only where they were offset by a reorganization of work in the enterprise. Reductions had be negotiated on a case-by-case basis in sectors and companies with the constant concern to improve overall performance. CNPF no longer favours the use of drastic general cuts in employers' social security contributions to create jobs as it has proved costly and ineffective in practice (see below). It does, however, still argue for reductions in contributions for lower-paid workers.

Unemployment and the Regulation of the Labour Market

State intervention in the labour market since the early 1980s has been overwhelmingly preoccupied with the high level of unemployment. France stands out among major OECD countries for the length and severity of its unemployment crisis, dating back to the first oil-price shock. A level of 6 per cent in 1979 was to reach 10.5 per cent in 1987, before falling back at the end of the decade. In 1990s, however, unemployment rose again, to reach a peak of 12.6 per cent in 1996. Unemployment has hit youth and women particularly hard. The unemployment rate among young people (those under 25) rose to 27 per cent in 1995 following a slight improvement in the second half of the 1980s. Moreover, young people's job opportunities have largely been confined to 'precarious' and badly paid work. Those with low educational levels are particularly affected. In 1995, French male unemployment was 9.5 per cent against 13.8 per cent for women, a differential that has scarcely changed in France since 1985. A serious aspect of the unemployment crisis is the severity of long-term unemployment (lasting more than a year): it rose from 21.6 per cent of the total in 1973 to 40.2 per cent in 1995. None the less, it remains below the EU average in proportional terms.

A 1994 report (CERC 1994) paints a picture of France as a country of precarious employment and where there is a high risk of social exclusion. The report estimated that only 51.6 per cent of the active population had 'stable non-threatened employment', whereas 'stable but threatened employment' accounted for 28.5 per cent and 'unstable employment' for 7.8 per cent. Those unemployed for less than 2 years were 6.8 per cent of the labour force, and those unemployed for more than 2 years were 5.3 per cent. A report by Senator Arthuis (Arthuis 1993) estimated that between three and five million French jobs in industrial and service activities, including new sectors such as information technology, were potentially at risk from relocation to low-labour-cost countries.

Increasing precariousness of employment is reflected in the increase in the use of part-time, temporary and fixed-term work. Part-time work rose from 8.5 per cent in 1984 to 16 per cent of jobs in 1995. Among women, especially in low-skilled jobs, it reached 30 per cent. The number of part-time jobs created between 1982 and 1992 – 845,000 – was almost equal to the total number of net new jobs. Between 1984 and 1993 the proportion of employees on 'precarious' (fixed-term and temporary) employment contracts tripled to 6 per cent of employment (excluding central and local government). The use of fixed-term contracts is more common in the service sector, while temporary work contracts are most often used in industry as a safety valve during and following large-scale redundancies, for example in the car industry.

In marked contrast to the deregulated approach in Britain, successive French governments have adopted an interventionist strategy towards unemployment, on the one hand to increase labour market flexibility and, on the other, to cushion the social consequences of deregulation and implement active employment creation measures.

In 1986, the Chirac government abolished the 1976 legislation requiring prior administrative authorization for redundancies. This allowed employers greater freedom to carry out rationalization programmes entailing job losses. Legislation has also promoted the increase in flexible employment patterns; 1992 provisions, for example, encourage the spread of part-time working on open-ended contracts as a way of facilitating the entry of young people into employment and of easing the transition from work to retirement for older workers.

Other legislation, however, has placed restrictions on labour market flexibility. First, the loosening of redundancy restrictions was followed by the 1993 'Aubry' law which provided tighter control over enterprise social plans in the event of redundancies, and stipulated the provision of concrete redeployment measures (such as better internal and external redeployment and more training initiatives). A judgement by the court of appeal in May 1995 insisted that social plans must contain 'serious' and 'real' redeployment measures. In July 1996, the government announced that state financial support for early retirement measures would not be granted in future if social plans did not seriously examine possibilities for reducing working time and hence facilitating employment creation. The socialist party currently favours reintroducing the 1976 law on prior administrative authorization of redundancies, a move opposed by the government.

Second, measures have been introduced to tighten controls over precarious employment. In July 1990, following a sharp rise in the proportion of precarious jobs, legislation increased costs to employers of the use of precarious work. An evaluation of the law by the Ministry of Labour in 1992 concludes that it helped to reduce employers' recourse to fixed-term contracts and to limit the rise in temporary contracts. However, the report also found numerous infringements of the legal regulations, notably the use of precarious forms of work as probationary or pre-recruitment periods. It concludes that employers have failed to turn precarious employment into stable jobs and are still focusing on external rather than internal flexibility.

Throughout the two last decades, both socialist and conservative government policies have been directed to the stabilization of unemployment through special programmes for the unemployed rather than through macro-economic policies. Public spending on employment policies has quadrupled since the mid-1970s to reach FF 300 billion in 1995 (4 per cent of GDP), of which FF 122 billion was devoted to 'active' measures. The latter cover those reducing employers' indirect employment costs, incentives to recruitment, training and the reorganization of working time, and measures to promote to industrial restructuring. A third of the active employment measures were directed at specific categories, mainly the young and long-term unemployed.

From 1988, the Rocard government launched three successive 'employment plans' with a vast array of policy measures. By the late 1980s, however, it was clear that the government had abandoned its expectation that unemployment would disappear with economic recovery, and now believed that the existence of a significant level of unemployment was unavoidable.

A key legislative measure of recent years is the complex 'five year' employment law enacted by the conservative government of Balladur in December 1993 (see EIRR 1994a and 1994b). The legislation aimed to remove rigidities perceived as barriers to job creation. Vehement trade union opposition to initial proposals led to a number of government concessions. The law has been implemented through subsequent decrees and through collective bargaining at various levels, a process that is continuing.

The law's first major objective was to increase employment. In the first place it reduced employers' social security contributions especially for low-paid and less-skilled employees as well as those in areas of high unemployment. Employers' social contributions would be progressively transferred to taxation, starting with the system of family allowances. The law also simplified employee representation structures (while protecting employees' rights), reducing their cost to employers (see below). In the second place, it reorganized existing schemes – e.g. 'return to work' contracts and 'employment solidarity contracts' – targeted at problematic groups such as the long-term unemployed, the young jobless, the unemployed over 50 and those on low incomes. The most controversial measure was the new 'vocational integration contract' for young people (*contrat d'insertion profession-nelle*). This was withdrawn following massive opposition from trade unions and the young who saw it as a form of 'youth SMIC' (a youth minimum wage below the normal legal minimum wage or 'SMIC'). In its place the government introduced new financial incentives for hiring and training the young unemployed on fixed-term contracts, allowing young people initial work experience combined with vocational training. In the third place, the act tightened control of job seekers. The short duration of a contract was no longer a legitimate reason for refusing a job, nor was the requirement of geographical mobility; refusal would lead to the loss of benefit. A proposal to top up the earnings of unemployed people accepting a job paying less than unemployment benefit was opposed by the social partners, who feared it might exert a downward pressure on pay. Instead a national agreement was reached in 1994 which sought to encourage a return to employment by other means, such as combining unemployment benefit with part-time paid work.

In June 1996, a new measure known as the 'Robien law' was passed, providing financial incentives to employers to reduce their employees' working time. Despite fierce opposition by CNPF on the grounds of the high cost of the provisions, the Robien law has surprised even the government by its success. By December 1996, some 160 agreements covering 100,000 employees had already been signed.

The second objective of the law was to encourage bargaining at sector and company level over working time reductions. It granted substantial financial support, in the form of reductions in employers' social security contributions, to companies concluding such agreements. The reduction in working time had to be of at least 15 per cent (subsequently reduced to 10 per cent), offset by compulsory new hirings which must be maintained for 3 years (reduced to 2 years). Implementation of working time provisions proved difficult, as it relied on sectoral negotiations and on a general decree for those sectors which had not concluded an agreement. The reform ambitiously attempted to replace 75 individual decrees dating back to the 1930s, an initiative which had already been unsuccessfully attempted in 1983 and 1985. In the 2 years following the introduction of the law, there were only 13 company agreements under the provisions. The law also encourages bargaining over more working-time flexibility through annualized hours agreements, which had to be linked to working-time reductions. Its impact in this respect appears limited: of 68 company agreements on annualization between early 1994 and the end of 1995, only 9 carried job creation provisions (see below).

Numerous other provisions aimed to provide alternatives to redundancy by encouraging part-time work, employee leave schemes, continuous working, Sunday opening times, and reductions in overtime. The very high cost of early retirement has reduced its attraction as a way of increasing employment opportunities, but the legislation promoted part-time early retirement schemes. (A September 1995 agreement between the peak employers associations and the union confederations aimed to provide jobs for 100,000 young unemployed as replacements for early retiring employees.)

The third objective of the 1995 law was to strengthen vocational training, whose inefficiency, fragmentation and wastefulness had been criticized in a parliamentary report in 1994. The legislation strengthened control of the financing and quality of vocational training and promoted regional decentralization of training for young people, the reform of apprenticeships and life-time learning measures.

A new 'emergency programme' for jobs was introduced by the Juppé government in summer 1995 (EIRR 1995b). The programme was expected to create 700,000 jobs by the end of 1996. The new 'employment initiative contract' (*contrat initiative-emploi*) was aimed at the long-term unemployed, those on minimum benefits, and people with disabilities. The measures offered subsidies and tax exemptions to employers providing new permanent jobs or fixed-term contracts for a minimum period. A further scheme aimed to create 100,000 new jobs by combating youth unemployment in deprived areas (where it reaches an average of 43 per cent against the national average of 27 per cent): some 30 areas (*zones franches*) were granted complete exemption from fiscal and social charges for 4 years.

In the parliamentary elections of May 1997 the socialists won an unexpected victory, campaigning on an ambitious programme to combat unemployment. In June the new government of the left announced plans to create 350,000 jobs for young people in the public sector, at the level of the national minimum wage (itself increased by 4 per cent); the social partners were urged to match this in the private sector. There were also projected measures to reduce the standard working week gradually to 35 hours, and to encourage early retirement through changes to the pension system.

The judgement on the active employment approach of successive French governments must remain guarded. The 1996 report of the *Commission d'enquête sur les aides à l'emploi* (Assemblée Nationale 1996) criticized measures for being too numerous and too complex to be understood by the unemployed and employers, and for tending to change too often in response to political contingencies. The whole system was adjudged costly and inefficient, creating only 100,000 additional jobs in 1995. In particular, the strategy of linking employment creation to reductions in employer fiscal and social charges has proved controversial. Even CNPF has denounced the expense of a policy that had failed to have a great impact on employment creation. Many employers benefited from state subsidies for employment measures which they would have taken in any case. In some instances employers used schemes to replace employees on normal employment contracts. This debate has surfaced on various occasions in recent years, with the Juppé government accusing employers of not meeting their responsibilities on employment creation. Perhaps the Jospin government will stimulate greater progress: at the time of writing it is far too early to judge.

Collective Bargaining

Background

Although collective bargaining in France predates the creation of a legal framework, the characteristics of the bargaining system have been largely shaped by successive pieces of legislation from 1919 onwards. The Popular Front's 1936 law in particular established a enduring framework of bargaining based on the primacy of the industrial sector level. The law also established the extension procedure under which the Minister of Labour may make a collective agreement binding on all employers in a given industry, regardless of their membership of employers' associations. Industry-level bargaining suited weak unions, since it maximized the proportion of the workforce covered by agreements and promoted equality of treatment across companies. It also appealed to employers in establishing only minimum industry standards, leaving individual enterprises considerable autonomy in setting terms and conditions and allowed them to marginalize union workplace organization.

Following the social and political unrest of 1968, new legislation strengthened the role of multi-industry bargaining, leading to innovative agreements on issues such as job security, vocational training and redundancy provisions. The plant level was highlighted by measures to strengthen union workplace representation and to give union delegates a bargaining function, and the 1970s witnessed the rise of plant-level agreements. These tendencies were consolidated by the major wave of legislation enacted by the socialist government in the early 1980s, known collectively as the Auroux laws. These embodied the government's efforts to reform workplace relations and to provide employees with real 'citizenship within the firm'. The Auroux laws were intended to foster a mutual learning process within the enterprise, with employers becoming more aware of their social employment responsibilities and unions more attentive to the firm's economic constraints. One of the key provisions was the imposition on employers of the obligation to bargain annually with company-level unions on pay and working time. Following the Auroux laws, the volume of plant-level agreements increased sharply, a reflection also of changing employer strategies and their pursuit of improved productivity, quality and flexibility.

As a result of this evolution, the French collective bargaining system is now structured around the three levels of multi-industry, industry and company bargaining. At multi-industry level agreements are concluded between central employers and trade union organizations. These agreements are not directly binding but set the framework within which industry and company bargaining can take place. In the late 1980s, CNPF and some unions (especially CFDT) favoured the development of a consensual approach to the modernization of French enterprises by means of a series of multi-industry 'orientation agreements', intended to encourage bargaining at sectoral and company levels on issues linked to the modernization of companies and various forms of labour flexibility.

At industry level, there is a statutory obligation (under the Auroux laws) to negotiate annually on minimum rates of pay, although with no obligation to reach agreement. The parties at industry level are also obliged by statute to review job classification systems every five years. At company level, as mentioned, employers are required to negotiate (although not to conclude agreements) annually with union representatives on pay and working time issues.

Industry and company agreements are binding once they have been signed by one or more so-called 'representative' unions and employer organizations or individual employer. Thus an agreement is reckoned valid even if signed by a minority union. However, non-signatory unions may veto a company agreement if it contradicts one reached at a higher level, and providing that non-signatory opponents gather more than half of the votes in the works committee or employee delegate elections. Giving opposition unions such veto rights was expected to lead to more legitimate agreements, but in practice the provision has rarely been used.

A characteristic of French collective bargaining dating from the 1936 law is that collective agreements can be extended by ministerial decree to all companies, whether they have signed them or not, within the same sector and geographical area (*procédure d'extension*) or to all companies in the same sector but in a different geographical area (*procédure d'élargissement*). These procedures enable employees to benefit from the terms of an agreement even where they are not directly covered by it. The annual report of the Ministry of Labour records an average of 400 agreements per year subject to these procedures.

Collective Bargaining Developments

Multi-industry Agreements

After a spate of agreements in the early 1970s, multi-industry bargaining faded away until the late 1980s when it received a new boost as result of the Rocard government's support for broad national enabling agreements, and of a more consensual approach by the social partners at national level. Seven major issues were the subject of multi-industry agreements in this second wave of multi-industry bargaining: technological change, working time, sexual equality, working conditions, vocational training, employment conditions for precarious forms of work – all directly linked to the issue of flexibility and the modernization of enterprises – and social protection (unemployment benefit and pension systems). CGT and FO have been reluctant partners in multi-industry bargaining and have refused to sign some agreements, while CFDT, CGC and CFTC have been warm supporters of such deals with CNPF. The employers' confederation believed that a consensus approach on modernization issues would strengthen French enterprises in the face of the single market and the challenge of internationalization. However, the modernization initiatives launched at multi-industry level have not been followed up at sectoral level, largely as a result of the reluctance of some industry employer federations.

More recently, the 'five-year employment' law of 1993 provided a new impetus for multi-industry bargaining, as for bargaining at other levels. Thus a joint declaration in February 1995, signed by all the social partners, ushered in a series of talks at central level on the fight against unemployment, the integration of young people in the labour market, the organization of working time and the articulation of bargaining levels. Five intersectoral agreements relating to employment were reached in 1995: on vocational training; the vocational integration of young people (not signed by CGT); early retirement in exchange for recruitment; the relaunching of sectoral bargaining on the reorganization of working time (not signed by CGT); and the articulation of bargaining levels and bargaining in companies without union representatives (not signed by CGT or FO).

The enabling agreement on the 'reorganization of working time' (October 1995) aims to develop sectoral bargaining on working time. Among the measures covered are the introduction of annual hours in exchange for working-time reductions, cuts in overtime, the provision of incentives to move from full-time to part-time work, and the promotion of 'time saving accounts' (see above). Special attention is also paid to companies not covered by an agreement. The agreement is important in marking the employers' recognition for the first time that working-time reductions are a serious element in the fight against unemployment. By November 1995, employers in nine industry sectors covering around a third of the private sector workforce had drawn up 'employment charters', some with quantified job creation targets. However, the failure of intersectoral agreements over the past 10 years to stimulate bargaining at sectoral level, and the opposition of certain sectoral employer federations to the CNPF deal, mean the real impact of the agreement is in doubt. A tripartite 'social summit' in December 1995 in the wake of the strike wave aimed to accelerate the bargaining process, and the government threatened the social partners with legislation if collective agreements were not reached. However, by mid-1996, agreements had been reached in only seven sectors. The government initiated negotiations in the public sector and state-owned companies on working-time issues, leading to an agreement in July 1996 on 'early retirement for youth employment' in government and the health service.

The multi-industry procedural agreement on 'the articulation of bargaining levels and the possibility of negotiations in companies without union representatives' (October 1995) represents a significant development in the structure of collective bargaining in France. The agreement entails two quite revolutionary changes. First, it establishes a complementary rather than a hierarchical relationship between the three traditional bargaining levels. The intention is to confer greater autonomy on company bargaining. Second, the 1995 accord aims to develop collective bargaining in small and medium-sized companies where there is often no union presence. Thus it allows company agreements to be signed, in the absence of union delegates, by employees specifically mandated by unions, or by elected employee representatives (works committee members or employee delegates). (However, a majority of the sector's trade unions would have the power to reject an agreement.) Draft legislation in May 1996 provided the necessary statutory backing for such agreements.

The 1995 agreement is for a 3-year experimental period. Along with the upsurge in multi-sector bargaining more generally, it may partly be seen as an attempt by the social partners to provide a counterweight to the tendency to increasing legislative intervention, especially in the context of state concern with employment.

Industry Bargaining

Industry bargaining has also been subject to development and renewal over the last 10 years and, despite the more spectacular growth of company and multi-industry bargaining, it remains essential. In 1981, 3.5 million workers were not covered by an industry agreement; although one of the objectives of the Auroux laws was to ensure comprehensive coverage, one million workers remained unprotected in 1990, in sectors such as sports, the media and leisure.

The number of national industry agreements rose from 365 in 1981 to 968 in 1995. FO and CFDT were the most prominent participants in industry bargaining (signing 72 per cent and 68 per cent of all agreements respectively, compared with 58 per cent for CGC and 60 per cent for CFTC 60). CGT was much less active, signing only 35 per cent.

Though pay is still the main subject of industry agreements and is the subject of more than 75 per cent of them, qualitative developments have been taking place. Bargaining increasingly deals with issues such as vocational training (12 per cent of agreements in 1995), retirement benefits (5 per cent), working time (3 per cent), and employment (2.6 per cent). The employment agreements have, in certain sectors, established joint committees to assess the impact on qualifications and jobs of an economic downturn.

Despite its failures in areas such as annualized hours, industry bargaining has had a significant impact on pay, most notably in the upgrading of low-paid workers. Employer federations at industry level were persuaded to take part in negotiations over low pay in order to avoid more onerous legislative measures. An assessment in June 1995 showed that 71 per cent of sectors had minimum pay scales above the rate of the statutory minimum wage (the 'SMIC'). A similar assessment a year later revealed a sharp deterioration, with minima above the SMIC in only 30 per cent of sectors. This was largely due to two consecutive SMIC increases linked to electoral pressures. The prevalence of company-level pay bargaining (see below) means that there is a discrepancy between sectoral minimum rates and actual pay (estimated to be around 30 per cent in engineering). Nevertheless, the sectoral level still plays a fundamental role in wage formation. There is a strong correlation between the hierarchy of conventional minima and the hierarchy of real wages (INSEE studies).

Despite its developments, industry bargaining remains on the whole rather weak. Some attribute such weakness to the declining representativity of union and employer organizations and to the lack of homogeneity of activities within sectors. Others point to the lack of articulation between bargaining levels, and to the growing prominence of company bargaining.

Company-level Bargaining

A study of the impact of the first decade of operation of the Auroux laws (Coffineau 1993) provides an optimistic assessment of the evolution of French collective bargaining, a picture confirmed by most recent developments. Company bargaining has become the key factor in regulating company industrial relations. The number of company agreements rose sixfold between 1982 and 1995, from 1,410 to 8,550. More than 3 million employees – around 20 per cent of the workforce – in both private and public sectors are covered. However, in smaller firms and those without unions, collective bargaining is often non-existent. The bargaining obligation is very difficult to enforce in smaller companies: among those with less than 100 employees, only 55 per cent respect the annual obligation to negotiate; overall, about two-thirds of companies comply with the law. This has accentuated the already large gap between large and small enterprises. Agreements are reached in around 70 per cent of companies where negotiations take place.

According to Ministry of Labour figures for 1995, the largest number of company agreements (49 per cent) deal with pay, followed by the organization of working time (42 per cent). The importance of traditional pay items has been slowly falling relative to working-time and employment issues, although 1995 saw an exceptional 20 per cent increase in agreements on pay. A Ministry of Labour study (DARES 1994) found, surprisingly, that two-thirds of employers believed that the negotiation process had not affected pay outcomes, and that the same pay increases would have been conceded without it. The union side was less pessimistic but even so, half of union delegates judged that negotiations had no effect on the employer's initial decision. It could be argued, however, that the annual obligation to negotiate has pushed employers to make more reasonable pay offers than they would have done in the absence of such an obligation.

The DARES study found that the existence of pay individualization schemes (found in more than 50 per cent of establishments) or profit-sharing schemes (in 44 per cent) was no obstacle to successful agreements on collective pay increases. Pay individualization was mostly linked with changes in work organization, reflecting the employers' wish to increase employee acceptance of organizational and technological change. Twenty-five per cent of company pay agreements contained an individualization clause in 1985, rising to more than 30 per cent in the early 1990s. Another striking trend is the growth of financial participation agreements. Between 1986 and 1993, the number of French employees covered by voluntary profit-sharing schemes (*accords d'intéressement*) had more than tripled to 2.5 million. In addition, agreements on employee participation in company results or growth through share ownership, known as *accords de participation*, are compulsory. Legislation in 1990 reduced the company size threshold for such 'capital-sharing' schemes. This has led to an increase in the number of such agreements, which covered 5 million employees in 1993.

The high volume of company agreements on working-time issues is all the more notable in that sector-level framework agreements are lacking in most cases. Traditional working-time issues such as annual and bank holidays have lost ground to agreements on working-time reorganization. From 1994, annualized hours, the variable working week (through extended operating times), hours reductions and shift-working have constituted the majority of agreements. Part-time work has been the subject of one out of ten agreements, reflecting the possibility for part-timers to work overtime and the provision under the 1993 employment legislation for part-time working to be annualized. Such agreements are most frequent in the health, finance and distribution sectors. Agreements on time off in lieu or on so-called 'time saving accounts' (which allow bonuses, profit-sharing payments, overtime etc. to be converted into paid time off) remain limited. The rise in agreements on the reorganization of working time reflects not only employer flexibility strategies but also legislative changes such as the highly successful 'de Robien' law of 11 June 1996, aiming to reduce unemployment. Innovative 'employment agreements' (a different category from working-time agreements) have doubled since 1992 although they are still relatively infrequent, accounting for 8 per cent of the total. These agreements, both 'defensive' aimed at avoiding redundancies and 'offensive' aimed at increasing employment levels, have been introduced in companies such as Thomson–CSF, the insurance companies UAP, AXA and the GAN, and the French gas and electricity company EDF–GDF. Agreements have used hours reductions, in some case with partial loss of pay, partial early retirements, and more flexible working-time arrangements as a key means of safeguarding or creating jobs (cf. EIRR 1996) However, economic difficulties or company take-overs have called some agreements into question as companies have been unable to meet their employment commitments.

Other issues such as technological change, qualifications, working conditions, training or job classifications have been less subject to negotiations than might have been expected, suggesting that unilateral employer implementation of workplace change remains the rule in these areas. The number of agreements on the right of direct expression also remains very low (around 2 per cent), even though in 1995 such agreements were supposed to be subject to renewal for a 3-year period. On the whole, the content of company agreements remains fairly poor and innovative provisions are rare, with the exception of some well-publicized agreements on the reform of work organization (e.g. the accords at Renault and in the chemical firm Péchiney) or employment creation. However, there has been a tendency in some company agreements towards the 'globalization' of bargaining topics (linking pay, the duration and organization of working time, employment levels, training, and so on) (see EIRR 1995a).

The sectoral distribution of company agreements is skewed towards industry. In 1995, 60 per cent of all agreements were reached in manufacturing, 29 per cent in services, 8 per cent in distribution and 3 per cent in building and civil engineering. However, the proportion of agreements reached in industry is slowly decreasing. In 1995, the largest union, CFDT, signed 57 per cent of all agreements, CGT 47 per cent, FO 41 per cent, CFTC 21 per cent and CGC 36 per cent. As these figures suggest, despite its strong oppositional attitudes at national level and its low propensity to sign agreements at industry level, CGT tends to sign numerous company agreements. A study by the Ministry of Labour (DARES 1994) on company pay bargaining found that company negotiations, where they take place, are mostly conducted by union delegates (as required by law). So-called 'quasi agreements' (agreement reached informally with works committee representatives in the absence of union delegates) remain the exception, accounting for only 16 per cent of agreements signed.

In conclusion, growing competitive pressures, reinforced by legislative changes in the 1980s and 1990s have encouraged unions and employers to develop greater flexibility in work organization, working time, wages, employment practices and company employee representation procedures. It is principally at the level of company bargaining that these various challenges of corporate modernization have been met – particularly in view of the limited success of initiatives by progressive union and employer groups to encourage economic modernization through multi-industry enabling agreements. Thus, as in most European countries, there has been a significant trend towards decentralized bargaining. However, it remains to be seen whether company deals produce positive outcomes for employees. Working-time flexibility deals have generally meant increasing constraints rather than greater freedom, and the success of flexibility measures in creating or maintaining jobs is open to question. Finally, the fragmentation of collective bargaining implied by the increasing role of company bargaining may make it more difficult for the social partners to take account of societal effects, and in particular to deal with the problems of social exclusion.

▌Employee Representation at Company Level

A major characteristic of the French system of industrial relations is the multitude of representative institutions at the workplace, each reflecting social and political pressures at a particular period. Employee delegates (*délégués du personnel*), compulsory in companies with 10 or more workers, were instituted by the Popular Front in 1936 to deal with individual employee grievances and to make sure labour laws and collective agreements were enforced. Works committees (*comités d'entreprise*), set following the Liberation in 1945, have information and consultation rights and are responsible for developing social and cultural activities. *Comités d'entreprise* are compulsory in companies of 50 or more employees. Workplace union branches (*sections syndicales*) and trade union delegates in companies (*délégués syndicaux*) were introduced in 1968 to carry out union activities and to participate in plant-level bargaining. In 1982, the Auroux laws widened the powers of these bodies on economic issues and gave them additional resources. 'Group committees' (*comités de groupe*) were also created, enabling works committees to intervene in corporate decision centres beyond their own establishment. Recent research (Hege and Dufour 1995) suggests that workplace representation is likely to be more effective where representatives are able to maintain close links with strong unions, both within the enterprise and at sectoral or regional levels. Where workplace union organization is ineffectual, statutory workplace institutions tend to have little impact, and representatives lack legitimacy in the eyes of employees. In such cases, the *comité d'entreprise* tends to retreat into purely social and cultural activities.

Employee delegates and works committee representatives are elected by the whole workforce. Election is by secret ballot on lists of candidates proposed in the first instance by the five national unions (CGT, CFDT, FO, CFTC, CGC). By giving unions a monopoly on proposing candidates in the first round of elections, the state aimed to strengthen national unions at enterprise level, and successful candidates are generally elected on a union slate. (See table 13.3.)

The 1993 'five-year employment' law sought to simplify the legislation on employee representation and to make it less burdensome for employers, especially small and medium-sized companies. The duration of the mandate of employee delegates was extended from one year to two to bring it into line with that of works committee representatives, enabling elections to be held at the same time and thus reducing the administrative burden for the employer. The law also reduced paid time off for employee delegates in small firms from 15 to 10 hours a month. Enterprises with under 300 employees became entitled to provide information in a single annual document rather than in four written reports as before. And in firms with under 150 employees, works committees could be held every two months rather than every month as before. Finally, firms with between 50–199 employees may opt for a single representative structure instead of two, with employee delegates taking over the works committee representatives' role. The government estimated that around 60 per cent of firms with works committees and 25 per cent of those with 50 and more employees would benefit from these measures, leading to a 40 per cent reduction in the cost to employers of workplace representative structures.

A major innovation of the Auroux laws was the workers' right of expression (*droit d'expression*), introduced in 1982 and amended in 1986. This gave all employees in the public and private sectors the right to express their view within a group, concerning the content, conditions and organization of work. As framework legislation, it was followed by plant-level agreements specifying issues such as the size of the 'expression groups', the frequency of meetings, whether they are chaired by a trade unionist or a manager, and procedures for dealing with issues raised by the group. Initially very reluctant, employers came to see advantages for management in the new bodies. Assessments of the working of the groups have been fairly negative, though they have contributed to an improvement in working conditions and workstations.

Both companies and employees regarded quality circles, which expanded rapidly in the mid-1980s, more favourably than the statutory expression groups. Quality circles were better resourced, and were seen as better able to tackle specific problems, often with a direct impact on the individual's job. The number of expression groups declined in the late 1980s and early 1990s, but this was also the case for quality circles. The Ministry of Labour estimates that 3.5 million people in 10–12,000 enterprises were covered by expression groups in 1990.

▌ Conflict

In their analysis of French strikes, Shorter and Tilly (1974) distinguished three types of developments: linear trends, mini-strike waves around bread and butter issues, and exceptional strike peaks where workers take to the streets with their demands for political participation. Among the 'political' strikes they identify the waves of 1899, 1906, 1919–20, 1936 (the Popular Front strike), 1947–8 (when the Communist party was a major political force) and the 1968 movement. Jefferys (1996b) adds 1995 to the list. Mini-strike waves are 1953 (in which public sector workers played a major role), 1971 (the height of a period of militancy involving new claims of a more qualitative nature and new categories of employees such as women, immigrants and the unskilled), 1976 and 1982 (in protest against government austerity plans), and 1989 (a peak in public sector strikes).

In terms of long-term strike trends, there was, first, a drastic decline in the number of days lost from an average of 3.6 million per year in the trading sector in the 1970s to 1.2 million in the 1980s and less than 600,000 in the 1990s (excluding 1995). Second, the proportion of 'generalized conflicts' (multi-employer general strikes) decreased sharply in the 1980s and 1990s (excluding 1995) compared with the 1970s. This may be attributed to the combined effects of rising unemployment, low union density, weak inter-union solidarity, and the declining importance of sectoral collective bargaining for local wages (Jefferys 1996b: 519).

Third, the public non-market sector was more strike-prone than the private sector: 'throughout the period since 1982, public sector workers were on average between half (1980s) and one-third (1990s) more likely to experience strikes than their fellow market sector workers' (Jefferys 1996b: 521). In 1986 and 1987, civil servants accounted for 45 per cent of days lost. In 1986, for example, there were strikes in the civil service, on the railways (SNCF), the Paris metro, and in gas and electricity; while in 1987, strikes in SNCF alone amounted to a third of the total number of days lost and other public sector groups such as school teachers, air traffic controllers and pilots also went on strike. The late 1980s also saw serious stoppages in the health service, the prisons, central government and education. In 1989, civil servant strikes accounted for 72 per cent of total days lost. After 1990 civil service strikes declined until the huge strike wave of autumn 1995, although large state enterprises remained in the forefront of conflict during the 1990s.

One of the chief causes of public sector unrest in the 1980s was government adherence to a policy of strict pay guidelines. Despite a fairly high union density of 25 per cent in the sector, wage levels and increases for public employees remained considerably lower than those in the private sector. Pay restraint has continued to provoke conflict in the public services in the 1990s, most notably on the eve of the 1995 wave of protest. The public sector strike of 10th October 1995 in opposition to Juppé's announcement of a pay freeze attracted three million civil servants and state enterprise employees. In the public enterprise sector, labour unrest has stemmed from fears among employees about restructuring – as with plans to split SNCF into two parts – rationalization and job loss, continuing privatization, and the liberalization and deregulation of public utilities, especially as a result of EU directives in sectors such as telecommunications and electricity supply. Among employee demands have been the preservation of the specific statutes of public sector workers and the safeguarding of jobs. Sales of shares in France Telecom and Renault, fears about job losses in the banks, and successive reform plans at Air France and at SNCF led to a series of strikes in those enterprises in the 1990s, and there have been major strikes in the electricity and gas industries and in the postal service. However, the private sector has also witnessed some major conflicts in recent years, an example being the highly effective 12-day lorry-drivers' strike over pay and working hours which paralysed the country in November 1996.

A key characteristic of public sector strikes in the 1980s was the setting up of rank-and-file 'co-ordination groups' to organize strike action either alongside or in opposition to official union channels (as in the railway workers' and nurses' strikes in 1987 and 1988). The *co-ordinations* were largely a phenomenon of the public sector. Under charismatic (often extreme left-wing) leaders, they questioned the traditional and often bureaucratic negotiating practices of the union confederations and tried to bridge what they saw as a gap between the demands of the rank and file and the proposals of official union representatives. The *co-ordinations* also saw mass meetings as a way of exerting greater control over strike committees and negotiating bodies. *Co-ordinations* were a clear reflection of some of the deficiencies of French union activity in the 1980s. Unions have subsequently learnt some of the lessons and have tended to consult employees more frequently about negotiating priorities and about the conduct of strikes and negotiations.

The 1995 Strike

Several background conditions made the 1995 strike wave possible: the bottoming-out of the economic recession with wage increases remaining below productivity increases; greater trade union unity and the rank-and-file desire for less union rivalry with the advent of right-wing government from 1993; deep government unpopularity over nuclear testing, tax increases and failures in the fight against unemployment; a general threat to the welfare state consensus; and a lack of confidence in the future in a context of high unemployment (Jefferys 1996b).

Before the November–December strikes, strike activity had been on the increase, both in the private and public sector. In the private sector, conflicts tended to be concentrated in enterprises with a high proportion of precarious workers, no wage increases despite productivity gains, and increased stress at work (Pernot 1996).

The strike wave took the form of three different but overlapping forms of mobilization (Jefferys 1996b): a series of one-day public sector protest strikes, several indefinite strikes by public sector workers, and street demonstrations particularly in provincial cities such as Bordeaux, Marseilles and Toulouse. Protest demonstrations were generally led by public sector strikers but supported by students and non-striking sympathizers from the private sector. The strikes were spread over a two-month period and brought the country to a halt for almost a month. There were nine one-day strikes and demonstrations, culminating in that of 12th December which attracted some five million participants. Among the longer strikes, the 25-day SNCF stoppage was prominent as railway workers fought against the threat to their jobs from yet another rescue plan. A strike by city transport workers lasted 23 days, that by postal and telecommunications workers 16 days, and a stoppage in EDF–GDF 10 days. Strikes also affected schools, hospitals, air traffic, ports and the Bank of France. Significantly, unlike the unrest of the late 1980s, the strikes remained under the control of the major unions, principally CGT and FO, and did not give rise to spontaneous 'co-ordinations'.

The December strike movement began in the traditional manner, in response to government attempts to put an end to acquired rights. In the context of the Maastricht timetable for meeting public expenditure and deficit targets, Alain

Juppé unveiled plans in mid-November to reform the social security system by reducing expenditure, raising taxes (the RDS – *remboursement de la dette sociale* – to pay off the £33 billion social security debt for the period 1992–96), and transferring to Parliament part of the unions' responsibility for managing the social security system. He also announced the alignment of special public sector pension schemes with the scheme introduced in the private sector. This harmonization would have meant a deterioration in pension conditions for 4.5 million public employees in organizations such as SNCF or EDF–GDF. The Juppé plan provided a rallying point for employee grievances throughout the public sector. The strike wave ended when Juppé convened a tripartite summit of all the social partners on 21 December 1995, from which his social security reform emerged more or less intact, and a timetable was drawn up for future negotiations on employment issues such as young people and working time.

On the whole, the December strike movement may be judged a victory for the striking groups. Special pension regimes were maintained, the restructuring plan for SNCF was withdrawn. The episode was notable for the high degree of solidarity shown by private sector workers. Although they did not join the strike movement, many took part in demonstrations and accepted without serious protest the inconvenience caused by the disruption of public services. The relative job security and advantageous employment conditions of public sector workers did not provoke the hostility that might have been expected, nor were they perceived as major causes of unemployment. Indeed, the unrest was tagged a 'proxy strike' on behalf of the private sector. This solidarity between the public and private sectors added to the pressures on the government and was a significant factor in its retreat.

The strike was, as Jefferys (1996b) argues, 'political' in the Shorter and Tilly sense, as much as industrial, in that it could be seen as a way of extending workers' political participation at a critical moment in which feelings of political exclusion were strong. But although it represented a movement of radical opposition to the government's liberal economic choices, it never turned into a social movement: in contrast to May 1968, neither the strikers nor the political parties of the left were able to use the events to articulate an alternative vision for the future of French society. The strike remained essentially a movement of *refus*, of rejection of existing policies, but provided no new answers to the challenges of European integration and globalization (Touraine et al. 1996).

One outcome of the government's proposals for social security reform has been the intensification of union divisions at national level. CFDT supported some elements of the plan, provoking a major confrontation with FO which was the plan's strongest opponent. As a result, FO moved closer to its former enemy CGT in the course of the strike movement. The unrest has generated considerable tensions within FO and CFDT. Some federations (such as food, telecommunications, posts) have accused their confederal leadership of lacking political independence and of being subject to excessive Trotskyist or communist influences. In CFDT, the left opposition attacked the general secretary Nicole Notat for supporting part of the Juppé plan and for seeking to become the privileged partner of government and employers.

▌Conclusions

The basic paradox of French industrial relations in the 1980s and 1990s is that collective bargaining has never been so intense, while trade unions have never been weaker. Over the past 15 years the traditional industrial relations actors – unions principally, but also employers to some extent – have experienced considerable organizational turmoil, uncertainty over aims, and a broader crisis of legitimacy. At the same time, collective bargaining has finally become established in France as the major means of employment regulation. The institutional framework has been provided largely by the Auroux laws of the left and the five-year employment law of the right.

Inter-union rivalry has been increasing as have internal organizational tensions. Inter-union disagreements have been manifested in divergent attitudes to employers' flexibility strategies and to government policy, particularly in the reform of the social security system. While FO has become a much more combative union, moving closer to CGT, CFDT seems to be seeking a new role as the privileged partner of government and employers. The prospects for a united union front in France look bleak. Union weakness and divisions have encouraged the emergence of a new union organization, the 'Group of Ten' which has argued for a more unitary, democratic and efficient model of representation, premised on the incorporation of the growing number of 'excluded' social groups. At the same time, growing fragmentation is visible, especially in the public sector, for instance among the teacher unions. Thus one detects ambivalent and contradictory tendencies towards the renewal of organization and strategy, but also the stubborn defence of 'acquired rights'. Public sector strikes have frequently triggered a resurgence of inter-union rivalry and internal division. At the same time employees in the public sector have sought to protect their particular sectoral interests against the challenges of liberalization and deregulation. Yet paradoxically, this apparently privileged group obtained the support of its private sector counterparts during the massive strikes of December 1995.

The employer organization, CNPF, has also suffered from internal divisions between modernizing forces and more traditional ones. Yet again, its representativeness with respect to small and medium-sized enterprises has been called into question. Its decreasing capacity to act centrally has been exposed by its inability to offer job creation guarantees in exchange for cuts in employers' social and fiscal costs, and it has failed to generate convincing strategies and ideas in the fight against unemployment.

While collective bargaining has evolved into the key method of regulating industrial relations, there appears to be a disjunction between the increasing volume of bargaining and the rather poor content of the vast majority of agreements. This is true both at sectoral and company levels. Innovative deals on issues such as employment, working time and training remain a small minority, albeit affecting some of the most prominent employers. In any event, the effectiveness of such agreements in terms of job creation is still an open question despite the extensive and costly array of financial incentives provided by successive governments in recent years.

The role of the state, under governments of both left and right has been one of active support for modernization of economic structures and for the flexibility strategies of employers. On the one hand, recent years have seen increasing intervention to consolidate a strong regulatory framework of industrial relations; to reduce labour market constraints on employers as regards redundancy, working time and employee representation; to reform social protection systems; and to confront the challenge of chronic mass unemployment. On the other hand, however, the state has also encouraged trade unions and employers to reach negotiated agreements on key issues of flexibility and employment, partly in order to increase their legitimacy but also in order to reduce the burden of legislation and to shift the responsibility for regulation on to the social actors. One reason for this ambivalence, perhaps, is the rather disappointing outcome of much government intervention. In particular, new employment measures have repeatedly been introduced without any serious assessment of their impact in practice on employers' recruitment strategies, and most policy instruments have proved fairly ineffective in maintaining or creating jobs.

Over the past decade, the state's margin of manoeuvre in economic policy has been greatly reduced by the impact of internationalization. The policy of the *franc fort*, resulting from the pressures of European Monetary Union and the need to meet the convergence criteria of the single currency, has severely constrained the range of solutions available to the government in the social field. The emphasis of economic policy has been on the reduction of the public deficit (which lay behind the massive reform of social security) and on the gradual deregulation of public enterprise (posts, telecommunications, energy, air transport, television) in response to EU liberalization directives (Cohen 1996). However, a new approach was adopted by the Jospin government, elected just before the Amsterdam summit of the European Council. On its insistence a 'Resolution on Employment and Growth' was adopted, committing the EU (at least symbolically) to giving more active priority to reducing unemployment.

The public sector conflict around the preservation of public services *à la française*, and the more general opposition to social security reforms, reflect a widespread malaise arising from slowing economic growth, the worsening crisis of unemployment and a resulting lack of confidence. This has been reinforced by the negative public perception of politicians and politics and the growing distance between 'state elites' and the citizen, and between union elites and their rank and file. Some observers have seen the December 1995 movement as signalling a renewed capacity for organization and resistance among the rank and file, while others regard it as one more symptom of the inability of the French public sector and the social welfare system to modernize themselves. More generally, however, the strike wave, with its overtones of political challenge, must cast doubt on the thesis that the 'French model' is finally converging on the more stable patterns of its European partners. It can be seen, above all, as a reflection of the continuing exceptionalism of the French. Perhaps the one safe forecast for future developments is that more such 'surprises' may be expected.

Abbreviations

CFDT *Confédération française démocratique du travail* – French Democratic Confederation of Labour

CFE–CGC *Confédération française de l'encadrement – Confédération générale des cadres* – French Confederation of Managerial Staffs – General Confederation of Managerial Staffs

CFTC *Confédération française des travailleurs chrétiens* – French Confederation of Christian Workers

CGC *see* CFE–CGC

CGPF *Confédération générale de la production français* – General Confederation of French Production

CGPME *Confédération générale de petites et moyennes entreprises* – General Confederation of Small and Medium Enterprises

CGT *Confédération générale du travail* – General Confederation of Labour

CGT-FO see FO

CGTU *Confédération générale du travail unitaire* – Unitary General Confederation of Labour

CNPF *Conseil national du patronat français* – National Council of French Employers

CSL *Confédération des syndicats libres* – Confederation of Free Trade Unions

FEN *Fédération de l'éducation nationale* – Federation of National Education

FGAF *Fédération générale autonome des fonctionnaires*

FO *Force ouvrière* – Workers' Strength

FSU *Fédération syndicale unitaire de l'enseignement, de la recherche et de la culture*

SMIC *Salaire minimum interprofessionel de croissance* – national minimum wage

SNPMI *Syndicat national de la petite et moyenne industrie* – National Union of Small and Medium-sized Industries

UCC *Union confédérale des ingénieurs et cadres* – Confederation of Engineers and Managers

UNSA *Union nationale des syndicats autonomes* – National Federation of Autonomous Unions

References and Further Reading

Arthuis, J. 1993: Rapport Arthuis sur les délocalisations hors de France, *Liaisons Sociales*, doc. R, no. 59/93, 14 June 1993.

Assemblée Nationale 1996: *Commission d'enquête*. Rapport no. 2943 sur 'les aides à l'emploi'.

Batstone, E. 1978: Arms' length bargaining: Industrial relations in a French company. Unpublished typescript. Coventry: Industrial Relations Research Unit.

Bevort, A., Labbé D. 1992: *La CFDT: Organisation et Audience depuis 1945*. Paris: La Documentation Française.

Bibes, G. and Mouriaux, R. (eds) 1990: *Les Syndicats Européens à l'épreuve*. Paris: FNSP.

Boyer, R. 1985: *La Flexibilité du Travail en Europe*. Paris: La Découverte.

Caillé, A., Le Goff, J-P. 1996: *Le Tournant de Décembre*. Paris: La Découverte.

CERC (*Centre d'Etudes et de Recherches sur les Coûts*) 1994: *Précarité et risque d'exclusion en France*. Paris: La Documentation Française.

Coffineau, A. 1993: Report to the French Prime Minister on the Auroux laws "Ten years after", *Liaisons Sociales*, 29.

Cohen, E. 1996: *La Tentation Hexagonale*. Paris: Fayard.

Croisat, M. and Labbé D. 1992: *La Fin des Syndicats ?* Paris: L'Harmattan.

Crouch, C. and Streeck, W. 1996: (eds), *Les Capitalismes en Europe*. Paris: La Découverte.

Denis, J-M. 1996: Le Groupe des Dix, Working document, Paris: IRES.

EIRR (European Industrial Relations Review) 1994a: 'France – Five-year employment law: part one', *EIRR* **242**, March 1994: 16–21.

EIRR 1994b:'France – Five-year employment law – part two', EIRR 243, April 1994: 20–23.

EIRR 1995a: France. Innovating for employment – a new wave of company agreements, *EIRR* **253**, February 1995: 15–18.

EIRR 1995b: France: Emergency government plan for employment, *EIRR* **259**, August 1995: 14–16.

EIRR 1996: 'France. Reorganizing and reducing working time – company agreements take the initiative', *EIRR* **267**, April 1996: 13–17.

ETUI 1996a: (ed.) Fajetag, G., *Collective Bargaining in Western Europe*. Bruxelles: ETUI.

ETUI 1996b: *European Trade Union Book*. Bruxelles: ETUI.

Goetschy, J. 1991: 'An appraisal of French research on direct participation' in (eds) Russel R. and Rus V.*, International Yearbook of Participation in Organizations*, Oxford: OUP.

Goetschy, J. 1995: 'Major developments and changes in French industrial relations since 1980s', in Mesch, M., *Sozialpartnershaft und Arbeitsbeziehungen in Europa*, Vienna: Manz Verlag.

Goetschy, J. and Linhart, D. 1990: *La crise des syndicats en Europe occidentale*. Paris: La Documentation Française.

Groux, G. and Mouriaux, R. 1994: 'Syndicalisme sans syndiqués: dimensions at dilemnes', in Perrineau (ed.), *L'engagement politique: déclin ou mutations?*, Paris: FNSP.*

Hege, A. and Dufour, C. 1995: 'Decentralization and legitimacy in employee representation: a Franco-German comparison', *European Journal of Industrial Relations*, 1(1), 83–99.

Jefferys, S. 1996a: 'Down but not out: French unions after Chirac', *Work, Employment and Society*, 10(3), 509–27.

Jefferys, S. 1996b: 'France 1995: The backward march of labour halted?', *Capital and Class*.

Jobert, A. 1990: 'La négociation collective dans les entreprises multinationales en Europe', in Devin G., *Dimensions Internationales*, Nanterre: Erasme.

Jones, G. 1995: *The Evolution of International Business*. London: Routledge.

Labbé, D. 1994: La crise du syndicalisme français, *La revue de L'Ires*, Automne, 75–101.

Labbé, D. 1996: *Syndicats et syndiqués en France depuis 1945*. Paris: L'Harmattan.

Lallement, M. 1996: *Sociologie des relations professionnelles*. Paris: La Découverte.

Lane, C. 1989: *Management and Labour in Europe. The Industrial Enterprise in Germany, Britain and France*. Aldershot: Edward Elgar.

Lange, P., Martin, A., Ross, G. and Vannicelli, M. 1982: *Unions, Change and Crisis: French and Italian Union Strategy and Political Economy*. London: Allen and Unwin.

Leisink, P., Van Leemput, J. and Vilrokx, J. 1996: *The Challenge of Trade Unions in Europe*. Cheltenham: Edward Elgar.

Linhart, D. and Malan, A. 1988: 'Individualisme professionnel des jeunes et action collective', *Travail et Emploi*, 36–7, June-September, 9–18.

Lipietz, A. 1991: Governing the economy in the face of international challenge. In Hollifield, J. and Ross, G. (eds), *Searching for the New France*, London: Routledge, 17–42.

Lipietz, A. 1996: *La Société en Sablier*. Paris: La Découverte.

Maurice, M., Sellier, F. and Sylvestre, J-J. 1986: *The Social Foundations of Industrial Power. A Comparison of France and Germany*. London/Cambridge, Mass.: MIT.

Méda, D. 1995: *Le Travail: Une Valeur en Voie de Disparition*. Paris: Aubier.

Ministère du Travail (DARES) 1996: Enquête 'délégués du personnel 1994', *Premières Synthèses*, 96, October.

Morville, P. 1985: *Les Nouvelles Politiques Sociales du Patronat*. Paris: La Découverte.

Mouriaux, R. 1986: *Le Syndicalisme Face à la Crise*. Paris: La Découverte.

Mouriaux, R. 1993: *Les Syndicats dans la Société Français*. Paris: Foundation Nationales des Sciences Politiques.

Mouriaux, R. 1994: *Le Syndicalisme en France Depuis 1945*. Paris: La Découverte.

Observatoire Social Européen 1995: (ed.) Pochet, P., *Pactes Sociaux Européens*, Bruxelles: Vie ouvrière.

Pernot, J-M. 1996: 'Les syndicats à l'épreuve du mouvement social', *Regards sur l'actualité*, 222.

Perret, B. 1996: *L'avenir du Travail*. Paris: Seuil.

Petit, P. 1985: Heurs et malheurs face au rapport salarial. In Boyer R. (ed.), *La Flexibilité du Travail en Europe*, Paris: La Découverte.

Reynaud, J-D. 1975: *Les Syndicats en France*. Paris: La Découverte.

Rojot, J. 1988: The myth of French exceptionalism. In Barbash, J. and Barbash, K. (eds), *Theories and Concepts in Comparative Industrial Relations*, Columbia: South Carolina Press.

Rojot, J. 1990: Human resource management in France. In Pieper, R. (ed.) *Human Resource Management: An International Comparison*. Berlin/New York: Walter de Gruyter.

Rosanvallon, P. 1988: *La Question Syndicale*. Paris: Seuil.

Rozenblatt, P. 1991: 'La forme coordination: une catégorie sociale révélatrice de sens', *Sociologie du Travail*, 33(2), 239–54.

Sally, R. 1995: *States and Firms. Multinational Enterprises in Institutional Competition*. London: Routledge.

Schmidt, V. 1993: An end to French economic exceptionalism? The transformation of business under Mitterand, *California Management Review*, Fall, 75–98.

Sellier, F. and Sylvestre, J-J. 1986: 'Unions' policies in the economic crisis in France', in (eds) Edwards et al., *Unions in Crisis and Beyond*, London: Auburn House.

Shorter, E. and Tilly, C. 1974: *Strikes in France 1830–1968*. Cambridge: CUP.

Siweck-Pouydesseau, J. 1993: *Les Syndicats des Grands Services Publics et l'Europe*. Paris: L'Harmattan.

Touraine, A. et al. 1996: *Le Grand Refus*. Paris: Fayard.

Visier, L. 1990: 'A l'épreuve des coordinations', *CFDT Aujourd'hui*, July, 1997, 21–32.

Visser, J. 1990: *In Search of Inclusive Unionism*. Deventer: Kleuver.

14 Portugal: Industrial Relations under Democracy

JOSÉ BARRETO • REINHARD NAUMANN

Introduction

Since the revolution of 1974–5 which put an end to four decades of an authoritarian corporatist regime, Portuguese industrial relations have undergone several stages of development. Despite the intense efforts of governments and employers over the last 20 years to 'normalize' industrial relations, the heritage of authoritarian regulation and of the revolutionary turmoil in the early years of democratization is still a major influence at all levels of the emerging system. With the defeat of the liberal–conservative social democratic party (PSD) in the elections of autumn 1995 an 8-year period of government based on absolute parliamentary majorities came to an end. During the era of prime minister Cavaco Silva (1985–95) Portugal advanced a long way down the path to a capitalist social and economic order corresponding to Western European patterns.

The legal and institutional changes which have taken place since the revolutionary period have had considerable but still limited effects on the behaviour and ideological orientation of the actors in Portuguese industrial relations. The antagonistic relationship between employers and unions, and ideological divisions within the labour movement between 'class-oriented' and 'concertation-oriented' bodies continue to be determining features of industrial relations, obstructing the creation of a pattern based on class compromise and trust relations. Polarization is more marked in Portugal than in neighbouring Spain and reflects the birth of post-fascist labour relations in Portugal in the context of revolutionary mass mobilization. The hegemonic forces within the labour movement aspired not only to the democratization of class relations but also to the elimination of capitalism. Today's generation of employers and union leaders was formed during this exceptional period of revolutionary struggle and is still marked by it.

In the first decade of democracy, the dominant pattern was one in which workers mobilized at company, sector and national levels to defend the gains made through national collective agreements and labour legislation during the revolutionary period. Trade union bodies and workers' commissions within companies were able to negotiate settlements that improved upon the provisions of sectoral agreements. Relatively high union density, a widespread web of militant union activists, and the readiness of workers to take industrial action were fundamental to the unions' ability to engage in strong – even aggressive – activity at all levels.

The decay of this pattern based on 'mass mobilization' began in the first half of the 1980s, against the background of a shift in power relations in favour of employers and of neo-liberal political forces. Union density and mobilization capacity fell. Bargaining at sector and company levels declined, while tripartite national negotiations gained in importance. Agreements on incomes policy during the second half of the 1980s and at the beginning of the 1990s became the central influence on wage bargaining at sector and company level. Decentralization took the form of increasing employer discretion at company level, rather than the devolution of bargaining to the micro-level. Tripartite national negotiations failed to lead to a real reform of industrial relations but functioned primarily as a means of gaining political acceptance for the overall process of liberalization and restructuring.

The most recent stage in the 'normalization' of Portuguese industrial relations under the Cavaco Silva governments had a marked neo-liberal character. The wider context of this process was the liberalization of the semi-developed Portuguese economy and its growing integration into the European and world economy. The pressures of growing competition and deregulation have had ambiguous consequences for the Portuguese industrial relations actors. While there are pressures for a convergence between competing trade union organizations, and in certain areas even between the 'social partners', the historical contradictions between the actors persist. The ambiguities are seen, for example, in the opposition to the Maastricht convergence criteria by both the class-oriented union confederation, CGTP, and (to a lesser extent) the industrial employers' organization, CIP, and recent inter-union conflicts over responses to functional and working-time flexibility.

Despite the continuing weakness of Portuguese industrial relations, gradual change is perceptible at different levels. In a growing number of companies, the unions' traditionally inflexible approach is being challenged by modern HRM which is undermining the unions' centrality in work relations within companies. Employees – who think increasingly in terms of the relationship between change, competition and job security – are demonstrating a growing acceptance of change in work organization. Thus unions feel under considerable pressure to adapt to the new conditions. Even CGTP unions are, beneath the surface of class struggle rhetoric and political agitation, adopting a more pragmatic approach. These trends may encourage a renewal in industrial relations practice, not only at company level but in industry bargaining as well. At the macro-level, tripartite social 'concertation' could provide the impetus for a more ambitious reform of industrial relations but, given the polarization between CGTP and CIP and the contradictions within the trade union camp, expectations should be realistically modest.

▌Political and Economic Background

In April 1974 the authoritarian corporatist regime of the dictator Salazar and his successor Marcelo Caetano, who between them had ruled the country for more than 40 years, was overthrown by a military coup enthusiastically supported by the population. The right of free association was restored, political parties were created or emerged from the underground. There followed a revolutionary period of uncontrolled radicalization which brought major changes in Portugal's political economy and left the country on the brink of violent conflict. The revolutionary forces – including the Communist Party and the trade union confederation, Intersindical (which was to become CGTP) – suffered political defeat in the 'hot summer' of 1975, and the left wing in the armed forces was disarmed. Portugal resumed the path of democratization based on the market economy and parliamentary institutions. In 1975 and 1976 free elections based on universal suffrage were held for the first time in the country's history.

The years 1976–80 were characterized by democratic institution-building, the financial crisis of the state, and political instability. With the legacy of the revolution still strong, this period saw the creation of large state-owned companies which dominated the economy, radical agrarian reform in the southern Alentejo region, and a 1976 Constitution which called for the creation of a socialist state. The nationalized sector (in electricity, transport and communications) and the agrarian co-operatives contributed greatly to the development of infrastructures and to job creation. However, despite the continuing influence of revolutionary rhetoric on Portuguese political discourse, the first constitutional governments, caught between the Scylla of the IMF and the Charybdis of the revolutionary opposition, were too concerned with their own political survival even to attempt a coherent reform programme.

The first half of the 1980s saw the emergence of a strong political *centro*, constituted by the Social-Democratic Party (PSD) and by the Socialist Party (PS). From 1980 the PSD (a liberal–conservative party despite its name, with populist traits and particularly strong in Portugal's densely populated rural north) was in government continuously, first in changing coalitions and then, after a short period of minority government, with an absolute majority (1987–95). A strategic alliance between PS and PSD emerged on major political issues, notably the first revision of the constitution in 1982 which expunged the revolutionary references, and Portugal's entry into the European Community in 1986. The immediate trigger for the creation of this 'central bloc' was the dramatic social crisis of the early 1980s which provoked major political unrest. Strategic co-operation between the two parties encouraged political stability and the steady convergence of the Portuguese economy and polity with western models.

The strategic alliance continued in the era of majority PSD governments. By agreeing to a second revision of the constitution in 1989 the Socialist Party opened the way to the government's extensive privatization and liberalization programme. Subsequently, the socialists supported the government austerity policy geared to meeting the Maastricht criteria for European Monetary Union. Following the socialists' victory in the elections of October 1995 this bipartisanship on European integration continued, with the PS government pursuing the same economic strategy as its predecessor. PS–PSD co-operation consigned other political parties to a marginal role in the political process. This was the case with both the CDS (renamed PP, Partido Popular), which includes the most important leaders of CIP, and the communist party, which has a dominant position in CGTP.

Economic Development and the Labour Market

The pace of industrialization, which had been very slow in the first half of the twentieth century, accelerated after the Second World War. By the end of the 1960s manufacturing and services had become the leading sectors of employment. Mass emigration in the 1960s and early 1970s (involving around 1.5 million people, over half of them of working age) resulted in labour shortages that strengthened the employees' position in the labour market and led to marked improvements in wages and work conditions even before the end of the dictatorship. This started to change with economic crisis and stagnation after 1974 coupled with the massive influx of white colonists following decolonization in 1975. The crisis deepened in the early 1980s, bringing a dramatic rise in unemployment. A symptom was that in many companies, employers paid employees' wages only after long delays, or suspended payment altogether.

Simultaneously, however, the volume of employment has grown much faster than elsewhere in western Europe, partly as a result of the rapid growth in female employment, from 26 per cent of total employment in 1970 to 45 per cent in 1995. Female employment is dominant in educational and health services and in some traditional labour-intensive industries – its share is over 80 per cent in the strongest exporting industry, clothing, and over 60 per cent in textiles, both with wage levels below the average for manufacturing. The virtual prohibition of redundancies under rigid labour laws, the narrow definition of fair dismissal, and the legal procedures relating to conflicts on this matter meant that adjustment to the crisis in the late 1970s took the form of a reduction in real wages rather than in employment, largely the opposite of what happened in Spain.

In the 1980s, new legislation allowed the hiring of workers on fixed term contracts and by 1996, 15 per cent of all employees were on such contracts. As a result of rationalization and restructuring in both public and private firms in the late 1980s and 1990s, the proportion of employees in the active population fell. A new stratum of independent workers emerged doing the same kind of work as before, often for their former employers, but as 'independent' contract workers. In 1995, 'workers on their own account' without employees represented about 20 per cent of the workforce. Sectors with the highest levels were retail trade, restaurants, and personal services.

Since the 1970s, employers' organizations have insistently demanded the complete overhaul of legislation on dismissals, seeing it as a major obstacle to domestic and foreign investment and to resolving the problems of unemployment, unpaid wages, absenteeism, low productivity and poor employee motivation. After the legislation on the introduction of fixed term contracts, a major revision of the law on dismissals was initiated by the Cavaco Silva government in 1988. The project was fiercely opposed by the unions and provoked the first (and only) general strike called simultaneously, though not jointly, by both CGTP and UGT. Passed with minor amendments in 1989, the law broadened the criteria of fair dismissal to include the worker's inability to adapt to changes in the nature of the job.

The 1980s and 1990s brought a major fall in agricultural employment and a continuation of the 'tertiarization' of labour (see tables 14.1–14.3). A major reason was the particularly strong growth of public services. Total employment in manufacturing stagnated. The metal and textile industries lost a considerable proportion of their workforce while employment in clothing and footwear rose strongly. The rationalization of companies under the pressure of competition and European integration, and the restructuring and privatization of large state-owned companies accentuated the preponderance of smaller firms in the economy (see table 14.4).

In the first decade after the country's entry into the European Community, a massive programme of investment in basic infrastructure, technological development, vocational training, and industrial innovation has been implemented by the Portuguese state with the help of European social and structural funds. But no serious progress has been made in transforming Portugal's status as a provider of mainly unskilled and low paid labour. The huge investments in vocational training lacked a comprehensive strategy and their results were disappointing. In terms of industrial innovation the country continues to have one of the poorest records in Europe. Foreign investment has tended to flow into privatized firms in the financial sector, although there have been some major manufacturing investments, notably the Ford–Volkswagen joint venture, 'AutoEuropa'.

Industrial Relations in Twentieth-century Portugal

Historical Background

Developments in the industrial relations system since the revolution must be seen against the background of earlier historical developments. The evolution of industrial relations in twentieth-century Portugal falls into three broad periods, resulting from two great divides in the country's contemporary political history: the establishment of an authoritarian corporatist regime in 1933 and the foundation of a modern democratic state after the 1974–5 revolution.

The Early Years

Economic underdevelopment hindered the emergence of strong working-class interest organizations and employers associations until the early decades of this

Table 14.1 Structure of employment

	Primary Sector	Secondary sector	Tertiary sector	Total employment (000s)	Wage and salary earners (000s)	Unemployment (000s)
1989	18.9	35.2	45.9	4395	3076	233
1995	11.3	32.3	56.4	4225	3040	325

Source: INE.

Table 14.2 % GDP by sector

	Primary	Secondary	Tertiary
1993	6	38	56

Source: OECD.

Table 14.3 Wage employment by main sectors (1995) % of all wage and salary earners

Primary sector	2.2
Manufacturing industry and mining	28.9
Electricity, gas and water	1.1
Construction	8.2
Commerce, restaurants and hotels	15.8
Transportation and communication	5.4
Banking, insurance and real estate	4.3
Central and local administration	10.4
Public and private education and health services	12.7
Other services (incl. informatics, research and development)	11
Total	100

Source: INE.

Table 14.4 Company size and employment in Portugal, 1989–94

Employees	No. Companies (000s)		% of companies		Average staff		Share of employment	
	1989	1994	1989	1994	1989	1994	1989	1994
1–9	99.1	147.1	75.3	79.8	4	3.4	17.3	22.9
10–19	16.2	19.5	12.3	10.6	13	13	10.3	11.7
20–49	10.3	11.6	7.8	6.3	30	30	14.7	15.7
50–99	3.36	3.49	2.6	1.9	69	69	10.9	10.9
100–199	1.51	1.54	1.1	0.8	138	138.5	9.8	9.6
200–499	0.85	0.78	0.6	0.4	298	301.8	12.0	10.7
500+	0.35	0.28	0.3	0.2	1,510	1,469	25.0	18.5
Total	131.7	184.3	100	100	16	12	100.0	100.0

Source: QdP DEMESS 1989, QdP DEMQE 1994 (Statistics Department of Portuguese Labour Ministry).

century. CGT, formed in 1919, was the first well-organized union confederation. Strongly influenced by French-style anarcho-syndicalism, it advocated direct class struggle and repudiated links with political parties. It was never able to realize its strategy of provoking a revolutionary general strike, while its rejection of bourgeois institutions led it to neglect collective bargaining. After its early ascendancy within the labour movement, it went into decline. The communist current which split from CGT in 1925 was still too small to represent an alternative to anarcho-syndicalism, when in 1926 a military coup – supported by political groups linked to business – suspended liberal–democratic institutions and paved the way for almost five decades of dictatorship.

The Period of Authoritarian Rule, 1926–74

The period of military rule opened the way to the Salazar dictatorship (1933–68). Strikes were banned (1927), the CGT was dissolved, and the multi-party system was suppressed. Existing independent unions were tolerated until a new Constitution (1933) and the *Estatuto do Trabalho Nacional* (National Labour Statute), a version of its Italian namesake, introduced the compulsory framework that was to regulate labour relations and interest representation for the next four decades.

Salazar's regime was characterized by direct state intervention in the economy and by the authoritarian regulation of labour relations through corporatist institutions. The government directly controlled all activities of the so-called *sindicatos nacionais* (national trade unions) and *grémios* (employers' guilds) which had a legal monopoly of representation. Employers saw little necessity to enter into serious negotiations on collective work regulation, obliging the government to regulate sectors and occupational groups by statute. Even in periods of less direct state intervention, the *sindicatos nacionais* were at best supplicants, with the ministry drawing up so-called 'collective agreements' and compelling reluctant employers to concede basic minimum wage levels and working conditions. The corporatist system excluded single-class peak organizations, but the regime's bias was evident in its suppression of any form of autonomous workers' mobilization and organization while allowing employers to retain their old interest associations alongside the corporatist network.

Authoritarian corporatism suspended for almost half a century the free development of industrial relations. The state's attempt to oversee a project of class co-operation failed completely, and antagonisms between workers and employers deepened behind the corporatist façade. The structures created by the regime failed to generate real bargaining relations between workers and employers. The tradition of direct state intervention in collective work regulation continued during and after the revolution – now favouring the workers – and only ceased in 1985.

In its final years, the authoritarian regime under Caetano attempted to make corporatism more compatible with industrialization, economic growth and internationalization. It conceded limited union autonomy, and fostered more responsible and regular collective bargaining which was made legally compulsory. The law admitted the concept of industrial disputes, although strikes remained illegal, and state-sponsored conciliation and arbitration were introduced. Collective bargaining was revitalized by the reforms, but generated new tensions for the government. Communists and progressive catholics operating within the *sindicatos nacionais*, under the co-ordination of the semi-clandestine trade union confederation, Intersindical, mobilized workers against the regime. An unprecedented number of militant activists and increasingly self-confident workers gave their support to a movement linking broad grass roots demands for better wages and working conditions with the struggle for free unionism and democratic rights. The repression directed against this movement in the regime's final years contributed to the dramatic radicalization of class relations in the transition period. Ironically, developments were spearheaded by the white-collar unions which the regime had fostered in an attempt to ensure middle-class support and to provide a model of 'constructive unionism' for the working class. Thus the attempted reform of corporatism turned into a severe setback for the regime.

The Fall of the Authoritarian Regime and the Democratic Transition

The turbulent transition after the fall of the authoritarian regime influenced the evolution of industrial relations at all levels. During 1974–5 a spiral of political radicalization and militant action was directed towards the construction of a socialist society, rather than the transition to liberal democracy. For the employers, used to the absolute authority in their companies, the first few years of free collective bargaining were a traumatic experience. The pressure exerted by radicalized workers, including intimidation and physical violence, led to situations in which employers' associations could only avoid signing agreements they disagreed with by disbanding themselves. The shift in the balance of power in favour of labour resulted in a spectacular increase in pay and social security benefits in this period, although this was short-lived and since the beginning of the 1980s, the unions have been unable to prevent a steady fall in wage-earners' share of national income.

Far from fostering trust relations, the democratic transition deepened mutual resentment between workers' representatives and employers. The outburst of pent-up grievances created a profound break with the past and impeded the establishment of a class compromise around which a new bargaining culture could be created. At the same time, and partly as a consequence of these traumatic political developments, the economic situation was rapidly worsening. Mass unemployment combined with high inflation, huge budget deficits and recession exerted overwhelming pressure on the labour market, placed heavy burdens on enterprises, and compelled successive governments to adopt deflationary economic policies and an interventionist role in labour matters.

The state intervened extensively in the economy during the revolutionary period. Successive impasses at the negotiating table led the unions to demand increasing government intervention. Labour legislation and the direct regulation of working conditions mushroomed, both in the public and private sectors. A revolutionary law from 1975, only partially revised since, made individual and collective dismissals extremely difficult. Shortly after the revolution a universal and compulsory system of social security was extended to the whole population. Thus the role of the state in industrial relations expanded considerably, even when compared to the corporatist period. This legacy continued to influence post-revolutionary industrial relations. In 1978 the great majority of wage earners were covered by direct statutory regulation in individual industries. A national minimum wage, introduced in 1974, has been revised every year since then. Successive legislation also reduced the scope of collective bargaining and during the late 1970s maximum rates for all statutory and collectively bargained pay increases, known as 'wage ceilings', were imposed by the government.

The 1980s: Shifting Power Relations and Worker De-mobilization

In the 1980s, the statist trend began to decline. The unemployment crisis weakened trade unions relative to employers and the state, and the emerging strategic alliance between the PS and PSD strengthened the ability of the political system to resist political mobilization by the 'class-oriented' CGTP unions. By 1985 the state had largely withdrawn from an active role in collective bargaining. However it failed to introduce the necessary framework of regulation to permit employers and unions to develop alternative, more autonomous bargaining relations. The emergence of UGT as a moderate alternative to CGTP, and the beginnings of cautious change in CGTP, favoured a new climate in industrial relations. In 1984, institutionalized negotiations were initiated in the tripartite CPCS, which were expected to encourage a new dynamism in industrial relations. Following EC membership in 1986 and the landslide victory of the neo-liberal prime minister Cavaco Silva in the general elections the following year, the CPCS took on a more important role in the political arena. In 1990 a major tripartite agreement on a wide range of issues was signed by all the social partners except CGTP. Nonetheless, implementation of the agreement was patchy and, with collective bargaining remaining limited in content and coverage, a fundamental change in industrial relations was slow to materialize. These themes are dealt with in greater detail in the following sections.

Employers

Characteristics of Portuguese Employers

One of the overall priorities of the Cavaco Silva governments was the restoration of the Portuguese capitalist class which had been drastically weakened by the radical nationalization process of 1975. Before the revolution, seven large corporate groups had dominated the Portuguese economy, from the financial sector to industry and colonial trade. The groups had grown up under the protection of the 'New State', forming oligopolies in sectors sheltered from external competition. The distinguishing feature of the nationalizations of 1975, compared to Italy or

France, was the expropriation of the whole domestic financial sector, giving the state a central strategic role in the economy.

Cavaco Silva's comprehensive privatization programme started with the reprivatization of the financial sector. With the important exception of the largest bank, the Caixa Geral de Depósitos, by 1995 almost all public banks and insurance companies had been privatized, stimulating a large influx of direct foreign investment and giving rise to a number of private financial–industrial corporate groups. With government help and in partnership with foreign investors several former owners were able to re-acquire their financial institutions and use them as the base for the reconstitution of large new corporate groups.

Among the state-owned industrial and service companies some of the most profitable were the first to be reprivatized. The state sold a part of its shares in Petrogal (oil refining and distribution), the largest Portuguese company in terms of turnover, and the two largest breweries (UNICER and Centralcer) were completely privatized. The large national companies in bus transport (Rodoviária Nacional), chemicals (Quimigal) and steel (Siderurgia Nacional) were broken up and reprivatized. In the telecommunications sector a new monopoly company (Portugal Telecom) was created and partly privatized. By 1994, reprivatized firms accounted for 34 per cent of total business volume on the Portuguese stock market compared to less than 3 per cent at the beginning of the privatization process in 1989. This proportion will rise further with the privatization of large companies in paper, concrete and tobacco industries and in electricity.

Privatizations are an integral part of the broader process of liberalization and the opening of national markets to foreign competitors and investors. Liberalization has been shaped by the context of European Union regulation, as for example in the restructuring of the country's steel industry and in current European negotiations on the opening up of the telecommunications sector. The financial services sector has been almost completely liberalized and opened to foreign competitors.

Privatization, and the full compensation of the 'victims' of the 'wildcat' nationalizations of 1975, were key demands of the industrial employers' confederation, CIP. The Cavaco Silva government largely satisfied these claims, helping to restore a national capitalist class. In this the government could count on the support of the Socialist Party (not to mention that of the ultra-conservative CDS) and the acquiescence of UGT. The Communist Party and CGTP unions were unable to mobilize effective resistance to the privatization programme. In some companies there was joint opposition by CGTP and UGT unions to restructuring plans, but even in these cases the unions' influence was very limited.

By the time the Cavaco Silva era had come to an end, the aim of rebuilding large domestic economic groups had been achieved. With a few exceptions (the postal service, rail and air transport) almost all large state-owned firms had been or were soon to be privatized. The public sector's share of the total labour force was drastically reduced. In the banking sector, the share of public enterprises in total employment fell from over 90 per cent in 1988 to less than 30 per cent in 1994.

The break-up of large state enterprises on privatization contributed an increase in the proportion of small firms. Firms employing fewer than 10 workers accounted for 75 per cent of the total at the end of the 1980s, a proportion already higher than anywhere else in the EC. This rose to almost 80 per cent in 1994. Over the same period, in which there was an enormous increase in the total number of companies, the proportion of firms with 100 and more workers fell and their share in employment was cut from 46.8 to 38.8 per cent (see table 14.4). The drop was sharpest in large companies (with 500 and more workers), from 25 to 18.5 per cent.

Foreign multinationals are the leading companies in several industrial sectors, notably cars, electrical equipment and electronics, chemicals, petrochemicals, food and clothing. As a rule, they can afford better wages and conditions, well above the minima established by industry agreements; but they have successfully resisted union demands for these better conditions to be formalized in company agreements as was the case in the former state-owned companies. Local export-oriented firms, predominantly small or medium-sized, have experienced major difficulties in responding to the challenges of the European single market and the global liberalization of trade. Improvements in technology, management and commercial strategies have been sporadic. Increased productivity has been achieved in many cases by workforce reductions rather than by the introduction of new technology and organizational rationalization. This has resulted in an intensification and extension of work. Unpaid overtime has become a generalized phenomenon in Portuguese companies. The ability of many firms to go on exporting still largely depends on low wages (especially for women workers) and the resources of the black economy. Increased competition in the domestic market has marginalized many local firms which have lost ground to foreign investors and a few larger national competitors.

Restructuring and Change at Company Level

While Portuguese industry and state agencies have sometimes been slow to respond to the increasingly pressing challenges of European economic and monetary integration and of international competition, recent research suggests that some firms have made a considerable effort to adapt. Modern management methods have been introduced by foreign multinationals and some innovative domestic companies. Re-engineering, human resource management, total quality management and marketing have been propagated by the consulting firms whose number and activity have grown considerably over the last 10 years. A modern entrepreneurship is gaining ground, although it is still far from being the predominant pattern amongst Portuguese employers.

A survey of companies with 100 and more employees (Stoleroff 1995) indicates that restructuring over the past 5 years has largely taken the form of technological modernization, vocational training, reorganization of company structures and workforce reductions. Functional flexibility has been introduced in a considerable proportion of companies. However, explicit deregulation – in the sense of freedom for employers from previous constraints upon the management of labour – has been of limited importance. (See table 14.5.)

Table 14.5 Elements of restructuring in medium-sized and large enterprises (%)

		Employees	
Changes made	Total	< 500	> 500
Investment in more modern technology and equipment	78	76	89
Investment in occupational training and qualifications	61	57	87
Reorganization of enterprise structures	68	67	75
Reduction of workforce	53	51	68
Flexibility of work	38	38	41
Deregulation of labour relations	11	12	8

Source: Stoleroff 1995.

Rigid legislation on dismissals encouraged the use of early retirement and voluntary redundancy – 32 per cent of all companies surveyed and 55 per cent of large companies reduced their workforce through these means. In public and foreign companies, where workforce reductions were much more frequent (83 and 73 per cent respectively), these 'soft' measures of redundancy were implemented much more than average (77 per cent and 70 per cent respectively). Other forms of numerical flexibility were also common: fixed-term contracts were used in over half of companies, sub-contracting in around a third (43 per cent of large companies) and part-time work in around a quarter. Only 5 per cent had introduced home-working, but in the textile and metal industries it was double that.

Sixty-nine per cent (88 per cent of large companies) introduced so-called *polivalência* (task flexibility). However, the formal integration of occupational categories took place in only 32 per cent of the companies (46 per cent of large). In companies where some kind of flexibility was introduced, three main methods were used: the derogation of the provisions of collective agreements (26 per cent), the introduction of alternative labour relations outside collective agreements (32 per cent), and individualization of the employee relationship (32 per cent). Only in a very few cases was flexibility negotiated with workers' representatives. Most managers perceived little significant change in the nature of union demands in response to the challenge of flexibility, with the important exception of job security; 28 per cent of managers perceived increasing union flexibility in negotiations.

Explicit deregulation was rare (11 per cent), but since the role of collective bargaining in regulating the employment relationship has declined, a process of implicit deregulation has been taking place. The absence of negotiations on flexibility supports this supposition.

Employers' Organizations

The three employers' confederations are organized according to sectoral criteria: CIP for industry; CCP for trade and services, and CAP for agriculture. CIP, created in June 1974, is the dominating force in the employers' camp; CCP and CAP have only limited influence. CIP is in general more cohesive and representative than its counterparts in services and agriculture. It has begun to move beyond the confines of manufacturing industry to compete in the service sector with CCP.

The three confederations may be seen as the successors of the old vertical or mixed 'corporations'. CIP's collective bargaining staff in the turbulent years after the revolution was largely recruited from among the former officials of the Ministry of Corporations who had been purged by Intersindical activists in 1974. The confederation was established immediately after the revolution by influential members of the major industrialists' associations, AIP Lisbon and AIP Oporto, which had survived state corporatism. It was seen as a means of protecting employer interests against the threat of the revolutionary movement. Its leadership of the employers' struggle for 'survival', gave CIP a measure of enduring legitimacy.

CIP at first adopted a reformist approach, but its proposals were ignored by the radicalized Intersindical unions which treated it with hostility. From 1976, as employers began their slow recovery from the shock treatment of 1974–5, CIP opted for a more offensive strategy. It waged campaigns against the economic section of the new constitution, legislation on dismissals, industrial disputes and 'workers' commissions', soaring budget deficits, 'Marxist' economic planning, and the inefficiency of public enterprises (which were not affiliated to CIP). In the early 1980s, the new CIP leadership began openly to demand an end to state monopolies, the privatization of the economy and a new constitution. CIP increasingly intervened directly in politics, supporting or opposing government coalitions. Although it lacked representativeness and provided few services to its members, it was nonetheless a powerful pressure group. Its priorities were reducing the state's role in the economy and improving the competitiveness of Portuguese enterprises (Pinto 1990).

There are no reliable data on membership of employers' associations. Since the early 1980s, CIP has claimed to represent 35,000 private companies, nearly 75 per cent of the total. However, an empirical study (Cardoso et al. 1990) covering companies with at least ten employees indicates a 60 per cent rate of affiliation to the primary associations, which are not all members of the CIP; while according to union sources, overall membership density of employers' associations may be even lower than the figure of around 30 per cent for unionized workers.

Inside CIP, the old regional multi-sector trade associations provide a wide range of services to member firms. They leave industrial relations functions almost entirely to the regionally based sectoral associations, but they are politically very influential and far better organized than the latter. CIP's legitimacy was significantly boosted by the entry of AIP Oporto and later AIP Lisbon in the late 1980s and early 1990s. Divergent attitudes towards state intervention, economic policy, European integration, international competition and privatization, as well as deep-rooted regional rivalries (notably between Lisbon and Oporto), which had long impeded AIP's entry into CIP, are now contained within the confederation; thus it may now be considered representative of employers in manufacturing, despite its low membership density. One of the most important issues facing the organization, however, is the struggle for influence between the confederal leadership on the one hand, and the powerful Lisbon and Oporto associations on the other.

The other two confederations have much more serious internal problems. CCP is structurally divided between wholesalers and retailers. In the early 1990s, a new problem arose when the 'hypermarkets' created their own association, APED, outside the confederation. Retailers within CCP have waged a campaign for legal constraints on the activities of the hypermarkets. Government resisted the retailers' demands and in 1996 wholesalers and 'moderate' retailers marginalized the 'radical' current in the leadership and prepared to negotiate with APED on possible co-operation. The crisis of representativeness facing CCP is reflected in its failure to recruit new members in services other than commerce despite the formal extension of its area of operation in the early 1990s. The important employers' associations in banking, insurance and transport continue to be outside the confederal structure.

CAP's social basis and legitimacy amongst agricultural employers have been in decline in the 1990s and it is being challenged by a dynamic new confederation, CNA, organizing primarily among the small and medium-sized firms who constitute the bulk of employers in agriculture. CNA is demanding to be recognized as a partner in social concertation. At present, however, only CIP, CCP and CAP are recognized by the state as legitimate employers' representatives in peak-level bodies such as the CPCS.

The Unions

The restoration of free trade unions in 1974–6 coincided with communist hegemony of the labour movement. This provoked the emergence of deep ideological and political cleavages, leading eventually to union pluralism (Barreto 1991). Since the late 1970s, the labour movement has been dominated by two contrasting national trade union confederations, CGTP and UGT. The two organizations have pursued radically different strategies and tactics in industrial relations. While CGTP represents the large majority of the unionized workforce and bases its activity on a widespread web of militant activists and 'mass mobilization', UGT's power resources are concentrated in the political arena, through its strong influence in the two main political parties, PS and PSD.

The Phase of Communist Dominance of the Labour Movement

In the final years of the old regime, opposition activists led by the communists had gained control of a number of *sindicatos nacionais*, which subsequently came together in Intersindical, a strongly politicized co-ordinating body soon banned by the government. Emerging from the underground following the revolution of 1974, Intersindical sought recognition as the legitimate peak organization of the emerging union movement. The old *sindicatos nacionais* were rapidly transformed into democratic unions with organizational autonomy from the state and the right to strike. The communists were able to extend their control over large parts of the union movement.

The socialist and 'social democratic' parties had at first only very limited influence in the unions. The PS, founded in 1875, had virtually disappeared in the 1930s, and it began to re-emerge only in 1973. The PSD was founded shortly after the fall of the old regime. Only the illegal PCP had managed to survive as an organized opposition force during the dictatorship. Its strategy of infiltrating the corporatist unions gave it considerable room for manoeuvre in the transition to democracy, when the unions were at the forefront of the political process. Intersindical was the first organization to demand large-scale nationalizations.

In 1974–5, two-thirds of existing unions joined Intersindical. The confederation won a legal monopoly of representation, from workplace up to confederal level, under the union law of 1975. At Intersindical's request compulsory contribution and check-off systems were maintained until 1975/77. Thus the framework of the corporatist unionism was in some respects perpetuated by the revolutionary governments. New union structures were created to co-ordinate local unions in each branch (*federações*) and in each region (*uniões*). The *federações* later co-ordinated the transformation of occupationally based CGTP unions into sectoral bodies, a complicated process involving the transfer of members between several unions. Intersindical also promoted new unions in areas where unionization had not been allowed before, notably public services, agriculture, fishery and domestic services.

While the communists dominated the leadership of the union movement, real control of the rank and file was much more problematic, particularly as unions attempted to moderate workers' demands and channel them towards the government, in which the PCP participated. Moreover, new workplace representative bodies, the *comissões de trabalhadores* (workers' commissions) began to emerge more or less spontaneously outside union control. Competing in some areas directly with union workplace organizations, they negotiated over a wide range of issues, called strikes in the face of union opposition, frequently demanded purges of management and even took over the running of hundreds of small companies. The workers' commissions were supported by various factions opposed to the PCP and for a while were seen as an alternative to Intersindical. After the revolution, the *comissões* were recognized by the constitution (1976) and regulated by law (1979), which confined them to the 'supervision of management' (a dead letter in practice) and to participation in the administration of welfare matters within the firm (see below).

The Emergence of Parallel Unions

The struggle against the legal monopoly of Intersindical became a central political issue for the parties opposed to the communists' revolutionary objectives and following the defeat of the radical forces in the summer and autumn of 1975, moderate socialist and 'social democrat' (liberal–conservative) factions won the elections in a series of important, mainly white-collar, unions, which had previously been strongly represented in the Intersindical leadership. At the same time, the new constitution of 1976 removed Intersindical's monopoly and allowed the free establishment of trade unions at any level. From 1976 on, new ('parallel') unions were created in almost every sector, occupation and professional category, with the exception of banking and insurance, which continued to be unitary. In 1978, the groups opposed to Intersindical and PCP domination of the union movement founded a second union confederation, UGT. The initiative was led by the unions for banking, insurance and office employees and had the formal support of the PS and the PSD. UGT started out with 30 unions and currently has 60, against 150 for Intersindical (also known since 1977 as CGTP, *Confederação Geral dos Trabalhadores Portugueses*). It failed to attract the majority of existing independent unions.

Despite numerous mergers among CGTP unions, there are now 370 unions, compared with 328 in 1974. This reflects the rapid rise in the number of small occupational unions during the 1980s, frequently as a result of the fragmentation of larger organizations. There are now more than 150, mostly small, occupational or even grade-based independent unions among groups such as airline pilots, train drivers, dockers and civil servants. Operating either as labour market cartels or as lobbying groups or both, a proportion of them are highly cohesive and effective organizations, though they do not see themselves as part of the wider union movement. They share a common desire to avoid integration in broader organizations, to defend their particular interests, and to preserve their autonomy from government and from political parties and ideologies. They reject egalitarian policies, narrow wage differentials and inter-occupational solidarity. CGTP and UGT sectoral unions view them largely as egocentric interest organizations serving privileged minorities, but UGT's attitude is ambivalent as in some sectors it is largely dependent on this type of organization.

UGT has pursued the creation of a new organizational structure with a limited number of national industrial unions on the German or Austrian model (UGT has always had close links with the union movements of central Europe and Scandinavia – though not with its namesake, the Spanish UGT). However, the plan has made little real progress. Existing UGT unions have defended traditional demarcations and have resisted even the most obvious mergers in banking, insurance, services, transport, education, and fisheries. The new national industry-based UGT unions in textiles and clothing, metal, chemicals, telecommunications, construction, etc. are all weaker than Intersindical's corresponding industrial federations; and, with white-collar groups and their unions resisting absorption into large sectoral organizations, they have been unable to achieve the 'vertical' integration of different groups of workers. Other occupational and territorial divisions also persist, sometimes nourished by the rivalry between socialists and 'social democrats'.

At the end of the 1980s, the PSD labour organization, TSD, decided to end the alliance with the Socialists and to create a third confederation of their own. TSD tried to split several UGT unions in the service sector (insurance, energy and telecommunications) in order to create a nucleus of unions for a new confederation. But the majority of PSD activists in UGT rejected the TSD project and remained inside UGT. Thus the so-called Convention of Independent Unions, CSI, was limited to a very narrow social base. UGT and CGTP opposition blocked CSI's attempt to win representation on the tripartite CPCS. In 1995, CSI had only seven small occupational unions and five sector unions with extremely low representativeness.

Thus the evolution of trade union structures during the 1980s and 1990s was contradictory. On the one hand, there have been moves to consolidation and rationalization. CGTP has gradually succeeded in reorganizing structures along federal ('vertical') and regional lines, and it continues to intregate the numerous smaller organizations into larger units. (For practical reasons some particularly dynamic occupational unions such as the teachers and the nurses are not integrated into vertical structures.) On the other hand, the fragmentation in Portuguese unionism has been fostered by the emergence of small new occupational unions. This contradictory picture is reflected in UGT's structure, an uneasy mix of 'vertical' sector unions and occupational unions.

Up to 1987–8, competition and open hostility between Intersindical and UGT hindered joint action in collective bargaining and dealings with government. With the simultaneous call for a general strike in March 1988 against the liberalization of redundancy legislation, and with the beginning of regular contacts in the context of the tripartite negotiations at the CPCS, some kind of reconciliation seemed to emerge. However, collaboration continued to be patchy. Differences in strategy, structure and practice continue to impede closer relations between the two confederations. Co-operation, in collective bargaining and in industrial disputes, between individual unions from different political camps is still the exception, particularly at industry level. In many sectors the growth of separate negotiations with independent unions has contributed to the fragmentation of bargaining.

The absence of legal recognition procedures or criteria of representativeness (the few legal requirements are not enforced, on the grounds that they may be unconstitutional) means that all unions are considered to be representative and have the same rights. Thus collective bargaining depends largely on the employers' willingness to negotiate with a particular union. This has permitted the employers, including public enterprises and the government, to help new UGT or independent unions establish themselves by rapidly reaching agreements with them. As a result, Intersindical's virtual 'bargaining monopoly' in manufacturing, construction, electricity, road and urban transport, post and telecommunications and large sections of the civil service, has been broken. UGT is dominant only in banking, insurance, and in white-collar occupations in several industries and services. It represents considerable parts of the workforce in electricity, education and transport and has a lesser presence in public administration and communications. The independent unions organize professional and managerial staff and several categories of higher-paid workers with special bargaining power, mainly in the public sector.

Union Membership

According to an in-depth study of union structures and density (Stoleroff and Naumann 1993; 1994), about one million Portuguese workers were organized in 1990, roughly a third of total wage-earners, but with a very unequal distribution between public and private sectors and between large and small enterprises. This places Portugal in the group of western European countries with low-medium union density, and significantly ahead of France and Spain. CGTP organizes 71 per cent of unionized workers, UGT 23 per cent and the independent unions about 6 per cent. All the largest organizations belong to CGTP or UGT, notably CGTP unions in public services, textiles, footwear and metal manufacturing, distribution and education, and UGT unions for banking and office employees.

Overall membership has fallen continuously since the late 1970s, although the effects of political mobilization and of the old system of compulsory dues, abolished in 1975, kept density high until about 1977. One factor in decline was the abolition of the compulsory check-off system by the socialist government in 1977, explicitly as a way of weakening Intersindical. While many public enterprises have agreed to deduct dues since then, private sector employers' associations have opposed co-operation in this field and contributions are now mostly collected by the unions. Several other factors are more important in explaining declining membership. Since 1976 there has been a very significant rise in temporary work and in informal employment in the black economy. The phenomenon, as in Spain, reflects the pressure of high unemployment, but has been aggravated in Portugal by the persistence of rigid regulations on dismissals. The estimated proportion of informal employment in construction is 50 per cent, consisting overwhelmingly of (often illegal) immigrants from the former African colonies, but it is also significant in the clothing and footwear industries and certain services. Probably as a consequence, construction (the largest industry in employment terms, with over 300,000 wage-earners) has a union density of barely 10 per cent, the lowest in the country. The loss of many thousands of jobs in union strongholds and the restructuring of the labour market, the weakening of the network of shop stewards, poor member services, inter-union competition, union politicization and factionalism, the reluctance of younger workers to join unions, and employer pressures, are also commonly cited by union officials as explanations for falling membership (Ribeiro et al. 1993).

Finances and Organization

The unions have experienced increasing financial difficulties. The effects of low union density and declining membership, the low level of dues, and the lack of resources inherited by most corporatist unions, are considerably worsened by the dispersion of scarce resources as a result of union pluralism. One consequence is that strike funds are relatively rare. Only small, cohesive, mostly independent unions with comparatively well-paid memberships (pilots, air traffic controllers, train drivers and so on) have such funds, and they use them to great effect.

Delays in union restructuring have meant that a considerable number of unions are unable to pay their affiliation fees to confederal and intermediate structures. As aid from foreign union movements has largely dried up, confederations rely increasingly heavily on the financial contributions of a small number of member unions, and on funds from national and European state agencies. In 1990, over 50 per cent of UGT's income from union contributions came from just one of its 61 affiliates, the Union of Banking Employees of Southern Portugal. In 1987, the government paid UGT an 'allowance' for its participation in the CPCS corresponding to 9 per cent of the confederation's total income in that year.

The Lisbon-based banking union is the richest and, with CGTP's local authority workers' union, the largest primary organization in the country, with more than 40,000 members (including retired workers). It was prominent in the creation of Intersindical in 1970, and subsequently of UGT in 1978, has been governed successively by all the main factions and since 1988 has been led by an unusual alliance of socialists and communists. The singular success of banking unionism in Portugal (unionization still today approaches 90 per cent) is partly due to relatively privileged treatment under the corporatist regime, but membership has more than doubled since the revolution, in sharp contrast to the general trend. Only CGTP-affiliated unions in public services have increased their membership as much. By contrast, most large manual workers' unions in manufacturing have suffered a drastic and continuous loss of members. In the banking unions, services to members are well developed, and the conduct of collective bargaining and industrial disputes has been very effective. Strikes are subject to ballots, internal factions cover the whole political spectrum, and the governing bodies are directly elected in well-contested elections with high turnouts. Very few unions combine the same features. The arrival of new domestic and foreign banks since the 1980s and the restructuring of the newly established private corporate groups pose a serious threat to the banking unions. Although union density remains high, these banks have undermined the effectiveness of collective agreements through new policies in personnel management and work organization. These include greater job mobility, more flexible working hours (including the regular practice of unpaid overtime), and, in the case of the largest new private bank, the Banco Comercial Português, the rejection of female employment.

The changes taking place in the banking sector are likely to be seen in other industries as state monopolies are dismantled and privatized. In the medium term, however, a drastic fall in unionization in privatized enterprises seems unlikely.

The number of full-time officials in Portuguese unions is very low – only 300 out of Intersindical's 5,000 officers are union employees, though some 'lay' representatives in large, mainly public, enterprises also work full-time for the union – and in general they are poorly qualified. A lack of resources and discrimination against activists (in the form of loss of pay and promotion) make union jobs extremely unattractive, at least to skilled workers. Most activists within Intersindical and even in UGT are motivated primarily by strong political commitment. Religious motivation is also still important. Although the church failed in its attempts to promote catholic unions, a considerable number of union activists, including confederal officers, began their careers in the 'schools' of the *Juventude Operária Católica* and the *Liga Operária Católica*, particularly prior to the 1970s.

Union leaders and activists are given party responsibilities and political jobs (and even appointed to party executive bodies, although this is formally prohibited under the union law). Formally, only personal ties exist between unions and parties; the unions do not provide financial support to the parties, nor have they any right of representation in party bodies. During the 1980s, 5–9 per cent of members of parliament were UGT and Intersindical union officers or confederal leaders. In theory, the three political parties with significant influence in the union confederations are all pro-labour (Socialists, Communists and 'social democrats'). None of them emerged historically out of the union movement, but the communists gained a strategic advantage as a result of their successful clandestine work during the dictatorship. With the advent of democracy, all the main parties sought to establish roots in the working class, and party activists played a large part in building and running the emerging union movement. Consequently, the unions have functioned largely as vehicles of political influence. Over the last decade, union action has become less ideologically determined, but the links between unions and party politics still prevail, even in the case of many so-called independent unions.

Under the dominant communist influence, CGTP has a more centralized, cohesive and disciplined culture than UGT, where the main tendencies are more balanced and the ideological cement is far less important. The UGT leadership finds it much harder than CGTP to lay down common positions for its member unions on issues such as political action, collective bargaining and union structure (demarcations, mergers, etc.).

In the confederal bodies of UGT and in most of its affiliated unions there are formally organized political factions (*tendências*). They have constitutional rights such as the nomination of candidates to the leadership, and they are generally represented on union bodies on a proportional basis; in practice, the union's top executive body (the *comissão executiva*) is composed of an equal number of socialists and 'social democrats'. The factions are nevertheless considered to be independent of the corresponding party leaderships. Intersindical rejects organized factions, but permits a limited pluralism in confederal bodies, with a clear majority of communists and a minority of left-wing socialists, catholics and other small groups.

The predominance of political action in Portuguese trade unionism results from several structural features: the historically minor role of societal self-regulation (including collective bargaining) compared to statutory regulation, partisan control of the unions, the prevailing weakness of unions and a chronic bias of employers' associations towards lobbying and reliance upon government. Following the 1974 revolution, these factors were reinforced by economic crisis and a much larger state role in the economy. Unable to prevent the rise in unemployment or the fall in real wages between 1976 and 1985, the unions directed their energies to defending labour legislation passed after the revolution, a legal framework which

Intersindical praised as the most advanced in western Europe. The unions used political action, including a successful general strike in 1988, to secure what may well be their major achievement in the 1980s: the maintenance of union rights and the protection of the main legal provisions on job security and the right to strike. For UGT, the creation of the CPCS by the PS–PSD coalition government in 1984 and the signing of the Economic and Social Agreement in 1990 were two other outstanding achievements.

Union pluralism, which does not have solid traditions in Portugal, was largely a reflection of the deep political divisions of the revolutionary period. Subsequent domestic and international developments have reduced the grounds for those divisions, but the existence of two politically opposed union organizations creates significant institutional inertia. The common struggle of socialists and communists against the policies of the PSD government (1985–95) and the growing autonomy of CGTP from the Communist Party have opened the way to reconciliation, though as noted above, a breakthrough in inter-confederal relations has yet to occur.

Membership and Organization at Company Level

In some medium-sized enterprises and in the majority of larger companies, a dual model of workers' representation exists. As noted above, side-by-side with trade union representation (shop-stewards, joint shop-steward committees) there is a representative body elected by all employees: the workers' commission. This pattern of representation is exceptional, because *comissões de trabalhadores* exist in a considerably smaller proportion of companies than do trade union organiz- ations. Moreover, an Intersindical survey based on 1993 Labour Ministry data revealed that about 60 per cent of the 1,076 registered commissions were inactive. General workers' commissions depend on the political orientation and financial resources of the dominant trade union in the company.

According to the results of the first comprehensive survey of industrial relations in large and medium-sized companies (Stoleroff 1995), the presence of trade union bodies (*comissões sindicais*, i.e. shop steward committees) in the companies is related to membership density. Density is low (less than 20 per cent) in almost half medium-sized and large companies, and is high in a quarter of them. Density is higher in large enterprises (with 500 and more employees), state-owned companies and in firms which belong to large corporate groups (whether national or foreign). Transport, chemicals, paper and metal industries and financial services are the sectors with the highest densities. Density is lower in companies with higher numbers of female or young employees, employees on fixed-term contracts, and those with below average length of service.

The existence of representative bodies like shop stewards, shop steward com- mittees and workers' commissions seems to depend largely upon company size and only to a lesser extent upon union membership density in the company. Shop- stewards (*delegados sindicais*) exist in 72 per cent of large companies, and workers' commissions in 40 per cent. In medium-sized companies these figures fall to 34 and 11 per cent, respectively. These numbers indicate that the dual system of workers' representation stipulated by law is the exception in practice. Workers' commissions in companies with high union density tend to pursue the same objectives as the dominant union.

An influential view amongst union analysts is that union capabilities would become increasingly independent of membership density. This is contradicted by the survey findings that management's evaluation of the trade unions' role is more positive in companies where density is higher. A similar correlation exists between union density and the 'negotiation index' (based on the regularity of union–management meetings, the existence of substantial negotiations, etc.). In the context of union pluralism, this may in practice mean that the strength of one union in terms of membership and mobilization capacity is translated into another union's leading role in negotiations with management.

Direct negotiations take place between management and workers' representatives on wages and working conditions in 25 per cent of medium-sized and 43 per cent of large enterprises. Approximately half of companies implement industry-level collective agreements without further consultation with representative bodies in the companies. Regular informative meetings take place in 15 per cent of medium-sized and 45 per cent of large enterprises. In 18 per cent and 29 per cent, respectively, they are sporadic and in 56 per cent and 23 per cent, respectively, they do not exist at all. The only bipartite bodies at company level are the health and safety committees which exist in 38 per cent of medium-sized and 77 per cent of large enterprises. Thus in general the degree of institutionalized workers' participation in Portuguese firms is low.

The differences outlined between large and medium-sized companies suggest that there is a dual system of industrial relations: on the one hand a smallish group of large and some medium-sized companies which practise institutionalized industrial relations, on the other hand a huge mass of small and medium-sized companies where labour relations are regulated by informal – and largely unresearched – methods and where institutionalized systems are largely irrelevant.

▌ Collective Bargaining

From the late 1970s, the newly created UGT unions challenged CGTP's hegemony in sectoral level collective bargaining as well as in some large, mostly state-owned, companies. Despite UGT's success in taking the initiative in some important sectors, the content of collective bargaining did not change fundamentally. Indeed, by the mid-1980s collective bargaining had entered a period of stagnation. This reflected a deadlock between the employers' demands for the radical revision of agreements made during the revolution, and the unions' insistence on retaining their gains. As power relations shifted in favour of employers, CGTP unions refused to agree to general revisions of agreements under disadvantageous conditions while UGT unions entered into limited concession bargaining. Negotiations became largely limited to pay issues. The main level of bargaining continues to be the sector, and the role of the company level remains limited. However, an important development of the 1980s was the formalization of tripartite national 'social concertation' which set a framework both for institutional arrangements and the substance of negotiation at lower levels.

In 1993, more than 90 per cent of the 2.15 million workers in legal employment in public and private enterprises were nominally covered by some kind of 'instrument for work regulation'. Eighty-three per cent were covered by collective agreements or government extensions at sector level, almost 5 per cent by direct statutory regulations, 7 per cent by company agreements and 4 per cent by multi-company agreements. A further half a million employees in unregistered companies had to be added to the workforce not covered by collective agreements, amounting to approximately one-third of the total number of wage earners. During the 1980s, the government gradually ceased to issue direct statutory regulations to break bargaining deadlocks, a legal expedient dating from the corporatist system when strikes were prohibited. The 600,000 employees in public administration, local authorities and services such as health and education are covered by statutory civil service regulations. In January 1996, a major agreement between the government, UGT and CGTP opened the way to negotiations on the introduction of collective bargaining in parts of the public sector.

Collective bargaining is voluntary, since few sanctions can be imposed on parties unwilling to negotiate or to participate in mediation or arbitration. However, once both sides agree to bargain formally, they must comply with all legal requirements. When an agreement is reached, it has to be registered and published by the Ministry of Employment, thus becoming legally enforceable and extendable to other employers and workers or related industries. Its remains in force until it is replaced by a new agreement, which legally may not be less favourable overall to the workers than the existing one. The first negotiation of a formal company agreement is viewed by individual employers as a step with far-reaching implications, since once an agreement is concluded, it is likely to form the basis of further union claims.

The legal position on the applicability of collective agreements is somewhat confused. In theory, agreements apply only to the workers represented by the signatory unions. In practice, however, since only one agreement is enforceable for the same group of employees within a company (conditions cannot be differentiated according to union membership), workers may find themselves covered by an agreement reached by a union of which they are not members. Moreover, in the absence of recognition procedures or criteria of representativeness, this union may be in a minority position in the sector. The current legal ambiguity has allowed UGT and some independent unions – even where they are in a minority – to oust Intersindical from the bargaining process of several large enterprises and sectors.

A deadlock in collective bargaining is usually followed by voluntary, though legally regulated, 'conciliation' procedures before a strike is called. Conciliation and mediation services, established by the corporatist regime in 1969, are provided free of charge by officials of the Ministry of Employment. The procedure gives unions and employers the opportunity to involve the government in their disputes, a traditional practice largely unchanged by the revolution. The arbitration mechanism is private (no permanent arbitration service exists) and expensive, and it became increasingly unpopular during the 1970s, especially with employers. In the 1980s, very few disputes were submitted to arbitration, even in public enterprises, where the government had the power to order it.

The tension between an over-regulated and highly legalistic framework and voluntary collective bargaining may help explain why formal company bargaining is so rare in the private sector, and why industry bargaining has so little impact on working conditions and terms of employment in leading or even average enterprises. The role of government extensions, the dominance of industry collective bargaining relative to company bargaining and the lack of articulation between the two levels are also legacies of the corporatist system.

The emergence of union pluralism and independent unions has led to the multiplication of bargaining processes and agreements. There has also been a move from regional to national industry agreements in a few cases. Despite the attempts made by large industry-based unions to unify the bargaining process within each sector, office employees and such occupations as sales representatives, drivers, managers, technicians, engineers and other professionals are very often covered by separate industrial agreements. The same occurs in several public and private enterprises: in the national railway company, for example, the various occupations are covered by five different company agreements, instead of only one in the 1970s.

Company-level Bargaining

Unlike other European countries, Portugal has not seen a significant devolution of bargaining to the company level. Indeed, since the end of the 1980s, the coverage of company and multi-company agreements has decreased and these agreements are almost entirely limited to public or privatized enterprises. As mentioned, the proportion of employees covered by company agreements is small. The limited bargaining at this level reflects employer hostility. Private employers and employers' associations have consistently opposed formal company-level bargaining, so as to discourage union activity within the enterprise and maximize employer control over employment conditions.

The privatization policy of the Cavaco Silva governments has resulted in a crisis of formal bargaining at company level in the one area in which it was previously significant, posing a major challenge to previously powerful public enterprise unions. Agreements in state firms were often regarded as models of company bargaining, but the restructuring and downsizing of firms prior to privatization was accompanied by management pressure for a radical revision of agreements. Unions usually insisted on maintaining existing provisions and conflict became inevitable. Bargaining in these companies tended to become less regular, and in several cases ended in complete deadlock. In several companies, like Petrogal (oil-refining and distribution) and Portugal Telecom, unions lost their battle against the revision of agreements. In other cases they succeeded in defending existing agreements even after large companies had been broken up into smaller units. In general, restructuring and privatization have encouraged a significant shift in collective bargaining at company level, putting an end to traditional 'Fordist' bargaining and opening the way to more flexible types of agreements although, as mentioned, increased flexibility is usually the result of unilateral management decision rather than collective agreement.

The rigidities of official collective bargaining can be evaded at company level by a variety of 'informal' or unofficial practices: avoiding written agreements or not complying with other legal requirements. The 'social contracts' concluded in several private and public enterprises in difficulties during the 1980s, despite being written agreements, should also be put in this category, as they temporarily suspended certain provisions and rights (the law prohibits such abrogations by collective agreements). These negotiations were conducted by the workers' commissions, not the unions, although the former are not legally entitled to bargain. Generally, however, informal bargaining involves the negotiation of a 'list of demands' or *caderno reivindicativo* submitted by workers' representatives. Frequently, management will only deal with the workers' commissions which, unlike the unions, are exclusively internal to the enterprise; moreover, only one workers' commission may be elected in each enterprise or establishment, while there may be several unions. The concessions made by the employer in informal bargaining are embodied in management minutes, avoiding the appearance of bilateral agreements. Demands are frequently backed up by different forms of union action, including stoppages.

Informal bargaining practices are not as widespread and regular as formal bargaining, but they are much more flexible and fill a visible gap in industrial relations by providing a complement to industry bargaining. A sharp distinction between the two practices is that informal bargaining is totally dependent on union strength and bargaining power in each company, while in formal industry bargaining the unions can rely on government extensions. In several industries informal company bargaining has not developed at all.

Tripartite Social Concertation

A major innovation of the 1980s was the introduction of tripartite national level bargaining or 'social concertation'. The principal forum was the *Conselho Permanente de Concertação Social*, created by the government, UGT and employers' confederations in 1984. CGTP opposed the creation of the CPCS from the beginning, denouncing it as a 'corporatist' intrigue to undermine the 'working class's struggle against capitalist exploitation'. In the aftermath of the 1987 liberal–conservative landslide, however, CGTP agreed to take its seats on the Council, seeing it as the only means of channelling union demands direct to government. The CPCS concluded a series of macro-level agreements on pay and incomes policy which laid down 'guide figures' for pay bargaining at lower levels.

In 1990 an attempt was made in the CPCS to reshape the institutional structures of Portuguese industrial relations. The 'Economic and Social Agreement' of 1990,

Table 14.6 Industrial disputes

	No. of strikes	Workers involved/strike	Working days lost (total)	Average duration (days)
1975	340	–	–	–
1980	374	1,066	734,536	1.8
1985*	504	478	335,664	1.4
1990	171	476	146,532	1.1
1991	262	455	123,838	1
1992	409	322	189,895	1.4
1993	231	361	79,942	1
1994	300	315	96,831	1

* From 1986, public administration and public services not included.
Source: MESS, INE.

signed by all CPCS members except the CGTP (which had actively participated in the negotiations), prepared the ground for the reform of the legal framework of collective bargaining with the objective of enlarging union and employer negotiating autonomy and introducing effective mechanisms for conciliation and arbitration. In fact, the Cavaco Silva governments failed to reform the restrictive legal framework regulating bargaining procedures and content, and the compulsory arbitration system was obstructed by CIP and CGTP (see below). In 1991 two 'sub-agreements' on occupational training and health and safety were signed by all CPCS members including CGTP, although their practical impact was limited. Peak-level bargaining has continued with the 1996 'Strategic Concertation Agreement' (*Acordo de Concertação Estratégica*, ACE). ACE comprises a catalogue of macro-economic aims and an ambitious programme for employment and competitiveness. It includes the definition of targets and measures in a vast range of policies.

Strikes

Following the legalization of strikes, strike activity reached its peak in the period 1980–83 against a background of deep economic and social crisis and of CGTP opposition to the right-wing government (see table 14.6). After 4 years of intense mobilization, the strike movement lost its momentum: the average duration of strikes in public and private enterprises fell from 3.6 days in 1978 to an average of 1.1 in the first half of the 1990s, probably the lowest figure since 1974. Other indicators fell in line with this. The trend reflected such factors as the dramatic crisis in employment, the emerging struggle between CGTP and UGT, and the ineffectiveness of the strike weapon in preventing real wage decreases or in forcing governments to adopt economic policies to alleviate the effects of recession.

The main sectors in terms of total working days lost between 1986 and 1994 were transport and communications, engineering, banking, textiles and clothing. The statistics exclude public administration, health and the state education sector for which reliable strike data are unavailable; in 1986 the government even ceased to issue statistics on strikes in the civil service. It is nevertheless possible to say that the public sector as a whole is much more affected by strikes than the private sector. The civil service has had a high strike frequency and there have been recurring industrial disputes in chronically loss-making public enterprises, particularly in the transport sector. In several public enterprises, there has been fierce union opposition to privatization and restructuring and this has resulted in an increase in strike action.

Conclusions: Peak-level Negotiations and European Regulation vs 'Grass-roots' Industrial Relations and Economic Liberalization

Social Concertation

Because of the stagnation of collective bargaining and an extremely low level of workers' involvement in the regulation of work relations at company level, peak-level tripartite bargaining has become the subject of major public and scientific interest. The CPCS has been the vehicle for a regular process of political exchange between state and industrial relations actors. With the signing of the AES in 1990, a new phase of social concertation appeared to have been initiated. Both the negotiation process in itself – involving all members of the CPCS including CGTP – and the broad range of issues broached by the agreement seemed to justify the view that a 'new paradigm of an industrial relations sub-system' was emerging, signalling the imminent arrival of a new wave of what might be called 'liberal corporatism'. Developments did not measure up to expectations, however, and a profound reform of Portuguese industrial relations is still pending. The main reason is that concertation failed to achieve a rapprochement between the principal antagonists of the system, the industrialists employers' confederation, CIP, and CGTP. The latter did not sign the 1990 agreement.

Moreover, continuing tensions between the two union confederations and their member associations at sector and local level have frustrated reform of the system. Two examples illustrate this problem. First, under the AES it was agreed to reduce the working week to 40 hours by 1995 and to introduce compensating flexibility measures by collective agreements at sector and company level. Some UGT unions concluded such agreements. However, CGTP unions (who opposed the link between working time reduction and flexibility) were able to win working-time reductions in several sectors while successfully resisting employers' attempts to introduce greater flexibility. Thus these provisions were often ineffective. In 1996, the signatories to the AES agreed to enforce the provisions by legislation, effectively undermining CGTP's stance. A second example concerns the introduction of compulsory arbitration under the AES. This provision was seen as a way of breaking the deadlock in collective bargaining in most sectors. The implementation of the measure proved to be impossible because CGTP and CIP failed to nominate representatives for the arbitration bodies, demonstrating their lack of confidence in a mechanism which would give decision-making powers to a body other than themselves.

The most recent concertation agreement, ACE 1996, perpetuates the pattern of a 'consensus' from which CGTP is excluded. Given the experience of the AES, the unresolved problem of CGTP's non-involvement, and CIP's explicitly-stated 'limited commitment' to the agreement, the likely impact of ACE 1996 'on the ground' is open to question. A failure once again to implement the agreed measures by direct negotiation between the 'social partners' at the sector and company levels may provoke enforcement through legislation. This would maintain the state as the key 'locus of action' (Stoleroff 1988) in the Portuguese system, and make it more difficult for the actors to regulate their relations autonomously.

Thus the impetus for a more coherent and dynamic model of industrial relations may be expected to come from other less 'visible' levels of the system, through the collective bargaining process and bilateral co-operation between employers and workers' representatives on particular issues. In some sectors, employers have cautiously demonstrated a growing interest in reaching regular agreements (even if only on pay issues) with unions of both UGT and CGTP. This may represent a first step towards more far-reaching settlements on the renewal of the general framework of employment regulation. This 'bottom-up' approach to reform is bound to be an extremely contradictory and protracted process, and its outcome is largely uncertain. Unlike tripartite concertation, it takes place away from the glare of publicity, but its potential should not be underestimated.

Europe

The European context exerts strong pressure on unions and employers to develop a new pattern of industrial relations. The key influence is not the relatively weak European regulation of social affairs but rather the opening up of the domestic economy to foreign competition and investment. Thus in the banking sector, European legislation on equal opportunities proved completely ineffective in the case of systematic and generalized discrimination by the *Banco de Comércio Português* (BCP) against women. The real changes in banking have resulted from the privatization, liberalization and internationalization of the sector in the context of European integration. After a phase of large-scale investment, the domestic market has become saturated and the newly constituted financial groups have initiated a process of drastic downsizing, rationalization and internal restructuring. This poses a serious challenge to banking unions and promises to become a major test for the existing pattern of industrial relations in the sector. The outcome will be vital not only for UGT, which depends heavily on the resources of these unions. The banking sector has been in the vanguard of the process of liberalization and privatization and its strong unions have encompassed the whole spectrum of political currents in the Portuguese trade union movement. As a result, current developments will also have a major impact on the direction and pace of the evolution of the industrial relations system as a whole.

The likely impact of the country's entry into the European Monetary Union (or, indeed, of its exclusion from the first wave) is difficult to assess. Even in the public sector, where increasing conflict might be expected to result from implementing the Maastricht convergence criteria, the current situation is too complex to allow such a simplistic extrapolation. Thus the comprehensive reform of public administration – including the introduction of real collective bargaining and binding agreements into the sector – currently being negotiated between the Socialist government and the trade unions may compensate for the EMU-induced potential for conflict.

▌Portugal in International Perspective

The specific characteristics of the democratic transition – particularly the explosion of most varied forms of revolutionary mass mobilization – distinguish the Portuguese case from the fall of the other dictatorships in southern Europe (Spain and Greece). This history has had a decisive impact on the industrial relations patterns that have emerged. In all three former dictatorships, the creation of relationships of trust was seriously constrained by activists' recent experience of employer authoritarianism backed by state repression, but in Spain and Greece the moderate and gradual process of democratization favoured an equally moderate change in the relationship between the emerging workers' organizations and the employers. The Spanish unions (including the communist-dominated *Comisiones Obreras*) submerged their ambitions in the overall project of gradual reform, while the Greek trade union confederation, GSEE, continued far beyond the transition period under control of conservative forces partly linked to the old regime. In Portugal, the revolutionary form of the political process fostered workers' radicalization and deepened class antagonism. The highly politicized approach and the dominance of relationships of distrust between the actors is a legacy of the transition period whose impact is felt in the still halting steps towards the modernization of the Portuguese industrial relations system.

▌Abbreviations

AES	*Acordo Económico e Social* – Economic and Social Agreement, signed in 1990
AIP	*Associação Industrial Portuguesa* – Portuguese Association of Industry
CAP	*Confederação da Agricultura Portuguesa* – Confederation of Portuguese Agriculture
CCP	*Confederação do Comércio Português* – Confederation of Portuguese Commerce

CDS/PP	*Partido do Centro Democrático e Social/Partido Popular* – Democratic and Social Centre Party, also known as Christian Democrats
CGT	*Confederação Geral do Trabalho* – General Confederation of Labour (outlawed in 1927)
CGTP (CGTP-IN)	*Confederação Geral dos Trabalhadores Portugueses* – General Confederation of Portuguese Workers, usually known as *Intersindical*
CIP	*Confederação da Indústria Portuguesa* – Confederation of Portuguese Industry
CNEP	*Conselho Nacional das Empresas Portuguesas* – National Council of Portuguese Enterprises
CPCS	*Conselho Permanente de Concertação Social* – Permanent Council for Social Concertation
INE	*Instituto Nacional de Estatística* – National Statistical Institute
MESS	*Ministério do Emprego e Segurança Social* – Ministry of Employment and Social Security
PCP	*Partido Comunista Português* – Portuguese Communist Party
PS	*Partido Socialista* – Socialist Party
PSD	*Partido Social Democrático* – Social Democratic Party
UGT	*União Geral de Trabalhadores* – General Workers' Union

| References and Further Reading

Barreto, J. 1991: *A Formação das Centrais Sindicais e do Sindicalismo Contemporâneo Português (1968–1990)*, Doctoral thesis, Lisbon.

Barreto, J. 1992: Portugal. In Ferner, A., and Hyman, R. (eds), *Industrial Relations in the New Europe*, 1st edn. Oxford: Blackwell Publishers, 445–81.

Campos Lima, M. (forthcoming): Balance of social concertation and social pacts in Portugal. In ETUI (ed.), *Social Pacts in Europe*. Brussels: ETUI.

Cardoso, J. L., Brito, J., Mendes, F. and Rodrigues, M. 1990: *Empresários e Gestores da Indústria em Portugal*. Lisboa: Dom Quixote.

Conceição Cerdeira, M., and Padilha, E. 1986–1988: *As Estruturas Sindicais Portuguesas (1933–1985)*, 3 Vols. Lisbon: MESS.

Kovács, I. 1994: Participação no trabalho no contexto de competitividade, *Organizações & Trabalho*, 12, October, 11–29.

Lucena, M. de, and Gaspar, C. 1991: Metamorfoses corporativas? – associações de interesses económicos e institucionalização da democracia em Portugal (I–II), *Análise Social*, 114, 847–903, and 115, 135–87.

Naumann, R. 1991: Portugal, in Däubler, W., and Lecher, W. (eds), *Die Gewerkschaften in dern 12 EG-Ländern*. Cologne: Bund Verlag, 81–87.

Naumann, R. 1993: Portugal. In Bispinck, R. and Lecher, W. (eds), *Tarifpolitik und Tarifsysteme in Europa (Handbuch)*. Cologne: Bund Verlag, 313–43.

Naumann, R. 1995a: Country-Report on Portugal. In ETUI (ed.) *Collective Bargaining in Western Europe 1994–5*. Brussels: ETUI, 123–39.

Naumann, R. 1995b: *Privatizações e Reestruturações. O Desafio para o Movimento Sindical em Portugal*. Lisbon: Friedrich Ebert Foundation.

Naumann, R. 1996: Country-Report on Portugal. In ETUI (ed.), *Collective Bargaining in Western Europe 1995–6*. Brussels: ETUI, 203–19.

Naumann, R. forthcoming (a): Country-Report on Portugal. In ETUI (ed.), *Collective Bargaining in Western Europe 1996–7*. Brussels: ETUI.

Naumann, R. forthcoming (b): Present conditions for a social pact in Portugal. In ETUI (ed.), *Social Pacts in Europe*. Brussels: ETUI.

Naumann, R., and Stoleroff, A. 1996: Portugal. In *Handbook of the Trade Unions in Europe*. Brussels/ETUI.

Pinto, M. 1990: Trade union action and industrial relations in Portugal. In Baglioni, G. and Crouch, C. (eds), *European Industrial Relations. The Challenge of Flexibility*. London: Sage, 243–64.

Pinto, M. 1991: Ensaio sobre a concertação social e a mudança do paradigma sindical e social. In *Portugal em mudança. Ensaios sobre a actividade do XI Governo Constitucional*. Lisbon: INCM, 337–63.

Raby, D.L. 1988: *Fascism and Resistance in Portugal*. Manchester.

Ribeiro, J., Granjo, P., Leitão, N, and Harouna, A. 1993: *Posições face à Sindicalização, Desafios de Mudança*. Lisbon: Edições Cosmos.

Stoleroff, A. 1988: Estratégia sindical e comportamento organizacional: O caso da CGTP, *Análise Psiológica*, **3–4**, 429–40.

Stoleroff, A. 1995: Elementos do padrão emergente de relações industriais no contexto da reestruturação: Alguns resultados de um inquérito nacional às médias e grandes empresas, *Organizações & Trabalho*, **13**, April, 11–42.

Stoleroff, A. and Casaca, S. 1996: Produção magra e relações laborais: cadências verificadas num Greenfield em Portugal, *Organizações e Trabalho*, **15**, 83–103.

Stoleroff, A., and Naumann, R. 1993: A sindicalização em Portugal, Sociologia. *Problemas e Práticas*, **14**, 19–47.

Stoleroff, A., and Naumann, R. 1994: Der «Fall» Portugal. Zur Untersuchung des gewerkschaftlichen Organisationsgrades in einem Land der europäischen Peripherie, *WSI-Mitteilungen*, **2**, 94, 134–9.

Stoleroff, A. and Naumann, R. 1996: Unions and the restructuring of the public sector in Portugal. In Leemput, J. van, Leisink, P. and Vilrokx, J. (eds), *The Challenges to Trade Unions in Europe: Innovation or Adaptation*. Cheltenham: Edward Elgar, 205–20.

15 | Spain: Regulating Employment and Social Fragmentation

Introduction

In Spain as elsewhere, the system of employment regulation is the product of past strategies and choices (cf. Lange et al. 1982). Spain is distinctive, however, in that actors have had to shape organizational identities and to forge 'modern' and 'organized' industrial relations in the absence of a stable institutional environment. Since the end of the Francoist dictatorship over two decades ago, unions and employers have been drawn into a broader political role, playing a central part in the stabilization of the system. This context has posed a series of challenges to the development of industrial relations. In particular, employers and the state have shown, in common with their counterparts elsewhere, an interest in labour market deregulation; in the context of attempts to construct new stable institutional frameworks, the quest for deregulation has assumed a special significance.

The chapter starts with a summary of the historical evolution of Spanish industrial relations: this provides the key to understanding the nature of state intervention and the character of labour identity. This is followed by an overview of the labour market and economic environment and of the main institutions and actors of Spanish industrial relations. The argument then turns to the role of the actors in shaping the regulation of employment, both at the level of the national state, and through the system of collective bargaining. One of the key challenges for the actors has been to establish modern forms of joint regulation in a highly fragmented labour market. The chapter ends with a critical assessment of the belief that the regulation of Spanish industrial relations is becoming more institutionalized and effective.

The organization of industrial relations in a context of political and economic fragmentation – increasingly complicated by the new supranational imperatives arising from European integration and the activities of multinational corporations – is thus a defining characteristic of the Spanish case. One of the most important strategic responses has been the transfer of regulatory functions from the national state to unions, employers and regional state bodies in an attempt to construct a system of 'regulation from below'. This pattern appears contingent and unstable, dependent on shifting political relations and alliances between the industrial relations actors. In short, an understanding of the Spanish situation increasingly requires an appreciation of the operation of the 'political' within the industrial relations sphere.

Industrial Relations under Franco

Many of the characteristics of the current industrial relations system have their origins in the years of Francoist dictatorship (1939–75). The Nationalist victory in the civil war of 1936–9 brought a complete break with the traditions of the Second Republic. Hundreds of thousands of Spaniards fled into exile, and up to a quarter of a million supporters of the republic are believed to have been executed in the years immediately after the civil war. The old autonomous unions – notably the socialist-linked UGT and the anarcho-syndicalist CNT – were crushed and during the early years of the dictatorship resistance was minimal (Maravall 1978: 77–109; Preston 1976). The regime developed an authoritarian, hierarchical system of labour relations institutions whose point of departure was the 1938 Labour Charter, inspired by Italian fascist and native Spanish corporatist and 'social catholic' ideas (Fina and Hawkesworth 1984). The Francoist system was based on the OSE, comprising 'vertical' unions (*sindicatos verticales*) in different sectors of production. The vertical unions compulsorily organized employers and workers alike around the principles of 'unity, totality and hierarchy', and the submergence of class antagonisms. The OSE was run by a command structure of appointed officials at national, provincial and local levels (Amsden 1972; Fower-aker 1989). Even when indirect elections were introduced, they were tightly controlled by the Falangists.

In the new system, the traditional features of liberal-democratic industrial relations were rejected: strikes and collective bargaining were banned and independent labour representation was made illegal. The Ministry of Labour set wages through compulsory official norms (*reglamentaciones*), and it imposed a detailed and rigid regulation of all aspects of employment by means of labour ordinances (*ordenanzas laborales*). In short, the state penetrated deeply into civil society, preventing its autonomous organization in the sphere of production.

The burden of Francoist labour legislation was not solely repressive. The regime sought also to establish a certain legitimacy, balancing rigid state control with paternalism. In 1953, compulsory *jurados* or works councils were introduced in firms and establishments; their official function was, however, limited to advisory and administrative matters, and they acted as extensions of the official unions. A 1944 law made it formally difficult for employers to dismiss workers, while detailed labour ordinances restricted labour mobility in the workplace or enterprise.

This system came under pressure as a result of economic modernization. Having failed to trigger state-led 'autarchic' development, the regime introduced major reforms in the late 1950s. While the state retained an active role in the economy, the country was opened up to foreign capital and there was a move away from state regulation of prices and incomes. These reforms laid the basis for the so-called 'economic miracle' of the 1960s, based on the growth of tourism and rapid industrialization. Industrialization, and the large-scale internal migration that accompanied it, brought a new workforce into the expanding sphere of waged labour. In some areas, like Asturias, Madrid and Barcelona, new, sporadic, ad hoc forms of workers' organization developed. The mass meeting, or *asamblea*, was the main vehicle for collective action, achieving an almost mythological status in modern Spanish labour history. Autonomous action gradually crystallized into the so-called *comisiones obreras* (workers' commissions) in certain larger factories and public enterprises, and into *comisiones de barrio* (neighbourhood commissions) in local areas (Villasante 1984; Castells 1983). The *comisiones obreras* began to engage in informal negotiations with employers. For many employers, particularly in larger, more modern enterprises, informal bargaining with semi-clandestine but more representative groups was seen as a way of reducing workplace conflict.

Alongside these developments, the first cracks appeared in the monolithic mould of the national-syndicalist labour system. The 1958 Law on Collective Agreements permitted the controlled development of collective bargaining. The law created in effect a dual structure (Fina and Hawkesworth 1984: 6) of multi-firm bargaining (at local, provincial or regional levels) and of company or plant bargaining. The former was conducted by the vertical unions, and the latter by management and labour representatives of the *jurado*. But in all cases, the official unions and the Ministry of Labour retained close control. Subsequently, collective labour disputes through the courts were recognized, and strikes were decriminalized (although not legalized) in 1965.

Bargaining became quite extensive. Seeing the prospect of genuine bargaining, the *comisiones obreras* adopted a strategy of electing workers to the *jurado* and to regional bodies of the official union system (Giner and Sevilla 1979). Independent representatives and union activists negotiated formally and informally with management. The presence of workers' commission members and other independent activists was vexatious enough for the government to expel 1,800 elected representatives from the OSE in a 1968 crackdown.

Much of the clandestine labour movement was concentrated in the larger factories in key sectors such as shipbuilding, steel, cars and chemicals. The Spanish Communist Party (PCE), which dominated the workers' commissions by the late 1960s, saw these factories as the basis for the anti-Francoist struggle. The consequences were to become apparent when the economic crisis of the 1970s and 1980s eroded the importance of these sectors.

Another key sector was construction, which was often the first stopping-off point for the influx of agricultural labourers into industrial employment. These workers inhabited areas with the worst living conditions produced by rapid urbanization and industrialization; thus they acted as a bridge between the labour and urban struggles (Martínez Lucio 1989). This social–urban dimension was a pivotal aspect of the labour movement from the 1960s. The strategy of the PCE, which became central in both movements, was to link the two arenas of action together in the struggle against Francoism.

Certain characteristics of the pre-1975 period were to have a strong influence on the subsequent development of the Spanish industrial relations system. First, worker representation was strongly oriented to the workplace and company. While collective action at the workplace was integral to the anti-Francoist movement, this focus would later obstruct the construction of centralized national labour organizations. Second, liberalization in the late 1950s and 1960s prompted an uncoordinated and inefficient system of ritualistic collective bargaining which spawned a vast range of collective agreements. This too created subsequent problems in developing representative organizations. Third, rigid state regulation in areas such as employment termination and job classification caused problems for employers as they sought greater flexibility at work and in the labour market; this was to become a major battleground under democracy. Fourth, employers attempted to offset rigidities in employment through a wide array of bonuses and other special payments (Toharia 1988: 121). As a result central, institutional control over this element of employment was weak. Finally, this shifting, amorphous industrial relations environment was used by autonomous worker organizations and opposition forces for political purposes. As a consequence, economic, social and political demands were never clearly differentiated.

Political Transition and the Establishment of Democratic Industrial Relations

Franco's death in November 1975 was followed by an escalation of industrial and social militancy in which protests against government economic policies were combined with demands for political democracy. The outcome was the legalization of the opposition parties and the holding of free elections in 1977. In this transitional period, Spanish trade unionism acquired its contemporary shape. In 1976, the workers' commissions were transformed into a centralized trade union, the CCOO. Its hopes of sustaining a monopoly of representation were dashed, however, when UGT was re-established, and the rivalry between the two movements paralleled that between their associated parties, the PCE and socialist party, PSOE. Electorally, the socialists soon overshadowed the communists, winning a majority in the 1982 elections. PSOE was to dominate Spanish politics until its defeat by the right-wing Partido Popular in March 1996.

In the formative phase of trade union reconstruction, political mobilization and union demands went hand in hand. Economic demands were intensified by the emerging leadership's lack of real control over local activists, and by inter-union competition in factories and local areas. Until 1978, these lower-level union representatives had no legal basis. Local action developed informally and was still interwoven with the vestiges of Francoist labour organization. National leaderships tolerated this since 'mobilization' constituted the basis for national union action. From 1977, however, union strategy moved towards national political compromise and concertation. The resulting 'disenchantment' among the rank and file was reflected in sharply falling union membership levels – from around a quarter in the late 1970s to half that figure in the 1980s (Jordana 1996).

There was intensive internal debate over forms of worker representation and the relationship between different organizational levels. UGT was constructed 'from above' on the basis of groups of non-communist workers and activists, and it adopted more moderate strategies than its rival. CCOO favoured unitary representation at the workplace through workers' committees (*comités de empresa*) – the successors of the old *jurados* – and through the *asamblea*. At national level, differences of ideology and strategy between the socialist and communist-dominated wings of the movement obstructed, inevitably, a unified confederal organization.

Even CCOO, in its search for more permanent, institutionalized structures, was steadily redefining the *asamblea*. In the early years of the transition it had frequently been used as the vehicle of spontaneous workplace democracy and mobilization. However, participation in national concertation in the late 1970s obliged CCOO to dampen down worker mobilization. Local groups were brought under control by political cells within the union, and the traditional role of the *asamblea* was steadily undermined. It came to be used more as a channel of communication, and for taking decisions on specific issues. Increasingly, too, the alliance between union organization and local community action was broken and labour issues were disentangled from wider concerns. This 'demobilization' went against CCOO's 'trade union culture' (Aguilar and Roca 1989; Roca 1991), and clashed with the expectations of the rank and file and with emerging forms of representation both inside and outside the workplace (Martínez Lucio 1987). It failed, however, to eliminate the organizational and ideological resources that were to fuel a resurgence of rank-and-file activity in the mid- to late 1980s.

UGT's organizational strategy and practices emphasized 'negotiation' rather than 'mobilization'. Compared with CCOO, UGT's rank and file was less active and more dependent on the regional and industrial tiers of the organization. Politically, the union emphasized the role of national social wage negotiations as part of tripartite political exchange. UGT's higher industrial relations profile in these years also reflected its increasing closeness to the employers. This was symbolized by the 1980 multi-industry framework agreement, signed by the employers and UGT but not by CCOO. Such exclusionary tactics became a hallmark of UGT both nationally and in company agreements on redundancy and restructuring. They reflected UGT's objective of depoliticizing industrial relations and steering it in the direction of 'Nordic' models. The ironic result, for some observers, was to limit the scope of industrial relations and to subordinate it to broader political objectives (Martínez Alier 1983).

Modern Spanish Industrial Relations: The Economic Context

Spain, like Portugal, made the transition to democracy at a time of growing economic crisis, with rising inflation and unemployment, a worsening balance of payments and stagnating or even falling GDP. The recession knocked Spanish output per head back to 72 per cent of the European average. Unemployment – which had been insignificant in the early 1970s – rose sharply and remained high despite economic recovery.

These problems were seriously aggravated by the Francoist legacy of an economy that was 'peripheral' to the rest of Europe and based on an inefficient, backward productive structure (Fina 1987). Industry was labour-intensive, used outdated technology and had low levels of productivity and international competitiveness. Radical state-sponsored restructuring was carried out in steel, shipbuilding, and mining and also in consumer durables sectors. Traditional industrial regions such as the Basque country were badly hit. From the mid-1980s, Spain began a phase of economic recovery and growth, with annual growth rates of over 4 per cent, although the early 1990s again saw an extensive round of redundancies.

The structure of employment has been gradually approaching that of the 'advanced' European economies. The total working population in 1994 was 15.5 million of whom 9.7 million were men and 5.8 million women. Agriculture accounted for 1.2 million, which is high compared to the EU average. Services employed 7.1 million while industry and construction accounted for 2.5 million and 1.1 million respectively. Public administration has been a major area of expansion (up by more than 50 per cent as a proportion of total employment between 1976 and 1994), reflecting the long-delayed development of a welfare state, and the creation of new state structures in the autonomous regions or *autonomías* set up under the 1978 Constitution. For men, the participation rate was 63 per cent in 1995. Only 36 per cent of women were economically active, although the figure had been steadily increasing from less than a quarter at the beginning of the 1970s.

Spain has been notable for the very high proportion of the labour force in insecure employment, a reflection of attempts to tackle perceived problems of labour market rigidities and the chronic problem of unemployment, one of the critical issues in Spanish political debate since the advent of democracy. From 4.7 per cent in 1976 unemployment rose to 14.4 per cent in 1981; by the early 1990s the figure had reached well over 20 per cent and remained there, reaching 22.9 per cent in 1995. The unemployment rate for women was considerably worse than for men, peaking at 30.6 per cent in 1995 according to Ministry of Labour figures. A further feature, all the more significant given mass unemployment, is the poor coverage of state unemployment benefit. The extent of youth unemployment has seriously restricted young people's experience of liberal-democratic industrial relations and of jointly regulated workplaces. To some extent the impact of high levels of youth unemployment has been cushioned by young people staying on in the education system and by the continuing importance of family structures. Nonetheless, 42.5 per cent of citizens aged 16–24 were unemployed in 1995 (50 per cent of women in this age group) (Ministerio de Trabajo y Asuntos Sociales 1996).

A number of explanations have been put forward for the peculiar intensity of Spanish unemployment (Fina 1987; Comisión de Expertos 1988; Arasa Medina 1992; Aragón Medina 1993). Observers have pointed variously to the breakdown of the Francoist model of economic growth based on protected product markets, labour-intensive industries and strictly regulated labour markets; the archaic industrial relations legacy of the dictatorship, including labour market rigidities; the prioritizing of monetary policy at the expense of industrial policy in response to the demands of European integration; under-investment in education and training (Aragón Medina 1993; Miguélez 1995); and the rapid increase in Spain's population (from 34 million in 1970 to nearly 40 million two decades later). Responses by the state and the industrial relations actors to the unemployment question, in particular through the pursuit of labour market reform, are considered in a later section.

The Institutions and Actors of Modern Spanish Industrial Relations

The legacy of Francoism and of the transition to democracy has contributed to an industrial relations system with a peculiar set of characteristics. This section provides an overview of the industrial relations actors and institutions that have emerged over the past two decades.

Employers

Characteristics of Spanish Employers

Spain is an economy in which small firms predominate. At the beginning of the 1990s, 41 per cent of workers were in firms with under ten employees, and only 8 per cent in companies with over 500 employees (Sisson et al. 1991: 97). However, this does not necessarily imply that Spain is taking the 'Italian road' to economic growth based on flexible specialization and the dynamism of a modern small-firm sector. Despite the emergence of incipient 'industrial districts' in Catalonia and Madrid, conservatism and paternalistic employment relations, along with the attempted avoidance of regulation, remain the dominant characteristics of small-scale capital in Spain. Union membership and organization tend to be much weaker in small firms and workforces are generally dependent on union bodies external to the workplace, even where elected union representatives exist. The predominance of small-scale enterprise means that their industrial relations and personnel management practices are the prevalent pattern (cf. Prieto 1991: 193–4). Unfortunately, empirical data on the industrial relations of small firms remain relatively scarce; research has concentrated on large companies, and in particular on multinationals.

A second notable feature of Spanish employers is the relative weakness of domestic capital *vis-à-vis* foreign companies, again a legacy of the country's late and dependent pattern of industrialization. The extent of penetration of foreign capital in manufacturing was 29.3 per cent in 1985 rising to 44.5 per cent in 1993; for the economy as a whole, the figure rose from just under 11 per cent in 1985 to 16.4 per cent in 1993 (Martín and Velázquez 1996). By contrast, few Spanish companies are major players on the international scene. Foreign multinationals have been importers of new industrial relations, personnel and human resource management policies into Spanish industry. Under Franco, certain multinationals were in the forefront of developing de facto bargaining with their workforces, and they are among those currently adopting modern HRM practices such as teamworking (see below).

State enterprise, largely created in the 1940s under the Francoist strategy of economic autarchy, has traditionally played a key role in industrialization, notably through the state industrial holding company INI (*Instituto Nacional de Industria*) modelled on the Italian IRI. Some state companies played a symbolic role in the early years of the transition to democracy by developing models of successful democratic industrial relations. From the 1980s, the sector underwent massive rationalization and restructuring, INI was steadily run down as an organizational entity, and many companies were privatized. The Partido Popular government has announced plans to privatize a large proportion of the remaining state enterprises, which employed around 300,000 people in 1996 (EIRR 272, September 1996: 9–10). Public services such as the post office were steadily modernized through the use of temporary contracting and flexible employment measures. The decline of the state's productive role has deprived it of a means of direct regulation of the economy, and could be seen as weakening indigenous capital still further in relation to foreign capital.

Employers' Organizations

The organization of business interests in Spain is highly unitary in formal terms (Pardo and Fernández 1991). The CEOE established a near monopoly of representation following its foundation in 1977. It represents large and small, foreign and national, public and private firms alike, although there has been a tendency to rely on small and medium capital since the multinationals which dominate the large-firm sector tend to be less active in the organization.

CEOE was formed out of various territorial and sectoral organizations, some of them with their roots in the old OSE system. Its structure continues to be based on a mixture of territorial and sectoral bodies combining the economic functions of trade associations with the industrial relations role of employers' associations. Companies are generally members of provincial sectoral federations which in turn have membership of CEOE through provincial intersectoral groupings and through national–sectoral associations. The growth of regional government has encouraged a corresponding decentralization of employers' organizations, and the autonomous communities are an important arena of employer action; one of CEOE's most powerful members is the Catalonian FNT (*Fomento del Trabajo Nacional*).

CEOE's inclusive nature and the wide variety of employer interests that it represents have prompted an organizational style that leaves considerable autonomy to member associations and avoids conflict on issues sensitive to its diverse constituents; occasional breakaways have nevertheless occurred. Though CEOE has tended to follow a more directive line in industrial relations than in other matters, its loose organizational structure has sometimes created problems in getting its member organizations to follow central policy.

CEOE was very much a response to the political conditions of the transition. In the context of an explosion of industrial conflict, employers felt the need for an effective political voice to confront powerful and politicized unions and to deal with the state. It actively attempted to forge an employer identity around deregulatory labour market policies (Martínez Lucio 1991; Martínez Lucio and Blyton 1995) and has supported governments (both socialist and conservative) in their attempts to construct a more deregulated economy (see below).

The Confederation has played an important role in constructing the new framework of industrial relations, pursuing a strategy of collective bargaining and social concertation, and accepting the trade unions as valid partners. Through bipartite and tripartite social pacts in the late 1970s and early 1980s, the employers helped institutionalize industrial relations. The bipartite agreement of 1979 formalized mutual recognition of unions and employers' organizations, while that of 1980 established, for the first time, criteria of representative status in the application of collective agreements (see below). Indeed, for Pardo and Fernández (1991: 170), 'the policy of social concertation has ... been the most significant contribution of [CEOE] to the consolidation of the democratic order, by increasing the country's governability in this crucial and uncertain period'. However, this judgement glosses over CEOE's obsession with limiting the range and content of joint regulation (by confining the agenda of collective bargaining largely to pay issues), and with fragmenting labour representation at both macro- and micro-level by isolating CCOO and favouring the more pragmatic UGT.

The Unions

Structure and Membership

At the end of the 1970s, trade unionism was 'extraordinary complex' and politicized (Miguélez 1991: 214). Subsequently, the structure of representation was clarified by the increasing duopoly of UGT and CCOO. As described above, CCOO emerged out of the spontaneous semi-clandestine workplace organization of the dictatorship period. UGT has a much longer history. Founded in 1888, it has always been closely linked to the Socialist Party, PSOE, founded a few years earlier. Despite its near total eclipse during the dictatorship years, it regained a leading role following the transition to democracy, helped by the establishment of a favourable legal-institutional framework.

The once powerful anarcho-syndicalist tradition has not been able to recapture its dominant position of the early part of the century. It was best represented by CNT, founded in 1910, which claimed 1.2 million members at the time of the Second Republic. CNT has some influence in particular regions and individual plants; so too do breakaways such as CGT (*Confederación General del Trabajo*), which, with its more 'realistic' brand of anarcho-syndicalism, has had some notable successes in workers' committee elections. Other small unions – such as the catholic-influenced USO (*Unión Sindical Obrera*), founded in 1960 – were active during the transition, but their significance has tended to decrease.

More significant are the regional unions, especially ELA–STV (*Solidaridad de Trabajadores Vascos*) in the Basque country, and INTG (*Intersindical Gallega*) in Galicia. These have tended to play a central role in action against state-led restructuring projects in their regions. Their future depends on how regional state structures evolve, and on the political 'space' left to them by the growing unity of action since the late 1980s between UGT and CCOO, both of which are present in substantial numbers within their territories. Other regionally based organizations are important, particularly in agriculture, where the radical SOC (*Sindicato de Obreros del Campo*) was a serious rival to the main unions among Andalusian land labourers in the early 1980s. Another important development has been the growth of independent unions, especially among more skilled, highly paid occupational groups in air and rail transport, health, education and communications.

Union membership is, in the absence of widespread check-off arrangements, difficult to assess (see Miguélez 1991); unpaid dues are a serious problem. The high point of union membership was around 1977–8, when the two main unions had 2.6 million members between them. The unions' own figures and survey findings suggest that density in manufacturing reached 40–45 per cent of the working population in the period of mass mobilization of the late 1970s. Thereafter, unionization fell sharply, and it is currently believed to be below 15 per cent (Jordana 1996). Density appears to vary considerably between sectors and groups of employees, being lower among white-collar and technical staff, especially in private industry; workers in small firms and insecure employment, particularly women and new entrants to the labour market have a low density and, of course, in the burgeoning black economy there is none at all (Miguélez 1991). The reasons for the fall in unionization include mass unemployment, the decline of heavily unionized sectors (engineering, textiles and construction) and the rise in 'precarious' forms of employment, which have eroded the traditional base of union organization. Moreover, the benefits of bargaining extend to unionized and non-unionized workers alike, reducing the incentives for membership.

Plummeting density and financial difficulties have led to talk of a 'crisis of representation' in Spanish unions. However, membership figures give an incomplete picture of union influence. First, Jordana (1996) argues that union membership in the 1970s has been significantly overstated; thus the picture of subsequent decline is misleading. Second, as in France, formal union 'representativeness', for the purposes of reaching collective agreements and for participation in tripartite bodies, is judged according to the results in workplace elections (see below) in which all employees, whether union members or not, are entitled to vote.

Table 15.1 Results in workers' committee elections 1977–1990 (% of delegates)

	1978	1980	1982	1986	1990	1994
UGT	21.7	29.3	36.7	40.9	43.1	34.7
CCOO	34.5	30.9	33.4	34.5	37.6	37.8
ELA-STV	0.9	2.4	3.3	3.3	3.2	3.6
CIG/INTG	–	1.0	1.2	1.3	1.5	1.7
USO	3.9	8.7	4.6	3.8	3.0	5.0*
Other unions	20.8	13.1	8.7	9.5	6.4	n.a.
Non-members	18.2	14.6	12.1	6.7	3.6	n.a.

* Estimate.
Source: Ministry of Labour and Social Security.

Participation of the workforce in these elections is high. In companies where elections take place (in many smaller companies, elections are not held because of a lack of union resources), participation is around 80 per cent, and around three-quarters of the votes go to the two main unions (see table 15.1). Unlike in France, the two major unions have consolidated their position in workers' committee elections and non-union representation has fallen away. The combined share of UGT and CCOO rose from 56.2 per cent in 1978 to 80.6 per cent in 1990 (although it dropped back to 72.5 per cent in 1994, largely as a result of a sharp decline in support for UGT).

Thus the Spanish union movement has been labelled a 'voters' trade unionism' rather than a 'members' trade unionism' (Martín Valverde 1991: 24–5). In other words, influence depends on electoral success as much as on membership figures. In these terms, the main Spanish unions appear to be more favourably regarded and more widely supported by workers than their membership figures might indicate.

Union Organization and Political Relations

A notable feature of Spanish union organization is the close link with political parties and politics generally. CCOO has been relatively more tolerant of internal opposition – its constitution emphasizes the concept of pluralism – and the interplay of politics is more diverse and complex than initial appearances might suggest. The union has also had to adjust to the crisis of the non-PSOE left in Spain which has led to the fragmentation of the traditional communist party. Political factions have been active within UGT, organized on the basis of their degree of support for the PSOE; but factionalism has not been so sustained and formalized, or tolerated, as in CCOO.

Despite subsidies from the state and foreign union movements, and the distribution of the assets of the Francoist OSE and of the traditional unions seized by the Nationalists after the civil war, the financial and organizational resources of Spanish unionism are poor. The extensive network of local union offices has been substantially reduced, particularly affecting the ability of the unions to service members in smaller companies. Head office facilities for research and organizational support have developed, although they do not yet compare with those of German unions. At workplace level, there is a scarcity of able activists outside key sectors.

The union confederations are organized on a dual structure: industrial or sectoral, and territorial. Thus a particular union is a member of both a sectoral federation and geographical multi-sectoral body; though at provincial level there is considerable overlap of union activists. Generally, the sectoral structure has tended to assume the main responsibility for industry negotiations in a particular province, with the territory playing a larger role in the unions' area organization and in relation with regional and local government (Lawlor and Rigby 1986: 258–9). More recently, core industrial federations at territorial level have begun to dominate the regional and provincial structures.

Despite different nuances, the Spanish trade union picture resembles the French case. State institutional support – through representation in tripartite bodies, legally extendable collective agreements, state-defined representativeness, financial support, a legal framework of facilities – may have provided a minimum basis for union action and allowed the movement to consolidate in the aftermath of dictatorship. But at the same time, it has arguably weakened the unions' autonomous capacity to organize and mobilize workers (cf. Estivill and de la Hoz 1990: 284–9); their recognition, legitimacy and influence derive more from the state than from their own members. State-assisted consolidation was probably the only way for UGT to be re-established as a major force, given its extreme organizational weakness at the end of the Francoist period. Conversely, institutionalization has forced CCOO to play down the alternative model of organization that its successful grass-roots activism had made viable at the start of the transition. Moreover, the dominance of the two main confederations has closed off the space for viable alternatives.

None the less, there have been important developments in the dynamics of inter-union relationships over the past decade, particularly a certain rapprochement between UGT and CCOO. The reasons are diverse. One was the growing rift between UGT and PSOE: against a background of European integration and more recently the demands of monetary union, socialist governments of the 1980s and 1990s abandoned socially progressive policies and pushed through legislation to deregulate labour markets, cut state expenditure and reform social security systems. In 1988, UGT and CCOO jointly called a widely-supported 24-hour general strike, forcing concessions from the government. The changes in the communist left in the early 1990s have also removed barriers to co-operation between the two confederations, and in recent years there has been a more pragmatic involvement by CCOO in bargaining over work organization issues at company level. In 1996, in a major development in union relations, the two main confederations launched a co-ordinated joint collective bargaining strategy to extend the remit and content of bargaining, and to lay down bargaining priorities aimed at maintaining employment levels and improving employment security.

The Institutional Framework of Industrial Relations

The period since 1976 has witnessed the establishment of liberal–democratic institutions of industrial relations, and an appropriate legal framework (e.g. Baylos 1991; Falguera i Baró 1991). The system was not created entirely from scratch; the influence of history was strong, for example, in the key role of the labour courts in the regulation of conflict, in employee representation at the workplace, in the role of labour ordinances and in the regulation of collective agreements. The process of institutionalization has been intricately bound up with the political struggles of the transition and with each actor's vision of its place in the system. Labour legislation was based on formal and informal negotiation involving unions and employers as well as political parties. The PSOE government and CEOE were generally able to ensure that the organizational interests of UGT prevailed and were embodied in legislation: a notable example is the legislative support for the workplace union branch, a form of organization favoured by UGT.

The first step towards the new industrial relations was the legalization of unions and recognition of the right to strike in 1977, subsequently embodied in the 1978 Constitution which also provided for a basic framework in the shape of the Workers' Statute (*Estatuto de los Trabajadores*). The Statute was finally passed in March 1980. Amended on several occasions, it still constitutes the 'centrepiece of Spanish labour law' (Martín Valverde 1991: 89). It is concerned, first, with the individual employment relationship, introducing some flexibility into the rigid Francoist system of regulation. Second, it lays down the procedures and scope of collective bargaining, consolidating the *erga omnes* principle whereby agreements apply to all workers and employers in a given bargaining domain. This type of agreement has been the most common throughout Spanish labour history. Third, the Statute formalized workers' participation within the enterprise through workers' committees and delegates, bodies which yet again have their historical antecedents in the Francoist institutions of *jurados* and *delegados sindicales*.

A second major statute is the Law of Trade Union Freedom (LOLS – *Ley Orgánica de Libertad Sindical*) of 1985 which develops the right of freedom of association and regulates the activities of unions. It provides statutory support for workplace union branches (*secciones sindicales*). Most importantly, it extends the notion of union representativeness by granting the status of 'most representative union' to unions gaining at least 10 per cent of representative posts nationally in workplace elections (or 15 per cent at regional state level). The 'most representative' unions are entitled to certain facilities within the enterprise and have the right to negotiate generally applicable collective agreements. They are represented on tripartite public bodies such as the National Employment Institute (INEM) which runs unemployment offices and administers the benefit system. The 'most representative' status has also been a major criterion for redistributing the accumulated assets of the old Francoist vertical unions.

A further notable feature of the institutional framework is the continuing role of labour law in the conduct of industrial relations. Recourse to the labour courts rather than (or in addition to) internal company disputes procedures has been a common form of individual grievance-handling on matters ranging from overtime pay to compensation for dismissals; more recently, however, extra-judicial mechanisms have been used more. The courts also play a large part in the settlement of collective disputes of rights, for example over the application or interpretation of collective agreements. However the legal framework in areas such as health and safety, the labour ordinances and employment contracting was, until the early 1990s, dysfunctional and bureaucratic; traditional and understaffed institutions have found it difficult to deal with the growing workloads created by increasing democratic demands. This framework has been steadily reformed through a transfer of state functions such as health and safety, and of work organization issues covered by labour ordinances, to the industrial relations actors themselves (see below).

As in Germany and France, there is a regulatory framework of workplace industrial relations, built around the institution of the *comité de empresa*. Elections for workers' committees and workers' delegates (*delegados de personal*) take place every four years (see table 15.1). The system of workplace representation, while formally separate from the structure of union representation, has come to be closely linked with it. The unions are very strongly represented on the *comités* and among workers' delegates, and have a key role in the electoral process; this is important since it is the workers' committee that is empowered to reach collective agreements with the company (Escobar 1995). Union branch organization at the workplace is generally linked closely with the workers' committee.

In most companies, the workers' committee is under the majority control of the two main unions although it is common for neither union to have a majority. As a result, the effectiveness of the committees has varied with the quality of the relationship between the two unions. This is particularly important when it comes to negotiating formal company collective agreements, since under the Workers' Statute, agreements must be signed by more than 50 per cent of workers' committee members in order to be legally binding on all employees. When relations between the two major unions are strained, as in the mid-1980s, the role of the committees is therefore weakened. In such circumstances UGT in particular has sometimes used the trade union workplace branch as the vehicle for negotiations with management, isolating CCOO and fragmenting worker representation (Martínez Lucio 1989).

Macro-level Relations between State, Labour and Capital

One of the key elements of the institutionalization process in Spain is the complex nature of political concertation between state, capital and labour. With the democratic transition, the uneven character of Spanish capitalism and state organization became increasingly apparent, as did the peculiar character of Spanish

Fordism (Barbiano 1993). The state had to be developed along northern European lines – just when the northern European model was itself entering crisis. A double transition was therefore required. Emerging political elites had to manage diverse regional, social and economic demands and to reorganize the economic system at a time of mounting 'disorganizaton', to use Lash and Urry's term (1987). At the same time, the unions were conscious of the need to strengthen the legitimacy of the new social and economic system, in the face of uncertainties and dangers. The response was to impart a peculiar set of characteristics to Spanish industrial relations at the macro-level. Between 1977 and 1986, there was a process of national concertation which involved, at various times, the government, political parties, CEOE, and the union confederations. The agreements of this period of 'weak neo-corporatism' can be seen as an attempt at tripartite or bipartite exchange in which wage control was accepted by the unions in return for government or employer concessions in areas like trade union law and job creation.

Against a background of a wage explosion and escalating industrial conflict, the Moncloa Pacts of October 1977 (signed by the political parties alone, but with the backing of the main union confederations) established a framework for policies on pay, employment and social security during the transition years. However, as with many later agreements, the wage controls were generally implemented effectively but the broader reforms were either delayed or ignored.

Concertation was also an arena of inter-union rivalry, and complex three-way politics were played out as the actors fought to consolidate their position. CCOO became increasingly marginalized, allowing UGT to establish itself institutionally and politically. This partly reflected CEOE's policy of favouring UGT. CCOO was excluded from the Basic Interconfederal Agreement (ABI) of 1979 and the Interconfederal Framework Agreement (AMI) of 1980. CCOO had its own reservations about concertation, fearing it would undermine unity of action built upward from the workplace. But the 1981 National Agreement on Employment (ANE), signed following the attempted military coup d'état of February, was truly tripartite, involving government, employers and both major unions. It offered employment creation and a range of other social measures in return for wage moderation. CCOO also participated in the Interconfederal Agreement (AI) of 1983, following the socialists' election victory in 1982. But when PSOE invited all the economic actors to discuss a new tripartite agreement, the AES (Economic and Social Agreement), CCOO once again felt unable to sign, concerned at the failure of the agreement to ensure the implementation of social measures.

The unions supported concertation, first, as a means of consolidating democracy. Second, however, they saw it as a way of legitimizing themselves as actors and of institutionalizing the rules of industrial relations. Thus some of the unions' recompense for wage moderation took the form of 'organizational benefits' (Roca 1991). Both major confederations took part in the deliberations leading to the 1980 Workers' Statute and had a considerable influence on its content. Third, the unions hoped for social benefits. More often than not, they were disappointed, and this was one of the principal causes of the decline in union interest in concertation from the mid-1980s, and the growing rapprochement between the two major confederations. The break between UGT and the PSOE government was triggered by the governments' refusal to accede to union demands at the time of the AES of 1984–6 (Gillespie 1990). On the pay front, too, the unions felt disillusioned by concertation. Generally, lower-level collective agreements stayed within the bands established by successive national pacts (Roca 1991: 367). After the end of the neo-corporatist phase, pay bargaining took place without any effective national framework or wage bands for the private sector. However there continued to be piecemeal negotiations between government, employers and the unions over aspects of labour regulation.

As Roca (1991) argues, concertation was a rational employer response at a time of union strength when no actor wished to see an all-out confrontation in view of the political fragility of democracy. By the mid-1980s, however, the disadvantages were outweighing the benefits. From the late 1980s, recession and the unions' own organizational difficulties meant that employers (and government) had less incentive to contain union demands through concertation. Nor were employers keen to pay for wage moderation with improved social provision and possibly expansionist economic policies. Thus they favoured bipartite agreements that did not involve broader social policy commitments by the government. They felt that they had gained little by government involvement; CEOE argued that the government was failing to implement its agreed commitments in areas vital to the competitiveness of Spanish business, such as the reform of corporate taxation, the reduction of employers' social security contributions, and the deregulation of labour markets. Employers were motivated, too, by fear of an explosion in the public sector and an expanding welfare state. Finally, their agenda had changed. Corporate restructuring, flexibility and international competitiveness were replacing inflation as their principal concerns. National concertation was thought to help maintain labour market rigidities and centralized, standardized collective bargaining outcomes (López Novo 1991).

The employers' lack of commitment to concertation reflects a political as well as an economic rationale. From the outset, CEOE resisted strong forms of corporatist involvement in order to avoid the institutionalization of relations between state and labour, and to prevent the development of a strong social dimension (Martínez Lucio 1991; Martínez Lucio and Blyton 1995). CEOE's strategy, reflecting its difficulties in forging a political identity and 'voice' for a highly fragmented employer class, lay in depicting employers as a force for social progress prevented from fulfilling their mission by the restrictions imposed by labour and social democratic governments. The representation of employers' interests thus assumed a highly antagonistic quality, as in the vehement support for labour market deregulation.

For government, too, the value of concertation diminished from the mid-1980s. The long period of PSOE government under Felipe González provided political and economic stability and helped entrench democratic institutions (although well before the end of the PSOE era, mounting government corruption was calling political stability into question). The need for tripartite peak bargaining as a political stabilizer therefore diminished. The socialists felt secure enough following their second election victory in 1986 to risk their close alliance with UGT, and a softer variant of Thatcherite economic and monetary discipline emerged; strong concertation had no place.

The decline of concertation puts into perspective the academic debate on the subject. On the one hand, writers such as Pérez Díaz (1984) see concertation as evidence of the creation of a Spanish neo-corporatism, albeit of a weaker kind than in northern or central Europe. Roca (1983; 1991) by contrast has argued that corporatism was not the only rational response to the requirements of the transition. Rather, it had to be seen more as a 'strategy' for coping with social conflict and generating consensus, initiated by government in response to a particular conjuncture. The absence of corporatist arrangements after 1986 tends to support Roca's interpretation. Indeed, it may be argued that the success of neo-corporatism as a governmental strategy in Spain has resided precisely in its contingent, non-institutionalized character. There have been some indications of instutitionalization, chief among them the formation of the tripartite national consultative body, the Economic and Social Council (CES). There has also been formal participation by employers and unions in existing state bodies such as the National Employment Institute (INEM). A new tripartite-based body to regulate health and safety at work also potentially broadens the role of employers and unions in this critical area of industrial relations. However, such developments have tended to be limited and ritualistic: CES was repeatedly delayed and it was only established in 1992, over 15 years after its proposal in the Constitution.

The informality of corporatist arrangements has given the government considerable flexibility, allowing it to convene negotiations at some junctures and to keep its distance from them at others. This 'strategic displacement' in decision-making has been a central feature of economic policy in democratic Spain (Martínez Lucio 1983; Foweraker 1989). When national concertation did not accord legitimacy to government policy, the government sought legitimacy elsewhere: for example by exploiting its parliamentary majority, as it did in the crises over cutbacks in state pensions in 1985 and over the state-sponsored industrial restructuring programme of 1983. One implication of this fluidity is that when conditions are appropriate, the government is likely to turn once again to concertation as a political tool. Indeed, this seems to have been the case since the beginning of the 1990s (see below), in response to the challenge of European integration, and to changes in the balance of political power following the December 1988 general strike. The conservative PP government has continued this approach since 1996, developing a relationship with the labour movement on issues of immediate sensitivity, as with the agreements on stabilizing pensions and on subsidies to agricultural workers.

▌ Collective Bargaining

▌ The Structure of Bargaining

The politics of incomes was one of the principal obsessions of Spanish industrial relations in the 1980s. Arguments about the need to maintain Spain's international

Table 15.2 Collective bargaining in Spain, 1977–1994

	No. of agreements	Employees (000s)	Companies (000s)
1977	1,349	2,876	557
1980	2,564	6,070	878
1984	3,796	6,182	837
1988	4,039	6,805	958
1992	5,010	7,921	1,055
1994	4,581	7,502	950

Source: Ministry of Labour and Social Security.

competitiveness or, alternatively, about the need to improve workers' living standards, were wheeled out in ritualistic debates. Measures of inflation, past and forecast were a key reference point (e.g. Espina 1991), becoming part of the internal organizational politics of unions and employers' associations. Union branches showed their loyalty by achieving the percentages laid down by their national leadership, either by restraining increases as part of the 'social wage' logic of the UGT for most of the 1980s, or by breaking the national objectives set in tripartite or bipartite national bargaining between government, UGT and CEOE, as was the case of CCOO during the neo-corporatist period.

The official statistics of the Ministry of Labour and Social Security present a picture of apparently healthy collective bargaining in Spain. In 1980, around 6 million employees were covered by collective bargaining; by 1994, some 7.5 million workers were covered by over 4,500 collective agreements applying to 951,00 companies (see table 15.2). The statistics also suggest a relatively centralized pattern of bargaining. Although 3,235 of the agreements signed in 1994 (around 75 per cent of the total) were concluded at company level, these affected only just over a million workers, the remainder being covered by higher-level agreements. The annual process of collective bargaining is also relatively centralized: it has generally been directed from the head offices of employers' organizations and trade union confederations, although until recently the unions have rarely been able to co-ordinate their bargaining strategies at a national level. The two major confederations are the dominant bargaining agents on the union side: CCOO and UGT were involved in 96 per cent of all agreements, and 86 per cent of company agreements, in 1995.

Above the company level there were two main types of agreement: provincial–sectoral and national–sectoral. In numerical terms, the former has predominated, covering 4.1 million workers, compared with 1.8 million in national–sectoral agreements in 1995. Provincial–sectoral agreements are important in industries such as metalworking and in hotels and catering. In theory the provincial–sectoral level is the vital level for the millions of workers in small and medium-sized concerns who have no company agreement or effective and independent representation structures at the workplace. Paradoxically, despite its importance, it is also the least studied level of bargaining. Among the most important national–sectoral agreements are private-sector banking (covering 162,000), chemicals (160,000), metalworking in the Vizcaya and Guipúzcoa regions (108,000), and large department stores (100,000) (EIRR 1996a). Other industries with national agreements include construction and textiles.

For many trade unionists and employers, the national industry agreement for the chemicals sector served as a point of reference for sectoral bargaining. Running for much of the 1980s, the agreement allowed the 'social partners' to deal consistently with wages, working hours, and the replacement of aspects of the labour ordinances, and in so doing to develop a strong consensual relationship. The 1988 chemicals agreement was the first to replace the job classification system provided for under the ordinances.

For employers, sectoral agreements seemed an effective means of adjusting incomes and tying them to changes within an industry. Thus negotiated wage increases barely kept pace with inflation, even in the late 1980s, although there was considerable variation from sector to sector. For the unions the attraction of such agreements was that they 'regulated' small and medium-sized employers while also strengthening the sectoral dimensions of their organizations, the effectiveness of which had been limited by the territorial dimension.

But despite the extent and apparent health of collective bargaining, the system has suffered from a number of weaknesses. First, it is estimated that around 25 per cent of workers are not covered by collective agreements of any description. In several industries, including fishing, freight haulage, mining and wood industries, there are no sectoral agreements; this means that many employees, particularly in smaller firms, may not be covered by bargaining. The absence of sectoral bargaining in many cases reflects the weakness or non-existence of sectoral employer organization (EIRR 1995).

Second, there has been much talk of the 'poverty of bargaining', and agreements have often covered a narrow range of employment issues. Many agreements merely reproduce the provisions of legal regulations, or of labour ordinances (EIRR 1995a: 26). Most deal primarily with the regulation of pay rates and of basic working-time issues. This is true also at company level. The annual studies of collective bargaining in companies with over 200 workers, conducted by the Ministry for the Economy (Ministerio de Economía y Hacienda 1995), have pointed to a limited negotiating agenda, and to difficulties in bringing subjects other than pay and working time to the bargaining table. The area of training remains underdeveloped even in larger firms. In some companies, especially multinationals, extensive bargaining does take place over a wide range of issues: in recent years, for example, issues to do with the control of temporary contracting and numerical flexibility have increasingly become the subject of bargaining (Consejo Económico y Social 1996: 269), significantly extending the scope of negotiation. But 'rich' bargaining remains the exception.

Third, bargaining is extremely fragmented. Most industrial sectors are broken down into a multiplicity of sub-sectors; this is particularly the case in food, distribution, and transport.

Fourth, as in Italy, the 'articulation' between agreements at sector and company level has until recently been weak and confused, and the responsibilities of different levels have been ill-defined. The vast majority of the several thousand agreements signed annually were entirely uncoordinated with higher or lower agreements.

Finally, the bargaining effectiveness of union organization varies widely between provinces and regions. While Barcelona, Madrid, Valencia, and a few other regions are well organized, the unions are considerably weaker elsewhere. At establishment level, moreover, particularly in smaller companies, the representative arrangements vital for monitoring implementation appear to be inoperative; while even in larger ones, most workers' committee delegates fail to use their allocation of time for workplace activity. Even in a relatively well-organized region such as Madrid, employers in metalworking have tended to implement the wage element of the agreement while ignoring other provisions; in construction, resistance on the part of provincial employers has proved a stumbling block to implementing agreements. In short, the national and provincial sectoral agreements cannot be considered a fully effective system of bargaining.

Overall, therefore, collective bargaining has been less centralized and more uneven and fragmented than would at first appear. The strategy of both CCOO and UGT has been to promote the rationalization of bargaining structures, and to broaden bargaining content. CCOO has always been less hostile to decentralized bargaining, which it sees as enhancing the participation of workers, and as providing an impetus to union activity during workplace elections.

The employers and CEOE showed a growing interest in decentralized bargaining from the late 1980s – for rather different reasons. In their view higher-level agreements enforced excessively homogeneous conditions across a wide range of companies. One particular area of 'rigidity' was the limited flexibility of employers to award differential increases to different segments of the labour force (the chemicals industry agreement is one of the few that permits the negotiated pay increase to be applied to the total wage bill of a company, rather than to each occupational grouping). Employers saw this as a particular problem given the erosion of pay differentials in the transition (Dolado and Bentolila 1992). Companies responded with deals on the margins of formal negotiations, involving particular workplaces and occupational groups, in order to restore differentials for key groups of skilled employees (Ruesga 1991: 392). The Ministry of Economy survey for 1994 shows continuing widening of differentials in bargaining in large companies.

▌ The Reform of Bargaining Structures

In recent years, major reform of collective bargaining arrangements has taken place, with significant implications for bargaining scope, content and co-ordination. In 1994, revisions to the 1980 Workers' Statute (see EIRR 1995a) allowed unions and employers to negotiate freely on a range of issues previously fixed by law. These included the duration and remuneration of certain kinds of fixed-term contract, the length of probationary periods, assignment of workers to occupational categories, and the distribution of working time over the course of the year. This removal of statutory constraints on bargaining topics increased the potential for 'enriching' the content of bargaining. But it could also be seen as risking reductions in standards below legal minima in areas where unions were weak. Moreover, a controversial provision of the 1994 legislation made it compulsory for collective agreements to set out the conditions under which companies in economic difficulties could 'opt-out' of implementing the pay terms agreed. Such obligatory *cláusulas de descuelgue* could be judged to undermine the potential effectiveness of sectoral agreements. However, UGT concluded that in the 1995 round, bargaining had proved effective in maintaining labour rights and minimizing the deregulatory impact of the 1994 reform. Fears that more individualized and variable pay systems might be introduced appear to have proved groundless (EIRR 1996a: 21).

The 1994 reform also addressed the question of 'articulation' between bargaining levels by explicitly defining the issues to be reserved to each level. Multi-industry 'inter-professional' agreements had responsibility for setting out voluntary procedures for resolving disputes relating to the interpretation of agreements, and for defining the process of substitution of labour ordinances by collective agreements. In 1996, an important national level agreement between CEOE, CEPYME and the two major union confederations established provisions for compulsory mediation in sectoral industrial disputes. Issues for sectoral collective bargaining include procedures for the use of opt-out clauses and the duration of certain fixed-term contracts. Reserved to company level are the determination of pay rates under the opt-out clause, and the amendment of higher-level agreements in relation to working time, payment by results and work organization; company agreements may also regulate areas such as occupational classifications and daily working hours where these are not covered by higher level agreements.

A second area of reform has been the repeal of statutory labour ordinances. The gradual replacement of regulations by collective bargaining had been going on since the early 1980s, but in 1994 legislation decreed that the ordinances would no longer have the force of law, and set a timetable for replacing them in several dozen sectors and sub-sectors through national sectoral bargaining. Agreements had to cover (as a minimum) the areas of occupational grading, disciplinary measures, promotion, and pay structures (see EIRR 1996b). In the mid-1990s a range of agreements have been signed in sectors as diverse as cement, wood and cork, and hotel and catering (whose employers had resisted such developments) (UGT 1996). Some of these have supplemented existing national agreements in areas previously regulated by the ordinances; others have set up sectoral agreements for the first time.

The endpoint of these developments is still uncertain. On the one hand, they do appear to have opened up new possibilities for the bargaining system. The replacement of the ordinances, with their detailed regulation of work organization and internal labour market structures, widens the potential content of negotiation. There are indications that unions are prepared to enter into an exchange, particularly at company level, making concessions on issues of functional flexibility in return for more joint control and limitations on numerical flexibility (see below).

However, the unions are concerned about the uneven strength of labour negotiators in different sectors and regions, and the scope exists for a weakening of labour rights on questions such as geographical and functional mobility, particularly in areas where collective bargaining was able to undermine statutory provision. There were also internal dissenters in the unions who saw the emerging style of concession bargaining as weakening historic achievements of the labour movement. However, a greater obstacle to the dissemination of such trade-offs is likely to be the ambivalence of the employers and their organizations to a deepening of employee involvement. In general, while the unions see labour reforms as a way of widening the remit of negotiation, employers are interested in limiting its scope and in moving to a more voluntarist model of industrial relations (Consejo Económico y Social 1996: 233, 239).

The Development of Company-based Employment Strategies

Spain, like other southern European countries, exhibits increasing labour market duality and fragmentation. Many employers have called for further flexibility and company-oriented approaches. Multinational firms have been in the forefront of innovative industrial relations policies such as quality circles, individualized payment systems, teamworking and multiskilling, notably in motor manufacturing plants (e.g. Martínez and Weston 1994; Ortiz forthcoming). Smaller employers have also been looking to the techniques and practices of human resource management as a way of pre-empting strong and independent labour representation. However, the implementation of such techniques has been patchy and uneven, and numerical flexibility has had a higher priority than functional flexibility (Pérez Díaz and Rodríguez 1995: 181–2).

In recent years, the changes in the labour ordinances and the reform of the Workers' Statute have opened the way to the treatment of new work organization issues at company level. Workers' committee structures are in some cases facilitating a more enterprise-based strategy in what were once key bastions of the labour movement. As a result, as in many other European countries, company bargaining is increasingly seen as a way of addressing issues of corporate rationalization through company 'viability' plans, and strategies of greater flexibility.

In some larger firms, processes of 'micro-concertation' similar to those in Italy have been discernible. This was evident, for example, in the landmark agreement of 1994 in the state-owned metalworking enterprise (INI/TENEO) which replaced the labour ordinances with provisions on new job classifications, functional flexibility, and working-time arrangements. In exchange, the company granted broader employee involvement in issues never formally discussed before, such as functional flexibility.

Against the background of an unemployment rate approaching 23 per cent, another kind of exchange has concerned agreements to maintain employment levels, or to create jobs, in return for union concessions on pay. An example was the 1995 agreement in the Spanish subsidiary of the German multinational Benckiser, Cosméticos Cotyastor, to create 142 new jobs whose occupants would be paid 30 per cent less than normal company rates for the following 5 years (EIRR 1996a: 21). An innovative recent agreement is the March 1997 accord in Seat, the motor manufacturer owned by Volkswagen; under its provisions, only two hours of Saturday shifts are paid, the remainder being put into an 'hours account' which is used to provide paid time off and thus minimize recourse to lay-offs when production falls (*Vanguardia*, 2 March 1997).

In general, however, such developments have been patchy, and a wider debate on functional flexibility and on new worker rights and roles in Spain has not so far emerged. One reason for the limited development of company-based employment strategies is that multinational subsidiaries in Spain tend to be less interested in importing the involvement and skill formation dimensions of innovative working practices. CCOO, for example, argues that teamworking is being implemented without extensive attention to training and multiskilling, and with only minor emphasis on the participatory dimension (CCOO 1994; Blanco 1996). This reflects the structure of many multinationals in Spain: subsidiary plants are not always high value-added operations and their management structures are often subservient to the dictats of international headquarters.

A further obstacle to such practices is that line management in Spain has remained highly traditional and paternalistic in many cases. In a context of low or variable trust in industrial relations, managers are resistant to opening up dialogue with the workforce, fearing that it will be exploited by the unions. There is also concern that unions may subvert innovations such as teamworking by, for example, competing in team leader elections (Blyton and Martínez Lucio 1995). Research by the author in car manufacturing and postal services suggests very little interest amongst line managers in alternative management techniques that enhance worker involvement.

Collective Bargaining and the Institutionalization of Conflict

A final aspect of collective bargaining is its role in the institutionalization of conflict. In the late 1970s, the mass mobilizations that linked political and economic demands resulted in a major upsurge in conflict. At the 1979 peak, 5.7 million workers participated in 2,680 strikes (see table 15.3). Spain has continued to have one of the highest rates of strike action in Europe. Total working days lost in 1993 were, at 250 per 1000 employees, higher than for any other EU country except Greece. However, the trend in recent years, discounting the distorting effect of the 24-hour general strikes in certain years, appears to be downwards. From the mid-1980s the emergence of 'productivity coalitions' in larger private sector companies, and the use by multinationals of the lever of investment (or the threat of disinvestment) to secure workforce co-operation, have led to changes in the culture of conflict in such sectors as electronics and car manufacturing. Short but irregular stoppages around work organization issues are not uncommon – but they are very different from the broader picture of 'mobilization' apparent from the mid-1970s to mid-1980s.

Table 15.3 Industrial conflict in Spain 1976–1995

	Strikes	Participants (000s)	Working days lost (000s)
1976	1,568	3,639	13,752
1977	1,194	2,956	16,642
1978	1,128	3,864	11,551
1979	2,680	5,713	18,917
1980 .	1,365	1,710	6,178
1981	1,307	1,126	6,154
1982	1,225	875	2,788
1983	1,451	1,484	4,417
1984	1,498	2,242	6,358
1985	1,092	1,511	3,224
1986	914	858	2,279
1987	1,497	1,881	5,025
1988	1,193	6,692	11,641
	(1,192)	(1,894)	(6,853)
1989	1,047	1,382	3,685
1990	1,231	863	2,442
1991	1,552	1,944	4,421
1992	1,296	5,169	6,246
	(1,295)	(1,678)	(4,055)
1993	1,131	997	2,012
1994	890	5,427	6,254
	(889)	(452)	(1,279)
1995	827	511	1,261

Data in brackets exclude figures for general strikes.
Source: Ministry of Labour and Social Security.

Large, long-lasting strikes with significant economic impact still occur – a notable recent example being the 1997 lorry-drivers' strike, echoing the similar French action of late 1996. There have also been major outbreaks of conflict in traditional sectors affected by massive restructuring, such as mining, shipbuilding and steel. However, many strikes occur as an almost ritualistic accompaniment to the collective bargaining process, reflecting routine union pressure on the employer in the course of negotiations rather than the breakdown of negotiations. In addition, many public services are subject to limitations on industrial action through 'minimum service' provisions. Lockouts are rare in Spain, largely because of legal restrictions.

Fragmentation in the Labour Market: A Destabilizing Influence

One of the major issues facing the industrial relations actors has been the reorganization of the labour market. In the context of government attempts to address the unemployment problem, and of employers' pressure for liberalization, deregulation has been presented as the key to overcoming rigidities that have supposedly stifled enterprise and modernization.

One of the most impressive manifestations of this approach has been the explosion of atypical employment. Successive bouts of deregulation opened the way for a range of more flexible contracts; around 15 different kinds of contract have been introduced by governments since the early 1980s. Temporary employment was the main area of expansion. By 1995, 32 per cent of the labour force (28.6 per cent of men and 38 per cent of women) were on fixed-term contracts, up from 16 per cent in 1987.

The increase affected all industrial sectors, although it was uneven across the economy, with particularly notable rises in services and construction. In the public sector, the proportion of non-permanent employees was much lower but rising. Temporary contracts were also much more common in smaller firms, among women workers (EIRR 1995b: 28), and among new entrants to the labour force. Unlike other EU countries, part-time employment is little used – it affected 6 per cent of the wage-earning population in 1995 compared with 13 per cent in the Community as a whole; one reason is the relatively low rate of female participation in the labour force (see Cousins 1994 for a discussion of gender and flexibility in Britain and Spain).

Even these figures understate the degree of de facto deregulation. Thus, although formally employers were prohibited from keeping workers on temporary contracts for long periods, in practice they have been able to evade the restrictions of the law by switching between different kinds of short-term contract (including work experience, job training and work-sharing contracts); such means were used even by large public employers such as the Post Office.

The deregulatory trend has continued into the 1990s. In 1994, 'urgent measures to promote employment' were introduced by decree-law, despite bitter union opposition. These liberalized placement services and introduced yet another new kind of temporary contract – the so-called 'apprenticeship contract' of up to 3 years' duration, paid at rates below the national minimum wage. The measures also increased incentives for part-time work, reducing part-timers' social security protection and hence making it cheaper to employ them.

Such developments rest on, and reinforce, the problematic belief that controlling labour costs is the key to economic regeneration and employment and that labour market flexibility is a principal factor in this (Miguélez 1995). Trade unions, unsurprisingly, have regarded labour market deregulation as contributing to the extensive casualization of employment, and they fear that the explosion of atypical contracts is undermining observation of health and safety regulations and inhibiting the acquisition of skills (cf. Pérez Amorós and Rojo 1991). Moreover, the changing structure of employment may be detrimental to membership, since temporary employees are less likely than more secure workers to be in unions or to organize in support of claims.

Other observers, however, have taken a more sanguine view. Segura and Malo de Molina (1991: 110) suggest that temporary contracts can act as a transition to more stable employment, and a form of regulation of the conditions of non-core workers. Policy-makers saw greater flexibility in the employment relation as a way of avoiding the expansion of the uncontrolled submerged economy in sectors such as textiles and footwear, although in practice the submerged economy has been tolerated as a way of allowing new entrepreneurs a breathing space to establish their activities.

The profound qualitative and quantitative transformation of the labour market in Spain requires closer scrutiny, especially because of its potential to destabilize the evolving institutional framework of Spanish industrial relations in both social and political terms.

One major effect of labour market segmentation has been to reinforce the diversity of workers' employment experiences. In a peculiar manner this limits the impact of unemployment. The effect of state-sponsored restructuring in larger concerns in the 1980s was to exclude large groups of organized workers, in core sectors and segments of the workforce, from active involvement in the struggle against unemployment. In key sectors such as motor manufacturing, company 'viability' plans tied collective bargaining into broader agreements on restructuring (Martínez Lucio 1989). Higher than average redundancy payments, largely financed – directly or indirectly – by the state were a central element in these agreements. Innovations such as the Employment Promotion Funds, agreed by UGT and the PSOE in 1983, also helped limit potential conflict in key areas of industry undergoing change. The funds guaranteed redundant workers longer periods of unemployment benefit if they put their redundancy payments into a fund which subsequent employers could use to give them employment on the same terms and conditions as before; in practice they were little used.

In the crucial period of the early to mid-1980s, this approach to restructuring was underpinned by UGT's strategy of co-operation involving, in contrast to CCOO's rhetoric, a rejection of workers' mobilization and an emphasis on negotiation with the employer to establish long-term corporate viability. Thus the strategies of UGT, employers and the state helped isolate and defuse this potentially disruptive sphere of industrial relations. It was mainly CCOO and minority unions close to it that used the issue for worker mobilization and political engagement during the 1980s. The arena of redundancy, along with pay, became a focus of union politics.

The state's role in this area is also illuminating. There has been an ongoing obsession with the argument that labour market regulation impedes restructuring by putting obstacles in the way of redundancies. The compulsory special redundancy procedure (*expediente de crisis* or *expediente de regulación de empleo*), which like so many aspects of Spanish industrial relations has a long tradition in labour law, required redundancies to be officially authorized in the absence of agreement by workers' representatives. In addition, the high cost of shedding labour on permanent contracts was supposedly a further deterrent to employment 'adjustment' in firms. For this reason 'labour market reform', making it easier and cheaper for companies to dismiss workers has become the panacea for unemployment and low labour market involvement (Jimeno and Toharia 1993).

The 'urgent measures to promote employment' of 1994 extended the grounds for collective redundancies to include 'organizational and production' reasons.

However, employers regarded this reform as insufficient in practice: should a court find that dismissal was unjustified (*improcedente*), compensation was at a much higher rate than the statutory minimum: 45 days' pay per year of service, up to a ceiling of 42 months' pay, compared with the 20 days and twelve months ceiling where redundancies were justified on 'objective' economic grounds. Most companies preferred to pay the higher rate voluntarily rather than risk lengthy and costly legal action (EIRR 277, February 1997: 13). In April 1997, under intense pressure from the PP government, employers and unions signed a national agreement clarifying the grounds for dismissal, and in effect making it easier for companies at risk of losses to declare redundancies on economic grounds. The agreement, which will require legislative changes to the Workers' Statute, also allows companies to employ younger people on long-term contracts with much lower redundancy pay entitlements (33 days' pay per year of service, with a ceiling of 24 months' pay) compared to those already in permanent employment (*El País Digital*, 9th April 1997).

None the less, the issue of redundancy may be regarded as much one of political symbolism as of practical labour market reform, since in some regards the system has allowed greater flexibility than at first appears. The creation of IMAC in January 1979 was a response to union reactions to the use of redundancy procedures. Individualized contract terminations through IMAC became far more significant than the more collective *expediente de crisis*, which accounted for little more than a quarter of total redundancies and dismissals. The termination of a contract via IMAC allowed workers to reach an individual agreement with their employer. The employer recognized that the termination was unjustified and hence that the employee had a legal right to compensation; in return the worker was compensated and received statutory social security benefits without having to go through the usual route of the labour courts. Although redundancy payments were often relatively high, employers' costs were more predictable and the process more speedy than the legal route, permitting easier planning for the introduction of new technology and other changes. Employers also avoided the 'opening the books' and the more extensive union involvement traditionally associated with the *expediente de crisis*. In short, as Bilbao (1991) argues, conflict between labour and capital was individualized. A cumulative total of 3.1 million workers were dismissed from their jobs in the critical period between 1978 and 1988 when union responses to restructuring were at their greatest (Falguera i Baró 1991: 285). In 1995, according to CCOO, two million people lost their jobs and 63 per cent of these received no compensation owing to their temporary contract status. Of those redundancies involving employees on permanent contracts – some 247,000 – the majority took place through the individualized forum of UMAC (formally IMAC) and only 20 per cent passed through the tribunal system (*Gaceta Sindical*, September–October 1996: 29–30). The sheer volume of job loss, taken together with the rise in temporary contracts outlined earlier, suggests that the widely held view concerning the 'rigidity' of the Spanish labour market is something of a myth.

Union responses to the evolution of the labour market have been constrained by their own organizational dynamics. Both UGT and CCOO have developed structures for women and youth (and in the case of CCOO, immigrants as well).

But these have yet to be fully integrated into organizational power structures, for example through voting rights at conference. More recent trends, particularly the increasing importance of public sector members, often facing casualization of employment, may influence the internal politics of the unions on substantive issues such as welfare rights, and encourage them to give greater organizational weight to new interests and groups.

Criticism of the influence of core groups of workers in key industries and large companies, with their protectionist interest in permanent and protected employment (Recio 1991), may be valid; but such influence has to be understood in the context of complex organizational influences and the wider political strategies of the two major unions. The unions' strength is, as described earlier, still concentrated in a few key sectors and regions. In addition, their organizational emphasis has been on sectoral realignments and mergers. As a result, far-reaching industrial transformation has not in general challenged the internal order of the major unions. Their ability to initiate alternative organizational strategies is further constrained, first, by their engagement with the state's regulatory structures and their extensive relations with the party-political system; and second, by a process of bureaucratization that has undermined the 'historic' participation mechanisms of the assembly, workplace delegates, and involvement in external community relations and politics. All have helped reinforce the isolation of industrial relations action within an increasingly institutionalized sphere. This is exemplified by the willingness of the unions to negotiate the 1997 national agreement on labour market reform with CEOE.

Conclusions: Trade Unions, Employers and the Modernization of Industrial Relations – Operationalizing the State?

The strategies of industrial relations actors in Spain have to contend with a complex social and economic context on the one hand and an increasingly complex state form on the other. The PSOE government from 1982–96 helped consolidate some of the key features of industrial relations and the welfare state, although it embraced an uneasy mixture of progressive reform and liberal deregulation which soured relations between PSOE and UGT from 1988. The growing distance between union and party encouraged the development of a more coherent set of macro-economic and industrial relations policies – based around the pursuit of labour market deregulation and the containment of state social programmes – which the 1996 conservative PP government is deepening.

These political developments have encouraged increasingly stable and close relations between the two union confederations, leading in 1996 to a new joint programme on collective bargaining. This has given increased clarity and structure to the industrial relations strategy of the unions, although, at the expense of internal political discussion and workplace participatory processes. CCOO's 1996 conference provided further indications of a move away from its traditional 'socio-political identity' and 'open-participative' character, signalling its continuing transformation into an organization relatively similar to UGT.

The role of the unions in the political process has been narrowed down rather than expanded. Their participation is channelled into a formal role in state bodies such as the Economic and Social Council. Together with employers, they act as overseers of discreet and separate areas of state intervention – for example, monitoring employment contracts in public employment agencies. Initially suspicious of these developments, CEOE has realized that, with organized labour locked into its fragmented approach, a general union political response to economic and social change is not on the cards.

This new role for the industrial relations actors has developed further in recent years. First, the replacement of the labour ordinances has transferred key elements of the employment relationship to the collective bargaining arena. Second, policy areas such as health and safety are being managed through quasi-public tripartite forums. Third, the PP government appears to be developing an approach to bargaining based on the separation of negotiating forums and issues. The 1996 agreement between the unions and the government on the maintenance of pension levels until the year 2001 conforms to this pattern, as does the accord on social and employment protection for agrarian workers, and the agreement on redundancy payments and contracting of younger workers. The PP government was apparently willing to pay the economic price of such agreements in order to deny the unions a key focus of mobilization in the future. However, the age of the grand pact, tying together a range of policy areas and interventions, appears to be over.

These developments represent a 'socialization' of state functions, that is their transfer from the state itself to the industrial relations actors. This 'strategic displacement' also entails a fragmentation of the regulation of social policy which is now broken up between different agencies and issues. Such peculiarities in the state's role and in the distribution of regulatory functions are important in understanding the changes occurring in Spanish industrial relations since the 1980s. However, they also raise questions as to the viability of the form of regulation. First, the state will face intensifying pressures from a social structure evolving away from traditional forms of employment. In many areas, regulation is still not firmly rooted in the new realities of employment relations, nor have unions and employers developed structures and strategies capable of dealing with them. For example, the increasingly dominant foreign companies are still not active within employers' organizations, while unions have yet to accommodate newly emerging groups of workers – women, immigrants, and those in precarious employment. As Pérez Díaz and Rodríguez (1995) argue, the economic and labour market integration of key constituencies is still a major problem in Spain. Second, the state and its regulation of employment is likely to be exposed to new political pressures within the sphere of industrial relations as a result of the restraining effect of European monetary integration on social and economic policy. Third, the dominant union strategy of the mid-1990s has been to exchange functional flexibility for the moderation of numerical flexibility. This is to assume, on the one hand, that genuine functional flexibility is possible in the context of a weak training culture and primarily cost-based employer strategies; and on the other, that employers are able and willing to countenance constraints on a numerical flexibility that has emerged as a predominant cultural and organizational norm. The emerging sectoral and tripartite structures are not yet stable and embedded enough to allow such exchanges to be effectively implemented. Fourth, the workplace structures of management and unions are uneven, and sometimes based on problematic trust relations. As a result, new managerial initiatives may fail by default.

Overcoming the legacy of history is not straightforward even if remarkable progress is apparent in modernizing industrial relations. The stability of the new system of industrial relations is dependent on the political relations and alliances of its main actors and on their ability to develop coherent strategies. This is dependent in turn on the success of their evolving representative and democratic processes.

Acknowledgements

I would like to thank the following for their support in my work on Spain over the last 2 years: Juan Blanco, Luis Alonso, Lola Morillo, Javier Quintanilla, Elena Gutiérrez and Jorge Aragón. As usual may I thank Anthony Ferner for his sound advice and help.

I dedicated the chapter in the first edition to the memory of my father, Miguel Martínez Fernández: I dedicate this version to my mother, Aurora Lucio González, for never losing hope, even if, like many Spaniards, she had to wait at home and in exile until she was in her late sixties for her first chance to vote in free Spanish elections.

Abbreviations

CCOO	*Comisiones Obreras* – Workers' Commissions
CEOE	*Confederación Española de Organizaciones Empresariales* – Spanish Confederation of Employers' Organizations
CES	*Consejo Económico y Social* – Economic and Social Council
CEYPME	*Confederación Española de la Pequeña y Mediana Empresa* – Spanish Confederation of Small and Medium-sized Enterprises
CGC	*Confederación General de Cuadros* – General Confederation of Professional and Managerial Staff
CNT	*Confederación Nacional del Trabajo* – National Confederation of Labour
IMAC	*Instituto de Mediación, Arbitraje y Conciliación* – Institute of Mediation, Arbitration and Conciliation
INEM	*Instituto Nacional del Empleo* – National Employment Institute
OSE	*Organización Sindical Española* – Spanish Syndical Organization
PCE	*Partido Comunista Español* – Spanish Communist Party
PSOE	*Partido Socialista Obrero Español* – Spanish Socialist Workers' Party
UGT	*Unión General de Trabajadores* – General Workers' Confederation
USO	*Unión Sindical Obrera* – Workers' Trade Union Confederation

References and Further Reading

Aguilar, S. and Roca, J. 1989: 14-D. Economía política de una huelga. *Bulletí Informatiu 1989*. Barcelona: Fundación Jaume Bofill.

Alonso, L. 1991: Conflicto laboral y cambio social. Una aproximación al caso español. In Miguélez, F. and Prieto, C. (eds), 403–23.

Amsden, J. 1972. *Collective Bargaining and Class Conflict in Spain*. London: Weidenfeld & Nicolson.

Aragón Medina, J. 1993: Crisis económica y reformas laborales, *Economistas*, 57, 22–31.

Arasa Medina, C. 1992: 1982–1992: Diez años de política económica en España, *Revista de Economía Aplicada e Historia Económica*, 2, 77–120.

Barbiano, J. 1993: Las peculiaridades del fordismo español, *Cuadernos de Relaciones Laborales*, 3.

Baylos, A. 1991: La intervención normativa del estado en materia de relaciones colectivas. In Miguélez, F. and Prieto, C. (eds), 289–306.

Bilbao, A. 1991: Trabajadores, gestión económica y crisis sindical. In Miguélez, F. and Prieto, C. (eds), 251–71.

Blanco, J. 1996: Interview with Juan Blanco, CCOO, September 1996, Madrid.

Blyton, P. and Martínez Lucio, M. 1995: Industrial relations and the management of flexibility: A comparison of Britain and Spain, *International Journal of Human Resource Management*, May, 271–92.

Castells, M. 1983: *The City and Grassroots*. London: Edward Arnold.

CCOO 1994: *Cambio Tecnológico y Organización del Tabajo en la Industria del Automóvil*. Madrid: CCOO.

Comisión de Expertos sobre el Desempleo 1988: *El Paro: Magnitud, Causas, Remedios*. Madrid.

Consejo Económico y Social 1996: *Economía, Trabajo y Sociedad*. Madrid: CES.

Cousins, C. 1994: A comparison of the labour market position of women in Spain and the UK with reference to the 'flexible' labour debate, *Work, Employment and Society*, 8(1), 45–67.

Dolado, J.J. and Bentolila, S. 1992: *Who are the Insiders? Wage Setting in Spanish Manufacturing Firms*. Madrid: Banco de España.

EIRR *(European Industrial Relations Review)* 1995a: Impoverishment or enrichment? Bargaining after the reforms. *EIRR* 255, April, 25–8.

EIRR 1995b: The deregulation of the Spanish labour market, *EIRR* 262, November 1995: 28–30.

EIRR 1996a: Spain. Collective bargaining in 1995, *EIRR* 268, May, 21–2.

EIRR 1996b: Replacing the labour ordinances – the current state of play, *EIRR* 272, September, 29–31.

Escobar, M. 1995: Works councils or unions? In Rogers, J. and Streeck, W. (eds), *Works Councils: Consultation, Representation and Corporatism in Industrial Relations*, Chicago: University of Chicago Press, 153–88.

Espina, A. 1991: Política de rentas en España. In Miguélez, F. and Prieto, C. eds, 331–60.

Estivill, J. and de la Hoz, J. 1990: Transition and crisis: the complexity of Spanish industrial relations. In Baglioni, G. and Crouch, C. (eds), *European Industrial Relations*, 265–299. London: Sage.

Falguera i Baró, M. 1991: La legislación individual de trabajo. In Miguélez, F. and Prieto, C. (eds), 271–87.

Fina, L. 1987: Unemployment in Spain: its causes and the policy response. *Labour*, 1(2), 26–39.

Fina, L. and Hawkesworth, R. 1984: Trade unions and collective bargaining in post-Franco Spain, *Labour and Society*, 9(1), 3–27.

Foweraker, J. 1989: *Making Democracy in Spain*. Cambridge: CUP.

Gillespie, R. 1990: The breakup of the 'Socialist Family': party–union relations in Spain, *West European Politics*, 13(1), 47–62.

Giner, S. and Sevilla, E. 1979: From despotism to parliamentarism: class domination and political order in the Spanish state, *Iberian Studies*, Autumn, 69–82.

Jimeno, J.F. and Toharia, L. 1993: El mercado de trabajo: lo que hay que reformar y porque, *Economistas*, 57, 13–21.

Jordana, J. 1996: Reconsidering union membership in Spain, 1977–1994, *Industrial Relations Journal*, September, 211–24.

Lange, P. et al. 1982: *Unions, Change and Crisis*. London: Allen & Unwin.

Lash, S. and Urry, J. 1987: *The End of Organised Capitalism*. Oxford: Polity.

Lawlor, T. and Rigby, M. 1986: Contemporary Spanish trade unions, *Industrial Relations Journal*, 17(3), 249–65.

López Novo, J. 1991: Empresarios y relaciones laborales: una perspectiva histórica. In Miguélez, F. and Prieto, C. (eds), 131–47.

Maravall, J. 1978: *Dictadura y Disentimiento Político*. Madrid: Alfaguara.

Martín Valverde, A. 1991. *European Employment and Industrial Relations Glossary: Spain*. Luxembourg: Office for Official Publications of the European Communities.

Martín, C. and Velázquez, F. J. 1996: Una estimación de la presencia de capital extranjera en la economía española y de algunas de sus consecuencias, *Papeles de Economía Española*, 66, 160–75.

Martínez Alier, J. 1983: The old corporatist ideology and the new corporatist reality in Spain. Paper presented to Conference, European University Institute.

Martínez Lucio, M. 1983: Corporatism and Political Transition. MA thesis, University of Essex.

Martínez Lucio, M. 1987: El sindicalismo madrileño en un contexto de cambio. *Alfoz*, January/February, 44–51.

Martínez Lucio, M. 1989: The politics and discursive struggles of trade union development and the construction of the industrial relations arena. A reassessment of concepts and problems. Unpublished Ph.D. Dissertation. Coventry: University of Warwick.

Martínez Lucio, M. 1990: Trade unions and communism in Spain: the role of the CCOO in the political projects of the left, *Journal of Communist Studies*, 6(4), 80–102.

Martínez Lucio, M. 1991: Employer identity and the politics of the labour market in Spain. *West European Politics*, 14(1), 41–55.

Martínez Lucio, M. and Blyton, P. 1995: Constructing the post-fordist state? The politics of flexibility and labour markets in contemporary Spain, *West European Politics*, 18(2), 340–60.

Martínez Lucio, M. and Weston, S. 1994: New management practices in a multinational corporation: the restrucuting of worker representation and rights? *Industrial Relations Journal*, 25(2), 110–21.

Miguélez, F. 1991: Las organizaciones sindicales. In Miguélez, F. and Prieto, C. (eds), 213–32.

Miguélez, F. 1995: El mercado de trabajo en España y la persistencia de las diferencias con la Unión Europea. Un modelo de expansión, *Revista de Economía y Sociología del Trabajo*, March–June, 61–73.

Miguélez, F. and Prieto, C. (eds) 1991: *Las Relaciones Laborales en España*. Madrid: Siglo Veintiuno.

Ministerio de Economía y Hacienda 1995: *La Negociación Colectiva en las Grandes Empresas*. Madrid: Ministerio de Economía y Hacienda.

Ministerio de Trabajo y Asuntos Sociales 1996: *Anuario de Estadísticas Laborales y de Asuntos Sociales*. Madrid: Ministerio de Trabajo y Asuntos Sociales.

Ortiz, L. forthcoming: Union response to teamwork: the case of Opel Spain, *Industrial Relations Journal*.

Pardo, R. and Fernández, J. 1991: Las organizaciones empresariales y la configuración del sistema de relaciones industriales en la España democrática, 1977–1990. In Miguélez, F. and Prieto, C. (eds), 147–84.

Pérez Amorós, F. and Rojo, E. 1991: Implications of the single European market for labour and social policy in Spain, *International Labour Review*, 130(3), 359–72.

Pérez Díaz, V. 1984: Políticas económicas y pautas sociales en la España de la transición: la doble cara del neocorporatismo. In Linz, J. (ed.), *España: un presente para el futuro*. Madrid: Instituto de Estudios Económicos, 21–55.

Pérez Díaz, V. and Rodriguez, J.C. 1995: Intertial choices: an overview of Spanish human resources, practices and policies. In Locke, R., Kochan, T. and Piore, M. (eds), *Employment Relations in a Changing World Economy*, Massachusets: MIT, 165–96.

Preston, P. 1976: La oposición anti-franquista: la larga marcha hacia la unidad. In Preston, P. (ed.), *España en Crisis*. Madrid: Fondo de Cultura Económica, 217–64.

Prieto, C. 1991: Las prácticas empresariales de gestión de la fuerza de trabajo. In Miguélez, F. and Prieto, C. (eds), 185–210.

Recio, A. 1991: La segmentación del mercado de trabajo en España. In Miguélez, F. and Prieto, C. (eds), 97–115.

Roca, J. 1983: Economic analysis and neo-corporatism. Paper presented at European University Institute.

Roca, J. 1991: La concertación social. In Miguélez, F. and Prieto, C. (eds), 361–77.

Ruesga, S. 1991: La negociación colectiva. In Miguélez, F. and Prieto, C. (eds), 379–402.

Segura, R. and Malo de Molina 1991: *Análisis de la Contratación Temporal en España*. Madrid: Ministerio de Trabajo y Seguridad Social.

Sisson, K., Waddington, J. and Whitston, C. 1991: Company size in the European Community, *Human Resource Management Journal*, 2(1), 94–109.

Toharia, L. 1988: Partial fordism: Spain between political transition and economic crisis. In Boyer, R. (ed.), *The Search for Labour Market Flexibility. The European economies in transition*. Oxford: Clarendon Press, 119–39.

UGT 1996: *Balance Cualitativa de la Negociacion Sectorial Estatal*. Madrid: UGT.

Villasante, T. 1984: *Comunidades Locales*. Madrid: Instituto de Estudios de Administración Local.

16 | Italy: The Dual Character of Industrial Relations

IDA REGALIA • MARINO REGINI

Introduction: Turning-points and Continuities in Italian Industrial Relations

After almost 30 years, the 'hot autumn' of 1969 still seems to be the principal watershed in the evolution of Italian industrial relations since the Second World War. Other major turning-points have occurred, of course: the trade union splits of 1948–49; the birth in 1958–60 of associations representing public corporations; the 1970 'Workers' Statute' protecting individual and collective rights in the workplace; the 'Eur document' of 1978 whereby the largest union (CGIL) agreed for the first time to take account of macro-economic constraints on its action; and the tripartite agreement of 1993 on incomes policy and reform of the system of collective bargaining. But none of them has represented such a radical break with the previous industrial relations system, or had such major economic consequences or such symbolic significance, as the workers' mobilization of the period 1968–72 whose high-point was the 'hot autumn'.

Since 1969, the Italian unions have become powerful protagonists in industrial relations, as well as playing an important institutional role. Their power (which has diminished since then but is still substantial) has allowed them to exert influence: choices made by firms and institutions since the 'hot autumn' have been profoundly conditioned by changed power relations, as has labour-market and economic legislation. In addition, however, the unions have been confronted with the dilemmas typical of large-scale organizations: power and influence have brought responsibility for the consequences of their actions.

Of the other crucial turning-points in the evolution of Italian industrial relations, the most recent – the 1993 tripartite agreement on incomes policy and reform of the collective bargaining system – is probably the most important since the 'hot autumn'. Economic and political actors have interpreted it as a second watershed in Italian industrial relations, both because it has reintroduced on a more stable basis the concertation that largely failed in the 1970s and 1980s, and because it has rationalized the collective bargaining system and institutionalized relationships among actors.

This revival of concertation is a crucial development, providing stability for the political system and for management of the economy during a difficult transition phase. It stands in sharp contrast to the crisis of centralized bargaining over incomes policy in countries such as Sweden and Denmark (see Kjellberg and Scheuer in this volume; also Iversen 1996; Pontusson and Swenson 1996; Visser 1996). Moreover, the success of concertation in Italy in introducing cuts in social welfare contrasts markedly with the social crisis and breakdown of political consensus provoked by similar attempts at reform in France in the same period.

However, it is an open question as to whether the renewal of concertation is a crucial turning-point in industrial relations or whether it is a manifestation of a long-term – though informal and hidden – tradition of de facto co-operation between the social partners. This question relates to a peculiar and enduring feature of the Italian industrial relations system (and political system, for that matter): the apparent coexistence of drastic changes and deep-lying continuities (Regini and Lange 1990). We shall propose an interpretation of this odd combination below, after briefly describing the principal phases of industrial relations since the war. In subsequent sections we provide more detailed analysis of changes in the organization and strategies of the industrial relations actors, as well as their bilateral and trilateral relationships. However, to aid understanding of the various phases through which post-war Italian industrial relations have passed, we first outline their economic and institutional contexts.

Socio-economic and Political-institutional Background[1]

Italy is, in terms of population, the second largest country in western Europe. Its post-war history has seen an incomplete socio-economic transformation from the most industrially backward member of the original EEC to a successful modern economy. However, internal disparities are among the most extreme of any European country. Large-scale manufacturing is geographically concentrated; early post-war industrialization was firmly rooted in the 'industrial triangle' between Milan, Turin and Genoa, and while the dominance of the north-west is now less decisive, regional contrasts in industrial structure remain marked. Agriculture has declined in significance since the 1940s, when it occupied some 40 per cent of the labour force, to 14 per cent in 1980 and 7 per cent in 1996. However, in the Mezzogiorno – the six southern mainland provinces, together with Sicily and Sardinia – some 12 per cent still work on the land.

As elsewhere in southern Europe, a substantial service sector developed while industrial employment was still relatively small (table 16.1). In 1996, 61 per cent of the labour force worked in services, as against 32 per cent in manufacturing and construction. Labour force participation rates, particularly for women, are relatively low, though as in other countries the female rate has been rising in recent decades. There is little part-time employment, though the removal of obstacles to such employment has been an important recent policy objective. Self-

Table 16.1 Labour market indicators 1970–95

	1970	1980	1985	1990	1995
Total employment (000s)	18,956	20,487	20,894	21,304	20,010
Unemployment rate (%)	3.1	7.8	10.6	11.0	12.0
male	–	4.7	7.0	7.3	9.2
female	–	13.0	17.3	17.1	16.7
youth (16–24 years)	–	25.2	26.1	31.3	33.9
South sectoral share of employment (%)	4.9	11.5	14.7	19.7	21.0
agriculture, forestry and fishing	19.4	14.2	11.1	8.9	7.0
industry (incl. construction)	43.3	37.6	33.2	32.1	32.2
services	37.3	48.3	55.7	59.0	60.8

Sources: OECD *Economic Surveys;* ILO *Yearbook of Labour Statistics;* ISTAT *Rilevazione campionaria delle forze di lavoro.*

employment is exceptionally high, accounting for 29 per cent of the total occupied labour force (63 per cent in agriculture and 46 per cent in market services).

The structure of the Italian economy is markedly bipolar. On the one hand there is a significant group of large, often multi-plant and multinational enterprises, many of them until recently state holding companies; on the other, there is a very extensive number of small establishments. Artisan and small-firm production – what has been termed 'high-technology cottage industry' (Sabel 1982: 220) – has played an important role in the development of some of the most advanced sectors of Italian manufacturing. In particular, the 'Third Italy' (the provinces in the north-eastern and central parts of the country) has often been viewed as the exemplar of a modern economy based on 'industrial districts', in which a network of interdependent small producers permits flexible and innovative economic performance.

Accurate discussion of the labour force and its distribution is obstructed by the existence of an extensive 'black economy'. Particularly in the south, there exists 'a massive underground and irregular economy, with its concomitant tax and social security evasion and widespread illegal and undocumented employment, the violation of labour rights legislation and the limitation of economic freedom' (Ministero del Lavoro 1990: 27). It is estimated that the underground economy, which includes irregularly employed, illegal immigrant workers and several other groups, accounts for over 16 per cent of national employment, against 8 per cent for 'atypical' and 75 per cent 'standard' forms of employment (Censis 1996: 63).

Unemployment has been a serious problem. It was over 10 per cent for most of the 1980s and reached 12.1 per cent in 1996 (see table 16.1). Levels are particularly high among first-time job seekers – the proportion of young people among the unemployed is among the highest in the EU. Female unemployment is almost double the male rate, in part reflecting the growth in female labour force participation. Unemployment in the south is more than three times as high as the rate in the north. These figures have combined to produce an unemployment rate of over 55 per cent for women aged under 29 in southern Italy (Censis 1996: 234).

By contrast, the rate of unemployment for male breadwinners in the North (the bulk of the unionized labour force) has been negligible.

The political system in Italy is extremely complex. The Chamber of Deputies and the Senate – both elected by proportional representation until the electoral reform of the early 1990s – have coequal status; the legislative process therefore requires delicate co-ordination between the two chambers. The electoral system generates a multiplicity of parties with parliamentary representation; governments are invariably coalitions, and the inter-party alliances on which they rest lack stability. Thus there have been more than fifty governments since the war – though in practice changes of government rarely involved major alterations either in political composition or in personnel; so much so that, in a sense, the Italian political system up to the early 1990s enjoyed an extraordinary continuity, with little real alternation in power.

Until the major changes of the early 1990s, culminating in the dissolution of most of the traditional parties, the pivotal role in Italian government was played by the Christian Democrats (DC), who regularly achieved the largest vote in national elections. The DC benefited from their traditional links with the powerful catholic church, and from the system of patronage and clientelism associated with control of public agencies at national (and often regional and local) level. However, the DC were less an integrated ideological bloc with a common policy orientation than a coalition of factions covering a broad spectrum of right–left politics.

After the war the communists, whose standing was boosted by their prominent role in the wartime anti-fascist resistance, became the second main political force, and the largest and most influential communist party in western Europe. From the onset of the Cold War the Italian Communist Party (PCI) was excluded from government, but nevertheless attracted roughly a quarter of the popular vote throughout the 1950s and the 1960s, and won control of local government in a number of important cities. The Italian party was the first to question established communist orthodoxies, calling in the 1970s for a 'historic compromise' embracing progressive tendencies in other parties and the Catholic associations in order to defend democracy and achieve social and economic reform. In the 1980s, however, the party lost popular support while continuing to distance itself from the communist tradition, and in 1990–1 changed its name to the Democratic Left Party (PDS). The radical minority split and built a new party – *Rifondazione Comunista* (RC) – to the left of the PDS.

At the beginning of the 1990s, Italian politics entered a new phase of instability. In the 1992 general election, all the major parties lost support. The main beneficiary was the *Lega Nord*, an alliance of the various newly formed political 'leagues' in the northern provinces, which argued for autonomy within a formal federal structure, curbs on immigration and lower taxes.

In the space of a few years, radical changes have taken place in the political system: the judicial campaign against corruption which hit a large part of the old political class and hastened the disintegration of the DC and PSI; an electoral reform which introduced a majority rule system and the direct election of mayors at local level; the entry into the political arena of a new centre–right party under media entrepreneur Silvio Berlusconi, who won the general election of 1994 but was forced to resign at the end of the year; and, for the first time in Italy's history, the electoral victory of a 'left–centre' coalition in 1996.

The distinctive politics of Italian industrial relations have been shaped by the contradictory combination of a tradition of state interventionism in the economy and governmental weakness. 'Blocked democracy' led to permanent difficulties in achieving policy consensus within unstable and disparate coalitions. Change has typically occurred incrementally, requiring ad hoc compromises to ensure the consent of the interests affected (Lange and Regini 1989). This has meant, in particular, that industrial relations policy must normally be acceptable both to unions and to employers' organizations.

Traditionally, the Italian labour market has been subject to a complex web of legal regulation, which has evolved piecemeal rather than being shaped – with the dramatic exception of the 1970 Workers' Statute – by comprehensive legislative initiative. Giugni (1982: 383) refers to the Italian labour law as a *formazione alluvionale* (alluvial deposit); in a similar vein, Reyneri (1989: 135) writes of a 'geological stratification' of legal instruments, with a succession of new regulations being 'casually added onto the old norms'.

The individual employment relationship is thus governed by extensive legal norms and administrative mechanisms. The post-war regulative system prescribed, for example, that firms were required to recruit labour via the official employment exchange. Part-time and short-terms contracts were permitted only in narrowly specified circumstances. A variety of 'protective' restrictions – for example, the prohibition of night-work – applied to women workers. Considerable protection of individual employment was provided by a law of 1966 (Sciarra 1986).

The 1970 Workers' Statute radically expanded employee rights. This reflected the dramatic shift in power relationships following the 'hot autumn' of 1969, and was intended to stabilize Italian industrial relations within a new institutional framework. The Statute strengthened employment security, restricted unilateral changes in job definitions, tightly regulated disciplinary procedures and sanctions, prohibited various forms of surveillance, and provided for educational and other forms of leave. In sum, the 1970 Statute provided the most radical body of individual employment rights in Europe.

The Italian system also contains a variety of instruments and institutions designed to facilitate economic restructuring by supporting workers made redundant. The most notable is the *Cassa Integrazione Guadagni* (earnings maintenance fund). Dating from 1941, the fund is administered by the tripartite National Institute for Social Insurance (INPS), which also administers pensions. Its original purpose was to provide income support for employees affected by short-time working or lay-offs as a result of temporary market difficulties. Subsequently, the scope of the scheme was extended, and by the 1980s it was functioning increasingly as a form of redundancy compensation for those whose jobs were permanently eliminated by corporate restructuring. In the peak year of 1984, a total of over 800 million working hours were paid for under the scheme in manufacturing and construction, though the figure had fallen by more than half by the end of the decade (Tronti 1991: 128). Such concealed redundancy made it relatively easy for firms to agree restructuring initiatives. Though the system was tightened up from

1991 – for example, a 2-year limit on payments from the fund was imposed – it gave unions a far more favourable bargaining position in responding to radical restructuring of employment than in most other countries.

The legal and institutional framework has altered, however, in recent decades. Attempts have been made, from the late 1970s, to introduce greater flexibility, and hence some of the original labour market controls have been relaxed. This process has been more limited and gradual in Italy than in many countries, and deregulation has occurred in a regulated fashion. The trend to deregulation has sustained the dual features of reform by agreement and the mutual interaction of legislation and collective bargaining. Wedderburn (1991: 254) has referred to the process as 'articulated deregulation'.

Despite the elaborate system of individual labour law, collective aspects of industrial relations are subject to very little direct legal regulation. The 1948 Constitution defined Italy as 'a democratic republic founded on labour', and declared (articles 39 and 40) that employees have the rights to organize collectively and to strike; but subsequent governments failed to enact specific legislation giving detailed force to these principles. This partly reflected the fear of employers and the political right that such legislation would strengthen the unions; but there was also concern in some sectors of the labour movement that legally enshrined rights would be accompanied by unpalatable regulations and restrictions.

In general terms, therefore, trade union organization and action, as well as the employers' associations, are less regulated in Italy than elsewhere in Europe. If unions enjoy few specific rights they are subject to even fewer obligations. Their internal organizational arrangements and their objectives are not externally regulated. Until the 1990 law on disputes in essential public services (discussed below), strike action was virtually unconstrained by law. Trade unions derive rights from the legal concept of 'most representative union', which provides the basis for appointment to tripartite administrative agencies. The status lacks precise statutory definition, but in practice 'most representative' unions have long been considered to include the three main confederations and their affiliated sectoral organizations, and on occasion also the neo-fascist CISNAL. However, the growth of 'autonomous' trade unions in competition with the confederal unions in the 1980s, and the outcomes of the referenda held in June 1995 which penalized the latter (Giugni 1995), have made the situation even more uncertain. A new law to clarify the situation has been urged from various quarters, but so far without concrete results.

The most notable source of collective employment rights is the *Statuto dei lavoratori*, which established a new institution, the *rappresentanza sindacale aziendale* (RSA – 'workplace union representative structure') (see below). The fact that most rights pertain to individuals (as is true, in Italy, of the right to strike itself) rather than unions does not appear to weaken their effect, and may be seen as a reflection of the problems of trade union pluralism and inter-union rivalry.

The Main Phases of Italian Industrial Relations: An Overview

Industrial Relations before the 'Hot Autumn'

The Italian system of industrial relations in the 1950s and early 1960s has been described as 'highly centralized and with political predominance' (Pizzorno 1980; Lange, Ross and Vannicelli 1982). Unions were very weak and unable to articulate rank-and-file demands.

In the 1950s, both the labour market and the political situation were markedly unfavourable to workers. Moreover, the three union confederations were deeply divided along ideological lines. The strategy of the largest (CGIL) of protecting 'general class interests' entailed the strong centralization of bargaining and of union activity in general, and an inability to respond to ongoing changes in the workplace. Only at the end of the decade did the economic boom and a partial thaw in the Cold War permit a degree of unity of action by the unions, together with some attempts to set up shop-floor organizations in the factories. However, this was too little to enable the unions to harness the growing discontent of broad sectors of the labour force.

Worker discontent bred a period of severe conflict culminating in the 'hot autumn' of 1969. The strike volume in 1969 was three times higher than the already high level for the period 1959–67 (Benetti and Regini 1978). However, strike statistics (see below tables 16.3 and 16.4) fail fully to convey the impact of general collective mobilization. Workers' struggles assumed much more radical and ideologically charged forms than those traditionally envisaged by the unions. Demands, driven by egalitarian aspirations and fiercely critical of the existing organization of work, were highly innovative (Pizzorno et al. 1978).

Collective mobilization added to tensions in the relationship between workers and unions resulting from changes in the composition of the labour force. The impact of Fordist production methods in large firms – the speed-up of work, fatigue, deskilling and the loss of occupational identity – was neglected by unions dominated by skilled workers. At the same time, the cities of the booming north-west were flooded with a mass of mainly young and unskilled workers from the poorer regions, unused to urban life and factory discipline, or to the traditions of collective action and interest representation.

There are a number of reasons why the enormous potential for unrest was expressed in explosive form in Italy, rather than being channelled into more institutional outlets as in Germany or Sweden. In addition to the political isolation of the unions, a key factor was the weakness of institutional mechanisms – such as collective bargaining – to channel protest and new demands in a controlled fashion.

The Rise and Decline of Centralized Political Exchange and the Search for Flexibility at the Workplace

In the longer run, Italian unions were able to draw considerable benefit from the collective mobilization, strengthening their organization and achieving greater recognition from employers and the state. Their principal concern came to be that of conserving their power, while minimizing any harmful macro-economic consequences that might provoke the hostility of other actors. This concern led to a strategy – symbolized by the 'Eur turning-point' of 1978 – of moderating labour market demands in exchange for benefits in the political arena. One manifestation of the strategy was the decline in industrial conflict in the late 1970s.

Unions saw concertation as a means of cushioning the effects of growing unemployment, industrial restructuring, the decentralization of production, and the rising cost of living. It also helped compensate for their declining market power by providing them with institutional functions and political recognition. For their part, employers accepted some form of union participation in economic policy because of their awareness of the power of the unions to oppose a strategy of deregulation. Governments viewed the concertation of incomes policies as a useful instrument for curbing inflation and regulating widespread social conflict. Consequently, the second half of the 1970s and the early 1980s were characterized by the central importance of 'political exchange' (Pizzorno 1978). For none of the three actors concerned was this the preferred solution: it emerged as a second-best choice in the absence of viable alternatives (Regini 1987).

The collapse of concertation in the mid-1980s was due ultimately to the changing balance of costs and benefits for each of the three actors. The union movement was by now undergoing a crisis of representation which was attributed to the excessive isolation from the workplace entailed by concertation. The unions therefore shifted their attention from the political level to company-level negotiations as a way of restoring their relations with the rank and file. Meanwhile, firms were recovering the central importance that they had lost during the period of political exchange. National economic adjustment depended on the ability of companies to restructure; the firm consequently became the centre of gravity of collective labour relations, the locus not only of technological innovation but of organizational and social innovation as well. The aggregate level of social concertation could not provide solutions to the problems thrown up by the transition to post-Fordism (Kern and Schumann 1984; Piore and Sabel 1984) and the challenges of increased international competition, both of which demanded flexible, company-specific responses.

At the periphery of the industrial relations system, in the workplace and the industrial districts, pragmatic new forms of co-operation arose. The de facto acknowledgement by local unions or workers' councils that their companies were compelled to restructure in order to compete in international markets, and the willingness of management to use existing industrial relations institutions rather than try to by-pass them, led to the 'micro-concertation' of industrial adjustment (Regini 1995). The widespread and fragmented conflict typical of the public sector in this period failed to spread to the private sector. Thus, far from turning to extensive deregulation as widely predicted, actors in the lower tiers of the industrial relations system sought mutually beneficial solutions, made pragmatic adjustments to each other's needs, and made widespread use of bargaining to achieve their ends.

The Resurgence of Macro-concertation in the 1990s

Despite the signing of tripartite agreements in 1983 and 1984, attempts to conclude a 'social pact' were short-lived and failed to change the features of the industrial relations system. The 1980s, therefore, were characterized by tacit acceptance of the existence of two distinct spheres of action: the central and official level, where relationships continued to be difficult and often antagonistic, and the local level of the firm or the industrial district where the search for often informal and voluntaristic joint regulation prevailed.

It was only in the 1990s that political bargaining was resumed with vigour, and that a more stable solution was found to the problem of weak institutionalization. Legislation was informally negotiated with the unions to bring public sector employment more closely in line with the overall model of industrial relations; tripartite agreements were signed on incomes policy and collective bargaining structure; agreement between government and unions was reached – following the most serious social conflict of the last 20 years – on pensions reform; and finally a tripartite 'pact for employment' was concluded in 1996. The most important of these events are discussed in more detail in later sections.

The revival of concertation stems from the renewed importance of public policy in areas such as incomes and social security as a crucial factor in the international competitiveness of Italian industry. Governments have also been increasingly driven by the need to conform to the EMU convergence criteria.[2] Moreover, while 'micro-social regulation' of the economy is still able to ensure some degree of wage co-ordination and other collective goods for firms, the new economic context requires the greater stability and predictability of outcomes that incomes policies and macro-concertation may provide. Finally, the globalization of markets and the intensification of international competition make it more difficult for firms to compete solely on flexibility and product quality, and curbing labour costs has once again become a major concern. The relative strength of the Italian unions is an obstacle to the pursuit of wage restraint through market mechanisms but facilitates the use of concerted policies to achieve the same end; thus many Italian employers have become committed advocates of incomes policy.

Visible Change and Hidden Continuity: Dualism as the Interpretative Key of Italian Industrial Relations

In no other European country have industrial relations and trade union action seen such radical and profound change as in Italy. Although power relations have altered in similar manner everywhere (Regini 1992), French, British, German or Scandinavian unions have tended to persist with their traditional strategies.

Why have the Italian unions changed so dramatically? One reason may be the different ways in which, during each of these phases, they have been able to strengthen themselves organizationally. While during the phase of worker mobilization the unions could gain strength only by 'riding the tiger' of protest, during the late 1970s organizational benefits were to be gained by participating in the management of the expanding welfare state. The primacy of the firm during the 1980s made recognition by employers a crucial resource. In the 1990s, with incomes policy once again seen as necessary, the unions have been able to acquire a political role that has compensated for the weakening of their representative capacity.

However, such an explanation fails to take account of the complex, difficult and often fragile relationships between the central and the peripheral levels of unions, and between representatives and the represented. These relationships make it impossible for the top leadership to modify strategies without provoking damaging dissent. A more realistic explanation needs to take account of the fact that changes of strategy at the central and 'overt' level of industrial relations have not undermined the independence and vitality of a 'peripheral' and almost 'covert' level where action may sometimes be directly contrary to the official line (Regini and Lange 1990).

At the time of the 'hot autumn', this peripheral level played a crucial role in persuading the initially hesitant unions to adopt a strategy of radical mobilization. In the mid-1970s, however, faced with the problem of how to exercise their recently acquired organizational power responsibly, the unions assigned a key role to the national level, through centralized concertation, rather than to the company level. The unions thereby hoped to insulate their action against pressure from more radical rank-and-file elements. By contrast, from the late 1970s until the 1990s macro-concertation foundered, while in the more sheltered sphere of company-level industrial relations, forms of micro-concertation spontaneously asserted themselves.

The dualism between the central, 'overt' level and the peripheral, almost 'underground' level of union action, provides a possible explanation for the rapidity and profundity of change in union behaviour. Thus the strategy of centralized political exchange was adopted shortly after the phase of 'permanent conflict' in order *inter alia* to restrict the autonomy of the peripheral representative bodies, and its instability was at least partly a consequence of the failure to achieve this objective (Golden 1988). Subsequent developments in micro-concertation at the periphery were tacitly condoned, almost as a compensation for the breakdown in relationships at the centre. Away from the spotlight, company-level co-operation paved the way for the new turning-point: when, towards the end of the 1980s, the national unions came to accept flexibility as indispensable and proposed forms of co-determination, the change appeared less radical because co-determination was already being practised de facto in the periphery of the system.

The Actors

In the absence of an explicit and formal legal framework of regulation for interest organizations in Italy, unions and employers' associations are voluntary associations, and access to the arena of interest representation is relatively open. This has fostered a pluralist, diversified, not to say fragmented, system of representation. The structures of workplace representation have likewise been subject – at least until the inter-confederal agreement of December 1993 (see below) – to few (and vague) rules concerning their constitution, tasks and prerogatives, and operating procedures, despite numerous attempts at consolidation and reform. As for the state, its role in industrial relations rested on neutrality and non-interference in the autonomous action of the social partners.

This voluntarist and pluralist 'imprinting' profoundly influenced the evolution of the industrial relations actors for around half a century. It was only in the mid-1990s, in a greatly changed economic and political context, that the first signs appeared of a new phase, heralding a major overhaul of the system.

Trade Unions

Italian Trade Unions before Collective Mobilization

Under the Pact of Rome, concluded by the anti-fascist parties in 1944, free trade unionism was reconstituted as a unitary, class-oriented, centralized representative system.

Its unitary nature proved fragile. The central trade union body, CGIL, was internally divided along ideological lines into partisan factions. In 1948–9, with the onset of the Cold War, the Christian democratic, reformist socialist, and republican factions withdrew, and soon afterwards formed two further confederations: CISL, connected to the Christian Democrats and UIL, linked to the small lay parties, the Republicans and Social Democrats, and to the reformist wing of the Socialists.

Existing differences (Craveri 1977; Romagnoli and Della Rocca 1989) were thus externalized. The change was to have enduring effects on relationships between unions and workers, which thereafter tended to be based on ideology and political alignment. It also influenced a vision of union democracy as a choice between competing organizational alternatives, rather than as the adoption of the rules of formal democracy *within* organizations (Pizzorno 1980; Regalia 1988).

The reconstituted union movement was class-oriented in that it aspired to organize all the country's workers – blue-collar and white-collar, employed and unemployed, unionized and non-unionized – rather than to provide different organizational channels for specific occupational groups or sectors. This was in line with the class tradition of continental Europe unionism (Visser 1990), and it was consistent with an economy characterized at the time by high unemployment, the continuing importance of agriculture, and the scant development of industry. Consequently, attention was long focused on general issues, rather than on specific groups or on working conditions at the level of firms.

Union structure, particularly in CGIL, followed the dual geographical (horizontal) and industrial (vertical) pattern typical of southern European trade unionism. Throughout the 1950s, horizontal structures and representative logic predominated – both at the national–confederal level and the decentralized level (chambers of labour) – in parallel with strategies of centralized and co-ordinated collective bargaining (see below). CISL, by contrast to CGIL, emphasized a 'trade unionist' logic, an industry-based organizational structure, and a negotiation strategy oriented to more specific issues and which included company-level collective bargaining.

However, against the background of labour's vulnerability in the market and of the weakening of the left in the political arena, employers sought simply to avoid dealing with the unions (although they showed a general but lukewarm preference for CISL and UIL at the shop-floor). As a consequence, UIL and CISL developed in a manner substantially similar to CGIL. If anything, given their links with the government parties, they made greater direct or indirect use of party-political channels.

The logic of the specific representation of occupational groups was pursued instead by the 'autonomous' unions,[3] which spread through the public and private tertiary sector (Stefanelli 1980), fostered by the low cost of entering the arena of interest representation. This laid the basis for the subsequent development of highly particularist bargaining strategies (Regalia 1990; Bordogna 1994).

Prior to the split, membership of CGIL was high – an estimated 5.7 million in 1947 (Turone 1973: 159) – reflecting the climate of social mobilization in which free trade unionism had been restored. However, for more than a decade and a half from 1950 union membership declined even as the 'economic miracle' strengthened labour's market position. This was the result of union divisions and of the repression of the union rank and file in the workplace during the 1950s (Accornero 1973; Della Rocca 1976). The overall decline concealed a a sharp drop in CGIL membership (see table 16.3) of more than two million, while CISL gained around half a million new members. There were also notable geographical and sectoral differences (Romagnoli 1980; Romagnoli and Della Rocca 1989).

Organizational Expansion and Incomplete Consolidation after the 'Hot Autumn'

In the long phase of conflict until the mid-1970s, the relationship between unions and their members was profoundly redefined. Increasingly it centred on the collective identity and solidarity created during the mobilization (rather than as before on political affiliations), giving rise to demands for direct democracy and control from below. In consequence, the ideological distance between the unions tended to narrow, and reunification seemed to be within reach. For the first time, unions were successful in establishing their workplace structures within firms, proposing a new system of shopfloor delegates and factory councils (see below) in recognition of the informal, direct forms of worker involvement and participation that had emerged during the period of collective mobilization.

The institutional-legal framework also changed, although while the logic of 'movement' prevailed the unions regarded all forms of outside intervention and regulation with suspicion. However, the enactment of the Workers' Statute in 1970 provided recognition and stability for union organization independent of shifts in the labour market position.

In the aftermath of the 'hot autumn' the reunification of the confederations proved to be impracticable owing to diffuse opposition from the Christian democratic, republican and social democratic parties (Couffignal 1979). Instead, a less binding 'federative pact' was signed in 1972, which ratified the highly popular factory councils. Social mobilization and the introduction of new organizational forms of representation encouraged increases in unionization – in agriculture and the public sector as well as in industry – throughout the 1970s (Romagnoli 1980; Regalia 1981). Membership peaked in 1978, when the overall rate reached 49 per cent of the active labour force, a high level in a system of voluntary unionization and in an economy in which small firms predominated.

However, organizational consolidation was soon halted by the recession following the first oil crisis. The unions were compelled to recentralize their activity before a stable pattern of practices and rules could be defined at the decentralized level. This change, which gave rise to a bargaining strategy of restraint symbolized by the 'Eur turning-point', had the undesired effect of eroding support among workers and reopening ideological fault lines within the CGIL–CISL–UIL Federation.

Union membership declined gradually and employers were able to exploit episodes of worker protest and displays of intolerance by militants. The so-called 'march of the forty thousand' Fiat middle managers and white-collar workers against the unions – immediately interpreted by its leaders and by observers as signalling the 'defeat' of the unions (Baldissera 1988) – is perhaps the best-known of these episodes, but it was not the only one. Uncertainty in interpreting the attitudes of the rank and file exacerbated the already difficult relationship among the confederations, and in 1984 the Unitary Federation broke up over opposing views of wage restraint.

Trade Unions in the 1990s

At the beginning of the 1990s, the strength of confederal trade unionism in Italy had diminished compared with 10 years previously. The number of members in employment had fallen from 7.1 million in 1980 to 5.9 million in 1990, a decrease in union density from 49.0 to 39.2 per cent (see table 16.2). Another symptom

Table 16.2 Membership of the three main confederations 1950–93 (000s)

Year	Aggregate membership				Employed membership				
	CGIL	CISL	UIL	Total	CGIL	CISL	UIL	Total	Density %
1950	4,641	1,190	–	5,830					50.8
1951	4,491	1,338	–	5,829					50.9
1952	4,342	1,322	–	5,664					48.8
1953	4,075	1,305	–	5,380					45.6
1954	4,134	1,327	–	5,461					44.6
1955	4,194	1,342	–	5,536					43.9
1956	3,666	1,707	–	5,374					42.0
1957	3,138	1,262	–	4,400					34.2
1958	2,596	1,654	–	4,250					32.7
1959	2,601	1,284	–	3,885					29.7
1960	2,583	1,324	–	3,908					28.5
1961	2,531	1,399	–	3,930					28.2
1962	2,611	1,436	–	4,046					28.2
1963	2,626	1,504	–	4,129					28.6
1964	2,712	1,515	–	4,227					29.7
1965	2,543	1,468	–	4,011					28.5
1966	2,458	1,491	–	3,949					28.0
1967	2,424	1,523	–	3,946					27.7
1968	2,461	1,627	–	4,088					28.7
1969	2,626	1,641	–	4,268					29.4
1970	2,943	1,808	780	5,530					38.5
1971	3,138	1,973	825	5,937					41.1
1972	3,215	2,184	843	6,242					43.2
1973	3,436	2,214	902	6,553					44.6
1974	3,827	2,473	965	7,264					47.2
1975	4,081	2,594	1,033	7,708					48.5
1976	4,313	2,824	1,105	8,242					48.7
1977	4,475	2,810	1,160	8,445					49.0
1978	4,528	2,869	1,285	8,682					48.9
1979	4,584	2,906	1,327	8,817					48.4
1980	4,599	3,060	1,347	9,006	3,484	2,508	1,146	7,138	49.0
1981	4,595	2,989	1,357	8,941	3,387	2,371	1,143	6,901	47.6
1982	4,576	2,977	1,358	8,910	3,267	2,287	1,134	6,688	46.2
1983	4,556	2,953	1,352	8,860	3,134	2,224	1,121	6,479	45.2
1984	4,546	3,097	1,345	8,988	3,030	2,262	1,114	6,406	44.9
1985	4,592	2,953	1,306	8,851	2,939	2,056	1,064	6,059	42.0
1986	4,647	2,975	1,306	8,928	2,825	1,967	1,046	5,838	40.3
1987	4,743	3,080	1,344	9,167	2,768	1,952	1,069	5,789	39.9
1988	4,867	3,288	1,398	9,554	2,733	2,018	1,100	5,851	40.0
1989	5,027	3,379	1,439	9,845	2,718	1,994	1,104	5,815	39.5
1990	5,150	3,508	1,486	10,145	2,725	2,024	1,124	5,872	39.2
1991	5,222	3,657	1,524	10,403	2,706	2,071	1,136	5,913	39.1
1992	5,231	3,797	1,572	10,600	2,642	2,107	1,157	5,906	39.1
1993	5,237	3,769	1,588	10,594	2,529	2,007	1,125	5,661	38.5

Note: UIL membership not available before 1970. Density refers to the membership of the confederations listed, excluding retired, unemployed and self-employed members.
Sources: Romagnoli and Della Rocca (1989); Giacinto (1995).

was the deteriorating relationship with the rank and file, manifested in the growth from 1987 of the *Cobas* (radical rank-and-file organizations), especially in the public sector (Armeni 1988; Baldissera 1988; Bordogna 1994), and in the frequent outbreaks of dissent organized by factory councils in the private sector. The unions' difficulties were compounded by inter-union rivalry following the break-up of the Unitary Federation, blocking various attempts to reform workplace representation and measure union representativeness. At the same time there was growing disaffection with the role played by confederal trade unionism among the wider public and, to a lesser extent, employers and the state as well.

However, the evaluation of these developments is not straightforward. First, falling membership seems to have stemmed more from structural changes in the economy – an expansion of the services and small-firm sectors – than from explicit dissatisfaction with union strategies. Moreover, union density was still eminently respectable when compared with the European average. Second, although the deterioration in relations between unions and members was very evident in areas of the public sector, it was much more muted in the private sector, where confederal unionism remained well rooted in the workplace and played a major role in industrial readjustment. Third, although relations between the confederal organizations had been strained for some time, this did not prevent them from achieving substantial unity of action.

Until the early 1990s, the unions' role at the decentralized level remained dispersed and received little recognition, while inter-union divisions at the centre allowed direct intervention by the state on critical issues and impeded self-reform. Subsequently, however, a number of changes – notably the reform of the workplace representation system – revitalized the relationship with members and improved relations between unions. These changes strengthened confederal trade unionism and restored its public visibility and popularity.

A further innovation was the revival of debate on union reunification from the mid-1980s. This was accompanied by the resumption of united action and by CGIL's decision at the beginning of the 1990s to dissolve its internal party factions. More notably the reunification agenda has been helped by the collapse of the party system which ruled the country for almost 50 years. In the mid-1990s, outright reunification of the confederal unions has become a real prospect. Discussions have begun among executive bodies, although the outcome remains uncertain.

The process of reform that has been set in motion seems likely to consolidate confederal trade unionism and strengthen its role *vis-à-vis* employers and the government. Even the results of the referenda of June 1995 – which abolished some of the provisions of the Workers' Statute particularly favourable to the confederal unions – have not so far had the damaging impact that might have been anticipated. This is probably due in part to the fact that the issues affected (check-off and the attribution of 'union representativeness') are also regulated by collective agreements. But it is certainly significant that employers have not seized this opportunity to launch a campaign to draw attention to the unions' low level of popular support.

Forms of Workplace Representation

From Commissioni Interne *to* Consigli di Fabbrica: *The Italian Road to Works Councils*

As with other areas of industrial relations, workplace representation in Italy has long been characterized by the looseness of the rules governing its operation, a feature which has facilitated change. Three principal models can be identified.

The first was the *commissione interna* or internal commission, a body dating back to the beginning of the century and reintroduced after the fascist period by national agreement between employers' and workers' representatives. Free trade unionism had yet to be re-established. As a result, the commissions were initially assigned union competences, notably bargaining rights at the company level. After the establishment of CGIL and the subsequent splits into separate confederations, the rights and functions of such commissions were repeatedly redefined by inter-confederal agreements (never by law) which curtailed their powers and expanded those of the unions (Vais 1958; Craveri 1977; Regalia 1995).

This is the model that most closely corresponds to the works council typical of the European tradition (Rogers and Streeck 1995). The *commissione interna* (like the German *Betriebsrat*) was an elected body representing the workforce as a whole. It was not a union body, had no bargaining powers and could not call strikes. Operating within a framework of consensus and co-operation, its functions ranged from consultation with the employer to monitoring the implementation of collective agreements signed by external trade unions. Nevertheless, until the end of the 1960s, internal commissions in many companies provided worker protection against management and sometimes undertook embryonic forms of bargaining on company issues. This was despite a climate of union weakness and rivalry, and of widespread intimidation and repression of activists and workers by companies.

It was estimated that by the mid-1960s around 3000 *commissioni* with some 15,000 representatives had been active for nearly 20 years (Accornero 1976). It is difficult to estimate their effectiveness because experiences were heterogeneous and a thorough historical reconstruction is not yet available. In any case, while CGIL continued to support the general concept of representation embodied in the commissions, from the mid-1950s the other confederations were advocating (albeit with little success) a model based on workplace union branches (Treu 1971). At the beginning of the 1970s, in the context of collective mobilization, the commissions were labelled 'outdated', 'bureaucratic' and 'ineffective', and abruptly replaced by other models of representation.

The second model of workplace representation is the RSA, envisaged by the Workers' Statute of 1970, which authorized workers from the 'most representative' unions to establish workplace-based union representation. Accordingly, RSAs replaced the internal commissions. However, while the law granted them rights and entitled them to organizational resources, it did not regulate their constitution or operation. In consequence, the RSA assumed a variety of forms.

The third form of representation, and the most widespread from the 'hot autumn' until the early 1990s, was the *consiglio di fabbrica* or the *consiglio dei delegati* (factory council, council of delegates) which first appeared as an unexpected consequence of union initiatives to regain control over the spontaneous wave of worker mobilization. Following the enactment of the Workers' Statute, the unions had to decide how to reconcile the provisions of the law, vague as they were, with the realities of a protest movement which viewed any structured form of representation with suspicion. For example, the Statute provided for an equal – and small – number of representatives to be assigned to each of the 'most representative' unions. But the factory councils then being set up were broad and heterogeneous groupings of both union members and non-members elected by the workforce as a whole. In 1972, the federative Pact between CGIL, CISL and UIL (see above) officially defined factory councils as workplace-based institutions of worker *and* union representation. Thus the two functions, of representing the workforce as a whole and of representing the external union, were embodied in the single institution, which was entitled to the resources provided for the RSA. After acrimonious debate, the conflict was resolved by assuming that councils would respond both to workers and unions, and that they combined the characteristics of both internal commissions and union bodies.

Discussion of the effects of this dual nature of the *consigli* usually focuses on the unpredictability of their behaviour, on their internal instability, and on the unions' inability to control them (Accornero 1992, ch. 5). For around 20 years, the unions endeavoured to devise forms of regulation – notably electoral rules – to give them greater stability: with scant success, however, owing to their own divisions and rivalries. Yet little attention has been paid to the fact that this same ambivalence often proved to be an unexpected resource as well. In a highly informal context, it enabled councils rapidly to balance internal and external pressures, and general and specific demands, according to circumstances (Regalia 1995). Thus councils were able to maintain a degree of union control in periods of worker unrest; conversely, they could ensure a degree of continuity of union action at the workplace in periods of recentralization of industrial relations, or in the event of conflict between the confederations. One may also hypothesize that councils entered crisis when they were unable to perform this function of 'anticyclical counterbalancing'. A significant example is provided by Fiat in the late 1970s and early 1980s, when the workers' council (unlike other councils elsewhere) failed to adapt pragmatically to change (Bonazzi 1984). (For other examples, see Regini and Sabel 1989.)

The evolution of the councils in the 1970s and 1980s may be reinterpreted in terms of a shifting balance between functions. Three distinct phases can be identified. The first, lasting until the mid-1970s, was the phase of protest and collective mobilization. The newly-created councils enjoyed broad support among workers, who viewed them as an accessible channel for participation in the labour movement, and as a counterweight to the managerial discretion in the organization of work. At the same time, they provided unions with a channel of access to the workplace. Under the Workers' Statute, for example, union representative bodies at company level (i.e. the councils, when recognized as such by the unions) were authorized to convene workers' assemblies during working hours which the union representatives could attend. Moreover, insofar as they represented the workers *vis-à-vis* management, the councils performed a key role in aggregating, selecting and redefining worker demands, making it easier for the unions to regain control over protest. The outcome was a prolonged period of decentralized collective bargaining at plant level, which in turn reinforced the popularity of the representative institutions and of the unions more generally among workers.

The second period (from the mid-1970s to the mid-1980s) saw the recentralization of union action in a context of high unemployment and high inflation, culminating in the breakdown of union unity in 1984. These are generally considered to be the years of crisis and decline for the councils. However, in the light of existing research (Regalia 1984; Negrelli 1987), this phase can be more appropriately described as one of pragmatic adjustment to change. Issues concerning the internal organization of representation became more important; closer attention was paid to individual worker demands and to day-to-day action on working conditions; even some kind of collective bargaining continued to be conducted at shop or plant level. In the economically stronger regions of the country, at least, the continuity of union presence at the workplace was ensured, even after the break-up of the Federation. According to union figures, over 32,000 councils, consisting of some 206,000 delegates, represented some 5 million workers at the beginning of the 1980s. This means that around 50 per cent of the labour force – excluding the public sector and agriculture, where representation took the form of unelected RSAs appointed by the unions – was protected by councils. Given the extremely large number of workers employed in small firms, this was a very high percentage indeed. Although official figures are not available for subsequent years, various studies have confirmed the continuing importance, indeed the near ubiquitousness, of these bodies, even in smaller firms (Mortillaro 1984; 1986; Squarzon 1989; Regalia and Ronchi 1988–92).

The third period (from the mid-1980s until the early 1990s) saw increasing management initiatives to gain worker commitment to production goals, against a background of growing market competition and the increasing need for more flexible work. In this situation, especially where they continued to enjoy broad support among workers and sufficient backing by the unions, the councils assumed relatively innovative functions of collective representation within a framework of broadly co-operative relations at the workplace. The wide diffusion of formal agreements and informal understandings (Baglioni and Milani 1990), and the growing propensity of companies to involve delegates in the day-to-day management of production (Regalia and Ronchi 1988–92), signalled the widening and strengthening of the councils' functions.

Thus their dual nature and loose regulation permitted the councils to give all workers a voice while enabling the unions to exert final control over their activity (not least because they could withdraw their recognition). The system performed a variety of functions, acting as a channel for information disclosure between management and unions, and as a permanent mechanism for workplace negotiation, joint consultation or decision-making (if need be with the support of other committees specialized in particular issues)

However, the system had its costs: the lack of clear boundaries between the respective powers of councils and unions; the uncertainty of roles and procedures;

and the unpredictable behaviour of the parties. In the course of the 1980s these costs grew rapidly for all actors involved, but especially for the unions. On several occasions in the second half of the decade, the confederations sought to establish unambiguous rules. These initiatives invariably failed in the face of the power of veto that every organization, however minor, wielded by virtue of the Workers' Statute.[4] The difficulties of the confederations were confirmed in the early 1990s when their most comprehensive attempt at reform to date, the protocol agreement of March 1991, proved impracticable.

The Reform of the Representation System in 1993

Reform of the system finally became possible in 1993. With the tripartite accord signed in July, the social partners opted for a single body in all workplaces, the RSU (unitary union representative structure). Coined by the 1991 agreement, the name was chosen to emphasize that this was a single institution recognized by the unions. The aim was to put an end to the organizational vagueness and terminological confusion of the previous 20 years.

Like previous workplace representation, RSUs were bodies of both general and union representation. They continued to be elected by the whole workforce (not just union members), while unions had priority in nominating candidates. The novel feature was that under the reorganized bargaining system introduced by the July 1993 agreement, employers too had an interest in establishing workplace representation on a more solid footing, so as to have a more reliable partner in decentralized bargaining. Accordingly, in December 1993, unions and employers' associations reached a national-level agreement on the RSU (followed in early 1994 by a similar agreement for the public sector), the first on such matters after nearly 30 years of substantially informal arrangements. As a consequence, a body of coherent – and above all formally defined – rules on the constitution and operation of workplace representative bodies began to take shape.

After 1994, the unions could hold elections for workplace representative bodies to an extent unknown since the end of the 1970s, revitalizing their relationship with workers. The results were a resounding success for confederal trade unionism; publication in the press of figures on RSU elections further enhanced the public image of the confederal unions. According to figures issued by the *Osservatorio nazionale sulle Rsu* (Carrieri 1995a: 46–8), more than 70 per cent of those entitled to vote did so. The confederal unions obtained large majorities of votes and representatives (95 per cent and 96 per cent respectively). This gave rise to a broad, and perhaps unexpected, renewal of rank-and-file union activism: in Milan alone, 5000 delegates without previous experience were elected in the space of 2 years.

Thus effective channels were restored for the expression of 'voice' (from below) and for the consultation of the workforce (from above); this was to be an important feature of negotiations on reform of the pension system in May 1995.

Employers and their Associations

The system of employers' representation developed in an even more haphazard manner than union representation, and it was highly compartmentalized by sector, size, legal-institutional nature, and political affiliation (Becchi Collidà 1989; Lanzalaco 1990; Martinelli 1994). This fragmentation has complicated interest aggregation and the operation of the industrial relations system. Facilitated by low barriers to entry for new interest organizations, segmentation increased until the early 1990s. More recently, however, there have been signs of a move towards consolidation.

In part, segmentation of employer representation reflects the existence of a small number of large firms and a multitude of small ones, and also, until the early 1990s, of a substantial block of state-controlled enterprises and services (Bianco and Trento 1995). As a result, the basic differentiation of employers' representation by economic sector (agriculture, industry, commerce, craft activity) has been crosscut by further distinctions based on firm size and the nature of ownership (public–private; capitalist–co-operative).

By far the largest employers' organization is Confindustria. Formed after the First World War out of a looser confederation of associations, it supported fascism but was reconstituted at the end of the Second World War on a more 'apolitical' basis. In 1990 it had some 110,000 affiliated firms with 4.2 million employees. Confindustria organizes large private firms in manufacturing and construction but only some of the smaller ones. In the industrialized regions of the Third Italy (Bagnasco 1988) especially, small and medium-sized industrial firms are organized by Confapi. Set up in 1947, Confapi had around 30,000 member firms with 800,000 employees in 1987. Publicly-owned enterprises controlled by the IRI and Efim holding companies split from Confindustria in the late 1950s and were represented by their own organization, Intersind (created in 1958), while those controlled by ENI, the chemical and electrical public holding, belonged to ASAP (constituted in 1960). Co-operative manufacturing enterprises have their own organizations.

Added to these structural distinctions is political differentiation, especially in the representation of smaller firms. This stemmed largely from the differentiation of public policies by sector and social group (Pizzorno 1980) after the war, and from the links between firms and political parties. In agriculture, for example, besides Confagricoltura, which mainly organized larger firms, Coldiretti (traditionally linked to the Christian Democrats) and Confcoltivatori (closer to the parties on the left) organized smaller and family-owned businesses. In the commerce sector, Confcommercio was the organization traditionally associated with the Christian Democrats, while Confesercenti was more left-wing. Similarly, artisan and co-operative organizations were distinguished by their party allegiances.

The segmentation of the representation system is matched by a low level of functional specialization: many employer organizations are responsible for representing employers' interests in both economic and industrial relations fields. This tended to reinforce the political character of representation, at least at central level.

Employers' associations developed associative strategies that were formally highly centralized but in practice granted substantial autonomy to local organizations and individual firms (Alacevich 1996). The first sign of breakdown in the system was the withdrawal of state-owned companies from Confindustria at a time when labour's economic strength was increasing. This led to a long-lasting divergence between the strategies of state and private firms, which was to provoke serious tensions in industrial relations. The public sector associations played an innovative role, developing policies from the early 1960s of union recognition and the acceptance of company-level bargaining.

The private sector associations began to pay closer attention to industrial relations issues and to be more open to the unions only in the 1970s, in response to pressure from the large firms most vulnerable to competition. Confindustria attempted to move to a more proactive industrial relations strategy (Lanzalaco 1995), but it was hampered in doing so until the end of the 1980 by the difficulty of defining common positions.

At the beginning of the 1990s, the creation of new associations in the services sector, and uncoordinated bargaining with the unions by various sectoral employers' associations, emphasized the pluralist and fragmented nature of the system. However, the strong external constraints imposed by international competition and the single European market highlighted common goals that cut across many of the traditional cleavages. The crucial issues were cutting labour costs, curbing public expenditure, reducing the tax burden on firms, improving and rationalizing public services, aligning public and private sector employment practices, and introducing greater labour market flexibility. The emergence of such shared goals encouraged moves towards the rationalization of employers' interest representation, at least as regards negotiation or concertation with unions and government.

These two conflicting tendencies – towards the differentiation and the unification of interests – gave rise to constant changes of tack by employers' associations, especially with regards to relations with the unions. The strategic choice lay between gaining the commitment and involvement of unions and employees – as advocated by large and innovative firms – or eliminating external restraints and pursuing a *laissez-faire* approach, which was the preference of the majority of small firms.

Tensions surfaced between Confindustria and the public sector associations. In 1990, for instance, faced with a bill to defer abolition of the wage indexation mechanism (the *scala mobile*) until the end of 1991, and with what it deemed excessive union demands in negotiations on the renewal of national industry agreements, Confindustria controversially withdrew from the 1986 agreement on the *scala mobile*. Intersind did not follow suit, since it believed in a strategy of dialogue with the unions. Similar differences arose in the same year over the renewal of the metalworkers' agreement, during preparations for the tripartite negotiations of June 1991, and again during the negotiations leading up to the July 1993 agreement. In 1993–4, however, as a consequence of the privatization programme for publicly owned enterprises, Intersind and ASAP started a long and contradictory process of merger with Confindustria (Mascini 1995). The diversification of interests is tending therefore to be internalized within the enlarged Confindustria.

After the tripartite agreement of 1993, the priority of the new '*grande Confindustria*' was to co-ordinate and harmonize the bargaining policies of its affiliates. A central body was set up to monitor the progress of bargaining. Externally, Confindustria faced the pressures deriving from the political upheavals of the early 1990s: the *Tangentopoli* scandal, and the entry into the political arena of Silvio Berlusconi, whose strongly *laissez-faire* ideas were potentially at odds with concertation. Confindustria followed a strategy of explicit autonomy from parties and politics. Thus it adopted a neutral stance during the electoral campaigns of 1994 and 1996, and was pragmatic in its attitude towards both the Berlusconi government and the subsequent 'technocrat' and 'centre–left' administrations. Confindustria relied on this strategy to hold together a highly differentiated block of employers while at the same time preserving its co-operative and stable relationship with the unions.

Overall, the system of employer representation is stronger and more cohesive in the mid-1990s than it was at the beginning of the decade. Change is also apparent in employer organizations, all of which are to a greater or lesser extent committed to renewal, now that their privileged relationships with the party system have been severed.

The State as an Industrial Relations Actor and as an Employer

In Italy, the state has always played a secondary role in direct relations between capital and labour (Napoli 1989). However, if broader labour market and social welfare policies are taken into account, state intervention has been extensive. Since the early post-war period, social programmes and legislative measures have, on the one hand, ensured a minimum level of protection for workers in a period of rudimentary industrial relations, and, on the other, enabled firms to compete more freely in the market. The widespread involvement of the social partners in the administration of public programmes (Cammelli 1980) has also helped to stabilize contacts between them and to consolidate the industrial relations system.

On occasion the state has also intervened directly in industrial relations through legislative measures or the public mediation of labour disputes. Such intervention has, however, been conducted discreetly and according to a logic of subsidiarity, emphasizing the autonomy of the collective actors. The Workers' Statute (see above) has been the most conspicuous legislative intervention in industrial relations, and indeed marked a crucial turning-point in their evolution. In the 1980s, inter-union tensions, especially at central level, paved the way for direct government intervention to settle highly controversial questions like the *scala mobile*. The 1990 law regulating strike action in the public services constituted a symbolic break with the voluntarist tradition, although it was intended to encourage self-regulation rather than being directly prescriptive (see below).

Intervention in disputes has also taken the form of mediation by public bodies. Such mediation has never been compulsory or formally regulated, and is undertaken at the request of the parties. However, it has become increasingly routine, both nationally and locally, thereby lending stability to the system.

However, the most systematic and pervasive arena of state intervention in Italian industrial relations is as employer. In this connection a distinction should be drawn between state-controlled public enterprises and the public services sector. State enterprises have experimented with innovative and consensus-based models of industrial relations both at the central level and in the workplace. In the 1980s, the most important example of this approach was the *Protocollo IRI* of 1984, a framework agreement for companies belonging to the IRI group which inspired similar innovations in other public sector corporations. As Carinci (1986) has stressed, the overall philosophy of the *Protocollo* was close to that of German co-determination. The goal was to minimize conflict by instituting forums and procedures for discussion and by joint decision-making on a series of critical issues.

For many years the vast public services sector had a different framework of employment and industrial relations from the rest of the economy. Collective bargaining was not formally allowed, and conditions of employment were regulated by law. But with the expansion and diversification of public employment on the one hand, and the consolidation of collective bargaining on the other, the traditional system proved increasingly inadequate. The 'framework law' of 1983 introduced formal collective bargaining alongside the traditional principle of regulation by fiat. The outcome, however, was an escalation of expectations and demands, an excessive increase in spending, dissatisfaction among public employees, and the rebellion against the confederal unions among those groups most able to exert pressure.

A law of October 1992 and an associated government decree the following year initiated the so-called 'privatization' of the public employment relationship. As a result, the tripartite agreement of July 1993 was the first to apply simultaneously to both private and public sector employees (Barbieri 1995; Garofalo 1994). The project to 'privatize' public sector employment relations (i.e. to bring them into line with practices in the private sector) stemmed from proposals made by a group of union-appointed labour lawyers highly critical of the 1983 reform. The 1992 law was the outcome of systematic consultation and negotiation with the unions. This was almost inevitable given the high levels of unionization in the public sector (membership of the confederal unions represented nearly 50 per cent of the labour force), and the presence of powerful autonomous and rank-and-file unions. Under the new arrangements, the employment relationships of public employees were to be entirely regulated by collective bargaining. However, bargaining freedom was constrained by a legal framework which took account of the specific features of the sector; for example, the legislation included clauses to curb public expenditure. It also redefined the parties to bargaining, both unions and employer. The main innovation was the creation of a statutory 'Agency for Trade Union Relations', an administrative body which replaced ministerial 'delegations' as the representative of the government at central level. This had the twofold function of co-ordinating negotiations centrally, and of separating political from administrative responsibilities in order to eliminate clientelism and to reduce spending.

The Relationship between Trade Unions and Employers

Collective Bargaining: Structures and Changes

In keeping with the voluntarism of the Italian system, collective bargaining was long unregulated. Over time, three main negotiating levels emerged: the interconfederal national level, the national industry level, and the company or plant level. But until 1993, there was no formal specification of competences, procedures or issues. Consequently, relations between levels and the balance between centralization and decentralization changed frequently according to circumstances and power relations, and the same issues could be addressed at more than one level.

In the years immediately after the Second World War, bargaining was premised on strongly centralized and solidaristic co-ordination through agreements between the confederations and the employers on issues such as minimum wage levels or working hours for the economy as a whole or at least at the national industry level. This feature was not peculiar to Italy (Streeck 1993). However, whereas in some other countries of continental Europe centralized bargaining was accompanied by strong recognition of the unions by employers, in Italy it developed in the context of weak recognition and marginalization of the unions.

In manufacturing, especially in sectors exposed to competition, union action was closely bound up with their market power. In the late 1950s and early 1960s, bargaining become less centralized, more widespread and effective as the unions' labour market position improved. The next decade saw a greater role for company-level bargaining, on issues such as piecework and production bonuses, as a way of involving the labour force more closely in the growth of the economy. In the period of collective mobilization from the late 1960s, company-level bargaining developed to an extraordinary degree, and the provisions of agreements in the larger companies tended to shape the content of national bargaining. Through national industry agreements they spread to other sectors of the economy, thereby reversing the previous relationship between the bargaining levels (Giugni 1976). Demands centred on greater equality of treatment, the reduction of the intensity and discomfort of work, and the recognition of union and political rights at the workplace. This reflected the social base of the mobilization: mainly young, unskilled workers often unsocialized in the logic of the traditional shop-floor career. The key demands were for egalitarian flat rate increases, a narrower range of skill grades, the harmonization of conditions, and unified job classifications for blue- and white-collar workers. There were also widespread demands for reductions in working hours and the pace of work, the levelling of piecework rates (or the total elimination of piecework), improvement in the working environment, the right to hold shop-floor assemblies, and control over work organization (through delegates).

The years between the late 1970s and the early 1990s saw a new phase of centralization followed by another of decentralized union initiative. At first sight, these fluctuations were broadly connected to economic trends. In the period of recession and crisis, the centre of gravity of the industrial relations system shifted towards the centre, where it was easier to co-ordinate and moderate wage claims, while in the expansionary phase it tended to move once again to the periphery, where the unions could adapt better to the specific pressures exerted by firms and workers.

As Baglioni (1989) notes, this growing sensitivity of union action to the economic cycle signalled the increasing 'normalization' or institutionalization of industrial relations. However, there was no automatic mechanism of adjustment; changes in the level of union action came about, in the absence of a recognized regulatory framework, through a process of trial and error involving conflict, negotiation and agreement. Positive outcomes could by no means be taken for granted, especially since the new phase of centralization began at a time when union power was at its height, making it more difficult to adopt a strategy of wage restraint. By contrast, the decentralization phase began in the mid-1980s when the unions' representative capacity had diminished and it seemed more practicable for firms to try to regain the direct control over working conditions that they had enjoyed before the 1970s.

Two factors are important for a thorough understanding of the period. First, the confederations attempted to take firmer control of the centrifugal dynamic of union demands that gave a prominent role to industry unions and workplace organizations, and favoured the workforces of the large northern companies in relation to those in small firms, the unemployed, and precarious workers in the south. The second factor was government pressure on the unions to respond 'responsibly' to the crisis.

In the area of collective bargaining, the main novelty during the centralization phase was the consolidation of so-called 'rights to information'. These rights were included in national sector agreements in industry, services and public employment in 1979. They then spread gradually to the company level where they were seen as contributing to the extension and formalization of collective bargaining. Theorized at the time as the 'Italian road' to industrial democracy (Cella and Treu 1989b; Carrieri 1995b), information rights subsequently came to be viewed as ineffective. Nevertheless, they paved the way for more or less formalized union consultation practices, and created an arena for more systematic joint discussion (in ad hoc or permanent joint consultative committees) along the lines first introduced in the *Protocollo IRI*. When the centre of gravity of the industrial relations system shifted once again to the periphery, management, unions and works councils could use the emerging pattern of regular meetings as forums for the joint management of flexibility issues.

Analyses of company-level bargaining (Baglioni and Milani 1990) as well as surveys of company industrial relations (Mortillaro 1986; Regalia and Ronchi 1988–92) have shown that formal and informal negotiation was intense and pervasive, and often largely consensual, in manufacturing firms and private services in the 1980s. Traditional demands in areas such as pay and grading were still widespread. But in the larger and more innovative companies more complex bargaining patterns developed. These focused on procedural issues concerning relationships between the parties, and on working conditions. New methods of working and direct employee involvement, which in other countries were being introduced unilaterally by management, were often accompanied by information disclosure or by attempts to reach prior agreement with the unions (Regalia 1992; Carrieri 1995b).

The tendencies towards the 'proceduralization' of company bargaining relations and the de facto recognition of the unions in the workplace were embodied in the tripartite accord of July 1993. This agreement reformed the bargaining system and simplified its levels. For the first time, rules governing negotiation procedures, competences of different levels, the duration and renewal of agreements, and recourse to strike action, were explicitly defined. The structure of bargaining was built 'around the mainstay of the national industry agreement' (the CCNL) (Cella 1993: 7; Arrigo 1993; EIRR 1993), supplemented – as formally stipulated for the first time – by decentralized bargaining at company level (or by geographical area in the case of small firms). Company bargaining was to be conducted by RSUs and by the local structures of unions signing CCNLs. Any pay increases agreed at this level had to be linked to productivity and company performance. CCNLs would define the bargaining issues and procedures for the lower level; according to the agreement, company bargaining would deal with matters 'different from, and not overlapping with' pay-related provisions of sectoral contracts. The linkage between bargaining levels that had started to emerge with the introduction of information and consultation practices thus became explicit and generalized.

Strikes in the Private Sector and in Public Employment

In a system characterized by a substantial degree of voluntarism, recourse to conflict has always been a relatively easy option. In international comparisons, Italian strike figures are invariably near the top of the table (Bordogna and Provasi 1989; Franzosi 1995). However, the Italian propensity to industrial conflict has not only varied greatly over time, but has displayed markedly different patterns in the private and public sectors.

From the split of 1948–9 until the mobilization of the late 1960s, recourse to industrial action tended to reflect workers' power in the market. The average number of hours lost due to strikes per employee in the economy as a whole rose from 3.46 in the period 1952–58 to 7.26 in 1959–67, the period of the 'economic miracle' (Benetti and Regini 1978). However, the long phase of conflict from the late 1960s cannot be explained in terms of power relations in the market. Europe as a whole experienced an unexpected upsurge of industrial strife stemming from international economic trends (Crouch and Pizzorno 1978), but in Italy it was more radical and long-lasting, for the reasons discussed earlier: the low level of formalization and recognition of the unions' role in the economic sphere, and the influx into mass-production industries of young and unskilled migrant workers.

Table 16.3 Industrial disputes 1952–95

Years	Number	Workers (000s)	Days (000s)	Days per 100,000 employed
1952–58	1,810	1,982	4,755	44,527
1959–67	3,086	2,581	11,345	93,167
1968–73	4,243	5,087	19,307	148,506
1974–79	3,185	7,803	15,460	110,545
1980–84	1,890	5,330	8,683	59,481
1985–89	1,401	1,871	2,650	17,856
1990–94	936	920	1,747	11,420
1995	545	444	796	3,978

Note: Only 'industrial' disputes.
Sources: Bordogna (1995b); ISTAT *Bollettino mensile di statistica*, December 1996.

Table 16.4 Disputes by sector 1952–94 as percentage of all disputes

Years	Agriculture			Industry			Services		
	N	W	D	N	W	D	N	W	D
1952–58	6.80	17.87	31.91	76.77	64.10	50.90	19.24	18.02	17.19
1959–67	4.01	12.67	16.06	68.92	56.88	60.53	29.36	30.45	23.41
1968–73	2.29	8.26	7.89	63.93	64.78	64.90	35.08	26.96	27.21
1974–79	1.80	6.03	7.71	61.56	66.66	58.21	38.55	27.31	34.08
1980–84	2.66	6.74	5.61	61.14	64.08	62.10	39.35	29.83	32.29
1985–89	2.77	5.55	5.93	53.47	56.37	41.29	46.26	36.89	52.78
1990–94	2.78	12.50	4.97	54.75	60.62	60.50	42.47	33.83	34.53

Note: Only 'industrial' disputes. Totals may be slightly higher than 100 as a few disputes were registered in more than one sector.
Source: Bordogna (1995b).

From the second half of the 1970s, conflict in the industrial sector tended to diminish. This reflected, notably, the unions' involvement in concertation, and the increased de facto recognition of their role in the periphery of the industrial relations system (see tables 16.3 and 16.4).

In the public sector, sheltered from market forces, industrial conflict followed an independent pattern of evolution. In the second half of the 1980s, while the strike rate diminished in industry, the public sector witnessed the radicalization of 'tertiary'[5] conflict (Accornero 1985). There were frequent episodes of militant opposition by occupational groups to the actions of the confederal unions; opposition which bred the autonomous organizations known as 'Cobas' (Baldissera 1988; Bordogna 1994).

A law regulating strikes in essential public services was passed in June 1990 in an effort to soften the impact of tertiary conflict. As with the legislation 'privatizing' public sector employment relations, the law was the outcome of prolonged negotiation based on proposals by a group of union-appointed jurists.

While signalling a break with the long tradition of legislative non-intervention, the law emphasized union self-regulation and respected the constitutional principle that the right to strike attaches to all employees as individuals. Nevertheless, it introduced a minimal framework of rules on prior notice of the form and duration of industrial action, and on measures guaranteeing essential services. The activation of these rules was to be agreed between the parties, thereby strengthening the unions' role and promoting co-operation over the definition of legal rules. Finally a new agency was created to evaluate conflict and to mediate on a voluntary basis. The so-called *Commissione di garanzia dell'attuazione della legge* (Committee to Guarantee Implementation of the Law) consisted of experts appointed by presidential decree and accountable to parliament. The reform law undoubtedly contained several weaknesses, and proposals were immediately forthcoming for its amendment (Carinci 1992). But it was probably no coincidence that legislation was followed by a sharp fall in public sector strikes, reversing the anomalous trend of the 1980s towards increasing tertiary conflict (Bordogna 1995a).

Managerial Strategies of Flexibility and the Development of Micro-concertation

In the 1970s, company-level industrial relations in Italy were widely viewed as low-trust. The unions' power in the workplace grew rapidly, but their antagonistic culture persisted intact. Recognition of the rights and power of the unions appeared the only way for employers to obtain the minimum consensus necessary for the pursuit of corporate goals. Concessions were made in the often vain hope of gaining social peace and co-operation in return. A sort of 'negotiated management' of work thus became the rule in most large industrial firms. By contrast, unilateral management of the workforce was still widespread in the small traditional firms, where the search for consensus consisted at most of attempts at persuasion based on the ideology of shared interests. In the more dynamic industrial districts a strategy of individual employee involvement and direct participation in the firm could be observed, especially in the culturally and politically homogeneous areas of the Third Italy (Trigilia 1986). Finally, the state-controlled enterprises, and also a number of multinationals, had developed formal systems of information and consultation rights for workers' representatives (for example, the *Protocollo IRI*).

The first half of the 1980s marked a turning-point at company level, even against a background of adversarial national-level industrial relations. First, the more innovative and dynamic small firms, often with policies of employee involvement, proved to be those best equipped to cope with the increasing volatility of markets and the onslaught of international competition – to the point, indeed, that they were considered the sheet anchor of the Italian economy. Second, many large firms in crisis embarked on a long process of restructuring which required not only considerable technological innovation but also a radical reorganization of work in order to increase flexibility.

In this context two tendencies in personnel management and trade union relations came to the fore. First, measures to increase employees' involvement in and identification with the company were widely introduced. These included quality circles, collective incentives tied to company or departmental performance, and the definition of upgrading and career development paths based on collective rules. None of these phenomena was in itself entirely new. But the novel feature was the willingness of firms to accept a collective rather than merely individual dimension to personnel management and incentive schemes. In the Italian context, this almost invariably meant tolerance of a trade union presence. Also relatively new was the unions' acceptance, if not endorsement, of these phenomena.

The second trend was the spread of what we have called 'secluded micro-concertation' (Regini 1995: 116–20), that is, scattered, unobtrusive and often tacit co-operation between firms and trade unions in order to increase the flexibility of work rules through joint regulation. Unambiguous indicators of this trend are difficult to come by, precisely because they were often not explicit strategies. The pattern that emerges is of a wide-ranging search for mutually advantageous, rather than unilateral, solutions; or more simply the pragmatic adjustment of one party to the needs of the other. Case studies of adjustment by large firms (Regini and Sabel 1989; Colasanto 1987) have stressed such phenomena as informal bargaining on innovations, the flexible interpretation of existing work rules, and the creation of new, informal ones.

Why, after the 'rigidities' imposed by the unions in the 1970s and their weakening in the early 1980s, did the majority of employers not simply jettison previous rules? And why was union behaviour in the workplace so different from that at national level? The answer is probably that the extraordinarily high and politicized level of overt conflict in this period induced the actors to pursue pragmatic co-operation in their day-to-day interactions in order to avert paralysis. The centralization of formal industrial relations from the 1970s placed the national level constantly 'in the spotlight'. It was consequently the most visible level and the one with the greatest symbolic resonance. It was in this arena that adversarial relations, or at least a sharp distinction of roles, predominated, hampering attempts at concertation. But at the peripheral level, precisely because of its relative insulation from the centre, and therefore its lack of symbolic force, co-operation and the pursuit of common interests were generally possible. In short, in order to increase flexibility, employers no longer needed to by-pass the unions but could use them as agents of re-regulation.

Industrial Relations Actors and the Political System

The Changing Role of the State in the Economy

The crucial importance, and at the same time the extreme variability, of relationships between interest organizations and the state in Italy stem from two factors: the unusually broad role played by the state in the economic system compared with other Western countries; and its inefficiency and in particular its singular inability to implement coherent public policies capable of securing a stable consensus among the social partners (Amato 1976; Cassese 1987).

The extensive activities of the state as 'entrepreneur' have only recently, and with great difficulty, begun to be cut back by privatization. In addition, the Italian state has extraordinarily wide-ranging instruments of economic regulation, and considerable capacity to allocate economic resources directly as a result of an abnormally large public debt and a style of public spending giving priority to monetary transfers over public services.

However, despite extensive state intervention, a 'spoils system of pluralistic pressure' (Lange and Regini 1989) has weakened the ability of the public authorities to devise coherent long-term economic policies. Indeed, state decision centres are highly permeable to private interests, frequently giving rise to outright 'distributive collusion' which systematically thwarts attempts to create greater coherence. As a result, Keynesian policies have tended to be fragile and uncertain, and comparative studies talk of a 'weak version of Keynesianism' in Italy (Bordogna and Provasi 1984). This weakness has been reinforced by the minority role historically played by the reformist political forces that have most vigorously promoted such policies; government coalitions whose programmes incorporated significant elements of Keynesianism have led brief and stormy lives (Salvati 1980). Consequently, full employment has never been a truly binding public policy goal in Italy.

Figures on social spending as a percentage of GDP, which rank Italy in an intermediate position among the advanced industrial countries, seem to suggest that the development of the welfare state since the Second World War has brought major benefits for workers and for unions engaged in the political arena. But what sort of welfare state has come about? In the 1960s and 1970s the Italian system did acquire some universalistic-egalitarian features (for example, the extension of compulsory schooling, and the creation in 1978 of the national health service). But overall it preserved a particularist and corporatist character, as was very evident, for example, in the extension of pension coverage to different social and occupational groups at different times and in a wide variety of forms; and universalistic aspects were often implemented using clientelistic means (Ferrera 1984; Paci 1989). Social policy measures have generally been predicated on the provision of benefits for various social groups in order to secure their support. The Italian formula has thus entailed the extreme fragmentation of benefits and heavy welfare dependence by their beneficiaries, coupled with the dispersion of costs and widespread tax evasion (Ferrera 1984). These characteristics, which produced one of the most consensual models of welfare expansion in Europe, today lay the system open to attack not only by the government in its efforts to meet the EMU convergence criteria, but also by the unions, who view the shortcomings of the model more critically than their counterparts in the rest of Europe.

From Labour Exclusion to Collective Mobilization

In the 1950s, the relationships between industrial relations actors and the political-institutional system were conditioned above all by the weakness of the trade unions. The three union confederations lacked the conventional power resources: a high level of membership; a monopoly of workers' representation; and (with the partial exception of CISL and UIL) recognition by the government and employers. This compelled the unions to depend heavily on the support of friendly political parties, which provided them with militants, funds, and legitimacy. At the beginning of the 1950s, for example, four of the eleven members of the CGIL governing council were senior officials from the PCI, and four of the nine members of the CISL governing council had leading roles in the Christian Democratic party; a decade later, the proportions were the same (Alberoni et al. 1968). However, such dependence on the parties tended to divide the unions and alienate them from their rank and file (Pizzorno 1980).

Union weakness was compounded by the effects of the Cold War, which widened divisions and contributed to CGIL's political isolation. The unions' exclusion from economic policy choices also reflected the model of economic development pursued. Exclusion could be seen as the guarantee offered by the government to industrialists; in return the latter relinquished the traditional forms of state protection which conflicted with the decision to open up the Italian economy to international competition (Salvati 1980; Graziani 1979). The overall thrust of economic policy in those years was of non-interference in entrepreneurial decision-making, making it difficult to envisage union involvement in economic policy goals such as full employment.

In the early 1960s, the centre–left governments shifted from a strategy of union exclusion to one of limited union participation in experiments with incomes policy and labour market regulation, and, more generally, in economic planning. Having demonstrated a degree of united action and a moderate capacity for mobilization in negotiating a set of wage increases in 1962, the unions were now repeatedly consulted on a range of economic policy issues. Their dependence on the political parties diminished with the easing of the Cold War and the new Christian Democrat strategy of 'opening to the left', allowing greater attention to be paid to changes in the workplace and less to party-political allegiances.

Nevertheless, both the government's policy of union involvement and the unions' independence from the parties were frequently thwarted, and union influence on policy decisions was insubstantial. On the eve of the 'hot autumn' of 1969, therefore, change was still embryonic.

The Gradual Development of Political Exchange

In the early 1970s, at the height of mobilization, the unions launched a 'struggle for social reforms' which constituted an attempt to undertake direct political action in competition with the political parties (Giugni 1982). This stemmed partly from factors common to other European countries, notably the confederations' desire to regain control over mobilization, and their need to forge alliances with other social groups. In other respects, however, the situation was anomalous in European terms. It reflected the unusual inability of the Italian party system to implement reforms even where a degree of consensus on goals existed; and the unions' determination to employ the mobilization tactics typical of the period to combat their exclusion (even under relatively 'friendly' centre–left governments) from social and economic policy-making.

Although implemented in a conflictual manner, the strategy of reforms marked a transition from exclusion to involvement in the formation of economic and social policy in the phase of political exchange of the second half of the 1970s and the first half of the 1980s. The 'struggle for reforms' failed, however, to achieve significant results, both because the agreements reached with the government, for instance on housing policy, did not find their way into law, and because labour mobilization failed to engender major changes in voting patterns. This reduced the political weight of the unions *vis-à-vis* the political parties and the advantages accruing to the latter from supporting their demands.

From the mid-1970s, the unions' stance on economic and social policies changed; and there was an even more profound shift in the attitude of governments and employers. These developments took place against a background of international recession and spiralling inflation. Until the appearance of Margaret Thatcher on the international scene, any solution to the most serious economic slump since the Second World War seemed impossible without active state intervention and the co-operation of the large interest organizations. In the period 1976–9, governments of 'national solidarity', supported by a parliamentary majority including the PCI, attempted to handle the consequences of economic crisis through social pacts. The unions for their part were now prepared to engage in a wide-ranging process of political exchange involving wage restraint in return for full employment policies, controls on corporate restructuring and social reform. Exchange rested, therefore, on the unions' undertaking not to exploit fully the market power of the strongest workers. The change in union approach was illustrated most vividly by the Eur document of 1978, in which CGIL set out publicly its new strategy of recognizing macro-economic constraints on its actions.

This was undoubtedly an attractive arrangement, and other European countries adopted similar agreements in this period. But it proved difficult to implement. Neither unions nor government had sufficient control over the behaviour of the actors on whom the success of the pact ultimately depended. In a system such as Italy's, where industrial relations were not fully centralized and remained poorly institutionalized, dissenting groups of workers and union leaders at lower levels could advance demands at odds with the commitments made by the top leadership. Thus, although the unions exercised restraint by focusing on information rights rather than wages demands, this moderation was applied unevenly in different areas of the economy (Golden 1988), and in some cases it was vociferously opposed.

The government, for its part, while accepting that economic and social policy should take account of union objectives, could not guarantee that these goals would be achieved, since decisions had to be approved by an often hostile parliament and implemented by an equally hostile public administration (Regini 1984). In 1977 and 1978 the government for the first time sought the tacit prior consent of the unions to a number of important pieces of legislation, prompting some legal commentators to call them *leggi contrattate* (negotiated laws). Thus laws on industrial restructuring and youth employment in 1977, and a law on vocational training and a parliamentary bill to reform the pensions system in 1978, all to some extent took account of the unions' redistributive goals and their concern with boosting employment and exerting control over the economy. However, the pensions bill was blocked in parliament as a result of lobbying by the groups that it penalized. Moreover, legislation was only partially implemented: the public administration was often unwilling and unable to adopt the innovative behaviour required by the spirit of the measures, while the government frequently failed to introduce the further measures essential for implementation.

These factors led to a decline in concertation, and the PCI's withdrawal of support from the government in 1979 dealt the final blow to an experience already considered by its protagonists to have run its course.

Attempts at Social Pacts in the 1980s

The early 1980s saw prolonged and gruelling negotiations for an 'anti-inflation pact'. Initially proposed by the government in 1981, a tripartite accord was eventually concluded in January 1983. It was hailed by many as a breakthrough in relationships between industrial relations actors and the political system.

The 1983 accord marked a change in the government's role in social pacts. In exchange for a revision of the wage indexation mechanism and the more flexible use of the labour force it offered publicly financed benefits such as a partial transfer of employers' social charges to general taxation, the maintenance of workers' real incomes through fiscal means, and increased family allowances for workers. The government's role thus became more active but also more costly, since it had to compensate for the costs incurred by firms and workers in complying with the accord. This widely acclaimed agreement was based on an ad hoc exchange which did not constrain the future behaviour of the parties, rather than on an ambitious set of economic and social policies as in the previous decade.

The ad hoc nature of the agreement meant that subsequent concertation efforts could not start from an established base, and hence proved largely unsuccessful. Unable to draw on further public resources to persuade the social partners to conclude another agreement, the government stressed the general benefits of a reduction in inflation – a reduction which depended crucially on the actors' behaviour. It was therefore a proposal for an exchange based, not on the distribution of the benefits of the accord, but implicitly on a sharing of costs in order to achieve a common goal.

In 1984, this approach was accepted by the two smaller trade unions but not by CGIL, which did not sign the accord. Their respective decisions were influenced by their relationships with political parties, as well as by their differing assessments of its contents. The government reacted by converting the proposal into a decree to give it general efficacy. The issue acquired wider symbolic importance as a result of the PCI's decision to organize a referendum against the decree. The result of the referendum, held in June 1985, was a narrow defeat for the PCI, but it nevertheless marked the end of the period of anti-inflationary social pacts. The content of these pacts had by now shifted from economic matters to the predominantly symbolic exchange of legitimacy between interest organizations and government. Thus, inevitably, divergent political goals once again prevailed within trade union cultures no longer able to agree on the contents of bargaining.

The Novelties of the 1990s: The Success of Formal Tripartite Agreements

In the late 1980s and early 1990s, the resumption of tripartite concertation was also obstructed by the still unresolved and vital issue of the wage indexation mechanism. The *scala mobile* (sliding-scale mechanism) automatically linked wages to the inflation rate (the degree of linkage oscillating around 80 per cent before undergoing significant reductions from 1986). This was a major problem not only for firms, because of its impact on labour costs and competitiveness in a period of high inflation, but also for collective bargaining, given that the negotiable margins for wage increases and differentials were very narrow. On the other hand, it had high symbolic value for the unions, since it was the outcome of the waves of collective mobilization of earlier years and it was the principal indicator of the unions' ability to resist changes in power relationships.

However, the political situation changed markedly in 1992, the year in which the 'Clean Hands' anti-corruption investigation got under way. The April elections saw the collapse of the old political system, and the new 'technocratic government' faced a dramatic economic crisis. In an atmosphere of national emergency, the government was able to mobilize support for the most drastic programme to balance the budget since the war.

The tripartite accord of July 1992 was born in this climate. Aiming to achieve a drastic reduction in inflation, it abolished the *scala mobile* and froze company-level wage bargaining for the period 1992–3. Thus the core of the agreement was the curbing of wage increases without any of the traditional compensations that had accompanied political exchange in the early 1980s. It was hailed as the first real breakthrough in relations among the three actors. It was incomplete, however, in that it only blocked company-level bargaining temporarily, without introducing rules and procedures into the overall bargaining system. This problem was addressed a year later by a new 'technocratic government'. The July 1993 tripartite agreement was less of a short-term crisis measure. It set out a stable framework of pay determination and bargaining relations. First, besides confirming the abolition of the *scala mobile*, it introduced an incomes policy based on agreed but autonomous behaviour in compliance with the expected inflation rate. Second, as discussed above, it specified in detail for the first time the respective competences of the national-sector and company- or local bargaining levels.

Incomes policy and reform of the collective bargaining system have been the most important aspects of concertation in the 1990s, but not the only ones. A further key area is reform of the social security system. Spending on pensions has grown to dramatic proportions in Italy. Indeed, whereas the ratio of overall social spending to GDP is lower than the European average (25.8 per cent compared with the EU average of 28.5 per cent in 1993), the proportion of such spending on pensions – 15.4 per cent of GDP compared with an average of 11.9 per cent in the twelve countries of the EU in 1993 – is wholly anomalous.[6] If this figure is set against the background of an extremely high public deficit and debt on the one hand, and a declining population and labour force on the other, it is easy to understand why reform of the pensions system has become the principal concern of Italian policy-makers and a cornerstone of their strategies for economic renewal.

The Amato government was the first to tackle the problem with any degree of success. In 1992, it issued a decree raising the retirement age and the minimum number of years of contributions required to qualify for a pension. The measure also made it more difficult to combine a pension with other sources of income. There still remained, however, the problem of a 'structural' reform which would replace earnings-related pensions with a contributions-related scheme and abolish 'seniority pensions' (which allow employees to retire at any age after making 35 years of contributions). These issues profoundly affected the 'acquired rights' of many categories of workers, as well as the role and power of the trade unions, who control the INPS (the institute which administers the pension scheme for employees in the private sector).

The Berlusconi government introduced measures in the 1994 budget effectively scrapping seniority pensions. Berlusconi's attempt unilaterally to change the unwritten rules of the game on social security policy provoked widespread protests from the labour movement, even though the unions' proposals for reform did not differ greatly from the government's. The unions immediately called a successful general strike. The scale of the protest throughout the country weakened support for the government's position, and it was forced to concede an agreement with the unions under which the pensions measures were removed from the budget law and postponed until the following year. Confindustria, which had explicitly supported the measures, watched these developments with concern.

At the beginning of 1995, the Berlusconi administration was replaced by yet another 'technocratic' government, which set pensions reform as one of four objectives to be achieved before the next elections. The ensuing government–union negotiations took the union scheme as their starting point. The unions put the resulting agreement to a workplace ballot, achieving a narrow but significant majority in favour. Confindustria decided not to sign the accord on the grounds that the reform was not sufficiently radical, and that the envisaged savings would not come into effect rapidly enough. Nevertheless, the government converted the agreement into legislation. This new 'negotiated law' was hailed as one of the pillars of economic recovery, alongside the tripartite agreements of 1992 and

1993. The key factor in obtaining union support was the maintenance of the previous pension system (wholly or in part) for employees with greater seniority. This obviously meant that expected cuts in expenditure would take longer to come through. But it was the support from the unions, and their ability to secure the more or less grudging acceptance of the reform by workers, that allowed the outcome of the previous year to be reversed.

A final important area of tripartite concertation has been employment policy. In September 1996, a 'Pact for Employment' was signed to promote employment, especially in the less developed areas of the country. The most significant points of the agreement include reform of education and training systems, promotion of temporary work and of working-time reductions and – perhaps most important – the notion of 'territorial pacts' to promote new investment in areas with low rates of development and high unemployment. These agreements are to be signed by unions and employers' organizations, local authorities, banks and other private participants. They should involve greater wage and labour market flexibility; however, new divisions among the trade unions have emerged on this sensitive issue.

Conclusions

The Difficult Coexistence of Voluntarism and Institutionalization

The Italian industrial relations system has been conventionally described – at least until the July 1993 agreement – as having a low level of institutionalization, in the sense of lacking formalized and stable rules governing relations between the actors (Cella 1989; Napoli 1989; Accornero 1992). As we have repeatedly shown, this applies to the fundamental aspects of industrial relations narrowly defined: the structure and operation of the representation system, the forms of interaction between capital and labour, the role of the state in this interaction, and recourse to conflict. However, if the definition of labour relations is extended to include the ways in which public services and the public administration are regulated, especially in the fields of welfare and social security, the role of Italian interest organizations is much more formalized, while that of the public institutions appears to be diffuse and pervasive.

Thus one observes a pronounced voluntarism in relations between unions and employers (particularly in the private sector), coupled with the institutional involvement of industrial relations actors in the implementation of social policies and in the regulation of public sector employment. This is a structural feature of the Italian system of industrial relations which has never been substantially altered, even by the Workers' Statute. This structural dualism – supplementing that between the 'overt' central level and the 'covert' peripheral level of union action – helps explain the extraordinary stability of a system otherwise subject to constant change.

Before drawing a number of general conclusions, let us return briefly to the two aspects of this question. First, the low level of institutionalization of the Italian system of industrial relations is exemplified by the main features of the actors, their behaviour and their interactions. We have shown that Italian interest organizations are loosely regulated and operate in an arena of interest representation with few barriers to entry. This has favoured the emergence of a system of pluralistic representation for both unions and employers' organizations which is at once organizationally strong and unevenly representative. Workplace representative structures, too, are characterized by a high degree of informality which the interconfederal agreement of December 1993 on the RSU has only partly attenuated. We have stressed that this fluidity has permitted the growth of institutions sufficiently flexible to adapt to change with relative success. As regards collective action, the general lack of legislative restrictions on strikes and the absence of compulsory arbitration in labour disputes encourages conflictual behaviour even by small groups independent from, and sometimes hostile to, the major unions. Finally, collective bargaining in Italy is not subject to legal rules (as in Germany), nor is bargaining between the social partners compulsory (as in France). Consequently, at least until the accord of July 1993, the bargaining structure has moved back and forth between the centre and the periphery according to circumstances and power relations, without well-established rules accepted by both sides. This has given rise to overlaps in competences and in the issues addressed at different levels, and has hampered co-ordination by the union confederations.

However, this phenomenon is to some extent counterbalanced by the second fundamental aspect: the relatively formalized and stable involvement of the social partners in the implementation of public policies and by the indirect intervention of public institutions in labour relations. This side to the relationship, however, has remained largely concealed and its effects largely unobserved. A first element concerns the role assigned to the social partners. These have been active in public policy institutions since the period after the Second World War, when representatives of the interest organizations were involved in the administration of social security bodies and welfare programmes, from the pensions system to the Wages Guarantee Fund. Their role then expanded through participation in the numerous tripartite committees that intervene in labour market management at the national and local level. Added to these are the union representatives sitting on the administrative boards of ministries and public agencies, as well as on the hundreds of committees that regulate the employment relationship in the public sector (Cammelli 1980; Isap 1987; Reyneri 1989; Rusciano 1990). A second element is the intervention by public actors in the resolution of collective disputes, at both the centre and the periphery of the system. This type of intervention is not formally envisaged within the Italian industrial relations system, but its repeated occurrence has led to the definition of a framework for action to which the social partners can refer. Finally, industrial relations actors are frequently consulted by the public authorities on labour-related matters.

This dualism between voluntarism and informality, on the one hand, and involvement in and intervention by public institutions, on the other, undoubtedly stems from the unions' economic and political weakness, which for many years allowed other industrial relations actors simply to ignore them. Informality could ensure flexibility at low cost and without excessive risks; while institutional involvement (at least symbolic) by the social partners, and intervention by the state to ensure a minimum level of protection for the industrial labour force and to forestall organized protest, could substitute for a more developed and formalized industrial relations system, and thereby build social cohesion.

Over time, this arrangement has generated a number of unforeseen effects. First, the results of the unions' institutional involvement have been generally disappointing, as regards their ability to influence the administration's choices, and the efficiency and quality of services. Second, however, there have been a number of beneficial consequences for the industrial relations system. Institutional participation has created spaces for contact between the social partners even in periods when collective bargaining has faltered. A further effect has been the consolidation of the unwritten rule that implementation of major changes promoted by the public authorities requires the consent of the interest organizations (Treu 1987). This also means that the effective influence of the unions in Italy has always been somewhat greater than might appear from indicators such as membership levels or the results of collective bargaining. Institutional involvement has also provided interest organizations with opportunities to obtain benefits and resources which they can then convert into selective incentives for their members.

Overall, therefore, the informality and voluntarism of the Italian industrial relations system has increased its ability to adapt to changing circumstances. But this has been at the price of the unpredictable behaviour of actors, and their tendency to adopt a short-term perspective. On the other hand, the widespread institutional involvement of the interest organizations has helped to build social cohesion, as well as indirectly fostering industrial innovation and adjustment. At the same time, however, it has hampered reform of a welfare system whose unwieldy and haphazard structure has grown increasingly inefficient and inequitable.

It seems that, with the increased need for predictability, the advantages of informality and indirect institutionalization have diminished, and their costs have increased. Accordingly, at the beginning of the 1990s, there was increasing debate as to whether formal regulation should be imposed on processes that were still substantially hidden, implicit and under the control of largely autonomous actors.

The Turning-point of the 1993 Tripartite Agreement as an Attempt to Overcome the Dual Character of Italian Industrial Relations

The resumption of concertation in the 1990s has radically altered the traditional scenario of coexistence between voluntarism and indirect institutionalization. Not only has negotiation between unions, employers' associations and governments given rise to a large number of formal agreements, bilateral and trilateral; more importantly these actors have for the first time explicitly set out to impose a framework of formal regulation on the collective bargaining structure and on their own relationships. This commitment to the institutionalization of industrial relations was by no means inevitable, since it conflicted with the voluntarist tradition, and to an extent with the interests of the actors themselves, especially given the climate of profound uncertainty surrounding ongoing political change.

In practice, informality can offer considerable advantages, as shown by the good performance of the Italian industrial relations system during the economic adjustment of the 1980s. An informal system can be highly adaptive in phases of profound change, allowing arrangements adopted at the periphery of the system to be tailored to local conditions. It permits experimentation with innovations that would be difficult to introduce if they required institutional change. Moreover, formal regulation may have the effect of limiting interaction by removing from the agenda those issues not subject to regulation.

However, informality also has drawbacks, most notably the unpredictability of industrial relations and their vulnerability to shifts in power relations. In the current climate, the unions judged that there was a likelihood that sub-standard situations would multiply relative to those in which tradition and power relations would give rise to higher standards. Such considerations tipped the balance in favour of regulation. To offset the potential inflexibility of institutionalized relations, the normative framework provided by the tripartite agreement of 1993 was specifically designed to create spaces for interaction at the periphery of the system (company-level and local bargaining) rather than eliminate them.

These may be important factors in the stabilization of concertation. However, it is not yet clear to what extent the actors regard concertation as an institutionalized fact that will not be called into question with every shift in power relations or external circumstances. Confindustria's formal request to the President of the Republic before the 1994 elections – that whatever the winning coalition, it should commit itself to maintaining the 1993 tripartite agreement – signals a clear change of attitude among employers. But this change is still not firmly established, as is shown by the controversies between the social partners and with the government which have re-emerged since the centre–left coalition gained office.

Despite its importance, the tripartite accord of 1993 was an agreement on the rules, not a social pact committing the parties to a shared vision of economic development and priorities. Indeed, even agreement on rules may soon deteriorate if it is not injected with new content. By a 'shared vision of economic development' we do not mean the old exchange between employment and productivity, but instead a conception of the competitiveness of the national economy based on a partially shared programme for the development of human resources. Despite the importance of recent events, the relationships among employers, unions and state in Italy are still a long way from achieving this goal.

Abbreviations

ASAP	*Associazione Sindacale per le Aziende Petrolchimiche e Collegate a Partecipazione Statale* – Employers' Association for Public Sector Oil and Petrochemical Enterprises

CCNL	*contratto collettivo nazionale di lavoro* – national industry agreement
CGIL	*Confederazione Generale Italiana del Lavoro* – Italian General Confederation of Labour
CIG	*Cassa Integrazione Guadagni* – earnings maintenance fund
CISL	*Confederazione italiana sindacati dei lavoratori* – Italian Confederation of Workers' Unions
CISNAL	*Confederazione Italiana dei Sindacati Nazionali Lavoratori* – Italian Confederation of National Workers' Unions
cobas	*comitati di base* – rank-and-file committees
Coldiretti	*Confederazione Coltivatori Diretti* – Confederation of Self-employed Farmers
Confagricoltura	*Confederazione Generale dell'Agricoltura Italiana* – General Confederation of Italian Agriculture
Confapi	*Confederazione della Piccola e Media Industria* – Confederation of Small and Medium-Sized Industry
Confcoltivatori	*Confederazione Coltivatori* – Confederation of Farmers
Confcommercio	*Confederazione tra le Associazioni dei Commercianti* – Confederation of Commercial Associations
Confesercenti	*Confederazione esercenti attività commerciali e turistiche* – Confederation of Commercial and Tourist Operators
Confindustria	*Confederazione Generale dell'Industria Italiana* – General Confederation of Italian Industry
DC	*Democrazia Cristiana* – Christian Democracy/Christian Democrats
ENI	*Ente Nazionale Idrocarburi* – National Petrochemical Agency
INPS	*Istituto Nazionale per la Previdenza Sociale* – National Institute for Social Insurance
Intersind	*Associazione Sindacale Intersind* – employers' association for public sector enterprises
IRI	*Istituto per la Ricostruzione Industriale* – Institute for Industrial Reconstruction (state industrial holding company)
PCI	*Partito Comunista Italiano* – Italian Communist Party
PDS	*Partito Democratico della Sinistra* – Democratic Party of the Left
PSI	*Partito Socialista Italiano* – Italian Socialist Party
RC	*Rifondazione Comunista* – Communist Reconstruction Party
RSA	*Rappresentanza sindacale aziendale* – workplace union representation
RSU	*Rappresentanza sindacale unitaria* – Unitary workplace union representation
UIL	*Unione Italiana del Lavoro* – Italian Union of Labour

| Notes

1 This section draws freely on the chapter written by A. Ferner and R. Hyman for the previous edition of this volume. We wish to acknowledge their special sensitivity to what a foreign reader especially needs to know in order to capture the 'Italian enigma', and at the same time their sophisticated, insider-like understanding of how the Italian system of industrial relations works.

2 In 1992 and 1993, when tripartite agreements on incomes policies were signed, inflation

was about 5 per cent, public debt well above 110 per cent of GDP and the current budget deficit slightly below 10 per cent. In the following years, as a result both of these agreements and of rather strict budget laws aimed at meeting the 'Maastricht parameters', these indicators have dramatically improved. By the end of 1996, the inflation rate was down to 3.1 per cent and the budget deficit to 6.7 per cent of GDP (Censis 1996). Public debt was still 124.3 per cent of GDP, but decreasing for the first time in many years, and against the general trend in Europe.

3 Unions not affiliated to the CGIL, CISL and UIL confederations. Gradually the autonomous unions also created their own confederal-type organizations (Stefanelli 1980). A fourth confederation, which played a negligible role except in some areas of the public sector, is the neo-fascist CISNAL.

4 The power of veto depended on the right to withdraw from the accord. Each of the 'most representative' unions (and therefore the three central confederations and the autonomous unions signatories to the collective contracts) could independently set up their own company-level bodies (i.e. their own distinct RSAs providing associative rather than general representation).

5 The label is used to stress both that conflict takes place in the services (or 'tertiary') sector and involves 'third' parties (the customers) besides the two conflicting ones.

6 OECD and European Commission figures cited in *La Repubblica Affari & Finanza*, XI, 15 (22 April 1996), pp. 1–3.

▌ References and Further Reading

Accornero, A. 1973: *Gli anni '50 in fabbrica*. Bari: De Donato.

Accornero, A. 1976: Per una nuova fase di studi sul movimento sindacale. In A. Accornero (ed.), *Problemi del movimento sindacale in Italia 1943–1973*. Milan: Feltrinelli, 1–105.

Accornero, A. 1985: La 'terziarizzazione' del conflitto e i suoi effetti. In G.-P. Cella and M. Regini (eds), *Il conflitto industriale in Italia*. Bologna: Il Mulino, 275–313.

Accornero, A. 1992: *La parabola del sindacato*. Bologna: Il Mulino.

Alacevich, F. 1996: *Le relazioni industriali in Italia. Cultura e strategie*. Rome: La Nuova Italia Scientifica.

Alberoni, F. et al. 1968: *La presenza sociale del PCI e della DC*. Bologna: Il Mulino.

Amato, G. 1976: *Economia, politica e istituzioni in Italia*. Bologna: Il Mulino.

Armeni, R. 1988: *Gli extraconfederali*. Rome: Ed. Lavoro.

Arrigo, G. 1993: La riforma della contrattazione collettiva tra nuove regole e vecchi modelli organizzativi. *Prospettiva sindacale*, 84, 15–24.

Baglioni, G. (ed.) 1989: *Le relazioni industriali in Italia e in Europa negli anni '80*. Rome: Ed. Lavoro.

Baglioni, G. and Milani, R. (eds) 1990: *La contrattazione collettiva nelle aziende industriali in Italia*. Milan: Franco Angeli.

Bagnasco, A. 1988: *La costruzione sociale del mercato*. Bologna: Il Mulino.

Baldissera, A. 1988: *La svolta dei quarantamila. Dai quadri Fiat ai Cobas*. Milan: Comunità.

Barbieri, M. 1995: Le politiche contrattuali dopo il Protocollo di luglio: continuità e discontinuità degli assetti contrattuali nel pubblico impiego. In Cesos (ed.), 295–307.

Becchi Collidà, A. 1989: Le associazioni imprenditoriali. In G.-P. Cella and T. Treu (eds), 135–55.

Benetti, M. and Regini, M. 1978: Confronti temporali e spaziali sui conflitti di lavoro. In P. Alessandrini (ed.), *Conflittualità e aspetti normativi del lavoro*. Bologna: Il Mulino, 35–85.

Bianco, M. and Trento, S. 1995: Capitalismi a confronto: i modelli di controllo delle imprese. *Stato e Mercato*, 43, 65–93.

Bonazzi, G. 1984: La lotta dei 35 giorni alla Fiat: un'analisi sociologica. *Politica ed Economia*, 15(11), 33–43.

Bordogna, L. 1994: *Pluralismo senza mercato. Rappresentanza e conflitto nel settore pubblico*. Milan: F. Angeli.

Bordogna, L. 1995a: Tendenze recenti del conflitto industriale. Implicazioni per l'analisi e la regolazione. In A. Chiesi, I. Regalia and M. Regini (eds), 159–84.

Bordogna, L. 1995b: La conflittualità. In Cesos (ed.), 75–81.

Bordogna, L. and Provasi, G. 1984: *Politica, economia e rappresentanza degli interessi*. Bologna: Il Mulino.

Bordogna, L. and Provasi, G. 1989: La conflittualità. In G.-P. Cella and T. Treu (eds), 275–305.

Cammelli, M. 1980: *L'amministrazione per collegi*. Bologna: Il Mulino.

Carinci, F. 1986: Il Protocollo Iri nella dinamica delle relazioni industriali. In Cesos (ed.), 425–40.

Carinci, F. 1992: L'attività della commissione di garanzia (L.no.146/1990). *Giornale di diritto del lavoro e di relazioni industriali*, 55, 435–59.

Carrieri, M. 1995a: *L'incerta rappresentanza. Sindacati e consenso negli anni '90: dal monopolio confederale alle rappresentanze sindacali unitarie*. Bologna: Il Mulino.

Carrieri, M. 1995b: Alla ricerca della democrazia economica. In A. Chiesi, I. Regalia and M. Regini (eds), 185–207.

Cassese, S. 1987: Stato ed economia: il problema storico. In P. Lange and M. Regini (eds), *Stato e regolazione sociale*. Bologna: Il Mulino, 45–52.

Cella, G.-P. 1989: Criteria of regulation in Italian industrial relations: a case of weak institutions. In P. Lange and M. Regini (eds), 167–85.

Cella, G.-P. 1993: Luglio 1993: un passo avanti. *Prospettiva sindacale*, 84, 7–8.

Cella, G.-P. and Treu, T. (eds) 1989a: *Relazioni industriali. Manuale per l'analisi dell'esperienza italiana*. Bologna: Il Mulino.

Cella, G.-P. and Treu, T. 1989b: La contrattazione collettiva. In G.-P. Cella and T. Treu (eds), 157–217.

Censis 1996: *30° Rapporto sulla situazione sociale del paese 1996*. Milan: Franco Angeli.

Cesos (ed.)1982–95: *Le relazioni sindacali in Italia. Rapporto annuale*. Roma: Ed. Lavoro.

Chiesi, A., Regalia, I. and Regini, M. (eds) 1995: *Lavoro e relazioni industriali in Europa*. Rome: La Nuova Italia Scientifica.

Colasanto, M. (ed.) 1987: *Innovazione e regolazione nell'impresa*, Milano: Franco Angeli.

Couffignal, G. 1979: *I sindacati in Italia*. Rome: Editori Riuniti.

Craveri, P. 1977: *Sindacati e istituzioni nel dopoguerra*. Bologna: Il Mulino.

Crouch, C. and Pizzorno, A. (eds) 1978: *The Resurgence of Class Conflict in Western Europe Since 1968*. London: Macmillan, 2 vols.

Della Rocca, G. 1976: L'offensiva politica degli imprenditori nelle fabbriche. In A. Accornero (ed.), *Problemi del movimento sindacale in Italia 1943–1973*. Milan: Feltrinelli, 609–38.

EIRR (European Industrial Relations Review) 1993: Central agreement on incomes policy and bargaining reform. *European Industrial Relations Review*, 236, 15–19.

Ferrera, M. 1984: *Il welfare state in Italia*. Bologna: Il Mulino.

Franzosi, R. 1995: *The Puzzle of Strikes. Class and State Strategies in Postwar Italy*. CUP.

Garofalo, M.G. 1994: Legislazione e contrattazione collettiva nel 1992. *Giornale di diritto del lavoro e di relazioni industriali*, **61**, 163–95.

Giacinto, E. 1995: La sindacalizzazione. In Cesos (ed.), 82–98.

Giugni, G. 1976: Critica e rovesciamento dell'assetto contrattuale. In A. Accornero (ed.), *Problemi del movimento sindacale in Italia 1943–1973*. Milan: Feltrinelli, 779–807.

Giugni, G. 1982 Il diritto del lavoro negli anni '80. *Giornale di Diritto del Lavoro e di Relazioni Industriali*, **15**, 373–410.

Giugni, G. 1995 La rappresentanza sindacale dopo il referendum. *Giornale di Diritto del Lavoro e di Relazioni Industriali*, **67**, 357–68.

Golden, M. 1988: *Labor Divided: Incomes Policies, Trade Unions and the Italian Communist Party*. Ithaca: Cornell University Press.

Graziani, A. (ed.) 1979: *L'economia italiana 1945–1970*. Bologna: Il Mulino.

Isap (ed.) 1987: *Le relazioni fra amministrazione e sindacati*. Milan: Giuffré, 2 vols.

Iversen, T. 1996: Power, flexibility, and the breakdown of centralised wage bargaining. Denmark and Sweden in comparative perspective. *Comparative Politics*, July, 399–436.

Kern, H. and Schumann, M. 1984: *Das Ende der Arbeitsteilung? Rationalisierung in der Industriellen Produktion*. München: Beck.

Lange, P. and Regini, M. (eds) 1989: *State, Market and Social Regulation. New Perspectives on Italy*. Cambridge: CUP.

Lange, P., Ross, G. and Vannicelli, M. 1982: *Unions, Change and Crisis: French and Italian Union Strategy and the Political Economy 1945–1980*. London: Allen & Unwin.

Lanzalaco, L. 1990: *Dall'impresa all'associazione. Le organizzazioni degli imprenditori: la Confindustria in prospettiva comparata*. Milan: Franco Angeli.

Lanzalaco, L. 1995: L'evoluzione dell'azione imprenditoriale: il ruolo delle associazioni datoriali. In A. Chiesi, I. Regalia and M. Regini (eds), 111–32.

Martinelli, A. (ed.) 1994: *L'azione collettiva degli imprenditori italiani*. Milan: Ed. Comunità.

Mascini, M. 1995: Le organizzazioni imprenditoriali, in Cesos (ed.), 199–207.

Ministero del Lavoro 1990: *Report '89: Labour and Employment Policies in Italy*, Rome: IPZS.

Mortillaro, F. 1984: *Sindacati e no*. Milano: Ed. Sole-24 Ore.

Mortillaro, F. 1986: *Aspettando il robot*. Milano: Ed. Sole-24 Ore.

Napoli, M. 1989: Il quadro giuridico-istituzionale. In G.-P. Cella and T. Treu (eds), 47–83.

Negrelli, S. 1987: La contrattazione della flessibilità. *Prospettiva sindacale*, 18(66), 7–20.

Paci, M. 1989: *Pubblico e privato nei moderni sistemi di welfare*. Napoli: Liguori.

Piore, M. and Sabel, C. 1984: *The Second Industrial Divide*. New York: Basic Books.

Pizzorno, A. 1978: Political exchange and collective identity in industrial conflict. In C. Crouch and A. Pizzorno (eds), 277–98.

Pizzorno, A. 1980: *I soggetti del pluralismo*. Bologna: Il Mulino.

Pizzorno, A., Reyneri, E., Regini, M. and Regalia, I. 1978: *Lotte operaie e sindacato: il ciclo 1968–1972 in Italia*. Bologna: Il Mulino.

Pontusson, J. and Swenson, P. 1996: Labor markets, production strategies, and wage bargaining institutions. The Swedish employer offensive in comparative perspective. *Comparative Political Studies*, **29**(2), 163–79.

Regalia, I. 1981: Ipotesi sulla sindacalizzazione negli anni settanta. *Democrazia e Diritto*, **5**, 81–90.

Regalia, I. 1984: *Eletti e abbandonati. Modelli e stili di rappresentanza in fabbrica*. Bologna: Il Mulino.

Regalia, I. 1988: Democracy and unions: Towards a critical appraisal. *Economic and Industrial Democracy*, **9**, 345–71.

Regalia, I. 1990: *Al posto del conflitto. Le relazioni di lavoro nel terziario*. Bologna: Il Mulino.

Regalia, I. 1992: New forms of organization and direct involvement of the workers in Italy. Dublin: European Foundation for the Improvement of Living and Working Conditions, Working Paper No. 92/11.

Regalia, I. 1995: Italy: The costs and benefits of informality. In J. Rogers and W. Streeck (eds), 217–41.

Regalia, I. and Ronchi, R. 1988–92: Le relazioni industriali nelle imprese lombarde, Milano: IRES Papers nos. 14, 20, 24, 31, 34.

Regini, M. 1984: The conditions for political exchange: How concertation emerged and collapsed in Italy and Great Britain. In J. Goldthorpe (ed.), *Order and Conflict in Contemporary Capitalism*. Oxford: Clarendon Press, 124–42.

Regini, M. 1987: Social pacts in Italy. In I. Scholten (ed.), *Political Stability and Neo-Corporatism*. London: Sage, 195–215.

Regini, M. (ed.) 1992: *The Future of Labour Movements*, London: Sage.

Regini, M. 1995: *Uncertain Boundaries. The Social and Political Construction of European Economies*. CUP.

Regini, M. and Lange, P. 1990: Twenty years after the "hot autumn": Work and politics in Italy from rupture to change. *Labour*, **1**, 3–8.

Regini, M. and Sabel, C. (eds) 1989: *Strategie di riaggiustamento industriale*. Bologna: Il Mulino.

Reyneri, E. 1989: The Italian labor market: between state control and social regulation. In P. Lange and M. Regini (eds), 129–45.

Rogers, J. and Streeck, W. (eds) 1995: *Works Councils. Consultation, Representation, and Co-operation in Industrial Relations*. Chicago and London: The University of Chicago Press.

Romagnoli, G. (ed.) 1980: *La sindacalizzazione fra ideologia e pratica. Il caso italiano 1950–1977*. Roma: Ed. Lavoro.

Romagnoli, G. and Della Rocca, G. 1989: Il sindacato. In G.P. Cella and T. Treu (eds), 85–134.

Rusciano, M. 1990: Lavoro pubblico e privato: dalla "separatezza" all'"unificazione" normativa. In AA.VV., *Stato sociale, servizi, pubblico impiego*. Napoli: Jovene, 7–32.

Sabel, C. 1982: *Work and Politics*. CUP.

Salvati, M. 1980: *Alle origini dell'inflazione italiana*. Bologna: Il Mulino.

Sciarra, S. 1986: Restructuring labour in the enterprise: Italy. *Bulletin of Comparative Labour Relations*, **15**, 53–84.

Squarzon, C. 1989: I consigli dei delegati vent'anni dopo. *Prospettiva sindacale*, **73/74**, 151–71.

Stefanelli, R. (ed.) 1980: *I sindacati autonomi: particolarismo e strategie confederali negli anni '70*. Bari: De Donato.

Streeck, W. 1993: The Rise and Decline of Neo-corporatism. In IIRA (ed.), *Economic and Political Changes in Europe*. Bari: Cacucci Editore, 27–62.

Treu, T. 1971: *Sindacato e rappresentanze aziendali*. Bologna: Il Mulino.

Treu, T. 1987: Italian industrial relations in the past ten years. *Bulletin of Comparative Labour Relations*, **16**, 167–81.

Trigilia, C. 1986: *Grandi partiti e piccole imprese*, Bologna: Il Mulino.

Tronti, L. 1991: Employment protection and labour market segmentation. *Labour*, **5**, 121–45.

Turone, T. 1973: *Storia del sindacato in Italia 1943–1969*. Bari: Laterza.

Vais, M. 1958: *Le commissioni interne*. Rome: Ed. Riuniti.

Visser, J. 1990: *In Search of Inclusive Unionism*. Deventer: Kluwer.

Visser, J. 1996: Trends and variations in European collective bargaining. University of Amsterdam. Unpublished paper.

Wedderburn, K.W. (Lord) 1991: *Employment Rights in Britain and Europe*. London: Lawrence & Wishart.

17 | Greece: The Maturing of the System

NICOS D. KRITSANTONIS

In the 1990s, Greece continues its post-war social and economic transition: from political authoritarianism and dictatorship, and from profound economic backwardness, to integration within the European Union and a competitive international economy. Adaptation has required a comprehensive modernization of Greek institutions; and as part of the process, a transformation in industrial relations.

▍Historical background

The history of Modern Greece since the formation of an independent state in 1830 may be divided into four stages. Until 1890 the economy was pre-capitalist, and agriculture remained the dominant sector. Between 1890 and the 1920s a considerable inflow of capital facilitated the development of transportation and related infrastructure, as well as initial stages of industrialization. In the third phase – the 1920s and 1930s – the domestic economy expanded rapidly. However, the economy still remained primarily agrarian. Only since 1945 – and the crushing of the left in the civil war of 1944–9 – has Greece become a decisively capitalist economy.

The post-war years may in turn be perceived as four distinct phases. In the first, external capital investment under the Truman Doctrine and the Marshall Plan helped consolidate the Greek economy and integrate it within international trade. The state was closely involved in the process, undertaking infrastructural development, investing in strategic industries, and offering incentives for foreign investment.

The second phase, after 1960, saw impressive economic growth. The inflow of foreign capital continued; multinationals gained control of key sectors of the economy. At the same time, domestic capital formation was encouraged by state loan finance and other incentives. GNP increased rapidly – by 7 per cent a year between 1950 and 1973. Thus Greece was clearly a successful entrant to the international economy. Economic expansion, however, was achieved at the price of political repression, particularly following the military coup of 1967, when trade unions and opposition parties were driven underground.

The downfall of the military dictatorship in 1974 coincided with the global oil crisis. The policies of the conservative New Democracy (ND) government compounded the problems of the Greek economy. In the same period Greece entered the EEC. Unemployment and inflation both rose rapidly. Towards the end of the period a series of bankruptcies engulfed whole sectors of the economy.

The economic crisis helped encourage a mass movement which culminated in the election in 1981 of the PASOK (Panhellenic Socialist Movement) government. In this fourth phase, the new government attempted to raise workers' living standards, develop a welfare state, and modernize Greek institutions. But the inheritance of economic crisis and institutional backwardness frustrated the attempt (Vergopoulos 1986: 99). This in turn contributed to PASOK's defeat by the right in 1990. The neo-liberal policies of the ND government which succeeded PASOK caused economic instability, with increased unemployment and a fall in real wages.

In 1993, a new PASOK government was elected. PASOK had no choice but to adapt domestic economic policy to the constraints imposed by the Maastricht Treaty and Economic and Monetary Union. The new economic policy succeeded in improving a number of economic indicators: in 1996, inflation fell below 10 per cent for the first time since the 1970s, interest rates dropped significantly, manufacturing output and investment rose. However, unemployment rose to 10 per cent, while the trade deficit and public debt also worsened. PASOK's attempts to meet the criteria of European integration, its undertaking of major infrastructure projects particularly in the area of public transport, and its programme of partial privatizations may be seen as contributing to Greece's international competitiveness; but they have also imposed considerable costs on labour.

▌ Uneven Development

The Greek economy performed increasingly well for most of the post-war period, and in particular between 1955 and 1975, as measured by the growth of GNP, exports and invisible earnings. After 1975, however, the position deteriorated. And throughout the post-war decades, economic development has displayed considerable internal imbalance. This is evident if one compares the relative performance of the agricultural, manufacturing and service sectors.

Agriculture has always been important for the Greek economy. It accounted for 30 per cent of GNP in 1951, and though the figure had fallen to 12 per cent in 1993, this is still high by comparison with other EU countries. Traditionally farming has been based on small family units with low productivity. More modern methods have brought some improvement, but serious imbalances remain.

There are also imbalances within manufacturing. Production almost tripled between 1962 and 1978, rising as a proportion of GNP from 25 to 32.5 per cent. But manufacturing remains dominated by traditional industries such as textiles, clothing, and foodstuffs. Conversely, the engineering industry is very underdeveloped, and Greece depends almost totally on imports of machinery. The traditional industries were hit by crisis in the 1980s and 1990s, and their output dropped sharply. Manufacturing as a whole declined as a proportion of GNP – to 28.3 per cent in 1993. However, in the mid-1990s, it has recovered significantly, although investment levels remain low.

Since 1961 the service sector has accounted for more than half of GNP, and is currently around 60 per cent. The rapid expansion of banking, commerce, import–export services, as well as tourism, has not encouraged the development of the rest of the economy. On the contrary, the service sector has diverted resources from industrial production.

Despite impressive aggregate growth, the lack of structural integration is a fundamental weakness in the Greek economy. For example, the importance of agriculture is not matched by the development of an agricultural machinery industry. Similarly, the rapid expansion of electricity generation has depended on expensive imports of fuel and technology. Or again, there has been a successful development of metal mining, but not of associated processing and manufacturing activities; most of the output is exported in, at best, a semi-processed state. Hence Greek industry remains polarized between production of domestic consumer goods, and the export of primary commodities. This imbalance has combined with the openness of the Greek economy and the dominance of foreign capital to cause a deteriorating balance of payments. The visible trade deficit has more than doubled since 1988 to 26 per cent of the national income. External equilibrium has thus depended on invisible earnings – tourism, shipping, and remittances from Greek migrant workers overseas. This has made Greece particularly vulnerable to vicissitudes in the world economy, as is currently all too apparent.

▌ The Structure of Employment

The rapid expansion of the Greek labour force has steadied in recent years. The structure of employment reflects the characteristics of the national economy. In 1995, one worker in six was engaged in manufacturing; the combined workforce of mining, manufacturing, construction and public utilities was only 23.2 per cent of the economically active total (see table 17.1). The proportion working in agriculture dropped from 27 per cent in 1987 to around 20 per cent in 1995 – still three and half times higher than the EU average. (The low productivity of Greek agriculture is shown in the fact that the contribution of farming to GNP is almost half the proportion represented by agriculture in the labour force.) The workforce in the service sector has been rising continuously, and now stands at 56.4 per cent.

Female employment increased rapidly in the 1970s and 1980s before stabilizing at around 36 per cent. But the level is still low by comparison with other European countries. Over 60 per cent of women work in services, a figure that has expanded over the past decade; almost all these jobs are in retail, catering and public services; 24 per cent work in agriculture, and only 14 per cent in manufacturing.

Table 17.1 The sectoral distribution of the Greek labour force, 1995

	Male		Female		Total	
	(000s)	*%*	*(000s)*	*%*	*(000s)*	*%*
Agriculture, forestry, fishing	452.1	18.5	327.9	23.9	781.9	20.4
Mining	15.0	0.6	0.6	0.1	15.6	0.4
Manufacturing and handicraft	397.4	16.2	180.3	13.1	577.7	15.1
Electricity, gas and water	34.4	1.4	7.2	0.5	41.5	1.1
Construction and public works	249.4	10.2	2.9	0.2	252.3	6.6
Commerce, restaurants and hotels	535.2	21.8	313.5	22.9	848.7	22.1
Transport and communications	215.7	8.8	32.3	2.4	248.0	6.5
Financial and related services	142.3	5.8	98.6	7.2	240.9	6.3
Other services	408.9	16.7	408.3	29.7	817.3	21.5
Total	2,450.4	100	1,371.6	100	3,823.9	100

Source: NSSG, *Labour Force Survey for 1995*.

This relates to the most distinctive feature of the Greek labour force: only half (53.8 per cent) are employees (compared with an EC average of 82 per cent), while 27.3 per cent are self-employed, 12.3 per cent are unpaid family workers and 6.4 per cent are employers. Almost half the self-employed are in agriculture, and a quarter work in shops and tourism. These figures contribute to the unusually small size of work units: 94 per cent of establishments have fewer than 10 employees, only 0.2 per cent have over 100.

Finally, the labour market is highly urbanized: in 1995, 33 per cent of the labour force worked in the Athens area, and 30 per cent in other urban centres (i.e. locations with 10,000 or more inhabitants). But in this respect also, the imbalances are evident. At one extreme, 4 million workers – 41 per cent of the labour force – live in the four largest urban areas of Greece. But conversely 25.6 per cent live in rural settlements (under 2,000 inhabitants) and a further 11.7 per cent in semi-rural (under 10,000). Modern Greece is thus a contradictory mixture of milieux.

Multinational Companies and Large Employers

Despite the great preponderance of small enterprises, the dominant role in the economy is increasingly played by a small number of large, often foreign-owned enterprises, and in some sectors by state enterprises. Increasingly the dominant firms are conglomerates, straddling several sectors of the economy. The influx of foreign capital has increased rapidly over recent years: it constituted around a quarter of investment in the 1970s, two-fifths in the first half of the 1980s (Perakis 1987: 40), about half in the 1990s.

In 1972, foreign multinationals already dominated several sectors of industry

Table 17.2 The dominance of the 100 largest firms in Greek manufacturing

	Total number of firms with 10 or more employees	Stake of top 100 in total (%)			
		Assets	Sales	Profits	Employment
1973	1759	56	54	56	40
1981	3210	52	58	75	34
1994	3524	49	47	43	30

Source: Karantzas (1985: 39), ICAP (1996).

such as petroleum products, transport, steel, chemicals, and electrical equipment. They controlled 30 per cent of production in manufacturing as a whole (Karantzas 1985: 38). Foreign companies controlled 30 per cent of the assets of the 550 largest manufacturing firms in 1981, but received 61 per cent of total profits (Tolios 1987). In the service sector, foreign ownership is also substantial. In 1993, foreign banks controlled 15 per cent of loan capital, while foreign insurance companies controlled 18 per cent of the market. In the retail and tourist sectors, multinationals also have a significant and increasing stake especially with the invasion of foreign hypermarket chains.

The dominance of large companies has become increasingly marked in the last three decades (see table 17.2). In manufacturing, while the number of small firms has also increased rapidly, the 100 largest enterprises account for half the total assets and sales; their declining share of total employment reflects their success in rationalizing production. Highly concentrated ownership exists in mining, construction and civil engineering, in road haulage – where giant multinationals have increasingly taken over local small owners as subcontractors – and in shipping. In the service sector, the two main banking groups owned 69 per cent of total assets in 1993. Five companies controlled 69 per cent of the insurance market in 1993. The ten biggest exporting firms controlled over a third of foreign trade in the same year. Even in agriculture, with its proliferation of small farmers, there has been a rapid rise in the proportion of large units, most notably in livestock.

In the 1980s, state economic activity became very important as the PASOK government assigned publicly owned companies a key role in its 'strategic plan for national independence'. A State Business Reconstruction Organization was also established, to take over domestic firms in economic difficulties. Despite recent moves to privatize state assets – as with the recent partial privatization of telecommunications – state control is still extensive. The state has a monopoly in electricity supply, railways and the airline. In oil refining and distribution, the state company, together with a handful of multinationals, dominates the domestic market. The state also has majority control in banking and insurance. Of the 100 largest manufacturing firms in 1994, 20 were state-controlled.

Class Relations and the Greek State

The character of Greek economic development can be viewed in the context of the distinctiveness of Greek politics. For half a century – from the inter-war military dictatorships to the regime of the colonels between 1967 and 1974, authoritarian, anti-labour and pro-capitalist rule was the norm. The implications for the evolution of trade unionism and industrial relations will be discussed later in this chapter. Here the consequences for Greek capital will be indicated.

Between the wars, government policy had encouraged the development of the Greek manufacturing base, leading to the emergence of a significant class of industrial capitalists. But under German occupation a different type of capitalist emerged: described in 1947 by Paul Porter, head of the US Economic Mission in Greece, as a 'new generation of speculators, opportunists and black marketeers that emerged after the war with large fortunes and luxury' (Tsoukalas 1986: 19). This new breed dominated post-war reconstruction, and was closely linked to the Greek state throughout the 1949–67 period of 'restricted democracy'. The crushing of the left in the civil war gave political control to the extreme anti-communist right, many of whom had collaborated with the Nazis. The regime lacked a rational strategy for the development of the Greek economy. Its priorities were to implement policies attractive to foreign capital and to sustain a mutually advantageous relationship with local capitalists. This relationship operated largely through networks of personal bribery and patronage (Petmetzidou-Tsoulouvis 1984: 28).

In a context where Greek post-war economic expansion was driven by subsidies, incentives and state-sponsored monopoly prerogatives, the business culture encouraged the pursuit of easy profits. Capitalists turned primarily to non-productive activities because profits were higher.

After the restoration of democracy in 1974, Greek capitalists pursued a strategy which became known as 'autocratic modernization'. This involved a new basis for integration of the Greek economy within the international division of labour, symbolized by Greece's accession to the EC in 1981. Throughout the period of PASOK government (1981–9) Greek capital resisted policies of economic reconstruction by engaging in an effective investment strike – even though the government rapidly turned from its initial radicalism to more orthodox economic policies (Spourdalakis 1986). Having made significant gains in the period of right-wing government between 1989 and 1993, employers are currently pressing for further liberalization through the privatization of state activities and labour market deregulation.

Employers' Organizations

The organizations that represent employers in national collective bargaining are the Federation of Greek Industries (SEB), the National Confederation of Greek

Commerce (EESE), and the General Confederation of Greek Artisans and Handi-crafts (GSEBEE). In addition to the functional division between these groups there are other lines of division. The shipowners, traditionally a key section of Greek capital, have two separate organizations, one of them London-based. In commerce, EESE faces rivalry from strong breakaway groups, while it clashed with GSEBEE in 1987 over the latter's decision to recruit shopkeepers; GSEBEE insisted that EESE represented the interests of large concerns and neglected smaller trades, 80 per cent of whom were unorganized.

SEB was established in 1917 and included handicraft producers until they formed their own association in 1946. The present name was adopted in 1979, reflecting a change of rule permitting only corporate, and not individual member-ship. This seemingly minor change reflected a modernization strategy within SEB. Traditionally the organization had been largely a vehicle for the personal interests of the wealthy and powerful families who both owned and controlled the companies which dominated pre-war industrialization. Their leadership faced three challenges: the collapse or decline of many traditional family-owned firms; the growth of modern, professional management with a different conception of corporate interests; and growing popular denunciations in the 1970s (which culminated in PASOK's election victory) of the relationships of personal patronage between the state and leading industrialists.

The current structure of the SEB is complex, with some 550 directly affiliated companies, and a number of sectoral and geographical associations representing around 2200 firms. Every 2 years, a General Assembly of SEB elects the twenty-member Administrative Board, which in turn appoints a smaller Executive Committee. There are also a variety of sub-committees and consultative councils, including a General Council which meets monthly. SEB represents its member companies in centralized collective bargaining and negotiations with government; it also provides information services, seminars and conferences for member firms.

Influenced by progress in the economy, SEB and its members have changed their negative attitude towards investment. They have pressed for modernization of the system of industrial relations, and have promoted the creation of a more stable internal environment: thus they favour 'social dialogue' through the Economic and Social Committee, and have participated in European-level employers' bodies. At the same time, however, they have sought greater labour market flexibility. Currently, SEB is urging the government to reduce non-wage labour costs which are alleged to amount to over 50 per cent in some industries, and to relax the strict rules governing collective dismissals – particularly restrictions on the maximum number of employees who may be dismissed in one calendar month (EIRR 1996b: 7).

GSEBEE has existed since 1919 as a national confederation for the sector of small businesses and artisan producers, currently numbering nearly half a million. Under the corporatist arrangements established in 1946, it acquired a legal monopoly of representation. The situation changed in 1981 when the new government abolished compulsory affiliation payments, subsequently enforcing a more democratic structure through legislation. GSEBEE's total membership in 1990 was 131,548 but only 67,029 voted for their Congress, dropping to 36,000 in 1994, almost half affiliated via local artisan unions. A distinctive feature of GSEBEE is that factions associated with different political parties nominate slates, and the election is decided by proportional representation. In this way, a unitary organization is maintained despite the existence of ideological differences.

EESE is of relatively recent creation. Only in 1961 did local commercial associations form a loose umbrella body, the Co-ordinating Council of Greek Commercial Associations, comprising the 15 largest associations then in existence. Collective bargaining in the commercial sector was undertaken by the three largest local associations (Athens, Piraeus and Thessaloniki). National organizations have also operated in specialized sections of commerce, for supermarkets and for importers and wholesalers, and these remain outside EESE, which represents only around 15 per cent of eligible firms. However, EESE is certainly the most representative organization in the commercial sector. In 1994 it became a confederation, incorporating a tertiary-level federation representing ten district federations. As in GSEBEE, its governing bodies are elected from rival political slates, and political factionalism is often a divisive influence.

EESE is trying to project a new image for the Greek commercial sector. In negotiations for the national collective agreement in 1996 it tried to shape the pay strategy of the employers on the grounds that its sector covered the majority of the employees involved. EESE has responded to the internationalization of markets by upgrading research and information services to members, and by establishing a National Vocational Training Centre for employees in commerce. By contrast, GSEBEE which represents small firms directly threatened by competition from – or take-over by – larger Greek and foreign firms, has pressed for measures to protect its members from competition; collaboration with small-business representatives from other EU countries is one vehicle for such demands.

Overall, therefore, employers are marked by a wide diversity of interests. Their attitudes to labour, however, have had much in common, particularly demands for greater flexibility of the labour market.

Personnel Management and Industrial Relations in Greek Companies

The factors already discussed are reflected in the very limited development of personnel management in Greece. As in other countries of the Mediterranean periphery, the post-war alliance between the new capitalist class and the state allowed the marginalization of organized labour and the adoption of an autocratic and authoritarian management style. In addition, the dominant tradition – most obviously, but by no means exclusively, among small employers – was of owner-management; control was exercised by the owner, and perhaps other members of his immediate family.

In this context there was no space for personnel management as the function is understood in Britain: those given this title had little more than a policing role. Customarily the position was filled by a junior member of the owner's family, or by a retired military or police officer. Formalized personnel policies were very much the exception. Not until the 1970s did different management policies emerge. The restoration of political democracy in 1974 and the rapid growth of trade union organization helped stimulate more sophisticated labour relations practices, with the establishment of specialist personnel departments in larger firms. Nevertheless, a management consultancy survey found that in 1986 only 9 per cent of Greek companies with 100 or more employees had a separate personnel department; only 11 per cent had an explicit personnel planning policy. By contrast, 52 per cent of foreign-owned companies undertook personnel planning. A further weakness is that personnel departments tend to be staffed by managers without formal training in personnel and industrial relations; there is a complete lack of such courses in Greece, at least at graduate level. A study of Greek personnel managers by Kanellopoulos (1990) found that 61 per cent were graduates, but only 10 per cent had specific personnel qualifications. Companies have increasingly recognized this gap in management development and are investing, with the help of EU funding, in management training.

There has been a dramatic change in policies towards company industrial relations. The 1955 legislation (Act 3239/1955) which set the main framework for post-war labour law prescribed collective bargaining only at multi-employer level, and companies resolutely refused to recognize unions at workplace level. But after 1975, employers were forced to come to terms with the shopfloor strength of the resurgent trade union movement, legally underpinned in 1982 by Act 1264/1982 which established union rights in the workplace. Other legislation has also encouraged a shift in the focus of industrial relations to company or plant level. In the public sector, Act 1365/1983 provided for employee representation on company boards. In private companies, Act 1876/1990 has encouraged company negotiations by bringing these within the statutory framework of conciliation and arbitration.

It is unclear how far multinational companies are an exception to the trend, and perhaps an obstacle to its generalization. Certainly most foreign multinationals are non-union, and some have applied sophisticated human resource management programmes as a way of integrating employees within the company. However, the more modern generation of Greek managers does not object in principle to the formal rights of unions at company level, which do not seriously inhibit managerial prerogative in practice. In the 1990s, despite employer pressure, legislative measures to permit greater employment flexibility have not been introduced. Indeed, Act 2224/94 reversed certain provisions of earlier legislation, especially restrictions on union rights and curbs on the right to strike.

| Labour

As has already been noted, the Greek class structure is distinctive in the low proportion of employees and the high proportion of self-employed and family workers in artisan production, trade and agriculture. Not only are employees a minority of the active labour force, but the larger part of the wage-labour force is employed in the public sector and in state-controlled companies. This has important implications for working-class identity. In a context of employment insecurity throughout the post-war period, state employment was a source of patronage used by the government party to sustain clientelist relations. At the same time, wage levels were lower than in the private sector, encouraging dual job-holding, even though the law until 1990 in theory restricted part-time employment. Workers in such a position develop a 'split personality' (Tsoukalas 1986: 175) which can inhibit effective social and political mobilization.

Conversely, small-business owners and other self-employed form a relatively cohesive and effective socio-political group. They are almost as numerous as waged and salaried employees; moreover in most cases the self-employed are not simply individual economic actors but represent a family production unit. Hence, as Simitis (1989: 13) argues, it is very difficult to apply conventional notions of class structure and class politics to Greece. Rather, there exists a diversity of bases of interest and lines of division, which may cut across simple criteria of class in terms of locations in the production system. Correspondingly, groups relate to the state not as a protagonist in a struggle between capital and labour, but as the potential defender of their special rights and interests. Politics itself becomes primarily an arena for the mobilization of sectoral economic interests.

▎The Development of Greek Trade Unions

Contemporary Greek trade unionism has inevitably been shaped, both by the late and limited development of an industrial working class, and by the central role of the state in the formation of the modern economy.

Occupational and industrial union organization first emerged in the 1880s, with multi-union local federations being created in the early years of the present century. The Greek General Confederation of Labour (GSEE) was established in 1918. Though nominally the confederation has continued to function uninterrupt-edly since then, in fact its character and status have fluctuated repeatedly in the face of state regulation and repression, and the vagaries of internal union politics.

As in many other European countries, unions suffered internal political splits after 1920, notably between socialists and communists. The latter acquired considerable strength in Greece, but were outlawed by the Metaxas dictatorship in 1936 and legalized only after the restoration of democracy in 1974. After 1968 Greek communists themselves were split between 'Eurocommunists' and the orthodox communist KKE (Spourdalakis 1986: 263–5). As elsewhere in Europe, the 1990s have witnessed the fragmentation of the Greek communist parties. The complex patterns of internal political tendencies and tensions in GSEE itself are discussed below.

The initial formation of a national structure of trade unionism was the outcome of a period best described as one of state paternalism, when different political parties sought organized popular support, and a system of labour legislation was introduced between 1909 and 1922. In 1931, the state established a Workers' Housing Trust (*Ergatiki Estia* – literally Workers' Hearth) with a reserve fund drawn from compulsory contributions of 0.25 per cent of every employee's pay (with equivalent contributions from employers). The Minister of Labour received the power to distribute 8 per cent of this fund to trade unions. Under the Metaxas regime in 1936, this procedure was used to subordinate unions to the government. GSEE became, in effect, a state institution with exclusive jurisdiction. The Minister of Labour became responsible for appointing union officials, who were required to support government policies. Unions were thus transformed in this corporatist system into mere 'rubber-stamp' organizations.

An attempt after the war to reconstitute GSEE as an independent and pluralistic confederation broke down in 1946 when the new royalist government overturned the executive elected by conference and imposed its own nominees. Repressive state control was slightly relaxed two decades later under the Centre Union Party government, but reasserted with a vengeance after the colonels' coup. Thus over several decades up to 1974, supporters of independent trade unionism were subject to police surveillance, arrest, imprisonment and sometimes worse (see, for example, Catephores and Tzannatos 1986).

While genuine activists were persecuted, a caste of leaders developed who were ironically known as *ergatopateres* (workers' fathers). Sustained by government patronage, they also maintained a spurious legitimacy by convening rigged conferences, deregistering troublesome branches, and similar stratagems. Since their income came from government rather than members' subscriptions, they were under no real pressure to act effectively as workers' representatives.

Trade Unions under Democracy

The fall of the military dictatorship in 1974 brought important changes in the trade union situation, but some distinctive features persisted.

An important novelty was the rise of factory organization, independently of the official GSEE structures (OBES 1984). This provided for the first time a significant basis for rank-and-file initiative within Greek trade unionism, and a pressure point for greater union democracy. Factory unionism was a spontaneous movement, stemming both from the growing concentration of urban industrial workers and from the broader protest movement which resulted in the fall of the military dictatorship. The factory movement sought effective collective protection against dismissals (not provided by the existing unions), improvements in wages and working conditions, and a shorter working week. Autonomous factory unions emerged out of strike movements in 1975. A decree issued during the dictatorship, providing for the appointment of a tripartite mediation committee to resolve workplace disagreements, was utilized by the factory unions to press a far wider range of demands than specified under the law. The decisions of the tripartite committee then served as the de facto equivalent of company collective agreements. But the factory movement was to collapse in the face of political defeat, the hostility of the Communist Party to the movement's 'syndicalist' character, and the opposition of SEB, with victimization and blacklisting of union activists.

A second development was the collapse of totalitarian control of the unions and

Table 17.3 GSEE Congresses (1989–95) members voted

| | Congress | Members voted | | Total |
		Labour centre	Federation	
1989	25th	192,023	372,454	564,477
1990	26th	169,610	358,973	528,583
1992	27th	160,094	322,243	482,337
1995	28th	147,962	281,526	429,488
		(−22.9%)	(−24.4%)	(−23.6%)

Source: GSEE.

the introduction of explicit political factionalism in which all main left parties – newly legalized after 30 years – were represented. Maintaining a unitary organization despite these complex organized divisions has been a continuous, and not always resoluble, problem for GSEE since 1974 (see below).

While the corporatist character of union dependence on the state was modified after 1974, a close interrelationship persisted. Unions continued to receive finance from the state social welfare system. It was open to them to supplement their income through membership subscriptions, but most made no attempt to do so (major exceptions being unions for seafarers, bank employees and public utility workers – all of whom benefit from a check-off system). Hence in 1984, GSEE received a total income of 200 million drachma (£620,000), a mere 45,000 drachma (£140) coming from membership subscriptions (Koukoules 1988: 26). Local and sectoral unions obtained a higher proportion of income from subscriptions; but the contribution levels in Greek unions are remarkably low by international standards.

Trade union legislation in 1990 and 1992 abolished this system of state subsidy, which had provided 1.2 billion drachma to the trade union movement in 1991. GSEE notionally supported the abolition of state subsidy but most unions were reluctant to require realistic levels of contribution for fear of losing members. With the unions experiencing financial difficulties, a new law (Act 2224/94) re-established a version of the old system, and even increasing the financing ceiling to 25 per cent of the revenue of *Ergatiki Estia*.

The structure of Greek trade unionism has changed little since 1918. The basic level of organization consists of 'primary' unions, representing workers of a particular industry, occupation, craft or company in each locality. At the beginning of the 1980s almost 5,000 were registered, but at its 1989 Congress GSEE reported 3,020 and in 1995 only 2,361. The decline largely reflects the elimination of many of the 'ghost' unions which existed only on paper in the era of the *ergatopateres*. But it also reflects changes in occupational structure and the nature of work (e.g. outsourcing). Actual membership is difficult to determine; Katsanevas (1984: 13) estimated a density of between 27 and 33 per cent. This no longer seems realistic. According to official union data, unions have lost a quarter of their membership (see table 17.3). However, some sectors are far more strongly unionized than others; in banking, public utilities, local government and education density is probably 80 per cent or higher.

Traditionally, most primary unions were based on craft or occupation, reflecting the very limited development of mass-production industry in Greece. This form of organization was favoured by the authorities during the period of state paternalism, as less likely than industrial unionism to present a class–political challenge to the regime. However, craft organization has been weakened by technological change. Conversely, membership expanded in industrial or sectoral unions; by 57 per cent between 1975 and 1989 in the two largest industry federations, those of metal and textile workers. However, subsequent crisis in these sectors has led to a sharp drop in membership – by 40 per cent in metal-working and 29 per cent in textiles. A new type of primary union also came to prominence from 1975: the factory union (see above). The rapid growth of factory unionism in the 1970s was halted in the 1980s, largely because many were rooted in the so-called 'problematic' sectors of traditional manufacturing where heavy job losses have occurred. Membership of OBES, the national federation of factory unions formed in 1979, fell from 11,600 in 1983 to 6,300 in 1989 and only 2,287 in 1995. Finally, there exist some primary unions which are general in coverage, though at present their significance is slight.

Primary unions are able to affiliate to either of two types of secondary organization. One is the national federation, organized on the basis of sector, industry or occupation. GSEE contains 53 such federations, which represent 1,042 local unions – just under half the total number of primary organizations within its ranks. In membership terms, however, the national federations are the key component of GSEE. In 1995, the 15 largest federations accounted for 50 per cent of total GSEE membership of 430,000. The largest federations cover such sectors as construction, metalworking, banks, telecommunications, electricity, railways, health care and public services.

The alternative line of affiliation for primary unions is to 'labour centres', a type of local or regional body to some extent modelled on the French *bourses du travail*. Though such centres predate GSEE itself, their role has been marginalized by the development of collective bargaining. The 66 labour centres in 1995 encompassed the majority of primary unions, but only a third of total GSEE membership. Those in the three major cities – Athens, Piraeus and Thessaloniki – contain 10.6 per cent of the members of GSEE; the others are far smaller bodies, often in peripheral regions.

At national confederal level, GSEE is the one organization of note. A separate confederation – ADEDY – covers public employees whose status is formally defined in the Greek Constitution.

▌ Internal Organization

The internal organization of Greek unions has, from the outset, been subject to detailed legal regulation. Any association of workers with more than 20 members can register as a union. The governing body is an executive board, while an audit committee also exists to oversee financial administration. The main official positions (president, vice-president, and secretary/treasurer) must be open to election at least every 3 years, and no individual may hold more than one of these offices.

A worker is permitted to belong to two different primary unions (e.g. one occupationally and the other industrially based), but may vote or stand for office in only one of these. Members of primary unions have the right to vote, and stand for election, at secondary level (regional labour centre or national federation), according to how the union decides to affiliate.

Political Factionalism

With the relaxation of state control in 1974, a variety of organized political tendencies emerged within GSEE, attached to different political parties. Originally aiming to challenge the corrupt leadership of the *ergatopateres*, these political factions now act primarily as 'transmission belts' for their respective parties. The main political groupings are PASKE, linked to PASOK; DAKE, linked to the conservative New Democracy party; ESAK, orthodox communist; and AEM, linked to the Renewal Left. Following the split in PASKE in 1985 (see below), a new grouping – SSEK – was formed, but it is no longer significant.

Political factionalism could be seen as encouraging an active, campaigning democracy within Greek unions. But it may also be regarded as leading to an excessive politicization of unionism, with policy debates reflecting party-political loyalties rather than specifically trade union priorities. Recruitment can also be inhibited, if political activists are reluctant to 'dilute' the membership with non-partisans. Realistically, political factionalism may be considered the necessary price to pay for GSEE's survival as a unitary federation. Since union governing bodies are elected by proportional representation, all significant tendencies are able to achieve some positions of leadership. While disputes over the representation of specific tendencies are not uncommon, these have never gone so far as to threaten the breakup of GSEE itself. The links with political parties have increasingly been identified as a problem in recent years; the debate continues as to whether, and how, unions might attain greater independence – in terms of membership, structure, finance and policy formulation – from political institutions.

From the restoration of democracy until 1983, GSEE congresses were dominated by the right, partly because a number of left-oriented federations were excluded. In effect, the New Democracy government, within the framework of the 330/1976 law, was able to facilitate control of the unions by its own supporters. With the change of government in 1981, 'the Socialists inherited a markedly corporatist labour relations system in which compulsory government mediation, and other direct involvement in trade union procedures were the rule, and free collective bargaining and open-democratic trade union structures the exception' (Spourda-lakis 1988: 229–30). Law 1264/1982 on trade union democracy passed by PASOK provided the basis for a successful legal challenge to the GSEE leadership elected in 1981 (when key left unions were excluded). The court judgement gave a majority of seats on the executive to PASKE, leading to a boycott by the right at the 1983 congress.

In 1985, PASOK's austerity measures (see below) provoked a major crisis. A minority of the PASKE leadership, representing public sector unions, opposed the measures, and were promptly expelled from PASOK. Oppositionists held a majority on the GSEE administrative board but were outvoted on the governing council. With two rival ruling committees each claiming legitimacy, a court ruling backed the government supporters. Only in 1989 was the split finally overcome, when all main factions participated in the GSEE congress. The outcome was an administrative board in which no one faction was dominant. Since then PASKE has controlled a majority in all congresses.

▌ Workplace Representation

While statutory or voluntary machinery of workplace employee representation is an established part of most European industrial relations systems, there is no sustained tradition of such institutions in Greece.

Attempts to establish workplace structures with functions complementary to those of the unions can be identified at historical phases of trade union advance (Koutroukis 1987: 54), as for example, at the height of the national liberation struggle against the Nazis and the collaborationist government. The factory union movement after 1974 gave a major impetus to demands for worker participation, with both PASOK and the Eurocommunists supporting proposals for socialization and workers' self-management.

PASOK's 1982 legislation (1264/1982) was designed to encourage union-based workplace representation. Employers were obliged to provide facilities for union meetings at the workplace (outside working hours), and notice-boards for union announcements. Workers elected to representative positions in their local union were protected against dismissal and entitled to unpaid time off work to carry out their duties. Employers were also obliged to hold discussions with employee representatives, if so requested, at least once a month. Union representatives were also entitled to attend any workplace inspection by Ministry of Labour officials.

A subsequent law, 1586/1985, provides for statutory health and safety committees with employee representation. This was followed by a more general law, 1767/1988, prescribing workers' councils in all enterprises – both private and public – with more than 50 employees. The councils are only consultative, and all employees – whether or not union members – can vote and stand for election. In any difference between councils and unions, the latter are guaranteed precedence.

The introduction of workplace representatives in the 1980s occurred only slowly in the private sector, but much faster in public enterprises. A special law, 1365/1983, provided a number of new mechanisms of employee representation including a general assembly, a central workers' council, and representation on company boards and management committees. However, the implementation of the new institutions merely stimulated intense competition for representation among the different political factions and high hopes for employee democracy degenerated into petty antagonisms. Union leaders, of whatever political persuasion, came to view the new machinery as a threat, and the government itself diluted a number of the provisions. This sorry episode seems to support the conclusion of Metropoulos (1987: 101) that employee participation can function in a positive manner only where an institutionalized relationship between capital and labour already exists. It is yet to be seen whether the operation of European Works Councils will help promote a more successful culture of company-level worker representation in Greece.

Trade Unions and Politics

Greek unions are exceptional in Europe for the continued role of class politics as their dominant point of reference. In part this reflects the unusual degree of political polarization in Greece and – to some extent as a corollary – the intensity of industrial conflicts. The long heritage of political repression, and of autocratic employers, never made 'free collective bargaining' an option for Greek trade unions. Rather, 'industrial' and 'political' aspirations were interconnected and mutually conditioning. For example, the operation of compulsory arbitration prescribed in the 3239/1955 law, and the restrictive impact of government incomes policies meant that simple wage bargaining could readily lead to confrontation with the state. Unions could not avoid politics, and experience of the alliance between state and capital in post-war Greece encouraged most political tendencies in the unions to adopt a radical anti-capitalist stance.

This orientation was perhaps most clear-cut in the years 1976–81, between the fall of the dictatorship and the election of the PASOK government. Labour movement activists had played an important part in resistance to the colonels' regime, but saw themselves eclipsed by the New Democracy government which failed to make a complete break with the old regime and consolidated the existing economic order. After 1981, the unions were split between committed support for the PASOK government, and opposition – by PASOK dissidents and other leftists – to government policies if these appeared to contradict workers' interests.

The election of a conservative government in 1989 helped to reunite the political tendencies in the unions and sharpen their radicalism against the 'Balkan Thatcherite' policies it tried to implement. This period marks the beginning of a new era for the Greek trade unions. Since 1991, the development of the labour movement has been influenced by such issues as growing unemployment (together with a large, mainly illegal, immigrant workforce), the problems of the left after the collapse of communism, and the environment of accelerating European integration after Maastricht.

The control of GSEE by 'realists' has encouraged a logic of 'modernization' which emphasizes 'social dialogue' and 'responsible participation' in the development of strategy in areas such as employment policy, industrial development, and union rights. The change of approach has been seen in the structures of collective bargaining – for example, the introduction of novel 2-year agreements (in 1991–92, 1994–5 and 1996–7, see below) – and in its content, with agreements on the unemployed, training, and health and safety. There has also been a new attitude to the use of strike action, reflected in the remarkable drop in strike figures. Further, there are signs of an institutionalization of the unions' role with the emergence in the 1990s of new bipartite and tripartite bodies, notably the mediation and arbitration body, OMED; the Economic and Social Council (OKE), created in 1994 with the duty to express opinions on issues of social and economic policy prior to legislation; and the National Labour Institute (EIE), founded in 1993 by the social partners and the Ministry of Labour to assist policy-making in the areas of employment, labour relations and vocational training (EIRR 1996c).

The new European reality has brought to the fore many issues concerning the role of Greece and Greek labour in broader European developments. In recent years, GSEE has strengthened links with other European unions (it has been a member of ETUC since 1976), and has attempted to co-ordinate its responses to issues arising from the process of European integration – for example, the European Commission's White Paper on Employment.

For the first time, unions are also giving serious attention to the interests of women workers. In the past decade there have been important advances on such questions as maternity leave, parental allowances, insurance rights and legal protection. Nevertheless, women are still mainly confined to low-paid, low-skilled occupations, and have remained largely unrepresented in the governing bodies of the unions. There are signs of change, however: one women has recently been elected to the GSEE's 15-member executive committee while, in banking, the union recently agreed to ensure proportional representation for women on governing bodies.

State and Law

Industrial relations in Greece are subject to a comprehensive and complex framework of legal regulation. Ever since 1909 the law has defined in detail the relationships between employers, unions and the state, in ways which – according to the political context – have been sometimes progressive but more usually repressive.

For most of the post-war period, the rules of the game were defined by Law 3239/1955 which prescribed a centralized system of collective bargaining with provision for state intervention via compulsory arbitration. After 1974 New Democracy enacted some revisions, and PASOK initiated some more radical and pro-union changes, but without replacing the previous legal framework of collective bargaining.

The Law 1876/1990, passed under the conservative–socialist–communist coalition government, was a radical step towards industrial relations moderniza-tion. The 1955 law was abolished and a more voluntaristic set of procedures established, consolidating the independence of collective bargaining from the state. The rights and duty of the parties to engage in collective bargaining were legally enshrined. Compulsory arbitration was replaced by a new voluntary system of conciliation, mediation and – on the initiative of either party – arbitration by independent specialists under the direction of the tripartite OMED (Organization of Mediation and Arbitration) (see EIRR 1996c: 19–20).

In terms of other aspects of collective labour law, the Act 330/1976 soon after the fall of the dictatorship provided a very restrictive framework. Trade union rights were severely circumscribed, job security was reduced and strikes were subject to serious limitations. Law 1264/1982, passed in the early months of the PASOK government, radically enhanced trade union rights. As has been seen, the union position in the workplace was strongly reinforced. Extensive rights to strike were provided, and where a strike was called according to specified procedures the employer was prohibited from dismissing strikers, hiring strike-breakers, or imposing a lockout. However, the law imposed additional restrictions in the public sector and in certain essential services; and this was compounded between 1983 and 1988, under a legal provision specifying that strikes in newly nationalized services required a majority of all employees to vote in favour of action. Even more restrictive was the law 1915/1990 which, in effect, abolished most of the rights acquired by the unions in 1982, restricting the scope of lawful strikes, permitting the dismissal of unlawful strikers, and imposing new limitations on strikes in public services. When PASOK returned to power in 1993, this legislation was repealed.

Numerous changes in Greek labour law since the restoration of democracy have affected individual employment rights. The main issues involved have been working hours and holidays; the position of women and young workers; and health and safety. Regulation of the labour market has been another important area of intervention. The OAED (Labour Force Employment Organization) was authorized by law 1403/1983 to organize employment training. Under the Act 1545/1985, OAED acquired far more extensive powers of labour market regulation including administration of unemployment benefits. The provisions for vocational training were considerably expanded by law 1839/1989. To control job losses, the law 1387/1983 imposed rigid limits on collective dismissals. However, law 1892/1990, while maintaining constraints on the use of collective dismissals, introduced new forms of flexibility in the labour market, including the authorization – for the first time in Greece – of part-time employment.

▌ Public Sector Activity

As an agency of income distribution, the state in Greece is of considerable importance compared with other European countries: state expenditure was 40.6 per cent of GNP in 1980 and rose to 55.5 per cent in 1985. But in terms of business activity, the state is much more marginal in Greece. Public enterprises accounted for around 11 per cent of valued added in 1982.

State-owned firms employed 9 per cent of the wage-labour force in 1985. But for the public sector as a whole the figure was far higher, 32 per cent in 1985. Almost three-quarters of public employees are on fixed-term contracts: in part a reflection of the insecurity of Greek workers generally, but also an indication of the way that Greek governments have always used employment as a means of patronage.

Employment status varies in different parts of the public sector. Direct employees of the state have a status as civil servants specified in the Constitution. This imposes a number of obligations and restrictions, but also guarantees security of employment. Until 1981, public employees required a formal certificate of 'civic reliability' issued by the local police authority; and though this has been abolished, political acceptability still remains a significant influence on employment. However, there have been moves to modernize the system; a 1994 measure implemented an objective system for hiring civil servants. In other parts of the public sector – nationalized companies, banks, etc. – employment status is the same as in the private sector. In practice, however, employees have achieved considerable employment security irrespective of the formal contractual position.

Special legal regulations affect collective organization in the public sector. Trade unionism is prohibited in the police and fire service and the military. Permanent civil servants are not allowed to join the same trade unions as other workers. However, the 1982 legislation enabled the formation of civil service unions on the same structural basis as other unions. The primary unit of organization is the individual section with national federations for particular government departments. These 59 federations are in turn members of the Confederation of Civil Servants, ADEDY. Founded in 1945, ADEDY has a history of internal politics which parallels GSEE. Until 1983 it was controlled by a right-wing leadership unaccountable to the membership, but their position was eventually challenged successfully in the courts. As in GSEE, political factions linked to the various parties now compete for leadership positions.

Union density in the civil service is very high. In 1995, ADEDY claimed 220,000 members, representing 65 per cent of those with permanent contracts as civil servants. Density is particularly high among primary and secondary schoolteachers, whose federations together make up some 40 per cent of ADEDY membership.

Public servants in Greece are covered by a unitary grading system. Basic pay is supplemented by a variety of allowances, which serve to widen differentials. A reform in 1996 reduced the number of separate pay scales, and abolished many of the supplementary allowances. Until 1990, pay was adjusted automatically every four months on the basis of the official cost-of-living index; now the adjustment is decided unilaterally by the government.

Collective bargaining does not formally occur in the public service, and the right to strike is more restricted than for other types of employee. Unions can submit demands relating to terms and conditions of employment, but all governments have regarded it as an issue of state sovereignty that they retain absolute jurisdiction on these matters. Greece has not therefore ratified the relevant ILO conventions, despite repeated demands from the unions. In 1996, however, discussions started between ADEDY and the PASOK government, and it is anticipated that legislation will be enacted to allow free collective bargaining in the public sector. Such a development could in the future result in the unification of ADEDY and GSEE.

The issue of privatization and deregulation did not arise in Greece while PASOK was in government in the 1980s. On the contrary, state intervention played a central role in its economic strategy. The aim was to 'socialize' the existing public sector; rescue bankrupt sectors of the economy through state reconstruction, subsidies and protected markets; and build up a modern welfare state. But the grand strategy failed: rather than modernization, state intervention seemed to result in bureaucracy and low productivity. Later than in the rest of Europe, neo-liberal views eventually gained ground; the conservative government tried to implement an extensive programme of deregulation and privatization. Its efforts were not notably successful, but since the return of PASOK in 1993, the policy of modernization has continued, and partial privatization measures have been implemented in certain areas.

| Trends in Collective Bargaining

There has developed a variegated structure of collective bargaining in Greece, with four levels of negotiation: single-company; local craft or occupational; national industry-level; and national multi-industry. Until 1990 there was no legal right to negotiate at company level, apart from provisions for 'special collective agree-ments' for clearly specified organizations such as banks, public utilities or local government, belonging to the public or semi-public sector (Ioannou 1989: 209). The abolition in 1990 of the previous restrictive legislation appears to have stimulated a shift to company and sectoral bargaining as well as a considerable expansion in the scope of bargaining. Issues covered in recent agreements include trade union rights and facilities at the workplace, supplementary social welfare benefits, company investment and the introduction of new technology. National agreements set national minimum pay rates which are binding on the private sector and provide a floor for lower-level bargaining. However, there has been employer pressure in recent years for the provisions of national agreements to be treated flexibly, allowing the different positions of individual sectors or companies to be taken into account (EIRR 1996a: 8).

Table 17.4 shows the annual figures for agreements and arbitration awards in the last three decades. It indicates clearly the traditional weakness of 'free collective bargaining' in the Greek context. In most years until the late 1980s, more claims were resolved through arbitration than by negotiation (cf. Ioannou 1989: 211). Excluding from consideration the 'special' agreements in the public and semi-public sector, the weakness of 'voluntary' collective bargaining is even more obvious: during the 1970s and 1980s, an average of only some 50 agreements a year were concluded. In the last few years, however, there have been signs of a considerable increase in the effectiveness of bargaining. Up to 1991, over 50 per cent of collective agreements were issued by compulsory arbitration; since 1992 the number of arbitration decisions has been sharply reduced.

The articulation of the different levels of bargaining is a potential source of problems. In the past, agreements were negotiated mainly at two levels: centrally, between SEB and GSEE and locally, for individual occupational groups. The

Table 17.4 Collective agreements and arbitration decisions 1961–91 (Law 3239/55)

Year	C.A	A.D	National General	National Craft	Local Craft	'Special'	Company	Sector
1961	63	69	1	12	36	14		
1962	70	66	2	14	19	35		
1963	61	75	–	10	31	20		
1964	97	93	–	27	41	29		
1965	121	93	1	21	59	40		
1966	105	96	–	28	40	37		
1967	63	78	1	10	26	26		
1968	63	91	2	14	24	23		
1969	50	81	–	13	16	21		
1970	53	57	–	20	3	30		
1971	46	60	–	17	7	22		
1972	88	45	–	44	11	33		
1973	158	60	–	47	18	93		
1974	70	85	–	21	15	34		
1975	131	143	3	30	13	85		
1976	144	120	1	30	24	90		
1977	146	179	1	29	15	101		
1978	166	214	–	37	14	115		
1979	173	247	(2)**	42	15	116		
1980	221	299	(1)**	56	25	140		
1981	233	330	–	54	26	153		
1982	300	232	(1)**	70	42	188		
1983	57	80	–	7	8	40		
1984	252	264	1	47	22	182		
1985	175	167	1	51	29	194		
1986	44	82	1	18	7	18		
1987	76	84	(1)**	21	11	44		
1988	210	73	1	83	28	18		
1989	276	111	1	90	24	161		
1990	236	106	1	65	20	51	53	46
1991	283	87	1	37	33	–	123	89
(Law 1876/90) OMED								
1992	171	32	–	28	14		66	63
1993	280	30	1	51	26		97	105
1994	276	42	1	34	33		96	112

** National General agreements reached after Arbitration.
Source: Ministry of Labour.

recent growth of company and single-industry agreements is a prospective source of inter-union tension and rivalry – even though there are few signs that Greek employers are pursuing the decentralization strategy evident in other European countries.

Table 17.5 Strikes in Greece 1976–95

Year	Strikes	Strikers	Hours lost
1976	829	241,142	5,187,783
1977	401	393,572	8,217,864
1978	405	349,969	6,477,117
1979	372	638,635	9,950,074
1980	472	1,317,917	20,494,944
1981	313	361,106	5,341,961
1982	447	246,543	7,892,094
1983	361	148,174	2,986,957
1984	268	107,957	2,986,957
1985	453	785,725	7,660,879
1986	218	1,106,330	8,839,363
1987	235	1,576,520	16,353,463
1988	320	363,864	5,596,123
1989	202	765,115	8,903,863
1990	200	1,405,497	20,435,313
1991	161	476,582	5,839,663
1992	166	969,484	7,072,014
1993	83	501,274	3,509,044
1994	56	226,155	1,872,899
1995	43	120,250	660,630

Source: Ministry of Labour.

| Conflict

The exceptional political context of industrial relations in Greece, and the very limited institutionalization of 'free collective bargaining' in the past, were reflected in distinctive patterns of industrial conflict. Strikes have not, in the main, been used as a means of applying sustained pressure on employers in the course of collective bargaining. Unions do not have the resources for a trial of strength and their use of the strike is conditioned as much by political as by industrial relations considerations.

Greek unions resort to a variety of 'cut-price' sanctions on employers: short workplace stoppages, withdrawal of goodwill, go-slows, working-to-rule, refusal to perform specific duties, sit-ins.

The period up to 1981 was marked by an increase in the frequency and size, though not duration, of strikes (Ioannou 1989: 96) (see table 17.5). At the peak, almost one worker in two was involved in strike action. This reflected not bargaining strength but the escalating political radicalism of the years following the fall of the dictatorship and resistance to government attempts to impose pay constraint in a period of high inflation. Almost all these strikes were unsuccessful.

The early years of the PASOK government (1981–5) saw low strike figures, as the government met many of the unions' demands. But after the imposition of austerity measures in 1985 strikes escalated. A significant feature of this period

Table 17.6   State-owned companies' share of strike activity (1985–95) (%)

Year	Strikes	Strikers	Hours lost
1985	10	36	28
1986	18	37	37
1987	23	23	34
1988	19	23	39
1989	24	26	38
1990	33	43	49
1991	39	27	35
1992	34	62	61
1993	49	35	35
1994	14	34	44
1995	28	17	14

Source: Ministry of Labour.

was the key role of public employees in industrial conflict. The modernization of Greek industrial relations in train since 1991 has influenced strike activity. As table 17.5 shows, there has been a dramatic fall in the number of disputes, the number of strikers, and days lost. Public sector companies have been responsible for a significant share in strike activity (table 17.6), notably in 1992 when employees reacted defensively to the conservative government's plan for social security cuts and privatization policies. The government's strict economic policy and the reform of the civil service pay structure provoked a wave of public sector strikes in late 1996 and early 1997 (EIRR 1997: 8). Despite the drop in strike levels in recent years, Greece had an average of 3,729 days lost per 1,000 employees in 1985–95, the worst record of any OECD country (IRE 280, April 1996: 1).

Conclusion

Greece remains marked by an 'immature' system of industrial relations. Organized labour has not yet achieved a position of influence in socio-economic development. Workers and unions have therefore had to react, often destructively, against the policies of employers and governments, rather than being able to play a more positive role. Factional rivalry within the union movement and the considerable decentralization of power which has arisen are additional obstacles to the unions adopting a more 'responsible' role in Greek industrial relations.

However, the process of modernization that has been taking place over the past 5 years or so indicates that the actors within the Greek industrial relations system have begun to accept their responsibility for creating a context of social dialogue within which more stable change can take place in the future.

❙ Abbreviations

ADEDY   Confederation of Greek Civil Servants
EESE   National Confederation of Greek Commerce
GSEBE   General Confederation of Greek Artisans and Independent Handicraft Producers
GSEE   General Confederation of Greek Workers
OBES   Federation of Industrial Unions
SEB   Federation of Greek Industries

❙ References and Further Reading

Catephores G. and Tzannatos, Z. 1986: Trade unions in Greece: 1949–81 and 1981–83. In Z. Tzannatos (ed.) *Socialism in Greece*, Aldershot: Gower.

EIRR (*European Industrial Relations Review*) 1996a: Employers question role of national general agreement. *EIRR* **268**, May 1996: 8.

EIRR 1996b: Employers' organization urges more labour market flexibility. *EIRR* **274**, November 1996: 7–8.

EIRR 1996c: New social bodies shape industrial relations. *EIRR* **275**, December 1996: 19–20.

EIRR 1997: More strikes test economic policy. *EIRR* **277**, February 1997: 8.

Ioannou C. 1989: *Salaried Employment and Trade Unionism in Greece*. Athens: Foundation for Mediterranean Studies (in Greek).

Kanellopoulos, C. 1990: *Personnel Management and Personnel Managers in Greece*. Athens: ELKEPA (in Greek).

Karantzas, G. 1985: Data on the Greek Economy in '*Leaflet*' No. 4. Athens (in Greek).

Katsanevas, T. 1984: *Trade Unions in Greece*. Athens National Centre of Social Research (in Greek).

Koukoules, F. 1988: Seventy years of recent trade union history. *Trade Union Review*, **45**, September (in Greek).

Koutroukis, T. 1987: Worker participation in Greece 1910–1981. *Trade Union Review*, **34**, October (in Greek).

Mavrogordatos, G. 1988: *Between Pityokamptis and Prokroustis: The Occupational Organisations in Contemporary Greece*. Odysseus: Athens (in Greek).

Metropoulos, A. 1987: The future of the trade unions. *Positions*, **19** (in Greek).

NSSG 1985, 1987, 1995 : *Labour Force Surveys of Greece*. Athens.

OBES 1984: *The Factory Movement*. Athens: OBES (in Greek).

Perakis, C. 1987: Foreign capital in Greece. Types and evolution tendencies. *Scientific Thought*, **32**.

Petmetzidou-Tsoulouvis, M. 1984: Approaches to the issue of under-development of the Greek social pattern. *Contemporary Issues*, **22** (in Greek).

Simitis, C. 1989: Introduction. In N. Mouzelis et al. (eds), *Populism and Politics*, Athens: Gnosis (in Greek).

Spourdalakis, M. 1986: The Greek experience. *Socialist Register*, 1985–6, London: Merlin.

Spourdalakis, M. 1988: *The Rise of the Greek Socialist Party*. London: Routledge.

Tolios, C. 1987: The new phenomenon of monopoly sovereignty in the Greek economy. *Scientific Thought*, **32** (in Greek).

Tsoukalas, C. 1986: *State, Society and Labour in Post-War Greece*. Athens: Themelio (in Greek).

Vergopoulos, C. 1986: Economic crisis and modernisation in Greece and the European South. In *Les Temps Modernes, Greece in Evolution*, Athens: Exantas (in Greek).

Index